ADVANCED LEVEL
MATHEMATICS
(PURE AND APPLIED)

PHYSICAL SCIENCE TEXTS

General Editor
SIR GRAHAM SUTTON
C.B.E., D.SC., LL.D., F.R.S.

Advanced Level Applied Mathematics
C. G. LAMBE
B.A., PH.D.

Advanced Level Pure Mathematics
C. J. TRANTER
C.B.E., M.A., D.SC., F.I.M.A.

Techniques of Mathematical Analysis
C. J. TRANTER
C.B.E., M.A., D.SC., F.I.M.A.

Light
C. B. DAISH
M.SC.

Electricity and Magnetism
C. G. WILSON
M.SC., A.INST.P.

Experimental Physics
C. B. DAISH and D. H. FENDER
M.SC.   B.SC., PH.D.

Heat
A. J. WOODALL
O.B.E., PH.D., F.INST.P.

ADVANCED LEVEL
MATHEMATICS
(PURE AND APPLIED)

C. J. TRANTER, C.B.E., M.A., D.Sc., F.I.M.A.
Bashforth Professor of Mathematical Physics,
Royal Military College of Science, Shrivenham

C. G. LAMBE, B.A., Ph.D.
Formerly Associate Professor of Mathematics,
Royal Military College of Science, Shrivenham

HODDER AND STOUGHTON
LONDON SYDNEY AUCKLAND TORONTO

ISBN 0 340 21474 0

First printed 1966

Second edition 1970

Third edition 1973, reprinted 1975

Paperback edition 1976

Printed in Great Britain for
Hodder and Stoughton Educational,
a division of Hodder and Stoughton Ltd.,
Mill Road, Duntan Green, Sevenoaks, Kent TN13 2YD
at The Pitman Press, Bath

GENERAL EDITOR'S FOREWORD

THE present volume is one of a series on physics and mathematics for the upper forms at school and the first year at the university. The books have been written by a team of experienced teachers at the Royal Military College of Science where, among other things, students are prepared for London (External) Degrees in Natural Science and Engineering. The series therefore forms an integrated course of study based on many years' experience in the teaching of physics and mathematics.

In preparing their manuscripts the writers have been mainly guided by the examination syllabuses of London University, the Joint Board of Oxford and Cambridge and the Joint Matriculation Board, but they have also taken a broad view of their tasks and have endeavoured to produce works which aim to give a student that solid foundation without which it is impossible to proceed to higher studies. The books are suitable either for class teaching or self study; there are many illustrative examples and large collections of problems for solution, taken, in the main, from recent examination papers.

It is a truism too often forgotten in teaching that knowledge is acquired by a student only when his interest is aroused and maintained. The student must not only be shown how a class of problems in mathematics is solved but, within limits, why a particular method works, and, in physics, why a technique is especially well adapted for some particular measurement. Throughout the series special emphasis has been laid on illustrations which may be expected to appeal to the experience of the student in matters of daily life, so that his studies are related to what he sees, feels and knows of the world around him. Treated in this way, science ceases to be an arid abstraction and becomes vivid and real to the enquiring mind.

The books have therefore been written, not only to ensure the passing of examinations, but as a preparation for the exciting world which lies ahead of the reader. They incorporate many of the suggestions which have been made in recent years by other teachers and, it is hoped, will bring some new points of view into the classroom and the study. Last, but by no means least, they have been written by a team working together, so that the exchange of ideas has been constant and vigorous. It is to be hoped that the result is a series which is adequate for all examinations at this level and yet broad enough to satisfy the intellectual needs of teachers and students alike.

O. G. SUTTON

PREFACE

OUR previous books in this series were Advanced Level Pure Mathematics and Advanced Level Applied Mathematics. Here we have
collaborated to produce a text suitable for students who are preparing
to offer the joint subject Pure and Applied Mathematics at the Advanced
Level of the General Certificate of Education. The material included
covers the syllabus laid down for this subject by the major examining
boards and is intended to be equally suitable for class work or private
study.

The inclusion of Pure and Applied Mathematics in a single volume
has enabled us to avoid some repetition. It has also made it possible
to knit the subjects more closely together. Thus, for example, vectors
treated at an early stage make the principles of Statics more readily
comprehensible and much of the subject matter of the chapters on the
Calculus paves the way for Dynamics.

The book contains more than 2000 worked examples and exercises
(with answers). Most of these have been taken from recent papers set
by the various examining bodies and our thanks for permission to use
these questions (and, in some cases, to adapt them to the metric
system) are due to the Senate of the University of London, the Joint
Matriculation Board and the Oxford and Cambridge Schools Examination Board. In the case of the worked examples, we wish to make it
clear that the examining boards are in no way committed to approval
of the solutions given.

C. J. TRANTER
C. G. LAMBE

PREFACE TO THE SECOND EDITION

In preparing this edition, the opportunity has been taken to amend
the text so that the units used are those of the Système International
d'Unités (SI). This system, in which the basic units of length, mass
and time are the metre, kilogramme and second has many advantages;
its use by schools, universities and industry is being actively encouraged
and it is, in the words of the Royal Society Conference of Editors on
Metrication in Scientific Journals, destined to become the universal
currency of science and commerce.

PREFACE TO THE THIRD EDITION

The chief alteration in this edition is the introduction of a short chapter on matrices. This would preferably follow Chapter 6 on vectors and complex numbers but for practical printing reasons it has had to be put at the end of the previous text as Chapter 22. The use of matrices in scientific and engineering work has grown rapidly in recent years and some knowledge of the subject is likely to be required in sixth form work in the future.

CONTENTS

1. **Indices and Logarithms. Quadratic Equations. The Remainder Theorem. Undetermined Coefficients**   13

   Introduction. Positive integral indices. Fractional, zero and negative indices. Logarithms. Common logarithms. Quadratic functions and quadratic equations. Equations leading to quadratic equations. Equations in which the unknown occurs as an index. The remainder theorem. Undetermined coefficients.

2. **Arithmetical and Geometrical Progressions. Permutations and Combinations. The Binomial Theorem. Partial Fractions**   34

   Introductory. Sequences and series. Arithmetical progressions. Geometrical progressions. Convergent geometrical progressions. Permutations and combinations. The formula $^{n+1}C_r = {}^nC_r + {}^nC_{r-1}$. Similar and repeated objects. Probability. The binomial theorem for a positive integral index. The binomial theorem for fractional and negative indices. Partial fractions.

3. **Addition Formulae. Trigonometrical Equations. Small Angles. The Inverse Notation**   62

   Introduction. Basic definitions and formulae. The addition formulae. Multiple angles. Trigonometrical ratios of A in terms of $\tan \frac{1}{2}A$. The transformation of $a \cos x + b \sin x$. The equation $a \cos x + b \sin x = c$. The factor formulae. Small angles. The inverse notation.

4. **Relations between the Sides and Angles of a Triangle. The Solution of Triangles**   84

   Introduction. The sine formula. The cosine formula. Some other formulae for the triangle. The numerical solution of triangles. Practical applications.

5. **The Coordinate Geometry of the Straight Line**   107

   Introduction. Coordinates. The relation between Cartesian and polar coordinates. The distance between two points. A proof of the addition formulae. The coordinates of a point which divides the join of two given points in a given ratio. The area of a triangle whose vertices have given coordinates. Loci. The points of intersection of loci. The equation of a straight line. The angle between two straight lines. Conditions for parallelism and perpendicularity. Perpendicular distance of a given point from a line. Equation of line passing through the intersection of two given lines. The determination of laws from experimental data.

6. **Vectors and Complex Numbers**   143

   Introductory. Definition of a vector. Addition of vectors. The sum of two vectors. Vector algebra. Components of a vector. Addition by components. The scalar product of two vectors. Vector quantities. Complex numbers. Algebra of complex numbers. Modulus and amplitude. Modulus and amplitude of products and quotients. The Argand diagram. The cube roots of unity. Real and imaginary parts of a function.

7. **The Differential Calculus** 166

Introduction. Functions and functional notation. The gradient of a graph. The increment notation. The derivative of a function. The differential coefficient of x^n. The differential coefficients of sin x and cos x. Technical processes in the differential calculus. The differential coefficient of a constant. The differential coefficient of a sum. The differential coefficients of a product. The differential coefficient of a quotient. The differential coefficient of tan x, cot x, sec x and cosec x. The differential coefficient of a function of a function. The differential coefficients of inverse functions. Table of standard forms. The differentiation of parametric and implicit functions. Second and higher derivatives.

8. **Some Applications of the Differential Calculus** 196

Introduction. The derivative as a rate measurer. Some mensuration formulae. Some applications from dynamics. Approximations. Maximum and minimum values. Applications to practical problems. Points of inflexion. Curve sketching.

9. **The Integral Calculus** 223

Introductory. Standard integrals. A more general list of standard integrals. Integration by change of variable. The integration of products of sines and cosines. Integration by parts. Area as the limit of a sum. The integral as the limiting value of a sum. The relation between the definite and indefinite integral. The example of § 9.7 solved by integration. Some examples of the evaluation of definite integrals and calculation of area. Definite integrals by change of variable. Numerical integration.

10. **Some Applications of the Integral Calculus** 259

Introduction. Further examples of the calculation of area. Mean values. Volumes of solids of revolution. Centres of gravity. Some further examples of centres of gravity. Moments of inertia. Some examples of the calculation of moments of inertia. Some applications from dynamics. Motion with constant acceleration.

11. **The Logarithmic and Exponential Functions. Expansions** 286

Introduction. The integral $\int x^{-1}\, dx$. Some further properties of the function $f(u)$. The logarithmic function. The exponential function. An integral depending on $\int x^{-1}\, dx$. The integration of rational algebraic fractions. Further examples of integration by parts. Successive approximations and the Taylor-Maclaurin theorem. Series for e^x and $\log_e(1 + x)$. Newton's method of approximation to the root of an equation.

12. **Elementary Differential Equations** 307

Introduction. Some definitions. First order equations with variables separable. Homogeneous equations. An important second order differential equation. Some applications to practical problems.

13. **Elementary Coordinate Geometry of the Circle, Parabola, Ellipse and Hyperbola** 325

Introduction. The equation of a circle. The tangent to a circle at a given point. The equation of a parabola. The parametric equations of a parabola. The equation of an ellipse. The parametric equations of an ellipse. The equation of a hyperbola. The parametric equations of a hyperbola. The rectangular hyperbola.

14. The Equilibrium of a Rigid Body 350
Applied mathematics. Force. Forces acting on a particle. Forces acting on a rigid body. Resultant of parallel forces. Moment of a force. Line of action of the resultant. Couples. Centre of parallel forces. Conditions for equilibrium of a rigid body. Triangle of forces. Lami's theorem.

15. Solution of some Problems in Statics 386
Types of problem. Equilibrium under the action of four or more forces. Elastic strings. Centres of gravity. Toppling problems. Laws of friction. Equilibrium on an inclined plane. Problems involving friction. Problems involving two bodies.

16. Motion in a Straight Line 414
Velocity and acceleration. Units of velocity and acceleration. Motion with constant acceleration. Graphical methods for constant acceleration. Differentiation of a graph. Integration of a graph. Types of graph. Explicit expressions for the acceleration.

17. Motion in a Plane 433
Relative motion and parabolic motion. Frames of reference. Resultant velocity. Relative velocity. Relative path. Components of velocity and acceleration. Parabolic motion. Equations governing the motion. Range and time. Vertex and remaining velocity. Projection from a height. Condition for a point to lie on the trajectory.

18. Newton's Laws. Power. Work. Energy 459
Newtonian mechanics. Newton's laws. Newton's second law. Units of force. Motion of a rigid body. The inclined plane. Motion of connected masses. Work done by a force. Work done in lifting a body. Work done by a couple. Power. Efficiency. Kinetic energy. Kinetic energy and power. Potential energy.

19. Impulse. Impact. Units 485
Introduction. Impulse and momentum. Collision of particles. Impact of water jets. Coefficient of restitution. Impact of a sphere on a smooth fixed surface. Direct impact of spheres. Loss of kinetic energy. Units and dimensions. Change of units.

20. Motion in a Circle 507
Introduction. Normal acceleration. Effective normal force. Reversed effective force. Conical pendulum. Vehicles moving in a circle. Banking. Circular motion with variable velocity. Motion in a vertical circle.

21. Simple Harmonic Motion. Motion about an Axis 531
Introduction. Simple harmonic motion. Other initial conditions. Relation to uniform motion in a circle. The simple pendulum. Forces causing simple harmonic motion. Suspension by an elastic string. Motion of a body about an axis. Kinetic energy. The energy equation. The compound pendulum. Wheel turned by a falling weight.

22. Matrices 557
Introduction. The product of two 2×2 matrices. The product of two 3×3 matrices. Some general definitions. Some particular matrices. Determinants. The inverse matrix. The decomposition of a matrix. The inverse of a unit diagonal matrix. Reduction of a system of equations. Alternative method of reduction of the system of equations. Matrices as transforms.

CONTENTS

Answers to the Exercises   579

Index   603

THE sources from which some of the examples and exercises have been taken are indicated by the following abbreviations:—

[L.U.] University of London;

[N.U.] Joint Matriculation Board of the Universities of Manchester, Liverpool, Leeds, Sheffield and Birmingham;

[O.C.] Oxford and Cambridge Schools Examination Board.

CHAPTER 1

INDICES AND LOGARITHMS; QUADRATIC EQUATIONS; THE REMAINDER THEOREM; UNDETERMINED COEFFICIENTS

1.1 Introduction

In this chapter we introduce some ideas which have been important in the development of mathematics. We start by defining a^m, where m is a positive whole number, and develop rules for writing down the product, quotient, etc., of two such quantities. We then discover meanings for a^m when m is negative, zero, or fractional. This is an example of the concept of *generalisation* from simple to more complicated ideas and is typical of much of the mathematician's work. We deal next with logarithms whose basic theory follows on naturally from what has preceded.

We then consider the solutions of algebraical equations of the second degree (quadratic equations). Whereas equations of the first degree have but one solution, the formula derived for the solution of a quadratic equation shows that, provided we extend our ideas on numbers to include those whose square is negative, there are now two solutions. Although we do not pursue this idea of number extension in this chapter, it provides another example of generalisation and will form the basis of a later treatment (see § 6.10) of the so-called complex numbers.

The remainder theorem is then discussed. This is again an example of a type of generalisation as it enables the remainder to be found when certain algebraical expressions are divided without the necessity of having to perform the actual division. The chapter concludes with the principle of undetermined coefficients; this is of great importance in many algebraical processes.

1.2 Positive integral indices

When a quantity a is multiplied by itself a number of times, the resulting product is said to be a *power* of a. For example, $a \times a$ is the second power of a and the result is written a^2. Similarly $a \times a \times a$ is the third power of a and is written a^3. In general, if m is a positive integer, a^m *denotes the product of m factors each equal to a* and the number m, expressing the power, is called the *index*.

There are three fundamental laws for the combination of indices; these relate to multiplication, division, and the power of a power and are given below for the cases in which the indices (m and n) are positive integers.

(i) $a^m \times a^n = a^{m+n}$. $\hspace{4cm}$ (1.1)

From the definitions of a^m and a^n,

$$a^m = a \times a \times a \times \ldots \text{ to } m \text{ factors,}$$

$$a^n = a \times a \times a \times \ldots \text{ to } n \text{ factors,}$$

so that

$$a^m \times a^n = a \times a \times a \times \ldots \text{ to } (m + n) \text{ factors}$$

$$= a^{m+n}.$$

(ii) $a^m \div a^n = a^{m-n}$. $\hspace{4cm}$ (1.2)

Here

$$a^m \div a^n = \frac{a \times a \times a \ldots \text{ to } m \text{ factors}}{a \times a \times a \ldots \text{ to } n \text{ factors}}.$$

Assuming that $m > n$, the n factors in the denominator will cancel with n of the m factors in the numerator leaving $(m - n)$ factors, so that

$$a^m \div a^n = a \times a \times a \times \ldots \text{ to } (m - n) \text{ factors}$$

$$= a^{m-n}.$$

(iii) $(a^m)^n = a^{mn}$. $\hspace{4cm}$ (1.3)

In this case,

$$(a^m)^n = a^m \times a^m \times a^m \times \ldots \text{ to } n \text{ factors,}$$

$$= a^{m+m+m+\ldots \text{ to } n \text{ terms}}, \text{ by (1.1),}$$

$$= a^{mn}.$$

Example 1. *If* $\{(a^4)^2 \times a^5\}/a^{11} = a^p$, *find* p. $\hspace{2cm}$ [L.U.]

$$\frac{(a^4)^2 \times a^5}{a^{11}} = \frac{a^8 \times a^5}{a^{11}} = \frac{a^{8+5}}{a^{11}} = a^{8+5-11} = a^2,$$

so that $p = 2$.

1.3 Fractional, zero, and negative indices

It is convenient to be able to work also with indices which are not positive integers and for one set of laws to apply in all cases. The definition of a^m as the product of m factors each equal to a is clearly meaningless unless m is a positive integer. However, we can define its meaning when m is fractional, zero, or negative in such a way that the first fundamental law $a^m \times a^n = a^{m+n}$ is obeyed. It is then possible to show that, with the interpretation so derived, the other two fundamental laws of § 1.2 remain valid [see Example 3 below in the case of the law (1.2)].

(i) *The interpretation of fractional indices.*

Suppose p and q are positive integers and that the rule (1.1) is to be true. Then $a^{p/q} \times a^{p/q} = a^{2p/q}$, $a^{p/q} \times a^{p/q} \times a^{p/q} = a^{3p/q}$ and so on. Hence

$$a^{p/q} \times a^{p/q} \times a^{p/q} \times \ldots \text{ to } q \text{ factors}$$
$$= a^{p/q+p/q+p/q+\cdots \text{ to } q \text{ terms}} = a^{p},$$

and this implies that $(a^{p/q})^q = a^p$ so that, taking the qth root,

$$a^{p/q} = \sqrt[q]{a^p}, \tag{1.4}$$

that is, $a^{p/q}$ is the qth root of a^p.

(ii) *The interpretation of a^0.*

Since the fundamental law $a^m \times a^n = a^{m+n}$ is to remain true,

$$a^m \times a^0 = a^{m+0} = a^m.$$

Division by a^m then gives, provided that a is not zero,

$$a^0 = 1, \tag{1.5}$$

that is, any non-zero quantity with zero index is equivalent to unity.

(iii) *The interpretation of negative indices.*

Since the law $a^m \times a^n = a^{m+n}$ is to be true for all values of m and n, we can write $n = -m$ to give

$$a^m \times a^{-m} = a^{m-m} = a^0 = 1, \text{ using (1.5)}.$$

Again assuming that a is not zero, division by a^m leads to

$$a^{-m} = \frac{1}{a^m}, \tag{1.6}$$

showing that a^{-m} is the reciprocal of a^m.

Example 2. *If $y = 27^{2/3}$ and $x = 3^{-4}$, find (without using tables) the value of xy^2.*
[L.U.]

$$y = 27^{2/3} = \sqrt[3]{(27)^2} = 3^2$$

and hence

$$xy^2 = 3^{-4} \times (3^2)^2 = \frac{1}{3^4} \times 3^4 = 1.$$

Example 3. *With the interpretation of a^{-n} as $1/a^n$, show that the law $a^m \div a^n = a^{m-n}$ remains valid when n is negative.*

$$a^m \div a^n = \frac{a^m}{a^n} = a^m \times \frac{1}{a^n}$$
$$= a^m \times a^{-n}$$
$$= a^{m-n}.$$

the last step resulting from the first of the fundamental laws, $-n$ being positive.

Exercises 1 (a)

1. Simplify the expressions

$$\text{(i) } \frac{(x^3)^2 y^4}{x^6 y}, \quad \text{(ii) } \frac{a^2 b}{c^3} \div abc, \quad \text{(iii) } 5 \times 4^{3n+1} - 20 \times 8^{2n}.$$

2. Write down, in their simplest forms

        (i) the square root of $36 \ x^2 y^4$,
        (ii) the cube root of $27 \ x^6 y^3$.

3. Express with positive indices

$$\text{(i) } \frac{2x^{-3}a^2}{9y^{-4}b^2}, \quad \text{(ii) } \frac{\sqrt[3]{(x^{-a})}}{\sqrt[3]{(a^2)}}.$$

4. Evaluate (i) $10^{3/2} \div 10^{-1/2}$, (ii) $(16^{1/4})^3$.

5. If $a = 25$ and $b = 9$, find the values of

$$\text{(i) } a^{1/2} - b^{1/2}, \quad \text{(ii) } (a-b)^{1/2}, \quad \text{(iii) } (b/a)^{1/2}.$$

6. If $x = 1 \cdot 44$, find the values of $x^{1/2}$, x^0, $x^{-1/2}$ and $(x^{1/2} - x^{-1/2}) \div x^{-1/2}$.

7. If $x^3 z = 1$, $x^2 = y$ and $z = y^n$, find the value of n.

8. If $8^{2x} = 64 \times 4^{3y}$, express x in terms of y.

9. Find the values of x if

$$\text{(i) } 2^x = 4, \quad \text{(ii) } 4^x = 2, \quad \text{(iii) } (\tfrac{1}{2})^x = \sqrt{2}.$$

10. Find the value of x satisfying the equation $8x^{-2/3} = 2/9$.   [O.C.]

11. If $64x^{-3/4} = a$, find the value of x when $a = 27$.

12. Prove that

$$\left(x - \frac{1}{x}\right)(x^{4/3} + x^{-2/3}) = x^{1/3}\left(x^2 - \frac{1}{x^2}\right).$$

13. Simplify

$$\text{(i) } (4a^{7/3} - 8a^{4/3} + 4a^{1/3}) \div (4a^{1/3}), \quad \text{(ii) } \frac{1}{1-x^2} - \frac{1}{x^{-2}-1}.$$

14. If $a^b = b^a$, show that $(a/b)^{a/b} = a^{(a-b)/b}$. If $b = 2a$, find the value of b.
                                                          [L.U.]

15. Show that

$$\left\{\left(\frac{x^{3/2}}{a^{5/3}}\right)^2 \div \left(\sqrt[3]{\frac{a^{-1}}{x^{-3}}}\right)\right\} + \left\{\frac{\sqrt{(a^2 - x^2)}}{a} \div \left(\frac{a^3 + a^2 x}{a - x}\right)^{1/2}\right\} = \frac{x^3 + a^3}{a^3(x + a)}.$$

1.4 Logarithms

The logarithm of a positive quantity n to a given *base* a is defined as the power to which the base a must be raised to make it equal to the quantity n. Thus if x is the logarithm of n to base a,

$$a^x = n, \tag{1.7}$$

and x is written

$$x = \log_a n. \tag{1.8}$$

The two formulae (1.7) and (1.8) are equivalent statements expressing the relation between x, n and a. Substituting for x from formula (1.8) in (1.7), we have

$$n = a^{\log_a n}, \tag{1.9}$$

and this formula will be useful in what follows.

Writing $x = 0$ in (1.7), we obtain $n = a^0 = 1$ and formula (1.8) gives, with these values of n and x,

$$\log_a 1 = 0, \tag{1.10}$$

showing that *the logarithm of unity to any base is zero*. If we write $x = 1$ in equation (1.7), $n = a$, and (1.8) then gives

$$\log_a a = 1, \tag{1.11}$$

so that *the logarithm of the base itself is unity*.

To find the logarithm of the product of two positive quantities m and n, we have, using (1.9),

$$mn = a^{\log_a m} \times a^{\log_a n} = a^{\log_a m + \log_a n}$$

Hence, by the definition of a logarithm,

$$\log_a (mn) = \log_a m + \log_a n \tag{1.12}$$

showing that *the logarithm of the product of two positive quantities is equal to the sum of the logarithms of the separate quantities*. Similarly, in the case of three quantities m, n, p,

$$\log_a (mnp) = \log_a m + \log_a n + \log_a p,$$

and so on when more quantities are involved.

The logarithm of a quotient can be found in a similar way. Thus, equation (1.9) gives

$$\frac{m}{n} = \frac{a^{\log_a m}}{a^{\log_a n}} = a^{\log_a m - \log_a n},$$

showing that

$$\log_a \left(\frac{m}{n}\right) = \log_a m - \log_a n, \tag{1.13}$$

that is, *the logarithm of a quotient is the difference between the logarithm of the numerator and the logarithm of the denominator.*

A similar method can also be used to obtain the logarithm of m raised to the power p. Thus, again using formula (1.9),

$$m^p = (a^{\log_a m})^p = a^{p \log_a m},$$

giving

$$\log_a (m^p) = p \log_a m. \tag{1.14}$$

If we write $p = 1/q$ in this result, it becomes

$$\log_a (m^{1/q}) = \frac{1}{q} \log_a m, \tag{1.15}$$

and these formulae show that (i) *the logarithm of the pth power of a positive quantity is p times the logarithm of the quantity* and (ii) *the logarithm of the qth root of a positive quantity is 1/q times the logarithm of the quantity.*

Example 4. *If $\log_a q = 5 + \log_a b$ and $c = a^4$, prove that $q = abc$.* [L.U.]

The first of the given relations can be written $\log_a q - \log_a b = 5$ and, by equation (1.13), this is equivalent to

$$\log_a \left(\frac{q}{b} \right) = 5.$$

By the definition of a logarithm we therefore have $q/b = a^5$ and this can be written $q = a^5 b = a \cdot b \cdot a^4$. Replacing a^4 by c, it follows that $q = abc$.

Example 5. *Simplify (i) $a^{\log_a x}$, (ii) $a^{-2 \log_a x}$.*

(i) Let $y = a^{\log_a x}$ so that $\log_a y = \log_a (a^{\log_a x}) = \log_a x \times \log_a a$, by (1.14). Since, by (1.11), $\log_a a = 1$, it follows that $\log_a y = \log_a x$ and hence that $y = x$.

(ii) Let $z = a^{-2 \log_a x}$ giving $\log_a z = \log_a (a^{-2 \log_a x}) = -2 \log_a x \times \log_a a$. Hence $\log_a z = -2 \log_a x = \log_a (x^{-2})$ and $z = x^{-2} = 1/x^2$.

Example 6. *Prove that $\log_b n = \dfrac{1}{\log_a b} \times \log_a n$.*

Let $x = \log_b n$ so that $b^x = n$. Taking logarithms to base a,

$$\log_a (b^x) = \log_a n,$$

giving

$$x \log_a b = \log_a n.$$

Hence

$$\log_b n = x = \frac{1}{\log_a b} \times \log_a n. \tag{1.16}$$

The result proved in this example is of importance in that it relates logarithms to different bases. It shows that to transform logarithms from base a to base b we have to multiply by $1/(\log_a b)$.

1.5 Common logarithms

The logarithms generally used in numerical calculations are those to base 10. Such logarithms are called *common* logarithms and the base is often omitted in written work—thus log 32 is usually taken to mean $\log_{10} 32$. The reader is assumed to be familiar with the use of common logarithms in arithmetical work and only very few examples will be given here. Further examples involving the use of common logarithms occur throughout the book.

Example 7. *Given that log 2 = 0·3010 and log 3 = 0·4771 find the values of (i) log 5, (ii) log $\sqrt[3]{(0·3)}$.*   [O.C.]

(i) $\log 5 = \log \left(\dfrac{10}{2}\right) = \log 10 - \log 2 = 1 - \log 2$ (since log 10 = 1)

$\qquad = 1 - 0·3010 = 0·6990.$

(ii) $\log \sqrt[3]{(0·3)} = \dfrac{1}{3} \log (0·3) = \dfrac{1}{3} \log \left(\dfrac{3}{10}\right) = \dfrac{1}{3}(\log 3 - \log 10)$

$\qquad = \dfrac{1}{3}(0·4771 - 1) = \dfrac{1}{3} \times -0·5229 = -0·1743$

$\qquad = \bar{1}·8257,$

the last form meaning $-1 + 0·8257$.

Example 8. *Given that log 5 = 0·6990, find the number of digits in the integral part of* $(\sqrt{5})^{21}$.

$$\log (\sqrt{5})^{21} = \frac{21}{2} \log 5 = \frac{21}{2} \times 0·6990 = 7·3395.$$

Thus 10 has to be raised to more than the seventh power to give $(\sqrt{5})^{21}$ and this quantity will therefore contain 8 digits in its integral part.

Exercises 1 (b)

1. Write down the values of $\log_2 16$ and $\log_8 2$.

2. Given that $\log_b a = c$ and $\log_c b = a$, prove that $\log_c a = ac$.   [O.C.]

3. Prove that (i) $\log_q p = \dfrac{1}{\log_p q}$, (ii) $\log_q p \,.\, \log_r q \,.\, \log_p r = 1$.   [O.C.]

4. Prove that $\log_a N \log_b M = \log_b N \log_a M$.

5. If $\log_x 10·24 = 2$, find x.   [L.U.]

6. Without using tables, find the value of

$$\log_2 \left(\frac{5}{3}\right) + \log_2 \left(\frac{6}{7}\right) - \log_2 \left(\frac{5}{28}\right).$$ [L.U.]

7. If $\log_8 n = \frac{1}{2}p$, $\log_2 2n = q$ and $q - p = 4$, find n.   [L.U.]

8. Evaluate 5^x where $x = \log (\log 10)$.   [O.C.]

9. Find, without using tables, the values of x if

    (i) $\log x - \log 3 = 1$,   (ii) $\log \sqrt{x} = \dfrac{3}{2}$,   (iii) $x = \log_6 216$.

10. Find the values of (i) $10^{3 \log 2}$ and (ii) $\log \left(\dfrac{35}{8}\right) + 4 \log 2 - \log 7$.

    [O.C.]

11. Given $\log 2 = 0{\cdot}3010300$ and $\log 3 = 0{\cdot}4771213$ find the value of $\log (2^{-1} + 3^{-1})$ to six places of decimals.   [O.C.]

12. If $\log y = 2 - \log (x^{2/3})$, express y as a function of x not involving logarithms; hence show that, if $x = 8$, then $y = 25$.   [O.C.]

13. Solve the equation $\log x + \log x^2 + \log x^3 = 1$.   [O.C.]

14. Given that $\log 3 = 0{\cdot}4771$, find the number of digits in front of the decimal point in $(\sqrt{3})^{20}$ and find the value of x for which $3^x = 100$.

15. Express $\log \dfrac{125}{128}$ and $\log \dfrac{625}{512}$ in terms of $\log 2$. Hence show that $\log 2$ lies between $3/10$ and $4/13$.   [L.U.]

1.6 Quadratic functions and quadratic equations

The general form of the quadratic equation is

$$ax^2 + bx + c = 0 \qquad (1.17)$$

where a, b, c are given numerical coefficients and x is the quantity whose value is to be determined. If the factors of the quadratic function on the left-hand side of equation (1.17) can be found, the values of x (the *roots* of the equation) are most easily obtained by setting each of the factors in turn equal to zero and solving the resulting simple equations.

Example 9. *Solve the equations* $2x^2 - x - 3 = 0$.

The factors of the left-hand side are $(2x - 3)$ and $(x + 1)$. Hence the equation can be written in the form

$$(2x - 3)(x + 1) = 0$$

so that *either* $2x - 3 = 0$ giving $x = 3/2$ *or* $x + 1 = 0$ leading to $x = -1$.

Example 10. *Solve the equation* $\dfrac{6x}{x - 2} - \dfrac{2x - 1}{x + 2} + \dfrac{19}{3} = 0$.   [O.C.]

Clearing of fractions by multiplying through by $3(x - 2)(x + 2)$, the equation becomes

$$18x(x + 2) - 3(x - 2)(2x - 1) + 19(x - 2)(x + 2) = 0,$$

and this reduces to $31x^2 + 51x - 82 = 0$. This can be written

$$(x - 1)(31x + 82) = 0$$

so that the two required roots are $x = 1$ and $x = -82/31$.

A similar method can be used to determine the range of values of x for which the quadratic function $ax^2 + bx + c$ takes a prescribed sign. This is illustrated in Example 11 below.

Example 11. *For what range of values of x is $3x^2 - x + 1 < x + 2$?*   [L.U.]

The given inequality becomes, by transposing the two terms from the right,

$$3x^2 - 2x - 1 < 0,$$

and this can be written

$$(3x + 1)(x - 1) < 0. \tag{1.18}$$

For this inequality to be satisfied, the left-hand side must be negative and therefore the factors $(3x + 1)$, $(x - 1)$ must be of opposite signs. The required range is given by $3x + 1 > 0$ and $x - 1 < 0$, that is, by $-1/3 < x < 1$. [The inequality (1.18) is also satisfied by $3x + 1 < 0$ and $x - 1 > 0$ leading to $x < -1/3$ and $x > 1$ but these are clearly inconsistent.]

A general formula for the roots of the quadratic equation

$$ax^2 + bx + c = 0$$

can be found as follows. Dividing by a and transposing the term not containing x to the right-hand side, the equation can be written

$$x^2 + \frac{b}{a}x = -\frac{c}{a},$$

and by adding the term $b^2/(4a^2)$ to each side we have

$$x^2 + \frac{b}{a}x + \frac{b^2}{4a^2} = \frac{b^2}{4a^2} - \frac{c}{a},$$

or

$$\left(x + \frac{b}{2a}\right)^2 = \frac{b^2 - 4ac}{4a^2}.$$

Taking the square root of each side,

$$x + \frac{b}{2a} = \pm \frac{\sqrt{(b^2 - 4ac)}}{2a},$$

giving the two roots

$$x = \frac{-b \pm \sqrt{(b^2 - 4ac)}}{2a}. \tag{1.19}$$

If $b^2 > 4ac$, the two roots are real and unequal, if $b^2 = 4ac$ the roots are real and both equal to $-b/(2a)$. If $b^2 < 4ac$, the expression under the square root sign in (1.19) is negative and, since there is no real quantity whose square is negative, the roots are in this case said to be unreal or imaginary (see § 6.10).

Example 12. *Solve the equation $4x^2 - 12x + 7 = 0$.*

Comparing the given equation with the standard form $ax^2 + bx + c = 0$, $a = 4$, $b = -12$, $c = 7$. With these values of a, b and c, formula (1.19) gives

$$x = \frac{-(-12) \pm \sqrt{\{(-12)^2 - 4(4)(7)\}}}{2(4)} = \frac{12 \pm \sqrt{(144 - 112)}}{8}$$

$$= \frac{12 \pm \sqrt{32}}{8} = \frac{12 \pm 4\sqrt{2}}{8} = \frac{3 \pm \sqrt{2}}{2}$$

giving $x = 2 \cdot 207$ or $0 \cdot 793$.

Example 13. *Find the values of λ for which the equation $x^2 - x + 1 = \lambda(x^2 + x + 1)$, where $\lambda \neq 1$, has equal roots and find, also, the range of values of λ for which the roots are real and unequal.* [L.U.]

Arranged in the standard form, the given equation is

$$(1 - \lambda)x^2 - (1 + \lambda)x + 1 - \lambda = 0,$$

so that $a = 1 - \lambda$, $b = -(1 + \lambda)$, $c = 1 - \lambda$. The condition for equal roots, ($b^2 = 4ac$) gives

$$\{-(1 + \lambda)\}^2 = 4(1 - \lambda)(1 - \lambda),$$

or

$$(1 + \lambda)^2 = 4(1 - \lambda)^2,$$

so that $1 + \lambda = \pm 2(1 - \lambda)$. The solution of these two linear equations gives $\lambda = \frac{1}{3}$ or 3 and these are the required values of λ for equal roots. For real and unequal roots the condition $b^2 > 4ac$ leads to

$$(1 + \lambda)^2 > 4(1 - \lambda)^2,$$

that is, after a little reduction

$$3\lambda^2 - 10\lambda + 3 < 0.$$

This can be written $(3\lambda - 1)(\lambda - 3) < 0$ and hence $(3\lambda - 1)$ and $(\lambda - 3)$ must be of opposite signs. Consistent values of λ are given by $3\lambda - 1 > 0$ and $\lambda - 3 < 0$ leading to $\frac{1}{3} < \lambda < 3$ as the required range.

It is useful to obtain formulae for the sum $\alpha + \beta$ and the product $\alpha\beta$ of the roots α and β of the standard quadratic equation $ax^2 + bx + c = 0$ in terms of the coefficients a, b and c. The equation can be written

$$x^2 + \frac{b}{a}x + \frac{c}{a} = 0, \tag{1.20}$$

and, since the roots are α and β, it can also be written in factor form as

$$(x - \alpha)(x - \beta) = 0.$$

This is equivalent to

$$x^2 - (\alpha + \beta)x + \alpha\beta = 0 \tag{1.21}$$

and, comparing equations (1.20) and (1.21), it follows that

$$\alpha + \beta = -\frac{b}{a}, \qquad \alpha\beta = \frac{c}{a}, \tag{1.22}$$

or, expressed in words,

$$\left. \begin{array}{l} \text{sum of roots} = -\dfrac{\text{coefficient of } x}{\text{coefficient of } x^2}, \\[2mm] \text{product of roots} = \dfrac{\text{coefficient of term independent of } x}{\text{coefficient of } x^2}. \end{array} \right\} \quad (1.23)$$

Example 14. *If α and β are the roots of the equation $px^2 + qx + r = 0$, find in terms of p, q and r, the values of $\alpha^2 + \beta^2$ and $\alpha^3 + \beta^3$.*   [L.U.]
From (1.23),

$$\alpha + \beta = -\frac{q}{p}, \quad \alpha\beta = \frac{r}{p}.$$

Hence,

$$\alpha^2 + \beta^2 = (\alpha + \beta)^2 - 2\alpha\beta = \left(-\frac{q}{p}\right)^2 - \frac{2r}{p} = \frac{q^2 - 2pr}{p^2},$$

$$\alpha^3 + \beta^3 = (\alpha + \beta)(\alpha^2 - \alpha\beta + \beta^2) = -\frac{q}{p}\left(\frac{q^2 - 2pr}{p^2} - \frac{r}{p}\right) = \frac{3pqr - q^3}{p^3}.$$

Example 15. *The roots of $ax^2 + bx + c = 0$, where none of the coefficients a, b or c is zero, are α and β. The roots of $a^2x^2 + b^2x + c^2 = 0$ are 2α and 2β. Show that the equation whose roots are $n\alpha$ and $n\beta$ is $x^2 + 2nx + 4n^2 = 0$.*
Applying (1.23) to the two given equations we have

$$\alpha + \beta = -\frac{b}{a}, \quad \alpha\beta = \frac{c}{a},$$

$$2\alpha + 2\beta = -\frac{b^2}{a^2}, \quad 4\alpha\beta = \frac{c^2}{a^2}.$$

Division of these pairs of relations gives

$$\frac{b}{a} = 2, \quad \frac{c}{a} = 4.$$

For the equation whose roots are $n\alpha$ and $n\beta$,

$$\text{sum of roots} = n\alpha + n\beta = n(\alpha + \beta) = -n\frac{b}{a} = -2n,$$

$$\text{product of roots} = n^2\alpha\beta = n^2\frac{c}{a} = 4n^2.$$

From (1.23), when the coefficient of x^2 is unity,

coefficient of $x = -$ sum of roots $= 2n$,
coefficient independent of $x = $ product of roots $= 4n^2$,

so that the equation with roots $n\alpha$ and $n\beta$ is $x^2 + 2nx + 4n^2 = 0$.

Exercises 1 (c)

1. Solve the equations (i) $x^2 - 5x + 6 = 0$, (ii) $3x^2 + 5x - 12 = 0$.

2. Solve the equations

    (i) $\dfrac{x}{3} = \dfrac{1}{4 - x}$, (ii) $\dfrac{3x}{x - 4} + \dfrac{x - 2}{x + 1} + 3 = 0$.

3. Solve the equation $\log_a (x^2 + 3) - \log_a x = 2 \log_a 2$. [O.C.]

4. Solve the equations, giving the roots to two places of decimals
$$\text{(i) } x^2 - 7x + 8 = 0, \text{ (ii) } 3x^2 - x - 3 = 0.$$

5. Solve the quadratic equations
$$\text{(i) } 21x^2 - 17x = 8, \text{ (ii) } 4x^2 - 12x + 9 = 0.$$

6. Find the values of k if the equation $x^2 + x + 3 = k(x^2 + 5)$ has equal roots. Find also the range of values of k if the equation has real and distinct roots. [O.C.]

7. Show that there are two values of k for which the equation

$$\frac{3}{x + 1} - \frac{4k}{x} + \frac{27}{x - 1} = 0$$

has equal roots in x. Show further that the roots corresponding to the two values of k are reciprocal. [L.U.]

8. Prove that the expression $3x^2 - x + 1$, where x is real, can take any assigned value which is not less than $11/12$. [L.U.]

9. Find the range, or ranges, of values of the constant k for which the equation $x^2 + kx + 2k = 3$ has real distinct roots. [N.U.]

10. If $(2x^2 + 1)y = 2(x + 1)^2$, prove that $0 \leqslant y \leqslant 3$ for all real values of x. [O.C.]

11. If α and β are the roots of the equation $3x^2 + 2 = 8x$, find the values of $\alpha^2 + \beta^2$ and $\alpha^{-1} + \beta^{-1}$. [L.U.]

12. Given that α and β are the roots of the equation $x^2 - px + q = 0$, form the equation whose roots are $(\alpha + \beta)^2$ and $(\alpha - \beta)^2$. [N.U.]

13. If the roots of the equation $x^2 - ax + b = 0$ are p and q, prove that the equation whose roots are $(p - 1)/q$ and $(q - 1)/p$ is

$$bx^2 + (a + 2b - a^2)x + 1 - a + b = 0.$$ [L.U.]

14. If p and q are the roots of the equation $2x^2 - x - 4 = 0$ find (i) the value of $p^3 + q^3$ and (ii) the equation whose roots are $p - (q/p)$ and $q - (p/q)$. [O.C.]

15. Prove that, if a, b and c are real and non-zero, then the roots of the equation $(b^2 + c^2)x^2 + 2(a^2 + b^2 + c^2)x + a^2 + b^2 = 0$ are real and distinct. If the sum and product of the roots are -6 and $2\frac{1}{3}$ respectively, prove that $a^2 = 6b^2 = 3c^2$. [O.C.]

1.7 Some equations leading to quadratic equations

The solution of some types of equation can be made to depend on that of a quadratic. A few of the devices used in such solutions are illustrated in the examples given below.

Example 16. *Solve the equation* $x^{1/3} - 3x^{-1/3} = 2$. [O.C.]

Writing $x = y^3$, the given equation becomes $y - (3/y) = 2$. Multiplication by y and a slight rearrangement gives $y^2 - 2y - 3 = 0$ and this can be written $(y - 3)(y + 1) = 0$, leading to $y = 3$ and -1. Hence, since $x = y^3$, the required values of x are 27 and -1.

Example 17. *Solve the equation* $(2x^2 - x)^2 - 9(2x^2 - x) + 18 = 0$. [O.C.]

Writing $2x^2 - x = y$, the equation besomes $y^2 - 9y + 18 = 0$, or

$$(y - 3)(y - 6) = 0.$$

Hence $y = 3$ or 6 and x is then found from the quadratics (i) $2x^2 - x = 3$, (ii) $2x^2 - x = 6$. The first of these can be written

$$(2x - 3)(x + 1) = 0$$

leading to $x = 3/2$, -1 while the second gives

$$(2x + 3)(x - 2) = 0$$

or $x = -3/2, 2$. Hence the required roots are $-1, 2, \pm 3/2$.

Example 18. *Solve the equations* $x - 3y + 5 = 0$, $x^2 + 4xy + y + 3 = 0$. [O.C.]

When one of a pair of simultaneous equations is of the first degree, either unknown quantity is easily expressed in terms of the other. Substitution in the second equation then results in a single equation in one unknown. For the pair given here, the first equation gives $y = \frac{1}{3}(x + 5)$. Substituting in the second equation,

$$x^2 + \frac{4x}{3}(x + 5) + \frac{1}{3}(x + 5) + 3 = 0.$$

Multiplication by 3 and a slight reduction gives $7x^2 + 21x + 14 = 0$ and this can be written $7(x + 1)(x + 2) = 0$ leading to $x = -1$ and -2. Since $y = \frac{1}{3}(x + 5)$, the corresponding values of y are 4/3 and 1.

Example 19. *Solve the simultaneous equations* $x^2 + xy + y^2 = 3$, $x^2 + 2xy + 2y^2 = 5$.

When the two equations are of the same degree and when the separate terms involving the unknowns are all of this degree, a solution can be found by writing $y = \lambda x$ and solving the resulting equation for λ as shown below. With $y = \lambda x$, the given equations can be written

$$x^2(1 + \lambda + \lambda^2) = 3, \quad x^2(1 + 2\lambda + 2\lambda^2) = 5,$$

and, by division,

$$\frac{1 + \lambda + \lambda^2}{1 + 2\lambda + 2\lambda^2} = \frac{3}{5}.$$

This reduces to $\lambda^2 + \lambda - 2 = 0$ giving $(\lambda - 1)(\lambda + 2) = 0$ and hence $\lambda = 1$ or -2. With the root $\lambda = 1$, $y = x$ and the first of the given equations gives $x^2 + x^2 + x^2 = 3$ so that $x = \pm 1$, $y = \pm 1$ is one pair of solutions. With $\lambda = -2$, $y = -2x$ and the first equation leads to $x^2 - 2x^2 + 4x^2 = 3$ giving $x = \pm 1$, $y = \mp 2$ as a second pair.

1.8 Equations in which the unknown occurs as an index

When the unknown quantity in an equation occurs as an index, the laws of combination of indices and the use of logarithms usually enable the solution to be found. Some examples follow.

Example 20. *Solve the equation* $3^{2x}2^{-x} = (2{\cdot}67)^{1/x}$. [O.C.]

Taking logarithms,

$$2x \log 3 - x \log 2 = \frac{1}{x} \log 2{\cdot}67,$$

giving

$$x^2 = \frac{\log 2{\cdot}67}{2 \log 3 - \log 2}$$

$$= \frac{0{\cdot}4265}{2 \times 0{\cdot}4771 - 0{\cdot}3010}$$

$$= \frac{0{\cdot}4265}{0{\cdot}6532},$$

No.	log
0·4265	$\bar{1}$·6299
0·6532	$\bar{1}$·8150
x^2	$\bar{1}$·8149
x	$\bar{1}$·9075

and $x = \pm 0{\cdot}808$.

Example 21. *Find the values of x satisfying the equation* $2^{x^2} = 256 \times 4^{-x}$.

Since $256 = 2^8$ and $4 = 2^2$, the equation can be written

$$2^{x^2} = 2^8 \times (2^2)^{-x} = 2^{8-2x}.$$

Hence $x^2 = 8 - 2x$ giving $x^2 + 2x - 8 = 0$, or $(x + 4)(x - 2) = 0$. The required values of x are therefore 2 and -4.

Example 22. *Solve the equation* $3^{2x} - 3^{x+1} + 2 = 0$.

This equation can be written

$$(3^x)^2 - 3(3^x) + 2 = 0,$$

which is equivalent to

$$(3^x - 1)(3^x - 2) = 0.$$

No.	log
0·3010	$\bar{1}$·4786
0·4771	$\bar{1}$·6768
x	$\bar{1}$·8000

Hence either $3^x = 1$ leading to $x = 0$ [by equation (1.5)], or $3^x = 2$. Taking logarithms this gives

$$x \log 3 = \log 2,$$

so that

$$x = \frac{\log 2}{\log 3} = \frac{0{\cdot}3010}{0{\cdot}4771} = 0{\cdot}631.$$

Exercises 1 (d)

1. Solve the equation $x^{1/3} - 4x^{-1/3} = 3$.

2. Find values of x satisfying the equation

$$(3x^2 + 2x)^2 - 9(3x^2 + 2x) + 8 = 0.$$

3. Solve the equation $x^2 + 2x - 2 = 3/(x^2 + 2x)$.

4. Solve the equation

$$3\sqrt{\left(\frac{x}{x-1}\right)} + 6\sqrt{\left(\frac{x-1}{x}\right)} = 11.$$

5. Find two values of x satisfying the equation
$$\sqrt{(3x+4)} = 3 + \sqrt{(x-3)}.$$

6. Solve the simultaneous equations
$$x + y + 4 = 0, \ x^2 + 3xy + y^2 + 5 = 0.$$

7. Solve the simultaneous equations
$$x^2 - xy = 10, \ 3x + 2y = 0. \hspace{2cm} \text{[L.U.]}$$

8. Solve the equations
$$\frac{x}{2} + \frac{2}{y} = 1, \quad xy - 3x = 4. \hspace{2cm} \text{[O.C.]}$$

9. Solve the equations
$$(x - 3y)^2 = 1, \ x^2 - 4y^2 + 3x = 24. \hspace{2cm} \text{[O.C.]}$$

10. Solve the equations $x + y = 72$, $x^{1/3} + y^{1/3} = 6$. \hspace{1cm} [L.U.]

11. Given that x and y have opposite signs, solve the simultaneous equations
$$x + y + xy = -5, \ x^2 + y^2 + x^2y^2 = 49. \hspace{1.5cm} \text{[N.U.]}$$

12. Solve the equation $5^{2x} = 7^{x+1}$.

13. Find the values of x satisfying the equation $3^{x^2+1} = 27/3^x$.

14. Solve the equation $5^{2x} - 5^{x+1} + 4 = 0$.

15. Find the values of x and y from the simultaneous equations
$$2^{x+y} = 6^y, \ 3^x = 3 \times 2^{y+1}.$$

1.9 The remainder theorem

A polynomial of degree n in x is an expression of the form

$$c_0 x^n + c_1 x^{n-1} + c_2 x^{n-2} + \ldots + c_{n-1} x + c_n$$

where $c_0, c_1, c_2, \ldots, c_{n-1}, c_n$ are constants. It is convenient to denote such an expression by $P(x)$, a notation which will later be generalised (see § 7.2). With this notation, $P(a)$ is used to denote the value of $P(x)$ when $x = a$, so that

$$P(a) = c_0 a^n + c_1 a^{n-1} + c_2 a^{n-2} + \ldots + c_{n-1} a + c_n.$$

The remainder theorem states that *if a polynomial in x is divided by $(x - a)$, the remainder is given by writing a for x in the polynomial.*

The proof is as follows. Let $P(x)$ be the given polynomial in x, let $Q(x)$ be the quotient when $P(x)$ is divided by $(x - a)$ and let R be the remainder. Then, for all values of x,

$$P(x) = (x - a)\, Q(x) + R,$$

and R is independent of x. Putting $x = a$, we have

$$P(a) = R,$$

since the first term on the right-hand side vanishes because of the factor $(x - a)$. Hence the remainder is obtained by writing a for x in $P(x)$.

This theorem enables the remainder to be found without actually having to perform the division. An immediate consequence of the theorem is that if $P(x)$ vanishes when $x = a$, then $(x - a)$ is a factor of $P(x)$.

Example 23. *Find the values of the constants a and b if $(x - 1)$ and $(3x - 1)$ are both factors of the polynomial $3x^4 + ax^3 - 6x^2 + bx - 1$.*

Here $P(x) = 3x^4 + ax^3 - 6x^2 + bx - 1$ and, if $(x - 1)$ is a factor, $P(1) = 0$, giving

$$3 + a - 6 + b - 1 = 0,$$

or

$$a + b = 4.$$

If $(3x - 1)$ is a factor, so is $3(x - \frac{1}{3})$ and hence $P(\frac{1}{3}) = 0$, giving

$$3(\tfrac{1}{3})^4 + a(\tfrac{1}{3})^3 - 6(\tfrac{1}{3})^2 + b(\tfrac{1}{3}) - 1 = 0,$$

or

$$\frac{a}{27} + \frac{b}{3} = 1 + \frac{6}{9} - \frac{3}{81} = \frac{44}{27}.$$

The solution of these simultaneous equations for a and b is easily found to be $a = -1$, $b = 5$ and these are the required values of the constants.

Example 24. *Find the factors of $ab(a - b) + bc(b - c) + ca(c - a)$.*

If we set $a = b$, the given expression vanishes; in other words, there is no remainder when the expression is divided by $(a - b)$. Hence $(a - b)$ is a factor and, similarly, so also are $(b - c)$, $(c - a)$. The given expression is of the third degree so that, besides the factors $(a - b)$, $(b - c)$ and $(c - a)$, there can be no further factors involving a, b or c. There may, however, be a numerical factor, say N, so we write

$$ab(a - b) + bc(b - c) + ca(c - a) = N(b - c)(c - a)(a - b).$$

To determine N we can give a, b and c any convenient numerical values. Choosing $a = 0$, $b = 1$, $c = 2$, the left-hand side becomes equal to -2 and the right-hand side to $2N$. Hence $2N = -2$ giving $N = -1$ and the required factors are $-(b - c)(c - a)(a - b)$.

Example 25. *The equations $x^2 + 9x + 2 = 0$ and $x^2 + kx + 5 = 0$ have a common root. Find the quadratic equation giving the two possible values of k.*
[L.U.]

If the common root is α, $(x - \alpha)$ will be a factor of both $x^2 + 9x + 2$ and $x^2 + kx + 5$. Hence $\alpha^2 + 9\alpha + 2 = 0$ and $\alpha^2 + k\alpha + 5 = 0$. By subtraction, $(9 - k)\alpha - 3 = 0$ giving $\alpha = 3/(9 - k)$. Substitution in the equation $\alpha^2 + 9\alpha + 2 = 0$ then leads to

$$\frac{9}{(9 - k)^2} + \frac{27}{9 - k} + 2 = 0,$$

and this reduces to $2k^2 - 63k + 414 = 0$ as the required quadratic equation for k.

1.10 The principle of undetermined coefficients

We start by showing that if a polynomial expression of degree n in x vanishes for more than n different values of x, the coefficients of each power of x in the expression are zero. We write

$$P(x) = c_0 x^n + c_1 x^{n-1} + c_2 x^{n-2} + \ldots + c_{n-1} x + c_n,$$

where $c_0, c_1, c_2, \ldots, c_n$ are the coefficients and suppose that $P(x) = 0$ when x is equal to each of the unequal values $\alpha_1, \alpha_2, \alpha_3, \ldots, \alpha_n$. Hence $(x - \alpha_1), (x - \alpha_2), (x - \alpha_3), \ldots, (x - \alpha_n)$ are all factors of the expression $P(x)$ and we can write

$$P(x) = c_0(x - \alpha_1)(x - \alpha_2)(x - \alpha_3) \ldots (x - \alpha_n).$$

Let β be another value of x such that $P(x) = 0$, then

$$c_0(\beta - \alpha_1)(\beta - \alpha_2)(\beta - \alpha_3) \ldots (\beta - \alpha_n) = 0,$$

and since none of the factors $(\beta - \alpha_1), (\beta - \alpha_2), (\beta - \alpha_3), \ldots, (\beta - \alpha_n)$ vanishes, it follows that $c_0 = 0$. The expression $P(x)$ now reduces to

$$P(x) = c_1 x^{n-1} + c_2 x^{n-2} + \ldots + c_{n-1} x + c_n,$$

and, since this vanishes for more than n values of x, it can be shown in the same way that $c_1 = 0$. In a similar way it can be shown that each of the coefficients $c_2, c_3, \ldots, c_n$ must also vanish.

We can now show that if two polynomials of degree n in x are equal for more than n values of x, the n coefficients in the one are equal to the corresponding n coefficients in the other. If we take the two polynomial expressions

$$c_0 x^n + c_1 x^{n-1} + c_2 x^{n-2} + \ldots + c_{n-1} x + c_n,$$

and

$$d_0 x^n + d_1 x^{n-1} + d_2 x^{n-2} + \ldots + d_{n-1} x + d_n,$$

as equal for more than n values of x, then the polynomial

$$(c_0 - d_0)x^n + (c_1 - d_1)x^{n-1} + (c_2 - d_2)x^{n-2} + \ldots + (c_{n-1} - d_{n-1})x + c_n - d_n$$

vanishes or more than n values of x and its n coefficients are zero.

Hence
$$c_0 - d_0 = 0, \; c_1 - d_1 = 0, \; c_2 - d_2 = 0, \ldots, c_{n-1} - d_{n-1} = 0,$$
$$c_n - d_n = 0,$$
leading to
$$c_0 = d_0, \; c_1 = d_1, \; c_2 = d_2, \ldots, c_{n-1} = d_{n-1}, \; c_n = d_n.$$

We have established above the important result that *if two polynomials in x are equal to each other for more than n values of x, we may equate the coefficients of the like powers of x*. This result is often called the *principle of undetermined coefficients* and has important applications. Some examples of its use are given below.

Example 26. *Find three constants A, B and C such that*
$$2x^2 - x + 1 \equiv A(x - 1)^2 + B(x - 1) + C.$$

The sign $\equiv$ is used to denote equality between two expressions for all values of the variable involved. When two expressions are separated by such a sign we can, by the principle of undetermined coefficients, equate the coefficients of like powers of the variable.
In this example,
$$\begin{aligned} 2x^2 - x + 1 &\equiv A(x - 1)^2 + B(x - 1) + C \\ &\equiv A(x^2 - 2x + 1) + B(x - 1) + C \\ &\equiv Ax^2 - (2A - B)x + A - B + C. \end{aligned}$$

Equating in turn the coefficients of x^2, x and the term independent of x,
$$A = 2, \; -(2A - B) = -1, \; A - B + C = 1.$$

The solution of these simultaneous equations is $A = 2$, $B = 3$, $C = 2$ and these are the required values of the constants.

Example 27. *If $x^3 + ax^2 + bx + c$ is a perfect cube, show that $ab = 9c$.*
Let $x^3 + ax^2 + bx + c \equiv (x + \lambda)^3$
$$= x^3 + 3\lambda x^2 + 3\lambda^2 x + \lambda^3.$$

Equating the coefficients of x^2, x and the term independent of x,
$$3\lambda = a, \; 3\lambda^2 = b, \; \lambda^3 = c.$$

From the first two of these relations $ab = 9\lambda^3$, and substituting for λ^3 from the third relation, we have $ab = 9c$.

Exercises 1 (e)

1. Find the value of the constant λ if the remainder is 22 when the expression $3x^3 + \lambda x^2 - 4x + 6$ is divided by $(x - 4)$.

2. Find the value of the constant p for which the polynomial $x^4 + x^3 + px^2 + 5x - 10$ has $(x + 2)$ as a factor.   [N.U.]

3. When $x^4 + 3x^3 + Ax^2 + Bx + 43$ is divided by $(x + 4)$, the remainder is 3; when it is divided by $(x - 3)$, the remainder is 10. Find A and B.   [O.C.]

4. Find the values of λ and μ if $(x - 1)$ and $(2x - 4)$ are factors of $2x^3 + \lambda x^2 + 4x + \mu$. What is then the third factor?

5. If $(x - 1)$ and $(x + 2)$ are factors of $bx^3 + cx^2 - 2x + 1$, find the values of b and c; find also the remaining factor. [O.C.]

6. When $x^2 + px + q$ is divided by $x - h$ the remainder is the same as when the quadratic expression is divided by $x - 2h$. Find two possible values of h. [L.U.]

7. Find the values of a and b if the expression $ax^3 + bx^2 - 28x + 15$ is exactly divisible by $(x + 3)$ and leaves a remainder -60 when it is divided by $(x - 3)$. When a and b have these values, find all the values of x for which the expression is zero. [O.C.]

8. Use the remainder theorem to find the factors of

$$(x - y)^3 + (y - z)^3 + (z - x)^3.$$

9. Express $x^3(y - z) + y^3(z - x) + z^3(x - y)$ as the product of four linear factors.

10. Show that the quadratic equations $x^2 + bx + c = 0$, $x^2 + Bx + C = 0$ have a common root if $(C - c)^2 = (B - b)(bC - Bc)$.

11. Prove that, if the equations $x^2 + ax + b = 0$ and $cx^2 + 2ax - 3b = 0$ have a common root and neither a nor b is zero, then

$$b = \frac{5a^2(c - 2)}{(c + 3)^2}.$$ [O.C.]

12. Find the values of the constants A, B and C when

$$x^2 \equiv A(x - 1)(x - 2) + B(x - 1) + C.$$ [O.C.]

13. If $x^3 + 3ax^2 + bx + c$ is a perfect cube, prove that $b^3 = 27c^2$.

14. Find values of A, B and C such that

$$\frac{9}{(x - 1)(x + 2)^2} \equiv \frac{A}{x - 1} + \frac{B}{x + 2} + \frac{C}{(x + 2)^2}.$$

15. Find the values of a and b which make the quartic expression

$$x^4 - 2x^3 + 3x^2 + ax + b$$

a perfect square.

Exercises 1 (f)

1. If $a = xy^{p-1}$, $b = xy^{q-1}$ and $c = xy^{r-1}$, show that $a^{q-r}b^{r-p}c^{p-q} = 1$.

2. If $a^x = b^y = c^z$ and $b^2 = ac$, show that $(x + z)y = 2xz$.

3. Show that

   (i) $\left(\dfrac{a^x}{a^y}\right)^{x+y} \times \left(\dfrac{a^y}{a^z}\right)^{y+z} \times \left(\dfrac{a^z}{a^x}\right)^{z+x} = 1$,

   (ii) $\left(\dfrac{x^a}{x^b}\right)^{a+b} \div \left(\dfrac{x^{a+b}}{x^{a-b}}\right)^{a^2/b} = \dfrac{1}{x^{a^2+b^2}}$

4. Find the value of x from the equation $81^{3/x} = 27$ and find also the values of x and y satisfying the simultaneous equations

$$\log x + \log y = 1, \; x + y = 11.$$

5. Solve the equation $21^x = 2^{x+1} \times 5^x$. [O.C.]

6. If $\log_a (1 + \tfrac{1}{8}) = l$, $\log_a (1 + \tfrac{1}{15}) = m$ and $\log_a (1 + \tfrac{1}{24}) = n$, show that

$$\log_a (1 + \tfrac{1}{80}) = l - m - n.$$ [L.U.]

7. If $(\log_4 x)^2 = \log_2 x \log_a x$, find the value of a.

8. If $y = 5(x + 2)/(x^2 + 5)$ prove that, for real values of x, $-\tfrac{1}{2} \leqslant y \leqslant 2\tfrac{1}{2}$. [O.C.]

9. Find the range of values of k for which the equation

$$\frac{3x - 1}{x(x + 1)} = k$$

   has real roots. [N.U.]

10. If the roots of the quadratic equation $x^2 - px + q = 0$ are k, $k + 1$, find the relation independent of k which must hold between p and q. If $q = 6$, find the possible values of k. [N.U.]

11. The roots of the equation $ax^2 + bx + c = 0$ are α and β. If $\alpha = 4\beta$, find the relation between a, b and c. Deduce that α and β are both real if a and c are of the same sign. [L.U.]

12. The roots of the equation $x^2 + ax + b = 0$ are α, β. Find the equation whose roots are $\lambda\alpha + \mu\beta$, $\mu\alpha + \lambda\beta$. If the original equation is $x^2 - 4x - 5 = 0$, find the values of λ/μ so that the new equation shall have one zero root.

13. Find the range of values of k for which the equation $x^2 + 7x - 2 + k(x^2 - 5x + 2) = 0$ has real roots. Find the roots in the case where they are equal. Find also the values of k for which the roots are (i) reciprocals, (ii) equal in magnitude but opposite in sign, showing that in case (ii) the roots are not real. [L.U.]

14. Verify that $x^2 + \dfrac{1}{x^2} = \left(x + \dfrac{1}{x}\right)^2 - 2$. Hence find the roots of the equation

$$3\left(x^2 + \frac{1}{x^2}\right) - 16\left(x + \frac{1}{x}\right) + 26 = 0.$$ [O.C.]

15. Solve the equations

(i) $2.2^{2x} - 9.2^x + 4 = 0$, (ii) $4^{x+1} - 5.2^x + 1 = 0$.   [O.C.]

16. Solve the equations

(i) $\log(x^2 + 6) = 1 + \log(x - 1)$, (ii) $\sqrt{(3x + 4)} = 3 + \sqrt{(x - 3)}$.   [O.C.]

17. Show that the equation $20x^4 + 48x^3 - 65x^2 - 72x + 45 = 0$ can be written

$$\frac{x}{2x^2 - 3} - \frac{2x^2 - 3}{x} = \frac{24}{5}.$$ [O.C.]

Hence find the four roots of the equation.

18. Solve the simultaneous equations

(i) $4x + y = 5$, $4x^2 + y^2 + 24x - 4y = 10$,

(ii) $\dfrac{x}{y + a} + \dfrac{y}{x + a} = 1$, $x + y = 2a$.   [L.U.]

19. Prove that, if the equations $x^2 + 2x + p = 0$ and $x^2 - 2qx + 1 = 0$ have a common root, then

$$(1 - p)^2 + 4(1 - p)(1 + q) + 4p(1 + q)^2 = 0$$

and hence show that, if $p = \dfrac{2}{3}$, then $q = \dfrac{-15 \pm \sqrt{3}}{12}$.   [O.C].

20. A polynomial $P(x)$ is divided by $x^2 - x$ and the remainder is $A + Bx$. Determine the constants A and B.   [N.U.]

21. If $(x - 1)$ and $(x + 2)$ are factors of $P(x) \equiv x^5 + bx^3 + 4x^2 + cx - 4$, find the values of b and c. Show that, with these values of b and c, $(x + 1)$ is also a factor of $P(x)$ and find the fourth factor.

22. Find the value of c which will make $2x^4 - x^3 - 11x^2 + cx - 3$ exactly divisible by $(x + 1)$. Show that, with this value of c, the above expression is exactly divisible by $(x + 1)^2$ and hence solve the equation $2x^4 - x^3 - 11x^2 + cx - 3 = 0$.   [O.C.]

23. When a polynomial is divided either by $ax - b$ or $bx - a$, where a is not equal to b, the remainders are equal and the quotients are $Q_1(x)$ and $Q_2(x)$ respectively. Show that $(ax - b)$ is a factor of $Q_2(x)$ and that $(x - 1)$ is a factor of $Q_1(x) + Q_2(x)$.   [N.U.]

24. If $x^3 + 5x^2 - 2x - b$ and $x^3 + 12x^2 - x - 2b$ have a common factor and $b \neq 0$, find the two alternative values of b.   [O.C.]

25. If $x^4 + ax^3 - 3x^2 - 2ax + a^2$ is a perfect square and has a factor $(x + 2)$, find a. When a has this value, obtain the square root of the expression in its factorised form.   [O.C.]

2

ARITHMETICAL AND GEOMETRICAL PROGRESSIONS;
PERMUTATIONS AND COMBINATIONS; THE BINOMIAL
THEOREM; PARTIAL FRACTIONS

2.1 Introductory

Series of numbers or powers of x, each term of which is derived from
the preceding one by a definite law, are important in mathematics.
They are, in fact, encountered in elementary arithmetic without being
recognised as such. For instance, when a fraction such as $\frac{1}{3}$ is put into
decimal form, it is written $0\cdot\dot{3}$ which is simply a short way of writing
$\frac{3}{10} + \frac{3}{100} + \frac{3}{1000} + \ldots$ and this is an example of one of the two very
simple series discussed in the first part of this chapter. Although the
above series is "unending," it represents precisely the number $\frac{1}{3}$ and this
representation leads to the ideas of limits and convergence touched on
in § 2.5. Such ideas are of great value in more advanced work.

Another important topic in modern mathematics is the theory of
probability and a few of the simplest ideas on which it is based are
introduced in §§ 2.6–2.9. We then go on to a famous formula, first
discovered by Newton, known as the binomial theorem. This formula
not only permits the full or expanded form of expressions like
$(2x + 5y)^{12}$ to be written down without actually performing the successive multiplications involved, but it also enables us to represent
expressions such as $\sqrt{(1 + x)}$ by a series of terms in ascending powers
of x.

The chapter ends with a brief description of the method of splitting
up an algebraical fraction into two or more simpler fractions. This
process is of use in work involving the binomial theorem and it will also
be found to be of great value in later work in the integral calculus.

2.2 Sequences and series

A set of numbers or algebraical expressions each of which can be
obtained from the preceding one by a definite law is called a *sequence*
or a *progression*. Each of the numbers or expressions forming the set
is called a *term* of the sequence. For example, the sets

(i) $1, 2, 3, 4, \ldots$ .. (ii) $x, x^2, x^3, x^4, \ldots$ .. (iii) $1, 4, 9, 16, \ldots$ ..

are all sequences.

It is possible to give a simple formula for the nth or *general* term of
each of the above sequences. Thus for (i) the nth term is n, for (ii) it
is x^n and for (iii) it is n^2. When a formula for the nth term of a sequence

is known, successive terms can be written down by giving successive integral values to n. Thus the sequence whose nth term is n^3 is 1, 8, 27, 64, . . . while that with nth term $\left(1 + \dfrac{1}{n}\right)^n$ is 2, $\tfrac{9}{4}$, $\tfrac{64}{27}$, $\tfrac{625}{256}$, . . ., these sequences being found by writing $n = 1, 2, 3, 4, . . .$ in the formula for the general term. When the terms of a sequence are linked together with signs of addition or subtraction, the resulting expression is known as a *series*. Thus

(i) $1 + 3 + 5 + . . . + 20 + 21$,
(ii) $x - x^2 + x^3 - . . .$,

are both series. The first series ends at the term 21 while the absence of a last term in (ii) indicates that it is "unending."

2.3 Arithmetical progressions

A sequence in which each term is obtained from the preceding one by adding or subtracting a constant quantity is called an *arithmetical progression*. Thus the sequences,

$$1, 3, 5, 7, . . .,$$
$$a, a + d, a + 2d, a + 3d, . . .,$$

are such progressions. The difference between each term and the preceding one is called the *common difference* of the progression and, in the above two examples, the common differences are respectively 2 and d. When three quantities are in arithmetical progression, the middle one is called the arithmetic mean of the other two. Thus a is the arithmetic mean of $a - d$ and $a + d$.

In the progression

$$a, a + d, a + 2d, a + 3d, . . ., \tag{2.1}$$

it will be noted that the coefficient multiplying d in each term is one less than the number of the term in the sequence. Thus $a + 3d$ is the fourth term and the nth term will be given by

$$n\text{th term} = a + (n - 1)d. \tag{2.2}$$

To obtain the sum s_n of n terms of the sequence (2.1), we have

$$s_n = a + (a + d) + (a + 2d) + . . . + (l - 2d) + (l - d) + l, \tag{2.3}$$

where l is the last or nth term and is given by (2.2) as

$$l = a + (n - 1)d. \tag{2.4}$$

If we now write the terms on the right-hand side of (2.3) in the reverse order,

$$s_n = l + (l - d) + (l - 2d) + . . . + (a + 2d) + (a + d) + a. \tag{2.5}$$

Adding (2.3) to (2.5) and noticing that the sums of terms in corresponding positions are all $(a + l)$,

$$2s_n = (a + l) + (a + l) + (a + l) + \ldots \text{ to } n \text{ terms}$$
$$= n(a + l).$$

Hence

$$s_n = \tfrac{1}{2}n(a + l) \tag{2.6}$$

$$= \tfrac{1}{2}n\{2a + (n - 1)d\}, \tag{2.7}$$

when we substitute the value of l given by equation (2.4).

Example 1. *Sum the sequence* 3, 5, 7, 9, . . . *to* 200 *terms.* [O.C.]

Here the common difference, found by subtracting successive terms, is 2 and the first term is 3. Hence $a = 3$, $d = 2$, $n = 200$ and formula (2.7) gives

$$s_{200} = \tfrac{200}{2}\{2 \times 3 + (200 - 1) \times 2\}$$
$$= 100(6 + 398) = 40400.$$

Example 2. *Find three numbers in arithmetical progression such that their sum is 15 and their product is 45.*

Let the required numbers be $a - d$, a and $a + d$. Then the sum of the numbers is $3a$ and, since this is 15, $a = 5$. The product of the three numbers is

$$(a - d)a(a + d) \text{ or } a(a^2 - d^2).$$

Hence

$$a(a^2 - d^2) = 45,$$

and, since $a = 5$, $5(25 - d^2) = 45$ leading to $25 - d^2 = 9$, $d^2 = 16$ and $d = \pm 4$. Hence the required numbers are 5 ∓ 4, 5 and 5 ± 4, that is, 1, 5 and 9.

Example 3. *A polygon has 25 sides, the lengths of which starting from the smallest side are in arithmetical progression. If the perimeter of the polygon is 1100 cm, and the length of the largest side is ten times that of the smallest, find the length of the smallest side and the common difference of the arithmetical progression.*
  [L.U.]

If the shortest side is a cm and the common difference of the progression is d cm, the largest side (which is the 25th) is of length $a + 24d$. Since this is 10 times the shortest side,

$$a + 24d = 10a$$

giving $9a = 24d$ or $d = 3a/8$. Since the perimeter of 1100 cm is the sum of all 25 sides, substitution of $s_{25} = 1100$ and $n = 25$ in equation (2.7) gives

$$\tfrac{25}{2}\{2a + (25 - 1)d\} = 1100.$$

Writing $d = 3a/8$ and making a few reductions,

$$2a + \left(24 \times \frac{3a}{8}\right) = \frac{1100 \times 2}{25},$$

leading to

$$11a = \frac{1100 \times 2}{25}.$$

Hence $a = 8$ cm and the common difference d, being $3a/8$, is 3 cm.

2.4 Geometrical progressions

When each term of a sequence is obtained from the preceding one by multiplying by a constant quantity, the sequence is said to be a *geometrical progression*. Examples of such sequences are

$$2, 4, 8, 16, \ldots,$$

and

$$a, ar, ar^2, ar^3, \ldots.$$

The ratio of each term to the preceding one is called the *common ratio* and, in the above examples, the common ratios are respectively 2 and r. When three quantities are in geometrical progression, the middle one is said to be the geometric mean of the other two. Thus a is the geometric mean of a/r and ar, and $\sqrt{(ab)}$ is the geometric mean of a and b.

In the geometrical progression

$$a, ar, ar^2, ar^3, \ldots, \tag{2.8}$$

the index of r in each term is one less than the number of the term in the sequence. For example, ar^3 is the fourth term and the nth term is given by

$$n\text{th term} = ar^{n-1}. \tag{2.9}$$

To obtain the sum s_n of n terms of the progression (2.8), we have

$$s_n = a + ar + ar^2 + \ldots + ar^{n-3} + ar^{n-2} + ar^{n-1},$$

and, multiplying throughout by r,

$$rs_n = ar + ar^2 + ar^3 + \ldots + ar^{n-2} + ar^{n-1} + ar^n.$$

If we subtract and notice that all the terms except the first and last cancel in pairs,

$$s_n - rs_n = a - ar^n,$$

giving

$$s_n = \frac{a(1 - r^n)}{1 - r} \tag{2.10}$$

as the required formula for s_n.

Example 4. *Find three numbers in geometrical progression such that their sum is 26 and their product is 216.*

Let the numbers be a/r, a and ar. Their product is a^3 and, since this is 216, $a^3 = 216$ giving $a = 6$. Since the sum of the numbers is 26 we have

$$\frac{6}{r} + 6 + 6r = 26$$

so that $6r^2 - 20r + 6 = 0$ or $3r^2 - 10r + 3 = 0$. This gives $(3r - 1)(r - 3) = 0$ so that $r = \frac{1}{3}$ or 3. The required numbers are therefore 6/3, 6 and 6 × 3, or 6 × 3, 6 and 6/3, and each set leads to 2, 6 and 18.

Example 5. *A geometrical progression has a for its first term. Find its common ratio if eight times the sum of six terms is equal to nine times the sum of three terms.*
[O.C.]

If r is the common ratio, formula (2.10) gives for the sums s_3 and s_6 of three and six terms respectively

$$s_3 = \frac{a(1 - r^3)}{1 - r}, \; s_6 = \frac{a(1 - r^6)}{1 - r} = \frac{a(1 - r^3)(1 + r^3)}{1 - r}.$$

Since these are in the ratio of 8 to 9,

$$1 + r^3 = \tfrac{9}{8}$$

leading to $r^3 = \tfrac{1}{8}$ and $r = \tfrac{1}{2}$.

Example 6. *Starting with a square of side 10 cm, a series of squares is constructed with the diagonal of each square equal to the side of the previous one. The areas of successive squares are denoted by A_1 (A_1 being 100 cm^2), A_2, A_3, ... Find the smallest value of n for which $A_n < 1$ cm^2.* [O.C.]

The length of the side of the second square is $10/\sqrt{2}$ cm, that of the third square is $10/(\sqrt{2})^2$ cm and so on, the length of the side of the nth square being $10/(\sqrt{2})^{n-1}$ cm. The area A_n of the nth square is therefore given by

$$A_n = \left\{ \frac{10}{(\sqrt{2})^{n-1}} \right\}^2 = \frac{100}{2^{n-1}}.$$

Since $2^6 = 64$ and $2^7 = 128$, A_n will be less than unity when $n - 1 = 7$, that is when $n = 8$.

Exercises 2 (a)

1. Write down the first three and the sixth terms of the sequences whose nth terms are

    (i) $3n - 2$,   (ii) 4^{n-1},   (iii) $(-1)^n$,   (iv) $\dfrac{n + 1}{n}$.

2. Find the sum of 65 terms of the progression 1, 2·1, 3·2, 4·3, ...   [O.C.]

3. Given that a and c are the first and third terms of an arithmetical progression, find the common difference and the sum of the first nine terms. [O.C.]

4. The second term of an arithmetical progression is -4 and the sixth term is -24. Find the fifteenth term and the sum of the first fifteen terms. [L.U.]

5. Find how many terms of the progression 5, 9, 13, 17, . . . have a sum of 2414. [O.C.]

6. Find an expression for the sum of the first n terms of the arithmetical progression 8, 11, 14, ... Find the value of n if this sum is 385. [O.C.]

7. The sum of the first eight terms of an arithmetical progression is 60 and the sum of the next six terms (from the ninth to the fourteenth) is 108. Find the first term and the common difference. [O.C.]

8. If a^{-1}, b^{-1}, c^{-1}, d^{-1} are in arithmetical progression, prove that $b = 2ac/(a + c)$ and find b/d in terms of a and c. [L.U.]

9. Prove that $\log x + \log(xy) + \log(xy^2) + \ldots$ is an arithmetical progression and show, without using tables, that when $x = 160$ and $y = \frac{1}{2}$, the sum of the first nine terms of the progression is 9. [O.C.]

10. Given that 27 is the fourth term of a geometrical progression whose first term is 8, find the common ratio and the seventh term. [O.C.]

11. Sum the series $2 + 6 + 18 + 54 + \ldots$ to thirty terms; by using logarithms, verify that this sum is greater than 2×10^{14}. [O.C.]

12. The sum of the first three terms of a geometrical progression is 38 and the fourth term exceeds the first by 19. Find the values of the first term and of the common ratio. [O.C.]

13. Given that $x - 2$, $x - 1$ and $3x - 5$ are three consecutive terms of a geometrical progression, find the possible values of x and of the common ratio of the progression. [O.C.]

14. In a geometrical progression of increasing positive terms, the sum of the first six terms is nine times the sum of the first three terms. Find the common ratio of the progression. [N.U.]

15. The first term of a geometrical progression is a and the nth term is b. Obtain the common ratio and express the product of the first n terms as simply as possible in terms of a, b and n. [N.U.]

16. The sum of three consecutive terms of a geometrical progression is 3·5 and the middle one of these terms is unity. Find the other two terms. [L.U.]

17. The first n terms of a geometrical progression are a_1, a_2, a_3, $\ldots$, a_n. Prove that its sum is $(a_2 a_n - a_1{}^2)/(a_2 - a_1)$.

18. Show that the arithmetic and geometric means between the two positive quantities a and b are respectively $\frac{1}{2}(a + b)$ and $\sqrt{(ab)}$. Deduce that the arithmetic mean is greater than the geometric mean.

19. Three unequal numbers a, b, c are such that $1/a$, $1/b$, $1/c$ are in arithmetical progression and a, c, b are in geometrical progression. Prove that b, a, c are in arithmetical progression. [L.U.]

20. A geometrical progression and an arithmetical progression have each a first term of 32 and each a sixth term of 243. Find the common ratio of the geometrical progression and the common difference of the arithmetical progression. The sum of six terms of the geometrical progression can be written $3^6 - 2^x$; find x. Find also the sum of eleven terms of the arithmetical progression. [O.C.]

2.5 Convergent geometrical progressions

The sums of two, three and four terms of the geometrical progression $1, \frac{1}{2}, \frac{1}{4}, \frac{1}{8}, \ldots$ are respectively $\frac{3}{2}, \frac{7}{4}, \frac{15}{8}$ and these differ from 2 by $\frac{1}{2}, \frac{1}{4}, \frac{1}{8}$. In other words the sum of two terms differs from 2 by the second term of the progression, the sum of three terms differs from 2 by the third term and the sum of four terms differs from 2 by the fourth term. Similarly it will be found that the sum to n terms differs from 2 by the nth term. As the terms of the above progression are clearly getting progressively smaller, we can conclude that the sum of n terms never exceeds 2, never reaches 2 but can be made as close to 2 as we wish by taking n to be sufficiently large. The value 2 is called the *limit of the sum* of the progression and series for which such a limit exists are said to be *convergent*.

If we consider the general geometrical progression $a, ar, ar^2, \ldots$ the sum s_n of n terms is given by equation (2.10) as

$$s_n = \frac{a(1 - r^n)}{1 - r}.$$

This can be written in the form

$$s_n = \frac{a}{1 - r} - \frac{ar^n}{1 - r} \tag{2.11}$$

and, if r lies between 0 and 1, the value of r^n decreases as n increases. As, for the moment, we are assuming that r is positive, r^n cannot be negative and hence must tend to some positive limit l as n increases. Since $r^{n+1} = r \times r^n$, r^{n+1} and r^n are both ultimately equal to l and we have $l = rl$, showing that as $r \neq 0$, l must be zero. It can be shown in a similar way that if r lies between -1 and 0, the limiting value of r^n is also zero. Hence, provided $-1 < r < 1$, the value of the term $ar^n/(1 - r)$ in equation (2.11) becomes closer and closer to zero as n increases and the limit of the sum of the progression, denoted by s, is given by

$$s = \frac{a}{1 - r}, \tag{2.12}$$

for we can make s_n as near to $a/(1 - r)$ as we please by making n sufficiently large.

The last paragraph can be summarised by saying that the geometrical progression $a, ar, ar^2, \ldots$ is convergent when $-1 < r < 1$ and that the limit s of its sum is given by $s = a/(1 - r)$. Rather loose expressions are often used in connection with convergent series. For instance the limit of the sum is sometimes called "the sum to infinity" and a convergent geometrical progression is often referred to as an "infinite" geometrical progression. Such expressions are open to objection and it is best to avoid their use as far as is possible.

When the common ratio r of a geometrical progression lies outside the range -1 to 1, there is no limit to the sum of the progression. Thus the sum of the progression 1, 3, 9, 27, . . . in which $r = 3$ becomes more and more unmanageable as more and more terms are included. In such cases, the series involved are said to be *divergent*.

Example 7. *Evaluate* $0\cdot\dot{3}$ *as a fraction.*

$0\cdot\dot{3}$ means $\frac{3}{10} + \frac{3}{100} + \frac{3}{1000} + \ldots$ and this can be written

$$\frac{3}{10}\left(1 + \frac{1}{10} + \frac{1}{10^2} + \ldots\right).$$

The series in the brackets is a convergent geometrical progression with first term unity and common ratio $\frac{1}{10}$. By (2.12) the limit of its sum is $1/(1 - \frac{1}{10})$ or $\frac{10}{9}$. Hence we have

$$0\cdot\dot{3} = \tfrac{3}{10} \times \tfrac{10}{9} = \tfrac{1}{3}.$$

Example 8. *The first term of a convergent geometrical progression is 3/5. A new series is formed by taking the square of each term and the limit of the sum of the new series is nine-tenths the limit of the sum of the first series. Find the common ratio of the first progression.* [N.U.]

If the common ratio of the first progression is r, that of the second will be r^2 and their respective first terms are 3/5 and 9/25. By (2.12), the limits of their sums are

$$\frac{3/5}{1 - r} \quad \text{and} \quad \frac{9/25}{1 - r^2}$$

and hence we have

$$\frac{9/25}{1 - r^2} = \frac{9}{10}\left(\frac{3/5}{1 - r}\right).$$

This reduces to $3(1 + r) = 2$ giving $r = -1/3$.

Exercises 2 (b)

1. The second and fourth terms of a convergent geometrical progression of positive terms are respectively 36 and 16. Find the first term of the progression and the limit of its sum.

2. The limit of the sum of convergent geometrical progression is 6 and the first term is 4. Find the fourth term and the sum of the first four terms.

3. By expressing $5\cdot2\dot{7}$ in the form of a series, show that it is equal to $5\frac{5}{18}$.

4. The limit of the sum of a convergent geometrical progression is m and the limit of the sum of the squares of its terms is n. Show that the first term of the progression is given by $2mn/(m^2 + n)$.

5. Show that the limit of the sum of the convergent geometrical progression whose first two terms are $\sqrt{3}/(\sqrt{3} + 1)$ and $\sqrt{3}/(\sqrt{3} + 3)$ is 3/2.

6. Find for what values of x the geometrical series

$$\text{(i)} \quad \frac{1}{1+x} - \frac{1-x}{(1+x)^2} + \frac{(1-x)^2}{(1+x)^3} - \cdots,$$

$$\text{(ii)} \quad \frac{1}{1+3x} + \frac{1+x}{(1+3x)^2} + \frac{(1+x)^2}{(1+3x)^3} + \cdots,$$

converge and prove that the limit of the sum of the first series is $\frac{1}{2}$.

7. The sum of the first two terms of a convergent geometrical progression is unity and the nth term is equal to twice the difference between the limit of the sum and the sum of n terms. Find the first term and the common ratio of the progression.

8. A convergent geometrical progression has a positive common ratio r. If the sum of the first n terms differs from the limit of the sum by less than 1 per cent., prove that $n \log (1/r) > 2$. If $r = \frac{1}{2}$, determine the least value of n satisfying this condition.   [L.U.]

9. The first three terms of a convergent geometrical progression are

$$\frac{1}{2-x}, \quad \frac{x}{(2-x)^2}, \quad \frac{x^2}{(2-x)^3}$$

where $-1 < x < 1$. Find the sum of all the other terms.   [L.U.]

10. The third term of a geometrical progression is equal to the sum of the first two terms. Find, in surd form, the possible values of the common ratio. If the first term of the progression is now taken to be 2, find in its simplest surd form, the limit of the sum of the progression in the case in which it is convergent.   [N.U.]

2.6 Permutations and combinations

Possible selections of groups of two letters from the four letters A, B, C and D are AB, AC, AD, BC, BD and CD. Each *selection* is called a *combination* and it is possible therefore to make 6 different combinations from four objects taken two at a time. If, however, we are concerned with the arrangements of the four letters A, B, C and D taken two at a time, these are

$$AB, AC, AD, BC, BD, CD,$$

$$BA, CA, DA, CB, DB, DC,$$

and there are therefore 12 such arrangements. Each *arrangement* is called a *permutation* and there are 12 different permutations from four objects taken two at a time. Thus in forming combinations only the number of objects contained in each selection is important, whereas in forming permutations, the order of the component objects also has to be considered.

We now obtain a formula giving the number of permutations which can be made from n dissimilar objects taken r at a time. Here we have to fill r places from n objects and the first place can clearly be filled in n ways. When the first place has been filled, the second place can be filled in $(n - 1)$ ways for now we have only $(n - 1)$ objects with which to fill it. Each way of filling the first place can be associated with each way of filling the second so that there are $n(n - 1)$ ways of filling the first two places. Proceeding in this way, the first three places can be filled in $n(n - 1)(n - 2)$ ways and the r places in

$$n(n - 1)(n - 2) \ldots (n - r + 1)$$

ways. A convenient notation for the number of permutations of n objects taken r at a time is ^nP_r and hence

$$^nP_r = n(n - 1)(n - 2) \ldots (n - r + 1) \tag{2.13}$$

the number of factors being r (the number in the suffix of the symbol ^nP_r). The number of permutations of n objects taken all at a time, or the number of arrangements of n objects among themselves, is given, on writing $r = n$ by

$$^nP_n = n(n - 1)(n - 2) \ldots 3.2.1,$$

there now being n factors. The product $n(n - 1)(n - 2) \ldots 3.2.1$ is called "factorial n" and written $(n)!$, or sometimes, $\lfloor n$.

To find the number of combinations which can be made from n dissimilar objects taken r at a time, let ^nC_r (a notation similar to that of ^nP_r) be the required number. Each of these ^nC_r combinations consists of a selection of r objects which can be arranged among themselves in ^rP_r or $(r)!$ ways. Hence the product of $(r)!$ and ^nC_r is the total number of arrangements ^nP_r of n objects taken r at a time, so that

$$(r)! \times {}^nC_r = {}^nP_r$$
$$= n(n - 1)(n - 2) \ldots (n - r + 1)$$

giving

$$^nC_r = \frac{n(n - 1)(n - 2) \ldots (n - r + 1)}{(r)!}. \tag{2.14}$$

An alternative formula for ^nC_r can be obtained by multiplying the numerator and denominator of the right-hand side of (2.14) by $(n - r)!$. Since $(n - r)! = (n - r)(n - r - 1) \ldots 3.2.1$, the numerator will now contain all the numbers n, $(n - 1)$, $(n - 2)$, $\ldots$ down to unity and will therefore be $(n)!$. Hence

$$^nC_r = \frac{(n)!}{(r)!(n - r)!}. \tag{2.15}$$

Example 9. *How many different arrangements can be made by taking (i) five, (ii) all, of the letters of the word* numbers *?*

(i) Here we require the number of permutations of 7 letters taken 5 at a time. This is

$$^7P_5 = 7 \times 6 \times 5 \times 4 \times 3 = 2520.$$

(ii) In this case we require the number of permutations of 7 letters taken 7 at a time, that is,

$$^7P_7 = (7)! = 7 \times 6 \times 5 \times 4 \times 3 \times 2 \times 1 = 5040.$$

Example 10. *A sub-committee of five, including a chairman, is to be chosen from a main committee of ten members. If the chairman is to be a specified member of the main committee, in how many ways can this be done?*

As the specified member of the main committee always has to be included, we have to find the number of ways in which selections of 4 can be made from the remaining 9. This is $^9C_4$ and, using (2.14), the required number is

$$\frac{9 \times 8 \times 7 \times 6}{4 \times 3 \times 2 \times 1} = 126.$$

2.7 The formula $^{n+1}C_r = {}^nC_r + {}^nC_{r-1}$

The method of Example 10 above can be used to obtain a formula which will be required later in this chapter (§ 2.10). Suppose we have $(n + 1)$ objects; the number of selections from these objects taken r at a time such that a specified object is always *excluded* is ^nC_r for we have to make selections of r objects from only n. The number of selections taken r at a time such that a specified object is always *included* is $^nC_{r-1}$ for now we have to select from n objects for the remaining $(r - 1)$ places in each selection. The sum of ^nC_r and $^nC_{r-1}$ will therefore give the number of selections with the specified object excluded *and* included and this is $^{n+1}C_r$, the number of selections taken r at a time from $(n + 1)$ objects. Hence

$$^{n+1}C_r = {}^nC_r + {}^nC_{r-1}. \tag{2.16}$$

This formula can also be obtained by substituting (2.15) and the corresponding result when r is replaced by $r - 1$ in the right-hand side and showing that this reduces to (2.15) with $n + 1$ replacing n. The details are left as an exercise for the reader.

2.8 Similar and repeated objects

So far it has been assumed that the objects of which arrangements have been made or from which selections have been taken are all dissimilar. Formulae for the number of permutations or combinations when the objects are not all dissimilar are rather complicated and such cases are probably best treated on their merits. Some examples are given in the following paragraphs.

To find the number of permutations of n objects taken all at a time when p of the objects are exactly alike, let x be the required number.

Then if the p like objects were replaced by p dissimilar objects (different from the remaining $(n - p)$ objects), from any one of the x permutations we could form $(p)!$ new permutations without altering the position of any of the remaining objects. If this change were made in each of the x arrangements, we should obtain $x \times (p)!$ permutations. With this change, the objects are all different and can be arranged among themselves in $(n)!$ ways, so that

$$x \times (p)! = (n)!$$

giving

$$x = \frac{(n)!}{(p)!}. \tag{2.17}$$

Similarly the number of permutations of n objects taken all at a time when p are alike of one kind, q alike of a second kind, r alike of a third kind and so on is

$$\frac{(n)!}{(p)!(q)!(r)! \ldots}.$$

Example 11. *How many different arrangements of letters can be made by using all the letters of the word* algebra? *In how many of these arrangements will the* a's *be separated by at least one other letter?*

Here we have 7 letters of which two are similar. The required number of arrangements is therefore, by (2.17),

$$\frac{(7)!}{(2)!} = \frac{7 \times 6 \times 5 \times 4 \times 3 \times 2 \times 1}{2 \times 1} = 2520.$$

If we treat the two a's as one letter, the number of arrangements in which the a's are together is

$$(6)! = 6 \times 5 \times 4 \times 3 \times 2 \times 1 = 720.$$

The number of arrangments in which the a's are separated is the difference, $2520 - 720$, or 1800.

Sometimes the number of arrangements of n objects taken r at a time is required when each object may be repeated up to r times in any arrangement. Here, the first place may be filled in n ways and, when it has been filled, the second place may also be filled in n ways for we are allowed, if we wish, to use the same object again. The first two places can therefore be filled in $n \times n$ or n^2 ways. Similarly the first three places can be filled in n^3 ways and so on. The total number of arrangements is therefore n^r.

Example 12. *How many entries must be made in a football pool of eight matches to ensure a correct forecast?*

The result of each match may be a home win, an away win or a draw so that a forecast of the result of the first match can be made in three ways. The result of the second match can similarly be entered in three ways so that, to cover all possibilities, the first two matches will require 3^2 entries. For the first three matches, 3^3 entries will be necessary and so on. Hence for all eight matches, the number of entries required to ensure a correct forecast will be 3^8 or 6561.

2.9 Probability

The probability of an event in a single trial is defined as its relative frequency in a large number of trials. If a coin is tossed 1000 times, we would expect it to fall head upwards about 500 times and tail upwards about 500 times giving a relative frequency of heads of about 500/1000, or $\frac{1}{2}$, and we say that the chance of a head in a single trial is $\frac{1}{2}$. The theory of probability is based on the axiom that, as the number of trials increases, the relative frequency of an event tends to a limit and this limit may often be deduced by considering the nature of the event. Thus we can see no reason why the limit of the relative frequency of heads when a coin is tossed should be anything but $\frac{1}{2}$. Similarly if a symmetrical six-sided die shows the numbers 1 to 6, there is no reason why the relative frequency of one number should be greater than that of another—in (say) 6000 trials we would expect each number to turn up about 1000 times giving a limiting relative frequency forecast of $\frac{1}{6}$.

If an event occurs m times in a large number $(m + n)$ trials, the probability p of it occurring in a single trial is given by the limiting value of $m/(m + n)$ when m and n become large. Similarly the chance q of it not occurring is the limiting value of $n/(m + n)$, so that $p + q = 1$ and $q = 1 - p$. Probabilities therefore range between 0 and 1, 0 indicating impossibility and 1 certainty. Sometimes percentages are used in this connection, a two per cent. chance meaning a probability of two in a hundred. If the chances for and against an event are p and q, the *odds* for and against are respectively p to q and q to p. Thus odds of 5 to 2 against an event happening implies that the probability of it occurring is 2/7 and of it not occurring is 5/7.

If the probability of an event occurring is p and that of another independent event occurring is p', the probability of both occurring is pp'. The probability of the first occurring and of the second not occurring is $p(1 - p')$, that of the second occurring and not the first is $(1 - p)p'$, while the probability of neither occurring is $(1 - p)(1 - p')$. All these results follow directly from the definition of probability.

Example 13. *Find the probability that a hand of thirteen cards dealt from a pack shall contain only black cards.*

The number of possible hands is $^{52}C_{13}$ and the number of favourable hands is $^{26}C_{13}$, for selections of 13 cards have to be made only from the 26 black cards in the case of the favourable hands. The required probability is therefore

$$^{26}C_{13}/^{52}C_{13} = 1/61055, \text{ approximately.}$$

(a) Success at the second throw only implies failure at the first and hence the
required chance $= (1 - p)p' = (1 - \frac{1}{9}) \times \frac{1}{9} = \frac{8}{81}$.

(b) The chance for failure at both throws

$$= (1 - p)(1 - p') = (1 - \frac{1}{9})(1 - \frac{1}{9}) = \frac{64}{81}.$$

Exercises 2 (c)

1. How many different four-digit numbers can be made from the digits
6, 4, 2, 7 and how many of these will be between 2000 and 3000?

2. In how many ways can a team of eleven players be picked from fourteen
possible players?

3. In how many ways can three prizes be distributed to six candidates when
each candidate can have all the prizes?

4. Find the number of different arrangements of eight letters that can be
formed from the letters of the word *nineteen*.   [L.U.]

5. Seven men volunteer to dig a trench. Find the number of ways in which
some or all of the men may be chosen for the job.   [L.U.]

6. In how many ways can a car registration number be made by arranging
the letters A, M, S and the figures 4, 4, 1 if the letters and figures must
each occur in groups of three.

7. How many numbers of four digits can be formed from the digits 1, 2,
3, 4 when each digit can be repeated four times. Calculate the sum of all
these numbers.   [L.U.]

8. There are six boys and twelve girls at a party. If each boy dances with a
girl, in how many different ways may the six mixed couples be selected?
If the remaining six girls also join the dance in pairs, find also the
number of different ways in which the nine couples can be selected.
                                                                      [L.U.]

9. Find how many different numbers can be formed with the digits 0, 1, 2,
2, 2, 3, 3, 4, each number containing eight digits and not beginning with
0. Find also how many of these numbers are odd.   [L.U.]

Example 14. *Show that the chance of scoring a total of 9 in a single throw with two
ordinary dice is 1/9. If, in attempting to score 9 in a single throw, two throws are
made (each with two dice), find the chance of* (a) *succeeding at the second throw
only,* (b) *failing at both throws.*   [L.U.]
The total number of combinations of numbers which can be thrown with two
dice is 36, for any one of six different numbers can be thrown with each dice.
The only combinations which give a total of 9 are $4 + 5$, $5 + 4$, $3 + 6$, $6 + 3$
and the number of favourable combinations is 4. Hence the required chance
$p = 4/36 = 1/9$.
If p and p' are respectively the chances of throwing a total of 9 in the first and
second throws, $p = p' = 1/9$.

10. The odds against a student solving a certain problem are 4 to 3 and the odds in favour of a second student solving the same problem are 7 to 5. Find the chance that the problem will be solved if both students attempt it.

11. A box of ten radio valves are all apparently sound although four of them are actually substandard. Find the chance that, if two valves are taken from the box together, they are both substandard.   [N.U.]

12. When three marksmen take part in a shooting contest, their chances of hitting the target are $\frac{1}{2}$, $\frac{1}{3}$ and $\frac{1}{4}$. Calculate the chance that one, and only one, bullet will hit the target if all three men fire at it simultaneously.   [N.U.]

13. Five books on mathematics and four books on physics stand in a row. Find the probability that there will be a mathematics book at each end of the row.

14. A committee of four is to be chosen from a number of people, of whom two are women. If the probability of both women being on the committee is twice that of neither being on it, find the number of people available. Find also the probability of only one woman being on the committee.   [L.U.]

15. Smith and Brown are two of eight men who seat themselves in a railway carriage, four men sitting on each side. What is the chance that they will be seated next to one another?   [L.U.]

2.10 The binomial theorem for a positive integral index

The binomial theorem gives the expansion in a series of ascending powers of x of the two-termed or *binomial* expression $(1 + x)$ when this expression is raised to the nth power. We start by giving the results, which can easily be verified by actual multiplication, for the cases when the index n takes the positive integral values 2, 3 and 4. These are

$$\left.\begin{aligned}
(1 + x)^2 &= 1 + 2x + x^2 = 1 + \frac{2}{1}x + x^2, \\[2mm]
(1 + x)^3 &= 1 + 3x + 3x^2 + x^3 = 1 + \frac{3}{1}x + \frac{3.2}{1.2}x^2 + x^3, \\[2mm]
(1 + x)^4 &= 1 + 4x + 6x^2 + 4x^3 + x^4 \\[2mm]
&= 1 + \frac{4}{1}x + \frac{4.3}{1.2}x^2 + \frac{4.3.2}{1.2.3}x^3 + x^4.
\end{aligned}\right\} \quad (2.18)$$

The reason for the apparently complicated way in which the coefficients of the various powers of x have been written in the final expressions on the right of (2.18) is that this enables a forecast to be made for the coefficients in the expansion of $(1 + x)^n$ when n is *any* positive integer.

By inspecting (2.18), it can be seen that

(i) the indices of x in the various terms on the right successively increase by unity, the index of the last term being the same as the power to which $(1 + x)$ is raised,

(ii) the first term and the coefficient of the last term are each unity; those of the other terms are, in the notation of equation (2.14), $^2C_1$ in the expression for $(1 + x)^2$, $^3C_1$ and $^3C_2$ in those of $(1 + x)^3$ and $^4C_1$, $^4C_2$, $^4C_3$ in those of $(1 + x)^4$.

This suggests that the result for any positive integral value for the index n will be

$$(1 + x)^n = 1 + {}^nC_1x + {}^nC_2x^2 + \ldots + {}^nC_rx^r + \ldots + x^n.$$
(2.19)

Assuming that the result (2.19) is valid, multiplication by $(1 + x)$ and collection of the terms in like powers of x gives

$$(1 + x)^{n+1} = 1 + ({}^nC_1 + 1)x + ({}^nC_2 + {}^nC_1)x^2 + \ldots$$
$$+ ({}^nC_r + {}^nC_{r-1})x^r + \ldots + x^{n+1}.$$

Since, by equation (2.16), $^nC_1 + 1 = {}^{n+1}C_1$ and $^nC_r + {}^nC_{r-1} = {}^{n+1}C_r$, this can be written

$$(1 + x)^{n+1} = 1 + {}^{n+1}C_1x + {}^{n+1}C_2x^2 + \ldots + {}^{n+1}C_rx^r + \ldots + x^{n+1}.$$
(2.20)

Hence if the assumption made in (2.19) is true for a positive integral index n, equation (2.20) shows that it is true also when n is increased to $n + 1$. But we know from (2.18) that the assumption is true when $n = 2$, 3 and 4, and hence we can infer it is true also when $n = 5$, therefore it is true when $n = 6$, and so on. Hence the result (2.19) is true for any positive integer n. This method of establishing the truth of the theorem contained in (2.19) is known as proof by *induction* and is a powerful method used in many branches of mathematics.

If the expansion of $(a + x)^n$ is required, we can write

$$(a + x)^n = a^n \left(1 + \frac{x}{a}\right)^n$$

$$= a^n \left(1 + {}^nC_1\frac{x}{a} + {}^nC_2\frac{x^2}{a^2} + \ldots + {}^nC_r\frac{x^r}{a^r} + \ldots + \frac{x^n}{a^n}\right)$$

$$= a^n + {}^nC_1 a^{n-1}x + {}^nC_2a^{n-2}x^2 + \ldots$$
$$+ {}^nC_ra^{n-r}x^r + \ldots + x^n.$$
(2.21)

The numerical coefficients in the binomial expansion are conveniently given by the following table (*Pascal's arithmetical triangle*)

Index	Coefficients
1	1 1
2	1 2 1
3	1 3 3 1
4	1 4 6 4 1
5	1 5 10 10 5 1
6	1 6 15 20 15 6 1
. . .	. . . .

The first and last entries in each line of coefficients are unity and the other entries are formed by summing the one immediately above that required and the next entry on the left. Thus the first of the entries 10 in the fifth line is the sum of 6 and 4 and so on. The coefficients in the expansion of $(1 + x)^7$ are therefore obtained from the last line given in the above table as 1, 7, 21, 35, 35, 21, 7, 1 and, when these are available, the coefficients in the expansion of $(1 + x)^8$ can be found in a similar way.

Example 15. *Expand $(c + 2y)^5$ by the binomial theorem and apply your result to evaluate $(1·02)^5$ correct to 4 places of decimals.*

Writing c for a, $2y$ for x and taking $n = 5$, equation (2.21) gives

$$(c + 2y)^5 = c^5 + 5c^4(2y) + 10c^3(2y)^2 + 10c^2(2y)^3 + 5c(2y)^4 + (2y)^5,$$

the coefficients 5, 10, 10, 5 being taken from Pascal's triangle (or calculated from the formulae for ^5C_r, $r = 1, 2, 3, 4$). This reduces to

$$(c + 2y)^5 = c^5 + 10c^4y + 40c^3y^2 + 80c^2y^3 + 80cy^4 + 32y^5.$$

Taking $c = 1$, $y = 10^{-2}$, $c + 2y = 1·02$ and hence

$$(1·02)^5 = 1 + 10 \times 10^{-2} + 40 \times 10^{-4} + 80 \times 10^{-6} + 80 \times 10^{-8} + 32 \times 10^{-10}$$

$$= 1·000000 + 0·100000 + 0·004000 + 0·000080 + \ldots$$

$$= 1·104080 = 1·1041 \text{ (to four places).}$$

Example 16. *If the first three terms in the expansion of $(1 + x)^p(1 - x)^q$, where p and q are positive integers, are $1 + 3x - 6x^2$, find the values of p and q.* [L.U.]

Equation (2.19) gives directly

$$(1 + x)^p = 1 + px + \tfrac{1}{2}p(p - 1)x^2 + \ldots,$$

while, replacing p by q and x by $-x$,

$$(1 - x)^q = 1 - qx + \tfrac{1}{2}q(q - 1)x^2 + \ldots$$

Multiplying these results,

$$(1 + x)^p(1 - x)^q = 1 + (p - q)x + \{\tfrac{1}{2}p(p - 1) + \tfrac{1}{2}q(q - 1) - pq\}x^2 + \ldots,$$

the terms not written down being powers of x above the second.

Identifying these terms with $1 + 3x - 6x^2$,

$$p - q = 3, \tfrac{1}{2}p(p - 1) + \tfrac{1}{2}q(q - 1) - pq = -6.$$

Substituting $q = p - 3$ from the first of these equations in the second, we find after a little reduction, $p = 12$ and it then follows that $q = 9$.

Example 17. *In the expansion of* $(1 - 2x + ax^2)^4$ *as a series of powers of* x, *the coefficient of* x^3 *is zero. Prove that* $a = -4/3$ *and find the coefficient of* x^4.

[O.C.]

Replacing x by $x(-2 + ax)$, equation (2.19) gives with $n = 4$,

$$(1 - 2x + ax^2)^4 = 1 + 4x(-2 + ax) + 6x^2(-2 + ax)^2 + 4x^3(-2 + ax)^3 + x^4(-2 + ax)^4.$$

As we are only interested in terms up to x^4, this can be written

$$(1 - 2x + ax^2)^4 = 1 + 4x(-2 + ax) + 6x^2(4 - 4ax + a^2x^2)$$
$$+ 4x^3(-8 + 12ax + \ldots) + x^4(16 + \ldots)$$
$$= 1 - 8x + (4a + 24)x^2 - (24a + 32)x^3$$
$$+ (6a^2 + 48a + 16)x^4 + \ldots$$

If the coefficient of the term in x^3 is zero, $24a + 32 = 0$ giving $a = -4/3$. The coefficient of x^4 is $6a^2 + 48a + 16$ and, with $a = -4/3$, this is

$$6(-\tfrac{4}{3})^2 + 48(-\tfrac{4}{3}) + 16,$$

that is, $-112/3$.

Exercises 2 (d)

1. Write down in its simplest form the complete expansion of $(x - \tfrac{1}{2})^6$. By taking $x = 1/400$ in this expansion, show that

$$(\tfrac{199}{400})^6 = 0 \cdot 01516,$$

correct to five places of decimals. [O.C.]

2. Employ the binomial theorem to evaluate $(0 \cdot 998)^{40}$ correct to four places of decimals. [O.C.]

3. Find the term independent of x in the expansion of $\left(\dfrac{x^2}{2} - \dfrac{2}{x}\right)^9$. [L.U.]

4. In the expansion of $(ax - bx^{-2})^8$, the coefficients of x^2 and x^{-1} are the same. Show that $a + 2b = 0$. [L.U.]

5. In the expansion of $(1 + px)^7(1 + qx)$, where p and q are numerical coefficients and $p \neq 0$, the coefficients of x and x^2 are -4 and 0 respectively. Find the coefficient of x^3. [L.U.]

6. Find a positive integer p such that the coefficients of x and x^2 in the expansion of $(1 + x)^{2p}(1 - x)^p$ are equal. [L.U.]

7. In the binomial expansion of $(1 + x)^n$, where n is a positive integer, the coefficient of x^4 is $1\tfrac{1}{2}$ times the sum of the coefficients of x^2 and x^3. Find the value of n and determine these three coefficients. [L.U.]

8. The ratio of the third to the fourth term in the expansion of $(2 + 3x)^n$ in ascending powers of x is $5 : 14$ when $x = 2/5$. Find n.   [L.U.]

9. The sum of the first four terms in the expansion of $(1 - 2x)^4$ is equal to the sum of the first three terms in the expansion of $(1 - x)^8$. Show that this is true only if $x = 0$ or $-1/8$.   [O.C.]

10. It is known that a, b, n are positive integers and that the first three terms in the binomial expansion of $(a + b)^n$ are 729, 2916 and 4860 respectively. Find a, b and n.   [O.C.]

11. Find the values of n for which the coefficients of x^4, x^5 and x^6 in the expansion of $(1 + x)^n$ are in arithmetical progression.

12. Prove that if x and y are positive integers the expression $(x + y)^5 - x^5 - y^5$ is always exactly divisible by 5. Show also that if the integers x and y are even it is divisible by 160 and that if x and y are the same integer it is divisible by 30.   [L.U.]

13. The first three terms in the expansion in ascending powers of x of $(1 + 2x + ax^2)^n$, where n is a positive integer, are $1 + 2nx + \lambda x^3$. Show that

$$a = 2(1 - n), \quad \lambda = -\tfrac{4}{3} n(n - 1)(2n - 1).$$

14. The expansion of $(1 + x)^{10}(1 + ax + bx^2)$ in ascending powers of x begins with the terms $1 + x + x^2$. Find the numerical values of a and b.   [L.U.]

15. Prove that in the binomial expansion of $(1 + 0.03)^{12}$, the rth term is less than one-tenth of the $(r - 1)$th term if $r > 4$.   [L.U.]

2.11 The binomial theorem for fractional and negative indices

When the index n is fractional or negative, it can be shown (but the proof is outside the range of this book) that the series

$$1 + nx + \frac{n(n - 1)}{(2)!} x^2 + \frac{n(n - 1)(n - 2)}{(3)!} x^3 + \ldots \qquad (2.22)$$

converges* if $-1 < x < 1$ and that the limit of its sum is $(1 + x)^n$. This result is known as the binomial theorem for fractional and negative indices. The points of difference between it and the theorem for a positive integral index [equation (2.19)] are

(i) when n is a positive integer, the series (2.22) terminates at the term in x^n and its sum is $(1 + x)^n$ for *all* values of x;

(ii) for fractional and negative values of n, the series (2.22) does *not* terminate and it is only convergent with the limit of its sum as $(1 + x)^n$ when x lies between -1 and 1.

* For certain values of n, the series also converges when $x = 1$ or when $x = -1$.

The following particular cases should be noted. Putting $n = -1$ in (2.22), we deduce that the series $1 - x + x^2 - x^3 + \ldots$ converges when $-1 < x < 1$ and the limit of its sum is $(1 + x)^{-1}$. Changing x into $-x$, it follows that the series $1 + x + x^2 + x^3 + \ldots$ converges when $-1 < x < 1$ and that the limit of its sum is $(1 - x)^{-1}$. These two series are geometrical progressions with first terms unity and common ratios $\mp x$ respectively and the limits of their sums as given here are in agreement with those given by (2.12). Putting $n = \frac{1}{2}$ in (2.22), we find that the series $1 + \frac{1}{2}x - \frac{1}{8}x^2 + \frac{1}{16}x^3 - \ldots$ converges when $-1 < x < 1$ and the limit of its sum is $\sqrt{(1 + x)}$. Finally, putting $n = -2$ and writing $-x$ in place of x in (2.22) shows that the series $1 + 2x + 3x^2 + 4x^3 + \ldots$ converges when $-1 < x < 1$ and the limit of its sum is $(1 - x)^{-2}$.

When x is small compared with unity, the values of $x, x^2, x^3, \ldots$ are progressively smaller, and successive terms of a convergent series in ascending powers of x contribute less and less to the limit of its sum. Thus a first approximation to $(1 + x)^n$ for small x is given by

$$(1 + x)^n \simeq 1 + nx,$$

a better approximation being

$$(1 + x)^n \simeq 1 + nx + \tfrac{1}{2}n(n - 1)x^2,$$

and so on. Similarly

$$\frac{1 + ax}{1 + bx} = (1 + ax)(1 + bx)^{-1}$$

$$= (1 + ax)\{1 - bx + \tfrac{1}{2}b(b - 1)x^2 - \ldots\}$$

$$\simeq 1 + (a - b)x,$$

when the terms in $x^2, x^3, \ldots$ are neglected.

Example 18. *Obtain the first four terms in the expansion of $(1 + x)^{\frac{1}{3}}$. Hence find the cube root of $1 \cdot 012$ correct to seven decimal places.* [L.U.]

Writing $n = \frac{1}{3}$ in (2·22),

$$(1 + x)^{\frac{1}{3}} = 1 + (\tfrac{1}{3})x + \frac{\tfrac{1}{3}(\tfrac{1}{3} - 1)}{1.2}x^2 + \frac{\tfrac{1}{3}(\tfrac{1}{3} - 1)(\tfrac{1}{3} - 2)}{1.2.3}x^3 + \ldots$$

$$= 1 + \frac{x}{3} - \frac{x^2}{9} + \frac{5x^3}{81} - \ldots$$

$$\sqrt[3]{(1 \cdot 012)} = (1 + 0 \cdot 012)^{\frac{1}{3}}$$

$$= 1 + \frac{0 \cdot 012}{3} - \frac{(0 \cdot 012)^2}{9} + \frac{5(0 \cdot 012)^3}{81} -$$

$$= 1 + 0 \cdot 0040000 - 0 \cdot 0000160 + 0 \cdot 0000001 - \ldots = 1 \cdot 0039841.$$

Example 19. *Show that, if x is so small in comparison with unity that x^3 and higher powers can be neglected*

$$\frac{(1-4x)^{\frac{1}{2}}(1+3x)^{\frac{1}{3}}}{(1+x)^{\frac{1}{2}}} = 1 - \frac{3}{2}x - \frac{33}{8}x^2.$$ [L.U.]

The given expression can be written $(1-4x)^{\frac{1}{2}}(1+3x)^{\frac{1}{3}}(1+x)^{-\frac{1}{2}}$ and, using appropriate values for n and x in (2.22) this is equal to

$$\left\{1 + \tfrac{1}{2}(-4x) + \frac{\tfrac{1}{2}(\tfrac{1}{2}-1)}{2}(-4x)^2 + \ldots\right\}\left\{1 + \tfrac{1}{3}(3x) + \frac{\tfrac{1}{3}(\tfrac{1}{3}-1)}{2}(3x)^2 + \ldots\right\}$$

$$\times \left\{1 + (-\tfrac{1}{2})x + \frac{(-\tfrac{1}{2})(-\tfrac{1}{2}-1)}{2}x^2 + \ldots\right\}$$

$$= (1 - 2x - 2x^2 - \ldots)(1 + x - x^2 + \ldots)(1 - \tfrac{1}{2}x + \tfrac{3}{8}x^2 - \ldots)$$
$$= (1 + x - x^2 + \ldots - 2x - 2x^2 - \ldots - 2x^2 - \ldots)(1 - \tfrac{1}{2}x + \tfrac{3}{8}x^2 - \ldots)$$
$$= (1 - x - 5x^2 + \ldots)(1 - \tfrac{1}{2}x + \tfrac{3}{8}x^2 - \ldots)$$
$$= 1 - \tfrac{1}{2}x + \tfrac{3}{8}x^2 + \ldots - x + \tfrac{1}{2}x^2 - \ldots - 5x^2 + \ldots = 1 - \tfrac{3}{2}x - \tfrac{33}{8}x^2,$$

when terms in x^3 and above are neglected.

2.12 Partial fractions

The process of simplifying a group of algebraical fractions separated by addition or subtraction signs is assumed to be well known. For example, the expression

$$\frac{1}{x-1} - \frac{1}{x+2} - \frac{3}{(x+2)^2}$$

can be simplified to give the simple fraction $9/\{(x-1)(x+2)^2\}$. In work involving expansions, and later in the integral calculus, it is often useful to be able to carry out the reverse process. In other words, we require to be able to split up a single fraction whose denominator can be factorised into two or more *partial* fractions.

This reverse process, called resolution into partial fractions, depends on the following rules

(i) if the degree of the numerator of the given fraction is equal to or greater than that of the denominator, divide the numerator by the denominator until a remainder is obtained which is of lower degree than the denominator;

(ii) to every linear factor like $(ax + b)$ in the denominator, there corresponds a partial fraction of the form $A/(ax + b)$;

(iii) to every repeated factor like $(ax + b)^2$ in the denominator, there correspond two partial fractions of the form $A/(ax + b)^2$ and $B/(ax + b)$; similarly for factors like $(ax + b)^3$, there are three partial fractions $A/(ax + b)^3$, $B/(ax + b)^2$, $C/(ax + b)$ and so on;

(iv) to every quadratic factor like $(ax^2 + bx + c)$, there corresponds a partial fraction $(Ax + B)/(ax^2 + bx + c)$ and repeated quadratic factors are treated as in (iii) above.

The application of these rules is illustrated in the examples which follow.

Example 20. *Resolve $4/(x^2 - 4)$ into partial fractions.*

The factors of $x^2 - 4$ being $(x - 2)$ and $(x + 2)$, we assume that

$$\frac{4}{x^2 - 4} \equiv \frac{A}{x - 2} + \frac{B}{x + 2} \equiv \frac{A(x + 2) + B(x - 2)}{(x - 2)(x + 2)}.$$

The denominators of the expressions on the left and right being the same, the numerators must be the same and hence

$$A(x + 2) + B(x - 2) \equiv 4. \qquad (2.23)$$

The values of A and B can be found from this identity by the principle of undetermined coefficients. Thus, equating the coefficients of x and of the term independent of x,

$$A + B = 0, \quad 2A - 2B = 4,$$

and the solution of this pair of equations is $A = 1$, $B = -1$.

Another and, in the case of linear factors such as we have here, simpler method of evaluating A and B from the identity (2.23) is to give x suitable numerical values so that A and B can be found separately. Thus by putting $x = 2$ in (2.23) we have $4A = 4$ giving $A = 1$, and, by putting $x = -2$, $-4B = 4$ leading to $B = -1$. Hence

$$\frac{4}{x^2 - 4} \equiv \frac{1}{x - 2} - \frac{1}{x + 2}.$$

Example 21. *Express $(2x + 1)/\{(x - 1)(x + 2)^2\}$ as the sum of three partial fractions. When x is small, so that x^3 and higher powers of x may be neglected, obtain the expansion of the given function in the form $a + bx + cx^2$. State the range of values of x for which the expansion is valid.* [O.C.]

Here we have a repeated linear factor and we assume

$$\frac{2x + 1}{(x - 1)(x + 2)^2} \equiv \frac{A}{x - 1} + \frac{B}{(x + 2)^2} + \frac{C}{x + 2}$$

$$\equiv \frac{A(x + 2)^2 + B(x - 1) + C(x - 1)(x + 2)}{(x - 1)(x + 2)^2}.$$

The identity from which A, B and C are to be determined by equating coefficients is

$$A(x + 2)^2 + B(x - 1) + C(x - 1)(x + 2) \equiv 2x + 1,$$

and this can be written

$$(A + C)x^2 + (4A + B + C)x + 4A - B - 2C \equiv 2x + 1.$$

Hence $A + C = 0, 4A + B + C = 2, 4A - B - 2C = 1$, giving $A = -C = \frac{1}{3}$, $B = 1$, and

$$\frac{2x + 1}{(x - 1)(x + 2)^2} \equiv \frac{\frac{1}{3}}{x - 1} + \frac{1}{(x + 2)^2} - \frac{\frac{1}{3}}{x + 2}.$$

This can be written

$$\frac{2x + 1}{(x - 1)(x + 2)^2} \equiv \frac{1}{4}\left(1 + \frac{x}{2}\right)^{-2} - \frac{1}{3}(1 - x)^{-1} - \frac{1}{6}\left(1 + \frac{x}{2}\right)^{-1},$$

and it is now in a form in which the binomial expansion of (2.22) can be applied.

Thus

$$\frac{2x + 1}{(x - 1)(x + 2)^2} = \frac{1}{4} \left\{ 1 + (-2) \left(\frac{x}{2}\right) + \frac{(-2)(-2 - 1)}{1.2} \left(\frac{x}{2}\right)^2 + \ldots \right\}$$

$$- \frac{1}{3} \left\{ 1 + (-1)(-x) + \frac{(-1)(-1 - 1)}{1.2} (-x)^2 + \ldots \right\}$$

$$- \frac{1}{6} \left\{ 1 + (-1) \left(\frac{x}{2}\right) + \frac{(-1)(-1 - 1)}{1.2} \left(\frac{x}{2}\right)^2 + \ldots \right\}$$

$$= \frac{1}{4} \left(1 - x + \frac{3}{4} x^2 - \ldots \right) - \frac{1}{3} (1 + x + x^2 + \ldots)$$

$$- \frac{1}{6} \left(1 - \frac{x}{2} + \frac{x^2}{4} - \ldots \right)$$

$$= -\frac{1}{4} - \frac{1}{2} x - \frac{3}{16} x^2 - \ldots$$

In the above we have expanded the binomial expressions $(1 + x/2)$ and $(1 + x)$. The expansions are valid when $-1 < \frac{1}{2}x < 1$ and when $-1 < x < 1$; taking these inequalities together, all the expansions are valid when $-1 < x < 1$.

Example 22. *Express* $\dfrac{x^4 + 5x^3 + 9x^2 + 6x + 5}{(x + 2)(x^2 + 1)}$ *in partial fractions.*

In the previous examples, the numerator was of lower degree than the denominator. Here the numerator is of degree 4 and the denominator of degree 3 so that preliminary division is necessary. This division gives a quotient of $x + 3$ and a remainder of $2x^2 + x - 1$. Hence

$$\frac{x^4 + 5x^3 + 9x^2 + 6x + 5}{(x + 2)(x^2 + 1)} \equiv x + 3 + \frac{2x^2 + x - 1}{(x + 2)(x^2 + 1)}.$$

We now assume that

$$\frac{2x^2 + x - 1}{(x + 2)(x^2 + 1)} \equiv \frac{A}{x + 2} + \frac{Bx + C}{x^2 + 1}$$

$$\equiv \frac{A(x^2 + 1) + (Bx + C)(x + 2)}{(x + 2)(x^2 + 1)},$$

the numerator of the fraction with quadratic denominator $(x^2 + 1)$ being chosen in accordance with rule (iv). The identity from which A, B and C are to be found is therefore $A(x^2 + 1) + (Bx + C)(x + 2) \equiv 2x^2 + x - 1$. This can be written

$$(A + B)x^2 + (2B + C)x + A + 2C \equiv 2x^2 + x - 1,$$

and, equating the coefficients of like powers of x,

$$A + B = 2, \ 2B + C = 1, \ A + 2C = -1.$$

The solution of these simultaneous equations is $A = 1$, $B = 1$, $C = -1$ and hence the given expression can be written in the form

$$x + 3 + \frac{1}{x + 2} + \frac{x - 1}{x^2 + 1}.$$

Exercises 2 (e)

1. If x^4 and higher powers of x are neglected, find by how much $\sqrt[3]{(1 + x)}$ differs from $1 + \frac{1}{3}x - \frac{1}{9}x^2$ and hence evaluate $\sqrt[3]{(1010)}$ to five decimal places.
   [L.U.]

2. Calculate by means of the binomial theorem, the value of $(16 \cdot 32)^{-\frac{1}{4}}$ to five places of decimals.
   [O.C.]

3. Expand $(1 + 3x)^{-\frac{2}{3}}$ by the binomial theorem up to the term in x^3 and calculate, to four places of decimals, the value of $(0 \cdot 97)^{-\frac{2}{3}}$.
   [O.C.]

4. Obtain the first three terms in the binomial expansion of $(1 + \frac{1}{2}x)^{\frac{1}{3}}$ in ascending powers of x. By writing $x = \frac{1}{4}$, find the cube root of 9, giving your answer to three decimal places.
   [L.U.]

5. Prove that

$$\frac{x}{1 + x + \sqrt{(2x + 1)}} = \frac{1}{x}\{1 + x - \sqrt{(2x + 1)}\}$$

   and show that, if x is small, the expression is approximately equal to $\frac{1}{2}x(1 - x)$.
   [O.C.]

6. If x^6 and higher powers of x can be neglected, show that

$$(4 - x)^{\frac{1}{2}} + (4 + x)^{\frac{1}{2}} = 4 - \frac{1}{2^5}x^2 - \frac{5}{2^{13}}x^4.$$
   [L.U.]

7. If $-1 < tx < 1$ and $t \neq 0$, find the values of a, b and t for which the expression $(1 + x + \frac{1}{2}x^2)(1 + ax) + (1 - x + \frac{1}{2}x^2)(1 + bx)$ is the same as the expansion of $2(1 + tx)^{-2}$ as far as the term in x^3.
   [L.U.]

8. In the expansion of $(1 - kx)^{-k}$, $-1 < kx < 1$, $k \neq 0$, $k \neq -1$, in ascending powers of x, the coefficients of x^2 and x^3 are equal. Find the two values of k and the coefficients of x^4 corresponding to these values.

9. Prove that if $a^2 > 2$, then

$$\sqrt{(a^2 - 2)} = \sqrt{(a^2 - 1)}\left\{1 - \frac{1}{2(a^2 - 1)} - \frac{1}{8(a^2 - 1)^2} - \frac{1}{16(a^2 - 1)^3} - \cdots\right\}$$

   Use this result when $a^2 = 51$ to show that $140/99$ is a close approximation to the value of $\sqrt{2}$.
   [O.C.]

10. Find the relation between a and b if the coefficients of x^4 in the expansions of $(1 + ax + x^2)^3$ and $(1 - bx^2)^{-\frac{1}{3}}$ are equal.
    [O.C.]

11. If $-1 < x < 1$, find in its simplest form the coefficient of x^n in the expansion of

$$\left(\frac{1 + x}{1 - x}\right)^3$$

    in ascending powers of x.
    [N.U.]

12. Express in partial fractions

$$\text{(i) } \frac{1}{x^2 + 5x + 6}, \quad \text{(ii) } \frac{x}{(x + 1)(x - 1)^2}, \quad \text{(iii) } \frac{1}{x^3 - 1}.$$

13. Express in partial fractions

$$\text{(i) } \frac{x^2 + 2x + 1}{x^2 + x - 2}, \quad \text{(ii) } \frac{5x^3 + 2x^2 + 5x}{x^4 - 1}.$$

14. Express the function

$$\frac{7x + 2}{(x + 2)^2(x - 2)}$$

in partial fractions and hence obtain the expansion of the function in ascending powers of x as far as the term in x^4, stating the necessary restrictions on the values of x. [O.C.]

15. Express

$$\frac{10(x + 1)}{(x + 3)(x^2 + 1)}$$

in partial fractions. Hence obtain the expansion of the given function in ascending powers of x as far as the term in x^3, stating the necessary restrictions on the value of x. [O.C.]

Exercises 2 (f)

1. An arithmetical progression has 2 for its first term. Find its common difference if the sum of 33 terms is equal to six times the sum of 13 terms. [O.C.]

2. The pth and qth terms of an arithmetical progression, where $p \neq q$, are in the ratio $2p - 1 : 2q - 1$. Show that the sum of the first p terms is to the sum of the first q terms as p^2 is to q^2. [L.U.]

3. Find the difference, if any, (a) between 3^{16} and the sum of sixteen terms of the geometrical progression 2, 6, 18, etc., (b) between 3^{16} and half the seventeenth term. [O.C.]

4. The nth term of a series is $(an + 5r^n)$ where a and r are constants and $r \neq 1$. State the sum of the first n terms. In the series $18 + 36 + 64 + \ldots$, it is given that the nth term is of the form stated above. Find a and r and the sum of the first ten terms. [N.U.]

5. The sum of the first n terms of a series is $2n + 3n^2$. Show that the series is an arithmetical progression and find the sum of the first m terms occupying odd places in the series. [N.U.]

6. Show that there are two geometrical progressions in which the second term is $-4/3$ and the sum of the first three terms is 28/9. Show also that one of these progressions is convergent and, in this case, find the limit of its sum. [L.U.]

7. If a geometrical progression with common ratio $(1 + c)/(1 - c)$ is convergent, prove that c must be negative, but that it is otherwise unrestricted. Two such progressions, one with $c = c_1$ and the other with $c = c_2$, each have their first terms unity. If S_1 and S_2 are the corresponding limits to their sums, show that

$$S_1 - S_2 = (c_1 - c_2)/2c_1c_2.$$

Hence deduce that $S_1 > S_2$ when c_1 is less than c_2 numerically. [L.U.]

8. Find the limit of the sum of the series

$$1 + r + (1 + a)r^2 + (1 + a + a^2)r^3 + \ldots,$$

where a, r are both less than unity and the coefficient of the term in r^n in the series is $1 + a + a^2 + \ldots + a^{n-1}$.

9. Using all the digits 1, 2, 3, 4, 5, 6, how many arrangements can be made (i) beginning with an even digit, (ii) beginning and ending with an even digit?

10. How many different six figure numbers can be made from the six digits 1, 2, 2, 3, 3, 3? Find also how many different five figure numbers can be made from these digits.

11. A touring cricket party consists of 14 players, 5 of whom can bowl. How many distinct teams of 11 players can be selected containing at least 3 bowlers and how many of these contain one specified bowler? [L.U.]

12. Four different positive integers, each less than 10, are chosen at random. Find the probability that their sum is even. [L.U.]

13. Three stamps are taken at random from a box containing 5 orange, 4 brown and 3 blue stamps. Find the probability that (i) three are of the same colour, (ii) all three are of different colours, (iii) two are of the same colour and the third is of a different colour. [L.U.]

14. An entry in a football pool contains 27 different forecasts of 8 matches. Find the odds in favour of the entry containing an all-correct forecast.

15. Show that, if the order of the groups is immaterial, the number of ways in which $4n$ different objects can be divided into 4 groups of n each is $(4n)!/\{(n!)^4(4)!\}$. Deduce that the number of different sets of four bridge hands which can be dealt from an ordinary pack is $52!/(13!)^4$.

16. In the expansion of $(1 + ax + 2x^2)^6$ in powers of x, the coefficients of x^2 and x^{11} are 27 and -192 respectively. Find a and the coefficients of x^3 and x^{10}. [L.U.]

17. Obtain in its simplest form, the binomial expansion of $(1 - x)^{\frac{1}{4}}$ as far as the term in x^3. Use your result to evaluate the fourth root of 77 to five significant figures. [L.U.]

18. Show that for a certain range of values of x,

$$\frac{(1 + x)^2}{1 + x^2} = 1 + 2x - 2x^3 + 2x^5 - 2x^7 + \ldots$$

and prove that the error in using $1 + 2x - 2x^3$ as an approximation for the function is $2x^5(1 + x^2)^{-1}$.

19. The expansion, in ascending powers of x, of the expression

$$\frac{ax^2 + bx + c}{(1 - x)^4}$$

begins with the terms $1^3 + 2^3x + 3^3x^2$. Find the values of a, b, c and verify that, when a, b, c have these values, the coefficient of x^r is $(r + 1)^3$.   [L.U.]

20. If $-1 < x < 1$, find the coefficient of x^n in the expansion in ascending powers of x of

$$\frac{A + Bx + Cx^2}{(1 - x)^3}.$$

Determine A, B and C so that this expansion reduces to

$$1^2x + 2^2x^2 + 3^2x^3 + \ldots + n^2x^n + \ldots$$

Show also that

$$\frac{1^2}{2} + \frac{2^2}{2^2} + \frac{3^2}{2^3} + \ldots + \frac{n^2}{2^n} + \ldots = 6. \qquad \text{[N.U.]}$$

21. Write down and simplify the first three terms in the binomial expansions of $(1 + x)^{\frac{1}{2}}$ and $(1 + x)^{-\frac{1}{2}}$.

AB is a chord, of length $2ka$, of a circle of radius a. The tangents to the circle at A and B meet in C. Show that, if k is so small compared with unity that k^7 is negligible, the area of the triangle ABC is $a^2k^3 + \frac{1}{2}a^2k^5$.   [L.U.]

22. Use the binomial theorem to write down the first four terms of the expansion of $(1 + y)^{-\frac{1}{2}}$ in a series of ascending powers of y. Hence find, in terms of $\cos \theta$, the coefficients c_1, c_2, c_3 in the expansion of $(1 - 2x \cos \theta + x^2)^{-\frac{1}{2}}$ in the form $1 + c_1x + c_2x^2 + c_3x^3 + \ldots$ Prove that, when $\theta = 0$, every coefficient in the series is equal to $+1$. [You may assume throughout that the expansions are valid.]   [N.U.]

23. If x is so small that cubes and higher powers may be neglected and if

$$\frac{(2x + 1)^{\frac{3}{4}}}{1 + (3x^2 + 1)^{-\frac{1}{2}}} = P + Qx + Rx^2,$$

determine the values of P, Q and R.   [L.U.]

24. Express in partial fractions the function E given by

$$E \equiv \frac{4x + 1}{(x - 3)(x^2 + x + 1)}.$$

Hence expand E as a series in ascending powers of x as far as the term in x^3.   [O.C.]

25. Express in partial fractions

$$E \equiv \frac{2x^2 + 7}{(x + 2)^2(x - 3)}.$$

Hence, if x is so *large* that x^{-5} can be neglected, prove that

$$E = \frac{1}{x^4}(2x^3 - 2x^2 + 25x - 17).$$ [O.C.]

CHAPTER 3

ADDITION FORMULAE; TRIGONOMETRICAL EQUATIONS; SMALL ANGLES; THE INVERSE NOTATION

3.1 Introduction

This chapter opens with a brief recapitulation of elementary trigonometry starting from the definitions of the trigonometrical functions as the ratios of the sides of a right-angled triangle. This is probably the simplest way of starting a study of trigonometry and one which leads directly to its use in problems involving heights and distances.

It should be noted, however, that the use of the trigonometrical functions in mathematics is by no means confined to problems of this type. Many natural phenomena (for instance, the phases of the moon or of the tides) are periodic in the sense that they repeat themselves in a regular way and the trigonometrical functions, which are themselves periodic, are very useful in representing such occurrences. Such applications are probably best left until the student is adept in manipulating elementary trignonometrical formulae and it is the purpose of the remaining part of the chapter to provide an opportunity to acquire the necessary skill.

3.2 Basic definitions and formulae

The reader is assumed to be familiar with the basic definitions and formulae of elementary trigonometry and this paragraph is intended simply to be one of recapitulation.

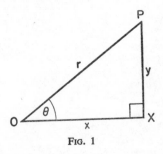

Fig. 1

The trigonometrical ratios of an acute angle are defined in terms of the sides x, y, r of a right-angled triangle POX (Fig. 1) by

$$\sin \theta = y/r, \qquad \cos \theta = x/r, \qquad \tan \theta = y/x, \tag{3.1}$$

and

$$\operatorname{cosec}\theta = \frac{1}{\sin\theta}, \qquad \sec\theta = \frac{1}{\cos\theta}, \qquad \cot\theta = \frac{1}{\tan\theta}. \qquad (3.2)$$

Immediate consequences of these definitions are

$$\tan\theta = \frac{\sin\theta}{\cos\theta}, \qquad \cot\theta = \frac{\cos\theta}{\sin\theta}, \qquad (3.3)$$

$$\sin^2\theta + \cos^2\theta = 1, \qquad (3.4)$$

$$\sec^2\theta = 1 + \tan^2\theta, \qquad \operatorname{cosec}^2\theta = 1 + \cot^2\theta. \qquad (3.5)$$

By considering the elementary geometry of right-angled triangles in which the angle θ is respectively 45° and 60°, it is easy to show that

$$\left.\begin{array}{l} \sin 45° = \cos 45° = \dfrac{1}{\sqrt{2}}, \quad \tan 45° = 1, \\[2mm] \sin 60° = \cos 30° = \tfrac{1}{2}\sqrt{3}, \quad \tan 60° = \cot 30° = \sqrt{3}, \\[2mm] \sin 30° = \cos 60° = \tfrac{1}{2}, \qquad \tan 30° = \cot 60° = \dfrac{1}{\sqrt{3}}. \end{array}\right\} \quad (3.6)$$

These values are conveniently summarised in the following table, which also gives the values of the ratios for 0° and 90°.

θ	$\sin^2\theta$	$\cos^2\theta$	$\tan^2\theta$
0°	0	1	0
30°	$\frac{1}{4}$	$\frac{3}{4}$	$\frac{1}{3}$
45°	$\frac{1}{2}$	$\frac{1}{2}$	1
60°	$\frac{3}{4}$	$\frac{1}{4}$	3
90°	1	0	∞

This table is worth remembering as is also the relation

$$x \text{ degrees} = \frac{\pi x}{180} \text{ radians}. \qquad (3.7)$$

The trigonometrical ratios of the general angle are also given by the above relations but appropriate signs have to be given to x and y according to the quadrant in which P lies. These signs are the same as those used in ordinary graphical work; for example, when P lies in the second quadrant as shown in Fig. 2, x is negative and y is positive.

The length of OP $(= r)$ is always taken to be positive. Positive angles are those swept out when OP rotates in an anti-clockwise direction (Fig. 2) and angles generated when OP rotates clockwise as in Fig. 3

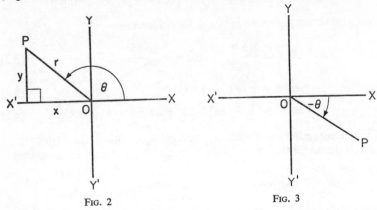

FIG. 2   FIG. 3

are called negative angles. The following can be deduced from diagrams such as those shown below

$$\left.\begin{array}{ll}
\sin (180° \pm \theta) = \mp \sin \theta, & \cos (180° \pm \theta) = -\cos \theta, \\
\sin (360° \pm \theta) = \pm \sin \theta, & \cos (360° \pm \theta) = \cos \theta, \\
\sin (90° \pm \theta) = \cos \theta, & \cos (90° \pm \theta) = \mp \sin \theta, \\
\sin (270° \pm \theta) = -\cos \theta, & \cos (270° \pm \theta) = \pm \sin \theta, \\
\sin (-\theta) = -\sin \theta, & \cos (-\theta) = \cos \theta.
\end{array}\right\} \quad (3.8)$$

The corresponding relations for the tangent, cosecant, secant and cotangent are then easily found from equations (3.2) and (3.3). Fig. 4

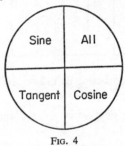

FIG. 4

shows which of the fundamental trigonometrical ratios is positive in each quadrant and should be a useful aid to memory.

Graphs of the fundamental trigonometrical ratios $\sin \theta$, $\cos \theta$ and $\tan \theta$ are shown in Figs. 5 and 6. These graphs show the periodic nature of the trigonometrical ratios; the value of each ratio is repeated after a certain interval called the *period*. The periods of sin θ and cos θ are both 360° (or 2π radians) while that of tan θ is 180° (or π radians).

Equations involving the trigonometrical ratios differ from algebraical

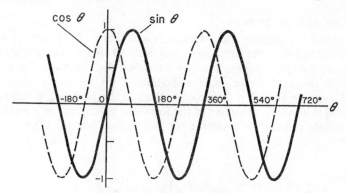

FIG. 5. Graphs of sin θ and cos θ

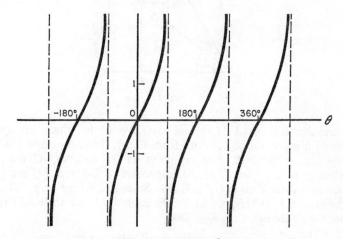

FIG. 6. Graph of tan θ

equations in that they often have an unlimited number of solutions. For example, consider the equation $2 \cos^2 \theta = 1 + \sin \theta$. By using equation (3.4) and writing $\cos^2 \theta = 1 - \sin^2 \theta$, the given equation reduces to $2 \sin^2 \theta + \sin \theta - 1 = 0$ and this can be written

$$(2 \sin \theta - 1)(\sin \theta + 1) = 0$$

leading to $\sin \theta = \frac{1}{2}$ or $\sin \theta = -1$. From (3.6), $\sin 30° = \frac{1}{2}$ and, glancing at Fig. 5, other angles whose sine is $\frac{1}{2}$ are . . ., $-210°$, 150°,

390°, ... Similarly sin θ = —1 when θ = . . ., —90°, 270°, 630°, ... If, as often happens, only those solutions which lie between 0° and 360° are required, the appropriate solutions are 30°, 150° and 270°.

3.3 The addition formulae

Formulae expressing the trigonometrical ratios of the sum of two angles in terms of the trigonometrical ratios of the separate angles are known as *addition formulae* and we start by deriving them for a restricted range of angles. Generalisation of the results to cover all angles can be made but the process is rather troublesome: a compact general method of derivation of the formulae making use of a result in coordinate geometry is available and this is given later (§ 5.5).

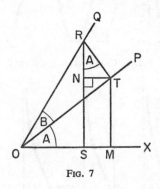

FIG. 7

Formulae for sin $(A + B)$ and cos $(A + B)$ in which the angle $(A + B)$ is *acute* can be obtained from Fig. 7. Here the angle POX is A, the angle QOP is B, R is any point on OQ and RS, RT are perpendicular to the lines OX, OP respectively. TM and TN are perpendiculars from T on to OX and RS. Since RS, RT are perpendicular to the arms OX, OP respectively of the angle POX, the angle SRT is A. From the right-angled triangle SRO

$$OR \sin (A + B) = SR = SN + NR = MT + NR, \qquad (3.9)$$

since $SMTN$ is a rectangle by construction. The right-angled triangle OMT gives $MT = OT \sin A$, and the right-angled triangle OTR gives $OT = OR \cos B$. Hence $MT = OR \sin A \cos B$. Also from the right-angled triangle RNT, $NR = RT \cos A$, while the triangle ORT gives $RT = OR \sin B$. Thus $NR = OR \cos A \sin B$. Substituting for MT and NR in (3.9) and dividing by OR, we have

$$\sin (A + B) = \sin A \cos B + \cos A \sin B. \qquad (3.10)$$

The corresponding formula for $\cos(A + B)$ is obtained similarly; thus, from Fig 7,

$$OR\cos(A + B) = OS = OM - SM = OM - NT.$$

Also,

$OM = OT\cos A$ and $OT = OR\cos B$ so that $OM = OR\cos A \cos B.$

Again,

$NT = RT\sin A$ and $RT = OR\sin B$ giving $NT = OR\sin A \sin B.$

Substitution and division by OR then leads to

$$\cos(A + B) = \cos A \cos B - \sin A \sin B. \tag{3.11}$$

Equations (3.10) and (3.11) give the fundamental addition formulae. By writing $-B$ in place of B and using the last result listed in (3.8), they become

$$\sin(A - B) = \sin A \cos(-B) + \cos A \sin(-B)$$
$$= \sin A \cos B - \cos A \sin B, \tag{3.12}$$

and

$$\cos(A - B) = \cos A \cos(-B) - \sin A \sin(-B)$$
$$= \cos A \cos B + \sin A \sin B. \tag{3.13}$$

By division of equations (3.10) and (3.11),

$$\tan(A + B) = \frac{\sin(A + B)}{\cos(A + B)} = \frac{\sin A \cos B + \cos A \sin B}{\cos A \cos B - \sin A \sin B}$$
$$= \frac{\tan A + \tan B}{1 - \tan A \tan B}, \tag{3.14}$$

dividing the numerator and denominator by $\cos A \cos B$. This is the addition formula for the tangent and, replacing B by $-B$, we also have

$$\tan(A - B) = \frac{\tan A + \tan(-B)}{1 - \tan A \tan(-B)} = \frac{\tan A - \tan B}{1 + \tan A \tan B}. \tag{3.15}$$

Example 1. *If A and B are acute angles such that $\sin A = \frac{1}{5}\sqrt{5}$ and $\tan B = \frac{1}{3}$, find the value of $(A + B)$ by means of the addition formula for $\sin(A + B)$.* [O.C.]

From the given values of $\sin A$ and $\tan B$, it is easily seen that A and B are the angles of two right-angled triangles whose sides are of the lengths shown in Fig. 8. The remaining sides of the two triangles are found by Pythagoras'

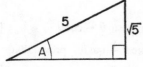
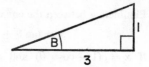

FIG. 8

theorem to be of lengths $2\sqrt{5}$ and $\sqrt{10}$ respectively and hence we have

$$\sin A = \frac{1}{5}\sqrt{5}, \quad \cos A = \frac{2}{5}\sqrt{5}, \quad \sin B = \frac{1}{\sqrt{10}}, \quad \cos B = \frac{3}{\sqrt{10}}.$$

Substitution in formula (3.10) then gives

$$\sin(A + B) = \frac{1}{5}\sqrt{5} \cdot \frac{3}{\sqrt{10}} + \frac{2}{5}\sqrt{5} \cdot \frac{1}{\sqrt{10}} = \frac{5\sqrt{5}}{5\sqrt{10}} = \frac{1}{\sqrt{2}}$$

and hence $A + B = 45°$.

Example 2. *If* $\tan \alpha = \frac{1}{8}$, $\tan \beta = \frac{4}{19}$ *and* $\tan \gamma = \frac{2}{5}$, *show that* $\tan(\alpha + \beta + \gamma) = 1$.
[O.C.]

Using the addition formula (3.14) and the given values of $\tan \alpha$ and $\tan \beta$,

$$\tan(\alpha + \beta) = \frac{\frac{1}{8} + \frac{4}{19}}{1 - \frac{1}{8} \cdot \frac{4}{19}} = \frac{39}{91} = \frac{3}{7}.$$

Writing (3.14) in the form

$$\tan(\alpha + \beta + \gamma) = \tan\{(\alpha + \beta) + \gamma\} = \frac{\tan(\alpha + \beta) + \tan \gamma}{1 - \tan(\alpha + \beta)\tan \gamma},$$

and substituting for $\tan(\alpha + \beta)$ and $\tan \gamma$ we have

$$\tan(\alpha + \beta + \gamma) = \frac{\frac{3}{7} + \frac{2}{5}}{1 - \frac{3}{7} \cdot \frac{2}{5}} = \frac{29}{29} = 1.$$

Exercises 3 (a)

1. Find the angles x between $0°$ and $360°$ which satisfy the equations
   　　(i) $\tan x = -0.4560$, (ii) $\sin \frac{3}{2} x = -0.5678$. [O.C.]

2. Solve the equations, giving values between $0°$ and $360°$
   　　(i) $\cos \frac{2}{3} x = \tan 155°$, (ii) $\sin \frac{3}{4} x = \cot 108°$. [O.C.]

3. Find the values of θ between $0°$ and $360°$ which satisfy the equation $\tan \theta = \frac{3}{4}$. Which of these values satisfies the pair of equations
   $$\sin \theta = -\frac{3}{5}, \cos \theta = -\frac{4}{5}?$$

4. Find values of x, between $0°$ and $360°$, which satisfy the equations
   　　(i) $6 \sin^2 x - 5 \cos x - 2 = 0$, (ii) $4 \tan x - 2 \cot x = 5 \operatorname{cosec} x$.
   [O.C.]

5. Solve the equation $\tan(45° + x) + \cot(45° + x) = 4$ for those values of x which lie between $0°$ and $360°$. [O.C.]

6. Eliminate θ between the equations
   $$x = \tan \theta + \cot \theta, \, y = \sin \theta - \cos \theta. \qquad \text{[O.C.]}$$

7. If $x = a(1 - \operatorname{cosec} \theta)$ and $y = a(\sec \theta + \tan \theta)$, prove that
   $$xy^2 + a^2(2a - x) = 0. \qquad \text{[O.C.]}$$

8. If $\tan \alpha = \dfrac{a\sqrt{3}}{2b - a}$ and $\tan \beta = \dfrac{2a - b}{b\sqrt{3}}$, find the values of $(\alpha - \beta)$ between $0°$ and $360°$. [L.U.]

9. If $\tan \alpha = \frac{1}{8}$, $\tan \beta = \frac{3}{4}$ and $\tan \gamma = \frac{1}{3}$, prove that $\tan(\alpha + \beta - \gamma) = \frac{4}{3}$. [O.C.]

10. Use the addition formulae for the sine and cosine to show that
$$\cot(A - B) = \frac{1 + \cot A \cot B}{\cot B - \cot A}.$$
Deduce that, if $\cot A = \frac{1}{2}$, $\cot B = 2$ and $\cot C = 3$, then
$$\cot(A - B - C) = 3. \qquad \text{[O.C.]}$$

11. If $F(\cos \alpha + \mu \sin \alpha) = \mu W$ where $\mu = \tan \lambda$, prove that
$$F = \frac{W \sin \lambda}{\cos(\alpha - \lambda)}.$$

12. If $\tan \alpha \tan \beta = k$, show that
$$(1 + k) \cos(\alpha + \beta) = (1 - k) \cos(\alpha - \beta).$$

13. If $x \cos \alpha + y \cos \beta = c$ and $x \sin \alpha - y \sin \beta = 0$, show that
$$\frac{x}{\sin \beta} = \frac{y}{\sin \alpha} = \frac{c}{\sin(\alpha + \beta)}.$$

14. If $A + B + C = 180°$, show that
$\sin A \sin(A + 2C) + \sin B \sin(B + 2A) + \sin C \sin(C + 2B) = 0$.

15. Show that $\sin(A + B + C)$
$= \cos A \cos B \cos C \,(\tan A + \tan B + \tan C - \tan A \tan B \tan C)$.

Deduce that, if A, B and C are the angles of a triangle, then
$$\cot A \cot B + \cot B \cot C + \cot C \cot A = 1. \qquad \text{[L.U.]}$$

3.4 Multiple angles

The trigonometrical ratios of $2A$ are easily found in terms of those of A by writing $B = A$ in formulae (3.10), (3.11) and (3.14). Thus, from (3.10),
$$\sin(A + A) = \sin A \cos A + \cos A \sin A,$$
giving
$$\sin 2A = 2 \sin A \cos A. \qquad (3.16)$$
Also, from (3.11), we have similarly
$$\cos 2A = \cos^2 A - \sin^2 A. \qquad (3.17)$$
By writing $\sin^2 A = 1 - \cos^2 A$, this can be written in the alternative form
$$\cos 2A = 2 \cos^2 A - 1, \qquad (3.18)$$

and, by writing $\cos^2 A = 1 - \sin^2 A$, yet another form of (3.17) is

$$\cos 2A = 1 - 2 \sin^2 A. \tag{3.19}$$

Sometimes, especially in the integral calculus, it is useful to be able to express $\cos^2 A$ and $\sin^2 A$ in terms of $\cos 2A$. This can be done by rearranging the last two formulae in the forms

$$\cos^2 A = \tfrac{1}{2}(1 + \cos 2A), \quad \sin^2 A = \tfrac{1}{2}(1 - \cos 2A). \tag{3.20}$$

Finally, writing $B = A$ in (3.14),

$$\tan 2A = \frac{2 \tan A}{1 - \tan^2 A}. \tag{3.21}$$

Formulae for the sine, cosine and tangent of $3A$ can be found in terms of those of A as follows. Writing $B = 2A$ in (3.10),

$$\sin 3A = \sin A \cos 2A + \cos A \sin 2A.$$

Substitution of $\cos 2A = 1 - 2 \sin^2 A$ and $\sin 2A = 2 \sin A \cos A$ from (3.19) and (3.16) then gives

$$\begin{aligned}
\sin 3A &= \sin A(1 - 2 \sin^2 A) + 2 \cos^2 A \sin A \\
&= \sin A(1 - 2 \sin^2 A) + 2(1 - \sin^2 A) \sin A \\
&= 3 \sin A - 4 \sin^3 A,
\end{aligned} \tag{3.22}$$

where we have used $\cos^2 A = 1 - \sin^2 A$ in the second step. Similarly

$$\begin{aligned}
\cos 3A &= \cos A \cos 2A - \sin A \sin 2A \\
&= \cos A(2 \cos^2 A - 1) - 2 \sin^2 A \cos A \\
&= \cos A(2 \cos^2 A - 1) - 2(1 - \cos^2 A) \cos A \\
&= 4 \cos^3 A - 3 \cos A.
\end{aligned} \tag{3.23}$$

Starting from (3.14) with $B = 2A$,

$$\tan 3A = \frac{\tan A + \tan 2A}{1 - \tan A \tan 2A};$$

substitution for $\tan 2A$ from (3.21) and a little reduction then leads to

$$\tan 3A = \frac{3 \tan A - \tan^3 A}{1 - 3 \tan^2 A}. \tag{3.24}$$

Example 3. *Show that $\cos^6 \theta + \sin^6 \theta = 1 - \tfrac{3}{4} \sin^2 2\theta$.* [L.U.]

$$\begin{aligned}
\cos^6 \theta + \sin^6 \theta &= (\cos^2 \theta + \sin^2 \theta)(\cos^4 \theta - \cos^2 \theta \sin^2 \theta + \sin^4 \theta) \\
&= (\cos^2 \theta + \sin^2 \theta)\{(\cos^2 \theta + \sin^2 \theta)^2 - 3 \cos^2 \theta \sin^2 \theta\} \\
&= 1 - \tfrac{3}{4} \sin^2 2\theta,
\end{aligned}$$

since $\cos^2 \theta + \sin^2 \theta = 1$ and $\sin 2\theta = 2 \sin \theta \cos \theta$.

Example 4. *Find all the values of x between 0° and 360° for which cos 2x = sin x.*
[L.U.]

Using formula (3.19) in the form $\cos 2x = 1 - 2 \sin^2 x$, the given equation is $1 - 2 \sin^2 x = \sin x$ or $2 \sin^2 x + \sin x - 1 = 0$. This can be written $(2 \sin x - 1)(\sin x + 1) = 0$ leading to $\sin x = \frac{1}{2}$ or $\sin x = -1$. The angles between 0° and 360° for which $\sin x = \frac{1}{2}$ are 30°, 150° and those for which $\sin x = -1$ are 270° only. Hence the required values of x are 30°, 150°, 270°.

3.5 The trigonometrical ratios of A in terms of tan ½A

Formulae (3.16) and (3.17) can, with a little manipulation and use of the relation $\sec^2 A = 1 + \tan^2 A$, be written

$$\sin 2A = 2 \sin A \cos A = 2 \tan A \cos^2 A$$

$$= \frac{2 \tan A}{\sec^2 A} = \frac{2 \tan A}{1 + \tan^2 A}, \tag{3.25}$$

and

$$\cos 2A = \cos^2 A - \sin^2 A = \cos^2 A(1 - \tan^2 A)$$

$$= \frac{1 - \tan^2 A}{\sec^2 A} = \frac{1 - \tan^2 A}{1 + \tan^2 A}. \tag{3.26}$$

Writing $A = \frac{1}{2}x$ and $t = \tan \frac{1}{2}x$, these become

$$\left.\sin x = \frac{2t}{1 + t^2}, \quad \cos x = \frac{1 - t^2}{1 + t^2}\right\}$$

and, by division,

$$\tag{3.27}$$

$$\left.\tan x = \frac{2t}{1 - t^2}.\right\}$$

These formulae are useful in the solution of certain trigonometrical equations (see § 3.7) and have other applications.

Example 5. *If tan ½x = cosec x − sin x, prove that tan² ½x = −2 ± √5.* [L.U.]

Writing $t = \tan \frac{1}{2}x$ and using (3.27), the given equation becomes

$$t = \frac{1 + t^2}{2t} - \frac{2t}{1 + t^2}.$$

This reduces to $t^4 + 4t^2 - 1 = 0$ and, solving as a quadratic in t^2, we have $t^2 = \frac{1}{2}\{-4 \pm \sqrt{16 + 4}\} = -2 \pm \sqrt{5}$.

Exercises 3 (b)

1. Prove that $\dfrac{2 \sin \theta + \sin 2\theta}{1 - \cos 2\theta} = \dfrac{\sin \theta}{1 - \cos \theta}$. [L.U.]

2. Find the values of x between 0° and 360° which satisfy the equation $\cos 2x + 7 \sin x + 3 = 0$. [O.C.]

3. Show that $\sin (A + 60°) \sin (A + 120°) = \sin 3A/(4 \sin A)$.   [L.U.]

4. Find the angles between $0°$ and $360°$ satisfying the equation
$$\cos 3x - 3 \cos x = \cos 2x + 1.$$ [O.C.]

5. Prove that $\dfrac{\cot \theta - \tan \theta}{\cot \theta + \tan \theta} = \cos 2\theta.$ [N.U.]

6. Show that $(2 \cos \theta + 1)(2 \cos \theta - 1)(2 \cos 2\theta - 1) = 2 \cos 4\theta + 1.$ [O.C.]

7. Prove that $\cos 2\theta \sec \theta - 2 \sin 3\theta \operatorname{cosec} 2\theta + 2 \cos \theta = 0.$ [O.C.]

8. Prove that $(2 \cos 2\theta - 1) \tan 3\theta = (2 \cos 2\theta + 1) \tan \theta.$ [O.C.]

9. By writing $x = 2 \cos \theta$, verify that the equation $x^3 - 3x - 1 = 0$ reduces to $\cos 3\theta = \frac{1}{2}$ and hence find the three roots of the equation in x correct to two decimal places.   [L.U.]

10. Find the solution of the equations $\sin (x + y) = 2 \sin (x - y)$,
$2x = \frac{1}{2}\pi - y$, for which x and y are positive acute angles.   [L.U.]

11. If $\sin 3\theta = p$ and $\sin^2 \theta = \frac{3}{4} - q$, prove that $p^2 + 16q^3 = 12q^2$.   [L.U.]

12. If $\sec \theta - \tan \theta = x$, prove that $\tan \frac{1}{2}\theta = (1 - x)/(1 + x)$.   [L.U.]

13. If $\tan \frac{1}{2}x = b/a$, find the value of $a \cos x + b \sin x$ in terms of a and b.

14. Given that $\tan x = 3/4$, find the values of $\sin 2x$, $\tan 2x$ and $\sin 4x$.

15. Find the square root of $(1 + \sin \theta)(3 \sin \theta + 4 \cos \theta + 5)$ in terms of $\tan \frac{1}{2}\theta$.   [L.U.]

3.6 The transformation of $a \cos x + b \sin x$ into the form $R \cos (x - \alpha)$

It is often useful to be able to express $a \cos x + b \sin x$ in the form $R \cos (x - \alpha)$ where R and α are quantities to be found. We start by writing

$$a \cos x + b \sin x = \sqrt{(a^2 + b^2)} \left\{ \frac{a}{\sqrt{(a^2 + b^2)}} \cos x + \frac{b}{\sqrt{(a^2 + b^2)}} \sin x \right\},$$
$$(3.28)$$

and then introduce an acute angle α whose tangent is b/a. This is the angle shown in the right-angled triangle of Fig. 9, the base and height

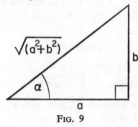

FIG. 9

of this triangle being a and b respectively. The hypotenuse of the triangle is clearly $\sqrt{(a^2 + b^2)}$ and

$$\cos \alpha = \frac{a}{\sqrt{(a^2 + b^2)}}, \quad \sin \alpha = \frac{b}{\sqrt{(a^2 + b^2)}}.$$

Substitution in (3.28) then gives

$$a \cos x + b \sin x = \sqrt{(a^2 + b^2)}(\cos x \cos \alpha + \sin x \sin \alpha)$$
$$= \sqrt{(a^2 + b^2)} \cos (x - \alpha),$$

when use is made of (3.13). Hence

$$a \cos x + b \sin x = R \cos (x - \alpha) \tag{3.29}$$

where

$$R = \sqrt{(a^2 + b^2)} \text{ and } \tan \alpha = b/a. \tag{3.30}$$

In a similar way $a \cos x + b \sin x$ can be expressed in the form $R \sin (x + \beta)$ where $R = \sqrt{(a^2 + b^2)}$ as before but $\tan \beta = a/b$.

Example 6. *Find the maximum and minimum values of $\cos x + \sqrt{3} \sin x$ and show that the smallest positive value of x for which this expression takes its maximum value is 60°.*

We have

$$\cos x + \sqrt{3} \sin x = 2 \left(\frac{1}{2} \cos x + \frac{\sqrt{3}}{2} \sin x \right)$$
$$= 2(\cos x \cos 60° + \sin x \sin 60°) = 2 \cos (x - 60°).$$

The maximum and minimum values of the given expression are therefore those of $2 \cos (x - 60°)$; since the cosine varies between 1 and -1, these are therefore ± 2. The expression is a maximum when $\cos (x - 60°) = 1$ and this occurs when $x - 60° = 0°$, $\pm 360°$, $\pm 720°$, ..., the smallest positive value of x being given by $x = 60°$.

3.7 The equation $a \cos x + b \sin x = c$

The equation $a \cos x + b \sin x = c$, where a, b and c are known numerical quantities often occurs in practical problems. Here we consider two methods of solution.

In the first method, $a \cos x + b \sin x$ is transformed as in § 3.6 into the form $R \cos (x - \alpha)$ and we therefore have $R \cos (x - \alpha) = c$ giving

$$\cos (x - \alpha) = \frac{c}{R} = \frac{c}{\sqrt{(a^2 + b^2)}}.$$

Provided c is less than $\sqrt{(a^2 + b^2)}$ in absolute value, $x - \alpha$ can then be found by the use of a table of natural cosines and, as the value of α can be found from the relation $\tan \alpha = b/a$, values of x can be deduced. If c exceeds $\sqrt{(a^2 + b^2)}$ in absolute value, there are no real solutions.

The second method of solution makes use of the formulae (3.27) expressing $\sin x$ and $\cos x$ in terms of $t = \tan \frac{1}{2}x$. Using these formulae, the equation $a \cos x + b \sin x = c$ transforms into

$$a \left(\frac{1 - t^2}{1 + t^2}\right) + b \left(\frac{2t}{1 + t^2}\right) = c$$

and this reduces to

$$(a + c)t^2 - 2bt + c - a = 0.$$

The roots of this quadratic give values of $t = \tan \frac{1}{2}x$ from which appropriate values of x can be found.

Details of the two methods are given in Example 7 below.

Example 7. *Find the values x between $0°$ and $360°$ which satisfy the equation*

$$8 \cos x + 9 \sin x = 7 \cdot 25.$$

Method (i). By § 3.6, $8 \cos x + 9 \sin x = R \cos (x - \alpha)$ where

$$R = \sqrt{(8^2 + 9^2)} = \sqrt{145} = 12 \cdot 04 \text{ and } \tan \alpha = 9/8 = 1 \cdot 125.$$

The acute angle whose tangent is $1 \cdot 125$ is $48° \, 22'$ and hence the given equation can be written

$$12 \cdot 04 \cos (x - 48° \, 22') = 7 \cdot 25$$

giving

$$\cos (x - 48° \, 22') = 7 \cdot 25/12 \cdot 04 = 0 \cdot 6021.$$

Angles whose cosines are $0 \cdot 6021$ are $52° \, 58'$, $307° \, 2'$, . . . and hence $x = 52° \, 58' + 48° \, 22' = 101° \, 20'$, $x = 307° \, 2' + 48° \, 22' = 355° \, 24'$ and a series of other angles which are outside the range required.

Method (ii). Writing $t = \tan \frac{1}{2}x$, the given equation becomes

$$8 \left(\frac{1 - t^2}{1 + t^2}\right) + 9 \left(\frac{2t}{1 + t^2}\right) = 7 \cdot 25$$

and this reduces to $15 \cdot 25 t^2 - 18t - 0 \cdot 75 = 0$. The roots of this quadratic equation are $1 \cdot 220$ and $-0 \cdot 0403$. Hence $\tan \frac{1}{2}x = 1 \cdot 220$ or $\tan \frac{1}{2}x = -0 \cdot 0403$ and these lead to $\frac{1}{2}x = 50° \, 40'$ and $177° \, 42'$. Hence $x = 101° \, 20'$ and $355° \, 24'$ as before.

3.8 The factor formulae

The factor formulae derived below express the sum (or difference) of two sines (or cosines) as the product of sines and cosines. We start with formulae (3.10) and (3.12),

$$\sin (A + B) = \sin A \cos B + \cos A \sin B,$$
$$\sin (A - B) = \sin A \cos B - \cos A \sin B,$$

and, by addition and subtraction, obtain

$$\sin (A + B) + \sin (A - B) = 2 \sin A \cos B, \qquad (3.31)$$
$$\sin (A + B) - \sin (A - B) = 2 \cos A \sin B. \qquad (3.32)$$

In the same way, formulae (3.11), (3.13) for $\cos (A + B)$ and $\cos (A - B)$ lead to

$$\cos (A + B) + \cos (A - B) = 2 \cos A \cos B, \qquad (3.33)$$

$$\cos (A + B) - \cos (A - B) = -2 \sin A \sin B. \qquad (3.34)$$

Writing $A + B = C$, $A - B = D$, it follows by addition and subtraction that $A = \frac{1}{2}(C + D)$, $B = \frac{1}{2}(C - D)$. Making these substitutions in formulae (3.31) to (3.34), the required factor formulae are given as

$$\left.\begin{array}{l} \sin C + \sin D = 2 \sin \frac{1}{2}(C + D) \cos \frac{1}{2}(C - D), \\[4pt] \sin C - \sin D = 2 \cos \frac{1}{2}(C + D) \sin \frac{1}{2}(C - D), \\[4pt] \cos C + \cos D = 2 \cos \frac{1}{2}(C + D) \cos \frac{1}{2}(C - D), \\[4pt] \cos C - \cos D = -2 \sin \frac{1}{2}(C + D) \sin \frac{1}{2}(C - D), \end{array}\right\} \quad (3.35)$$

and the negative sign on the right-hand side of the last of these formulae should be noted.

Example 8. *Show that*

$$\cos \theta + \cos 3\theta + \cos 5\theta + \cos 7\theta = 4 \cos \theta \cos 2\theta \cos 4\theta. \qquad \text{[L.U.]}$$

Applying the third of formulae (3.35) to $\cos \theta + \cos 3\theta$ and $\cos 5\theta + \cos 7\theta$, we have

$$\cos \theta + \cos 3\theta + \cos 5\theta + \cos 7\theta = 2 \cos 2\theta \cos \theta + 2 \cos 6\theta \cos \theta$$
$$= 2 \cos \theta \,(\cos 2\theta + \cos 6\theta)$$
$$= 4 \cos \theta \cos 4\theta \cos 2\theta,$$

when, in the last step, (3.35) is applied to $\cos 2\theta + \cos 6\theta$.

Example 9. *Find the values of y between $0°$ and $360°$ such that, for all values of x,*
$sin (x + y) + sin (x - y) = sin x$. [N.U.]
By the first of formulae (3.35) $\sin (x + y) + \sin (x - y) = 2 \sin x \cos y$. Hence $2 \sin x \cos y = \sin x$ and, if this is to be true for all values of x, $2 \cos y = 1$ leading to $\cos y = \frac{1}{2}$. Angles between $0°$ and $360°$ for which this is true are $60°$ and $300°$.

Exercises 3 (c)

1. Express $\cos x + \sin x$ in the form $R \cos (x - \alpha)$ giving the values of R and α. Hence find the maximum and minimum values of $\cos x + \sin x$.

2. Express $W(\sin \alpha + \mu \cos \alpha)$ in the form $R \cos (\alpha - \beta)$ giving the values of R and $\tan \beta$. Show that the maximum value of the expression is $W\sqrt{(1 + \mu^2)}$ and that this occurs when $\tan \alpha = 1/\mu$.

3. Find a positive number S and an angle β between $0°$ and $360°$ such that $21 \cos \theta - 20 \sin \theta = S \sin (\theta + \beta)$. [N.U.]

Find the values of x between $0°$ and $360°$ which satisfy the equations

4. $3 \cos x + \sin x = 1$.   [L.U.]

5. $\cos x + 7 \sin x = 5$.

6. $7 \cos x - 6 \sin x = 2$.   [O.C.]

7. $5 \sin x - 6 \cos x = 4$.   [O.C.]

8. $12 \cos x - 5 \sin x + 3 = 0$.   [O.C.]

9. Prove that
$$\text{(i)} \cos 20° + \cos 100° + \cos 140° = 0,$$
$$\text{(ii)} \sin 85° - \cos 55° = \sin 25°.$$

10. Show that $\sin \theta (\cos 2\theta + \cos 4\theta + \cos 6\theta) = \sin 3\theta \cos 4\theta$.   [O.C.]

11. Show that $\sin^2 (A + B) - \sin^2 (A - B) = \sin 2A \sin 2B$.   [L.U.]

12. If A, B, C are the angles of a triangle, show that
$$\sin A + \sin B + \sin C = 4 \cos \tfrac{1}{2}A \cos \tfrac{1}{2}B \cos \tfrac{1}{2}C.$$

13. Find the values of x between $0°$ and $180°$ which satisfy the equation
$\cos x = \cos 2x + \cos 4x$.   [L.U.]

14. Show that
$\sin \theta \sin 3\theta + \sin 2\theta \sin 6\theta + \sin 3\theta \sin 9\theta = 2 \sin 3\theta \sin 7\theta \cos 2\theta$.
     [L.U.]

15. If $\cos \theta + \cos \phi = a$, $\sin \theta + \sin \phi = b$, prove
(i) $\cos (\theta - \phi) = \tfrac{1}{2}(a^2 + b^2 - 2)$,   (ii) $\tan \tfrac{1}{2}(\theta + \phi) = b/a$.
Hence solve the simultaneous equations $\cos \theta + \cos \phi = -1$,
$\sin \theta + \sin \phi = 1 \cdot 5$ for values of θ and ϕ between $0°$ and $180°$.   [L.U.]

3.9 Small angles

Fig. 10 shows the graphs of $y = \sin x$, $y = x$ and $y = \tan x$ plotted

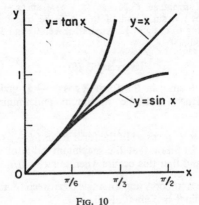

Fig. 10

on the same diagram for values of x in radian measure. It is apparent that, for $0 < x < \frac{1}{2}\pi$,

$$\sin x < x < \tan x \tag{3.36}$$

and that these quantities are approximately equal to each other for small values of the angle x. Thus when x is measured in radians and when it is *small*, we can write

$$\sin x \simeq x, \tan x \simeq x \tag{3.37}$$

and, by division,

$$\cos x \simeq 1. \tag{3.38}$$

Some idea of the order of these approximations can be obtained by taking, as an example, an angle of $4°$ whose radian measure is $0 \cdot 0698$: the values of the sine, tangent and cosine are respectively $0 \cdot 0698$, $0 \cdot 0699$, $0 \cdot 9976$. Even for an angle as large as $10°$ ($0 \cdot 1745$ radians) the percentage errors of the approximations are only about $\frac{1}{2}$, 1 and $1\frac{1}{2}$ respectively.

The above inequalities and approximations can also be inferred from Fig. 11 in which the chord AB subtends an angle x radians at the centre O of a circle of radius r. The tangent to the circle at B meets OA

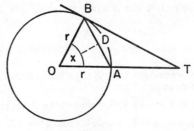

Fig. 11

produced at T. If OD is the bisector of the angle AOB, it will bisect the base AB of the isosceles triangle AOB at right-angles at D. Hence $OD = r \cos \frac{1}{2}x$, $AB = 2BD = 2r \sin \frac{1}{2}x$ and the area of the triangle $AOB = \frac{1}{2} OD \cdot AB = \frac{1}{2}(r \cos \frac{1}{2}x \cdot 2r \sin \frac{1}{2}x) = \frac{1}{2}r^2 \sin x$. The area of the sector AOB is $\frac{1}{2}r^2 x$ and since OBT is a right angle, $BT = r \tan x$ and the area of the triangle $OTB = \frac{1}{2} OB \cdot BT = \frac{1}{2}r^2 \tan x$. It is clear that area of triangle $AOB <$ area of sector $AOB <$ area of triangle OTB, so that

$$\tfrac{1}{2}r^2 \sin x < \tfrac{1}{2}r^2 x < \tfrac{1}{2}r^2 \tan x,$$

and the inequalities (3.36) follow on division by $\frac{1}{2}r^2$. It is also clear that the area of the three figures approach equality as the angle AOB diminishes. so that the approximations (3.37) can also be established by a consideration of these areas.

Dividing the inequalities (3.36) by $\sin x$, we have

$$1 < x/\sin x < 1/\cos x.$$

These can be written

$$1 > (\sin x)/x > \cos x$$

and these in turn can be expressed in the form

$$0 < 1 - \frac{\sin x}{x} < 1 - \cos x.$$

Now, $1 - \cos x = 2 \sin^2 \tfrac{1}{2}x$ and, since $\sin x < x$ (implying that $\sin \tfrac{1}{2}x < \tfrac{1}{2}x$), we have $1 - \cos x < 2(\tfrac{1}{2}x)^2$ or $1 - \cos x < \tfrac{1}{2}x^2$. Hence,

$$0 < 1 - \frac{\sin x}{x} < \tfrac{1}{2}x^2,$$

and $1 - (\sin x)/x$ can therefore be made as small as we please by making x sufficiently small. Another way of expressing this is to write

$$\frac{\sin x}{x} = 1 - \varepsilon$$

where ε is a positive quantity which can be made as small as we please by taking x to be sufficiently small. Yet another way of expressing the same thing is to say that the *limiting value of* $(\sin x)/x$ *as* x *tends to zero is unity*.

Example 10. *Find an acute angle which approximately satisfies the equation* $\sin x = 0{\cdot}48$.

Since $\sin x$ is nearly equal to $0{\cdot}5$, x is nearly equal to $\tfrac{1}{6}\pi$ radians. Let $x = \tfrac{1}{6}\pi + \varepsilon$ where ε is therefore small. Then

$$0{\cdot}48 = \sin(\tfrac{1}{6}\pi + \varepsilon) = \sin \tfrac{1}{6}\pi \cos \varepsilon + \cos \tfrac{1}{6}\pi \sin \varepsilon.$$

Since $\sin \tfrac{1}{6}\pi = \tfrac{1}{2}$, $\cos \tfrac{1}{6}\pi = \tfrac{1}{2}\sqrt{3}$ and, because ε is small, $\cos \varepsilon \simeq 1$, $\sin \varepsilon \simeq \varepsilon$ we have

$$0{\cdot}48 = \frac{1}{2} + \frac{\sqrt{3}}{2}\varepsilon$$

giving

$$\varepsilon = -\frac{2}{\sqrt{3}} \times 0{\cdot}02 = -0{\cdot}0231.$$

Hence $\varepsilon = -0{\cdot}0231$ radians $= -1° \ 19'$ and $x = 30° - 1° \ 19' = 28° \ 41'$.

Example 11. *Assuming that* $\sin x = x - kx^3$, *where k is a numerical constant, is a sufficient approximation to the value of $\sin x$ when x is a small angle, use the formula for $\sin 3x$ to show that $k = \tfrac{1}{6}$.*

From (3.22), $\sin 3x = 3 \sin x - 4 \sin^3 x$ and writing $\sin 3x = 3x - k(3x)^3$, $\sin x = x - kx^3$, this gives

$$3x - 27kx^3 = 3(x - kx^3) - 4(x - kx^3)^3$$
$$= 3x - 3kx^3 - 4x^3,$$

when we neglect terms of higher order than x^3 in the last term on the right-hand side. This gives, after division by x^3, $27k = 3k + 4$ leading to $k = \tfrac{1}{6}$.

3.10 The inverse notation

If $\sin \theta = x$ where x is a given quantity numerically less than or equal to unity, we know that θ can be any one of a series of angles. For example, if $\sin \theta = \frac{1}{2}$, $\theta = \pi/6$, $5\pi/6$, $13\pi/6$, ... or $\theta = -7\pi/6$, $-11\pi/6$, ... The inverse notation $\theta = \sin^{-1} x$ is used to denote the angle whose sine is x and the *numerically smallest angle* satisfying the relation $x = \sin \theta$ is said to be the *principal value* of $\sin^{-1} x$. In what follows we shall deal only with principal values and hence we shall understand the notation $\theta = sin^{-1} x$ *to mean that θ is the angle between* $-\frac{1}{2}\pi$ *and* $\frac{1}{2}\pi$ *radians whose sine is x* and hence, for example, $\sin^{-1} \left(\frac{1}{2}\right) = \frac{1}{6}\pi$.

In a similar way, $\theta = \cos^{-1} x$ will be taken to denote the smallest angle whose cosine is x. Since the cosine takes the same values for negative as for the corresponding positive angles and a notation is required which gives an unique value to θ when x is given, it is conventional to take θ *to be the angle between* 0 *and* π *radians whose cosine is x.* For example, $\cos^{-1} \left(\frac{1}{2}\right) = \frac{1}{3}\pi$ and $\cos^{-1} \left(-\frac{1}{2}\right) = \frac{2}{3}\pi$.

The similar notation $\theta = tan^{-1} x$ *is taken to mean that θ is the smallest angle between* $-\frac{1}{2}\pi$ *and* $\frac{1}{2}\pi$ *radians, whose tangent is x.* Thus $\tan^{-1} (1) = \frac{1}{4}\pi$, $\tan^{-1} (-1) = -\frac{1}{4}\pi$ and, since the tangent can take all values, it is no longer necessary to restrict x to the range $-1 \leqslant x \leqslant 1$ as in the case of $\sin^{-1} x$ and $\cos^{-1} x$. Similar definitions apply to the inverse cosecant, secant and cotangent.

It follows from these definitions that

$$\sin (\sin^{-1} x) = x, \ \cos (\cos^{-1} x) = x, \ \tan (\tan^{-1} x) = x \quad (3.39)$$

and these relations are used in some of the exercises which follow. Care should be taken to avoid confusion between the inverse sine, cosine and tangent and the reciprocals of the sine, cosine and tangent. The latter should always be written $1/(\sin x)$ or $\operatorname{cosec} x$, $1/(\cos x)$ or $\sec x$ and $1/(\tan x)$ or $\cot x$.

Example 12. *Show that* $2 \tan^{-1} \left(\frac{1}{2}\right) - tan^{-1} \left(\frac{1}{7}\right) = \frac{1}{4}\pi$. [O.C.]

Let $\alpha = \tan^{-1} \left(\frac{1}{2}\right)$, $\beta = \tan^{-1} \left(\frac{1}{7}\right)$ so that $\tan \alpha = \frac{1}{2}$, $\tan \beta = \frac{1}{7}$. Also

$$2 \tan^{-1} \left(\tfrac{1}{2}\right) - \tan^{-1} \left(\tfrac{1}{7}\right) = 2\alpha - \beta$$
$$= \tan^{-1} \{\tan (2\alpha - \beta)\}$$
$$= \tan^{-1} \left\{\frac{\tan 2\alpha - \tan \beta}{1 + \tan 2\alpha \tan \beta}\right\}.$$

Since $\tan \alpha = \frac{1}{2}$,

$$\tan 2\alpha = \frac{2 \tan \alpha}{1 - \tan^2 \alpha} = \frac{1}{1 - \frac{1}{4}} = \frac{4}{3},$$

so that substituting $\tan 2\alpha = 4/3$, $\tan \beta = 1/7$, we have

$$2 \tan^{-1} \left(\tfrac{1}{2}\right) - \tan^{-1} \left(\tfrac{1}{7}\right) = \tan^{-1} \left\{\frac{\frac{4}{3} - \frac{1}{7}}{1 + \left(\frac{4}{3}\right)\left(\frac{1}{7}\right)}\right\}$$
$$= \tan^{-1} \left(\tfrac{25}{25}\right) = \tan^{-1} (1) = \tfrac{1}{4}\pi.$$

Example 13. *Find x from the equation* $2 \sin^{-1}x + \sin^{-1}(x^2) = \frac{1}{2}\pi$.   [O.C.]

Let $\sin^{-1} x = \alpha$, $\sin^{-1} (x^2) = \beta$ so that $\sin \alpha = x$, $\sin \beta = x^2$. The given equation can be written $2\alpha + \beta = \frac{1}{2}\pi$ giving $\cos (2\alpha + \beta) = \cos \frac{1}{2}\pi = 0$, and this can be written

$$\cos 2\alpha \cos \beta - \sin 2\alpha \sin \beta = 0.$$

Now $\cos 2\alpha = 1 - 2 \sin^2 \alpha = 1 - 2x^2$, $\sin 2\alpha = 2 \sin \alpha \cos \alpha$

$= 2 \sin \alpha(1 - \sin^2 \alpha)^{\frac{1}{2}} = 2x (1 - x^2)^{\frac{1}{2}}$,

$\sin \beta = x^2$, $\cos \beta = (1 - \sin^2 \beta)^{\frac{1}{2}} = (1 - x^4)^{\frac{1}{2}}$. Hence

$$(1 - 2x^2)(1 - x^4)^{\frac{1}{2}} - 2x(1 - x^2)^{\frac{1}{2}} x^2 = 0.$$

Hence either $(1 - x^2)^{\frac{1}{2}} = 0$ leading to $x = \pm 1$, or $(1 - 2x^2)(1 + x^2)^{\frac{1}{2}} = 2x^3$. Squaring this second equation and making a few reductions we obtain $3x^2 = 1$ and hence $x = \pm 1/\sqrt{3}$. Of the four values of x given above, it will be found on substitution in the given equation that only $x = 1/\sqrt{3}$ satisfies it when we limit ourselves to principal values of the terms $\sin^{-1} x$ and $\sin^{-1} (x^2)$.

Exercises 3 (d)

1. Find the limit as ϕ tends to zero of $(\tan \phi)/\phi$ where ϕ is measured in *degrees*.   [L.U.]

2. Use the approximations $\sin x \simeq x$, $\cos x \simeq 1$ to show that when x is small and in radians,

    (i) $\dfrac{\sin px}{\sin qx} \simeq \dfrac{p}{q}$,   (ii) $\cos (\frac{1}{4}\pi + x) \simeq \dfrac{1}{\sqrt{2}}(1 - x)$,

    (iii) $\tan (\alpha + x) \simeq \tan \alpha + x \sec^2 \alpha$.

3. If θ is a small angle measured in radians, find the limit as θ tends to zero of $(\sin 3\theta + \tan 2\theta)/\theta$.

4. If $\sin (\alpha + \theta) = k \sin \alpha$ and θ is small, show that $\theta \simeq (k - 1) \tan \alpha$.

5. In a right-angled triangle ABC, C is the right angle, $BC = a$ and $AC = b$. Show that the angle ABC lies between $b/\sqrt{(a^2 + b^2)}$ and b/a radians.

6. A star whose distance from the earth is $1\cdot61 \times 10^9$ km subtends at the earth an angle of 15 seconds. Find the approximate value of its diameter.

7. Without using trigonometrical tables, find in degrees and minutes an angle x near $90°$ such that $\cos x = 0\cdot0364$.

8. Given that $\sqrt{3} = 1\cdot73205$, find without the use of any tables, the value of θ (in radians) which satisfies the equation $\sin (\frac{1}{3}\pi + \theta) = 0\cdot87$. [L.U.]

9. The elevations to the top Q of a flagstaff PQ from three *distant* points A, B, C which are in a horizontal line with P are θ, 2θ and 3θ respectively. Prove that $AB \simeq 3BC$.   [L.U.]

10. Evaluate $\sin^{-1} (1/\sqrt{2})$, $\cos^{-1} (-\sqrt{3}/2)$, $\tan^{-1} (-2)$, $\sec^{-1} 2$.

11. Show that

    (i) $\sin^{-1} (\frac{3}{5}) - \sin^{-1} (\frac{5}{13}) = \sin^{-1} (\frac{16}{65})$,
    (ii) $\tan^{-1} (\frac{1}{2}) + \tan^{-1} (\frac{2}{3}) + \tan^{-1} (\frac{4}{7}) = \frac{1}{2}\pi$.

12. If $\tan^{-1} a + \tan^{-1} b + \tan^{-1} c = \pi$, show that $a + b + c = abc$.

13. Show that $\sin^{-1} x + \cos^{-1} x = \frac{1}{2}\pi = \tan^{-1} x + \cot^{-1} x$.

14. Find a positive value of x satisfying the equation

$$\tan^{-1}(2x) + \tan^{-1}(3x) = \tfrac{1}{4}\pi.$$

15. Solve the equation $\cos^{-1}(x\sqrt{3}) + 2\sin^{-1} x = \frac{1}{2}\pi$.

Exercises 3 (e)

1. Find the values of x, between $0°$ and $360°$ which satisfy the equations
    (i) $\tan(5x/3) = -0.5620$,   (ii) $\tan(x + 45°) + 3\tan(x - 45°) = 0$.

2. If $\tan \alpha = (x \cos \theta)/(1 - x \sin \theta)$ and $\tan \beta = (x - \sin \theta)/\cos \theta$, show that $\sin(\theta + \beta)\cos(\theta - \alpha) = \sin \alpha \cos \beta$. Deduce that, if α and β are acute angles $(\alpha > \beta)$, then $\theta = \alpha - \beta$ or $90°$.   [O.C.]

3. If A, B and C are the angles of a triangle, show that

$$\sin^2 A + \sin^2 B + \sin^2 C = 2 + 2\cos A \cos B \cos C. \qquad \text{[O.C.]}$$

4. Given that $\tan \theta = x$, show that $\tan \frac{1}{2}\theta = \{\sqrt{1} \pm \sqrt{(1 + x^2)}\}/x$ and use this result to prove that $\tan 15° = 2 - \sqrt{3}$ and that $\tan 105° = -2 - \sqrt{3}$.   [O.C.]

5. Show that if $x = 18°$, then $\cos 2x = \sin 3x$. Hence find the exact value of $\sin 18°$ and prove that $\cos 36° - \sin 18° = \frac{1}{2}$.   [L.U.]

6. Without using tables, evaluate $\cos^4 15° + \sin^4 15°$.   [L.U.]

7. If $t = \tan \frac{1}{2}x$, find the values of t which satisfy the equation

$$(a + 2)\sin x + (2a - 1)\cos x = 2a + 1$$

where a is a non-zero constant. Hence find two acute angles which satisfy the equation when $a = \sqrt{3}$.   [O.C.]

8. Express the function $4 \sin x - 3 \cos x$ in the form $R \sin(x - \alpha)$ where R is positive, stating the values of R and α. Deduce the solution of the equation $8 \sin x - 6 \cos x = 5$ in the range $0°$ to $180°$.   [O.C.]

9. Express $4 \cos(\theta - \beta) - 3 \sin(\theta - \beta)$ in the form $R \cos(\theta - \alpha)$, finding the numerical value of R and expressing $\tan \alpha$ in terms of $\tan \beta$. Show that $\tan(\beta - \alpha) = \frac{3}{4}$.

10. Show that the equation $6 \sin^2 x - 3 \sin x \cos x + \cos^2 x = 2$ can be written in the form $5 \cos 2x + 3 \sin 2x = 3$. Hence, or otherwise, find values of x between $0°$ and $360°$ which satisfy the equation.

11. If A and B are acute angles such that $\tan A = \frac{1}{5}$ and $\tan B = \frac{1}{239}$, show without the use of tables that $4A - B = 45°$.   [L.U.]

12. Find pairs of angles between $0°$ and $180°$ satisfying the equations $\sin A + \sin B = 0.95$, $A - B = 120°$.   [L.U.]

13. Simplify the fraction

$$\frac{\cos \alpha + \cos 2\alpha + \cos 3\alpha + \cos 4\alpha}{\sin \alpha + \sin 2\alpha + \sin 3\alpha + \sin 4\alpha}$$

and find all the solutions of the equation

$\cos x + \cos 2x + \cos 3x + \cos 4x = 0$ which lie between $0°$ and $360°$.

[L.U.]

14. Show that a triangle ABC in which

$$\sin A (\cos C - \cos B) = \sin B - \sin C$$

is either isosceles or right-angled.   [L.U.]

15. If $x = \cos \theta + \cos 2\theta + \cos 3\theta$ and $y = \sin \theta + \sin 2\theta + \sin 3\theta$, prove that

(a) $x = y \cot 2\theta$,
(b) $xy = \frac{1}{2} \sin 2\theta + \sin 3\theta + \frac{3}{2} \sin 4\theta + \sin 5\theta + \frac{1}{2} \sin 6\theta$,
(c) $x^2 + y^2 = 3 + 4 \cos \theta + 2 \cos 2\theta$.   [L.U.]

16. By expressing $\sec 2x$ and $\tan 2x$ in terms of $\tan x$, find the values of x between $0°$ and $180°$ such that $\sec 2x + 2 \tan 2x = 4$.   [L.U.]

17. Find the values of θ in the range 0 to 2π radians which satisfy the equation $\sin 2\theta + \cos 2\theta = \sin \theta + \cos \theta$.   [O.C.]

18. If $\tan \theta$, $\tan 2\theta$ and $\tan \phi$ are in arithmetical progression, show that $\tan (\phi - \theta) = \sin 2\theta$.

19. The angles of elevation to an aeroplane observed at instants separated by half a minute in time are θ and 2θ where θ is a *small* angle. If the aeroplane is flying directly towards the observer at a constant height of 152 m and with constant speed of 146 m/s, show that θ is approximately $1°$.

20. Assuming the diameter of the moon to be 3475 km and her distance from the earth to be 386,160 km find to the nearest minute the angle subtended by the moon at a point on the earth's surface. Find also the distance at which the mean radius of the earth's orbit (15×10^7 km) subtends an angle of one second, giving your answer correct to two significant figures. (Take 1 radian as 3438 minutes.)   [L.U.]

21. Use the relation $\sin^2 x + \cos^2 x = 1$, the binomial theorem and the approximation $\sin x \simeq x$ to show that $\cos x \simeq 1 - \frac{1}{2}x^2$, where x is small and in radian measure. Deduce that $\cos 4° \simeq 0.9976$.

22. Find a value of x near 0.74 which satisfies the equation $\cos x = x$.

23. Show that

(i) $\cos^{-1} (\frac{63}{65}) + 2 \tan^{-1} (\frac{1}{5}) = \sin^{-1} (\frac{3}{5})$,
(ii) $2 \sin^{-1} (x - a + \frac{1}{2})^{\frac{1}{2}} = \cos^{-1} 2 (a - x)$.

24. If $\cos^{-1}\alpha + \cos^{-1}\beta + \cos^{-1}\gamma = \pi$, show that
$$\alpha^2 + \beta^2 + \gamma^2 + 2\alpha\beta\gamma = 1.$$

25. Find x from the equations

(i) $\sin^{-1}\left(\dfrac{a}{x}\right) + \sin^{-1}\left(\dfrac{b}{x}\right) = \dfrac{1}{2}\pi$,

(ii) $\tan^{-1}(x+1) = 3\tan^{-1}(x-1)$.

CHAPTER 4

RELATIONS BETWEEN THE SIDES AND ANGLES OF A TRIANGLE; THE SOLUTION OF TRIANGLES

4.1 Introduction

A triangle has six parts—three sides and three angles. If A, B and C are used to denote the angles of the triangle, it is usual to denote the sides opposite these angles by the corresponding small letters a, b and c respectively (see Fig. 12).

The lengths of the sides are independent of one another except that the sum of any two of them is greater than the third. The angles,

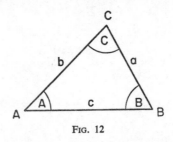

FIG. 12

however, are not independent for their sum is 180° and hence the magnitude of the third angle is known if those of any two are given. There are therefore five independent parts of a triangle and, if any three parts are given (one of which is the length of a side), formulae can be obtained which enable the remaining parts to be found.

In the early part of this chapter, some basic relations between the angles and sides of a triangle are derived and here the reader should have a further opportunity to acquire skill in manipulating trigonometrical formulae. We then go on to suggest ways in which the necessary computations might be arranged when undertaking numerical work involving these formulae. Finally, some examples are given in which the formulae can be used in practical problems in heights and distances.

4.2 The sine formula

In Figs. 13 and 14, which apply respectively when the angle A of the triangle ABC is acute or obtuse, O is the centre of the circumscribing circle and BO meets this circle again at D. In both diagrams, the angle BCD, being the angle in a semi-circle, is a right-angle. In Fig. 13, the angle BDC is equal to the angle BAC in the same segment, while in

Fig. 14 the angle BDC is equal to the supplement of BAC as the points A, B, C and D are concyclic. If R is the radius of the circumscribing circle, $BD = 2R$ and the right-angled triangle BDC gives,

in Fig. 13, $BC = 2R \sin A$,

in Fig. 14, $BC = 2R \sin (180° - A) = 2R \sin A$,

so that in both cases $a = BC = 2R \sin A$.

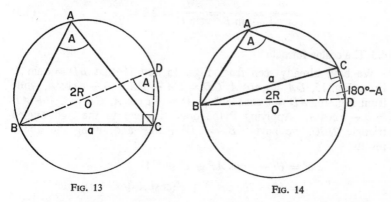

FIG. 13   FIG. 14

By joining AD instead of CD, we could show similarly that $c = 2R \sin C$ and, by starting the construction from C instead of B, that $b = 2R \sin B$. These three results can be displayed in the formula

$$\frac{a}{\sin A} = \frac{b}{\sin B} = \frac{c}{\sin C} = 2R, \qquad (4.1)$$

and this result is usually known as the *sine formula* for the triangle.

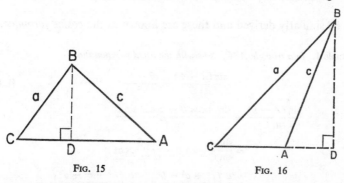

FIG. 15   FIG. 16

In Figs. 15 and 16, BD is the perpendicular from B on to the base CA, or CA produced, of the triangle ABC. The first diagram applies when the angle A is acute and the second when it is obtuse. In each case, the right-angled triangle DAB gives $BD = c \sin A$. The area Δ of the triangle ABC is then given by

$$\Delta = \tfrac{1}{2}CA \cdot BD = \tfrac{1}{2}bc \sin A, \qquad (4.2)$$

and this can be written in the form $a/(\sin A) = (\tfrac{1}{2}abc)/\Delta$. Hence we can rewrite the sine formula (4.1) as

$$\frac{a}{\sin A} = \frac{b}{\sin B} = \frac{c}{\sin C} = 2R = \frac{abc}{2\Delta}. \qquad (4.3)$$

4.3 The cosine formula

We have already seen from Figs. 15 and 16 that $BD = c \sin A$. From Fig. 15, $DA = c \cos A$, $CD = CA - DA = b - c \cos A$, while from Fig. 16, $AD = c \cos (180° - A) = -c \cos A$, $CD = CA + AD = b - c \cos A$. Applying Pythagoras' theorem to the right-angled triangle DBC, we have $CB^2 = CD^2 + BD^2$ and, using the above results,

$$a^2 = (b - c \cos A)^2 + c^2 \sin^2 A$$
$$= b^2 - 2bc \cos A + c^2(\cos^2 A + \sin^2 A),$$

which, using the result $\sin^2 A + \cos^2 A = 1$, reduces to

$$a^2 = b^2 + c^2 - 2bc \cos A.$$

The two similar formulae

$$\left.\begin{array}{l} b^2 = c^2 + a^2 - 2ca \cos B, \\ c^2 = a^2 + b^2 - 2ab \cos C, \end{array}\right\} \qquad (4.4)$$

can be similarly derived and these are known as the *cosine formulae*.

Example 1. *In a triangle ABC, show with the usual notation that*

$$\frac{\sin (A - B)}{\sin C} = \frac{a^2 - b^2}{c^2}. \qquad \text{[L.U.]}$$

$$\frac{\sin (A - B)}{\sin C} = \frac{\sin A \cos B - \cos A \sin B}{\sin C}$$

$$= \frac{\sin A}{\sin C} \cdot \cos B - \frac{\sin B}{\sin C} \cdot \cos A$$

$$= \frac{a}{c} \left(\frac{c^2 + a^2 - b^2}{2ca} \right) - \frac{b}{c} \left(\frac{b^2 + c^2 - a^2}{2bc} \right),$$

when we substitute from (4.3) and (4.4), and this is easily found to reduce to $(a^2 - b^2)/c^2$.

Example 2. *A triangle has sides of lengths* $m - n$, m, $m + n$ *where* $m > n > 0$. *Use the cosine formula to show that, if the triangle is obtuse-angled, then* $\frac{1}{4}m < n < \frac{1}{2}m$. [L.U.]

Writing $a = m - n$, $b = m$, $c = m + n$, the sides a, b and c are in ascending order of magnitude and the greatest angle, being opposite the greatest side, will be the angle C. As a triangle can only contain one obtuse angle, this will therefore be the angle C and cos C will be negative. Hence, using (4.4),

$$0 > \cos C = \frac{a^2 + b^2 - c^2}{2ab}$$

$$= \frac{(m - n)^2 + m^2 - (m + n)^2}{2m(m - n)} = \frac{m^2 - 4mn}{2m(m - n)}$$

$$= \frac{m - 4n}{2(m - n)}.$$

As $m > n$, it follows that $m - 4n < 0$ and $\frac{1}{4}m < n$. Since the sum of the lengths of the two shorter sides of a triangle is greater than the length of the longest side $(m - n) + m > (m + n)$, leading to $m > 2n$ and $n < \frac{1}{2}m$.

Exercises 4 (a)

1. Show that, in a triangle ABC,

$$c(a^2 - c^2) \sin (A - B) = b(a^2 - b^2) \sin (A - C).$$ [O.C.]

2. In a triangle ABC, $B = \frac{1}{3}A$. Show that $2 \sin B = \sqrt{(3 - a/b)}$.

3. In a triangle ABC, show that $a = b \cos C + c \cos B$. Deduce that, if θ is any acute angle,

$$c \cos (B + \theta) + b \cos (C - \theta) = a \cos \theta,$$
$$c \sin (B + \theta) - b \sin (C - \theta) = a \sin \theta.$$ [O.C.]

4. If the sides a, b and c of a triangle are in arithmetical progression, show that $\cos \frac{1}{2}(A - C) = 2 \cos \frac{1}{2}(A + C)$.

5. D is a point on the side BC of a triangle ABC such that $2BD = 3DC$ and the angle $ADB = 60°$. Prove that

$$AD = \{a^2 + 5(b^2 - c^2)\}/5a.$$

If, further, the angle $ABD = 60°$ and ϕ denotes the angle DAC, prove that $\tan \phi = \frac{1}{4}\sqrt{3}$. [O.C.]

6. Δ is the area of a triangle ABC and E is the middle point of the side CA. Prove that

$$b^2 + c^2 = a^2 + 4\Delta \cot A$$

and that

$$4\Delta \cot AEB = a^2 - c^2.$$ [L.U.]

7. In the triangle ABC, the angle ACB is double the angle ABC. Prove that

$$\frac{c}{b} = \frac{a + b}{c} = 2 \cos B.$$ [L.U.]

8. With the usual notation for a triangle ABC, prove that

$$a \cos A + b \cos B = c \cos (A - B).$$ [L.U.]

9. In an acute angled triangle ABC, a semi-circle is drawn on BC as diameter cutting AB in D and AC in E. Prove that the area of that part of the semi-circle which lies outside the triangle is

$$\tfrac{1}{8}a^2(2A - \sin 2B - \sin 2C).$$ [L.U.]

10. If Δ is the area of a triangle ABC and R is the radius of the circumscribing circle, prove that

    (i) $\Delta = 2R^2 \sin A \sin B \sin C,$
    (ii) $4\Delta = b^2 \sin 2C + c^2 \sin 2B.$

11. D is the mid-point of the side AB of a triangle ABC and CD is perpendicular to AC. Prove that $2 \tan A + \tan C = 0$.

12. Prove that the area Δ of the triangle ABC is given by

$$\Delta = \tfrac{1}{2}aR\{\cos (B - C) + \cos A\}$$

where R is the radius of the circumscribing circle.

13. In an acute angled triangle ABC, BE and CF are the perpendiculars from B and C to the opposite sides. Find the magnitude of the angle A such that the area of the triangle AEF shall be half that of the triangle ABC.

14. If, in the usual notation for the triangle ABC, $b = a + \lambda c$ show that $\lambda \cos \tfrac{1}{2}C = \cos (A + \tfrac{1}{2}C)$.

15. Find the largest angle in the triangle whose sides are $\alpha^2 + \alpha + 1$, $2\alpha + 1$ and $\alpha^2 - 1$ where $\alpha > 1$.

4.4 Some other formulae for the triangle

The fundamental sine and cosine formulae for the triangle derived in §§ 4.2, 4.3 are not always the best ones to use in numerical work and we give below some of the other forms into which these formulae may be recast.

(i) The half-angle formulae

The cosine formula (4.4) can be written in the form

$$b^2 + c^2 - a^2 = 2bc \cos A$$

and, using the relations

$$\cos A = 1 - 2 \sin^2 \tfrac{1}{2}A = 2 \cos^2 \tfrac{1}{2}A - 1,$$

we have

$$b^2 + c^2 - a^2 = 2bc(1 - 2\sin^2 \tfrac{1}{2}A) = 2bc(2\cos^2 \tfrac{1}{2}A - 1).$$

Solving for $\sin^2 \tfrac{1}{2}A$ and $\cos^2 \tfrac{1}{2}A$, this gives

$$4bc \sin^2 \tfrac{1}{2}A = 2bc - b^2 - c^2 + a^2 = a^2 - (b - c)^2$$
$$= (a - b + c)(a + b - c),$$

and

$$4bc \cos^2 \tfrac{1}{2}A = 2bc + b^2 + c^2 - a^2 = (b + c)^2 - a^2$$
$$= (b + c - a)(b + c + a).$$

If s is the semi-perimeter of the triangle, $2s = a + b + c$, $2s - 2a = b + c - a$, $2s - 2b = a + c - b$, $2s - 2c = a + b - c$, and the above can be written in the form

$$bc \sin^2 \tfrac{1}{2}A = (s - b)(s - c), \quad bc \cos^2 \tfrac{1}{2}A = s(s - a),$$

giving

$$\sin \tfrac{1}{2}A = \sqrt{\left\{ \frac{(s - b)(s - c)}{bc} \right\}}, \qquad \cos \tfrac{1}{2}A = \sqrt{\left\{ \frac{s(s - a)}{bc} \right\}}. \quad (4.5)$$

On division these give

$$\left. \begin{array}{c} \tan \tfrac{1}{2}A = \sqrt{\left\{ \dfrac{(s - b)(s - c)}{s(s - a)} \right\}}, \\[2mm] \text{and the two similar formulae} \\[2mm] \tan \tfrac{1}{2}B = \sqrt{\left\{ \dfrac{(s - c)(s - a)}{s(s - b)} \right\}}, \qquad \tan \tfrac{1}{2}C = \sqrt{\left\{ \dfrac{(s - a)(s - b)}{s(s - c)} \right\}}, \end{array} \right\} \quad (4.6)$$

can be similarly derived.

(ii) *The area formula*

A formula for the area Δ of a triangle in terms of the lengths of its sides can be derived from the formulae (4.2) and (4.5). Thus

$$\Delta^2 = (\tfrac{1}{2}bc \sin A)^2 = b^2 c^2 \sin^2 \tfrac{1}{2}A \cos^2 \tfrac{1}{2}A$$
$$= s(s - a)(s - b)(s - c),$$

giving

$$\Delta = \sqrt{\{s(s - a)(s - b)(s - c)\}}. \quad (4.7)$$

(iii) *The included angle formulae*

Starting from the sine formulae (4.3) in the form $b = 2R \sin B$, $c = 2R \sin C$, we have after division of numerator and denominator by $2R$,

$$\frac{b - c}{b + c} = \frac{\sin B - \sin C}{\sin B + \sin C}$$

$$= \frac{2 \cos \frac{1}{2}(B + C) \sin \frac{1}{2}(B - C)}{2 \sin \frac{1}{2}(B + C) \cos \frac{1}{2}(B - C)}$$

$$= \cot \frac{1}{2}(B + C) \tan \frac{1}{2}(B - C).$$

Since $B + C = 180° - A$, $\cot \frac{1}{2}(B + C) = \cot (90° - \frac{1}{2}A) = \tan \frac{1}{2}A$, this can be written,

$$\tan \tfrac{1}{2}(B - C) = \left(\frac{b - c}{b + c}\right) \cot \tfrac{1}{2}A,$$

and the two corresponding formulae

$$\tan \tfrac{1}{2}(C - A) = \left(\frac{c - a}{c + a}\right) \cot \tfrac{1}{2}B,$$

$$\tan \tfrac{1}{2}(A - B) = \left(\frac{a - b}{a + b}\right) \cot \tfrac{1}{2}C$$

(4.8)

can be obtained in the same way.

Example 3. *If in a triangle ABC, $2a \cos^2 \frac{1}{2}C + 2c \cos^2 \frac{1}{2}A = 3b$, show that the sides of the triangle are in arithmetical progression.*

Using the second of formulae (4.5) and the corresponding formula for $ab \cos^2 \frac{1}{2}C$,

$$3b = 2a \cos^2 \tfrac{1}{2}C + 2c \cos^2 \tfrac{1}{2}A$$

$$= \frac{2s(s - c)}{b} + \frac{2s(s - a)}{b}$$

$$= \frac{2s(2s - a - c)}{b} = 2s,$$

since $2s - a - c = b$. Hence $3b = 2s = a + b + c$ giving $2b = a + c$, and this shows that the sides a, b and c are in arithmetical progression.

Example 4. *Prove, with the usual notation for a triangle, that*

$$c \cos \tfrac{1}{2}(A - B) = (a + b) \cos \tfrac{1}{2}(A + B).$$

Using the sine formulae in the form $a = 2R \sin A$, $b = 2R \sin B$, $c = 2R \sin C$ and dividing numerator and denominator by $2R$,

$$\frac{a + b}{c} = \frac{\sin A + \sin B}{\sin C} = \frac{\sin A + \sin B}{\sin (A + B)}, \text{ since } C = 180° - A - B,$$

$$= \frac{2 \sin \tfrac{1}{2}(A + B) \cos \tfrac{1}{2}(A - B)}{2 \sin \tfrac{1}{2}(A + B) \cos \tfrac{1}{2}(A + B)} = \frac{\cos \tfrac{1}{2}(A - B)}{\cos \tfrac{1}{2}(A + B)},$$

and the required result follows by cross multiplication.

Exercises 4 (b)

1. In any triangle ABC, prove that $\tan \frac{1}{2}A \tan \frac{1}{2}B \tan \frac{1}{2}C = \Delta/s^2$ where Δ is the area of the triangle and s the semi-perimeter. [L.U.]

2. If the sides a, b, c of a triangle ABC are in arithmetical progression, show that $\sin \frac{1}{2}A \sin \frac{1}{2}C = \frac{1}{2} \sin \frac{1}{2}B$.

3. In a triangle ABC prove that

$$\frac{a+b-c}{a+b+c} = \tan \frac{1}{2}A \tan \frac{1}{2}B.$$

Hence calculate the perimeter of the triangle, correct to the nearest millimetre, given that $a + b = 0.1175$ m, $A = 46° 52'$, $B = 69° 36'$.

[O.C.]

4. Prove that in a triangle ABC,

$$4bc \cos^2 \tfrac{1}{2}A + 4ca \cos^2 \tfrac{1}{2}B + 4ab \cos^2 \tfrac{1}{2}C = (a + b + c)^2.$$

5. In a triangle ABC, prove that

$$(a + b + c)(\tan \tfrac{1}{2}A + \tan \tfrac{1}{2}B) = 2c \cot \tfrac{1}{2}C.$$

6. The area of a triangle is 3.36×10^{-2} m², the sum of the three sides is 0.84 m and one side is 0.28 m. Calculate the lengths of the other two sides. [L.U.]

7. Prove that in any triangle ABC, $a \sin \frac{1}{2}(B - C) = (b - c) \cos \frac{1}{2}A$.

8. If in a triangle ABC, $(b - c) \tan \theta = (b + c) \tan \frac{1}{2}A$, prove that $a = (b - c) \cos \frac{1}{2}A \sec \theta$. [L.U.]

9. In a triangle ABC show that $(a + b) \sin B = 2b \sin (B + \frac{1}{2}C) \cos \frac{1}{2}C$.

10. With the usual notation for a triangle, show that

$2\sqrt{(ab)} \cos \frac{1}{2} (A + B) = c \sin \theta$ where $c \cos \theta = a - b$.
Show further that $2\sqrt{(ab)} \cos \frac{1}{2} (A - B) = (a + b) \sin \theta$.

11. If in a triangle $a = 5$, $b = 4$ and $\cos (A - B) = \frac{31}{32}$, prove that $\cos C = \frac{1}{8}$. [O.C.]

12. The angle A of a triangle ABC is $60°$ and the area of the triangle is equal to that of an equilateral triangle with sides of length x. Show that $b^2 + c^2 - a^2 = x^2$.

4.5 The numerical solution of triangles

When three of the six parts of a triangle are given numerically and when one at least of these is a side, the other three parts can be found. In principle this can be done by the use of the fundamental sine and cosine formulae (4.3) and (4.4) but some improvement in the numerical work involved can often be made by using the formulae (4.6) or (4.8).

It is recommended that the computational work be set out in a systematic manner and that checks be employed whenever these are possible. Some suggested lay-outs are shown in the examples which follow.

(i) *One side and two-angles given*

Here the remaining angle can be found at once from the fact that the sum of the three angles is 180°. If the side c, for example, is given the diameter $2R$ of the circumscribing circle of the triangle can be found from (4.3) as

$$2R = \frac{c}{\sin C} = c \operatorname{cosec} C.$$

Once $2R$ has been computed, the remaining sides a and b can then be calculated from the sine formulae in the forms

$$a = 2R \sin A, \; b = 2R \sin B,$$

and the adaptation of the above when a or b is given instead of c should cause no difficulty.

Example 5. *Solve the triangle in which* $c = 1.414 \, cm$, $A = 117°$, $B = 45°$.

	No.	log
$C = 180° - (A + B)$		
$\quad = 180° - (117° + 45°) = 180° - 162°$	1.414	0.1504
$\quad = 18°.$	$\operatorname{cosec} 18°$	0.5100
$2R = c \operatorname{cosec} C = 1.414 \operatorname{cosec} 18°.$	$2R$	0.6604
$a = 2R \sin A = 2R \sin 117°$	$\sin 63°$	$\bar{1}.9499$
$\quad = 2R \sin (180° - 117°) = 2R \sin 63°.$	$a = 4.077$	0.6103
$b = 2R \sin B = 2R \sin 45°.$	$2R$	0.6604
	$\sin 45°$	$\bar{1}.8495$
The required solution is therefore	$b = 3.235$	0.5099
$\quad C = 18°, \quad a = 4.077 \text{ cm}, \quad b = 3.235 \text{ cm}.$		

(ii) *Two sides and the non-included angle given*

To fix ideas, suppose b and c are the given sides and B the given angle. The angle C can be found from the sine formula in the form

$$\sin C = \frac{c \sin B}{b} \qquad\qquad (4.9)$$

and various possibilities can arise

(a) If b is less than $c \sin B$, the value of $\sin C$ given by (4.9) will be greater than unity and no triangle will exist for the given values of b, c and B, see Fig. 17.

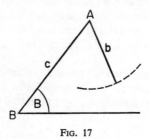

FIG. 17

(b) If $b = c \sin B$, equation (4.9) shows that $\sin C = 1$ and hence that $C = 90°$. In this case the triangle is right-angled at C as shown in Fig. 18. Since, when one angle of a triangle is $90°$, the other two angles are necessarily acute, this case can only occur when $B < 90°$.

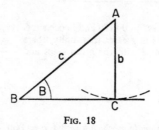

FIG. 18

(c) If b is greater than $c \sin B$, the value of $\sin C$ given by (4.9) will be less than unity and there will be two possible values of C less than $180°$. If C_1 is the acute and C_2 the obtuse angle having this value of $\sin C$, we have now to discover if both these angles give possible solutions.

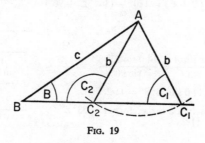

FIG. 19

If B is greater than $90°$, there cannot be another obtuse angle in the triangle and the angle C_2 must be excluded as a possible solution. If B is less than $90°$, values of C greater than $90°$ are not immediately excluded. If, however, the given side b is greater than the other given side c, such values are excluded because the greater angle would then be opposite the lesser side. In the remaining case in which $B < 90°$, $b < c$, there are two possible values C_1, C_2 of C and this is often called the *ambiguous case*, see Fig. 19.

Once the angle C has been found, the remaining angle and side can be found as in Example 5. In the ambiguous case there will be two values a_1, a_2 of the side corresponding to the two values A_1, A_2 deduced for the angle A.

Example 6. *Solve the triangle in which $b = 9$, $c = 13$, $B = 65°$.*

The magnitude of the angle C is given by

$$\sin C = \frac{c \sin B}{b} = \frac{13 \sin 65°}{9}.$$

This leads to log sin $C = 0.1170$ and hence sin C $= 1.309$. Since this is greater than unity, there is no possible triangle with the given sides and angle.

No.	log
13	1·1139
sin 65°	$\bar{1}$·9573
	1·0712
9	0·9542
sin C	0·1170

Example 7. *Solve the triangle in which $b = 8.4$, $c = 14.0$, $B = 36° 52$.*

Here the sine formula gives

$$\sin C = \frac{c \sin B}{b} = \frac{14.0 \sin 36° 52}{8.4}.$$

This gives log sin $C = 0$, sin $C = 1$ and $C = 90°$. The remaining angle A is given by

$$A = 180° - (B + C) = 180° - (36° 52' + 90°)$$

$$= 53° 8'.$$

For the side a,

$$a = \frac{c \sin A}{\sin C} = \frac{14.0 \sin 53° 8'}{\sin 90°}$$

$$= 14.0 \sin 53° 8' = 11.2.$$

The required solution is therefore $A = 53° 8'$ $C = 90°$, $a = 11.2$.

No.	log
14·0	1·1461
sin 36° 52′	$\bar{1}$·7782
	0·9243
8·4	0·9243
sin C	0·0000
14·0	1·1461
sin 53° 8′	$\bar{1}$·9031
a	1·0492

Example 8. *Solve the triangle in which $b = 107 \cdot 2$, $c = 76 \cdot 69$, $B = 102° 25'$.*

Here

$$\sin C = \frac{76 \cdot 69 \sin 102° 25'}{107 \cdot 2} = \frac{76 \cdot 69 \sin 77° 35'}{107 \cdot 2},$$

since $\sin 102° 25' = \sin (180° - 102° 25')$.

Hence $\log \sin C = \bar{1} \cdot 8442$ giving $C = 44° 19'$, an obtuse value for C being impossible as $B > 90°$.

$$A = 180° - (B + C)$$
$$= 180° - (102° 25' + 44° 19')$$
$$= 33° 16'.$$

$$a = \frac{c \sin A}{\sin C} = c \sin A \operatorname{cosec} C$$

$$= 76 \cdot 69 \sin 33° 16' \operatorname{cosec} 44° 19' = 60 \cdot 21,$$

and the full solution is $A = 33° 16'$, $C = 44° 19'$, $a = 60 \cdot 21$.

No.	log
$76 \cdot 69$	$1 \cdot 8847$
$\sin 77° 35'$	$\bar{1} \cdot 9897$
	$1 \cdot 8744$
$107 \cdot 2$	$2 \cdot 0302$
$\sin C$	$\bar{1} \cdot 8442$
$76 \cdot 69$	$1 \cdot 8847$
$\sin 33° 16'$	$\bar{1} \cdot 7392$
$\operatorname{cosec} 44° 19'$	$0 \cdot 1558$
a	$1 \cdot 7797$

Example 9. *In a triangle ABC, $B = 60°$, $b = 14$ and $c = 16$. Calculate the two possible values of the side a.* [L.U.]

From the sine formula

$$\sin C = \frac{16 \sin 60°}{14}.$$

This gives $\log \sin C = \bar{1} \cdot 9955$ and $C_1 = 81° 48'$, $C_2 = 180° - 81° 48' = 98° 12'$, since this is the ambiguous case in which $B < 90°$ and $b < c$. If we denote the angles BAC_1, BAC_2 respectively by A_1 and A_2 (Fig. 20),

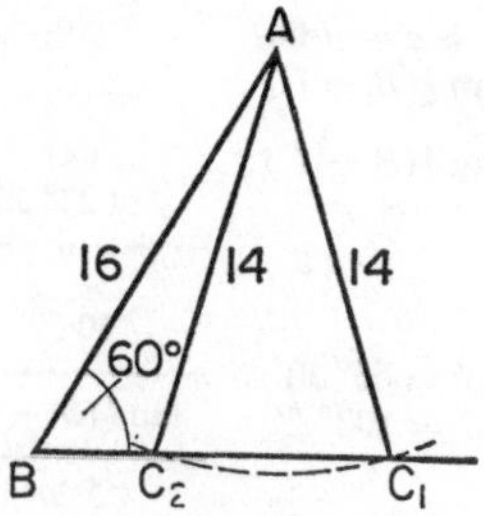

No.	log
16	$1 \cdot 2041$
$\sin 60°$	$\bar{1} \cdot 9375$
14	$1 \cdot 1416$
	$1 \cdot 1461$
$\sin C$	$\bar{1} \cdot 9955$
16	$1 \cdot 2041$
$\sin 38° 12'$	$\bar{1} \cdot 7913$
$\operatorname{cosec} 81° 48'$	$0 \cdot 0045$
a_1	$0 \cdot 9999$
16	$1 \cdot 2041$
$\sin 21° 48'$	$\bar{1} \cdot 5698$
$\operatorname{cosec} 98° 12'$	$0 \cdot 0045$
a_2	$0 \cdot 7784$

FIG. 20

$A_1 = 180° - (60° + 81° 48') = 38° 12'$ and
$A_2 = 180° - (60° + 98° 12') = 21° 48'$.

Hence if BC_1 and BC_2 are denoted respectively by a_1 and a_2,

$$a_1 = \frac{c \sin A_1}{\sin C_1} = c \sin A_1 \operatorname{cosec} C_1 = 16 \sin 38° \, 12' \operatorname{cosec} 81° \, 48',$$

$$a_2 = \frac{c \sin A_2}{\sin C_2} = c \sin A_2 \operatorname{cosec} C_2 = 16 \sin 21° \, 48' \operatorname{cosec} 98° \, 12';$$

these formulae lead to $a_1 = 10·0$ and $a_2 = 6·0$, correct to one decimal place.

(iii) *Two sides and the included angle given*

Again, to fix ideas, we suppose that the sides b, c and the angle A included between them are given. The side a can be calculated from the cosine formula

$$a^2 = b^2 + c^2 - 2bc \cos A,$$

tables of squares and square roots being useful in the numerical work. The remaining angles B and C can then be found from the sine formulae

$$\sin B = \frac{b \sin A}{a}, \quad \sin C = \frac{c \sin A}{a}.$$

Since all the sides of the triangle are known, any question of the values of B and C being greater or less than 90° can be settled by choosing angles which are in the same order of magnitude as the sides opposite them.

When using logarithms it is preferable to use formula (4.8),

$$\tan \tfrac{1}{2}(B - C) = \frac{b - c}{b + c} \cot \tfrac{1}{2}A$$

to find $\tfrac{1}{2}(B - C)$. Since $A + B + C = 180°$, $\tfrac{1}{2}(B + C) = 90° - \tfrac{1}{2}A$ and the values of B and C then follow by addition and subtraction. The remaining side a can then be determined from the sine formula.

Both methods of solution are shown in Example 10 below.

Example 10. *Solve the triangle in which $b = 7·00$ cm, $c = 3·59$ cm and $A = 47°$.*

Method (i)

	No.	log
Since $b - c = 7·00 - 3·59 = 3·41$, $b + c = 7·00 + 3·59 = 10·59$ and $\tfrac{1}{2}A = 23° \, 30'$, $\tan \tfrac{1}{2}(B - C)$ $= \dfrac{3·41 \cot 23° \, 30'}{10·59}$, leading to $\log \tan \tfrac{1}{2}(B - C)$ $= \bar{1}·8696$ and $\tfrac{1}{2}(B - C) = 36° \, 32'$.	3·41 cot 23° 30'	0·5328 0·3617
		0·8945
Also	10·59	1·0249
$\tfrac{1}{2}(B + C) = 90° - \tfrac{1}{2}A = 90° - 23° \, 30' = 66° \, 30'$, and addition and subtraction gives $B = 103° \, 2'$, $C = 29° \, 58'$.	$\tan \tfrac{1}{2}(B - C)$	$\bar{1}·8696$
	3·59 sin 47° cosec 29° 58'	0·5551 $\bar{1}·8641$ 0·3014
The side a is then found from $$a = \frac{c \sin A}{\sin C} = 3·59 \sin 47° \operatorname{cosec} 29° \, 58'$$ $= 5·255$ cm.	a	0·7206

Method (ii)

$$a^2 = b^2 + c^2 - 2bc \cos A$$

$$= (7 \cdot 00)^2 + (3 \cdot 59)^2 - 2(7 \cdot 00)(3 \cdot 59) \cos 47°$$

$$= 49 \cdot 00 + 12 \cdot 89 - 34 \cdot 28 = 27 \cdot 61,$$

giving $a = \sqrt{(27 \cdot 61)} = 5 \cdot 255$ cm.

$$\sin B = \frac{7 \cdot 00 \sin 47°}{5 \cdot 255},$$

giving $\log \sin B = \bar{1} \cdot 9886$ and

$$B = 76° \, 58' \text{ or } 180° - 76° \, 58' = 103° \, 2'.$$

$$\sin C = \frac{3 \cdot 59 \sin 47°}{5 \cdot 255},$$

giving $\log \sin C = \bar{1} \cdot 6986$ and

$$C = 29° \, 58' \text{ or } 180° - 29° \, 58' = 150° \, 2'.$$

Since b, a, c are in descending order of magnitude, so must be B, A, C and their sum must be 180°. Hence the required solution is $a = 5 \cdot 255$ cm, $B = 103° \, 2'$, $C = 29° \, 58'$, giving the same solution as by Method (i).

No.	log
2	0·3010
7·00	0·8451
3·59	0·5551
cos 47°	$\bar{1}$·8338
2bc cos A	1·5350
7·00	0·8451
sin 47°	$\bar{1}$·8641
	0·7092
5·255	0·7206
sin B	$\bar{1}$·9886
3·59	0·5551
sin 47°	$\bar{1}$·8641
	0·4192
5·255	0·7206
sin C	$\bar{1}$·6986

(iv) *Three sides given*

When all three sides are given, the angle can be found from the cosine formula rearranged in the form

$$\cos A = \frac{b^2 + c^2 - a^2}{2bc},$$

with corresponding formulae for $\cos B$ and $\cos C$. Alternatively, one of the angles can be found in this way and the other two found by the sine formula.

When using logarithms it is, however, simpler to use formula (4.6),

$$\tan \tfrac{1}{2}A = \sqrt{\left\{ \frac{(s - b)(s - c)}{s(s - a)} \right\}}$$

and the two similar formulae for $\tan \tfrac{1}{2}B$ and $\tan \tfrac{1}{2}C$. To save repetition in the numerical work, these formulae can be written

$$\tan \tfrac{1}{2}A = \frac{1}{s - a} \sqrt{\left\{ \frac{(s - a)(s - b)(s - c)}{s} \right\}} \tag{4.10}$$

with corresponding expressions for $\tan \tfrac{1}{2}B$ and $\tan \tfrac{1}{2}C$. The logarithm for the expression under the square root sign has only to be worked out once and the logarithmic tangents of $\tfrac{1}{2}A$, $\tfrac{1}{2}B$, $\tfrac{1}{2}C$ then follow by subtracting $\log (s - a)$, $\log (s - b)$ and $\log (s - c)$.

Example 11. *Find all the angles of the triangle in which* $a = 10\cdot4$, $b = 12\cdot8$, $c = 17\cdot6 \ m$.

We first find s from the formula $2s = a + b + c$ and then form $s - a, s - b, s - c$. A check is provided by $(s - a) + (s - b) + (s - c) = s$. We then find $\log \{(s - a)(s - b)(s - c)/s\}$ by adding the logarithms of $(s - a)$, $(s - b)$, $(s - c)$ and subtracting that of s. The logarithm of the square root of this quantity follows by division by 2 and the angles are found from (4.10). From the working on the right we have

$\frac{1}{2}A = 17^\circ 54'$, $A = 35^\circ 48'$,
$\frac{1}{2}B = 23^\circ 1\frac{1}{2}'$, $B = 46^\circ 3'$,
$\frac{1}{2}C = 49^\circ 4\frac{1}{2}'$, $C = 98^\circ 9'$.

No.		log.
a	10·4	
b	12·8	
c	17·6	
$2s = $ sum	40·8	
s	20·4	
$s - a$	10·0	1·0000
$s - b$	7·6	0·8808
$s - c$	2·8	0·4472
$(s - a)(s - b)(s - c)$		2·3280
s	20·4	1·3096
$\{(s - a)(s - b)(s - c)/s\}$		1·0184
$\sqrt{\{(s - a)(s - b)(s - c)/s\}}$		0·5092
$s - a$		1·0000
$\tan \frac{1}{2}A$		$\bar{1}$·5092
$\sqrt{\{(s - a)(s - b)(s - c)/s\}}$		0·5092
$s - b$		0·8808
tab $\frac{1}{2}B$		$\bar{1}$·6284
$\sqrt{\{(s - a)(s - b)(s - c)/s\}}$		0·5092
$s - c$		0·4472
$\tan \frac{1}{2}C$		0·0620

There is a final check that the sum of the angles should be 180°.

Exercises 4 (c)

Solve the triangles in which

1. $c = 12$, $A = 70^\circ$, $B = 58^\circ 16'$.

2. $a = 57\cdot91$ m, $A = 27^\circ 28'$, $B = 103^\circ 19'$.

3. $a = 6\cdot91$ cm, $B = 60^\circ 3'$, $C = 47^\circ 57'$.

4. $b = 5$, $c = 6$, $B = 65^\circ$.

5. $a = 5$, $c = 7$, $A = 48^\circ 36'$.

6. $b = 5$, $c = 4$, $C = 53^\circ 8'$.

7. $a = 15$, $c = 39$, $A = 22^\circ 37'$.

8. $b = 9 \cdot 4$ cm, $c = 5 \cdot 2$ cm, $B = 119° \ 6'$.

9. $a = 0 \cdot 214$ m, $c = 0 \cdot 853$ m, $C = 128° \ 41'$.

10. $b = 50\sqrt{3}$, $c = 150$, $B = 30°$.

11. $a = 46 \cdot 8$ m, $c = 36 \cdot 9$ m, $C = 34° \ 20'$.

12. $b = 4$, $c = 6$, $A = 70° \ 32'$.

13. $a = 15$ km, $b = 40$ km, $C = 60°$.

14. $a = 7$ m, $b = 11$ m, $c = 12$ m.

15. $a = 16$ m, $b = 20$ m, $c = 33$ m.

4.6 Practical applications

Elementary trigonometry is often useful in the solution of practical problems, particularly in those arising in survey work and in navigation. By measuring certain distances and angles it is sometimes possible to calculate other distances and angles which cannot be measured directly. Such calculations are usually simple applications of the formulae relating the angles and sides of a triangle and we give below a few typical examples.

Example 12. *The angle of elevation of the top of a vertical tower from a point A on the same horizontal level as the foot of the tower is α. From a point B, in a direct line between A and the foot of the tower and at distance d from A, the angle of elevation to the top of the tower is β. Find a formula giving the height of the tower in terms of d, α and β.*

In Fig. 21, TT' is the tower, ABT' is horizontal, the angle $AT'T$ is a right angle, the distance $AB = d$ and the angles of elevation α and β at A and B are as shown.

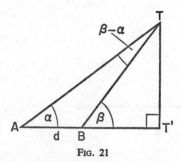

Fig. 21

Since the external angle of a triangle is equal to the sum of the two internal opposite ones, it should be clear that the angle ATB is $β - α$. Applying the sine formula to the triangle ATB

$$\frac{TB}{\sin α} = \frac{d}{\sin (β - α)}$$

so that $TB = d \sin \alpha \operatorname{cosec} (\beta - \alpha)$. The right-angled triangle BTT' now gives for the height of the tower

$$TT' = TB \sin \beta = d \sin \alpha \sin \beta \operatorname{cosec} (\beta - \alpha).$$

Thus, by measuring two angles and one distance, this formula enables the height of an inaccessible object to be found.

Example 13. *Two points on a shore are 777 m apart and the distances of a lighthouse from these points are 650 m and 525 m. The lighthouse radiates a narrow beam which revolves at a uniform rate, making one complete revolution in 15 seconds. Find the time taken for the beam to traverse the strip of shore between the two points.* [L.U.]

In Fig. 22, A, B are the two points on the shore and C is the lighthouse. The semi-perimeter s of the triangle ABC is given by $2s = 777 + 650 + 525$, leading to $s = 976$, $s - a = 451$, $s - b = 326$, $s - c = 199$. Hence

$$\tan \tfrac{1}{2}C = \sqrt{\left\{\frac{(s - a)(s - b)}{s(s - c)}\right\}} = \sqrt{\left\{\frac{451 \times 326}{976 \times 199}\right\}},$$

giving $\tfrac{1}{2}C = 41° 1'$, $C = 82° 2' = 1\cdot432$ radians. The beam rotates through 2π radians in 15 seconds, so that the time taken to traverse the strip of shore (the time taken to rotate through the angle C) is

$$\frac{1\cdot432 \times 15}{2\pi} = 3\cdot42 \text{ seconds.}$$

No.	log.
451	2·6542
326	2·5132
	5·1674
976	2·9894
199	2·2989
	5·2883
	5·1674
	5·2883
$\tan^2 \tfrac{1}{2}C$	$\bar{1}\cdot8791$
$\tan \tfrac{1}{2}C$	$\bar{1}\cdot9396$
1·432	0·1559
15	1·1761
	1·3320
2π	0·7982
	0·5338

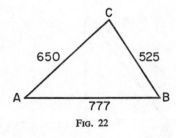

Fig. 22

Example 14. *A ship P is 15·7 km from a harbour H on a bearing of 048° (N 48° E) and a ship Q is 24·3 km from H on a bearing of 112° (S 68° E). Calculate the bearing of P from Q and the distance PQ.* [L.U.]

In Fig. 23, SN is due north and the angles PHN, QHS are respectively 48° and 68°. The angle H of the triangle PHQ is therefore $180° - 48° - 68° = 64°$ while the sides q and p are 15·7, 24·3. Hence formula (4.8) gives

$$\tan \tfrac{1}{2}(P - Q) = \left(\frac{24\cdot3 - 15\cdot7}{24\cdot3 + 15\cdot7}\right) \cot \tfrac{1}{2}(64°)$$

$$= \frac{8\cdot6}{40} \cot 32°$$

$$= 0\cdot215 \cot 32°.$$

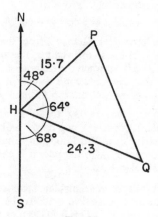

Fig. 23

This gives $\tfrac{1}{2}(P - Q) = 18° \, 59'$ and, since

$$P + Q + 64° = 180°,$$
$$\tfrac{1}{2}(P + Q) = 90° - 32° = 58°.$$

By subtraction, $Q = 58° - 18° \, 59' = 39° \, 1'$. QP therefore makes an angle of $68° - 39° \, 1' = 28° \, 59'$ with SN and the bearing of P from Q is $360° - 28° \, 59' = 331° \, 1'$. For the distance PQ, we have

$$PQ = \frac{15\cdot7 \sin 64°}{\sin 39° \, 1'} = 15\cdot7 \sin 64° \operatorname{cosec} 39° \, 1'$$

$$= 22\cdot42 \text{ kilometres.}$$

No.	log.
0·215 cot 32°	$\bar{1}$·3324 0·2042
$\tan \tfrac{1}{2}(P - Q)$	$\bar{1}$·5366
15·7 sin 64° cosec 39° 1'	1·1959 $\bar{1}$·9537 0·2009
PQ	1·3505

Exercises 4 (d)

1. The angle of elevation to the top of a vertical pole from an observation point at the same level as its foot is α. The angle of elevation to the top of the post from a point h metres vertically above the first point of observation is β. Show that the height of the post is

$$h \sin \alpha \cos \beta \operatorname{cosec} (\alpha - \beta) \text{ metres.}$$

2. A, B and C are three points on a level straight road, B being due East of A and C due East of B; also, $AB = BC$. From A the true bearing of a tower, whose base is on the same level as the road, is α North of East, from B the true bearing is β North of East and from C it is γ North of West. Prove that $2 \cot \beta = \cot \alpha - \cot \gamma$. [O.C.]

3. A and B are two points on one bank of a straight river, and the bottom of a vertical flagpole is at C on the other bank directly opposite A, all three points A, B and C being in a horizontal plane. The angles of elevation of the top of the flagpole from A, B and D (the mid-point of AB) are α, β and γ respectively. Prove that

$$4 \cot^2 \gamma = 3 \cot^2 \alpha + \cot^2 \beta.$$ [O.C.]

4. When a boat is at a horizontal distance x from the foot of a cliff on the edge of which is a light-house of height a, the angle subtended at the boat by the light-house is α; when the distance is $2x$, the corresponding angle is β. Prove that $3x = a(2 \cot \beta - \cot \alpha)$. Find the value of a, to the nearest metre, if $x = 240$ m, $\alpha = 15°$ and $\beta = 10°$.

5. A ship is steaming on a course 030° (N 30° E) at a certain speed. At 10.00 a.m. it is 5 kilometres due W of a port P and at 10.40 a.m. it is due N of P. Find its bearing from P at 11.00 a.m. Find also at what time the ship will lose radio contact with the port if it can only receive signals up to a radius of 25 kilometres. [L.U.]

6. AC is the longest side of a triangular field ABC. If $AB = 50$ m, $AC = 80$ m and the area of the field is $1000\sqrt{3}$ square metres, calculate the angle A and the length BC. This field lies on a plane hillside and A is the lowest corner of the field. If the sides AB and AC make angles of 29° and 21° respectively with the horizontal plane, calculate the angle which the side BC makes with that plane. [L.U.]

7. A is the base of a vertical flagpole AC which consists of two sections AB (of length H) and BC (of length p); W is an observation post at a vertical height $h(< H)$ above the level of A and at a horizontal distance d from A. Prove that, if the angle BWA is denoted by θ, then

$$H = \frac{(d^2 + h^2) \tan \theta}{d + h \tan \theta}.$$

If $h = 10$ m, $d = 100$ m and $\theta = 11°$, calculate to the nearest metre, (i) the value of H and (ii) the value of p if the angle CWA is $12\frac{1}{2}°$.

8. An aeroplane is observed flying on a constant course γ East of North at a constant height. When its true bearing is θ West of North, the angle of elevation is α, and when its true bearing is ϕ East of North, the angle of elevation is β. Prove that γ is given by

$$\tan \gamma = \frac{\sin \phi \tan \alpha + \sin \theta \tan \beta}{\cos \phi \tan \alpha - \cos \theta \tan \beta}.$$

Prove also that, if $\theta = \phi$, the angle of elevation δ when the true bearing is North is given by $\tan \delta = \frac{1}{2}(\tan \alpha + \tan \beta) \sec \theta$. [O.C.]

9. P and Q are two points on level ground on the same side of a level straight road, P being nearer the road than Q; A is a point on the road such that the road is the tangent at A to the circle through P, Q and A; B is the point on the road, at a distance a from A at which P and Q are seen in the same direction, which makes an acute angle β with the road. Prove that, if the angle PAQ is α, the distance between P and Q is

$$\frac{2a \sin \alpha \sin \beta}{\cos \alpha + \cos \beta}.$$

Prove also that, if $\alpha = \beta$ and $BP = 2PQ$, then $\tan \alpha = \frac{1}{2}\sqrt{2}$. [O.C.]

10. A and B are two towers, B being 4 km due East of A. The true bearings of a flagpole C from A and B are $\alpha°$ East of North and $\alpha°$ West of North respectively; the true bearings of a second flagpole D from A and B are $(\alpha + \beta)°$ East of North and $(\alpha - \beta)°$ West of North respectively. Assuming that A, B, C and D are on level ground, prove that D is $4 \sin^2 \beta \operatorname{cosec} 2\alpha$ km South of C and $2 \sin 2\beta \operatorname{cosec} 2\alpha$ km East of C. [O.C.]

11. From a point on the side line of a football field at a distance $2h$ from a corner flag the angle between the directions to the goal posts at the same end as the flag is α. Denoting the angle between the directions to the nearer post and the flag by θ, show that

$$\tan^2 \theta + \frac{d}{2h} \tan \theta + 1 - \frac{d}{2h} \cot \alpha = 0,$$

where d is the distance between the posts. If, when the distance $2h$ is changed to h, the angle α changes to 2α, determine d in terms of h and $\tan \alpha$. [N.U.]

12. D is the mid-point of the base BC of a triangular plate ABC. When the plate is freely suspended from the point A, the line AD is vertical and the side AB makes an angle α with this vertical. Using the usual notation for the triangle ABC, show that

$$\cot \alpha = (c/b) \operatorname{cosec} A + \cot A.$$

13. Two roads OA, OB cross at right angles on a level plain. Two trees A, B on the road side are at respective distances a and b from the cross-roads O. An observer at a point P in a field inside the angle AOB observes the angle APO to be α and the angle OPB to be β. If the angle AOP is θ, prove that

$$\tan \theta = \frac{a - b \cot \beta}{b - a \cot \alpha}.$$ [L.U.]

14. A radar tower leans towards the North. At equal distances North and South of its foot and in the same horizontal plane, the angles of elevation to the top of the tower are α and β ($\alpha > \beta$). Show that the angle of inclination θ of the tower to the vertical is given by

$$2 \tan \theta = \cot \beta - \cot \alpha.$$

Calculate θ when $\alpha = 42°$, $\beta = 32°$.

15. A flat triangular metal sheet is attached at one corner to a small peg on horizontal ground. A second corner is fixed to the top of a vertical post 4 m high, the foot of the post being 8 m North of the peg. The remaining corner is attached to a vertical pole, which is 6 m West of the post, at a point 7 m above the ground. Determine the angle of inclination of the plane of the sheet to the horizontal. [L.U.]

Exercises 4 (e)

1. The internal bisector of the angle BAC of a triangle ABC meets BC at D. Prove that $AD = c \sin B \sec \frac{1}{2}(B - C)$. [O.C.]

2. If Δ is the area of the triangle ABC, show that
$$4\Delta = b^2 \sin 2C + c^2 \sin 2B.$$

3. Prove that in any triangle ABC, $b(\cot A + \cot B) = c \operatorname{cosec} A$.

4. In a triangle ABC, perpendiculars from the vertices to the opposite sides are AD, BE, CF. Find the angles of the triangle DEF in terms of those of the triangle ABC and prove that the perimeter of the triangle DEF is $a \cos A + b \cos B + c \cos C$. [L.U.]

5. The angle C of a triangle ABC is $60°$. Show that
$$\frac{1}{a+c} + \frac{1}{b+c} = \frac{3}{a+b+c}.$$

6. D is the mid-point of the side BC of a triangle ABC and the angles BAD, CAD are respectively θ and ϕ. Show that
$$\tan \tfrac{1}{2}(\theta - \phi) = \left(\frac{b-c}{b+c}\right) \tan \tfrac{1}{2}A.$$

7. Prove, in the usual notation for a triangle, that if
$$\frac{b+c}{11} = \frac{c+a}{12} = \frac{a+b}{13},$$
then
$$\frac{\sin A}{7} = \frac{\sin B}{6} = \frac{\sin C}{5}, \quad \frac{\cos A}{7} = \frac{\cos B}{19} = \frac{\cos C}{25} \qquad \text{[L.U.]}$$

8. O is the centre and R the radius of the circle circumscribing the triangle ABC. AO, BO and CO meet the opposite sides in L, M, N respectively. Show that

(i) $AL \cos (B - C) = b \sin C$,

(ii) $\dfrac{1}{AL} + \dfrac{1}{BM} + \dfrac{1}{CN} = \dfrac{2}{R}.$ [L.U.]

9. If Δ is the area of the triangle ABC, show that
$$2\Delta(\tan B + \tan C) = a^2 \tan B \tan C.$$

10. Calculate the angles B and C of a triangle ABC given that $A = 64° 28'$, $b = 11·56$ m and $c = 14·68$ m, and find the area of the triangle.

11. Find the smallest angle of the triangle in which $a = 12·34$ m, $b = 14·56$ m, $c = 8·58$ m.   [O.C.]

12. Calculate the largest angle of the triangle for which $a = 8·75$ m, $b = 10·32$ m, $c = 7·39$ m.   [O.C.]

13. In a triangle ABC, $b = 91$, $c = 125$ and $\tan \frac{1}{2}A = 17/6$. Show that $a = 204$.   [O.C.]

14. Two sides of a triangle are of lengths 5 km and 6 km and the sum of the angles opposite them is $100°$. Find the angles and the radius of the circumscribing circle of the triangle.   [L.U.]

15. In a triangle ABC, the angle C is given and $5c = 4a$; prove that there are two possible values of b if $\cos C > 3/5$ and find the corresponding values of B if $\cos C = \frac{1}{6}\sqrt{13}$.   [O.C.]

16. If in a triangle ABC, $a < b$ and $\sin A < a/b$, show that the difference between the two values of c is $2\sqrt{(a^2 - b^2 \sin^2 A)}$.   [N.U.]

17. Find the third side of the triangle in which two sides are of lengths $\sin \theta$ and $\sin (120° - \theta)$ and the angle included between these sides is $60°$.

18. In the triangle ABC, prove that $c \cos \frac{1}{2}(A - B) = (a + b) \sin \frac{1}{2}C$. If the sum of the lengths of two sides of a triangle is 21 m, the length of the third side is 15 m and the angle opposite the third side is $52°$, solve the triangle completely.   [L.U.]

19. In a triangle ABC, the sides AB, AC are equal and contain an angle 2θ. The circumscribing circle of the triangle has radius R. Show that the sum of the lengths of the perpendiculars from A, B, C to the opposite sides of the triangle is $2R(1 + 4 \sin \theta - \sin^2 \theta - 4 \sin^3 \theta)$.   [N.U.]

20. A horizontal tunnel AB is bored through a ridge in a direction perpendicular to the line of the ridge, and a path goes from A to B over the ridge. Show that if l is the length of the tunnel and α, β are the inclinations of the two portions of the path to the horizontal, the height of the ridge above the tunnel is $l \sin \alpha \sin \beta \operatorname{cosec} (\alpha + \beta)$. What is the length of the path if $l = 1000$ m, $\alpha = 10°$ and $\beta = 7\frac{1}{2}°$?

21. A vertical tower AB stands on the top of a hill which may be assumed to be a plane inclined at $8°$ to the horizontal. BCD is the line of greatest slope of the hill through B, the foot of the tower. The angles of elevation, above the horizontal of A from C and D are $29°$ and $20°$ respectively and the length of CD is 125 m. Find the height of the tower.   [L.U.]

22. A man walking along a straight horizontal road from which the spire of a church in an adjoining field is always visible, notes that the angle of elevation is α. After a distance a the angle of elevation is β and after a

further distance b the angle of elevation is again β. Show that the greatest angle of elevation is θ, where

$$4a(a + b) \cot^2 \theta = (2a + b)^2 \cot^2 \beta - b^2 \cot^2 \alpha. \qquad \text{[L.U.]}$$

23. $ABCD$ is a trapezium in which the parallel sides are AD, BC and the side CD is perpendicular to them. If the angle ABD is α, show that

$$AD = \frac{(BC^2 + CD^2) \sin \alpha}{BC \sin \alpha + CD \cos \alpha}.$$

24. A statue h metres high, standing on the top of a tower, subtends at a point distant d metres in a horizontal line from the base of the tower the same angle as that subtended at the same point by a man $\frac{1}{3}h$ metres high standing at the base of the tower. Show that the height H of the tower is given by the equation $H^2 + hH - 4d^2 = 0$.

25. The angles of elevation to a stationary balloon measured by three observers are θ, θ and ϕ. The observers are positioned in a straight horizontal line, the middle observer being at equal distances d metres from each of the others. Show that the height of the balloon above the observers is given by the formula

$$(d \sin \theta \sin \phi)\sqrt{\{2 \operatorname{cosec} (\theta + \phi) \operatorname{cosec} (\theta - \phi)\}} \text{ metres.}$$

CHAPTER 5

THE COORDINATE GEOMETRY OF THE STRAIGHT LINE

5.1 Introduction

In this chapter we apply algebraical methods to the solution of certain geometrical problems involving straight lines. We start by explaining the coordinate systems usually adopted and go on to develop formulae for the distance between two given points, the area of a triangle with given vertices, and so on.

A brief section is devoted to the determination of the equation relating the coordinates x and y of a point which moves so as to satisfy prescribed conditions and we then show that, when this equation is of the first degree in x and y, the path of the point is a straight line. Special forms of this first degree equation are then discussed with relation to specific properties possessed by the line. Formulae are derived for the angle between two lines whose equations are given, for the distance of a given point from a given line and conditions are established so that two given lines may be parallel or perpendicular.

Finally, the fact that a first degree equation in the variables concerned implies a straight line graph is used to deduce mathematical formulae from sets of physical measurements.

5.2 Coordinates

The reader is assumed to be familiar with the way in which points are plotted in elementary graphical work. Thus, the position of a point

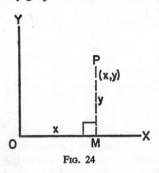

Fig. 24

P in a plane is specified by its perpendicular distances OM, MP from two fixed perpendicular lines OY, OX (Fig. 24). The point O is called the *origin*, the lines OX, OY are the *axes* and the distances OM, MP are referred to respectively as the *abscissa* and *ordinate* of the point P.

107

If $OM = x$, $MP = y$, the point P is said to have *coordinates* x and y, and the symbol (x, y) is used to denote the position of such a point. The sign convention used is briefly as follows; for a point to the right of the axis OY the abscissa is positive and for a point to the left it is negative, while the ordinate is positive or negative according as the point lies above or below the axis OX. Thus, in Fig. 25, the points

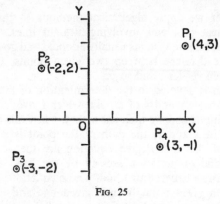

Fig. 25

P_1, P_2, P_3 and P_4 are those with coordinates $(4, 3)$, $(-2, 2)$, $(-3, -2$ and $(3, -1)$ respectively.

The above method of specifying the position of a point in a plane is due to the philosopher Descartes. It is not essential to use perpendicular axes as has been done in Figs. 24 and 25 but it is often convenient to do so and, in this book, we shall always take the axes to be mutually

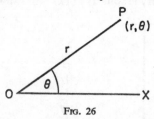

Fig. 26

at right-angles. When referred to such axes, the distances x and y of Fig. 24 are said to be the *rectangular Cartesian coordinates* of the point P. There are other coordinate systems, such as the one outlined below, but the Cartesian system is by far the most important.

Sometimes the position of a point P in a plane is conveniently specified by its distance OP from the origin and the angle which OP makes with some fixed direction OX. Thus, in Fig. 26, the length $OP = r$ and the angle $XOP = \theta$. The quantities r and θ are said to be the *polar co-*

ordinates of the point P referred to an *origin O* and an *initial line OX* and, in this system of coordinates the position of the point P is denoted by the symbol (r, θ).

5.3 The relation between Cartesian and polar coordinates

In Fig. 27, the point P has rectangular Cartesian coordinates (x, y) and polar coordinates (r, θ) and it is clear from the diagram that

$$x = OM = OP \cos POM = r \cos \theta, \\ y = MP = OP \sin POM = r \sin \theta. \tag{5.1}$$

These equations enable x and y to be found when r and θ are known and conversely, if x, y are known, the polar coordinates are given by

$$r^2 = x^2 + y^2, \quad \tan \theta = y/x. \tag{5.2}$$

Equations (5.2) do not, however, determine r, θ uniquely for $r = \pm\sqrt{(x^2 + y^2)}$ and θ can take an indefinite number of different

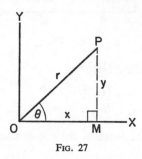

FIG. 27

values. To obtain an unique correspondence, we take $r = +\sqrt{(x^2 + y^2)}$ and determine θ as the angle which lies between 0 and 2π radians satisfying the two equations $\cos \theta = x/r$, $\sin \theta = y/r$.

Example 1. *Find (i) the rectangular Cartesian coordinates of the point whose polar coordinates are $(6, \pi/3)$ and (ii) the polar coordinates of the point whose Cartesian coordinates are $(-5, 12)$.*

(i) $r = 6$, $\theta = \pi/3$, so that
$x = 6 \cos (\pi/3) = 6 \times \frac{1}{2} = 3$,
$y = 6 \sin (\pi/3) = 6 \times \frac{1}{2}\sqrt{3} = 3\sqrt{3} = 5\cdot196$.

(ii) $x = -5$, $y = 12$, giving
$r = \sqrt{\{(-5)^2 + 12^2\}} = \sqrt{(25 + 144)} = \sqrt{(169)} = 13$,
$\cos \theta = -5/13$, $\sin \theta = 12/13$.

The last two equations lead to $\theta = 180° - 67° \, 23' = 112° \, 37' = 1\cdot9655$ radians.

5.4 The distance between two points with given coordinates

In Fig. 28, let P, Q be points with rectangular Cartesian coordinates (x_1, y_1) and (x_2, y_2). PM, QN are drawn perpendicular to the axis OX and QR is perpendicular to PM. Then

$$QR = NM = OM - ON = x_1 - x_2,$$
$$RP = MP - MR = MP - NQ = y_1 - y_2.$$

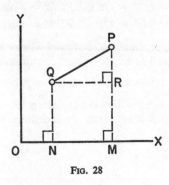

FIG. 28

The right-angled triangle PQR gives

$$PQ = \sqrt{(QR^2 + RP^2)}$$
$$= \sqrt{\{(x_1 - x_2)^2 + (y_1 - y_2)^2\}} \qquad (5.3)$$

and this is the required formula for the distance PQ in terms of the coordinates of P and Q.

In the derivation of formula (5.3), the coordinates of the points P and Q have been taken to be positive. When due regard is taken of the sign conventions for the coordinates, it will be found that the formula remains valid for all positions of the two given points.

Example 2. *Prove that the three points $A(5, 1)$, $B(6, 9)$, $C(-1, 5)$ are the vertices of an isosceles triangle.*   [O.C.]

Using formula (5.3), we have

$$AB^2 = (5 - 6)^2 + (1 - 9)^2 = 1 + 64 = 65,$$
$$AC^2 = (5 + 1)^2 + (1 - 5)^2 = 36 + 16 = 52,$$
$$BC^2 = (6 + 1)^2 + (9 - 5)^2 = 49 + 16 = 65.$$

Hence $AB = BC$ and the triangle ABC is isosceles.

5.5 A proof of the addition formulae of trigonometry

A compact derivation of the formula for $\cos(A - B)$ where A and B are angles of any magnitude can now be given. In Fig. 29, diagrams are given for (i) $90° < A < 180°$, $0 < B < 90°$, (ii) $0 < A < 90°$, $180° < B < 270°$ and corresponding diagrams can be constructed for angles of any size. OP, OQ are each of unit length and the rectangular Cartesian coordinates of P and Q are therefore respectively $(\cos A, \sin A)$ and $(\cos B, \sin B)$. In both cases shown in the diagram, the cosine of the angle POQ is equal to $\cos(A - B)$ and the cosine formula applied to the triangle POQ gives

$$PQ^2 = OP^2 + OQ^2 - 2OP \cdot OQ \cos POQ$$
$$= (1)^2 + (1)^2 - 2(1)(1) \cos(A - B)$$
$$= 2 - 2\cos(A - B).$$

Using formula (5.3) for the distance between the points P $(\cos A, \sin A)$ and $Q(\cos B, \sin B)$,

$$PQ^2 = (\cos A - \cos B)^2 + (\sin A - \sin B)^2$$
$$= 2 - 2\cos A \cos B - 2\sin A \sin B,$$

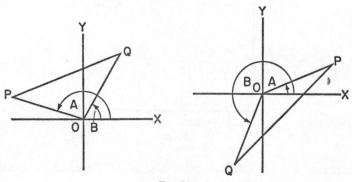

FIG. 29

when use is made of the relations $\cos^2 A + \sin^2 A = 1$, $\cos^2 B + \sin^2 B = 1$. Equating these values of PQ^2,

$$\cos(A - B) = \cos A \cos B + \sin A \sin B,$$

and the addition formulae for $\cos(A + B)$, $\sin(A + B)$, $\sin(A - B)$ can be deduced from this by replacing B by $-B$, $90° - B$ and $B - 90°$ respectively.

5.6 The coordinates of a point which divides the join of two given points in a given ratio

In Fig. 30, A and B are respectively points with coordinates (x_1, y_1) and (x_2, y_2) and we wish to find the coordinates (x, y) of a point P which divides the line AB in the ratio $m : n$. Draw AM, BN, PK

perpendicular to the axis OX and draw AS parallel to OX to meet PK, BN in R and S respectively. Then $OM = x_1$, $OK = x$, $ON = x_2$ and $AR = MK = OK - OM = x - x_1$, $RS = KN = ON - OK = x_2 - x$. Since PR and BS are parallel,

$$\frac{AR}{RS} = \frac{AP}{PB} = \frac{m}{n},$$

so that

$$\frac{x - x_1}{x_2 - x} = \frac{m}{n},$$

and, solving for x,

$$x = \frac{mx_2 + nx_1}{m + n}.$$

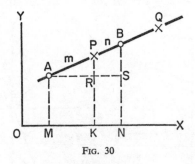

FIG. 30

By drawing AM', PK', BN' perpendicular to OY, we could show in the same way that the ordinate of P is given by

$$y = \frac{my_2 + ny_1}{m + n}.$$

Hence the coordinates (x, y) of a point P which divides the join of the points $A(x_1, y_1)$ and $B(x_2, y_2)$ *internally* in the ratio $m : n$ are given by

$$x = \frac{mx_2 + nx_1}{m + n}, \qquad y = \frac{my_2 + ny_1}{m + n}. \qquad (5.4)$$

If the point Q (Fig. 30) divides the line AB *externally* in the ratio $m : n$, its coordinates will be found in a similar way to be given by

$$x = \frac{mx_2 - nx_1}{m - n}, \qquad y = \frac{my_2 - ny_1}{m - n}. \qquad (5.5)$$

Example 3. *The points $A(x_1, y_1)$, $B(x_2, y_2)$, $C(x_3, y_3)$ are the vertices of a plane triangle and D is the mid-point of the side AB. Assuming that the centroid G of the triangle is a point in CD such that $CG : GD = 2 : 1$, find formulae for the co-ordinates of G in terms of those of the vertices of the triangle.*

Since D divides the join of A and B internally in the ratio $1 : 1$, its coordinates are, by formulae (5.4) with $m = n = 1$, given by

$$x = \tfrac{1}{2}(x_1 + x_2), \quad y = \tfrac{1}{2}(y_1 + y_2).$$

If the coordinates of G are $(\bar{x}, \bar{y})$, since G divides the join of C and D internally in the ratio $2 : 1$, formulae (5.4) give

$$\bar{x} = \frac{2\{\tfrac{1}{2}(x_1 + x_2)\} + 1(x_3)}{2 + 1}, \quad \bar{y} = \frac{2\{\tfrac{1}{2}(y_1 + y_2)\} + 1(y_3)}{2 + 1},$$

or

$$\bar{x} = \tfrac{1}{3}(x_1 + x_2 + x_3), \quad \bar{y} = \tfrac{1}{3}(y_1 + y_2 + y_3). \tag{5.6}$$

5.7 The area of a triangle whose vertices have given coordinates

Let the vertices of the triangle ABC be the points $A(x_1, y_1)$, $B(x_2, y_2)$ and $C(x_3, y_3)$. Draw AL, BM and CN perpendicular to the axis OX

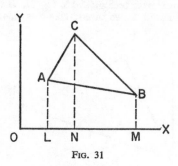

FIG. 31

(Fig. 31). Then each of the figures $ALNC$, $CNMB$ and $ALMB$ is a trapezium and the area of the triangle ABC is equal to the sum of the areas $ALNC$, $CNMB$ less the area $ALMB$. Hence

$$\text{area } \Delta ABC = \tfrac{1}{2}LN(AL + CN) + \tfrac{1}{2}NM(CN + BM)$$
$$- \tfrac{1}{2}LM(AL + BM)$$
$$= \tfrac{1}{2}(x_3 - x_1)(y_1 + y_3) + \tfrac{1}{2}(x_2 - x_3)(y_3 + y_2)$$
$$- \tfrac{1}{2}(x_2 - x_1)(y_1 + y_2)$$
$$= \tfrac{1}{2}\{x_1(y_2 - y_3) + x_2(y_3 - y_1) + x_3(y_1 - y_2)\}, \tag{5.7}$$

the last line being a slight rearrangement of the one above it. By taking $x_3 = y_3 = 0$, the point C coincides with the origin O and the above formula gives

$$\text{area } \Delta OAB = \tfrac{1}{2}(x_1 y_2 - x_2 y_1).$$

If the formula (5.7) is to give a positive value for the area, it should be noted that it is necessary to take the points A, B and C in a special order. This is such that, in starting from the point A and proceeding round the perimeter of the triangle in the order A, B, C, the area of the triangle must always be on the *left*.

The area of any plane polygon can be found in a similar way. Perpendiculars are drawn from the vertices of the polygon on to the axis OX (or on to a line parallel to OX through the vertex with the smallest ordinate) and the area can then be found in terms of those of various triangles and trapezia. A typical instance is shown in Example 5 below.

Example 4. *Find the area of the triangle whose vertices are the points* $(0, 2)$, $(2, 6)$ *and* $(6, 4)$.

The three given points have been plotted in Fig. 32. It will be seen that, if we take A to be the point $(0, 2)$, we have to take B as $(6, 4)$ and C as $(2, 6)$ if we

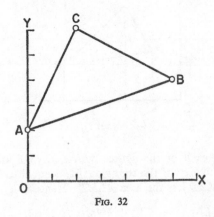

Fig. 32

are to keep the area on the left as we proceed round the triangle in the order A, B, C. Hence in formula (5.7),

$$x_1 = 0, y_1 = 2, x_2 = 6, y_2 = 4, x_3 = 2, y_3 = 6$$

and

$$\text{area } \Delta ABC = \tfrac{1}{2}\{0(2 - 6) + 6(6 - 2) + 2(2 - 4)\}$$

$$= 10 \text{ sq. units.}$$

Example 5. *Find the area of the quadrilateral whose vertices are the points* (1, 1), (3, 5), (−2, 4) *and* (−1, −5).

In Fig. 33, the four points (1, 1), (3, 5), (−2, 4) and (−1, −5) are denoted by *A*, *B*, *C* and *D*. Perpendiculars *AL*, *BM*, *CN* are dropped from *A*, *B*, *C* on to a

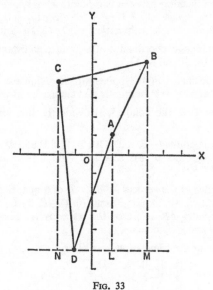

Fig. 33

line through *D* (the point with the smallest ordinate) parallel to *OX*. From the figure,

area *ABCD* = area trapezium *CNMB* − area triangle *CND* − area triangle *ADL* − area trapezium *ALMB*

$$= \tfrac{1}{2}(5)(9 + 10) - \tfrac{1}{2}(1)(9) - \tfrac{1}{2}(2)(6) - \tfrac{1}{2}(2)(6 + 10)$$

$$= 21 \text{ sq. units.}$$

Exercises 5 (a)

1. Find the rectangular Cartesian coordinates of the points whose polar coordinates are

   (i) $(\sqrt{2}, \tfrac{1}{4}\pi)$, (ii) $(2, \tfrac{2}{3}\pi)$, (iii) $(\sqrt{2}, \tfrac{5}{4}\pi)$, (iv) $(4, \tfrac{5}{3}\pi)$.

2. Plot the points with Cartesian coordinates

   (i) (1, 1), (ii) (−3, 2), (iii) (−3, −2), (iv) (1, −1),

   and find their polar coordinates.

3. Find the lengths of the sides of the triangle with vertices $A(-\tfrac{1}{2}, -\tfrac{1}{2})$, $B(0, 1)$, $C(\tfrac{1}{2}, \tfrac{1}{2})$ and show that the angle $A\widehat{C}B$ is a right angle.

4. When two points B, C are given, there exist two positions of a point A such that the triangle ABC is equilateral. Find the coordinates of these positions of A when

   (i) B is $(1, 1)$ and C is $(-1, -1)$,   (ii) B is $(5, 5)$ and C is $(3, 3)$.   [O.C.]

5. Show that the distance between two points whose *polar* coordinates are (r_1, θ_1) and (r_2, θ_2) is $\sqrt{\{r_1{}^2 + r_2{}^2 - 2r_1r_2 \cos(\theta_1 - \theta_2)\}}$ and find the perimeter of the triangle with vertices $(0, 0)$, $(2, \frac{1}{6}\pi)$ and $(4, \frac{1}{2}\pi)$.

6. Find the rectangular coordinates of a point equidistant from the three points $(2, 3)$, $(4, 5)$ and $(6, 1)$.

7. Find the coordinates of the points which divide the line joining the points $(2, 4)$ and $(1, -3)$ internally and externally in the ratio $2 : 1$.

8. In what ratio does the point $(3, 3)$ divide the line joining the points $(-6, 18)$, $(18, -22)$?

9. A, B, C are the points $(-6, -3)$, $(10, 5)$, $(7, 13)$ and D, E, F are respectively the mid-points of BC, CA and AB. Calculate the lengths of AD, BE and CF.

10. The coordinates of the vertices A, B, C, D of a quadrilateral $ABCD$ are respectively $(2, 5)$, $(8, 7)$, $(10, 3)$ and $(0, 1)$. E, F, G, H are the mid-points of the sides AB, BC, CD, DA respectively. Show that the mid-points of EG and FH coincide.

11. Find the area of the triangles with vertices

   (i) $(0, 0)$, $(2, -7)$, $(2, 3)$;
   (ii) $(-2, 3)$, $(-7, 5)$, $(3, -5)$.

12. Find the area of the triangle whose vertices are the points with *polar* coordinates $(1, \frac{1}{6}\pi)$, $(2, \frac{1}{3}\pi)$ and $(3, \frac{1}{2}\pi)$.

13. Show that the triangle with vertices $(0, 2)$, $(2, 6)$, and $(6, 4)$ is isosceles and right-angled: find its area.   [O.C.]

14. Find the area of the quadrilateral whose vertices are the points $(1, 1)$, $(2, 3)$, $(3, 3)$ and $(4, 1)$.

15. Show that the figure whose vertices are the points $(-1, 2)$, $(1, 0)$, $(3, 2)$ and $(1, 4)$ is a square and find the area of that part of the square which lies in the first quadrant.

5.8 Loci

When a point moves so that its position is restricted by a given condition or conditions, the path traced out by it is called a *locus*. For example, if a point moves in a plane so that it is always at distance 5 from the origin O, its coordinates (x, y) satisfy the relation $\sqrt{(x^2 + y^2)} = 5$, for the expression on the left is the distance between the points (x, y) and $(0, 0)$. This equation can be written $x^2 + y^2 = 25$ and is the *equation of the locus* of the point (x, y). In this particular example, the path traced out is clearly a circle, centre the origin and radius 5, and $x^2 + y^2 = 25$ is the equation of such a circle.

In general, if a point moves in a plane so as to satisfy some condition such as that given in the above example, the path of the point will be a definite locus or curve and the relation between the coordinates (x, y) of the point will only be true for points lying on the locus. Conversely, to every equation relating x and y there is, in general, a definite geometrical locus.

Two examples of the method of formation of equations of loci are given below.

Example 6. *The coordinates of the points A, B are (4, 0) and (0, 3) respectively. Find the equation of the locus of a point P(x, y) which moves so that PA = PB.* [O.C.]

The points A and B are shown in Fig. 34 and also three possible positions P_1, P_2, P_3 of the point P.

We have

$$PA^2 = (x - 4)^2 + y^2,$$

$$PB^2 = x^2 + (y - 3)^2,$$

and, since $PA = PB$,

$$(x - 4)^2 + y^2 = x^2 + (y - 3)^2.$$

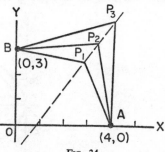

FIG. 34

This equation reduces to $8x - 6y = 7$ and is the required equation of the locus of P. On geometrical grounds, it is clear that the locus of P is the perpendicular bisector of the line AB and the equation $8x - 6y = 7$ therefore represents this bisector (shown dotted in Fig. 34).

Example 7. *Find the equation of the locus of a point which moves so that its distance from a line parallel to the axis OY through the point (−a, 0) is equal to its distance from the point (a, 0).*

In Fig. 35, AB is the line through the point $C(-a, 0)$ parallel to OY and S is the point $(a, 0)$. P is the point (x, y) and the distance PM is equal to the sum

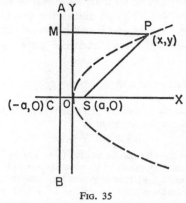

FIG. 35

of the abscissa x of P and the length a of OC. Hence $PM = x + a$ and, since P, S are respectively the points (x, y) and $(a, 0)$, $PS^2 = (x - a)^2 + y^2$. Since $PM^2 = PS^2$,

$$(x + a)^2 = (x - a)^2 + y^2$$

or, after a little reduction, $y^2 = 4ax$. This is the required equation of the locus of P and the shape of the curve, shown dotted in Fig. 35, can be obtained by plotting the graph of $y^2 = 4ax$. The curve is known as a parabola and is discussed in more detail in Chapter 13.

5.9 The points of intersection of loci

The coordinates of the points of intersection, or common points, of two loci will simultaneously satisfy the equations of the loci and the

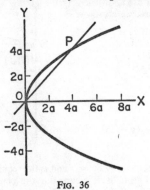

FIG. 36

problem of finding the coordinates of such points reduces to that of solving a pair of simultaneous equations. As an example, consider the loci whose equations are $y = x$ and $y^2 = 4ax$. Solving these as a pair of simultaneous equations by substituting for y from the first equation in the second, $x^2 = 4ax$ giving $x = 0$ or $x = 4a$. The corresponding values of y are also 0 and $4a$ so that the points of intersection are the points $(0, 0)$ and $(4a, 4a)$. Fig. 36 shows the graphs of the two loci plotted on the same diagram and it will be found that the coordinates of the common points O, P read from the graph agree with the calculated values.

Example 8. *Find the distance between the common points of the loci $y + x = 1$ and $y = x^2 - 6x + 7$.*

Substituting $y = -x + 1$ from the first equation in the second, the abscissae of the points of intersection are given by

$$-x + 1 = x^2 - 6x + 7$$

or, $x^2 - 5x + 6 = 0$. This can be written $(x - 2)(x - 3) = 0$ so that $x = 2$ or 3. The corresponding values of y, given by $y = -x + 1$, are -1 or -2 and the coordinates of the common points are therefore $(2, -1)$ and $(3, -2)$. The distance between these points is $\sqrt{\{(2 - 3)^2 + (-1 + 2)^2\}} = \sqrt{2}$.

Exercises 5 (b)

1. Find the equation of the locus of a point which moves so that its distance from the origin is always equal to its distance from the point $(10, 3)$. [O.C.]

2. Find the equation of the locus of a point which moves so that its distance from the point $(9, 12)$ is always twice its distance from the origin. [O.C.]

3. The point A is $(-6, 0)$ and B is $(0, 4)$. Find the locus of a point P which moves so that $PA^2 = 3PB^2$. [O.C.]

4. Find the equation of the perpendicular bisector of the line joining the points $(2, 3)$ and $(8, 5)$.

5. A and B are respectively the points $(2, 1)$ and $(6, 4)$. Find the equation of the locus of a point P which moves so that the angle APB is always $90°$.

6. A, B, C, D are respectively the points $(0, 1)$, $(0, 7)$, $(3, 0)$ and $(5, 0)$. Find the equation of the locus of a point P which moves so that the areas of the triangles PAB and PCD are equal in magnitude.

7. Find the coordinates of the points of intersection and the length of the common chord of the curves $y = 2x^2$ and $y^2 = 4x$.

8. Find the coordinates of the common points of the loci $x - 4 = 0$ and $x^2 + y^2 - 6x + 3y + 10 = 0$. Find also the coordinates of the mid-point of the line joining these common points.

9. The equations of the sides of a triangle are $x - 3y + 6 = 0$, $2x - y + 2 = 0$ and $x + 2y - 14 = 0$. Find the coordinates of its vertices. [O.C.]

10. Find the values of a and b if the loci $ax + 5y = 7$ and $4x + by = 5$ intersect at the point $(2, -1)$. If the loci meet the x-axis at A and B respectively, find the length of AB. [O.C.]

11. The equations of the sides AB, BC, CA of a triangle are $x + y = 6$, $x - y + 2 = 0$, $3x - y = 6$ and D is the mid-point of BC. Find the coordinates of A, B, C, D and verify that $AB^2 + AC^2 = 2AD^2 + 2BD^2$.

12. The vertices of a triangle are $A(1, 7)$, $B(-4, -3)$ and $C(5, -3)$. Find the equations of the perpendicular bisectors of the sides BC and CA. Deduce the coordinates of the centre of the circle circumscribing the triangle ABC and find its radius. [O.C.]

5.10 The equation of a straight line

We have already seen that an equation in x and y represents a definite locus or curve and it may have been noticed (e.g. Example 6)

that, when the locus is a straight line, its equation is of the first degree
in x and y. We now show that the general first degree equation

$$Ax + By + C = 0, \tag{5.8}$$

in which A, B and C are constants, always represents a straight line.

Let $P_1(x_1, y_1)$, $P_2(x_2, y_2)$, $P_3(x_3, y_3)$ be any three points lying on the
locus represented by the equation (5.8). Since the coordinates of the
points must satisfy (5.8) we have

$$Ax_1 + By_1 + C = 0, \quad Ax_2 + By_2 + C = 0 \text{ and } Ax_3 + By_3 + C = 0.$$

Subtracting the second of these equations from the first and the third
from the second,

$$A(x_1 - x_2) + B(y_1 - y_2) = 0 \text{ and } A(x_2 - x_3) + B(y_2 - y_3) = 0.$$

By equating the values of the ratio A/B given by these two equations
we have

$$\frac{y_1 - y_2}{x_1 - x_2} = -\frac{A}{B} = \frac{y_2 - y_3}{x_2 - x_3},$$

giving

$$(x_1 - x_2)(y_2 - y_3) = (x_2 - x_3)(y_1 - y_2),$$

and this can be rearranged in the form

$$x_1(y_2 - y_3) + x_2(y_3 - y_1) + x_3(y_1 - y_2) = 0.$$

Using formula (5.7), it follows that the area of the triangle formed by
the three points P_1, P_2, P_3 is zero. Since P_1, P_2, P_3 are *any* three points
on the locus represented by equation (5.8), the locus must be a straight
line (for a curved line could not be such that the area of the triangle
formed by any three points on it should be zero).

5.11 Special forms of the equation of a straight line

It is often useful to be able to write the general equation

$$Ax + By + C = 0$$

of a straight line in a form in which the constants A, B, C are
related to some geometrical properties of the line. These might be
the slope of the line and the coordinates of a point on it, the intercepts
made by the line on the axes OX, OY, etc., and it is the purpose of this
paragraph to develop special forms of the equation in terms of specific
properties possessed by the line.

(i) *In terms of the slope and intercept on the axis OY*

In Fig. 37, CP is the line, CQ is parallel to the axis OX and PP' is
parallel to the axis OY. The line makes an angle θ with the axis OX
and the intercept OC made by the line on the axis OY is taken to be c.

If the coordinates of any point P on the line are taken to be x and y, the figure shows that $CQ = OP' = x$, $PQ = PP' - QP' = PP' - OC = y - c$, and

$$\tan \theta = \frac{PQ}{CQ} = \frac{y - c}{x}.$$

The quantity $\tan \theta$ is called the *slope* of the line and if we write $m = \tan \theta$, we have

$$y = mx + c \tag{5.9}$$

as the relation between the coordinates x and y of any point P on the line; this is the required equation of the line in terms of its slope m and the intercept c made on the axis OY.

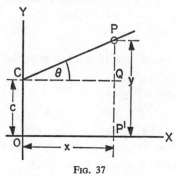

FIG. 37

By writing the general equation $Ax + By + C = 0$ in the form

$$y = -\frac{A}{B}x - \frac{C}{B}$$

and comparing it with equation (5.9), we see that the ratios A/B, C/B of the constants in the general equation can be expressed in terms of the slope m and intercept c by

$$\frac{A}{B} = -m, \qquad \frac{C}{B} = -c. \tag{5.10}$$

For a line of slope m passing through the origin O, $c = 0$ and the equation of such a line is $y = mx$. For a line parallel to the axis OX and at distance c from it, $m = 0$ and its equation is $y = c$. In the same way, the equation of a line parallel to the axis OY and distance d from it is $x = d$.

(ii) *In terms of the slope and coordinates of a point on the line*

By (5.9) the equation of any line of slope m is $y = mx + c$. If the point whose coordinates are (x_1, y_1) lies on the line, these values will satisfy the above equation and $y_1 = mx_1 + c$. By subtraction of these two equations,

$$y - y_1 = m(x - x_1) \qquad (5.11)$$

is the required equation of the line of slope m which passes through the point (x_1, y_1).

Example 9. *The point A has coordinates* $(6, -2)$. *Find the equation of the line through A which is parallel to the line* $4x - 3y = 5$. [O.C.]

The equation of the given line can be written

$$y = \tfrac{4}{3}x - \tfrac{5}{3}$$

showing that its slope is $\tfrac{4}{3}$. Since a parallel line will also have this slope, writing $m = \tfrac{4}{3}$, $x_1 = 6$, $y_1 = -2$ in (5.11), the required equation is

$$y + 2 = \tfrac{4}{3}(x - 6)$$

and this reduces to $4x - 3y = 30$.

(iii) *In terms of the coordinates of two points on the line*

If one of the given points has coordinates (x_1, y_1), the equation of a line passing through it is [equation (5.11)]

$$y - y_1 = m(x - x_1).$$

If the second of the given points has coordinates (x_2, y_2), the above equation will be satisfied by $x = x_2$, $y = y_2$ so that

$$y_2 - y_1 = m(x_2 - x_1).$$

By division, to eliminate m,

$$\frac{x - x_1}{x_2 - x_1} = \frac{y - y_1}{y_2 - y_1} \qquad (5.12)$$

is the required equation of the straight line passing through the points (x_1, y_1), (x_2, y_2).

Example 10. *The line joining the points* $(4, 0)$ *and* $(3, 2)$ *meets the axis* OY *at the point* $(0, b)$; *find b.* [O.C.]

Writing $x_1 = 4$, $y_1 = 0$, $x_2 = 3$, $y_2 = 2$ in (5.12), the equation of the line is

$$\frac{x - 4}{3 - 4} = \frac{y - 0}{2 - 0},$$

and this reduces to $2x + y = 8$. The ordinate of the point of intersection of this line with the axis OY is obtained by writing $x = 0$, and hence $b = 8$.

(iv) *In terms of the intercepts on the coordinate axes*

In Fig. 38, the line is shown as making intercepts of lengths a and b on the coordinate axes OX, OY respectively. The coordinates of the points A and B are respectively $(a, 0)$, $(0, b)$ and these coordinates will satisfy the general equation $Ax + By + C = 0$. Hence $Aa + C = 0$

and $Bb + C = 0$ giving $A = -C/a$, $B = -C/b$. The equation of the line is therefore

$$(-C/a)x + (-C/b)y + C = 0$$

and this reduces to

$$\frac{x}{a} + \frac{y}{b} = 1. \tag{5.13}$$

In working problems on the straight line, a suitable choice of the equation of the line often simplifies the algebraical work. We conclude this section with some illustrative examples.

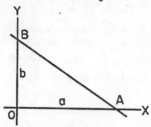

FIG. 38

Example 11. *A line MN which passes through the fixed point* (2, 3) *cuts OX at M and OY at N. Lines MP, NP, which are parallel to OY, OX respectively, intersect at P. Find the equation of the locus of P.* [O.C.]

The equation of a line of slope m through the point (2, 3) is, by (5.11), $y - 3 = m(x - 2)$. This can be written $mx - y = 2m - 3$ or, in the form of (5.13),

$$\frac{x}{\left(\dfrac{2m - 3}{m}\right)} + \frac{y}{-(2m - 3)} = 1.$$

Hence $OM = (2m - 3)/m$, $ON = -(2m - 3)$ and the equations of the lines MP, NP are, see Fig. 39, respectively

$$x = \frac{2m - 3}{m} = 2 - \frac{3}{m}, \quad y = -2m + 3.$$

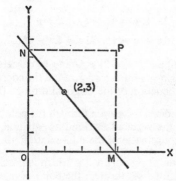

FIG. 39

The coordinates (x, y) of the point P satisfy these equations and the equation of the locus of P is given by eliminating m from them. The equations can be written $x - 2 = -3/m,\ y - 3 = -2m$ so that by multiplication

$$(x - 2)(y - 3) = 6.$$

This reduces to $xy = 3x + 2y$ and this is the required equation of the locus of P.

Example 12. *Find the coordinates of the point where the line $2y = 3x - 7$ meets the line joining the points $(4, -2)$ and $(-1, 3)$.*

By (5.12), the equation of the line joining the points $(4, -2)$, $(-1, 3)$ is

$$\frac{x - 4}{-1 - 4} = \frac{y - (-2)}{3 - (-2)}$$

and this reduces to $x + y = 2$. The coordinates of the point of intersection of this line with the line $2y = 3x - 7$ are the solution of the simultaneous equations

$$x + y = 2 \quad \text{and} \quad 3x - 2y = 7$$

and this is easily found to be $x = \frac{11}{5},\ y = -\frac{1}{5}$.

Exercises 5 (c)

1. Find the equation of the straight line which
   (i) passes through the points $(-8, 6)$ and $(4, -3)$;
   (ii) makes intercepts of -4 and 2 respectively on the axes OX, OY;
   (iii) cuts off an intercept of 2 units on the negative y-axis and makes an angle of $135°$ with the positive x-axis.

2. Find (i) the slope and (ii) the intercepts on the coordinate axes of the line $3x - 4y = 12$.

3. Find the coordinates of the point of intersection P of the straight lines $2x + y = 2$, $x - 2y = 6$. Find also the equation of the line joining P to the point $(4, 3)$.

4. Find the equations of the diagonals of the parallelogram whose sides have the equations

$$3x + y = 1, \quad 3y = 5x + 3,$$
$$3x + y = 15, \quad 3y = 5x - 11. \qquad \text{[L.U.]}$$

5. The points $(5, 10)$ and $(14, -2)$ are opposite corners of a parallelogram, of which the origin is a third corner. Find the coordinates of the fourth corner, and the equation of the diagonal through $(5, 10)$.   [O.C.]

6. A line whose gradient is $\frac{3}{4}$ passes through the point $(5, 2)$ and meets the x-axis at A and the y-axis at B. Find its equation, and also the length of AB and the coordinates of the mid-point of AB.   [O.C.]

7. Find the equation of a straight line which is parallel to the line $3x + 4y = 0$ and which passes through the point of intersection of the lines $x - 2y = a$ and $x + 3y = 2a$.

8. Three points A, B, C have coordinates $(8, 1)$, $(1, 2)$ and $(4, -2)$ respectively. Lines are drawn through A and C parallel respectively to BC and BA, and these lines meet at D. Find the equations of AD and CD, and hence find the coordinates of D, the fourth vertex of the parallelogram $ABCD$. Verify by calculation that the angle ACB is a right angle and find the area of the parallelogram.   [O.C.]

9. A straight line meets the axes OX, OY respectively at the points A, B and C is the point $(-5, 4)$ on the line. If $2AC = BC$, show that the equation of the line AB is $8x - 5y + 60 = 0$.

10. Find the equations of the sides of a triangle the middle points of whose sides are $(5, 3)$, $(2, 1)$ and $(3, 7)$.

11. The straight line $y = m(x - 2a)$ through a fixed point $(2a, 0)$ meets the lines $x = a$ and $y = b$ in P and Q respectively. If O is the origin and A the point $(a, 0)$ find the equations of the lines OP, AQ and the coordinates of their point of intersection R. If m varies, show that the locus of the point R is the straight line $2bx - ay = ab$.   [L.U.]

12. Find the equations of the two lines which pass through the point $(3, 3)$ and form with the positive x and y axes triangles of area 24 sq. units.

13. Two parallel lines AP, BQ pass through the points $A(5, 0)$ and $B(-5, 0)$ respectively. Find the slopes of these lines if they meet the line $4x + 3y = 25$ in points P and Q such that the distance PQ is 5 units.   [L.U.]

14. Show that the points $(-1, -2)$, $(3, 0)$ and $(7, 2)$ lie on a straight line. Find the slope of this line and the intercepts made by it on the axes OX, OY.

15. If O is the origin, A the point $(8, 0)$ and B the point $(0, 6)$ find the coordinates of the points P and Q where the line $3x + 2y = c$ meets OA and AB respectively. If the area of the triangle OPQ is half that of the triangle OAB, find the value of c.   [L.U.]

5.12 The angle between two straight lines

Fig. 40 shows the two lines AB, CD with equations $y = m_1x + c_1$ and $y = m_2x + c_2$. P is the point of intersection of the lines and the

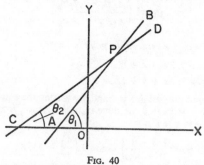

FIG. 40

angles made by the lines with OX are respectively θ_1, θ_2 so that $m_1 = \tan \theta_1$ and $m_2 = \tan \theta_2$. Since the external angle PAX of the triangle PCA is equal to the sum of the interior angles PCA and APC, the angle BPD between the lines is given by

$$\text{angle } BPD = \text{angle } APC$$
$$= \text{angle } PAX - \text{angle } PCA = \theta_1 - \theta_2.$$

Hence

$$\tan BPD = \tan (\theta_1 - \theta_2) = \frac{\tan \theta_1 - \tan \theta_2}{1 + \tan \theta_1 \tan \theta_2}$$

$$= \left(\frac{m_1 - m_2}{1 + m_1 m_2} \right),$$

when use is made of the relations $m_1 = \tan \theta_1$, $m_2 = \tan \theta_2$. The angle between the lines $y = m_1 x + c_1$ and $y = m_2 x + c_2$ is therefore

$$\tan^{-1} \left(\frac{m_1 - m_2}{1 + m_1 m_2} \right). \qquad (5.14)$$

It should be noted that if the quantity in brackets in (5.14) is positive, it is the tangent of the acute angle between the lines (the angle BPD of Fig. 40); if this quantity is negative, it is the tangent of the obtuse angle (the angle CPB).

If the angle between the two lines

$$A_1 x + B_1 y + C_1 = 0, \quad A_2 x + B_2 y + C_2 = 0$$

is required, we note that from (5.10) their respective slopes m_1, m_2 are given by

$$m_1 = - \frac{A_1}{B_1}, \qquad m_2 = - \frac{A_2}{B_2}.$$

Substitution in (5.14) and a little reduction then shows that the required angle is given by

$$\tan^{-1} \left(\frac{A_2 B_1 - A_1 B_2}{A_1 A_2 + B_1 B_2} \right). \qquad (5.15)$$

Example 13. *Find the angles between the pairs of lines*

(i) $y = 3x + 7$, $3y = x + 8$,

(ii) $x + 2y = 1$, $3x + y + 12 = 0$.

(i) The slope m_1 of the first line is 3 and, by writing the equation of the second line in the form $y = \frac{1}{3}x + \frac{8}{3}$, its slope m_2 is $\frac{1}{3}$. Hence, from (5.14), the angle between the lines is given by

$$\tan^{-1} \left\{ \frac{3 - \frac{1}{3}}{1 + 3(\frac{1}{3})} \right\} = \tan^{-1} \left(\frac{4}{3} \right) = 53° \, 8'.$$

(ii) Comparing the given lines with $A_1x + B_1y + C_1 = 0$, $A_2x + B_2y + C_2 = 0$, $A_1 = 1$, $B_1 = 2$, $A_2 = 3$, $B_2 = 1$, so that (5.15) gives the required angle as

$$\tan^{-1} \left\{ \frac{(3)(2) - (1)(1)}{(1)(3) + (2)(1)} \right\} = \tan^{-1}(1) = 45°.$$

Example 14. *Find the equations of the two straight lines which pass through the point* $(3, -2)$ *and make angles of* $60°$ *with the line* $\sqrt{3}x + y = 1$.

In Fig. 41, P is the point $(3, -2)$ and AB the line $\sqrt{3}x + y = 1$. This equation can be written $y = -\sqrt{3}x + 1$ so that the slope of the line AB is $-\sqrt{3}$. It is clear from the diagram that there are two possible lines PM, PN which make

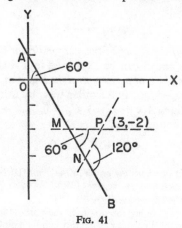

FIG. 41

angles of $60°$ with AB and the tangents of these angles are respectively $\tan 60° = \sqrt{3}$ and $\tan 120° = -\sqrt{3}$. Hence if m is the slope of the line PM, equation (5.14) gives

$$\sqrt{3} = \frac{m + \sqrt{3}}{1 - \sqrt{3}m},$$

leading to $m = 0$. Similarly if m' is the slope of PN,

$$-\sqrt{3} = \frac{m' + \sqrt{3}}{1 - \sqrt{3}m'},$$

leading to $m' = \sqrt{3}$. The required lines are therefore those which pass through the point $(3, -2)$ with slopes 0 and $\sqrt{3}$. By (5.11) the equations are

$$y + 2 = 0(x - 3) \quad \text{or} \quad y + 2 = 0,$$

and

$$y + 2 = \sqrt{3}(x - 3) \quad \text{or} \quad y - \sqrt{3}x + 3\sqrt{3} + 2 = 0.$$

5.13 The conditions for parallelism and perpendicularity

If the two straight lines $y = m_1x + c_1$, $y = m_2x + c_2$ are parallel, they have the same slope and hence

$$m_1 = m_2. \tag{5.16}$$

If the equations of the lines are given in the form $A_1x + B_1y + C_1 = 0$ and $A_2x + B_2y + C_2 = 0$, their slopes [by (5.10)] are $-A_1/B_1$ and $-A_2/B_2$. In this case the condition for parallelism is

$$\frac{A_1}{B_1} = \frac{A_2}{B_2}. \tag{5.17}$$

If the two lines $y = m_1x + c_1$, $y = m_2x + c_2$ are perpendicular, the angle between them is $90°$. Since the tangent of an angle of $90°$ is infinite, formula (5.14) shows that $1 + m_1m_2 = 0$. Hence the condition for perpendicularity is

$$m_1m_2 = -1, \tag{5.18}$$

that is, *the product of the slopes of two perpendicular lines is* -1. This is an important result and it can be expressed in a slightly different way by saying that *if the slope of a given straight line is* m, *the slope of a line perpendicular to it is* $-1/m$. In a similar way, by using (5.15), the condition for the two lines $A_1x + B_1y + C_1 = 0$, $A_2x + B_2y + C_2 = 0$ to be perpendicular is found to be

$$A_1A_2 + B_1B_2 = 0. \tag{5.19}$$

Example 15. *A straight line joins the origin to the point* (18, 24). *Find the equation of the line parallel to it through the point* (25, 0), *and also the equation of the line through* (18, 24) *perpendicular to these two lines.*   [O.C.]

The slope of the line joining the origin to the point (18, 24) is 24/18, or 4/3. The line parallel to this line and passing through the point (25, 0) is

$$y - 0 = \tfrac{4}{3}(x - 25), \quad \text{or} \quad 4x - 3y = 100.$$

The slope of the line perpendicular to these lines is $-3/4$ and the line passing through the point (18, 24) with this slope is

$$y - 24 = -\tfrac{3}{4}(x - 18), \quad \text{or} \quad 3x + 4y = 150.$$

Example 16. *A line parallel to* $3x + 4y = 0$ *meets the x-axis at A and the y-axis at B; the line through A drawn perpendicular to* $y - px = 0$ *meets at P the line through B drawn perpendicular to* $qx + y = 0$, *where p and q are constants. Prove that the locus of P is* $x(4q + 3) + y(3p - 4) = 0$.   [O.C.]

If A is the point $(a, 0)$ and B the point $(0, b)$, the equation of the line AB is $(x/a) + (y/b) = 1$ and its slope is $-b/a$. The slope of the line $3x + 4y = 0$ is $-3/4$ so that, since the two lines are parallel, $b/a = 3/4$. The slope of the line $y - px = 0$ is p and the slope of a line perpendicular to it is $-1/p$, so that the equation of the line PA is

$$y = -\frac{1}{p}(x - a), \quad \text{or} \quad py + x = a.$$

The slope of the line $qy + x = 0$ is $-1/q$, the slope of a line perpendicular to it is q, and the equation of the line PB is therefore

$$y - b = qx, \quad \text{or} \quad y - qx = b.$$

By division, and use of the relation $b/a = 3/4$, we have

$$\frac{3}{4} = \frac{b}{a} = \frac{y - qx}{py + x}$$

as the relation between the coordinates of the point of intersection of the lines PA and PB. This relation can be written $x(4q + 3) + y(3p - 4) = 0$ and is the required equation of the locus of P.

5.14 The perpendicular distance of a given point from a line

In Fig. 42, AB is the straight line $Ax + By + C = 0$ meeting the axes OX, OY in A and B. OR is drawn perpendicular to AB and is of

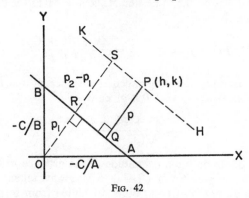

FIG. 42

length p_1. P is the point (h, k), PQ is perpendicular to AB and we require to find a formula for the distance $PQ = p$.

The intercepts OA, OB on the axes OX, OY are respectively $-C/A$ and $-C/B$ and the length of AB is given by

$$AB = \sqrt{\left\{ \left(-\frac{C}{A} \right)^2 + \left(-\frac{C}{B} \right)^2 \right\}} = \frac{C}{AB} \sqrt{(A^2 + B^2)}.$$

Since the area of the triangle OAB can be written as $\frac{1}{2}OA \cdot OB$ or as $\frac{1}{2}p_1 \cdot AB$ we have

$$\frac{p_1 C}{2AB} \sqrt{(A^2 + B^2)} = \frac{1}{2} \left(-\frac{C}{A} \right) \left(-\frac{C}{B} \right),$$

giving

$$p_1 = \frac{C}{\sqrt{(A^2 + B^2)}}.$$

If HK is a line parallel to AB, its equation will be $Ax + By + C' = 0$ and, in the same way, the perpendicular distance $p_2 = OS$ is given by

$$p_2 = \frac{C'}{\sqrt{(A^2 + B^2)}}.$$

5

If the line HK passes through the point $P(h, k)$, $Ah + Bk + C' = 0$ so that $C' = -(Ah + Bk)$ and

$$p_2 = -\frac{Ah + Bk}{\sqrt{(A^2 + B^2)}}.$$

By subtraction,

$$PQ = p = p_2 - p_1 = -\frac{Ah + Bk + C}{\sqrt{(A^2 + B^2)}}.$$

If the point P lies on the same side of the line AB as the origin O, we shall find similarly that

$$PQ = p = p_1 - p_2 = \frac{Ah + Bk + C}{\sqrt{(A^2 + B^2)}},$$

so that, summarising, the perpendicular distance of the point (h, k) from the line $Ax + By + C = 0$ is given by

$$\pm \frac{Ah + Bk + C}{\sqrt{(A^2 + B^2)}}. \tag{5.20}$$

It is usual to quote only the magnitude of the distance irrespective of its sign; if the positive root of $\sqrt{(A^2 + B^2)}$ is always taken, a difference in sign in the distances of two points calculated from formula (5.20) indicates that the points are on opposite sides of the given line. Formula (5.20) is best remembered by noticing that the numerator is obtained by substituting the coordinates of the given point in the left-hand side of the equation of the given line and that the denominator is simply the square root of the sum of the squares of the coefficients of x and y in the equation of the line.

Example 17. *Find the distances of the origin and the point* (4, 5) *from the straight line* $3x + 4y = 10$.

Writing the equation of the line in the standard form $3x + 4y - 10 = 0$, the distance of the origin (0, 0) from the line is, by (5.20),

$$\frac{3(0) + 4(0) - 10}{\sqrt{(3^2 + 4^2)}} = -\frac{10}{5} = -2.$$

The distance of the point (4, 5) is similarly

$$\frac{3(4) + 4(5) - 10}{\sqrt{(3^2 + 4^2)}} = \frac{22}{5}.$$

These distances would usually be quoted as 2 and 22/5 respectively; the calculated results show that the origin and the point (4, 5) are on opposite sides of the line $3x + 4y = 10$ (as can be seen if the line and points are plotted).

Example 18. *Find the equations of the bisectors of the angles between the lines* $Ax + By + C = 0$ *and* $ax + by + c = 0$.

In Fig. 43, the given lines are shown as AB, CD and their point of intersection is R. If P is the point (x, y) on the bisector of the angle ARC, P will be equidistant from both lines and will be on *opposite* sides of the two lines from the origin. Hence, from (5.20), the coordinates (x, y) of P will satisfy

$$\frac{Ax + By + C}{\sqrt{(A^2 + B^2)}} = -\frac{ax + by + c}{\sqrt{(a^2 + b^2)}}. \tag{5.21}$$

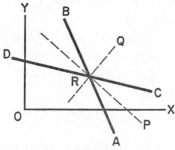

FIG. 43

If Q is the point (x, y) on the bisector of the angle ARD, Q will be equidistant from both lines and will lie on the *same* side of the lines as the origin. Hence the coordinates of Q will satisfy

$$\frac{Ax + By + C}{\sqrt{(A^2 + B^2)}} = +\frac{ax + by + c}{\sqrt{(a^2 + b^2)}}. \tag{5.22}$$

5.15 The equation of a straight line passing through the point of intersection of two given lines

Suppose the given lines are represented by the equations $Ax + By + C = 0$ and $ax + by + c = 0$. Consider the equation

$$Ax + By + C + k(ax + by + c) = 0, \tag{5.23}$$

where k is a constant. This equation represents a straight line for it is of the first degree in x and y. Further, the equation is satisfied by the coordinates of the point of intersection of the two given lines since these coordinates simultaneously satisfy the equations $Ax + By + C = 0$ and $ax + by + c = 0$. Hence equation (5.23) is the equation of a straight line passing through the common point of the given lines.

The argument used above is an example of one which is of great use in analytical geometry. It should be noted that the line given by equation (5.23) is not unique and that, by giving k different values, a family of lines all passing through the common point of the given lines can be obtained. In many examples, the line will be required to satisfy a second condition, such as to have a given slope or to pass through a second given point. This second condition enables the value of k to be fixed and an unique result to be obtained. Some illustrations follow.

Example 19. *Find the equation of the straight line which passes through the point of intersection of the lines $4x - 3y + 19 = 0$, $12x - 5y + 3 = 0$ and makes an intercept of $+ 2$ on the x-axis.* [O.C.]

Any line through the point of intersection of the given lines has the equation

$$4x - 3y + 19 + k(12x - 5y + 3) = 0,$$

and this can be written

$$(4 + 12k)x - (3 + 5k)y + 19 + 3k = 0. \tag{5.24}$$

This line meets the x-axis ($y = 0$) where

$$(4 + 12k)x + 19 + 3k = 0$$

and the intercept is $+2$ if

$$-\frac{19 + 3k}{4 + 12k} = 2.$$

The necessary value of k is easily found to be -1 and substitution in (5.24) gives $-8x + 2y + 16 = 0$. A slight reduction then gives $4x - y = 8$ as the required equation.

Example 20. *Find the equation of the straight line which is parallel to the line $3x + 4y = 0$ and which passes through the common point of the lines $x - 2y = 1$, $x + 3y = 2$.*

Any line through the intersection of the lines $x - 2y - 1 = 0$, $x + 3y - 2 = 0$ is $x - 2y - 1 + k(x + 3y - 2) = 0$, or

$$(1 + k)x - (2 - 3k)y - 1 - 2k = 0. \tag{5.25}$$

The slope of this line is $(1 + k)/(2 - 3k)$ and the slope of the line $3x + 4y = 0$ is $-\frac{3}{4}$. Hence if the lines are parallel,

$$\frac{1 + k}{2 - 3k} = -\frac{3}{4},$$

leading to $k = 2$. Substitution of this value of k in (5.25) then gives the required equation as $3x + 4y = 5$.

Exercises 5 (d)

1. At what angle are the lines whose equations are $ax + by + c = 0$ and $(a - b)x + (a + b)y + d = 0$ inclined to each other? [L.U.]

2. The vertices of a triangle are the points $A(1, 4)$, $B(5, 1)$, $C(-1, -1)$. Find the equations of its sides and the values of $\tan B$, $\tan C$. [L.U.]

3. Find the equation of the join of the points $(1, 2)$ and $(3, 4)$. Find also the coordinates of the middle point of the join and hence write down the equation of the perpendicular bisector of the join. [L.U.]

4. P, Q, R are three points with coordinates $(1, 0)$, $(2, -4)$, $(-5, -2)$ respectively. Determine
   (i) the equation of the line through P perpendicular to QR,
  (ii) the equation of the line through Q perpendicular to PR,
 (iii) the coordinates of the point of intersection of these lines.   [L.U.]

5. A line through the point $(2, 7)$ has a *positive* gradient and makes an angle of $45°$ with the line $x - 3y + 9 = 0$. Find the equation of the line.
    [O.C.]

6. The points $P(4, 2)$ and $R(-1, 0)$ are two opposite vertices of a square $PQRS$. The diagonal QS cuts the x-axis at M and θ is the acute angle between QS and PM. Show that $\tan \theta = 2\frac{1}{2}$.   [O.C.]

7. Find the coordinates of the point Q where the perpendicular from the point $P(1, 3)$ to the straight line $2x - 3y = 1$ cuts this line. If PQ is produced to a point R such that $PQ = QR$, find the coordinates of R.
    [O.C.]

8. Prove that the diagonals of the parallelogram formed by the lines $x + 2y = 2$, $2x + y = 2$, $x + 2y = 4$ and $2x + y = 4$ are at right angles to one another.

9. Find the equation of a line CP passing through the point $C(1, 2)$ and making an angle of $90°$ with the line $x - \sqrt{3}y + 4 = 0$. Find also the perpendicular distance of CP from the origin.

10. Show that the point $(1, 1)$ is equidistant from the lines $3x + 4y = 12$, $5x - 12y + 20 = 0$, $4x - 3y = 6$. By drawing a rough figure, decide whether the point is the centre of the inscribed or one of the escribed circles of the triangle formed by the above lines.   [O.C.]

11. A point P moves so that its perpendicular distance from the line $3x + 5y + 4 = 0$ is proportional to the square of its distance from the point $(1, 2)$. If the point $(2, -1)$ is one possible position of P, find the equation of its locus.

12. Find the equation of the straight line which is such that the x-axis bisects the angle between it and the line $2x + 5y = 18$.   [O.C.]

13. Find the equation of the line which passes through the point $(3, 2)$ and through the point of intersection of the lines $3x - 4y = 6$, $2x + 3y = 1$.

14. Find the equations of the lines through P, the point of intersection of the lines $x + 2y = 11$ and $2x - y = 2$ which are (i) parallel to and (ii) perpendicular to the line $x + 7y = 0$.   [L.U.]

15. Find the equation of the perpendicular from the vertex A of the triangle ABC to the opposite side BC, the equations of BC, CA and AB being respectively $x - y = 1$, $x + 2y + 1 = 0$ and $x - 2y = 3$. Find also the length of the perpendicular from B to AC.   [O.C.]

5.16 The determination of laws from experimental data

Relations between varying quantities, such as the voltage and current in an electrical circuit, can be shown graphically by plotting the results of experiments on squared paper. It is often useful to see if a formula can be deduced from such results, and formulae so deduced are said to be *empirical* (this simply means that they are deduced from experiment and not entirely from theory).

If the points plotted from the results of an experiment lie approximately on a straight line we know, from what has preceded, that the relation between the variables involved (say x and y) will be of the first degree and we can assume that the relation will be of the form

$$y = mx + c$$

where m and c are constants. Further, the values of these constants can be deduced by finding the slope of the line and the intercept made by it on the axis OY, or by substituting in the equation the coordinates (as read off from the graph) of two points on the line. The details are shown in Example 21 below.

Example 21. *In an experiment carried out at constant pressure, the volumes v cm³ of gas at temperature $\theta°C$ are given by the following table*

θ	10	21	33	50	65
v	103·7	107·7	112·0	118·4	123·9

By plotting v against θ, show that the approximate relation between these variables is $v = a\theta + b$ and determine values of the constants a and b.

Fig. 44 shows a plot of the recorded values of v and θ. In practice, this plot should be on a larger scale and it will be found that the points do not lie exactly

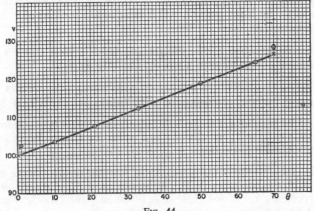

Fig. 44

along a straight line but that a line can be drawn from which none of the points deviates greatly. In drawing the line, its position should be fixed by ensuring that the plotted points are evenly distributed about it, some being above it and some below. This can be conveniently done by moving a stretched thread or a transparent scale with a fine line scratched on its lower surface and seeing that the points do not deviate systematically from the thread or line. Since the plotted points do here lie approximately along a straight line we can assume that v and θ approximately obey a formula of the type $v = a\theta + b$. Reading from the graph, we see that a rise of 70°C in temperature is accompanied by a rise of $125 \cdot 7 - 100 = 25 \cdot 7 \, cm^3$ in volume; the slope of the line is therefore $25 \cdot 7/70 = 0 \cdot 367$ and this is the required value of the constant a. We also see that the line cuts the v-axis when $v = 100$ so that $b = 100$. Alternatively, reading the coordinates of two points P and Q (chosen to be well spaced to minimise errors in reading from the graph), we find that P is (0, 100) and Q is (70, 125·7). Substituting these values of θ and v in the equation $v = a\theta + b$,

$$100 = b, \quad 125 \cdot 7 = 70a + b$$

and the values $a = 0 \cdot 367$, $b = 100$ are given by the solution of this pair of equations.

It should be noticed that if a law of the form $y = ax^n + b$, *where n is a known quantity*, is suspected of being true, this can be checked by seeing if a plot of y against x^n yields a straight line. If it does, the values of the constants a and b can be deduced as before. Cases in which n is not known are treated later.

Example 22. *Show that the data*

x	1	2	3	4
y	0·25	2·00	6·75	16·00

is satisfied by an equation of the form $y = ax^3 + b$ and find values of the constants a and b.

If the relation between x and y is $y = ax^3 + b$, there will be a linear relation between y and the *cube* of x. First forming a table of x^3 and the corresponding values of y, we have

x^3	1	8	27	64
y	0·25	2·00	6·75	16·00

and these values are plotted in Fig. 45. Since the plotted points lie on a straight line, the law relating x and y is of the form $y = ax^3 + b$. Reading from the graph, the slope of the line is given by

$$a = \tfrac{16}{64} = \tfrac{1}{4},$$

and, since the intercept on the y-axis is zero, $b = 0$.

The measurements of two related sets of physical quantities often obey a "power" law of the form $y = Ax^n$, where the multiplier A and the index n are constants. Taking logarithms, this relation gives

$$\log y = \log A + \log (x^n)$$
$$= n \log x + \log A,$$

showing that the graph of $\log y$ against $\log x$ will be a straight line of slope n and making an intercept $\log A$ on the axis of $\log y$. As it is possible, by using a stretched string or a transparent scale, to decide

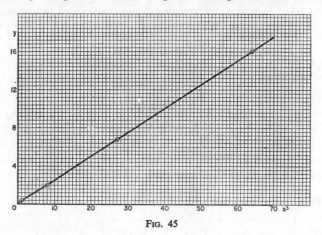

FIG. 45

if a set of points do or do not lie along a straight line, the graph of $\log y$ against $\log x$ will reveal if the given values of x and y do or do not obey a law of the form $y = Ax^n$. If they do, the values of n and $\log A$ can be deduced as before.

Example 23. *The following table shows the values of a quantity p obtained experimentally for the given values of a quantity v*

v	2	3	4	5
p	3·54	1·92	1·25	0·89

Show that the relation between p and v is of the type $pv^b = c$, where b and c are constants and determine approximate values of b and c. [L.U.]

Tabulating $\log p$ against $\log v$ from the data

$\log v$	0·301	0·477	0·602	0·699
$\log p$	0·549	0·283	0·097	−0·051

it should be remembered that the logarithms of numbers less than unity are negative, so that

$$\log 0 \cdot 89 = \bar{1} \cdot 9494 = -1 + 0 \cdot 9494 = -0 \cdot 0506;$$

this, and the other entries in the above table, have been rounded off to three places of decimals for the purpose of plotting. If we assume a relation between p and v of the form $pv^b = c$, $\log p + b \log v = \log c$, or $\log p = -b \log v + \log c$, and the plot of $\log p$ against $\log v$ should give a straight line. That this is so is shown by Fig. 46 and the slope $(-b)$ of the line is

$$-\frac{1 \cdot 0}{0 \cdot 67} = -\frac{3}{2} \text{ (approximately)},$$

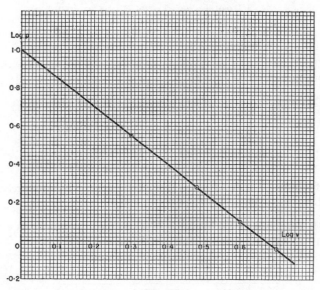

Fig. 46

the negative sign being affixed as the line makes an obtuse angle with the positive direction of the axis of $\log v$. Hence $b = \frac{3}{2}$ and, since the intercept made on the axis of $\log p$ is unity, it follows that $\log c = 1$, leading to $c = 10$.

Exercises 5 (e)

1. In a certain experiment, the recorded values of the load P lifted by an effort E were given by

P	100	200	300	400	500
E	5·60	8·65	11·85	14·88	18·00

Show that E and P are approximately related by the equation $E = aP + b$ and find the values of the constants a and b.

2. Show that the points whose coordinates are given by

x	0	1	2	3	4	5	6
y	−10·0	−7·7	−5·4	−3·1	−0·8	1·5	3·8

lie on the straight line $y = mx + c$ and determine the values of m and c.

3. Corresponding values of x and y are given by

x	0·0	1·0	1·6	2·5	3·2
y	−2·00	−1·50	−0·72	1·13	3·12

Show that x and y are related by an equation of the form $y = ax^2 + b$ and deduce values for a and b.

4. Corresponding values of two variables θ and t are given by

t	0·5	0·8	1·0	1·4	2·0
θ	4·08	4·21	4·33	4·65	5·33

By plotting θ against t^2, show that θ and t are approximately related by $\theta - c = \alpha t^2$ and find the values of α and c.

5. Measurements of the coefficient of friction μ of steel tyres on a rail at speeds V gave the following results

V	30	38	49	55	60
μ	0·066	0·051	0·041	0·036	0·033

Show that these results approximately follow a law of the form $V = (a/\mu) + b$ and find values of a and b. Use your result to calculate the coefficient of friction μ when $V = 45$.

6. Variables x and y are related by a law of the form $y = kx^n$. Approximate values of y for various values of x are given by the table

x	3	$4\frac{1}{4}$	$5\frac{1}{2}$	8	10	11	12
y	22	26	30	36	40	42	44

From the graph of $\log y$ against $\log x$, deduce the values of k and n.

[L.U.]

7. The following table shows some values of V obtained experimentally for the given values of t

t	5	9	16	20	25
V	0·45	0·6	0·8	0·89	1·0

By plotting log V against log t show that, allowing for small errors of observation, there is probably a relation between V and t of the type $V = At^n$ and find approximate values of A and n. [L.U.]

8. Given that x and y are related by a law of the form $y = Ax^n$, complete the following table

x	0			1·5	3	6
y		1·265	2·000	2·449		4·898

9. When a quantity of air is compressed to pressure p, the corresponding temperature t (degrees Centigrade) is given by

p	10	20	40	70	80
t	146	243	362	478	509

Verify that the law $T = kp^n$, where $T = t + 273$ is the absolute temperature of the air, is satisfied by the data and find values of the constants k and n.

10. The values of two variables y and z are given in terms of a third variable x by the table

x	$\frac{1}{3}$	$\frac{4}{3}$	$\frac{5}{3}$	6
y	1·061	1·732	2·371	3·673
z	1·250	1·667	2·250	4·000

Verify that relations of the form $y = Ax^n$ and $z = mx + c$ apply and find the values of A, n, m and c. Use your results to find two values of x for which $y = z$.

11. Two variables x and y are related approximately by the equation $y/A = 10^{kx}$ and corresponding values of x and y are

x	1·1	1·3	1·42	1·68	1·70
y	$4·99 \times 10^3$	$1·99 \times 10^4$	$4·55 \times 10^4$	$2·74 \times 10^5$	$3·15 \times 10^5$

By plotting log y against x, determine the values of A and k.

12. The following readings were recorded in an experiment

x	2	3	4	5
y	8	20	43	83

x and y are known to satisfy a relationship of the form $ay = b^x$ where a and b are constants. By plotting $\log y$ against x, draw a graph and from it determine probable values of a and b (to two figures) consistent with these readings.   [L.U.]

Exercises 5 (f)

1. Given the points $A(2, 14)$, $B(-6, 2)$, $C(12, -10)$, verify that the triangle ABC is right-angled. Calculate the coordinates of the point D on AB produced such that $AC = CD$.   [N.U.]

2. Find the distance between the point $(2, 4)$ and the point of intersection of the straight lines $4x - 3y + 4 = 0$, $5x + 7y + 8 = 0$.   [O.C.]

3. Find the coordinates of the fourth vertex of the parallelogram $ABCD$ given that A, B, C are the points $(-1, 6)$, $(-2, -2)$, $(5, 2)$ respectively. Prove that the parallelogram is a rhombus and find its area.   [O.C.]

4. The vertices of a triangle are the points $(3, 4)$, $(9, -4)$ and $(-3, -8)$. Calculate the area of the triangle and the coordinates of the centre of the circumscribing circle.   [L.U.]

5. ABC is a triangle in which A is $(1, 1)$, $B(6, 5)$ and $C(4, 7)$. AD and BE are the medians drawn from A and B. Find the coordinates of the two points of trisection of BE and verify that one of these lies on AD.

          [L.U.]

6. A variable straight line passes through the fixed point (h, k) and meets the axes OX, OY at P and Q; prove that the locus of the mid-point of PQ is $(h/x) + (k/y) = 2$.   [O.C.]

7. Show that the lines $y = mx + 1$ and $x + my = 9m + 6$ meet at right angles. Find the equation of the locus of their point of intersection.

          [L.U.]

8. O is the origin, Q is (a, b) and P is a variable point: R divides PQ in the ratio $m : n$ where m and n are positive; S divides PQ in the ratio $m : (-n)$. Prove that, if OR is perpendicular to OS, the equation of the locus of P is $n^2(x^2 + y^2) = m^2(a^2 + b^2)$.   [O.C.]

9. The vertices A, B of a triangle ABC are on the axes OX, OY respectively. The triangle is right-angled at A and AB, AC are of lengths 3 and 4 units respectively. If AC makes an angle θ with OX, show that the locus of C as θ varies is given by the equation $16x^2 - 24xy + 25y^2 = 256$.

          [L.U.]

10. Prove that the three points $(2, 3)$, $(-4, 7)$ and $(5, 1)$ lie on a straight line. Calculate the intercepts which this line makes with the axes.

    [O.C.]

11. Find the equations of the two straight lines drawn through the point $(4, 3)$ which make an isosceles right-angled triangle with the straight line $2x + 3y = 6$, having the right angle at the point $(4, 3)$.   [O.C.]

12. AB is the line $(x/a) + (y/b) = 1$. Write down the equation of the line CD whose intercepts on OX, OY are a^2/h and b^2/k respectively. Find the coordinates of Q, the point of intersection of AB and CD. Prove that, if the point (h, k) lies on AB, the equation of the line joining Q to the origin is $kx + hy = 0$.   [O.C.]

13. Find the reflection of the line $x - y = 4$ in the line $2x + y = 1$. [L.U.]

14. The line $2x - 3y = 5$ bisects at right angles a line PP'. If P is the point $(-1, 2)$, find the coordinates of P'.   [L.U.]

15. Verify that the two points $(a \cos \alpha, a \sin \alpha)$ and $(a \cos \beta, a \sin \beta)$ lie on the line $x \cos \frac{1}{2}(\alpha + \beta) + y \sin \frac{1}{2}(\alpha + \beta) = a \cos \frac{1}{2}(\alpha - \beta)$ and are at distance $2a \sin \frac{1}{2}(\alpha - \beta)$ from each other. Find the distance of the line from the origin.   [L.U.]

16. In the triangle LMN, the coordinates of L and M are $(2, 3)$ and $(4, -6)$ respectively. If N lies on the straight line $x + 2y + 3 = 0$, prove that the locus of the centroid of the triangle is $x + 2y + 1 = 0$. Find also the perpendicular distance between the locus and the given line. [O.C.]

17. A line CP is drawn through the point $C(6, 3)$ perpendicular to the line joining the points $A(1, 2)$ and $B(5, 5)$ meeting it in P. Another line CQ is drawn to pass through the mid-point Q of AB. Calculate the angle PCQ and the area of the triangle PCQ.   [L.U.]

18. The straight lines OA, OB through the origin and of slopes m_1, m_2 respectively meet the line $y = a$ at the points H and K; the perpendiculars to the lines at H and K intersect at P. Prove that the coordinates of P are

$$\left\{ \frac{a(m_1 + m_2)}{m_1 m_2}, \quad \frac{a(m_1 m_2 - 1)}{m_1 m_2} \right\}.$$

If the length HK is $3a$, prove that P lies on the curve $4ay + x^2 = 13a^2$.

    [O.C.]

19. Show that the straight line l whose equation is

$$(1 + 2\lambda)y - (2 + 3\lambda)x + 2\lambda - 3 = 0$$

always passes through the point $A(-8, -13)$. The line l meets the line $x + y = 1$ at the point P; calculate the coordinates of P and show that the values $\lambda = -5$ and $\frac{1}{2}$ give the points H, K respectively where the line $x + y = 1$ meets the axes OX, OY. Find the value of λ such that the line l passes through the mid-point of HK.   [O.C.]

20. Find the equations of two perpendicular straight lines, both of which pass through the point of intersection of the line $3x + 4y - 7 = 0$, $5x - 12y + 7 = 0$ and one of which passes through the point $(2, 9)$.

21. It is thought that two variables p and v are related by the formula

$$p = \frac{c}{v - b},$$

where b and c are constants. Show that the truth of this can be decided by testing if either the graph of v against $1/p$ or that of pv against p is a straight line.

22. Corresponding values of x and y are given by

x	1	2	3	4	5	6	7
y	0·56	1·25	2·14	3·33	5·00	7·50	11·67

By calculating y/x for each value of x and plotting a graph of y/x against y, show that the relation between x and y is $(10y/x) - y = 5$.

23. The quantity Q of a liquid passing per second through an orifice under a head H is given by the formula $Q = KH^n$. Determine the constants K and n from an experiment in which

H	0·0833	0·167	0·250	0·333	0·417
Q	0·00060	0·00088	0·00104	0·00120	0·00134

24. The following table shows a series of pressures p at corresponding volumes v for steam and air

v	2	4	6	8	10
p (steam)	68·7	31·3	19·8	14·3	11·5
p (air)	18·8	7·07	4·00	2·66	1·95

Verify that a law of the type $p = C/v^n$ holds for both steam and air, and find the value of n in each case.

25. Quantities x and y are connected by the relation $y = \log(a + bx)$, where a and b are constants. Plot 10^y against x from the table of values

x	1	2	3	4	5	6
y	0·857	0·924	0·982	1·033	1·079	1·121

and hence find estimates for a and b.   [L.U.]

CHAPTER 6

VECTORS AND COMPLEX NUMBERS

6.1 Introductory

In Statics and Dynamics it is necessary to establish theorems concerning the compounding and resolution of forces, velocities, accelerations and other quantities. Much repetition is avoided by showing that these are all vector quantities which can be represented by a straight line or vector, and proving some general theorems for vectors as such.

These theorems on vectors constitute a sort of algebra with rules similar to those of ordinary algebra. The use of vector symbols also leads to compactness which is of great value in more advanced parts of applied mathematics. The first part of this chapter can be regarded then as an application of what has been learned in Trigonometry as well as a preparation for later work in Statics and Dynamics.

The second part of the chapter is an introduction to the theory of complex numbers which involve the imaginary number $\sqrt{(-1)}$. It will be shown that such numbers can be manipulated in much the same way as real numbers and that they provide a valuable extension of the concept of number. The method of representing complex numbers graphically can be interpreted in terms of vectors and in the theory of complex numbers, as in the theory of vectors, we are able to represent a pair of numbers by a single symbol.

6.2 Definition of a vector

A *vector* is a straight line of a given magnitude drawn in a given direction.

If I walk 5 kilometres due East and then 4 kilometres due North-East my displacement can be shown diagrammatically. A line AB of length

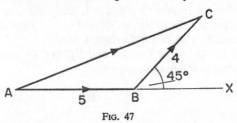

Fig. 47

5 cm drawn parallel to the top of the page represents the displacement to the East and a line BC of length 4 cm inclined at 45° to AB produced represents the second displacement (Fig. 47).

Here the lines *AB* and *AC* are vectors. They are marked with **arrows** in the diagram to show their *sense*, that is that they are drawn from *A* to *B* and from *B* to *C* rather than the reverse. The sense of a vector is usually indicated by the order of the letters and this is sometimes confirmed by an arrow. Thus we may write the above vectors as $\overrightarrow{AB}$ and $\overrightarrow{BC}$. Times bold type is used to denote a vector. Thus we may write a vector as **AB**, or it may be referred to by a single letter such as **a**. In written work it is convenient to underline the letters, writing $\underline{AB}$ or $\underline{a}$. The magnitude of a vector is called its *modulus*. Thus the modulus of the vector **AB** is the length *AB*, which is 5. The modulus of a vector **a** is denoted by the letter *a* (in italics). The direction of a vector may be given as its inclination to a fixed direction such as *AX* (Fig. 47). The vector whose direction is that of a given vector **a** and whose modulus is unity is called the *unit vector* in the direction of **a** and is denoted by the symbol **â**.

A vector as such is not considered as having any definite location and equal and parallel vectors are equivalent. Thus the statement **a** = **b** means that the vectors **a** and **b** are equal in magnitude and are parallel.

When dealing with vectors one refers to ordinary numbers, that is numbers not associated with a direction, as *scalars*. The effect of multiplying a vector by a scalar is to alter its magnitude while leaving its direction unaltered. Thus 2**AB** is a vector whose direction is the same as that of **AB** but whose modulus is twice that of **AB**. Hence, since **â** has unit modulus, *a***â** is a vector whose modulus is *a* and whose direction is that of **a**, and *a***â** is, in fact, merely an alternative way of writing **a**. Thus **a** = *a***â**.

6.3 Addition of vectors

In Fig. 47 the vectors **AB** and **BC** represent displacements to the East and North-East respectively and it is clear that the result of the two displacements is a displacement from *A* to *C*. Thus the vector **AC** represents the total or resultant displacement.

AC is called the *vector sum* of **AB** and **BC** and by an analogy with ordinary algebraical summation we write

$$\mathbf{AC} = \mathbf{AB} + \mathbf{BC}. \tag{6.1}$$

The vector sum of two vectors is thus defined as the third side of a triangle of which the given vectors are two sides. By measurement on an accurate diagram it will be found that *AC* = 8·32 cm and angle *CAB* = 19° 52′. This gives the magnitude and direction of **AC** and shows that the resultant displacement is 8·32 kilometres in a direction E 19° 52′ N.

If an additional vector **CD** is drawn from C (Fig. 48) it is easily seen that

$$\mathbf{AD} = \mathbf{AC} + \mathbf{CD}$$
$$= \mathbf{AB} + \mathbf{BC} + \mathbf{CD}. \tag{6.2}$$

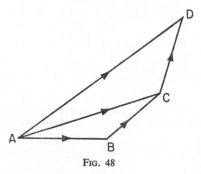

FIG. 48

Thus any number of vectors can be summed by placing them end to end and their sum is the vector drawn from A to close the polygon that they form.

6.4 Calculation of the sum of two vectors

Let **AB** be a vector whose modulus is AB and whose direction makes an angle α with a fixed direction AX; let **BC** have modulus BC and be inclined at an angle β to AX (Fig. 49). Then the angle between the

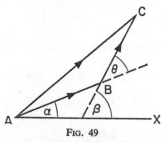

FIG. 49

positive directions of the vectors is θ, where $\theta = \beta - \alpha$, and θ is an external angle of the triangle ABC.

Applying the cosine rule to the triangle ABC, we have

$$AC^2 = AB^2 + BC^2 - 2AB \cdot BC \cdot \cos ABC,$$

and, since $\cos ABC = \cos(180° - \theta) = -\cos \theta$,

$$AC^2 = AB^2 + BC^2 + 2AB \cdot BC \cdot \cos \theta. \tag{6.3}$$

This gives the modulus AC of the vector $\mathbf{AC}$. The positive sign of the term containing $\cos\theta$ should be noted.

Applying the sine rule to the triangle ABC we have

$$\frac{BC}{\sin CAB} = \frac{AC}{\sin ABC},$$

and hence, since $\sin ABC = \sin(180° - \theta) = \sin\theta$,

$$\sin CAB = \frac{BC\sin\theta}{AC}. \tag{6.4}$$

This gives the direction of the vector $\mathbf{AC}$, since its inclination to AX is $\alpha + CAB$.

Example 1. *ABC is an equilateral triangle. A vector of modulus 3 has the direction of the side AB and a vector of modulus 2 has the direction of BC. Find the sum of these vectors.*

Let the side AB have length 3 units (Fig. 50); mark off D on BC so that

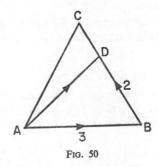

Fig. 50

$BD = 2$ units. Then AD is the sum of the vectors $\mathbf{AB}$ and $\mathbf{BD}$. By the cosine rule

$$AD^2 = 3^2 + 2^2 - 2.3.2.\cos 60° = 7,$$

giving

$$AD = 2\cdot646 \text{ units.}$$

By the sine rule

$$\frac{\sin DAB}{2} = \frac{\sin 60°}{2\cdot646}.$$

Hence

$$\sin DAB = \frac{1\cdot732}{2\cdot646} = 0\cdot6545,$$

and

$$DAB = 40° 53'.$$

Thus the sum has modulus $2\cdot646$ and is inclined at an angle $40° 53'$ to AB.

6.5 Vector algebra

We have used the summation sign of algebra to indicate the vector sum of vectors. This usage can be justified by showing that this kind of summation obeys the laws of ordinary algebraical summation.

The *commutative law* of algebra states that the order in which two quantities are summed is irrelevant, that is $a + b = b + a$. This law

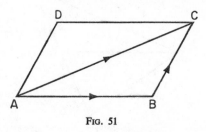

FIG. 51

holds for vector summation. Let **AB** and **BC** be two vectors and **AC** their vector sum (Fig. 51). Complete the parallelogram *ABCD*. Then since opposite sides of a parallelogram are equal and parallel the vectors **AD** and **BC** have the same modulus and direction, and so have the vectors **AB** and **DC**. That is **AD** = **BC**, **DC** = **AB**. Now by vector addition

$$AC = AB + BC \text{ and } AC = AD + DC.$$

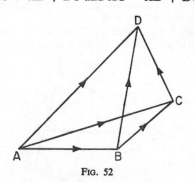

FIG. 52

Hence, replacing **AD** and **DC** in the second equation, we have

$$AB + BC = BC + AB.$$

The *associative law* of algebra states that $a + (b + c) = (a + b) + c$, where the quantities in brackets are added first. This also holds for vector summation. From Fig. 52 it is easily seen that

$$AD = AB + (BC + CD) = (AB + BC) + CD.$$

Subtraction is included in vector algebra by defining the vector $-\mathbf{b}$ as a vector whose modulus and direction is the same as that of $\mathbf{b}$ but which is drawn in the opposite sense to $\mathbf{b}$. Then

$$\mathbf{a} - \mathbf{b} = \mathbf{a} + (-\mathbf{b}).$$

The vectors $\mathbf{a} + \mathbf{b}$ and $\mathbf{a} - \mathbf{b}$ are shown in Fig. 53.

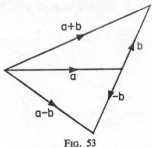

FIG. 53

The student may also wish to verify that the associative and distributive laws of algebraical multiplication apply to the multiplication of vectors by scalar quantities. Thus if m and n are scalars,

$$m(n\mathbf{a}) = n(m\mathbf{a}) = mn\mathbf{a},$$
$$(m + n)\mathbf{a} = m\mathbf{a} + n\mathbf{a},$$
$$n(\mathbf{a} + \mathbf{b}) = n\mathbf{a} + n\mathbf{b}.$$

Example 2. *Prove that, if λ and μ are positive scalar quantities, $\lambda AB + \mu AC = (\lambda + \mu)AD$ where $\lambda DB + \mu DC = 0$.*

Since $\lambda DB + \mu DC = 0$ the directions of DB and DC must be the same but in opposite sense. Therefore D (Fig. 54) is a point on BC which divides BC in the

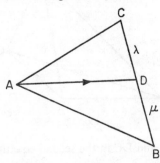

FIG. 54

ratio of λ to μ. Now $AB = AD + DB$ and $AC = AD + DC$, therefore

$$\lambda AB = \lambda AD + \lambda DB, \quad \mu AC = \mu AD + \mu DC.$$

Adding we have

$$\lambda AB + \mu AC = (\lambda + \mu) AD + \lambda DB + \mu DC$$
$$= (\lambda + \mu) AD.$$

6.6 Components of a vector

Let $r = OP$ join the origin of coordinates to a point P whose co-ordinates are (x, y) (Fig. 55). The vector **r** is called the position vector of the point P. The angle POX is θ, where $\tan \theta = y/x$, and (r, θ) are the polar coordinates of P so that $x = r \cos \theta$, $y = r \sin \theta$. Then

$$OP = ON + NP, \tag{6.5}$$

where **ON** has modulus $x(= r \cos \theta)$ and direction OX and **NP** has modulus $y(= r \sin \theta)$ and direction OY. The vectors **ON** and **NP** are

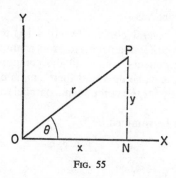

FIG. 55

called the *components* of the vector **OP** in the directions OX and OY respectively and **OP** is the vector sum of its components.

A unit vector in the positive direction of the x-axis is denoted by the symbol i (italics) and a unit vector in the positive direction of the y-axis by j (italics). With this notation **ON** $= xi$, **NP** $= yj$, and the equation (6.5) becomes

$$\mathbf{r} = \mathbf{OP} = xi + yj. \tag{6.6}$$

Alternatively we may write

$$\mathbf{r} = r \cos \theta \,.\, i + r \sin \theta \,.\, j,$$

and, since the modulus r is a scalar quantity,

$$\mathbf{r} = r(i \cos \theta + j \sin \theta). \tag{6.7}$$

In this form the modulus r is shown as multiplying the unit vector $i \cos \theta + j \sin \theta$ which is $\hat{\mathbf{r}}$. Thus, for example, a vector **r** whose modulus is 4 units and whose direction makes an angle of 30° with OX has components

$$4 \cos 30° = 3\cdot464, \quad 4 \sin 30° = 2.$$

and we may write

$$\mathbf{r} = 3\cdot464i + 2j.$$

If a vector is given in terms of its components, its modulus and direction are easily found. For example, let $\mathbf{r} = 3i + 4j$. Then

$$r^2 = 3^2 + 4^2 = 25,$$
$$r = 5,$$
$$\tan \theta = 4/3 = 1\cdot333,$$
$$\theta = 53° \ 8'.$$

Thus $\mathbf{r}$ has modulus 5 units and its direction is inclined at $53° \ 8'$ to OX.

6.7 Addition by components

When the sum of several coplanar vectors has to be found this is most easily done by expressing each vector as a sum of its components and adding the components. Since all the components parallel to a direction OX have the same direction their sum is obtained by simple addition, and similarly for the components parallel to the perpendicular direction OY.

Let the vectors to be summed be

$$\mathbf{r}_n = x_n i + y_n j,$$

where $n = 1, 2, 3, \ldots$ .. Then

$$\mathbf{r}_1 + \mathbf{r}_2 + \mathbf{r}_3 + \ldots = (x_1 + x_2 + x_3 + \ldots)i$$
$$+ (y_1 + y_2 + y_3 + \ldots)j.$$

Thus if R is the modulus of the sum and θ its inclination to OX, we have

$$R = \sqrt{\{(x_1 + x_2 + x_3 + \ldots)^2 + (y_1 + y_2 + y_3 + \ldots)^2\}}, \quad (6.8)$$

and

$$\tan \theta = \frac{y_1 + y_2 + y_3 + \ldots}{x_1 + x_2 + x_3 + \ldots}. \quad (6.9)$$

Example 3. *Vectors whose moduli are 3, 4, 6 and 7 act in directions making angles 30°, 90°, 135° and 240° respectively with a direction OX. Find their sum.*

The vectors in terms of their components parallel to and perpendicular to OX are

$$3(i \cos 30° + j \sin 30°) = 2\cdot598i + 1\cdot5j,$$
$$4(i \cos 90° + j \sin 90°) = \qquad\qquad 4j,$$
$$6(i \cos 135° + j \sin 135°) = -4\cdot243i + 4\cdot243j,$$
$$7(i \cos 240° + j \sin 240°) = -3\cdot5i - 6\cdot062j.$$

Adding the components we find for the sum

$$\mathbf{R} = -5\cdot145i + 3\cdot681j.$$

Hence

$$R = \sqrt{\{5\cdot145^2 + 3\cdot681^2\}} = 6\cdot326,$$

and

$$\tan \theta = -\frac{3 \cdot 681}{5 \cdot 145} = -0 \cdot 7153,$$

$$\theta = 180° - 35° \ 34' = 144° \ 26'.$$

Thus the sum has modulus $6 \cdot 33$ and its direction makes an angle of $144° \ 26'$ with OX.

6.8 The scalar product of two vectors

The scalar product of two vectors **a** and **b** is defined as the number $ab \cos \theta$, where a and b are the moduli of the vectors and θ the angle between their directions. The scalar product is denoted by **a . b**.

Since $\cos 0° = 1$ and $\cos 90° = 0$, it follows that the scalar product of parallel vectors is the product of their moduli and the scalar product of perpendicular vectors is zero. So for the unit vectors i and j

$$i.i = j.j = 1, \quad i.j = j.i = 0. \tag{6.10}$$

The square of a vector **a** is defined as **a . a** and written as $\mathbf{a}^2$, and we have $\mathbf{a}^2 = a^2$.

Since $b \cos \theta$ is the magnitude of the projection of the vector **b** on the direction of **a**, the scalar product of two vectors is the product of the modulus of one and the projection of the modulus of the other on its line. Since the projection of the modulus of **b + c** on any direction is the sum of the projections of **b** and **c** on that direction, it follows that

$$\mathbf{a} . (\mathbf{b} + \mathbf{c}) = \mathbf{a} . \mathbf{b} + \mathbf{a} . \mathbf{c},$$

and hence the distributive law of multiplication holds for scalar products. Hence

$$(x_1 i + y_1 j) . (x_2 i + y_2 j)$$
$$= x_1 x_2 i^2 + y_1 y_2 j^2 + x_1 y_2 i . j + y_1 x_2 j . i$$
$$= x_1 x_2 + y_1 y_2,$$

when we use the relations (6.10). Therefore if θ is the angle between the directions of these two vectors, we have

$$\sqrt{(x_1^2 + y_1^2)}\sqrt{(x_2^2 + y_2^2)} \cos \theta = x_1 x_2 + y_1 y_2. \tag{6.11}$$

Example 4. *Find the angle between the directions of the vectors $3i + 4j$ and $5i - 12j$.*
Here

$$x_1^2 + y_1^2 = 25, \quad x_2^2 + y_2^2 = 169,$$

$$x_1 x_2 + y_1 y_2 = -33,$$

so that, from (6.11)

$$5 \times 13 \times \cos \theta = -33,$$

giving

$$\cos \theta = -33/65 = -0 \cdot 5077$$

and

$$\theta = 120° \ 31'.$$

6.9 Vector quantities

A vector quantity is one that can be represented in magnitude and direction by a vector, and which is such that two or more such quantities can be added by vector summation. We have seen that displacement can be represented by a vector and the effect of two displacements is obtained by vector addition. Therefore displacement is a vector quantity.

Now velocity is defined (see § 8.2) as displacement in unit time and the sum of two velocities is the sum of two displacements in unit time. Therefore velocity is a vector quantity.

Similarly, acceleration is defined (see § 8.2) as change of velocity in unit time and the sum of two velocity changes can be obtained by vector addition. Therefore acceleration is a vector quantity.

The basic law of Dynamics is Newton's second law (see § 18.3) $F = ma$ which states that force is the product of mass and acceleration. Since the mass is a scalar quantity this implies that the force has the same direction as the acceleration. Hence, since acceleration is a vector quantity so is force, and Newton's law can be written in vector form as

$$\mathbf{F} = m\mathbf{a}.$$

Strictly, this applies to forces acting on a particle of negligible dimensions and further consideration is necessary before applying this equation to a rigid body.

The implications of this important principle will be considered later. For the moment it is sufficient to note that the vectors we have been considering in this chapter may represent displacements, velocities, accelerations or forces acting on particles.

Example 5. *A bomb which is falling vertically with velocity 200 m/s explodes and breaks into fragments. Each fragment is given an additional velocity of 100 m/s in some direction by the explosion. Prove that the fragments continue to move downwards within a cone of semi-vertical angle* 30°.

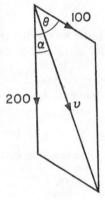

FIG. 56

Let a fragment be thrown in a direction inclined at θ to the downward vertical. Let v be its new velocity inclined at an angle α to the downward vertical (Fig. 56); v is obtained by vector addition of the velocities of 200 m/s and 100 m/s. Then

$$v^2 = 200^2 + 100^2 + 2 \cdot 200 \cdot 100 \cos \theta,$$

giving

$$v = 100\sqrt{(5 + 4 \cos \theta)},$$

and

$$\sin \alpha = \frac{100}{v} \sin \theta = \frac{\sin \theta}{\sqrt{(5 + 4 \cos \theta)}}.$$

The maximum value of sin α occurs (see § 8.6, Example 9) when $\cos \theta = -1/2$, $\theta = 120°$, and then

$$\sin \alpha = \frac{\sin 120°}{\sqrt{(5-2)}} = \frac{1}{2}.$$

Therefore, the maximum value of α is 30° and no fragment will deviate by more than 30° from the vertical.

Exercises 6 (a)

1. The medians of a triangle ABC meet at G. Prove that
$$\mathbf{AG} = \tfrac{1}{3}(\mathbf{AB} + \mathbf{AC}).$$
Hence show that $AG = \tfrac{1}{3}\sqrt{(2b^2 + 2c^2 - a^2)}$.

2. Express as a product of its modulus and a unit vector the sum of the vectors $i - 3j$, $3i + 3j$, $-3i + 4j$, $4(i + 2j)$.

3. If $\mathbf{OP} = i - 3j$ and $\mathbf{OQ} = 4i - 5j$, find the vector $\mathbf{PQ}$ and calculate its modulus. If $\mathbf{OR} = 4i + 5j$ and $\mathbf{OS} = 2i + 2j$ prove that $\mathbf{PQ}$ and $\mathbf{RS}$ are perpendicular.

4. If $\mathbf{OA} = ai + bj$, $\mathbf{OB} = ci + dj$, prove that the area of the triangle OAB is $\pm0{\cdot}5(ad - bc)$.

5. Find the area of a triangle formed by the vectors $2i + 3j$, $3i + 4j$.

6. D, E, F are the mid-points of the sides BC, CA, AB of a triangle. Prove that $\mathbf{AD} + \mathbf{BE} + \mathbf{CF} = 0$.

7. Show that the triangle ABC, where A is the point $(5, 7)$, B is $(7, 4)$, C is $(8, 9)$, is right-angled at A and find its area.

8. If $\mathbf{a} + \mathbf{b} = a\hat{c}$ and $\hat{\mathbf{a}} \cdot \hat{\mathbf{c}} = 0$, show that $b = a\sqrt{2}$.

9. E and F are the mid-points of the diagonals AC and BD of a quadrilateral $ABCD$. Prove that $\mathbf{AB} + \mathbf{AD} + \mathbf{CB} + \mathbf{CD} = 4\mathbf{EF}$.

10. P is a point in the side BC of a triangle ABC and Q is another point. Prove that, if $\mathbf{AP} + \mathbf{PB} + \mathbf{PC} = \mathbf{PQ}$, $\mathbf{AB} = \mathbf{CQ}$.

11. In any triangle ABC, $\mathbf{CB} = \mathbf{AB} + \mathbf{CA}$. By squaring both sides of this equation prove that $BC^2 = CA^2 + AB^2 - 2CA \cdot AB \cos A$.

12. $ABCD$ is a square. Prove that
$$3\mathbf{AB} + 4\mathbf{BC} + 5\mathbf{CD} + 8\mathbf{DA} + 3\mathbf{AC} = \mathbf{DB}.$$

13. The resultant of two intersecting forces P and $2P$ is $P\sqrt{3}$. Find the angle between the forces and the angle made by the resultant with the force of magnitude P. [L.U.]

14. Forces 3, 2, 1, 4 newton act at a point along the lines OA, OB, OC, OD respectively. $AOB = 60°$, $AOC = 150°$, $AOD = 270°$. Find the magnitude of the resultant and its inclination to OA.

15. *ABCDEF* is a regular hexagon. Find the sum

$$4AB + 5BD + 2CD + 3DE + 6EF + 3FA.$$

6.10 Complex numbers

We have seen (§ 1.6) that the quadratic equation $ax^2 + bx + c = 0$ has roots given by

$$x = \frac{-b \pm \sqrt{(b^2 - 4ac)}}{2a},$$

which are real and distinct if $b^2 > 4ac$ and coincident if $b^2 = 4ac$. If $b^2 < 4ac$ we can still find two solutions of the quadratic by introducing an imaginary number whose square is -1. This number is denoted by the symbol i, so that

$$i = \sqrt{(-1)}, \quad i^2 = -1.$$

With this notation we have the solution, when $b^2 < 4ac$,

$$x = \frac{-b \pm i\sqrt{(4ac - b^2)}}{2a}.$$

Thus the equation $x^2 - 4x + 13 = 0$ has the roots $2 + 3i$ and $2 - 3i$. If either of these two values is substituted for x in the quadratic and i^2 is replaced by -1 it will be found that the result is zero.

An expression of the form $a + ib$, where a and b are real numbers, is called a *complex number* and a and b are called the real and imaginary parts of the number respectively. Such numbers can be manipulated in the same way as rational or irrational numbers according to the fundamental rules of algebra and they provide an extension of the concept of number which is of enormous value in more advanced mathematics.

We may think of the complex number $a + ib$ as being an *ordered pair* of numbers which may represent, for example, the x and y coordinates respectively of a point in a plane. We speak of an *ordered* pair meaning that $a + ib$ is not the same number as $b + ai$, just as the point $(4, 5)$ is not the same point as $(5, 4)$.

Thus two complex numbers $a + ib$ and $c + id$ are equal if, and only if, $a = c$ and $b = d$. The sum of the numbers is defined as

$$(a + ib) + (c + id) = (a + c) + i(b + d). \tag{6.12}$$

The product of the numbers is defined as

$$\begin{aligned} (a + ib) \times (c + id) &= ac + iad + ibc + i^2bd \\ &= (ac - bd) + i(ad + bc). \end{aligned} \tag{6.13}$$

From this it is clear that the product of any number of complex numbers will always reduce to an expression such as $a + ib$ when i^2 is replaced by -1 wherever it occurs.

6.11 Algebra of complex numbers

The fundamental rules of algebra which are used in the manipulation of real numbers are

(*a*) the commutative law of addition

$$a + b = b + a,$$

(*b*) the associative law of addition

$$(a + b) + c = a + (b + c),$$

(*c*) the commutative law of multiplication

$$ab = ba,$$

(*d*) the associative law of multiplication

$$(ab)c = a(bc),$$

(*e*) the distributive law of multiplication

$$(a + b)c = ac + bc.$$

In each case the operation enclosed in brackets is understood to be performed first. It is easily seen that the operations of addition and multiplication of complex numbers defined in § 6.10 can be carried out in accordance with these laws. So, for example

$$(a + ib) \times (c + id) = (c + id) \times (a + ib),$$

and similarly for the other laws. Thus complex numbers are a logical extension of the concept of real numbers and can be manipulated in the same way.

Division by complex numbers presents no further difficulty. We define the quotient $1/(a + ib)$ as

$$\frac{1}{a + ib} = \frac{a - ib}{(a + ib)(a - ib)} = \frac{a - ib}{a^2 + b^2} = \frac{a}{a^2 + b^2} - i \frac{b}{a^2 + b^2}.$$

Thus division by a complex number is equivalent to multiplication by another complex number.

Example 6. *Show that* $\dfrac{2 + 3i}{4 + 5i} = \dfrac{1}{41} (23 + 2i).$

Multiplying numerator and denominator of the expression by $4 - 5i$, we have

$$\frac{2 + 3i}{4 + 5i} = \frac{(2 + 3i)(4 - 5i)}{(4 + 5i)(4 - 5i)} = \frac{8 - 15i^2 + 12i - 10i}{16 - 25i^2}$$

$$= \frac{23 + 2i}{16 + 25} = \frac{23 + 2i}{41}.$$

6.12 Modulus and amplitude

The *modulus* of a complex number $a + ib$ is defined as the positive real number $r = \sqrt{(a^2 + b^2)}$. The modulus is written as $|a + ib|$.

The *conjugate* of a complex number $a + ib$ is defined as the complex number $a - ib$. The product of a number and its conjugate is the square of its modulus, since on multiplying out $(a + ib)(a - ib) = a^2 + b^2$. Thus we have seen

$$\frac{1}{a + ib} = \frac{a - ib}{a^2 + b^2} = \frac{a - ib}{r^2}.$$

Also

$$|a + ib| = \sqrt{(a^2 + b^2)} = |a - ib|.$$

The *amplitude* of a complex number $a + ib$ of modulus r is defined as the angle θ which is such that

$$r \cos \theta = a, \quad r \sin \theta = b, \tag{6.14}$$

and hence

$$\tan \theta = \frac{b}{a}. \tag{6.15}$$

The two equations (6.14) are consistent since they give

$$\cos^2 \theta + \sin^2 \theta = \frac{a^2}{r^2} + \frac{b^2}{r^2} = \frac{a^2 + b^2}{r^2} = 1.$$

The angle θ may have any value from 0 to $360°$ or from 0 to 2π radians and the quadrant in which it lies depends on the signs of a and b. Thus, for example, $|3 + 4i| = 5$ and we have

$$5 \cos \theta = 3, \quad 5 \sin \theta = 4, \quad \tan \theta = \frac{4}{3},$$

and $\theta = 53° 8'$ since both $\sin \theta$ and $\cos \theta$ are positive. For $-3 + 4i$, $\cos \theta = -3/5$, $\sin \theta = 4/5$, $\theta = 180° - 53° 8' = 126° 52'$; for $3 - 4i$, $\cos \theta = 3/5$, $\sin \theta = -4/5$, $\theta = 360° - 53° 8' = 306° 52'$; for $-3 - 4i$, $\cos \theta = -3/5$, $\sin \theta = -4/5$, $\theta = 180° + 53° 8' = 233° 8'$. Thus the four numbers $\pm 3 \pm 4i$ all have the same modulus but different amplitudes.

It follows that any complex number can be written in the form $r \cos \theta + ir \sin \theta = r(\cos \theta + i \sin \theta)$. Thus

$$(3 + 4i) = 5(\cos 53° 8' + i \sin 53° 8').$$

Example 7. *Find the modulus and amplitude of* $(2 + i)^2(1 - i)/(1 + 3i)$.

By multiplication

$$(2 + i)^2 = 3 + 4i,$$

so that

$$(2 + i)^2(1 - i) = (3 + 4i)(1 - i) = 7 + i.$$

Hence

$$\frac{(2 + i)^2(1 - i)}{1 + 3i} = \frac{7 + i}{1 + 3i}.$$

Multiplying numerator and denominator by $1 - 3i$ we have

$$\frac{7 + i}{1 + 3i} = \frac{(7 + i)(1 - 3i)}{(1 + 3i)(1 - 3i)} = \frac{10 - 20i}{10} = 1 - 2i.$$

The modulus is given by $\sqrt{(1 + 2^2)} = \sqrt{5}$ and the amplitude θ by

$$\sqrt{5} \cos \theta = 1, \sqrt{5} \sin \theta = -2, \tan \theta = -2.$$

The angle satisfying these equations is, since $\sin \theta$ is negative and $\cos \theta$ positive, $\theta = 360° - 63° 26' = 296° 34'$.

6.13 Modulus and amplitude of products and quotients

The modulus of the product of two complex numbers is the product of their moduli and the amplitude of the product is the sum of their amplitudes. This can be seen as follows.

Let the moduli of the numbers be r_1, r_2 and their amplitudes θ_1, θ_2. Then

$$r_1(\cos \theta_1 + i \sin \theta_1) \times r_2(\cos \theta_2 + i \sin \theta_2)$$
$$= r_1 r_2(\cos \theta_1 \cos \theta_2 - \sin \theta_1 \sin \theta_2 + i \sin \theta_1 \cos \theta_2 + i \sin \theta_2 \cos \theta_1)$$
$$= r_1 r_2 \{\cos (\theta_1 + \theta_2) + i \sin (\theta_1 + \theta_2)\}$$

Hence the product has modulus $r_1 r_2$ and amplitude $\theta_1 + \theta_2$.

Similarly the quotient of two complex numbers has modulus equal to the quotient of their moduli and amplitude equal to the difference of their amplitudes. This follows since

$$\frac{1}{r_2(\cos \theta_2 + i \sin \theta_2)} = \frac{\cos \theta_2 - i \sin \theta_2}{r_2(\cos \theta_2 + i \sin \theta_2)(\cos \theta_2 - i \sin \theta_2)}$$

$$= \frac{\cos \theta_2 - i \sin \theta_2}{r_2}.$$

Therefore

$$\frac{r_1(\cos \theta_1 + i \sin \theta_1)}{r_2(\cos \theta_2 + i \sin \theta_2)} = (r_1/r_2)(\cos \theta_1 + i \sin \theta_1)(\cos \theta_2 - i \sin \theta_2)$$

$$= (r_1/r_2)(\cos \theta_1 \cos \theta_2 + \sin \theta_1 \sin \theta_2$$
$$+ i \sin \theta_1 \cos \theta_2 - i \sin \theta_2 \cos \theta_1)$$
$$= (r_1/r_2)\{\cos (\theta_1 - \theta_2) + i \sin (\theta_1 - \theta_2)\}.$$

Hence the quotient has modulus r_1/r_2 and amplitude $\theta_1 - \theta_2$.

6.14 The Argand diagram

Complex numbers may be shown graphically and compared on what is called the *Argand diagram* or, more simply, the *complex plane*. This merely consists of rectangular axes OX and OY with the complex number $a + ib$ represented by the point P whose coordinates are (a, b) (Fig. 57). With $r = \sqrt{(a^2 + b^2)}$ and $\tan \theta = b/a$, the polar coordinates of P on the same diagram, with OX as the initial line, are (r, θ). Thus at the same time the real and imaginary parts a and b of the number are shown and also by joining the representative point to the origin the modulus r and the amplitude θ are shown. OX is called the real axis of the diagram and OY the imaginary axis.

Many geometrical problems can be solved by the use of the Argand diagram. Thus we may consider a variable complex number z whose

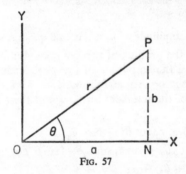

Fig. 57

real and imaginary parts are x and y, so that $z = x + iy$, and the equation of a curve on the diagram may sometimes be expressed in terms of z. For example, the equation of a circle of radius r about the origin may be written as $|z| = r$. Similarly, if the amplitude of z has a constant value α, which is written as am $z = \alpha$, we have the equation of a straight line through the origin. The equation am $(z - z_1) = \alpha$ is the equation of a straight line through the point representing z_1.

If z_1 and z_2 are the complex numbers $x_1 + iy_1$ and $x_2 + iy_2$ respectively, then

$$z_1 - z_2 = (x_1 - x_2) + i(y_1 - y_2)$$

and

$$|z_1 - z_2| = \sqrt{\{(x_1 - x_2)^2 + (y_1 - y_2)^2\}},$$

so that $|z_1 - z_2|$ is the distance between the points representing z_1 and z_2. Further, if $z_1 - z_2 = z_3 - z_4$, we know that $|z_1 - z_2| = |z_3 - z_4|$ and am $(z_1 - z_2) = $ am $(z_3 - z_4)$, so that the line joining the points representing z_1 and z_2 is equal and parallel to that joining the points representing z_3 and z_4.

The sum of two complex numbers z_1 and z_2 is shown on the Argand diagram as a sum of vectors which are the lines drawn from the origin to the points representing the numbers. Let P and Q represent the numbers z_1 and z_2 respectively and R represent z_3 which is their sum (Fig. 58). Then the equation

$$z_3 - z_1 = z_2 - 0$$

shows that the lines PR and OQ are equal in length and parallel, and so $OPRQ$ is a parallelogram. The vectors joining the origin to the

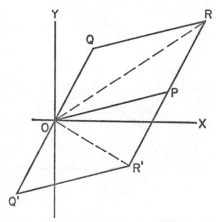

FIG. 58

points P, Q and R are OP, OQ and OR, and OR is therefore the vector sum of OP and OQ. The difference of the two complex numbers z_1 and z_2 is obtained in the same way by addition of the vectors representing z_1 and $-z_2$. Thus in Fig. 58, Q' is the point representing $-z_2$ and OR' which is the vector sum of OP and OQ' gives the point R' representing $z_1 - z_2$.

It is seen here that, as represented on the Argand diagram, complex numbers can be treated as vectors, with magnitudes given by their moduli and directions given by their amplitudes, whose sums and differences can be obtained by vector addition and subtraction.

Example 8. *Complex numbers z_1, z_2, z_3 are represented by points P, Q, R respectively on the Argand diagram and O is the origin; $z_1 = 3 + 4i$, $z_2 = 4 + 6i$, $z_3 = 1 + 2i$. Prove that $OPQR$ is a parallelogram and find its area.*

Here $z_2 - z_3 = z_1$, so that RQ and OP are equal and parallel and the figure is therefore a parallelogram (Fig. 59). Also, in terms of moduli and amplitudes,

$$z_1 = 5(\cos \theta_1 + i \sin \theta_1)$$

where $\cos \theta_1 = 3/5$, $\sin \theta_1 = 4/5$, and

$$z_3 = \sqrt{5}(\cos \theta_3 + i \sin \theta_3)$$

where $\cos \theta_3 = 1/\sqrt{5}$, $\sin \theta_3 = 2/\sqrt{5}$.
Hence

$$\sin(\theta_3 - \theta_1) = \frac{2}{\sqrt{5}} \cdot \frac{3}{5} - \frac{1}{\sqrt{5}} \cdot \frac{4}{5} = \frac{2}{5\sqrt{5}},$$

and the area of the parallelogram is $OR \cdot OP \cdot \sin(\theta_3 - \theta_1) = 2$.

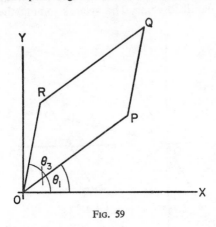

Fig. 59

6.15 The cube roots of unity

The equation $x^3 = 1$ may be solved by writing

$$x^3 - 1 = (x - 1)(x^2 + x + 1) = 0,$$

giving

$$x = 1 \text{ or } x = \frac{-1 \pm i\sqrt{3}}{2}.$$

There are thus one real cube root and two complex cube roots of unity. The modulus of each complex root is unity and the amplitudes are given by

$$\cos \theta = -\frac{1}{2}, \qquad \sin \theta = \pm \frac{\sqrt{3}}{2},$$

so that $\theta = 120°$ or $240°$, that is $2\pi/3$ or $4\pi/3$.
Since $x^3 + 1 = (x + 1)(x^2 - x + 1)$, the cube roots of -1 are

$$x = -1 \text{ or } x = \frac{1 \pm i\sqrt{3}}{2}.$$

THE CUBE ROOTS OF UNITY

In this case the modulus is again unity but the amplitudes are 60° and 300°, that is $\pi/3$ and $5\pi/3$. The cube roots in each case are shown on the Argand diagram (Fig. 60).

A more general theorem gives the real and complex roots of quantities directly. We have seen (§ 6.13) that the amplitude of a product of complex numbers is the sum of their amplitudes and hence, if n is a positive integer,

$$(\cos\theta + i\sin\theta)^n = \cos n\theta + i\sin n\theta. \tag{6.16}$$

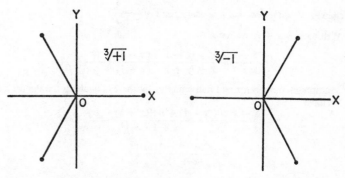

FIG. 60

This is known as *Demoivre's theorem* for positive integer index. Writing $\phi = n\theta$ this becomes

$$\left(\cos\frac{\phi}{n} + i\sin\frac{\phi}{n}\right)^n = \cos\phi + i\sin\phi$$

and hence

$$\cos\frac{\phi}{n} + i\sin\frac{\phi}{n} = \sqrt[n]{(\cos\phi + i\sin\phi)}. \tag{6.17}$$

We can use this formula to find the roots of unity. Thus if $n = 3$, $\cos\phi + i\sin\phi = 1$ if $\phi = 2r\pi$, where $r = 0, 1, 2, \ldots$ etc. Therefore a cube root of unity is $\cos(2r\pi/3) + i\sin(2r\pi/3)$, and taking $r = 0$, 1, 2 in succession we find the values

$$1, \quad \cos\frac{2\pi}{3} + i\sin\frac{2\pi}{3}, \quad \cos\frac{4\pi}{3} + i\sin\frac{4\pi}{3}.$$

Similarly, if $\cos\phi + i\sin\phi = -1$, $\phi = (2r + 1)\pi$ where $r = 0, 1, 2, \ldots$, so that a cube root of -1 is $\cos(2r + 1)\pi/3 + i\sin(2r + 1)\pi/3$, and taking $r = 0, 1, 2$ gives the values

$$-1, \quad \cos\frac{\pi}{3} + i\sin\frac{\pi}{3}, \quad \cos\frac{5\pi}{3} + i\sin\frac{5\pi}{3}.$$

The cube root of a, where a is any real number, is $a^{1/3}$ multiplied by one of the cube roots of unity.

6.16 Real and imaginary parts of a function

If z is a complex number we may write it as $z = x + iy$, where x and y are real numbers. It is sometimes necessary to find the real and imaginary parts of functions of z. Some examples of the procedure follow.

Example 9. *Find the real and imaginary parts of* $\dfrac{z-1}{z+1}$.

Writing $z = x + iy$ we have

$$\frac{z-1}{z+1} = \frac{x+iy-1}{x+iy+1} = \frac{(x-1)+iy}{(x+1)+iy}.$$

Multiplying numerator and denominator by the conjugate of the denominator we have

$$\frac{z-1}{z+1} = \frac{\{(x-1)+iy\}\{(x+1)-iy\}}{(x+1)^2+y^2}$$

$$= \frac{(x^2+y^2-1)+2iy}{(x+1)^2+y^2}.$$

In this form the real and imaginary parts are separated.

Example 10. *If $Z = (z - 6i)/(z + 8)$ and $z = x + iy$ where x and y are real, find the real and imaginary parts of Z. Prove that if Z is purely imaginary the locus of Z on the Argand diagram is a circle, whereas, if Z is real, the locus is a straight line.*
[O.C.]

Here
$$Z = \frac{x + i(y-6)}{(x+8)+iy}$$

$$= \frac{\{x+i(y-6)\}\{(x+8)-iy\}}{(x+8)^2+y^2}$$

$$= \frac{(x^2+y^2+8x-6y)+i(-6x+8y-48)}{(x+8)^2+y^2}.$$

This shows the real and imaginary parts of Z. If Z is imaginary, $x^2 + y^2 + 8x - 6y = 0$, that is, $(x+4)^2 + (y-3)^2 = 25$, so that the locus of z is a circle with centre at the point $-4 + 3i$ on the Argand diagram and radius 5. If Z is real, $-6x + 8y - 48 = 0$, and this is the equation of a straight line on which z lies.

Exercises 6 (b)

1. Express in the form $a + ib$
   (i) $(2 + i)^2$, (ii) $(2 - 3i)(3 + 4i)$, (iii) $(1 - i)/(1 + i)$, (iv) $(1 + i)^4$.

2. Express in the form $a + ib$
   (i) $(1 - i)^2/(1 + i)$, (ii) $(1 - i)^3/(1 + i)$, (iii) $1/(1 - i)^2$,
   (iv) $1/(1 + i) + 1/(1 - 2i)$.

3. Find the modulus and amplitude of

   (i) $(1 - i)^3$, (ii) $(1 - i)^{-2}$, (iii) $(1 + 2i)(3 + 4i)$, (iv) $(2 + i)^4$.

4. Find the modulus of

   (i) $\dfrac{(2 - 3i)(3 + 4i)}{(6 + 4i)(15 - 8i)}$, (ii) $\dfrac{(6 - 9i)(4 + 7i)(2 + 3i)}{(12 - 5i)(9 - 18i)}$.

5. If ω is a cube root of unity show that ω^n, where n is a positive integer, is also a root. If $x = a + b$, $y = a\omega + b\omega^2$ and $z = a\omega^2 + b\omega^4$, show that $x^2 + y^2 + z^2 = 6ab$.

6. Find the roots of the equation $(1 - x)^3 = x^3$.

7. By equating $\sqrt{(5 + 12i)}$ to $a + ib$, where a and b are real, find the value of the square root.

8. Prove that, if P and Q represent complex numbers z_1 and z_2 in the Argand diagram where O is the origin and $|z_1 - z_2| = |z_1 + z_2|$, then OP is perpendicular to OQ.

9. If ω is a cube root of unity form the quadratic equation whose roots are ω and $1/\omega$.

10. Find the four roots of the equation $z^4 - 4z^2 + 16 = 0$.

11. Find the modulus and amplitude of the roots of the equation $z^3 + 27 = 0$.   [O.C.]

12. Find the modulus and amplitude of
    $(2 + i)^2(1 - i)/(1 + 3i)$ and of $(2 - i)^2(3i - 1)/(i + 3)$.   [O.C.]

13. Find the roots of the equation $z^8 - 16 = 0$.

14. Prove that, if $|z + 1| = 2|z - 1|$, z lies on a circle whose radius is 4/3.   [O.C.]

15. Find the modulus and amplitude of
    $z_1 = (2 - i)/(3i - 1)$, $z_2 = (i - 3)/(2 + i)$ and of $z_1 + z_2$.   [O.C.]

Exercises 6 (c)

1. An aeroplane flies 50 kilometres on bearing $45°$, then 80 kilometres on bearing $300°$, and finally 60 kilometres on bearing $240°$. Find its distance and bearing from its starting point.

2. In a triangle ABC let the perpendiculars from B and C to the opposite sides meet in D. Prove that $AC \cdot (DA + AB) = 0$, $AB \cdot (DA + AC) = 0$, and hence that $DA \cdot BC = 0$, showing that the perpendiculars drawn from the vertices to the opposite sides are concurrent.

3. ABC is a triangle in which $AB = 7$ m, $BC = 3$ m, $CA = 5$ m. Find the sum $BC + 3AC + 2BA$.

4. $ABCD$ is a quadrilateral; P, Q, R, S are the mid-points of its sides and O is any point in its plane. Show that the system of forces represented by **OA**, **OB**, **OC**, **OD** has the same resultant as the system represented by **OP**, **OQ**, **OR**, **OS**. [L.U.]

5. Two forces are completely represented by the sides AB, AC of a triangle ABC. Show that their resultant is completely represented by $2AD$, where D is the mid-point of BC. A point O within a given triangle PQR is such that forces completely represented by OP, OQ, OR are in equilibrium. Prove that O is the centroid of the triangle. [L.U.]

6. L, M, N are the mid-points of the sides BC, CA, AB of a triangle. The perpendiculars from M and N to CA and AB respectively meet at K. Prove that **AB**.$(\mathbf{AK} - \frac{1}{2}\mathbf{AB}) = 0$, **AC**.$(\mathbf{AK} - \frac{1}{2}\mathbf{AC}) = 0$, and hence that **BC**.$(\mathbf{AK} - \mathbf{AL}) = 0$, and that the perpendiculars to the sides BC, CA, AB from L, M, N, respectively, are concurrent.

7. R is the resultant of forces P and $2P$ acting at O, the angle between their lines of action being $60°$. A third force S is greater than R and also acts at O. If the maximum and minimum values of the resultant of all three forces are 26 and 12 newton find P in newton. [O.C.]

8. When moving East at 10 km/h the wind seems to blow from due North. When the speed is doubled it appears to come from the North-East. Find the speed and true direction of the wind.

9. Five wires radiating from the top of a telephone pole produce the following horizontal pulls; 2000 N due South, 1900 N due East, 2050 N due North-East, 1850 N at 30° East of North and 2100 N due North-West. Find the magnitude and direction of the total pull on the post.

10. Given that $f(z) = (7 - z)/(1 - z^2)$, where $z = 1 + 2i$, show that $|z| = 2|f(z)|$.

11. If $z = 1 + i$, mark on an Argand diagram the points A, B, C, D, representing z, z^2, z^3, z^4. Find the moduli and amplitudes of $z^3 - z^4$ and $z^2 - z^4$. Show that the angle BDC is am $\{(z^3 - z^4)/(z^2 - z^4)\}$ and that the angles BDC and ACB are equal. [L.U.]

12. If $z_1 = 2 + i$, $z_2 = -2 + 4i$ and $1/z_3 = 1/z_1 + 1/z_2$, find z_3. If z_1, z_2 and z_3 are represented on an Argand diagram by P, Q and R respectively and O is the origin, show that R is the foot of the perpendicular from O to the line PQ.

13. In an Argand diagram points P, Q, R represent respectively the complex numbers α, β, $(1 - k)\alpha + k\beta$, where k is real. Prove that R lies on PQ and $PR/RQ = k/(1 - k)$.

14. Find the three roots of the equation $8x^3 = (2 - x)^3$.

15. Find the modulus of
    (i) $(1 - 2i)^{11}/(1 - 2i)^8$, (ii) $(1 - k^2 + 2ik)/(1 + k^2)$, k real.

16. Prove that, if $(z - 2i)/(2z - 1)$ is purely imaginary, the locus of z in the Argand diagram is a circle and find its centre and radius. [O.C.]

17. Prove that, if $(z - 6i)/(z + 8)$ is real, the locus of the complex number z in the Argand diagram is a straight line. [O.C.]

18. If $z_1 = (1 + 7i)/(1 - i)$ and $z_2 = (17 - 7i)/(2 + 2i)$, find the moduli and amplitudes of z_1, z_2, $z_1 + z_2$, $z_1 z_2$. [O.C.]

19. Show that if z is a complex number and the real part of $(z - i)/(z - 1)$ is zero, the locus of z in the Argand diagram is a circle and find its centre and radius. [O.C.]

20. Prove that, if $Z = X + iY = (z - 1)/(z + 2)$ and z is a complex number with modulus 1 and amplitude θ,

   (i) $Y/X = -3 \cot \tfrac{1}{2}\theta$,   (ii) $(X + 1)^2 + Y^2 = 1$.   [O.C.]

CHAPTER 7

THE DIFFERENTIAL CALCULUS

7.1 Introduction

We now commence the study of a subject in which the chief operation is rather different from the operations of addition, subtraction, multiplication, etc., used in elementary algebra. The subject concerned is the CALCULUS (the word is derived from the Latin term for a pebble used in reckoning) and the operation involved is that of taking a *limit*. Such an operation has already been briefly mentioned in connection with convergent geometrical progressions (§ 2.5) and again in connection with small angles (§ 3.9) but from now on it will be used continually.

Two limits are of special importance in the calculus. The first of these is the so-called *derivative* and its study forms the subject of the *differential calculus* of which the basic ideas are given in this chapter. The other is the *integral* and this will be introduced in Chapter 9. Both of these concepts have a wide variety of applications and have been significant in the development of many scientific theories.

In laying the foundations of the calculus it is necessary to be precise about what exactly is meant by terms like small, large, etc. For example, "small" is a purely relative term—a million is usually considered to be a large number but a million grains of sand is a small amount when compared with all the sand on our coasts. A reference standard is therefore essential when defining "a small quantity" and it is only by starting with precise definitions that the calculus can be developed into a tool which can be used with confidence. The reader is therefore advised to pay particular attention to the fundamental concepts—once these have been understood, he will then find that the technical processes involved are not at all difficult to use.

7.2 Functions and functional notation

When two variable quantities x and y are so related that the value of one quantity y depends on some values of the other quantity x, then y is said to be a *function* of x. The relation between the two variable quantities may be given by a simple formula such as

$$y = 5x^2 + 3x + 2$$

or $y = \cos x$, or the relation may be given by a graph or by a table of numerical values. In many practical cases a graph or table relating two variable quantities is available but it is often impossible, or very difficult, to express the relationship by a mathematical formula. For example, a recording barometer plots the atmospheric pressure p against the time t and, although p is a function of t, it is usually not possible (because of the complexity of the weather) to express p in terms of t by a mathematical formula.

When general, rather than particular, functions of x are under consideration, it is convenient to write $y = f(x)$, $F(x)$ or $\phi(x)$ . . .. This notation does not mean that y is the product of f, F, ϕ, . . . and x but is simply an abbreviation for the words "y is a function of x". The different letters f, F, ϕ, . . . are used to denote different functions.

If $y = f(x)$ and we wish to specify the value of y corresponding to a given value, say $x = 4$, we write the result as $f(4)$. For example, if $f(x) = 5x^2 + 3x + 2$,

$$f(4) = 5(4)^2 + 3(4) + 2 = 80 + 12 + 2 = 94$$

and this is the value of y when $x = 4$. Similarly if $\phi(x) = \cos x$, $\phi(\tfrac{1}{4}\pi) = \cos(\tfrac{1}{4}\pi) = 1/\sqrt{2}$.

Functions such as $y = 5x^2 + 3x + 2$ and $y = \cos x$ possess the property that y is determined for all values of x (this is usually expressed by saying that the function is *defined* for all values of x) and there is one, and only one, value of y corresponding to each value of x. Many functions do in fact possess this property but it is not in any way essential. For instance, if x is positive, the function $y = 2\sqrt{x}$ is not single-valued, since to each positive value of x, there correspond two real values of y. If $x = 0$ there corresponds only the single value $y = 0$, while if x is negative there are no real values of y satisfying the relation.

Functions such as we have considered above are called *explicit* functions. The variable quantity x is termed the *independent* variable and the second variable y, whose value depends on that given to x, is referred to as the *dependent* variable. Sometimes the relation between the two quantities x and y is given in a form such as

$$x^2 - 2xy^2 + 4 = 0, \text{ or } x^2 + y + \tan y = 3;$$

these are called *implicit* functions. In the first of these examples, we could solve for y to obtain

$$y = \pm\sqrt{\left(\frac{x^2 + 4}{2x}\right)}$$

and in this form y is an explicit function of x. In the second example it is not possible to express y explicitly in terms of x. Although implicit functions are important in mathematics, we shall be almost entirely concerned with explicit functions in this book.

Example 1. *If* $f(x) = x^2 + 5x + 6$, *find the values of* $f(1)$ *and* $f(0)$. *What values of* x *make* $f(x) = 0$?

To find the value of $f(1)$, we write $x = 1$ in the expression $x^2 + 5x + 6$. Thus

$$f(1) = (1)^2 + 5(1) + 6 = 12.$$

Similarly

$$f(0) = (0)^2 + 5(0) + 6 = 6.$$

$f(x) = 0$ when $x^2 + 5x + 6 = 0$ and this can be written in the form $(x + 2)(x + 3) = 0$ giving $x = -2$ and -3.

Example 2. *If* $f(x) = x^2 + \cos x$, *find the values of* $f(0)$ *and* $f(\pi)$. *For what value of* x, *between* 0 *and* π *radians, is* $f(x) = \frac{1}{4}\pi^2$?

$$f(0) = (0)^2 + \cos 0 = 1,$$
$$f(\pi) = (\pi)^2 + \cos \pi = \pi^2 - 1 = 8\cdot870.$$

When $f(x) = \frac{1}{4}\pi^2$, we have $x^2 + \cos x = (\frac{1}{2}\pi)^2$, and this equation is satisfied by $x = \frac{1}{2}\pi$.

7.3 The gradient of a graph

The variation of a function is conveniently shown by plotting its graph. This is illustrated in Fig. 61 by the graph of the simple explicit

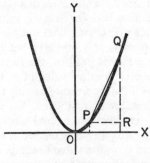

Fig. 61

function $y = x^2$. It will be seen that as the independent variable x increases from zero through positive values, the dependent variable y also increases. The reverse is true when x increases to zero from negative values. We could describe this change by saying that y decreases for increasing x so long as $x < 0$ and that y increases when $x > 0$.

In Fig. 61, P is the point with coordinates (x_1, y_1) and Q the point (x_2, y_2). The difference in the values of the ordinates at P and Q is $y_2 - y_1$ while the difference in their abscissae is $x_2 - x_1$ and the *average rate of change of* y as x changes from x_1 to x_2 is defined as

$$\frac{y_2 - y_1}{x_2 - x_1}. \tag{7.1}$$

From the diagram this is seen to be the tangent of the angle QPR, PR being parallel to the line OX, and this quantity is called the *slope* of the chord PQ.

To fix ideas, take the abscissae x_1 and x_2 of the points P and Q to be respectively 2 and 3. The ordinate of P, which is given by the formula $y = x^2$ with $x = 2$, is $y_1 = 2^2 = 4$ while that of Q is similarly $y_2 = 3^2 = 9$. The slope of the chord PQ is then given by formula (7.1) as

$$\frac{9 - 4}{3 - 2} = 5.$$

If we take another point Q_1, nearer to P than Q, say one whose abscissa is 2.3, its ordinate is $(2.3)^2$ or 5·29 and the slope of the chord PQ_1 will be

$$\frac{5\cdot29 - 4}{2\cdot3 \ - 2} = \frac{1\cdot29}{0\cdot3} = 4\cdot3.$$

Taking other points Q_2, Q_3, Q_4, . . ., each one nearer to P than the preceding one, and taking their abscissae to be 2·2, 2·1, 2·05, . . ., the

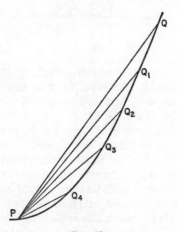

FIG. 62

slopes of the chords PQ_2, PQ_3, PQ_4, . . ., calculated in the same way, will be found to be 4·2, 4·1, 4·05, ...

A rough sketch (not to scale) of that part of the curve of Fig. 61 which lies between the points P and Q is shown in Fig. 62. It will be seen that as the points Q_1, Q_2, Q_3, Q_4, . . . approach nearer and nearer to the point P, the slopes of the chords PQ_1, PQ_2, PQ_3, PQ_4, . . . decrease. The calculated values 4·3, 4·2, 4·1, 4·05, . . . of these slopes suggest that they may be approaching a limiting value which might well be of magnitude 4.

The truth of the conjecture that the slope of the chord PQ approaches a limiting value of magnitude 4 as Q approaches P can be decided as follows. Let the abscissa of the point Q be $2 + h$ so that its ordinate is $(2 + h)^2$ and the slope of the chord PQ is given by

$$\frac{(2 + h)^2 - 2^2}{(2 + h) - 2} = \frac{h(4 + h)}{h} = 4 + h.$$

As the point Q approaches P, the value of h becomes smaller and smaller and the limiting value of the expression $4 + h$, as h decreases to zero, is 4. Put in another way, we can find h and the abscissa $2 + h$ of a

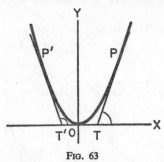

Fig. 63

point Q so that the slope $4 + h$ of the chord PQ differs from the value 4 by as little as we please. For example, if we wish to find the abscissa of Q such that the slope of the chord PQ is 4·0001, we take $h = 0·0001$ and the abscissa of Q as 2·0001.

The line through the point P of slope 4 is the *limiting position* of the chord PQ as Q approaches closer and closer to P and is the *tangent* to the graph at the point P. The slope of this tangent is defined as the *gradient* of the graph at P. The sign of the gradient should be noted. If the shape of the graph is such that the tangent makes an acute angle with the positive direction of the axis OX, the gradient is positive while it is negative at points for which this angle is obtuse. This is illustrated in Fig. 63 which again shows the graph of $y = x^2$. The gradient of the graph is positive at the point P where the tangent PT makes an acute angle PTX with OX. At the point P', the angle between the tangent $P'T'$ and the line OX is the obtuse angle $P'T'X$ and the gradient at P' is negative.

7.4 The increment notation

In finding the gradient of the graph of $y = x^2$ in § 7.3 we used the letter h to denote the difference between the abscissae of the points

P and Q and then allowed the value of h to decrease to zero. In what follows we shall often be concerned with operations of this nature and it is convenient to introduce here a notation for a small change in the value of a variable quantity.

We use the symbol δx, called "delta x", to denote a small increase, or *increment*, in the value of a variable x. This notation does not mean δ multiplied by x but implies that $\delta x = x_1 - x$ where x_1 differs from x by a small quantity. When y is a function of x, the symbol δy is used to denote the change in the value of the dependent variable y corresponding to a change δx in the value of the independent variable x.

In Fig. 64, P is the point (x, y) on the graph of a function $y = f(x)$

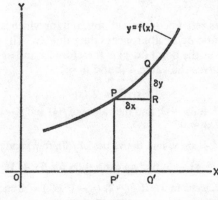

FIG. 64

and Q is a neighbouring point $(x + \delta x, y + \delta y)$. P' and Q' are the projections of P and Q on the line OX and PR is parallel to this line. Then $OP' = x$, $PP' = y$, $OQ' = x + \delta x$, $QQ' = y + \delta y$. It follows that

$$QR = QQ' - RQ' = QQ' - PP'$$
$$= y + \delta y - y = \delta y,$$

and that

$$PR = P'Q' = OQ' - OP'$$
$$= x + \delta x - x = \delta x.$$

The average rate of change of y as x changes to $x + \delta x$ is measured by the tangent of the angle QPR and this is the ratio $\delta y/\delta x$. The gradient of the graph at the point P, or the slope of the tangent at P to the graph, is the limiting value of this ratio as δx approaches zero.

As an example of the use of this notation, the gradient of the graph of $y = x^2$ at the point P with coordinates (x, y) would be found as follows. At the point P, we have

$$y = x^2$$

and at the neighbouring point Q with coordinates $(x + \delta x, y + \delta y)$,

$$y + \delta y = (x + \delta x)^2.$$

By subtraction,

$$\delta y = (x + \delta x)^2 - x^2 = (2x + \delta x)\,\delta x$$

and hence

$$\frac{\delta y}{\delta x} = 2x + \delta x.$$

As δx approaches zero (a convenient notation for which is "as $\delta x \to 0$"), we see that the ratio $\delta y / \delta x$ approaches the value $2x$. The gradient of the graph of $y = x^2$ at the point (x, y) is therefore $2x$ and at the point with abscissa 2, this gives the value 4 found in § 7.3.

Exercises 7 (a)

1. If $f(x) = 2x^2 + 3x - 2$, find the values of $f(\frac{1}{2})$ and $f(-\frac{1}{2})$. What values of x make $f(x) = 0$?

2. If $f(x) = 3x^2 + \sin x$, find the values of $f(0)$, $f(\frac{1}{2}\pi)$ and $f(-\pi)$.

3. If $f(x) = x^2 + 4x + 3$, find an expression for $f(x + 1)$.

4. $F(x)$ is a quadratic in x. If $F(-2) = -1$, $F(0) = 1$ and $F(1) = 5$, find this quadratic.

5. Given that $f(x) = (x - 1)/(x^2 + 1)$, find $f(0)$ and $f(x + h)$.

6. If $F(x) = \log x$, show that $F(ab) = F(a) + F(b)$ and that $F(a^3) = 3F(a)$.

7. Express y explicitly in terms of x when
   (i) $x^2 + 4y^2 = 2x$ and (ii) $xy + y^2 = x^2$.

8. Find the slope of the chord joining the points with abscissae 1 and 2 respectively on the graph of the function $y = 8 + 3x^2$.

9. P is the point (x, y) and Q the point $(x + \delta x, y + \delta y)$ on the graph of $y = 8 - 5x^2$. Show that

$$\frac{\delta y}{\delta x} = -10x - 5(\delta x)$$

   and deduce the gradient of the curve at the points where $x = 0$ and $x = 1$.

10. Show that the gradient of the graph of $y = -1 + 3x - \frac{1}{4}x^2$ when $x = 2$ is double that when $x = 4$. Find the abscissa of the point on the graph at which the gradient is -1. [O.C.]

11. An expression of the second degree is denoted by $f(x)$. If $f(1) = 7$, $f(2) = 23$ and $f(3) = 17$, find the gradient of the graph of $f(x)$ at $x = 2$.
[O.C.]

12. Calculate the gradient at the point $(2, \frac{1}{4})$ of the curve whose equation is $y = 1/x^2$. [N.U.]

13. Find the gradients of the graph of $y = 5x - x^2 - 6$ at the two points where the graph intersects the axis of x.

14. Find the coordinates of the point at which the tangent to the graph of $y = x^2 - 8x + 14$ is parallel to the axis of x.

15. Draw a graph, using the same scales for x and y, of $y = x^2 - 4x + 3$ for values of x between $x = 2.8$ and $x = 3.2$. Draw the tangent to the graph at $x = 3$ and measure its slope. Compare this with the limiting value of $\delta y/\delta x$ at $x = 3$ as δx approaches zero.

7.5 The derivative of a function

In § 7.4 we found that, for the function $y = x^2$, the limiting value of the ratio $\delta y/\delta x$ as δx approached zero was $2x$. Such limiting values are the central point of the differential calculus and they are known as *derivatives* or *differential coefficients*. For the general function $y = f(x)$, the derivative of y with respect to x is denoted by the symbols

$$\frac{dy}{dx} \quad \text{or} \quad y' \quad \text{or} \quad f'(x),$$

and its definition is

$$\frac{dy}{dx} = \lim_{\delta x \to 0} \left\{ \frac{f(x + \delta x) - f(x)}{\delta x} \right\} \tag{7.2}$$

where the expression on the right means the limiting value of the quotient inside the brackets as δx approaches zero. In evaluating this limiting value, we start with $f(x + \delta x) - f(x)$ which represents the change in value of y corresponding to a change δx in the value of x and this is the quantity previously denoted by δy. This quantity divided by δx is evaluated and the limiting value is found by ignoring all the terms containing δx, $(\delta x)^2$ and higher powers in the resulting expression.

Thus equation (7.2) can be written in the equivalent form

$$\frac{dy}{dx} = \lim_{\delta x \to 0} \left(\frac{\delta y}{\delta x} \right), \tag{7.3}$$

and we deduce that, when δx is small,

$$\frac{\delta y}{\delta x} \simeq f'(x) \quad \text{or,} \quad \delta y \simeq f'(x)\delta x \tag{7.4}$$

is an approximation which improves as δx becomes progressively smaller.

The operation of finding the derivative of a function by calculating the limit in equation (7.2) will be referred to as "differentiating from the definition" or as "differentiating from first principles" and we give some examples of this process. Before doing this, however, we shall give a geometrical interpretation of the approximation of (7.4). Fig. 65 gives an enlarged view of part of Fig. 64 and P, Q are neighbouring points with coordinates (x, y), $(x + \delta x, y + \delta y)$ on the graph of the function $y = f(x)$. PR is parallel to the axis OX and PT is the tangent to the graph at P. The gradient of the graph is the tangent of the angle (ψ) which the tangent PT makes with the line OX; it is also the derivative $f'(x)$ of the function $f(x)$. From Fig. 65, it will be seen that

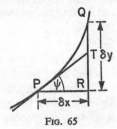

Fig. 65

$TR = PR \tan \psi$ and, since $\tan \psi = f'(x)$ and $PR = \delta x$, it follows that $TR = f'(x)\delta x$. QR is the change in the value of the ordinate of a point on the graph $y = f(x)$ as the abscissa changes from x to $x + \delta x$ so that $QR = \delta y$. The approximation (7.4) can therefore be written in the form $QR \simeq f'(x)\delta x$ or $QR \simeq PR \tan \psi$. Fig. 65 shows that the error in this approximation is the distance QT and makes it clear that this error decreases as the distance PR diminishes.

As an example of finding the derivative from its definition, consider the function $y = 2x^2 + 3x + 4$. Here

$$f(x) = 2x^2 + 3x + 4 \text{ and } f(x + \delta x) = 2(x + \delta x)^2 + 3(x + \delta x) + 4.$$

Hence

$$\delta y = f(x + \delta x) - f(x)$$
$$= 2(x + \delta x)^2 + 3(x + \delta x) + 4 - (2x^2 + 3x + 4)$$
$$= (4x + 3)\delta x + 2(\delta x)^2,$$

and

$$\frac{\delta y}{\delta x} = 4x + 3 + 2(\delta x). \tag{7.5}$$

The limiting value of this ratio as δx approaches zero is $4x + 3$ showing that the derivative of the function $2x^2 + 3x + 4$ is $4x + 3$. Except when $x = -\frac{3}{4}$, for which value $4x + 3$ vanishes, we can choose a range of values of δx so that $2(\delta x)$ is negligible in comparison with $4x + 3$ and the terms $4x + 3$ are called the principal part of the expression on the right-hand side of equation (7.5). Thus for the function $y = 2x^2 + 3x + 4$, the derivative (dy/dx) is the principal part of the ratio $(\delta y/\delta x)$ and this is a general property of all functions which can be differentiated.

7.6 The differential coefficient of x^n

If $y = x^n$, then $y + \delta y = (x + \delta x)^n$ and, by subtraction,

$$\delta y = (x + \delta x)^n - x^n.$$

Assuming that n is a positive integer, $(x + \delta x)^n$ can be expanded in a terminating series by the binomial theorem to give

$$\delta y = x^n + nx^{n-1}(\delta x) + \frac{n(n - 1)}{1.2} x^{n-2}(\delta x)^2 + \ldots + (\delta x)^n - x^n$$

so that a slight reduction and division by δx leads to

$$\frac{\delta y}{\delta x} = nx^{n-1} + \frac{n(n - 1)}{1.2} x^{n-2}(\delta x) + \ldots + (\delta x)^{n-1}.$$

Neglecting all the terms in (δx), $(\delta x)^2$, ..., $(\delta x)^{n-1}$, the limiting value as δx approaches zero of the expression on the right is nx^{n-1}. This limiting value is the required differential coefficient and hence

$$\text{if } y = x^n, \quad \text{then} \quad \frac{dy}{dx} = nx^{n-1}. \tag{7.6}$$

Although we have assumed in the above that n is a positive integer, the result (7.6) remains true when n is negative or fractional. A proof for such values of n will not be given here but we shall use the result (7.6) for negative and fractional values of n when this is called for.

Example 3. *Differentiate $1/x$ from first principles.*

Here $y = 1/x$ and $y + \delta y = 1/(x + \delta x)$, so that

$$\delta y = \frac{1}{x + \delta x} - \frac{1}{x}$$

$$= \frac{x - (x + \delta x)}{x(x + \delta x)} = \frac{-\delta x}{x(x + \delta x)}.$$

Thus

$$\frac{\delta y}{\delta x} = \frac{-1}{x(x + \delta x)}$$

and the limit of this expression as δx approaches zero is $-1/x^2$. [If we express this by saying that the derivative of x^{-1} is $-x^{-2}$, we see that the result $dy/dx = nx^{n-1}$ when $y = x^n$, proved only for positive n, is true in the case $n = -1$.]

7.7 The differential coefficients of sin x and cos x

If $y = \sin x$ then $y + \delta y = \sin (x + \delta x)$ and, by subtraction,

$$\delta y = \sin (x + \delta x) - \sin x$$
$$= 2 \cos (x + \tfrac{1}{2}\delta x) \sin (\tfrac{1}{2}\delta x),$$

by the second of formulae (3.35). Division by δx and a slight re-arrangement gives

$$\frac{\delta y}{\delta x} = \cos (x + \tfrac{1}{2}\delta x) \left\{ \frac{\sin (\tfrac{1}{2}\delta x)}{\tfrac{1}{2}\delta x} \right\}.$$

By § 3.9, the limiting value as δx approaches zero of the expression in $\{\ \}$ is unity and the limiting value of $\cos (x + \tfrac{1}{2}\delta x)$ is $\cos x$. Hence the limiting value of $\delta y/\delta x$ is $\cos x$ and we have established the result

$$\text{if } y = \sin x, \quad \text{then} \quad \frac{dy}{dx} = \cos x. \tag{7.7}$$

Similarly if $y = \cos x$, $y + \delta y = \cos (x + \delta x)$,

$$\delta y = \cos (x + \delta x) - \cos x$$
$$= - 2 \sin (x + \tfrac{1}{2}\delta x) \sin (\tfrac{1}{2}\delta x).$$

Hence

$$\frac{\delta y}{\delta x} = - \sin (x + \tfrac{1}{2}\delta x) \left\{ \frac{\sin (\tfrac{1}{2}\delta x)}{\tfrac{1}{2}\delta x} \right\}$$

showing that

$$\text{if } y = \cos x, \quad \text{then} \quad \frac{dy}{dx} = - \sin x. \tag{7.8}$$

Example 4. *Differentiate $3x + \sin 2x$ from first principles.*

Let $y = 3x + \sin 2x$, so that $y + \delta y = 3(x + \delta x) + \sin 2(x + \delta x)$, and by subtraction

$$\delta y = 3(x + \delta x) + \sin 2(x + \delta x) - 3x - \sin 2x$$
$$= 3\delta x + 2 \cos (2x + \delta x) \sin (\delta x).$$

Hence

$$\frac{\delta y}{\delta x} = 3 + 2 \cos (2x + \delta x) \left\{ \frac{\sin (\delta x)}{\delta x} \right\}$$

and the limiting value of this as δx approaches zero is $3 + 2 \cos 2x$.

Exercises 7 (b)

Differentiate from first principles:

1. x^3.

2. $x^2 + 3x + 4$.

3. $x^4 - x^2$.

4. $1/x^2$. [O.C.]

5. $1/x^3$.   [O.C.]   6. $1/(x + 1)$.

7. $1/(1 - x)$.   8. $1/(2x + 1)$.

9. $x + \sin x$.   10. $\sin 3x$.

11. $(\cos ax)/a$, a constant.   12. $\sec x$.   [L.U.]

13. $\tan x$.   14. $(1 - x)(2 - 3x + x^2)$.   [O.C.]

15. $(6x^3 - 4x)/x^2$.   [O.C.]   16. $(x + 1)^2/x$.   [O.C.]

17. If $y + x = \cos x$, find the value of dy/dx.

18. If $y = 2x^2 - 4x - 2$, find the value of x for which dy/dx vanishes.

19. Differentiate $2x^2 + 5 + 4x^{-2}$ with respect to x and find the value of the derivative when $x = 4$.   [O.C.]

20. If $y(x + 1) = 3$, find dy/dx.

7.8 Technical processes in the differential calculus

So far we have only considered the derivatives of very simple functions. Those of more complicated expressions can be found from the definition given in § 7.5 but the labour involved is often considerable. Fortunately a set of general rules can be obtained and these, together with the derivatives of a small number of standard functions, enable the differential coefficients of more complicated functions to be found readily.

It is the purpose of the next few sections to deal with the technical processes involved in finding the derivatives of functions which can be considered as sums or differences, products or quotients, etc., of simpler functions. These processes are of great importance and the reader is recommended to work through a large number of exercises until he is thoroughly familiar with them.

7.9 The differential coefficient of a constant

The graph of the function $y = C$, where C is a constant, is a straight line parallel to the axis of x. Its gradient is clearly zero and hence

$$\text{if } y = C \text{ (constant), then } \frac{dy}{dx} = 0. \tag{7.9}$$

7.10 The differential coefficient of a sum

Suppose that $y = u + v$ where $u = f(x)$ and $v = F(x)$ are two functions of x. When x changes to $x + \delta x$, u changes to $u + \delta u = f(x + \delta x)$, v changes to $v + \delta v = F(x + \delta x)$ and y changes to $y + \delta y$. Hence

$$y + \delta y = u + \delta u + v + \delta v$$

and, subtracting $y = u + v$, we have $\delta y = \delta u + \delta v$ giving, after division by δx,

$$\frac{\delta y}{\delta x} = \frac{\delta u}{\delta x} + \frac{\delta v}{\delta x}.$$

In the limit as x approaches zero, $\delta y/\delta x$, $\delta u/\delta x$ and $\delta v/\delta x$ become respectively dy/dx, du/dx and dv/dx so that

$$\frac{dy}{dx} = \frac{du}{dx} + \frac{dv}{dx}, \qquad (7.10)$$

showing that *the differential coefficient of the sum of two functions is the sum of the differential coefficients of the separate functions.* It is clear that the plus sign can be replaced throughout the above by a minus sign and the differential coefficient of the difference of two functions is therefore the difference of the differential coefficients of the separate functions.

These results are easily extended to cases in which three or more functions are involved. For instance, if u, v and w are three functions of x and $y = u + v - w$, then

$$\frac{dy}{dx} = \frac{du}{dx} + \frac{dv}{dx} - \frac{dw}{dx}.$$

Example 5. *If $y = x^4 - \cos x + 5$, find dy/dx.*

By §§ 7.6, 7.7 and 7.9, the differential coefficients of x^4, $\cos x$ and 5 are respectively $4x^3$, $-\sin x$ and zero. Hence

$$\frac{dy}{dx} = 4x^3 - (-\sin x) + 0 = 4x^3 + \sin x.$$

7.11 The differential coefficient of a product

Let $y = uv$ where $u = f(x)$ and $v = F(x)$ are two functions of x. As in § 7.10 when x changes to $x + \delta x$, u, v and y change respectively to $u + \delta u$, $v + \delta v$ and $y + \delta y$. Hence

$$y + \delta y = (u + \delta u)(v + \delta v) = uv + v\delta u + u\delta v + (\delta u)(\delta v)$$

and, subtracting $y = uv$, we have $\delta y = v\delta u + u\delta v + (\delta u)(\delta v)$ giving, after division by δx,

$$\frac{\delta y}{\delta x} = v\frac{\delta u}{\delta x} + (u + \delta u)\frac{\delta v}{\delta x}.$$

In the limit as δx approaches zero, $\delta u/\delta x$, $\delta v/\delta x$, $\delta y/\delta x$ approach respectively du/dx, dv/dx, dy/dx and the term $\delta u(\delta v/\delta x)$ tends to zero. Hence

$$\frac{dy}{dx} = v\frac{du}{dx} + u\frac{dv}{dx} \qquad (7.11)$$

showing that *the differential coefficient of the product of two functions is equal to the second function multiplied by the differential coefficient of the first plus the first function multiplied by the differential coefficient of the second.*

An important special case of formula (7.11) is that in which the first function u is a constant C. The differential coefficient of a constant being zero, we then have

$$\frac{dy}{dx} = (v \times 0) + C \frac{dv}{dx}.$$

Thus if $y = Cv$, $dy/dx = C(dv/dx)$ and *the differential coefficient of the product of a constant and a function is equal to the product of the constant and the differential coefficient of the function.* Thus if $y = 5x^6$, $dy/dx = 5(6x^5) = 30x^5$.

Example 6. *If $y = (2 + x)(3 + x^2)$, find dy/dx.*

Here $u = 2 + x$, $v = 3 + x^2$, $du/dx = 0 + 1 = 1$, $dv/dx = 0 + 2x = 2x$ and (7.11) gives

$$\frac{dy}{dx} = (3 + x^2)(1) + (2 + x)(2x)$$

$$= 3 + 4x + 3x^2.$$

Example 7. *Find dy/dx when (i) $y = x^3 \cos x$, (ii) $y = x \sin x \cos x$.*

$$\text{(i) } \frac{dy}{dx} = \cos x \frac{d}{dx}(x^3) + x^3 \frac{d}{dx}(\cos x)$$

$$= \cos x(3x^2) + x^3(-\sin x)$$

$$= x^2(3 \cos x - x \sin x).$$

$$\text{(ii) } \frac{dy}{dx} = \sin x \cos x \frac{d}{dx}(x) + x \frac{d}{dx}(\sin x \cos x).$$

Also

$$\frac{d}{dx}(\sin x \cos x) = \cos x \frac{d}{dx}(\sin x) + \sin x \frac{d}{dx}(\cos x)$$

$$= \cos^2 x - \sin^2 x.$$

Hence

$$\frac{dy}{dx} = \sin x \cos x + x(\cos^2 x - \sin^2 x).$$

7.12 The differential coefficient of a quotient

Let $y = u/v$ where $u = f(x)$, $v = F(x)$ are two functions of x. By cross-multiplication, $u = yv$ so that, by applying formula (7.11) to the product yv,

$$\frac{du}{dx} = v \frac{dy}{dx} + y \frac{dv}{dx},$$

and this may be written in the form

$$\frac{dy}{dx} = \frac{1}{v}\frac{du}{dx} - \frac{y}{v}\frac{dv}{dx}.$$

Since $y = u/v$, it follows that $y/v = u/v^2$ and we have

$$\frac{dy}{dx} = \frac{1}{v}\frac{du}{dx} - \frac{u}{v^2}\frac{dv}{dx}$$

$$= \frac{v\dfrac{du}{dx} - u\dfrac{dv}{dx}}{v^2} \qquad (7.12)$$

as the formula giving the differential coefficient of the quotient u/v.

Example 8. *If* $y = \dfrac{x^2}{4-x}$, *find* $\dfrac{dy}{dx}$. [L.U.]

Here $u = x^2$, $v = 4 - x$, $du/dx = 2x$, $dv/dx = -1$ and formula (7.12) gives

$$\frac{dy}{dx} = \frac{(4-x)(2x) - x^2(-1)}{(4-x)^2} = \frac{8x - x^2}{(4-x)^2}.$$

It was shown in § 7.6 that, if n is a positive integer, the derivative with respect to x of x^n is nx^{n-1}. The rule (7.12) for differentiating a quotient enables us to show that the same result is true when n is a negative integer. Thus $y = x^n = 1/x^m$ where $m = -n$ is a positive integer; hence by (7.12), since m is a positive integer and its derivative is therefore mx^{m-1}, we have

$$\frac{dy}{dx} = \frac{x^m \times 0 - 1 \times mx^{m-1}}{x^{2m}}$$

$$= -\frac{m}{x^{m+1}} = -mx^{-m-1}$$

$$= nx^{n-1}, \text{ since } n = -m.$$

7.13 The differential coefficients of tan x, cot x, sec x and cosec x

The differential coefficients of $\tan x$, $\cot x$, $\sec x$ and $\operatorname{cosec} x$ can be derived from those of $\sin x$, $\cos x$, and the rule (7.12) for differentiating a quotient. Thus

$$\frac{d}{dx}(\tan x) = \frac{d}{dx}\left(\frac{\sin x}{\cos x}\right)$$

$$= \frac{\cos x \dfrac{d}{dx}(\sin x) - \sin x \dfrac{d}{dx}(\cos x)}{\cos^2 x}$$

$$= \frac{\cos x \, (\cos x) - \sin x \, (-\sin x)}{\cos^2 x}$$

$$= \frac{\cos^2 x + \sin^2 x}{\cos^2 x}$$

$$= \frac{1}{\cos^2 x} = \sec^2 x. \tag{7.13}$$

Similarly

$$\frac{d}{dx} (\cot x) = \frac{d}{dx} \left(\frac{\cos x}{\sin x} \right)$$

$$= \frac{\sin x \dfrac{d}{dx} (\cos x) - \cos x \dfrac{d}{dx} (\sin x)}{\sin^2 x}$$

$$= \frac{\sin x \, (-\sin x) - \cos x \, (\cos x)}{\sin^2 x}$$

$$= - \frac{\sin^2 x + \cos^2 x}{\sin^2 x}$$

$$= - \frac{1}{\sin^2 x} = - \operatorname{cosec}^2 x. \tag{7.14}$$

Also

$$\frac{d}{dx} (\sec x) = \frac{d}{dx} \left(\frac{1}{\cos x} \right)$$

$$= \frac{\cos x \dfrac{d}{dx} (1) - (1) \dfrac{d}{dx} (\cos x)}{\cos^2 x}$$

$$= \frac{\sin x}{\cos^2 x} = \sec x \tan x, \tag{7.15}$$

and it is left as an exercise for the reader to show in the same way that

$$\frac{d}{dx} (\operatorname{cosec} x) = - \operatorname{cosec} x \cot x. \tag{7.16}$$

Exercises 7 (c)

Differentiate the following functions with respect to x:

1. $x^5 + 5x^4 + 10x^2 + 8$.   2. $5x^4 - \cos x + 2$.

3. $3x^3 - (1/x^2)$.   [L.U.]   4. $2x^{\frac{1}{2}} + 2x^{-\frac{1}{2}} - 3$.

5. $(x + 2)(x^2 + 3)$.   [O.C.]   6. $(1 + x^2)(1 - 2x^2)$.

7. $(x^2 - 3)^2$.   [O.C.]   8. $(x^2 - 1)^2/x$.   [O.C.]

9. $(1 - x)^3$.   10. $(3x + 2)^3$.

11. $(3 + x)(4 - x)$.   [O.C.]   12. $\sin x \cos x$.

13. $x \sin x + \cos x$.   [O.C.]   14. $\frac{1}{2}(x^2 - 2)\sin x + x\cos x$. [L.U.]

15. $(x^2 + 1) \tan x$.   [L.U.]   16. $\sec x \tan x$.   [L.U.]

17. $\operatorname{cosec} x \cot x$.   [L.U.]   18. $x \sec x + \cos x$.

19. $\dfrac{x}{1 - x^2}$.   [O.C.]   20. $\dfrac{1 + x^2}{1 - x}$.   [O.C.]

21. $\dfrac{x^2}{(x - 1)(x + 2)}$.   [O.C.]   22. $(5 - 2x^2)^{-1}$.

23. $\dfrac{x^4}{x^4 + 1}$.   [L.U.]   24. $\dfrac{\sin x}{x}$.   [L.U.]

25. $\dfrac{\sin x}{1 + \cos x}$.   [O.C.]   26. $\dfrac{5 + 3 \sin x}{3 + 5 \sin x}$.   [O.C.]

27. $\dfrac{2 + 7 \cos x}{3 + 5 \cos x}$.   [O.C.]   28. $\dfrac{\sin x}{1 + \tan x}$.   [O.C.]

29. $\dfrac{x}{\tan x}$.   30. $\dfrac{x^4}{(1 + x^2)^2}$.   [O.C.]

7.14 The differential coefficient of a function of a function

A function like $y = (x + 2)^2$ is a function of a function since $(x + 2)^2$ is a function of $(x + 2)$ and $(x + 2)$ is a function of x. Other examples are $\sqrt{(x^2 + 1)}$, $\sin 3x$, $\tan (x^2)$, etc., and the purpose of this section is to give a simple rule by which the derivatives of such functions can be found.

The differential coefficient of the first of the examples given above can, of course, be found by multiplying out the expression $(x + 2)^2$ [or by treating it as the product $(x + 2)(x + 2)$]. Thus,

$$y = (x + 2)^2 = x^2 + 4x + 4$$

and

$$\frac{dy}{dx} = 2x + 4 = 2(x + 2).$$

It should be noticed that the result is exactly the same as if we had treated $(x + 2)$ as if it were x and used the standard result for the differential coefficient of x^2. Similarly if $y = (x + a)^3$, where a is a constant,

$$y = (x + a)^3 = x^3 + 3ax^2 + 3a^2x + a^3$$

giving

$$\frac{dy}{dx} = 3x^2 + 6ax + 3a^2 = 3(x^2 + 2ax + a^2) = 3(x + a)^2,$$

and again the result is the same as if we had treated $(x + a)$ as if it were x and used the standard result for the differential coefficient of x^3.

Now consider $y = (3x + 2)^2$. Working as before

$$y = (3x + 2)^2 = 9x^2 + 12x + 4$$

and

$$\frac{dy}{dx} = 18x + 12 = 6(3x + 2),$$

so that the result is not now $2(3x + 2)$ but three times this. A rough explanation is that whereas $(x + 2)$ changes at the same rate as x, $(3x + 2)$ changes three times as fast. Similarly if $y = (ax + b)^2$ where a and b are constants,

$$y = (ax + b)^2 = a^2x^2 + 2abx + b^2,$$

$$\frac{dy}{dx} = 2a^2x + 2ab = 2a(ax + b),$$

and we notice the result is the same as if we had treated $(ax + b)$ as if it were x, used the standard result for the differential coefficient of x^2 and then multiplied by a, the differential coefficient of $(ax + b)$.

The above examples suggest that if y is a function of u where u is a function of x, the formula for the differential coefficient might well be

$$\frac{dy}{dx} = \frac{dy}{du} \times \frac{du}{dx}. \tag{7.17}$$

If we apply this formula to some of the above examples, we have

(i) $y = (x + 2)^2$, or $y = u^2$ where $u = x + 2$.

$$\frac{dy}{du} = 2u, \quad \frac{du}{dx} = 1,$$

$$\frac{dy}{dx} = \frac{dy}{du} \times \frac{du}{dx} = 2u \times 1 = 2u = 2(x + 2).$$

(ii) $y = (x + a)^3$, or $y = u^3$ where $u = x + a$.

$$\frac{dy}{du} = 3u^2, \quad \frac{du}{dx} = 1,$$

$$\frac{dy}{dx} = \frac{dy}{du} \times \frac{du}{dx} = 3u^2 \times 1 = 3u^2 = 3(x + a)^2.$$

(iii) $y = (ax + b)^2$, or $y = u^2$ where $u = ax + b$.

$$\frac{dy}{du} = 2u, \quad \frac{du}{dx} = a,$$

$$\frac{dy}{dx} = \frac{dy}{du} \times \frac{du}{dx} = 2u \times a = 2au = 2a(ax + b).$$

The formula (7.17) therefore gives the correct differential coefficients in the above examples and it does, in fact, hold generally. A strict proof of (7.17) is rather beyond the scope of the present book and the following, which assumes a theorem on limits not already proved, must suffice. If y is a function of u and u is a function of x, let δu be the increment in u corresponding to an increment δx in x and let δy be the increment in y corresponding to the increment δu in u. Then, provided $\delta u \neq 0$,

$$\frac{\delta y}{\delta x} = \frac{\delta y}{\delta u} \times \frac{\delta u}{\delta x}$$

and, assuming that the limit of a product is the product of the limits, this gives

$$\frac{dy}{dx} = \frac{dy}{du} \times \frac{du}{dx}, \tag{7.17}$$

since dy/dx, dy/du and du/dx are respectively the limiting values of $\delta y/\delta x$, $\delta y/\delta u$ and $\delta u/\delta x$ as δx approaches zero.

The formula (7.17) is an important one and the student is advised to work through a large number of exercises involving its use. At first it is probably wise to introduce the auxiliary function u as in the worked examples below but, with practice, this soon becomes unnecessary and the results can be written down directly.

Example 9. *Find dy/dx when* (i) $y = (2x + 1)^{-3/2}$, (ii) $y = \sin 3x$.

(i) Let $u = 2x + 1$ so that $y = u^{-3/2}$. Then

$$\frac{dy}{du} = -\frac{3}{2} u^{-5/2} \text{ and } \frac{du}{dx} = 2.$$

Hence

$$\frac{dy}{dx} = \frac{dy}{du} \times \frac{du}{dx} = -\frac{3}{2} u^{-5/2} \times 2$$

$$= -3u^{-5/2} = -3(2x + 1)^{-5/2}.$$

(ii) Let $u = 3x$ so that $y = \sin u$. Here

$$\frac{dy}{du} = \cos u \text{ and } \frac{du}{dx} = 3,$$

giving

$$\frac{dy}{dx} = \frac{dy}{du} \times \frac{du}{dx} = \cos u \times 3 = 3 \cos 3x.$$

Example 10. *Differentiate* $y = \sqrt{\left(\dfrac{x-1}{x+1}\right)}$ *with respect to* x. [L.U.]

Let $u = (x-1)/(x+1)$ so that $y = \sqrt{u} = u^{\frac{1}{2}}$ and $dy/du = \frac{1}{2}u^{-\frac{1}{2}}$.
To find du/dx we have to differentiate the quotient $(x-1)/(x+1)$. This gives

$$\frac{du}{dx} = \frac{(x+1)\dfrac{d}{dx}(x-1) - (x-1)\dfrac{d}{dx}(x+1)}{(x+1)^2}$$

$$= \frac{x+1-(x-1)}{(x+1)^2} = \frac{2}{(x+1)^2}.$$

Hence

$$\frac{dy}{dx} = \frac{dy}{du} \times \frac{du}{dx}$$

$$= \tfrac{1}{2}u^{-\frac{1}{2}} \times \frac{2}{(x+1)^2}$$

$$= \sqrt{\left(\frac{x+1}{x-1}\right)} \times \frac{1}{(x+1)^2} = \frac{1}{(x+1)\sqrt{(x^2-1)}}.$$

Example 11. *Find* dy/dx *when* $y = \sin^3(3x+4)$.

Let $u = 3x+4$ so that $y = \sin^3 u$ and this is still a function of a function.
Now let $v = \sin u$ so that $y = v^3$. Hence

$$\frac{dy}{dv} = 3v^2 \text{ and } \frac{dv}{du} = \cos u,$$

so that, applying (7.17) with v for u and u for x,

$$\frac{dy}{du} = \frac{dy}{dv} \times \frac{dv}{du} = 3v^2 \cos u.$$

Also

$$\frac{dy}{dx} = \frac{dy}{du} \times \frac{du}{dx}$$

$$= 3v^2 \cos u \times 3$$

$$= 9v^2 \cos u = 9 \sin^2 u \cos u$$

$$= 9 \sin^2(3x+4) \cos(3x+4).$$

Exercises 7 (d)

Differentiate the following functions with respect to x:

1. $(2x-3)^3$.

2. $\sqrt{(2x-1)}$.

3. $\cos 3x$.

4. $\sin(x^2)$.

5. $\tan(2x+1)$.

6. $\sec(x^3)$.

7. $\sin 2x \cos 2x$. [L.U.] 8. $\operatorname{cosec}\sqrt{x}$.

9. $\left(x+1-\dfrac{1}{x}\right)^3$. [N.U.] 10. $\dfrac{1+\sin^2 x}{1-\sin^2 x}$.

11. $\sin^3 x \sin 3x$.

12. $x\sqrt{(1+x^2)}$. [L.U.]

13. $x/\sqrt{(1 + x^2)}$.   [L.U.]   14. $\sqrt{(1 - x^2)}/x^3$.   [O.C.]

15. $\sqrt{(1 + x^3)}/x$.   [O.C.]   16. $\dfrac{\sqrt{(1 + x^2)} - x}{\sqrt{(1 + x^2)} + x}$.   [O.C.]

17. $\sqrt{(1 + \sin^2 x)}$.   [N.U.]   18. $(1 + x)^3 \tan 3x$.   [O.C.]

19. $\sec^2 x \,(\sec^2 x - 2)$.   [O.C.]   20. $\sin(\cos x)$.

21. $\sin^m x \cos^n x$.   22. $(\tan x + \sec x)^2$.

23. $x^n \cos^2 x$.   24. $2 \sin^2 x + \cos 2x$.

25.   If $y = \tan x \sin 2x$, show that $dy/dx = 2 \sin 2x$.

26.   If $y = \tan x + \frac{1}{3} \tan^3 x$, show that $dy/dx = \sec^4 x$.

27.   If $y = \sqrt{\{(1 + \sin x)/(1 - \sin x)\}}$, show that $(1 - \sin x)(dy/dx) = 1$.

28.   Prove that if $y = \sqrt{(1 + x^2)}$ then $y(dy/dx) = x$.

29.   If $y = \tan^2 x$, show that $dy/dx = 2(y^{\frac{1}{2}} + y^{\frac{3}{2}})$.

30.   If $y = (\cot x + \operatorname{cosec} x)^m$, show that $(dy/dx) + my \operatorname{cosec} x = 0$.

7.15   The differential coefficients of inverse functions

In Fig. 66, PT is the tangent at the point P to the curve representing the function $y = f(x)$. If PT makes an angle ψ with the axis OX, then

$$\tan \psi = \frac{dy}{dx}.$$

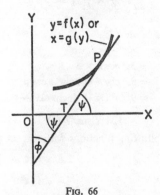

FIG. 66

If the equation $y = f(x)$ is written in the form $x = g(y)$, the curve shown in Fig. 66 also represents this function. If PT makes an angle ϕ with the axis OY, then

$$\tan \phi = \frac{dx}{dy}.$$

But, from the figure $\phi + \psi = 90°$ so that $\psi = 90° - \phi$ and

$$\tan \psi = \tan (90° - \phi) = \cot \phi = \frac{1}{\tan \phi}$$

giving

$$\frac{dy}{dx} = 1 \bigg/ \left(\frac{dx}{dy}\right). \qquad (7.18)$$

This formula is useful in the differentiation of inverse functions such as $\tan^{-1} x$, $\sin^{-1} x$, etc. Thus, if $y = \tan^{-1} x$, we have $x = \tan y$ and

$$\frac{dx}{dy} = \sec^2 y = 1 + \tan^2 y = 1 + x^2.$$

Hence, using (7.18),

$$\frac{dy}{dx} = 1 \bigg/ \left(\frac{dx}{dy}\right) = \frac{1}{1 + x^2}. \qquad (7.19)$$

Similarly, if $y = \sin^{-1} x$, then $x = \sin y$,

$$\frac{dx}{dy} = \cos y = \sqrt{(1 - \sin^2 y)} = \sqrt{(1 - x^2)},$$

and

$$\frac{dy}{dx} = 1 \bigg/ \left(\frac{dx}{dy}\right) = \frac{1}{\sqrt{(1 - x^2)}}. \qquad (7.20)$$

The differential coefficients of $\cos^{-1} x$, $\sec^{-1} x$, etc., can be found in a similar way and are left as exercises for the reader.

Example 12. *If* $y = \cos^{-1}\left(\dfrac{1-x}{1+x}\right)$, *find* $\dfrac{dy}{dx}$. [N.U.]

Let $u = (1 - x)/(1 + x)$, so that $y = \cos^{-1} u$ or $u = \cos y$.
Hence,

$$\frac{du}{dy} = -\sin y = -\sqrt{(1 - \cos^2 y)} = -\sqrt{(1 - u^2)}$$

$$= -\sqrt{\left\{1 - \left(\frac{1-x}{1+x}\right)^2\right\}} = -\frac{2\sqrt{x}}{1+x}.$$

Also

$$\frac{du}{dx} = \frac{d}{dx}\left(\frac{1-x}{1+x}\right)$$

$$= \frac{(1+x)(-1) - (1-x)(1)}{(1+x)^2} = \frac{-2}{(1+x)^2}.$$

But

$$\frac{dy}{dx} = \frac{dy}{du} \times \frac{du}{dx} = \left(1 \bigg/ \frac{du}{dy}\right) \times \frac{du}{dx}$$

$$= -\frac{1+x}{2\sqrt{x}} \times \frac{-2}{(1+x)^2} = \frac{1}{(1+x)\sqrt{x}}.$$

7.16 Table of standard forms

The formulae used in finding the derivatives of sums, products, quotients, etc., are of considerable importance. So also are the derivatives of certain "standard" functions like x^n, sin x, cos x, etc. For ease of reference, the formulae are collected in the table given below. In all cases C denotes a constant and u, v are functions of x.

$$\frac{d}{dx}(u \pm v) = \frac{du}{dx} \pm \frac{dv}{dx}.$$

$$\frac{d}{dx}(Cv) = C\frac{dv}{dx}.$$

$$\frac{d}{dx}(uv) = v\frac{du}{dx} + u\frac{dv}{dx}.$$

$$\frac{d}{dx}\left(\frac{u}{v}\right) = \frac{v\dfrac{du}{dx} - u\dfrac{dv}{dx}}{v^2}.$$

$$\frac{dy}{dx} = \frac{dy}{du} \times \frac{du}{dx}.$$

$$\frac{dy}{dx} = 1 \bigg/ \left(\frac{dx}{dy}\right).$$

$$\frac{d}{dx}(C) = 0. \qquad\qquad \frac{d}{dx}(x^n) = nx^{n-1}.$$

$$\frac{d}{dx}(\sin x) = \cos x. \qquad\qquad \frac{d}{dx}(\cos x) = -\sin x.$$

$$\frac{d}{dx}(\tan x) = \sec^2 x. \qquad\qquad \frac{d}{dx}(\cot x) = -\operatorname{cosec}^2 x.$$

$$\frac{d}{dx}(\sec x) = \sec x \tan x. \qquad\qquad \frac{d}{dx}(\operatorname{cosec} x) = -\operatorname{cosec} x \cot x.$$

$$\frac{d}{dx}(\tan^{-1} x) = \frac{1}{1 + x^2}. \qquad\qquad \frac{d}{dx}(\sin^{-1} x) = \frac{1}{\sqrt{(1 - x^2)}}.$$

7.17 The differentiation of parametric and implicit functions

Sometimes the two variables x and y are related by two equations of the form $x = f(t)$, $y = g(t)$ where f and g are functions of a so-called "parameter" t. In such cases we can regard y as being a function of a function, for y is a function of t and t is a function of x. Hence by (7.17),

$$\frac{dy}{dx} = \frac{dy}{dt} \times \frac{dt}{dx}$$

and, using equation (7.18) with t in place of y,

$$\frac{dt}{dx} = 1 \Big/ \left(\frac{dx}{dt}\right).$$

It follows that

$$\frac{dy}{dx} = \frac{(dy/dt)}{(dx/dt)} \tag{7.21}$$

and this formula is useful in finding the derivative when the equations are given in "parametric" form.

Example 13. *If $x = 4t^3 + 2t$ and $y = 3t^2 - t$, find dy/dx in terms of t.*   [O.C.]
  Here

$$\frac{dy}{dt} = 6t - 1, \qquad \frac{dx}{dt} = 12t^2 + 2$$

and

$$\frac{dy}{dx} = \frac{(dy/dt)}{(dx/dt)} = \frac{6t - 1}{12t^2 + 2}.$$

When finding the derivative dy/dx in cases in which the variables are related *implicitly*, it is not necessary (nor indeed is it usually possible) to start by expressing y explicitly in terms of x. Suppose, for example, that the implicit relation between y and x is $x^2 + y^2 = 4x$. Since y^2 is a function of y and y is a function of x, the rule (7.17) gives

$$\frac{d}{dx}(y^2) = \frac{d}{dy}(y^2) \times \frac{dy}{dx} = 2y\frac{dy}{dx}$$

and, differentiation of each term of the relation $x^2 + y^2 = 4x$ with respect to x leads to

$$2x + 2y\frac{dy}{dx} = 4$$

so that,

$$\frac{dy}{dx} = \frac{4 - 2x}{2y} = \frac{2 - x}{y}.$$

Example 14. *Find dy/dx when (i) $x + y + \sin y = 2$, (ii) $\sqrt{x} + \sqrt{y} = 1$.*

$$\text{(i) } 1 + \frac{dy}{dx} + \cos y\frac{dy}{dx} = 0$$

so that

$$\frac{dy}{dx} = \frac{-1}{1 + \cos y}.$$

(ii) $\dfrac{1}{2\sqrt{x}} + \dfrac{1}{2\sqrt{y}} \dfrac{dy}{dx} = 0$

leading to

$$\frac{dy}{dx} = -\sqrt{\left(\frac{y}{x}\right)}.$$

7.18 Second and higher derivatives

If y is a function of x, its derivative dy/dx will itself be a function of x and *its* derivative can be found by the usual rules. The result of differentiating dy/dx with respect to x is called *the second derivative of y with respect to x* or the *second differential coefficient*. Proceeding further, the derivative of the second derivative is called the *third derivative* and so on.

The usual notation for the second, third, . . . and nth derivatives of y with respect to x is

$$\frac{d^2y}{dx^2}, \quad \frac{d^3y}{dx^3}, \cdot \cdot \cdot, \frac{d^ny}{dx^n},$$

or, if we are using the notation $y = f(x)$, the symbols

$$f''(x), f'''(x), \cdot \cdot \cdot, f^{(n)}(x)$$

are often employed. There are but few cases in which the general expression for the nth derivative of a function can be found easily and here we shall be content to give some examples of the first few differential coefficients.

Example 15. *Find* $\dfrac{d^2y}{dx^2}$ *and* $\dfrac{d^3y}{dx^3}$ *when (i)* $y = x^4 + 3x^2 + 2$, *(ii)* $y = \sin 3x$.

(i) $\dfrac{dy}{dx} = 4x^3 + 6x, \quad \dfrac{d^2y}{dx^2} = 12x^2 + 6, \quad \dfrac{d^3y}{dx^3} = 24x.$

(ii) $\dfrac{dy}{dx} = 3 \cos 3x, \quad \dfrac{d^2y}{dx^2} = -9 \sin 3x, \quad \dfrac{d^3y}{dx^3} = -27 \cos 3x.$

Example 16. *Prove that, if* $y = x \sin x$, *then* $x^2 \dfrac{d^2y}{dx^2} - 2x \dfrac{dy}{dx} + (2 + x^2)y = 0$.

[O.C.]

$$y = x \sin x,$$
$$\frac{dy}{dx} = \sin x + x \cos x,$$
$$\frac{d^2y}{dx^2} = \cos x + \cos x - x \sin x = 2 \cos x - x \sin x$$

Hence,

$$x^3 \frac{d^2y}{dx^2} = 2x^2 \cos x - x^3 \sin x,$$

$$2x \frac{dy}{dx} = 2x \sin x + 2x^2 \cos x,$$

$$(2 + x^2)y = 2x \sin x + x^3 \sin x,$$

and it follows that

$$x^2 \frac{d^2y}{dx^2} - 2x \frac{dy}{dx} + (2 + x^2)y = 0.$$

Example 17. *A curve is given by the parametric equations $x = a \cos^3 \theta$, $y = a \sin^3 \theta$. Show that $dy/dx = - \tan \theta$ and find the value of d^2y/dx^2 where $\theta = \frac{1}{4}\pi$.* [O.C.]

Here

$$\frac{dx}{d\theta} = - 3a \cos^2 \theta \sin \theta, \quad \frac{dy}{d\theta} = 3a \sin^2 \theta \cos \theta,$$

so that

$$\frac{dy}{dx} = \left(\frac{dy}{d\theta}\right) \bigg/ \left(\frac{dx}{d\theta}\right) = \frac{3a \sin^2 \theta \cos \theta}{-3a \cos^2 \theta \sin \theta} = - \tan \theta.$$

The derivation of d^2y/dx^2 needs a little care. From the above we see that to differentiate y (a function of θ) with respect to x, we first differentiate y with respect to θ and then divide the result by the derivative of x with respect to θ. d^2y/dx^2 is found in exactly the same way except that y is replaced by dy/dx. Hence

$$\frac{d^2y}{dx^2} = \left\{\frac{d}{d\theta}\left(\frac{dy}{dx}\right)\right\} \bigg/ \left(\frac{dx}{d\theta}\right) = \left\{\frac{d}{d\theta}(- \tan \theta)\right\} \bigg/ \left(-3a \cos^2 \theta \sin \theta\right)$$

$$= \frac{- \sec^2 \theta}{-3a \cos^2 \theta \sin \theta} = \frac{1}{3a \cos^4 \theta \sin \theta}.$$

When $\theta = \frac{1}{4}\pi$, $\sin \theta = 1/\sqrt{2}$, $\cos \theta = 1/\sqrt{2}$ and $\cos^4 \theta \sin \theta = 1/(4\sqrt{2})$, so that

$$\frac{d^2y}{dx^2} = \frac{4\sqrt{2}}{3a}.$$

Exercises 7 (e)

Differentiate with respect to x:

1. $\sec^{-1} x$.
2. $\cot^{-1} x$.
3. $\sin^{-1} 2x$.   [N.U.]
4. $2 \tan^{-1} \sqrt{x}$.   [N.U.]
5. $x\sqrt{(1 - x^2)} + \sin^{-1} x$.   [O.C.]
6. $\tan^{-1} (\sin^2 x)$.   [O.C.]
7. If $x = at^2$ and $y = 2at$, find dy/dx in terms of t.
8. If $x = a(\theta - \sin \theta)$, $y = a(1 - \cos \theta)$ show that $1 + \left(\dfrac{dy}{dx}\right)^2 = \operatorname{cosec}^2 \frac{1}{2}\theta$.

9. Prove that if

$$x = \frac{1 - t^2}{1 + t^2}, \quad y = \frac{4t}{1 + t^2}$$

then

$$\frac{dy}{dx} = t - \frac{1}{t} = -\frac{4x}{y}.$$ [O.C.]

10. Find dy/dx when
   (i) $x^3y^2 = x + 2$, (ii) $xy^2 + \cos 2y = 4$.

11. If $x^2 + xy + y^3 = 0$, express dy/dx in terms of x and y.

12. Find the second differential coefficient with respect to x of $\tan ax$ where a is constant. [L.U.]

13. If $f(x) = \cos 2x$, find $f''(x)$ and $f'''(x)$.

14. If $y = x^2 \sin x$, prove that

$$x^2 \frac{d^2y}{dx^2} - 4x \frac{dy}{dx} + (x^2 + 6)y = 0.$$ [L.U.]

15. If $y = \sin^2 x$, prove that

$$\frac{d^2y}{dx^2} + 4y = 2.$$ [L.U.]

16. If $y = (\sin x)/x$ show that

$$\frac{d^2y}{dx^2} + \frac{2}{x}\frac{dy}{dx} + y = 0.$$ [N.U.]

17. Evaluate $\dfrac{d^2}{dx^2}\{(1 + 4x + x^2)\sin x\}$.

18. If $y + 1 = (ax + 1)(bx + 1)$ where a and b are independent of x, show that

$$x^2 \frac{d^2y}{dx^2} - 2x \frac{dy}{dx} + 2y = 0.$$ [L.U.]

19. If $x = (2 + t)/(1 + 2t)$ and $y = (3 + 2t)/t$, prove that

$$\frac{dy}{dx} = \frac{(1 + 2t)^2}{t^2},$$

and find the value of d^2y/dx^2 when $x = 0$. [O.C.]

20. If $x = 3t + t^3$ and $y = 3 - t^{5/2}$ express dy/dx in terms of t and prove that, when $d^2y/dx^2 = 0$, then x has one of the values 0, $\pm6\sqrt{3}$. [O.C.]

Exercises 7 (f)

1. $f(x)$ denotes a quadratic in x. If $f(-2) = 11, f(0) = 1$ and $f(1) = 8$ find the expression for $f(x)$. Find also the values of $f(2)$ and $f'(2)$.

2. If $f(x) = a \sin x + b \cos x, f(0) = 1$ and $f(\frac{1}{4}\pi) = \sqrt{2}$, find the values of the constants a and b. What are the values of $f'(0)$ and $f''(0)$?

3. Calculate the gradient of the curve $y = -x^3 + 4x^2 - 3x$ at each of the points where it crosses the axis of x. [L.U.]

4. Obtain from first principles the differential coefficient of $1/(x + 2)$ with respect to x. [L.U.]

5. Find dy/dx when (i) $y = \cos x + x \sin x$, (ii) $y = (3x - 1)(x - 3)$. [O.C.]

6. Differentiate with respect to x:

$$\text{(i) } \frac{1 + \tan x}{1 - \tan x}, \quad \text{(ii) } \frac{2 + x^2}{(1 - x)^2}, \quad \text{(iii) } \frac{x}{\sqrt{(1 - x^2)}}.$$

7. If $y = 3x^3 + \frac{1}{2}x + 6 \sin x - 6x \cos x - \frac{1}{4} \sin 2x$ show that
$$dy/dx = (3x + \sin x)^2. \qquad \text{[L.U.]}$$

8. Prove that
$$\frac{d}{dx}\left(\frac{1 + \sin x + \cos x}{1 - \sin x + \cos x}\right) = \frac{1}{1 - \sin x}. \qquad \text{[L.U.]}$$

9. If s_n denotes the sum of the first n terms of the geometrical progression $x + x^2 + x^3 + \ldots$, show that
$$(1 - x)\frac{ds_n}{dx} = (n + 1)\, s_{n-1} - ns_n + 1. \qquad \text{[N.U.]}$$

10. Differentiate with respect to x:

$$\text{(i) } x^2 \sin 3x, \quad \text{(ii) } \frac{x^2 + 3x}{x - 1}, \quad \text{(iii) } \cos\left(\frac{1}{x}\right). \qquad \text{[L.U.]}$$

11. If $u = (\sin x)/(\cos x + \sin x)$ and $v = \frac{1}{2}(\tan 2x - \sec 2x)$, show that du/dx and dv/dx are both equal to $1/(1 + \sin 2x)$. [L.U.]

12. If $y\sqrt{(1 - \sin x)} = \sqrt{(1 + \sin x)}$, show that
$$(1 - \sin x)\frac{dy}{dx} = 1.$$

13. If $y = \sin^{-1}(3x - 4x^3)$, show that
$$\sqrt{(1 - x^2)}\frac{dy}{dx} = 3.$$

14. Differentiate with respect to x:

$$\text{(i) } \sin^{-1}\left(\frac{1}{\sqrt{(1 + x^2)}}\right), \quad \text{(ii) } \tan^{-1}\left(\frac{1 - x^2}{1 + x^2}\right). \qquad \text{[O.C.]}$$

15. If $y = x^2 + (\sin^{-1} x)^2 - 2x\sqrt{(1 - x^2)}\sin^{-1} x$, show that

$$\sqrt{(1 - x^2)}\frac{dy}{dx} = 4x^2 \sin^{-1} x.$$

16. If $y = uvw$ where u, v and w are functions of x, prove that

$$\frac{dy}{dx} = vw\frac{du}{dx} + wu\frac{dv}{dx} + uv\frac{dw}{dx}.$$

Hence show that

$$\frac{d}{dx}(x^2 \sin x \cos x) = x(\sin 2x + x \cos 2x).$$

17. If $y^2(1 + x^2) = 1 - x^2$, show that

$$\left(\frac{dy}{dx}\right)^2 = \frac{1 - y^4}{1 - x^4}.$$

18. If $\sqrt{y} = \tan^{-1} x$, prove that

$$(1 + x^2)\frac{d}{dx}\left\{(1 + x^2)\frac{dy}{dx}\right\} = 2.$$

19. If $y^2 + x^2 = 2y\sqrt{(1 + x^2)}$, show that

$$\frac{dy}{dx} = \frac{x}{\sqrt{(1 + x^2)}}.$$

20. If $x = \sin 3t \cos t$ and $y = \cos 3t \sin t$, show that

$$\frac{d^2x}{dt^2} - \frac{d^2y}{dt^2} = 4(y - x). \qquad \text{[L.U.]}$$

21. Prove that if $y = (\cos x - \sin x)/(\cos x + \sin x)$ then

$$\frac{d^2y}{dx^2} + 2y\frac{dy}{dx} = 0. \qquad \text{[O.C.]}$$

22. If $y = (\sin x)/x^2$ find dy/dx and d^2y/dx^2. Prove that

$$x^2\frac{d^2y}{dx^2} + 4x\frac{dy}{dx} + (x^2 + 2)y = 0. \qquad \text{[L.U.]}$$

23. If $y = uv$ where u and v are functions of x, show that

$$\frac{d^2y}{dx^2} = v\frac{d^2u}{dx^2} + 2\frac{dv}{dx}\cdot\frac{du}{dx} + u\frac{d^2v}{dx^2},$$

and hence evaluate the second derivative of $x^3 \sin x$.

24. Given that $2x = t + t^{-1}$ and $2y = t - t^{-1}$, show that

$$\frac{dy}{dx} = \frac{t^2 + 1}{t^2 - 1} \quad \text{and} \quad \frac{d^2y}{dx^2} = -\frac{8t^3}{(t^2 - 1)^3}.$$

25. If $x = a(\theta + \sin \theta)$, $y = a(1 - \cos \theta)$, express dy/dx and d^2y/dx^2 in terms of trigonometrical functions of $\frac{1}{2}\theta$.

CHAPTER 8

SOME APPLICATIONS OF THE DIFFERENTIAL CALCULUS

8.1 Introduction

In this chapter we consider some of the applications of the differential calculus. These include the use of the derivative as a rate measurer and in specifying velocities and accelerations in dynamical problems, the derivation of approximate formulae, the calculation of maximum and minimum values and aids to curve tracing.

In developing the fundamental formulae of the differential calculus, the symbols x and y were employed for the independent and dependent variables. From now on the notation used will be that appropriate to the application under discussion. If, for example, x is given as a function of t, the first and second derivatives of x with respect to t will be denoted by dx/dt and d^2x/dt^2. The reader must therefore be prepared to use the results of Chapter 7 with appropriate changes of symbols where these are necessary.

8.2 The derivative as a rate measurer

Suppose that a body moves a distance x in a straight line in time t and that x is a function of t given by $x = f(t)$. If x and x_1 are the distances moved by the body in times t and t_1, the average velocity of the body over the time interval $t_1 - t$ is $(x_1 - x)/(t_1 - t)$, or in the increment notation of § 7.4 with $\delta t = t_1 - t$ and $\delta x = x_1 - x$, the average velocity over the time interval δt is $\delta x/\delta t$ and the limiting value of this as δt approaches zero is dx/dt. This is the rate of change of distance with respect to time and is the instantaneous *velocity* of the body at time t. Similarly if a body is moving in a straight line and its velocity is v at time t, the rate of change of velocity with respect to time is dv/dt and this is the *acceleration* of the body at the instant considered.

In general, if one variable y is a function of another variable x, the derivative dy/dx can be regarded as giving not only the gradient of the graph of $y = f(x)$ but also *the rate of change of y with respect to x*. It should be noted that y is increasing with x when the derivative dy/dx is positive and that y is decreasing as x increases when dy/dx is negative.

Example 1. *A spherical balloon is being inflated. When the diameter of the balloon is 10 cm its volume is increasing at the rate of 200 cm³/s. Find the rate at which its surface area is then increasing.* [L.U.]

Suppose the radius of the balloon at time t seconds is r cm. Its volume V is given by $V = \frac{4}{3}\pi r^3$ and, by the rule (7.17) for differentiating a function of a function,

$$\frac{dV}{dt} = \frac{dV}{dr} \times \frac{dr}{dt} = 4\pi r^2 \frac{dr}{dt}.$$

But dV/dt is the rate of increase of volume with respect to time, so that $dV/dt = 200$ when $2r = 10$. Hence

$$200 = 100\pi \frac{dr}{dt}$$

giving $dr/dt = 2/\pi$ as the rate of increase of the radius at the instant considered. The surface area S is given by $S = 4\pi r^2$, so that, again using equation (7.17),

$$\frac{dS}{dt} = \frac{dS}{dr} \times \frac{dr}{dt} = 8\pi r \frac{dr}{dt}.$$

When $2r = 10$, $dr/dt = 2/\pi$ so that

$$\frac{dS}{dt} = 4\pi \times 10 \times \frac{2}{\pi} = 80 \text{ cm}^2/\text{s}$$

as the required rate of increase of surface area.

Example 2. *A conical vessel of semi-vertical angle 30° is held with its vertex downwards and its axis vertical. Water enters at the rate of 1 cubic centimetre per minute. Find the rate at which the water level is rising when the depth of water is 6 cm and the rate at which the plane surface area is increasing at this instant.* [L.U.]

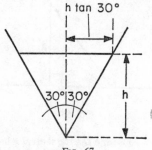

Fig. 67

At time t minutes let the depth of water be h cm and let the volume of water then be V cm³ (Fig. 67). The radius of the water surface is $h \tan 30° = h/\sqrt{3}$ and its area S is given by

$$S = \pi(h/\sqrt{3})^2 = \pi h^2/3.$$

The volume V of water is the volume of a cone of base radius $h/\sqrt{3}$ and height h, so that

$$V = \tfrac{1}{3}\pi(h/\sqrt{3})^2 \times h = \tfrac{1}{9}\pi h^3$$

and, by the rule for differentiating a function of a function,

$$\frac{dV}{dt} = \frac{dV}{dh} \times \frac{dh}{dt} = \frac{1}{3}\pi h^2 \frac{dh}{dt}.$$

Since the volume of water is increasing at the rate of 1 cubic centimetre per minute, $dV/dt = 1$ and we have

$$1 = \tfrac{1}{3}\pi h^2 \frac{dh}{dt}.$$

This gives

$$\frac{dh}{dt} = \frac{3}{\pi h^2} = \frac{3}{\pi \times 6^2} = \frac{1}{12\pi} \text{ centimetres per minute}$$

when $h = 6$ cm. From the formula $S = \pi h^2/3$, differentiation gives

$$\frac{dS}{dt} = \tfrac{2}{3}\pi h \frac{dh}{dt}$$

leading to, when $h = 6$ and $dh/dt = 1/(12\pi)$,

$$\frac{dS}{dt} = \tfrac{2}{3}\pi \times 6 \times \frac{1}{12\pi} = \tfrac{1}{3} \text{ square centimetres per minute}$$

as the rate at which the surface area of water is increasing.

Example 3. *The distance of a lighthouse from a straight shore is d metres. The beam from the lighthouse revolves at a constant rate of ω radians per second. Find formulae for the velocity and acceleration of the illuminated point along the shore when the beam makes an angle θ radians with the shore.* [L.U.]

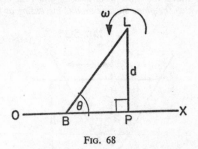

Fig. 68

In Fig. 68, L is the lighthouse and OX the shore, LP being perpendicular to OX and of length d. At time t, the beam meets the shore at a point B and the angle LBX is θ. The distance BP is given by $BP = d \cot \theta$ and the velocity (v) of the illuminated point is the rate of change of BP with respect to the time. Hence

$$v = \frac{d}{dt}(BP) = \frac{d}{dt}(d \cot \theta)$$

$$= -d \operatorname{cosec}^2 \theta \cdot \frac{d\theta}{dt}.$$

But $d\theta/dt$ is the angular velocity of the beam and this is equal to ω, so that the required formula for the velocity is $v = -\omega d \operatorname{cosec}^2 \theta$. The acceleration is given by

$$\text{acceleration} = \frac{dv}{dt} = \frac{d}{dt}(-\omega d \operatorname{cosec}^2 \theta)$$

$$= -\omega d \cdot 2 \operatorname{cosec} \theta \cdot (-\operatorname{cosec} \theta \cot \theta) \cdot \frac{d\theta}{dt}$$

$$= 2\omega^2 d \operatorname{cosec}^2 \theta \cot \theta.$$

8.3 Some mensuration formulae

In the set of exercises which follows, and later in the book, the following mensuration formulae will be found useful. They can be derived by the methods of the integral calculus and some of them will, in fact, be so derived in the chapters on that subject.

Circle

Circumference $= 2\pi r$. $\qquad$ r = radius.

Area $= \pi r^2$.

Length of arc $= r\theta$. $\qquad$ θ = angle between extreme radii.

Area of sector $= \frac{1}{2}r^2\theta$.

Trapezium

Area $= \frac{1}{2}(a + b)h$. $\qquad$ a, b the parallel sides,

h = altitude.

Prism

Volume $= Bh$. $\qquad$ B = area of base,

h = altitude.

Pyramid

Volume $= \frac{1}{3}Bh$. $\qquad$ B = area of base,

h = altitude.

Cylinder

Volume $= \pi r^2 h$. $\qquad$ r = radius of base,

Area of curved surface $= 2\pi rh$. $\qquad$ h = altitude.

Cone

Volume $= \frac{1}{3}\pi r^2 h = \frac{1}{3}\pi h^3 \tan^2 \alpha$. $\qquad$ r = radius of base,

Area of curved surface $= \pi rl$ $\qquad$ h = altitude,

$\quad = \pi h^2 \tan \alpha \sec \alpha$. $\qquad$ l = slant height,

α = semi-vertical angle.

Sphere

Volume $= \frac{4}{3}\pi r^3$. $\qquad$ r = radius.

Area of surface $= 4\pi r^2$.

Surface of zone $= 2\pi rh$. $\qquad$ h = height of zone.

Exercises 8 (a)

1. An excavator removes V cubic metres of soil in t minutes, where $V = 15t - (t^2/60)$. At what rate is the soil being removed after 20 minutes?   [L.U.]

2. A spherical balloon is being blown up, the volume increasing at the constant rate of 15 cm³/s. At what rate is the radius increasing when it is 10 centimetres long?   [L.U.]

3. The volume of a solid cube increases uniformly at k^3 cubic centimetres per second. Find an expression for the rate of increase of its surface area when the area of a face is b^2 square centimetres.

4. A block of ice in the form of a cube, whose edge is 2 metres, begins melting and its volume decreases at a constant rate, the block remaining cubical. If the rate of melting is such that the edge measures one metre after 28 hours, find

    (i) the length of edge after 16 hours,
    (ii) the rate at which the length of edge is decreasing at this time
                                                                                      [N.U.]

5. A man h m tall walks at the uniform rate of v m/s directly away from a lamp which is H m above the ground. Show that the length of his shadow is increasing at the rate of $(hv)/(H - h)$ m/s.

6. The inner and outer radii of a cylindrical tube of constant length change in such a way that the volume of material forming the tube remains constant. Find the rate of increase of the outer radius at the instant when the radii are 3 cm and 5 cm, and the rate of increase of the inner radius is $3\frac{1}{3}$ cm/min.

7. The sound of an explosion is propagated through the air as a sphere whose radius increases at the rate of 333 m/s. At what rate is the volume of the sphere increasing 2 seconds after the explosion?   [O.C.]

8. An aeroplane is flying at a constant height of h metres and at a constant speed of v m/s so that its path passes directly over a searchlight. Find a formula giving the rate (in degrees per second) at which the searchlight must be turned so that the aeroplane will be in the beam when its angle of elevation is θ degrees.

9. A ladder rests against a vertical pole. The foot of the ladder is sliding away from the pole along horizontal ground. Find the inclination of the ladder to the horizontal at the instant when the top of the ladder is moving three times as fast as its foot.   [L.U.]

10. A hollow circular cone with vertical angle 90° and height 36 cm is inverted and filled with water. This water begins to leak away through a small hole in the vertex. If the level of the water begins to sink at the rate of 1 centimetre in 2 minutes and the water continues to leak at the same rate, at what rate is the level sinking when the water is 24 cm from the top?

11. A trough 3 m long has its cross-section in the form of an isosceles triangle. The depth of the trough is 0·2 m and it is 0·25 m wide at the top. If water runs into it at the steady rate of 6×10^{-4} m^3/s, at what rate is the surface rising when the depth of water is 0·1 m.

12. A solid is formed by placing a hemisphere of radius x metres on one end of a cylinder of radius x metres and height 12 metres. Express the volume V as a function of x. If R_1 and R_2 are the rate of increase of V with x when $x = 9$ m and when $x = 10·5$ m, show that $5R_1 = 4R_2$.
[O.C.]

13. If an angle is increasing at a constant rate, find the magnitude of the angle at the instant when its tangent is increasing eight times as fast as its sine.

14. A vessel is constructed so that the volume of water contained in it is

$$\frac{\pi}{192} (x^3 + 24x^2 + 192x)$$

when the depth is x. What is the rate of increase of volume per unit increase of x when (i) $x = 2$, (ii) $x = 4$? How many times faster does the surface rise when $x = 2$ than when $x = 4$, if water is poured in at a constant rate? [O.C.]

15. A narrow beam of light radiating from a point O revolves at a constant rate, making one complete revolution every three minutes. At a certain instant a man standing at a point A 50 m from O is illuminated by the beam. He starts to run along a path at right angles to OA, adjusting his speed so as to keep in the beam. If his maximum speed is 6 m/s, show that he will be able to do this for between 28 and 29 seconds.
[L.U.]

8.4 Some applications from dynamics

We have already seen in § 8.2 that if a body, moving in a straight line, has travelled a distance x in time t, its velocity v at this time is given by

$$v = \frac{dx}{dt}. \tag{8.1}$$

We have also seen that the acceleration a acquired by the body in time t is

$$a = \frac{dv}{dt}. \tag{8.2}$$

It is often useful to have available alternative expressions for the acceleration a at time t and these can be found as follows. Firstly, combining equations (8.2) and (8.1)

$$a = \frac{d}{dt} \left(\frac{dx}{dt} \right) = \frac{d^2x}{dt^2}, \tag{8.3}$$

so that the acceleration is the second derivative of distance with respect to time. Secondly, since v is a function of x and x is a function of t,

$$a = \frac{dv}{dt} = \frac{dv}{dx} \times \frac{dx}{dt} = \frac{dv}{dx} \times v = v\frac{dv}{dx}. \qquad (8.4)$$

Thus the acceleration may be expressed in any one of the three equivalent forms

$$\frac{dv}{dt}, \quad \frac{d^2x}{dt^2}, \quad v\frac{dv}{dx}.$$

In dynamical applications, differential coefficients with respect to the time t are often denoted by dots placed above the dependent variable. Thus dx/dt, d^2x/dt^2, dv/dt are denoted by $\dot{x}$, $\ddot{x}$ and $\dot{v}$ respectively and, in this notation, equations (8.1), (8.2) and (8.3) would be written

$$v = \dot{x}, \quad a = \dot{v}, \quad a = \ddot{x}.$$

Example 4. *A particle P travels in a straight line AB, its distance x from A at the end of t seconds being given by $x = 2t^3 - 15t^2 + 36t + 20$. Prove that the velocity of P vanishes at two points C and D in AB and that its acceleration vanishes at one point E at a time mid-way between the times of arrival at C and D.* [O.C.]

The velocity v is given by

$$v = \dot{x} = \frac{d}{dt}(2t^3 - 15t^2 + 36t + 20)$$
$$= 6t^2 - 30t + 36 = 6(t - 2)(t - 3).$$

This vanishes when $t = 2$ and 3 seconds and these are the times of arrival at the two points C and D. The acceleration a is given by

$$a = \dot{v} = \frac{d}{dt}(6t^2 - 30t + 36) = 12t - 30 = 6(2t - 5)$$

and this is zero when $t = 2\frac{1}{2}$ seconds, showing that the acceleration vanishes at a time mid-way between the times to C and D.

Example 5. *If the velocity of a body varies inversely as the square root of the distance, prove that its acceleration varies as the fourth power of its velocity.*

Denoting the distance travelled by x and the velocity by v

$$v = k/\sqrt{x}, \text{ where } k \text{ is a constant.}$$

Using equation (8.4), the acceleration a is given by

$$a = v\frac{dv}{dx} = \frac{k}{\sqrt{x}} \times \frac{d}{dx}\left(\frac{k}{\sqrt{x}}\right) = \frac{k}{\sqrt{x}} \times \left(-\frac{k}{2x^{3/2}}\right)$$
$$= -\frac{1}{2}\frac{k^2}{x^2} = -\frac{1}{2}k^2 \times \frac{v^4}{k^4} = -\frac{v^4}{2k^2},$$

since $\sqrt{x} = k/v$, and we have established the required result.

8.5 Approximations

If y is a function of x given by $y = f(x)$ and if δy is the increment in y corresponding to an increment δx in the value of x, equation (7.4) of § 7.5 gives

$$\delta y \simeq f'(x)\delta x. \tag{8.5}$$

This is an *approximate* formula which can be used to find the effect on the value of a function of a *small* change in the value of the independent variable.

Example 6. *The pressure p units and the volume v units of an expanding gas are related by the law $pv^{1\cdot4} = k$, where k is a constant. If the volume increases by $0\cdot3$ per cent, estimate the percentage change in the pressure.* [N.U.]

Here $p = kv^{-1\cdot4}$ so that $f(v) = kv^{-1\cdot4}$ and $f'(v) = -1\cdot4\,kv^{-2\cdot4}$. Hence

$$\delta p \simeq -1\cdot4kv^{-2\cdot4}\delta v$$

giving

$$\frac{\delta p}{p} \simeq -\frac{1\cdot4kv^{-2\cdot4}}{kv^{-1\cdot4}}\,\delta v = -1\cdot4\,\frac{\delta v}{v}.$$

Now $\delta v/v$ is the ratio of the change in v to v and the percentage change in v is therefore $100\,\delta v/v$. Similarly the percentage change in p is $100\,\delta p/p$ and we can write

percentage change in $p \simeq -1\cdot4 \times$ percentage change in v.

The percentage increase in v being $0\cdot3$, the approximate percentage *decrease* (because of the minus sign) in v is $1\cdot4 \times 0\cdot3 = 0\cdot42$.

Example 7. *Find the approximate error made in calculating the area of a triangle in which two of the sides are accurately measured as 18 cm and 25 cm, while the included angle is measured as $60°$ but is $\frac{1}{2}°$ wrong.*

If the given sides and included angle are denoted by b, c and A, the area Δ of the triangle is given by equation (4.2) as $\Delta = \frac{1}{2}bc \sin A$. If the angle A is in error by a small amount δA, the error $\delta\Delta$ in Δ will be given by (8.5) as

$$\delta\Delta \simeq \frac{d}{dA}(\tfrac{1}{2}bc \sin A)\,\delta A$$

$$= \tfrac{1}{2}bc \cos A\,\delta A.$$

Now $b = 18$, $c = 25$, $A = 60° = \frac{1}{3}\pi$ radians and $\delta A = \frac{1}{2}° = \pi/360$ radians, so that

$$\delta\Delta \simeq \tfrac{1}{2} \times 18 \times 25 \times \cos\tfrac{1}{3}\pi \times \frac{\pi}{360}$$

$$= \frac{5\pi}{16}\ \text{cm}^2.$$

Exercises 8 (b)

1. The distance x m moved by a body in time t seconds is given by $x = 2t^4 + 3t + 2$. Find the velocity and acceleration of the body after 2 seconds.

2. The velocity v m/s of a particle at time t sec is given by the equation $v = ct + dt^2$ where c and d are numbers. If $v = 3$ when $t = 1$ and $v = 4$ when $t = 2$, find the values of c and d. Hence find the acceleration of the particle at time $1\frac{1}{2}$ sec. [N.U.]

3. A particle moves along the axis of x and at the end of time t its position is given by $x = 5 + 4\sin 2t + 3\cos 2t$. Prove that its acceleration is $20 - 4x$. Prove also that its velocity is zero when $x = 0$ and when $x = 10$. [O.C.]

4. A point P moves in a straight line so that after t seconds its distance x m from a fixed point O in the line is given by the equation

$$x = \sin t + 2\cos t.$$

Its velocity is then v m/s and its acceleration a m/s^2. Show that $v^2 = 5 - x^2$, $a = -x$ and find the velocity of P after 2 seconds (taking 1 radian as $57°\ 18'$). [N.U.]

5. If the velocity of a body varies as the square of the distance travelled, show that its acceleration varies as the cube of the distance.

6. A particle moves in a straight line and its distance x from a fixed point O on the line at time t is given by $x = a(1 + \cos^2 t)$. Show that the acceleration of the particle is $6a - 4x$ and find the values of x at the points where the velocity is zero. [O.C.]

7. The distance x moved in a straight line by a particle in time t is given by $x = at^2 + bt + c$, where a, b and c are constants. If v is the velocity of the particle at time t, show that $4a(x - c) = v^2 - b^2$. [L.U.]

8. A particle moves along the x-axis in such a way that its distance from the origin after t seconds is given by $x = t^4 - 5t^3 + 6t^2$. Show that its acceleration is negative for an interval lasting $1\frac{1}{2}$ seconds. [L.U.]

9. A particle moves along a straight line Ox in the time interval $0 \leqslant t \leqslant \pi$; after t seconds its displacement from O is x cm where $x = t + \sin 2t$. Calculate the values of t between 0 and π when the direction of motion changes and show that the particle always remains on the same side of O. Find also the time at which the acceleration is zero. [N.U.]

10. If $y = 4x^4$, find the approximate percentage change in y due to a change of $0 \cdot 2$ per cent. in the value of x.

11. A spherical soap bubble is of radius r and volume v. If r is subject to a slight variation, show that the percentage increase in r is approximately one-third of the percentage increase in v. If r increases from 1 cm to $1 \cdot 03$ cm, find (correct to two significant figures) the increase in v. [N.U.]

12. The base radius r and the semi-vertical angle α of a cone are measured to be $r = 6$ and $\alpha = 45°$. There is no error in the measurement of r but that in α is liable to be $\pm\frac{1}{4}°$. Show that the possible error in the calculated volume of the cone is a little less than $0 \cdot 9$ per cent.

13. The length l m of a simple pendulum is approximately related to its period of vibration t seconds by the equation $\pi^2 l = 2 \cdot 4 t^2$. If the length of the pendulum whose period is 3 seconds is increased by 0·006 m, find the resulting change in the period.

14. The angle C and the side b of a triangle ABC are accurately known to be 60° and 20 m respectively. The side a is measured as 30 m but there is a likely error of ±1 per cent in this measurement. Find the possible percentage error in the calculated value of the side c.

15. The current i passing through a certain galvanometer is proportional to the tangent of the angle of deflection θ of the needle. If there is a *small* error $\alpha°$ in the measured value of θ, show that the corresponding percentage error in the current is approximately 3·49 α cosec 2θ.

8.6 Maximum and minimum values

Fig. 69 shows the graph of the function $y = f(x)$. Points such as P, Q and R, at which the tangent to the graph is parallel to the axis

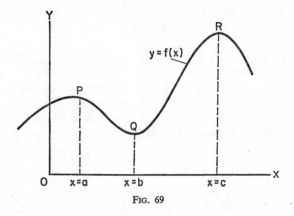

Fig. 69

OX, are called *turning points*. If a, b and c are the abscissae of P, Q and R respectively, the value of y increases as x increases to the value a, it decreases as x increases from a to b, it increases as x increases from b to c and then decreases again as x increases beyond c. At the points P, Q and R the value of y is *stationary* and is neither increasing nor decreasing.

The points P, Q and R are referred to as points of *maximum* and *minimum* values, maximum at P and R and minimum at Q. It should be noted that a maximum or minimum value is the greatest or least value in the *neighbourhood* but it need not be the absolutely greatest or least value. Thus there are points on the left of the graph of Fig. 69 where the values of y are less than the "minimum value" at Q and there are points on the right where the values are greater than the "maximum value" at P. Again in Fig. 70, which shows the graph of $y = x^2(8 - x^2)$, there are maximum values at the points P and Q where $x = \mp 2$ and these are also greatest values, but the minimum value at $x = 0$ is not a

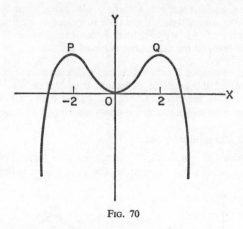

FIG. 70

least value for there are points on the graph with smaller values of y than at the origin O.

It has been pointed out in § 8.2, that y increases or decreases as x increases according as the derivative dy/dx is positive or negative. This is illustrated geometrically in Figs. 71 and 72 which show respectively parts of the graphs of functions which increase and decrease as

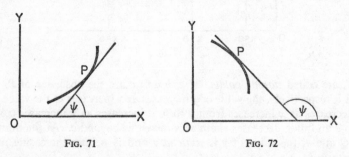

FIG. 71   FIG. 72

x increases. In Fig. 71, the tangent at a representative point P makes an acute angle ψ with the axis OX; since the tangent of an acute angle is positive and since $dy/dx = \tan \psi$, the derivative will be positive. In Fig. 72 the angle ψ is obtuse and, since such angles have negative tangents, the derivative will be negative. At turning points such as the points P, Q, R of Fig. 69, or P, O, Q of Fig. 70, the tangent to the graph is *parallel* to the axis OX and, since the tangent of a zero angle is itself zero, it follows that

$$\frac{dy}{dx} = 0 \qquad (8.6)$$

at such points.

Returning to Fig. 69, shown again in Fig. 73, the sign of the derivative has now been marked in. Immediately to the left of the point P, the function is increasing and its derivative is positive. At the point P, the function is neither increasing nor decreasing and the derivative is zero.

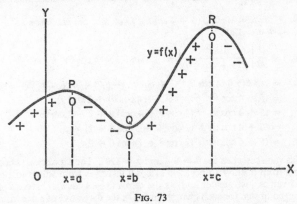

FIG. 73

Immediately to the right of P, the function is decreasing and has a negative derivative and so on. From these considerations it is possible to formulate the following rules for the determination of the position of turning points and for distinguishing between maximum and minimum values. Thus

(i) at a turning point, $dy/dx = 0$;

(ii) at a point giving a *maximum* value of y, the derivative dy/dx changes from *positive* to *negative* values as x increases from values just less to values just greater than the value at the turning point;

(iii) at a point giving a *minimum* value of y, the derivative dy/dx changes from *negative* to *positive* values as x increases from values just less to values just greater than the value at the turning point.

Example 8. *Find the coordinates of the turning points on the curve $y = x^3 - 3x$ and decide at which point y has a maximum value and at which point a minimum value.*

Since $y = x^3 - 3x$, $dy/dx = 3x^2 - 3$ and this vanishes when $x = \pm 1$. Hence the points $x = 1, y = 1 - 3 = -2$ and $x = -1, y = -1 + 3 = 2$ are turning points. For $x = 0.9$ (a value a little less than the value $x = 1$ at a turning point),

$$\frac{dy}{dx} = 3(0.9)^2 - 3 = -0.57,$$

while at $x = 1.1$ (a value a little greater than $x = 1$),

$$\frac{dy}{dx} = 3(1.1)^2 - 3 = +0.63.$$

The derivative therefore changes from negative to positive and hence the point $(1, -2)$ is one with a minimum value of y. It is left as an exercise for the redaer to show in the same way that the point $(-1, 2)$ is one with a maximum value of y.

Example 9. *If* $\sin \alpha = \sin \theta / \sqrt{(5 + 4 \cos \theta)}$, *show that the maximum value of* $\sin \alpha$ *occurs when* $\theta = 120°$.

$$\frac{d}{d\theta} (\sin \alpha) = \frac{d}{d\theta} \left\{ \frac{\sin \theta}{\sqrt{(5 + 4 \cos \theta)}} \right\} = \frac{d}{d\theta} \{ \sin \theta (5 + 4 \cos \theta)^{-1/2} \}$$

$$= \cos \theta (5 + 4 \cos \theta)^{-1/2} + \sin \theta . (-\tfrac{1}{2})(5 + 4 \cos \theta)^{-3/2}(-4 \sin \theta)$$

$$= (5 + 4 \cos \theta)^{-3/2} \{ \cos \theta (5 + 4 \cos \theta) + 2 \sin^2 \theta \}$$

$$= (5 + 4 \cos \theta)^{-3/2}(5 \cos \theta + 4 \cos^2 \theta + 2 - 2 \cos^2 \theta)$$

$$= (5 + 4 \cos \theta)^{-3/2}(2 \cos^2 \theta + 5 \cos \theta + 2)$$

$$= (5 + 4 \cos \theta)^{-3/2}(2 \cos \theta + 1)(\cos \theta + 2),$$

and this vanishes when $\cos \theta = -\tfrac{1}{2}$ and $\theta = 120°$. The expression $(2 \cos \theta + 1)$ changes from positive to negative as $\cos \theta$ increases from values just less than $-\tfrac{1}{2}$ to values just greater and, as the terms $(5 + 4 \cos \theta)^{-3/2}$, $(\cos \theta + 2)$ are unchanged in sign for such changes in $\cos \theta$, the derivative of $\sin \alpha$ with respect to θ changes from positive to negative near the turning point. The value of $\sin \alpha$ for $\theta = 120°$ is therefore a maximum value.

An alternative method of discriminating between maximum and minimum values can be obtained as follows. Fig. 74 shows the graphs of $y = f(x)$ and $y = f'(x)$, the derivative of y with respect to x, plotted

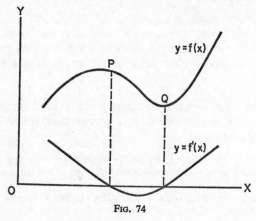

Fig. 74

on the same diagram. For points to the left of the maximum value at P, $y = f(x)$ is increasing and the derivative $f'(x)$ is positive. For points between P and Q, y is decreasing and the derivative $f'(x)$ is therefore negative, while for points to the right of Q, y is increasing and $f'(x)$ is again positive. For values of x corresponding to the two turning points P and Q, $f'(x)$ is zero as shown on the diagram. Considering now the graph of $y = f'(x)$, we see that $f'(x)$ is decreasing for the value of x corresponding to that of P and its derivative $f''(x)$ or d^2y/dx^2 is therefore negative for this value of x. Similarly for the value of x corresponding to that of Q, $f'(x)$ is increasing and $f''(x)$ is positive. Hence at a turning point such as P giving a *maximum* value,

$$\frac{d^2y}{dx^2} \text{ is } negative,$$

while at a point such as Q giving a *minimum* value,

$$\frac{d^2y}{dx^2} \text{ is } positive.$$

Thus a method of distinguishing between maximum and minimum values is given by calculating the numerical value of the second derivative for the values of x in question and considering its sign. Negative values of d^2y/dx^2 correspond to maximum values of y while positive values of d^2y/dx^2 correspond to minimum values of y. This method fails when the second derivative vanishes for the values of x under discussion and the previous method of examining the change in sign of the first derivative must be used in such cases.

Example 10. *Find the coordinates of the maximum and minimum points on the curve*
$y = x^3 - 9x^2 + 24x$ *and distinguish between them.* [L.U.]
Here

$$\frac{dy}{dx} = 3x^2 - 18x + 24 = 3(x^2 - 6x + 8) = 3(x - 2)(x - 4),$$

and

$$\frac{d^2y}{dx^2} = 3(2x - 6) = 6(x - 3).$$

dy/dx vanishes when $x = 2$ and when $x = 4$ and turning points occur at these values of x. When $x = 2$,

$$\frac{d^2y}{dx^2} = 6(2 - 3) = -6$$

and, as this is negative, $x = 2$ gives a maximum value of y. When $x = 4$,

$$\frac{d^2y}{dx^2} = 6(4 - 3) = 6$$

and, as this is positive, $x = 4$ gives a minimum value. The values of y when $x = 2$ and $x = 4$ are respectively

$$y = (2)^3 - 9(2)^2 + 24(2) = 20$$

and

$$y = (4)^3 - 9(4)^2 + 24(4) = 16,$$

so the required result is that the point $(2, 20)$ is a point of maximum y and the point $(4, 16)$ a point of minimum y.

Exercises 8 (c)

1. Calculate the maximum and minimum values of $y = x^2(1 - x)$ and distinguish between them.   [N.U.]

2. Find the values of x for which the expression $(x - 2)(x - 3)^2$ has turning points and decide which gives a maximum and which gives a minimum value.

3. The function $y = 2x^3 + ax^2 + bx$, where a and b are independent of x, has stationary values when $x = 1$ and $x = -2$. Find the values of a and b. For which of these values of x is the function a maximum and what is the maximum value?   [L.U.]

4. Prove that the function $(x^2 - 5x + 4)/(x^2 - 5x + 6)$ has a turning point at $x = 2\cdot5$.   [O.C.]

5. Find the coordinates of the turning points of the function

    $$(15 + 10x)/(4 + x^2),$$

    distinguishing between maximum and minimum values.   [O.C.]

6. Find the maximum and minimum values of the function

    $$(x + 2)/(x^2 + 1)^{1/3}.$$ [O.C.]

7. Find the maximum and minimum values of the function $4x - 3 \tan x$ in the range $0 < x < \pi$.   [L.U.]

8. Prove that the least value of $4 \sec \theta - 3 \tan \theta$ for $0 < \theta < \tfrac{1}{2}\pi$ is $\sqrt{7}$.   [O.C.]

9. Prove that the function $27 \sec \theta + 64 \operatorname{cosec} \theta$ has stationary values whenever $\tan \theta = \tfrac{4}{3}$. If θ is acute, calculate the stationary value and show that it is a minimum.   [L.U.]

10. Prove that the function

    $$y = \frac{\sin x \cos x}{1 + 2 \sin x + 2 \cos x}$$

has turning points in the range $0 \leqslant x \leqslant 2\pi$ when $x = \frac{1}{4}\pi$ and $x = \frac{5}{4}\pi$, distinguishing between maximum and minimum values.   [O.C.]

11. Find the maximum and minimum values of the function

$$y = (4x + 1)(x - 1)^4.$$ [O.C.]

12. Find the value of the function $x^3 - 6x^2 + 18x + 5$ when its rate of increase with x is a minimum.

13. Find the value of x for which the sum of the corresponding ordinates of the graphs of $y = 2x^3 - 15x^2 + 36x + 10$ and $y = x^2 - 4x + 6$ is a maximum. Show that, for this value of x, the ordinate of one graph is a maximum and that of the other is a minimum.

14. If the resistance of the air is neglected, the equation of the curve described by a particle projected with velocity V at elevation α is

$$y = x \tan \alpha - \frac{1}{2}(gx^2/V^2) \sec^2 \alpha$$

where x and y are measured horizontally and vertically from the point of projection and g is a constant. Show that the maximum height reached by the particle is $(V^2/2g) \sin^2 \alpha$.

15. Show that

$$\left(\frac{a}{p}\right)^{\frac{\gamma-1}{\gamma}} + \left(\frac{p}{b}\right)^{\frac{\gamma-1}{\gamma}},$$

where a, b and γ are constants, and $\gamma > 1$ is a minimum when $p = \sqrt{(ab)}$.

8.7 Applications to practical problems

Many practical problems can be solved by the method of the last section. In some cases the quantity whose maximum or minimum value is to be found appears at first sight to be a function of more than one independent variable. It is, however, often possible to eliminate all but one of these variables by using geometrical or other relations which exist. Once the quantity has been expressed in terms of a single variable, the method of finding its maximum or minimum value is identical with that given in § 8.6. We differentiate with respect to the single remaining variable and the resulting derivative is equated to zero. This leads to an equation whose solution gives stationary values to the quantity under discussion.

It is often unnecessary in practical problems to examine the change in sign in the first derivative (or the sign of the second derivative if that method is used) to distinguish between maximum and minimum values for it is usually possible to see at once on physical grounds whether the solution leads to a maximum or a minimum.

Some illustrative examples are given below.

Example 11. *A sector of a circle encloses an area of 25 cm². Find the least possible perimeter of the sector.* [L.U.]

Let the bounding radii of the sector be of length r centimetres and let the angle between them be θ (Fig. 75). Since the area of the sector is 25 cm², $\frac{1}{2}r^2\theta = 25$ giving $\theta = 50/r^2$. The perimeter P is given by

$$P = 2r + r\theta$$

and, substituting $\theta = 50/r^2$, P is given in terms of the single variable r by

$$P = 2r + \frac{50}{r}. \tag{8.7}$$

This expression takes a stationary value when

$$\frac{dP}{dr} = 2 - \frac{50}{r^2} = 0,$$

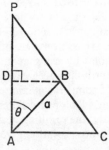

Fig. 75

that is, when $r = 5$ cm. Since $d^2P/dr^2 = 100/r^3 = 100/125$ and this is positive, the stationary value is a minimum. Substituting $r = 5$ in (8.7) the least perimeter is of length $2(5) + (50/5) = 20$ cm.

Example 12. *A rod AB of length a is hinged to a horizontal table at A. The rod is inclined to the vertical at an angle θ and there is a luminous point at a height h vertically above A($h > a$). Prove that the length, in fact, of the shadow of the rod on the table is $ah \sin \theta/(h - a \cos \theta)$. Prove also that the maximum length of the shadow is $ah/\sqrt{(h^2 - a^2)}$.* [O.C.]

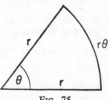

Fig. 76

In Fig. 76, P is the luminous point, AC the shadow and BD is drawn at right angles to AP. From the figure, $AD = a \cos \theta$, $PD = PA - AD = h - a \cos \theta$ and $BD = a \sin \theta$. Since the triangles PDB, PAC are similar,

$$\frac{AC}{BD} = \frac{AP}{PD}$$

giving

$$AC = BD \cdot \frac{AP}{PD} = a \sin \theta \left(\frac{h}{h - a \cos \theta} \right) = \frac{ah \sin \theta}{h - a \cos \theta}$$

as the required length of the shadow. This takes a maximum value when $d(AC)/d\theta = 0$, that is when

$$\frac{ah \cos \theta (h - a \cos \theta) - ah \sin \theta (a \sin \theta)}{(h - a \cos \theta)^2} = 0.$$

The expression on the left vanishes when $h \cos \theta - a \cos^2 \theta - a \sin^2 \theta = 0$ and, remembering that $\cos^2 \theta + \sin^2 \theta = 1$, this gives

$$\cos \theta = \frac{a}{h}, \quad \sin \theta = \sqrt{(1 - \cos^2 \theta)} = \frac{\sqrt{(h^2 - a^2)}}{h}.$$

Substituting these values of $\cos \theta$ and $\sin \theta$ in the formula for AC, the maximum length of the shadow is

$$\frac{ah \cdot \sqrt{(h^2 - a^2)}/h}{h - a(a/h)} = \frac{ah}{\sqrt{(h^2 - a^2)}}$$

Example 13. *A lighthouse A is 0·5 kilometre due South of B, a point on a straight coast running East and West. C is 3 kilometres due West of B. A man at A, wishing to reach C, rows a boat at 3 km/h, and lands somewhere between B and C, walking the rest of the distance to C at 3·25 km/h. How far from B must he land so as to accomplish the journey in the shortest possible time?*   [L.U.]

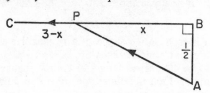

FIG. 77

In Fig. 77, P is the point of landing, x kilometres West of B. $AB = \frac{1}{2}$, $BP = x$ and $PC = 3 - x$ kilometres. Since ABP is a right angle, $AP = \sqrt{(x^2 + \frac{1}{4})}$ kilometres and the times taken to travel along AP, PC at 3 and $3\frac{1}{4}$ km/h respectively are

$$\frac{\sqrt{(x^2 + \frac{1}{4})}}{3} \quad \text{and} \quad \frac{4(3 - x)}{13} \text{ hours.}$$

The total time T for the journey is therefore given by

$$T = \frac{\sqrt{(x^2 + \frac{1}{4})}}{3} + \frac{4(3 - x)}{13},$$

and, for the journey to be accomplished as quickly as possible, this must be a minimum so that $dT/dx = 0$. Now

$$\frac{dT}{dx} = \frac{1}{3} \frac{x}{\sqrt{(x^2 + \frac{1}{4})}} - \frac{4}{13}$$

and this vanishes when $\sqrt{(x^2 + \frac{1}{4})} = \dfrac{13x}{12}$. This gives

$$x^2 + \frac{1}{4} = \frac{169}{144} x^2,$$

leading to $25x^2 = 36$, $5x = 6$ and $x = 1\frac{1}{5}$ kilometres.

Exercises 8 (d)

1. A 100 m fence completely encloses an area in the form of a sector of a circle. Calculate the angle between the bounding radii for which this area is a maximum and evaluate the maximum area.

2. An open cylindrical vessel is to be constructed from a given amount of uniform thin material. Show that it contains the greatest possible volume when its height is equal to the radius of its base.   [O.C.]

3. A rectangular tank, open at the top, is to have a capacity of 32 cubic metres. Prove that, if x m is its length, y m its width and A m^2 the area of its outer surface, then

$$A = xy + 64 \left(\frac{1}{x} + \frac{1}{y} \right).$$

   Prove that, if y remains fixed while x varies, the minimum value of A is $16\sqrt{y} + 64/y$. If now y is allowed to vary, find the minimum value of A.

4. A sports field is to have the shape of a rectangular area $ABCD$ with semicircular areas at opposite ends on BC and AD as diameters. Its perimeter is to be 400 metres long and the rectangular area $ABCD$ is to be a maximum. Find the dimensions of the rectangle.   [N.U.]

5. A rocket consists of a right circular cone, of semi-angle α and base radius r joined at its base to a circular cylinder also of radius r. The length of the cylinder is l and the total volume of the rocket is fixed. Prove that, if $\alpha = 30°$, the area of the curved surface is a minimum when $l/r = 2 - \sqrt{3}$.   [O.C.]

6. A tube of rectangular section is to be made by folding a strip of sheet metal 1 metre wide, one side of the tube being of two thicknesses. Find the maximum area of the section of the tube.   [L.U.]

7. A body is made up of a hemisphere of radius r with its plane face joined to one of the plane faces of a circular cylinder of radius r and length x. Prove that, if the volume of the body is 45π m^3, the least value of the total surface area is 45π m^2.   [O.C.]

8. The loss of heat from a closed full hot-water tank is proportional to its surface area. A cylindrical tank has flat ends and its volume is fixed.

Determine the ratio of the length to the radius for the heat loss to be a minimum. Find also whether such a tank would retain heat more efficiently than a cubical one of equal volume.   [N.U.]

9. A cone of semi-vertical angle θ is inscribed in a sphere of radius a. Prove that the volume of the cone is $\frac{8}{3}\pi a^3 \sin^2 \theta \cos^4 \theta$ and find the area of its curved surface. Prove that if a is fixed and θ allowed to vary, the maximum volume of the cone is 8/27 of the volume of the sphere. Prove further that if the volume of the cone is a maximum, the area of its curved surface is also a maximum.   [O.C.]

10. A beam of rectangular cross-section is to be cut from a cylindrical log of diameter d. The stiffness of such a beam is proportional to xy^3, where x is the breadth and y the depth of the section. Find the cross-sectional area of the beam (i) of greatest volume, (ii) of greatest stiffness, that can be cut from the log.   [O.C.]

11. Two corridors in a building, of widths a and b respectively, meet at right angles. Prove that the length of the longest ladder which can be carried in a horizontal position from one corridor to the other is $(a^{2/3} + b^{2/3})^{\frac{3}{2}}$. If $a = 2$ m, $b = 3$ m, evaluate your result to the nearest millimetre.   [L.U.]

12. A piece of wire, which forms the circumference of a circle of 0·3 metres radius, is cut and bent so as to form two new circles. Find the radius of each circle in order that the sum of the areas of the two circles shall be as small as possible.   [O.C.]

13. A despatch rider is in open country at a distance of 6 kilometres from the nearest point P of a straight road. He wishes to proceed as quickly as possible to a point Q on the road 20 kilometres from P. If his maximum speed, across country, is 40 km/h and, along the road, 50 km/h, find at what distance from P he should strike the road.   [L.U.]

14. Post Office regulations restrict parcels to a maximum length of 1·07 m and a maximum girth of 1·83 m. Find the maximum permissible volume of a rectangular parcel which satisfies these regulations.

15. A variable isosceles triangle is circumscribed about a circle of given radius. Prove that the area of the triangle is a minimum (and not a maximum) when the triangle is equilateral.   [O.C.]

8.8 Points of inflexion

At any point of a curve, the value of the second derivative d^2y/dx^2 gives the rate of change of the gradient. In Fig. 78, the gradient is increasing from P to Q and decreasing from Q to R. The value of d^2y/dx^2 is positive for points between P and Q and negative for points between Q and R. At the point Q the value of d^2y/dx^2 is *zero* and such a point is called *a point of inflexion.* At such points, the curve "crosses its tangent" as shown in the diagram and the coordinates of points like Q are found by finding the values of x which make

(i) $\dfrac{d^2y}{dx^2} = 0$,

(ii) the sign of $\dfrac{d^2y}{dx^2}$ change as we pass through the point.

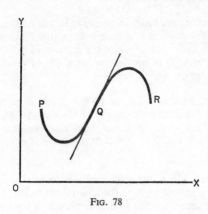

FIG. 78

Example 14. *Find the abscissae of the points of inflexion of the curve*

$$y = x^4 - 4x^3 - 18x^2 + 7x + 6.$$

Here

$$\frac{dy}{dx} = 4x^3 - 12x^2 - 36x + 7,$$

$$\frac{d^2y}{dx^2} = 12x^2 - 24x - 36 = 12(x^2 - 2x - 3)$$

$$= 12(x + 1)(x - 3).$$

The second derivative vanishes when $x = -1$, $x = 3$ and changes sign as x increases from just less than -1 to just greater than -1 and again as x increases from just less than 3 to just greater. Hence points of inflexion occur when $x = -1$ and when $x = 3$.

Example 15. *Find the turning points and points of inflexion on the graph of*

$$y = 3x^4 - 4x^3 + 1.$$

$$\frac{dy}{dx} = 12x^3 - 12x^2 = 12x^2(x - 1),$$

$$\frac{d^2y}{dx^2} = 36x^2 - 24x = 12x(3x - 2).$$

Here the first derivative vanishes when $x = 0$ and $x = 1$. When $x = 0$, the second derivative vanishes; when $x = 1$, the second derivative is 12. Hence $x = 1$ gives a minimum. The second derivative vanishes when $x = 0$ and $x = \frac{2}{3}$ and changes sign as x passes through these values: these two values of x therefore give points of inflexion. The values of y when $x = 0$, $\frac{2}{3}$ and 1 are respectively, 1, $\frac{11}{27}$ and 0 so that the point $(1, 0)$ is a minimum and the points $(0, 1)$, $(\frac{2}{3}, \frac{11}{27})$ are points of inflexion. As, when $x = 0$, both dy/dx and d^2y/dx^2 are zero, the tangent to the curve at the first of these points of inflexion is parallel to the x-axis.

8.9 Curve sketching

It is often convenient to be able to make a rough sketch of a curve without actually going to the trouble of calculating the coordinates of a large number of points and plotting them. The following procedure, carried out either wholly or in part, should lead to a general picture of the shape of the curve.

(i) Discover if there is symmetry about either or both axes of co-ordinates. Symmetry about the axis of x occurs if the equation of the curve contains only even powers of y and there is symmetry about the axis of y if only even powers of x occur.

(ii) Look for symmetry about the origin of coordinates—such symmetry occurs when a change in sign of x (or y) causes a change in sign of y (or x) without altering its numerical value.

(iii) Find values of x (or y) which make y^2 (or x^2) negative. No real points occur on the curve for such values of x (or y).

(iv) Find where the curve crosses the coordinate axes. It crosses the x-axis at points for which $y = 0$ and it crosses the y-axis where $x = 0$.

(v) Find values of x, if there are any, which make y very large and values of y which make x very large.

(vi) If the curve passes through the origin of coordinates, its behaviour near this point can be found by studying the value of dy/dx for small values of x and y. Since dy/dx measures the slope of the tangent to the curve, a small value of dy/dx means that the curve lies near the axis of x, a large value means it lies near the axis of y, and a value of dy/dx near to unity means that the tangent to the curve at the origin approximately bisects the angle between the axes.

(vii) Find the coordinates of the turning points and points of inflexion by the methods given in the last few sections.

Some worked examples illustrating this procedure follow.

Example 16. *Sketch the graph of $y = (x^2 - 5x + 4)/(x^2 - 5x + 6)$ indicating its main features and show that it cannot have a value between 1 and 9 for any real value of x.* [O.C.]

(i) Since odd powers of x and y occur in the equation there is no symmetry about the coordinate axes.

(ii) There is no symmetry about the origin.

(iii) Expressed as a quadratic in x, the equation can be written

$$(y - 1)x^2 - 5(y - 1)x + 6y - 4 = 0,$$

and the roots of this are imaginary when

$$\{-5(y - 1)\}^2 - 4(y - 1)(6y - 4) < 0,$$

that is, when

$$(y - 1)(y - 9) < 0.$$

This shows that y cannot take values between 1 and 9 for real values of x.

(iv) The curve crosses the x-axis where $x^2 - 5x + 4 = 0$, that is, where $x = 1$ and $x = 4$; it crosses the y-axis where $y = 4/6 = 2/3$.

(v) The equation to the curve can be written in the form

$$y = \frac{(x - 1)(x - 4)}{(x - 2)(x - 3)}$$

and hence y is infinite when $x = 2$ and $x = 3$.

(vi) The curve does not pass through the origin.

(vii) $\dfrac{dy}{dx} = \dfrac{(2x - 5)(x^2 - 5x + 6) - (2x - 5)(x^2 - 5x + 4)}{(x^2 - 5x + 6)^2} = \dfrac{2(2x - 5)}{(x^2 - 5x + 6)^2}$

so there is a turning point when $x = 2 \cdot 5$. As x changes from just less than to just greater than $2 \cdot 5$, dy/dx changes from negative to positive and hence there is a minimum value of y for this value of x. Substituting $x = 2 \cdot 5$ in the equation of the curve, we find that the minimum value of y there is 9.

A rough sketch of the curve built up from these observations is shown in Fig. 79.

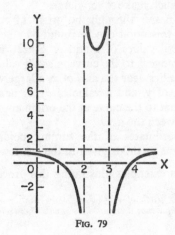

Fig. 79

Example 17. *Sketch the curve $y^2 = x^3$.*

Since only even powers of y occur in the equation, the curve is symmetrical about the axis of x. It is not symmetrical about the axis of y for an odd power of x is present. When x is negative, y^2 is negative and there are therefore no real points on the curve for such values of x. The curve passes through the origin and, since $y = \pm x^{3/2}$,

$$\frac{dy}{dx} = \pm \frac{3}{2} x^{1/2}.$$

This shows that, when x is small, the slope of the curve is small and the curve therefore lies close to the axis of x near the origin. As x becomes large, so does y and a sketch is given in Fig. 80.

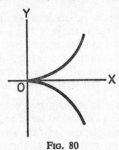

Fig. 80

Exercises 8 (e)

1. Find the abscissae of the points of inflexion on the curve
$$y = x^2(3x^2 - 10x - 12).$$

2. Show that the abscissa of the point of inflexion on the curve
$$y = \tfrac{1}{3}x^3 + 5x^2 + 24$$
is the mean of the abscissae of its turning points.

3. Show that turning points occur in the curve
$$y = (x - 1)^3(12x^2 - 9x - 43)$$
when $x = -1$, $x = 2$ and find the abscissae of the points of inflexion.

4. For what values of x are there points of inflexion on the curve $y = x + \sin x$ at which the tangent is parallel to the axis of x?

5. Discuss the nature of the points on the curve
$$y = 3x^4 - 8x^3 - 24x^2 + 96x$$
at which the tangent to the curve is parallel to the axis of x.

6. Sketch the graph of $y = x + (1/x)$ for $x > 0$. [N.U.]

7. Draw a rough sketch of the curve $y^2 = x(1 - x)^2$. [O.C.]

8. Sketch the curve $y^2 = x^2(x + 1)(2 - x)$. [L.U.]

9. Give a rough sketch of the curve $y = (15 + 10x)/(4 + x^2)$. [O.C.]

10. Indicate on a sketch the main features of the graph of

$$y = (x^2 + 1)/(x^2 + x + 1).$$ [N.U.]

Exercises 8 (f)

1. A solid cube of ice is melting, each edge decreasing at the constant rate of 0·25 cm/s. Find the rate of change of volume of the cube at the instant when the volume is 8 cm³. [L.U.]

2. The section of a trough is an isosceles triangle with its vertex downwards. The height of the triangle is 1 m, its base is 1·25 m and the length of the trough is 3 m. Water runs into the trough at the rate of 1·125 cubic metres per minute. Prove that, when the depth of water is x m, the volume of water is $\frac{15}{8}x^2$ cubic metres, and find in metres per minute the rate at which the level is rising after $1\frac{1}{2}$ minutes.

3. A chemical solution is passing through a conical filter 12 cm deep and 8 cm across the top into a cylindrical jar of radius 3 cm. At what rate is the level of solution rising in the jar if the level in the filter is falling at 3 centimetres per minute when its depth therein is 6 cm?

4. A spherical balloon is being inflated so that, at the time when the radius is 5 m, the radius is increasing at the rate of 0·15 m/s. Find the rate of increase of the volume at this time. If the rate of increase of volume thereafter remains constant, find the rate at which the radius is increasing when the balloon has a diameter of 12 m.

5. Two rings A and B connected by a rigid rod 2 m long slide along two fixed rods OX, OY at right angles and A moves along OX at the speed of 5 m/s. Find how far A is from O when B is moving at 2 m/s.

6. The distance x m moved in a straight line by a body in t seconds is given by $x = 16t(4 - t)$. Find the distance moved by the body when its velocity has dropped to half its initial value.

7. The displacement x at time t of a moving particle is given by

$$x = a \sin 2t + b \cos 2t.$$

If v is the speed at time t, prove that $v = 2\sqrt{(a^2 + b^2 - x^2)}$.

8. If a particle moves a distance x in time t such that $x^2 = at^2 + 2bt + c$ where a, b and c are constants, show that its acceleration is inversely proportional to x^3.

9. A height h is given in terms of a distance f and three angles θ, α and ϕ by the formula

$$h = \frac{f \sin \phi \tan \alpha}{\sin (\theta + \phi)}.$$

Show that when $f = 5400$ m, $\alpha = 45°$ and $\theta = \phi = 30°$, an error of $1°$ in θ leads to an error of about 31 m in the calculated height.   [N.U.]

10. In a triangle ABC, $a = 5$ and $A = 60°$. Find the percentage change in the radius of the circumscribed circle due to an increase of $0 \cdot 02$ radians in the angle A.

11. Find the values of x for which the function

$$y = \frac{a^2}{x} + \frac{b^2}{a - x} \quad (a > 0, b > 0)$$

has maximum and minimum values; discriminate between them.

12. Show that the function $x(x^2 + a^2)^{-5/2}$ has a maximum value when $2x = a$.

13. Find the values of x at the turning points of the graph of

$$y = \frac{x^2 - x + 1}{x^2 + x + 1}.$$

State which is a maximum and which is a minimum.

14. If turning points on the graph of $y = 2x^3 + ax^2 + bx + 8$ occur when $x = 0$ and when $x = 1$, determine the values of the constants a and b. Determine also the nature of the turning points.

15. Find the values of x in the range 0 to 2π for which the function $2 \sin x - x$ has a maximum or minimum value and distinguish between them.   [L.U.]

16. Prove that the function $(1 - \cos 2x)/\sqrt{(4 + 3 \cos 2x)}$ has turning points when $x = 0$ and $x = \frac{1}{2}\pi$. Find the maximum and minimum values of the function.   [O.C.]

17. If the graph of

$$y = \frac{ax + b}{(x + 1)(x - 2)}$$

has a stationary value when $x = 0$, $y = -1$, find the values of the constants a and b. Show that this stationary value is a minimum and find the value of x for which the function is a maximum.

18. A prism of square section contains 64 cubic metres of clay, the side of the square being x metres. Express the length of the prism in terms of x and find the total area of its faces. Show that the total area is a minimum when the prism is a cube.

19. $ABCD$ is a square ploughed field of side 132 m, with a path along its perimeter. A man can walk at 8 km/h along the path but only at 5 km/h across the field. He starts from A along AB, leave AB at a point P, and walks straight from P to C. Find the distance of P from A, if the time taken is the least possible.   [L.U.]

20. A piece of string 9 centimetres long has its ends tied to small rings which can slide on a fixed straight rigid wire. If the string is tautened so that, including the portion of the wire between the rings, the figure formed is (i) a rectangle, (ii) a right-angled triangle, the hypotenuse being one portion of the string, find in each case the lengths of the straight portions of the string when the area of the figure is a maximum. Show that the ratio of these maximum areas is $9 : 4\sqrt{3}$. [L.U.]

21. $PQRS$ is a rectangle inscribed in the area bounded by the curve $y = 4x - x^2$ and the x-axis; PQ being parallel to the x-axis and RS lying along that axis. Find the maximum area of $PQRS$. [L.U.]

22. Sketch the curve whose equation is $2y = x^4$. If O is the origin, show that the gradients of the tangent at any point P on the curve and of OP are in a constant ratio. Show also that, if P is in the first quadrant, the acute angle between the tangent at P and OP is a maximum at the point $(1, \frac{1}{2})$. Find this maximum value. [L.U.]

23. Find the values of the constants a and b if there is a point of inflexion on the graph of $y = ax^3 + bx^2 + 2x$ at the point $(1, 0)$.

24. Sketch the graph of $y = x/(x^2 + 1)$, finding the maximum and minimum values of y. Show that the graph lies entirely within the region bounded by the lines $y = \pm\frac{1}{2}$. [L.U.]

25. Sketch the curve $(2 - x)y^2 = (2 + x)x^2$.

CHAPTER 9

THE INTEGRAL CALCULUS

9.1 Introduction

The preceding chapters on the differential calculus have dealt with the rate of change of *known* functions. The integral calculus is concerned with the *inverse* problem—*if the rate of change of a function is known, what is the function itself?* In other words, a function y of x has to be found when the derivative dy/dx is given, that is, y has to be found from the equation

$$\frac{dy}{dx} = \phi(x), \tag{9.1}$$

where $\phi(x)$ is a given function of x.

As an example from dynamics, suppose a particle is moving in a straight line and that its velocity at time t is $u + at$ where u and a are constants. Suppose also that we require to find a formula giving the distance x travelled by the particle in this time. Since the velocity is given by dx/dt, we have to find x from the equation

$$\frac{dx}{dt} = u + at \tag{9.2}$$

and the solution of the problem lies in finding a function x of t whose derivative with respect to t is $u + at$. Anticipating the solution, it is easy to verify that equation (9.2) is satisfied by the formula

$$x = ut + \tfrac{1}{2}at^2,$$

for the derivative of this expression is indeed $u + at$. This solution is not, however, the only one since the formula

$$x = ut + \tfrac{1}{2}at^2 + C,$$

where C is *any* constant, also leads to $dx/dt = u + at$ and this solution is more *general* than the previous one.

The conventional way of writing the solution of equation (9.1) is

$$y = \int \phi(x)\, dx \tag{9.3}$$

and y is called *the indefinite integral of the function* $\phi(x)$ *with respect to* x. The origin of this notation will be explained later (§ 9.8) and at present it will merely be regarded as a means of expressing y when the derivative dy/dx is $\phi(x)$. In this notation, the general solution of equation (9.2) would be written

$$x = \int (u + at)\, dt$$

and we have seen already that this indefinite integral is $ut + \frac{1}{2}at^2 + C$ where C is an arbitrary constant.

There is a big distinction between *direct* and *inverse* operations in mathematics. Differentiation is a direct operation and can be performed according to definite rules to give an unambiguous result. Finding an indefinite integral (the operation known as integration) is an inverse operation; we seek a function whose derivative takes an assigned value. It has been seen in the foregoing example from dynamics that this does not lead to an unique solution—if there is one solution then there are an infinite number due to the presence of the arbitrary constant C in the general result. To discover under what circumstances there is a solution at all is outside the scope of the present book. We shall simply state here that there is a solution (that is, the indefinite integral exists) for a large class of functions and we shall, in this chapter, discuss some of the methods for finding it.

9.2 Standard integrals

There are no infallible rules by which an indefinite integral can be found. As integration is an inverse operation, we can only be guided by the direct operation of differentiation and this is the starting point for the list of standard integrals given below.

This list can be obtained from the list of standard forms for derivatives given in § 7.16. Each derivative in that list gives, on inversion, an indefinite integral as shown below, C being an arbitrary constant in each case.

$$\frac{d}{dx}(x^n) = nx^{n-1}, \qquad \int x^n \, dx = \frac{x^{n+1}}{n+1} + C,$$
$$\text{(except when } n = -1\text{)}.$$

$$\frac{d}{dx}(\sin x) = \cos x, \qquad \int \cos x \, dx = \sin x + C.$$

$$\frac{d}{dx}(\cos x) = -\sin x, \qquad \int \sin x \, dx = -\cos x + C.$$

$$\frac{d}{dx}(\tan x) = \sec^2 x, \qquad \int \sec^2 x \, dx = \tan x + C.$$

$$\frac{d}{dx}(\cot x) = -\operatorname{cosec}^2 x, \qquad \int \operatorname{cosec}^2 x \, dx = -\cot x + C.$$

$$\frac{d}{dx}(\tan^{-1} x) = \frac{1}{1+x^2}, \qquad \int \frac{dx}{1+x^2} = \tan^{-1} x + C.$$

$$\frac{d}{dx}(\sin^{-1} x) = \frac{1}{\sqrt{(1-x^2)}}, \qquad \int \frac{dx}{\sqrt{(1-x^2)}} = \sin^{-1} x + C.$$

Differentiating with respect to x the results given on the right of the second column of the above list, making use of the standard derivatives on the left, it will be seen that in each case the result is the function (called the *integrand*) included within the symbols $\int \ldots dx$. Thus, since

$$\frac{d}{dx}\left(\frac{x^{n+1}}{n+1} + C\right) = \frac{(n+1)x^n}{n+1} = x^n,$$

then

$$\int x^n \, dx = \frac{x^{n+1}}{n+1} + C.$$

Similarly, since

$$\frac{d}{dx}(\tan^{-1} x) = \frac{1}{1+x^2},$$

then

$$\int \frac{dx}{1+x^2} = \tan^{-1} x + C,$$

and so on. It should be noted that the result given for $\int x^n \, dx$ is invalid when $n = -1$; the integral $\int x^{-1} \, dx$ will in fact be discussed later (§ 11.2). It should also be noted that

$$\int \frac{dx}{1+x^2} \quad \text{and} \quad \int \frac{dx}{\sqrt{(1-x^2)}},$$

are convenient ways of denoting integrals which should strictly be written

$$\int \frac{1}{1+x^2} dx \quad \text{and} \quad \int \frac{1}{\sqrt{(1-x^2)}} \, dx.$$

Since, by § 7.10, the derivative of the sum (or difference) of two functions is the sum (or difference) of the derivatives of the separate functions, it follows inversely that *the indefinite integral of the sum (or difference) of two functions is the sum (or difference) of the indefinite integrals of the separate functions*. Thus, if $\phi_1(x)$ and $\phi_2(x)$ are two functions of x,

$$\int \{\phi_1(x) \pm \phi_2(x)\} \, dx = \int \phi_1(x) \, dx \pm \int \phi_2(x) \, dx, \qquad (9.4)$$

and the result can be generalised to three or more functions.

Also, by § 7.11, the derivative of the product of a constant and a function is equal to the product of the constant and the derivative of the function and it follows that *the indefinite integral of the product of a constant and a function is equal to the product of the constant and the indefinite integral of the function.* Thus, if a is a constant and $\phi(x)$ a function of x,

$$\int a\phi(x)\,dx = a \int \phi(x)\,dx. \tag{9.5}$$

The standard integrals and the two rules (9.4), (9.5) given above enable the indefinite integrals of quite a large number of functions to be found easily. Some typical examples follow.

Example 1. *Evaluate* $\int(1 + x)^2\,dx$.

$$\begin{aligned}
\int(1 + x)^2\,dx &= \int(1 + 2x + x^2)\,dx \\
&= \int dx + 2\int x\,dx + \int x^2\,dx \\
&= x + x^2 + \tfrac{1}{3}x^3 + C.
\end{aligned}$$

It should be noted that the given integral is first expressed as the sum of three separate integrals and that $\int dx = \int 1 \, . \, dx = \int x^0\,dx = x$. Also the three arbitrary constants from the three separate integrals can be combined into a single arbitrary constant C.

Example 2. *Evaluate* $\int \left(\dfrac{x^2 + 1}{x^2} \right) dx$. (L.U.)

Since $(x^2 + 1)/x^2$ can be written $1 + (1/x^2)$, we have

$$\begin{aligned}
\int \left(\frac{x^2 + 1}{x^2} \right) dx &= \int \left(1 + \frac{1}{x^2} \right) dx = \int (1 + x^{-2})\,dx \\
&= \int dx + \int x^{-2}\,dx \\
&= x - x^{-1} + C = x - (1/x) + C.
\end{aligned}$$

Example 3. *Integrate* $(x^2 - 4 + x^{-2})\sqrt{x}$ *with respect to x.* [N.U.]

$$\begin{aligned}
\int(x^2 - 4 + x^{-2})\sqrt{x}\,dx &= \int(x^{5/2} - 4x^{1/2} + x^{-3/2})\,dx \\
&= \int x^{5/2}\,dx - 4\int x^{1/2}\,dx + \int x^{-3/2}\,dx \\
&= \tfrac{2}{7}x^{7/2} - \tfrac{8}{3}x^{3/2} - 2x^{-1/2} + C.
\end{aligned}$$

Example 4. *Evaluate* $\int(2x + \sin x)\,dx$.

$$\begin{aligned}
\int(2x + \sin x)\,dx &= 2\int x\,dx + \int \sin x\,dx \\
&= x^2 - \cos x + C.
\end{aligned}$$

Exercises 9 (a)

Integrate the following functions with respect to x

1. $x^{2/3}$.

2. $3/x^2$.

3. $4 - 6x - x^4$.

4. $(3x + 1)^2$. [L.U.]

5. $(x + 1)/\sqrt{x}$. [L.U.]

6. $\left(x^2 + \dfrac{1}{x^2} \right)^2$. [O.C.]

7. $\left(x^2 + \dfrac{1}{x} \right)^2$. [L.U.]

8. $\left(x^2 - \dfrac{2}{x} \right)^2$. [O.C.]

9. $(1 + \sqrt{x})^2/\sqrt{x}$.

10. $3x + 2 \sin x + 4 \sec^2 x$.

11. $x^2 + \dfrac{2}{1 + x^2}$.

12. $\dfrac{4 + x^2}{1 + x^2}$.

Evaluate the following indefinite integrals

13. $\int (3x^2 - x + 7)\,dx$.

14. $\displaystyle\int \dfrac{ax^{-2} + bx^{-1} + c}{x^{-3}}\,dx$.

15. $\displaystyle\int \left(\dfrac{1}{x^3} + \dfrac{1}{x^2} - 4 \right) dx$.

16. $\int (\sin x + 3 \operatorname{cosec}^2 x)\,dx$.

17. $\int (1 - x)^2 \sqrt{x}\,dx$.

18. $\displaystyle\int \dfrac{x^4 + 1}{x^2}\,dx$.

19. $\displaystyle\int \left\{ 3x + \dfrac{2}{\sqrt{(1 - x^2)}} \right\} dx$.

20. $\displaystyle\int \dfrac{x^4 + 2x^2 + 1}{x^2}\,dx$.

21. By using the relation $\sec^2 x = 1 + \tan^2 x$, find the value of $\int \tan^2 x\,dx$. In a similar manner show that $\int \cot^2 x\,dx = C - x - \cot x$.

22. Use the relation $\cos x = 1 - 2 \sin^2 \frac{1}{2}x$ to evaluate $\int \sin^2 \frac{1}{2}x\,dx$.

23. Use the addition formula for $\cos (x + \alpha)$ to show that

$$\int \cos (x + \alpha)\,dx = \sin (x + \alpha) + C.$$

24. Evaluate

$$\text{(i)} \int \dfrac{x^3 + 1}{x + 1}\,dx \quad \text{and} \quad \text{(ii)} \int \dfrac{x^4 + x^2 + 1}{x^2 + x + 1}\,dx.$$

25. If $\sqrt{(1 - x^2)}(dy/dx) = 4$, find the general value of y.

9.3 A more general list of standard integrals

If the derivative of a function $f(x)$ with respect to x is $f'(x)$, the definition of the indefinite integral can be written in the form

$$\int f'(x)\,dx = f(x) + C, \tag{9.6}$$

where C is an arbitrary constant. The rule (7.17) for differentiating a function of a function shows that, if a and b are constants, the derivative with respect to x of $f(ax + b)$ is $af'(ax + b)$. Hence

$$\int af'(ax + b)\,dx = f(ax + b) + C$$

giving

$$\int f'(ax + b)\,dx = \dfrac{1}{a} f(ax + b) + C', \tag{9.7}$$

where $C' = C/a$ is another arbitrary constant.

A comparison of equations (9.6) and (9.7) enables the integral of a function of $(ax + b)$ to be written down when the integral of the *same* function of x is known. We can in fact say that *if the integral of a function of x is known, the integral of the same function of $(ax + b)$ is of the same form but it is divided by a.*

As an example,

$$\int (4x + 3)^3 \, dx = \tfrac{1}{16}(4x + 3)^4 + C$$

for the integral of x^3 is $\tfrac{1}{4}x^4$ and hence the integral of $(4x + 3)^3$ will be $\tfrac{1}{4}(4x + 3)^4$ *divided by* 4, the coefficient of x in $(4x + 3)$. Other examples are

$$\int (x + 2)^2 = \tfrac{1}{3}(x + 2)^3 + C,$$

$$\int (4 - x)^3 \, dx = -\tfrac{1}{4}(4 - x)^4 + C,$$

$$\int \frac{dx}{(3x + 4)^2} = - \frac{1}{3(3x + 4)} + C.$$

Applying (9.7) to the list of standard integrals given in § 9.2, the following more general list of integrals can be obtained. The integrals in this list are important and they should be memorized. In each entry a and b are constants and C is the arbitrary constant of integration.

$$\int (ax + b)^n \, dx = \frac{(ax + b)^{n+1}}{(n + 1) a} + C, \quad \text{except when } n = -1.$$

$$\int \cos (ax + b) \, dx = \frac{1}{a} \sin (ax + b) + C.$$

$$\int \sin (ax + b) \, dx = - \frac{1}{a} \cos (ax + b) + C.$$

$$\int \sec^2 (ax + b) \, dx = \frac{1}{a} \tan (ax + b) + C.$$

$$\int \operatorname{cosec}^2 (ax + b) \, dx = - \frac{1}{a} \cot (ax + b) + C.$$

$$\int \frac{dx}{a^2 + x^2} = \frac{1}{a} \tan^{-1} \frac{x}{a} + C.$$

$$\int \frac{dx}{\sqrt{(a^2 - x^2)}} = \sin^{-1} \frac{x}{a} + C.$$

The above all follow directly from those given in § 9.2 except the last two which are derived as follows

$$\int \frac{dx}{a^2 + x^2} = \int \frac{dx}{a^2\{1 + (x/a)^2\}}$$

$$= \frac{1}{a^2} \cdot \frac{1}{(1/a)} \tan^{-1}\left(\frac{x}{a}\right) + C = \frac{1}{a} \tan^{-1}\left(\frac{x}{a}\right) + C,$$

$$\int \frac{dx}{\sqrt{(a^2 - x^2)}} = \int \frac{dx}{a\sqrt{\{1 - (x/a)^2\}}}$$

$$= \frac{1}{a} \cdot \frac{1}{(1/a)} \sin^{-1}\left(\frac{x}{a}\right) + C = \sin^{-1}\left(\frac{x}{a}\right) + C.$$

It should be noticed that the method given above for generalising our first list of standard integrals only applies when x is replaced by $(ax + b)$, that is, by an expression of the *first* degree in x. It does *not* apply to integrals such as $\int (2x^2 + 3)^3 \, dx$ or $\int \sin(x^3 + 4x + 2) \, dx$ in which x is replaced by expressions of degrees higher than the first. It is also important not to omit the dividing factor a in the second list and in the early stages of this type of work it is advisable to check the correctness of an integration by differentiating the expression obtained. This should, of course, give back the function which was to be integrated.

One other point, which often calls for explanation in the early stages of integration, may be noticed here. If we evaluate the integral of $(x + 1)^2$ by using the first entry in our revised list, we have

$$\int (x + 1)^2 \, dx = \tfrac{1}{3}(x + 1)^3.$$

If, however, we evaluate this integral by first squaring $x + 1$,

$$\int (x + 1)^2 \, dx = \int (x^2 + 2x + 1) \, dx$$
$$= \tfrac{1}{3}x^3 + x^2 + x.$$

This can be written $\tfrac{1}{3}(x^3 + 3x^2 + 3x + 1) - \tfrac{1}{3}$ or $\tfrac{1}{3}(x + 1)^3 - \tfrac{1}{3}$ so that the two results differ by $\tfrac{1}{3}$. This apparent discrepancy can be removed when the arbitrary constant, which so far has been omitted, is included. The two results can be made identical by taking the arbitrary constant as C in the first result and as $C + \tfrac{1}{3}$ in the second. Expressions for indefinite integrals obtained by different methods often appear to differ at first sight; provided, however, that no error has been made, it will be found on examination that all the terms involving the variable of integration are identical and that the results only differ by a constant quantity.

Example 5. *Evaluate* $\int \cos\left(\tfrac{1}{4}\pi - x\right) dx$.

Since $\cos\left(\tfrac{1}{4}\pi - x\right) = \cos\left(-x + \tfrac{1}{4}\pi\right)$, this integral can be evaluated from the second entry of the revised list with $a = -1$, $b = \tfrac{1}{4}\pi$. This gives

$$\int \cos\left(\tfrac{1}{4}\pi - x\right) dx = \left(\frac{1}{-1}\right) \sin\left(\tfrac{1}{4}\pi - x\right) + C$$
$$= -\sin\left(\tfrac{1}{4}\pi - x\right) + C.$$

Example 6. *Evaluate* $\int \sqrt{(2x + 3)}\, dx$.   [L.U.]

From the first entry of the table with $a = 2$, $b = 3$ and $n = \tfrac{1}{2}$ we have

$$\int \sqrt{(2x + 3)}\, dx = \int (2x + 3)^{1/2}\, dx$$
$$= \frac{(2x + 3)^{3/2}}{(3/2)(2)} + C$$
$$= \tfrac{1}{3}(2x + 3)^{3/2} + C.$$

Example 7. *Integrate* $(5 + 4x - x^2)^{-\frac{1}{2}}$ *with respect to* x.   [O.C.]

We can write $5 + 4x - x^2 = 9 - (4 - 4x + x^2) = 3^2 - (x - 2)^2$, so that

$$\int \frac{dx}{\sqrt{(5 + 4x - x^2)}} = \int \frac{dx}{\sqrt{\{3^2 - (x - 2)^2\}}}$$
$$= \sin^{-1}\left(\frac{x - 2}{3}\right) + C,$$

using the last entry of the table with $a = 3$ and $(x - 2)$ in place of x.

Example 8. *Evaluate* $\displaystyle\int \frac{dx}{x^2 + x + 1}$.

Here

$$\int \frac{dx}{x^2 + x + 1} = \int \frac{dx}{(x + \tfrac{1}{2})^2 + \left(\dfrac{\sqrt{3}}{2}\right)^2}$$
$$= \frac{1}{(\sqrt{3}/2)} \tan^{-1}\left(\frac{x + \tfrac{1}{2}}{\sqrt{3}/2}\right) + C$$
$$= \frac{2}{\sqrt{3}} \tan^{-1}\left(\frac{2x + 1}{\sqrt{3}}\right) + C,$$

and we have worked in the same way as in Example 7 above but used the penultimate entry of the revised table.

Exercises 9 (b)

Evaluate the following indefinite integrals

1. $\int \sin(1 - x)\, dx$.

2. $\int \cos 4x\, dx$.

3. $\int \sqrt{(1 - 4x)}\, dx$.

4. $\displaystyle\int \left\{\frac{1}{\sqrt{(x + 2)}} + \sqrt{(x + 2)}\right\} dx$.

5. $\int (2 - x)^5\, dx$.

6. $\displaystyle\int \frac{dx}{\sqrt{(5x - 7)}}$.

7. $\int (2x - 3)^{-3/2} dx$.   [O.C.]   8. $\int \sqrt{(1 + 2x)} \, dx$.   [L.U.]

9. $\int \left\{ \dfrac{1}{(x - 1)^3} - \dfrac{1}{(2 - x)^3} \right\} dx$.   10. $\int \dfrac{dx}{x^2 + 9}$.

11. $\int \dfrac{dx}{\sqrt{(16 - x^2)}}$.   12. $\int \sec^2 2x \, dx$.

13. $\int \dfrac{dx}{9x^2 + 4}$.   14. $\int \dfrac{dx}{\sqrt{(7 + 6x - x^2)}}$.

15. $\int \dfrac{dx}{\sqrt{(25 - 16x^2)}}$.   16. $\int \dfrac{dx}{9x^2 + 6x + 5}$.

17. $\int \dfrac{2dx}{\sqrt{(11 + 4x - 4x^2)}}$.   18. $\int \dfrac{dx}{3x^2 - 4x + 7}$.

19. Show that $(\cos x - \sin x)^2 = 1 - \sin 2x$ and hence evaluate $\int (\cos x - \sin x)^2 \, dx$.

20. Show that

$$\int \frac{x^2 + 2x}{(x - 1)^2} \, dx = \frac{x^2}{x + 1} + C.$$

9.4 Integration by change of variable

Many integrals can be evaluated by changing the variable of integration. As will be seen from the derivation of formula (9.11) below, this method is essentially the inverse of the formula (7.17) for the derivative of a function of a function.

Suppose we change the variable from x to u in the indefinite integral

$$I = \int \phi(x) \, dx. \tag{9.8}$$

By the definition of the integral

$$\frac{dI}{dx} = \phi(x) \tag{9.9}$$

and, if x is a given function of u, formula (7.17) gives

$$\frac{dI}{du} = \frac{dI}{dx} \times \frac{dx}{du}.$$

Substitution of dI/dx from (9.9) then yields

$$\frac{dI}{du} = \phi(x) \frac{dx}{du} \tag{9.10}$$

and, if we again use the definition of the integral,

$$I = \int \phi(x) \frac{dx}{du} \, du. \tag{9.11}$$

The following are two important special cases of formula (9.11)

(i) *The integral $\int \phi(ax + b) \, dx$, a and b constants.*

Writing $ax + b = u$ so that $a(dx/du) = 1$ and $dx/du = 1/a$, formula (9.11) gives

$$\int \phi(ax + b) \, dx = \int \phi(u) \cdot \frac{1}{a} \, du = \frac{1}{a} \int \phi(u) \, du$$

and this is the symbolic expression of the rule given in § 9.3.

(ii) *The integral $\int x\phi(x^2) \, dx$.*

Here we substitute $x^2 = u$ so that $2x(dx/du) = 1$ and $dx/du = 1/2x$. Hence

$$\int x\phi(x^2) \, dx = \int x\phi(u) \left(\frac{1}{2x} \right) du = \frac{1}{2} \int \phi(u) \, du,$$

so that $\int x\phi(x^2) \, dx$ can be evaluated when $\int \phi(u) \, du$ is known. The presence of the "extra x" in $\int x\phi(x^2) \, dx$ should be noted. It is this term which enables the integral to be reduced to the simpler form $\frac{1}{2} \int \phi(u) \, du$. If the "extra x" were absent, the corresponding result would be

$$\int \phi(x^2) \, dx = \frac{1}{2} \int u^{-\frac{1}{2}} \phi(u) \, du$$

and this is not a very useful transformation.

Example 9. *Evaluate $\int 6x\sqrt{(1 - 2x^2)} \, dx$.*

Writing $1 - 2x^2 = u$, $-4x(dx/du) = 1$ giving $dx/du = -1/4x$, so that from (9.11),

$$\int 6x\sqrt{(1 - 2x^2)} \, dx = \int 6x\sqrt{u} \left(-\frac{1}{4x} \right) du = -\frac{3}{2} \int \sqrt{u} \, du$$

$$= -u^{3/2} + C$$

$$= -(1 - 2x^2)^{3/2} + C,$$

when we replace u by $1 - 2x^2$.

For other types of integral, the choice of a successful substitution is a matter of some judgment. It is only possible here to give a few hints and examples.

(*a*) If the integrand contains $(a^2 - x^2)$, it is often useful to use the substitutions $x = a \sin u$ or $x = a \cos u$.

(*b*) When the integrand contains $(a^2 + x^2)$, the substitution $x = a \tan u$ is often effective.

(c) Products of the form $\sin^m x \cos^n x$ where m and n are positive integers and one of them at least is odd can be integrated by the following devices

(i) If n is odd, $n - 1$ will be even and $\cos^{n-1} x$ can be expressed in terms of $\sin x$ by means of $\cos^2 x = 1 - \sin^2 x$; the substitution $\sin x = u$ will then enable the integral to be found:

(ii) If m is odd, $m - 1$ will be even and $\sin^{m-1} x$ can be expressed in terms of $\cos x$ by $\sin^2 x = 1 - \cos^2 x$; the substitution $\cos x = u$ should then be used.

(d) Other substitutions are effective in particular cases. For example, even positive integral powers of $\sec x$ may be integrated by writing $\tan x = u$ and those of cosec x by setting $\cot x = u$. The choice of a suitable substitution is, however, in many cases a matter of judgment and experience; hints are given in some of the exercises which follow.

Example 10. *Evaluate* $\int \dfrac{dx}{\sqrt{(a^2 - x^2)}}$ *by means of the substitutions* (i) $x = a \sin u$, *and* (ii) $x = a \cos u$.

(i) $x = a \sin u$, $dx/du = a \cos u$ and (9.11) gives

$$\int \frac{dx}{\sqrt{(a^2 - x^2)}} = \int \frac{1}{\sqrt{(a^2 - a^2 \sin^2 u)}} \, a \cos u \, du = \int du = u + C$$
$$= \sin^{-1} (x/a) + C,$$

for $\sqrt{(a^2 - a^2 \sin^2 u)} = a \cos u$ and $u = \sin^{-1} (x/a)$.

(ii) $x = a \cos u$, $dx/du = -a \sin u$,

$$\int \frac{dx}{\sqrt{(a^2 - x^2)}} = \int \frac{1}{\sqrt{(a^2 - a^2 \cos^2 u)}} (-a \sin u) du = -\int du = -u + C'$$
$$= - \cos^{-1} (x/a) + C',$$

for now $\sqrt{(a^2 - a^2 \cos^2 u)} = a \sin u$ and $u = \cos^{-1} (x/a)$.

The apparent discrepancy between these two results is explained by the relation $\sin^{-1} x + \cos^{-1} x = \frac{1}{2}\pi$ (see Exercises 3(d), 13). Using this relation, the second result can be written $\sin^{-1} (x/a) - \frac{1}{2}\pi + C'$ and agreement with the first result is secured by writing $C = -\frac{1}{2}\pi + C'$. This is another example of indefinite integrals evaluated by different methods differing by a constant quantity.

Example 11. *Evaluate* $\int \dfrac{dx}{4 + x^2}$ *by writing* $x = 2 \tan u$.

With $x = 2 \tan u$, $dx/du = 2 \sec^2 u$ and

$$\int \frac{dx}{4 + x^2} = \int \frac{1}{4 + 4 \tan^2 u} \, 2 \sec^2 u \, du$$
$$= \tfrac{1}{2}\int du = \tfrac{1}{2}u + C$$
$$= \tfrac{1}{2} \tan^{-1} (x/2) + C,$$

since $\sec^2 u = 1 + \tan^2 u$ and $u = \tan^{-1} (x/2)$.

Example 12. *Find* $\int \sin^5 x \cos x \, dx$.

Here the powers of sin x and cos x are both odd, so either of the methods suggested in (c) above can be used. Choosing the first (it is preferable here), we write sin $x = u$ so that cos $x \, (dx/du) = 1$ and $dx/du = \sec x$. Using (9.11) we therefore have

$$\int \sin^5 x \cos x \, dx = \int u^5 \cos x \sec x \, du = \int u^5 \, du$$
$$= \tfrac{1}{6} u^6 + C = \tfrac{1}{6} \sin^6 x + C.$$

Example 13. *Evaluate* $\int \sin^3 x \cos^2 x \, dx$.

Here the sine is raised to an odd power so we set cos $x = u$. This gives $-\sin x (dx/du) = 1$ and $dx/du = -\operatorname{cosec} x$. $\sin^3 x$ is written as sin $x(1 - \cos^2 x)$ and hence

$$\int \sin^3 x \cos^2 x \, dx = \int \sin x(1 - \cos^2 x) \cos^2 x \, dx$$
$$= \int \sin x(1 - u^2)u^2(-\operatorname{cosec} x) \, du$$
$$= -\int(u^2 - u^4) \, du = -\tfrac{1}{3}u^3 + \tfrac{1}{5}u^5 + C$$
$$= -\tfrac{1}{3}\cos^3 x + \tfrac{1}{5}\cos^5 x + C.$$

Example 14. *Integrate* $\sin^3 x$ *with respect to* x.

Here we use the second method given under (c) for $\sin^3 x$ is a particular case of the product $\sin^m x \cos^n x$ with $m = 3$ (odd) and $n = 0$ (even). Writing cos $x = u$, this gives $dx/du = -\operatorname{cosec} x$ (as in Example 13 above) and

$$\int \sin^3 x \, dx = \int \sin x(1 - \cos^2 x) \, dx$$
$$= \int \sin x(1 - u^2)(-\operatorname{cosec} x) \, du$$
$$= -\int(1 - u^2) \, du = -u + \tfrac{1}{3}u^3 + C$$
$$= -\cos x + \tfrac{1}{3}\cos^3 x + C.$$

Exercises 9 (c)

Integrate the following functions with respect to x

1. $x\sqrt{(1 - x^2)}$.   [O.C.]   2. $x(1 + x^2)^{3/2}$.   [O.C.]

3. $(\sqrt{x})/(x + 1)$.   [L.U.]   4. $\{x + \sqrt{(1 + x^2)}\}^2$.   [O.C.]

5. $x^2/\sqrt{(a^3 + x^3)}$ (Hint, put $a^3 + x^3 = u$).   [L.U.]

6. $x^3/(1 + x^8)$ (Hint, put $x^4 = \tan u$).

7. $\tan x \sec^2 x$ (Hint, put $\tan x = u$).   [O.C.]

8. $x^2/\sqrt{(1 - x^6)}$ (Hint, put $x^3 = \sin u$).

9. $x/(x^4 + 9)$ (Hint, put $x^2 = 3 \tan u$).

10. $(x + 1)/\sqrt{(x^2 + 2x - 9)}$ (Hint, put $x^2 + 2x - 9 = u$).

11. $\sin^2 x \cos^2 x$.   12. $\cos^4 x \sin^3 x$.

13. $\sin^3 x \cos^5 x$.   14. $\cos^3 x$.

15. $\sin^5 x$.   16. $\sin^3 x/\cos^2 x$.   [O.C.]

17. $\sin^3 2x$.   18. $\cos x/\sqrt{(\sin x)}$.

19. Evaluate $\int \dfrac{\cos x \, dx}{1 + \sin^2 x}$ by substituting $\sin x = u$.

20. By writing $3x = \sin u$, integrate $(x - 1)/\sqrt{(1 - 9x^2)}$ with respect to x.

9.5 The integration of products of sines and cosines

The product of two sines, two cosines or a sine and a cosine can be integrated by first expressing the product as a sum or difference by means of the formulae [§ 3.8, equations (3.34), (3.33) and (3.31)]

$$\left.\begin{array}{l} 2 \sin A \sin B = \cos (A - B) - \cos (A + B), \\ 2 \cos A \cos B = \cos (A - B) + \cos (A + B), \\ 2 \sin A \cos B = \sin (A - B) + \sin (A + B). \end{array}\right\} \quad (9.12)$$

Thus

$$\int \sin mx \sin nx \, dx = \tfrac{1}{2}\int\{\cos (m - n)x - \cos (m + n)x\} \, dx$$
$$= \frac{\sin (m - n)x}{2(m - n)} - \frac{\sin (m + n)x}{2(m + n)} + C,$$

$$\int \cos mx \cos nx \, dx = \tfrac{1}{2}\int\{\cos (m - n)x + \cos (m + n)x\} \, dx$$
$$= \frac{\sin (m - n)x}{2(m - n)} + \frac{\sin (m + n)x}{2(m + n)} + C,$$

$$\int \sin mx \cos nx \, dx = \tfrac{1}{2}\int\{\sin (m - n)x + \sin (m + n)x\} \, dx$$
$$= - \frac{\cos (m - n)x}{2(m - n)} - \frac{\cos (m + n)x}{2(m + n)} + C,$$

and these results are valid when $m \neq n$.

It is not recommended that these last three integrals should be committed to memory; it is better to remember the method and apply it to specific examples.

Example 15. *Integrate $\cos 4x \cos 2x$ with respect to x.*

$$\int \cos 4x \cos 2x \, dx = \tfrac{1}{2}\int(\cos 2x + \cos 6x) \, dx$$
$$= \tfrac{1}{2} \left(\frac{\sin 2x}{2} + \frac{\sin 6x}{6} \right) + C$$
$$= \tfrac{1}{4} \sin 2x + \tfrac{1}{12} \sin 6x + C.$$

The integrals of $\sin^2 mx$, $\cos^2 mx$ can be obtained from the double-angle formulae

$$\sin^2 mx = \tfrac{1}{2}(1 - \cos 2mx), \qquad \cos^2 mx = \tfrac{1}{2}(1 + \cos 2mx),$$

which can be deduced by writing $A = B = mx$ in the first two of equations (9.12) and which have also been given in equations (3.20).

Again it is better to use these identities with the particular example under discussion than to attempt to memorize the general integrals.

Example 16. *Evaluate* $\int sin^2 2x\,dx$.

$$\int \sin^2 2x\,dx = \tfrac{1}{2}\int(1 - \cos 4x)\,dx$$
$$= \tfrac{1}{2}(x - \tfrac{1}{4}\sin 4x) + C$$
$$= \tfrac{1}{2}x - \tfrac{1}{8}\sin 4x + C.$$

9.6 Integration by parts

A useful method of integration, known as *integration by parts*, results from the inverse of formula (7.11) for the derivative of the product uv of two functions u and v of x. This is

$$\frac{d}{dx}(uv) = v\frac{du}{dx} + u\frac{dv}{dx}$$

and, using the fundamental definition of the indefinite integral,

$$uv = \int\left(v\frac{du}{dx} + u\frac{dv}{dx}\right)dx.$$

This is easily transposed into

$$\int u\frac{dv}{dx}\,dx = uv - \int v\frac{du}{dx}\,dx \qquad (9.13)$$

and is a useful formula when the integral on the right can be evaluated.

Some judgment must be used in the choice of u and v when employing formula (9.13). For example, if one of the functions involved is an inverse trigonometrical function, this should be taken as u for then the term du/dx in the integral on the right often leads to the integral of a simple algebraical function. This and some other artifices useful in this method of integration are illustrated in the examples which follow.

Example 17. *Evaluate* $\int x\,tan^{-1}x\,dx$.

Take $u = \tan^{-1}x$ and $dv/dx = x$ so that $du/dx = 1/(1 + x^2)$ and $v = \tfrac{1}{2}x^2$. Formula (9.13) then gives

$$\int x\,\tan^{-1}x\,dx = \tfrac{1}{2}x^2\tan^{-1}x - \int(\tfrac{1}{2}x^2)\left(\frac{1}{1 + x^2}\right)dx.$$

The integral on the right can be written in the form

$$\tfrac{1}{2}\int\left(1 - \frac{1}{1 + x^2}\right)dx$$

and this is $\tfrac{1}{2}(x - \tan^{-1}x)$. Hence

$$\int x\,\tan^{-1}x\,dx = \tfrac{1}{2}x^2\tan^{-1}x - \tfrac{1}{2}(x - \tan^{-1}x) + C$$
$$= \tfrac{1}{2}(x^2 + 1)\tan^{-1}x - \tfrac{1}{2}x + C.$$

Example 18. *Integrate x sin x with respect to x.*

If we take $u = \sin x$ and $dv/dx = x$, we have $du/dx = \cos x$ and $v = \frac{1}{2}x^2$. In this case the integral on the right of equation (9.13) becomes $\int \frac{1}{2}x^2 \cos x \, dx$ and this is more complicated than the original integral. If, however, we take $u = x$ and $dv/dx = \sin x$, we have $du/dx = 1$ and $v = -\cos x$. Equation (9.13) then gives

$$\int x \sin x \, dx = -x \cos x - \int (1)(-\cos x) \, dx$$
$$= -x \cos x + \sin x + C.$$

Example 19. *Find $\int x^2 \cos x \, dx$.*

Take $u = x^2$, $dv/dx = \cos x$ so that $du/dx = 2x$ and $v = \sin x$. Then, by (9.13),

$$\int x^2 \cos x \, dx = x^2 \sin x - \int 2x \sin x \, dx$$

and we have related $\int x^2 \cos x \, dx$ to $\int x \sin x \, dx$. This latter integral can itself be evaluated by integrating by parts. Working as in Example 18 above we find

$$\int x \sin x \, dx = -x \cos x + \int \cos x \, dx,$$

and hence

$$\int x^2 \cos x \, dx = x^2 \sin x - 2(-x \cos x + \int \cos x \, dx)$$
$$= x^2 \sin x + 2x \cos x - 2\int \cos x \, dx.$$

Two applications of the rule for integration by parts have therefore related $\int x^2 \cos x \, dx$ with $\int \cos x \, dx$. As the latter is a known integral, we have finally

$$\int x^2 \cos x \, dx = x^2 \sin x + 2x \cos x - 2 \sin x + C.$$

In a similar way $\int x^n \cos x \, dx$ can be related to $\int x^{n-2} \cos x \, dx$ and the latter integral can be related to $\int x^{n-4} \cos x \, dx$ and so on. If n is a positive integer we shall be left with either $\int x \cos x \, dx$ or $\int \cos x \, dx$ to evaluate in order to determine completely the original integral. Both these integrals can in fact be found and integration performed in this way is known as "integration by successive reduction". Such a method is of considerable importance but it is beyond the scope of this book to pursue it except in very simple special cases.

Example 20. *Evaluate $\int \cos^2 x \, dx$ by the method of integration by parts.*

Although integration by parts is not the best method of evaluating $\int \cos^2 x \, dx$, the working shown below illustrates an artifice which is sometimes useful. Take $u = dv/dx = \cos x$ so that $du/dx = -\sin x$ and $v = \sin x$. Hence, by (9.13),

$$\int \cos^2 x \, dx = \cos x \sin x - \int \sin x (-\sin x) \, dx$$
$$= \cos x \sin x + \int \sin^2 x \, dx.$$

Since $\sin^2 x = 1 - \cos^2 x$, this can be written

$$\int \cos^2 x \, dx = \cos x \sin x + \int (1 - \cos^2 x) \, dx$$
$$= \cos x \sin x + \int dx - \int \cos^2 x \, dx,$$

giving, when the last term on the right is transposed to the left

$$2\int \cos^2 x \, dx = \cos x \sin x + x + C.$$

Hence

$$\int \cos^2 x \, dx = \frac{1}{2} \cos x \sin x + \frac{1}{2}x + C',$$

where $C' = \frac{1}{2}C$ is an arbitrary constant.

Exercises 9 (d)

Evaluate the following integrals

1. $\int \cos 3x \cos 2x \, dx$.

2. $\int \sin 3x \cos x \, dx$.

3. $\int \sin 3x \sin 2x \, dx$.

4. $\int \cos 4x \sin 2x \, dx$.

5. $\int x \cos x \, dx$.

6. $\int x\sqrt{(1 + x)} \, dx$.

7. $\int x^2\sqrt{(1 + x)} \, dx$.

8. $\int \sin^{-1} x \, dx$.

9. $\displaystyle\int \frac{x \sin^{-1} x}{\sqrt{(1 - x^2)}} \, dx$.

10. $\int x \sin 2x \, dx$.

11. $\int x^2 \sin x \, dx$.

12. $\int (\pi - x) \sin 3x \, dx$.

13. Use the method of integration by parts to find

$$\text{(i) } \int \sin^2 x \, dx, \quad \text{(ii) } \int \sin x \cos x \, dx.$$

14. By taking $u = \sqrt{(1 - x^2)}$ and $v = x$, use formula (9.13) to show that

$$\int \sqrt{(1 - x^2)} \, dx = \tfrac{1}{2}x\sqrt{(1 - x^2)} + \tfrac{1}{2} \sin^{-1} x + C.$$

15. If $U_n = \int x^n \cos x \, dx$ and $V_n = \int x^n \sin x \, dx$, show that

$$U_n = x^n \sin x - nV_{n-1} \text{ and } V_n = -x^n \cos x + nU_{n-1}.$$

Deduce that

$$U_n = x^{n-1} (x \sin x + n \cos x) - n(n - 1)U_{n-2}.$$

9.7 Area as the limit of a sum

As a preliminary to a second interpretation of the operation of integration, we give below an example of the calculation of an area by regarding it as the limiting value of a certain sum.

Fig. 81 shows the graph of $y = 1 + x$, A and B being two points on the graph with abscissae 0 and 10 respectively. B' is the projection of B on the axis OX and hence $OB' = 10$, $OA = 1$ and $BB' = 11$ units.

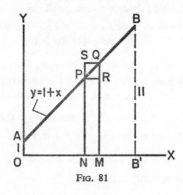

FIG. 81

The figure $OB'BA$ is a trapezium of base 10, mean height 6 and its area A is therefore 60 units.

The area A might also be calculated as follows. Divide it into n strips of equal width $10/n$ by lines parallel to the axis OY and suppose the rth strip is $PNMQ$. Since for the first of such strips PN lies along OY, for the second strip PN is distant $10/n$ from OY, for the third strip PN is at distance $2(10/n)$ from OY and so on, the distance of PN from OY for the rth strip will be $(r-1)(10/n)$. Similarly the distance of QM from OY for the rth strip will be $r(10/n)$. Thus for the strip shown in Fig. 81, the abscissa of P is $(r-1)(10/n)$ and, since P lies on the graph of $y = 1 + x$, the ordinate PN will be given by

$$PN = 1 + \frac{10(r-1)}{n} = 1 - \frac{10}{n} + \frac{10r}{n}. \qquad (9.14)$$

Similarly the length QM is given by

$$QM = 1 + \frac{10r}{n}. \qquad (9.15)$$

By drawing PR and QS parallel to OX, it can be inferred that the area of the trapezium $OB'BA$ is greater than the sum of the areas of n rectangles like $PNMR$ and that it is less than the sum of the areas of n rectangles like $SNMQ$. Since the length NM of the base of these rectangles is $10/n$,

$$\text{area rectangle } PNMR = \frac{10}{n}\left(1 - \frac{10}{n} + \frac{10r}{n}\right) = \frac{10}{n} - \frac{100}{n^2} + \frac{100r}{n^2},$$

$$\text{area rectangle } SNMQ = \frac{10}{n}\left(1 + \frac{10r}{n}\right) = \frac{10}{n} + \frac{100r}{n^2}.$$

The sum of n rectangles of which $PNMR$ is typical is therefore

$$\left(\frac{10}{n} - \frac{100}{n^2} + \frac{100}{n^2}\right) + \left(\frac{10}{n} - \frac{100}{n^2} + \frac{200}{n^2}\right) + \left(\frac{10}{n} - \frac{100}{n^2} + \frac{300}{n^2}\right) +$$

$$\ldots + \left(\frac{10}{n} - \frac{100}{n^2} + \frac{100n}{n^2}\right)$$

$$= \left(\frac{10}{n} - \frac{100}{n^2}\right)(1 + 1 + 1 + \ldots \text{ to } n \text{ terms}) + \frac{100}{n^2}(1 + 2 + 3 + \ldots$$

$$+ n)$$

$$= \left(\frac{10}{n} - \frac{100}{n^2}\right)(n) + \frac{100}{n^2}\left\{\frac{n(n+1)}{2}\right\} = 10 - \frac{100}{n} + \frac{50(n+1)}{n}$$

$$= 60 - \frac{50}{n}.$$

The sum of n rectangles of which $SNMQ$ is typical can be found in the same way to be $60 + (50/n)$, and hence

$$60 - \frac{50}{n} < A < 60 + \frac{50}{n}. \qquad (9.16)$$

By dividing OB' into 10 equal parts, that is by taking $n = 10$, we have from (9.16)

$$55 < A < 65,$$

while if we use 100 strips ($n = 100$),

$$59{\cdot}5 < A < 60{\cdot}5.$$

By taking $n = 1000$ we should find that the area A lies between $59{\cdot}95$ and $60{\cdot}05$ and equation (9.16) shows that the area A lies between $60 - \varepsilon$ and $60 + \varepsilon$ where ε can be made as small as we please by making n sufficiently large.

It should be noted that as the number n of rectangles such as $PNMR$ and $SNMQ$ increases, their width ($10/n$) decreases and the area A can be estimated with increasing precision. The area $OB'BA$ is, in fact, the limiting value to which the sum of the areas of the strips approaches as their number increases and their width decreases.

9.8 The integral as the limiting value of a sum

The method outlined in § 9.7 could be used to find the area below curves like $y = 3 + x^2$, $y = \sin 3x$, etc., but the summations involved would, of course, be more complicated. It is instructive, however, to apply a similar method to the general curve $y = \phi(x)$ and we shall find that this leads to the idea of regarding an integral as the limiting value of a certain sum.

To simplify matters, the graph of $y = \phi(x)$ shown in Fig. 82 is that of a function which is positive and which increases as x increases from $x = a$ to $x = b$. AA', BB' are the ordinates at $x = a$, $x = b$ and we consider the area $AA'B'B$. As in § 9.7, this area is divided into n strips of which $PNMQ$ is typical and we take $ON = x$, $OM = x + \delta x$, $PN = y$, $QM = y + \delta y$. The graph of $y = \phi(x)$ is assumed to meet the axis OY at the point H and we use the notation $A(x)$ to denote the area of the figure $HONP$ bounded by the curve, the coordinate axes and the line PN. When x increases to $x + \delta x$, the area $HONP$ increases to the area $HOMQ$ and we denote this area by $A(x) + \delta A(x)$. Hence

$$\delta A(x) = \text{area } HOMQ - \text{area } HONP = \text{area } PNMQ. \qquad (9.17)$$

It can be inferred from Fig. 82 that

$$\text{area } PNMR < \text{area } PNMQ < \text{area } SNMQ,$$

and, since

$$PN = y, \quad QM = y + \delta y, \quad NM = OM - ON = x + \delta x - x = \delta x,$$

$$\text{area } PNMR = y \, \delta x, \quad \text{area } SNMQ = (y + \delta y) \, \delta x,$$

giving, when substitution is made from these and (9.17),

$$y \, \delta x < \delta A(x) < (y + \delta y) \, \delta x. \tag{9.18}$$

These inequalities have been obtained by consideration of the strip $PNMQ$ and there will be $(n - 1)$ other inequalities of this type arising from similar consideration of the other $(n - 1)$ strips making up the

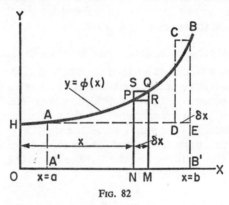

FIG. 82

area $AA'B'B$. Using the symbol Σ to denote the summation of the n results of which (9.18) is typical, we have

$$\Sigma y \, \delta x < \text{area } AA'B'B < \Sigma(y + \delta y) \, \delta x, \tag{9.19}$$

since $\Sigma \delta A(x)$ is the total area $AA'B'B$.

In Fig. 82, AE is drawn parallel to the axis OX and the rectangular strip $BCDE$ is constructed so that its width is δx. By sliding the rectangle $PRQS$ parallel to OX until QR lies along BE, it can be seen that the area $BCDE$ is equal to the sum of the areas of n rectangles of which $PRQS$ is typical. But this sum is the difference between the sum of the areas of n rectangles of which $SNMQ$ is typical and the sum of the areas of n rectangles of which $PNMR$ is typical. Hence

$$\Sigma(y + \delta y) \, \delta x - \Sigma y \, \delta x = \text{area } BCDE = BE \cdot \delta x,$$

giving

$$\Sigma(\delta y) \, \delta x = BE \cdot \delta x. \tag{9.20}$$

Since $\delta x = A'B'/n$, it can be made to be arbitrarily small by taking n to be sufficiently large and equation (9.20) shows that $\Sigma(\delta y) \, \delta x$ tends to zero as δx tends to zero. Thus $\Sigma(y + \delta y) \, \delta x$ and $\Sigma y \, \delta x$ tend to the same limit as δx tends to zero and, since (9.19) shows that the area $AA'B'B$ lies between quantities which tend to the same limit, it follows that

$$\text{area } AA'B'B = \lim_{\delta x \to 0} (\Sigma y \, \delta x). \qquad (9.21)$$

The limit on the right of equation (9.21) is denoted by the symbols $\int_a^b y \, dx$ and is called *the definite integral of y with respect to x taken over the range $x = a$ to $x = b$*. The symbol $\int$ is a specialised form of the letter S which was the symbol used for the operation of summation before the letter Σ was employed. The letters a and b are called respectively the *lower and upper limits of integration* and they indicate the range over which the summation is made.

9.9 The relation between the definite and indefinite integral

Except in very simple cases such as that considered in § 9.7, the method of § 9.8 is not a practical method of determining the area below a given curve because of the complicated summations involved. We can, however, relate the definition of the definite integral with that of the indefinite integral (given in § 9.1 as the inverse of the derivative) and this leads to a practical method for the calculation of area.

To establish this relation, we return to the inequalities (9.18) which, after division by δx, can be written

$$y < \frac{\delta A}{\delta x} < y + \delta y,$$

where, for brevity, A has been used in place of $A(x)$. Assuming* that δy tends to zero as δx tends to zero, this shows that

$$y = \frac{dA}{dx} \qquad (9.22)$$

and, since y is the derivative of A, A is the indefinite integral of y.

Now, in § 9.8, A measures the area $HONP$ of Fig. 82, and

$$\text{area } AA'B'B = \text{area } HOB'B - \text{area } HOA'A = A(b) - A(a);$$

hence

$$\int_a^b y \, dx = \lim_{\delta x \to 0} (\Sigma y \, \delta x) = \text{area } AA'B'B$$

$$= A(b) - A(a). \qquad (9.23)$$

---

* For the functions used in this book δy always tends to zero with δx. The reader is, however, warned that there are functions used in more advanced mathematics where this is not so.

This equation relates the definite integral $\int_a^b y\,dx$ with the indefinite integral A given by (9.22). Writing $y = \phi(x)$, equation (9.23) shows that $\int_a^b \phi(x)\,dx$ *measures the area enclosed by the curve* $y = \phi(x)$, *the axis of* x *and the two ordinates at* $x = a$, $x = b$.

In § 9.8 it was assumed that the graph of $y = \phi(x)$ was one in which y was positive and increasing with x. If y decreases as x increases, a similar argument will show that the inequality signs in (9.18) are reversed but it is still true that $\delta A/\delta a$ will lie between y and $y + \delta y$ and equations (9.22), (9.23) remain valid. If y increases while x increases for part of the range in x and then decreases as x increases over the other part of the range, the integral or area can be found in two parts and the results summed. If y is negative for certain values of x, say between $x = \alpha$ and $x = \beta$, the value of $\int_\alpha^\beta y\,dx$ will be negative (see § 10.2).

9.10 The example of § 9.7 solved by integration

The area enclosed by the graph of $y = 1 + x$, the axis of x and ordinates at $x = 0$, $x = 10$ is, by (9.23), $A(10) - A(0)$ where $A(x)$ is the indefinite integral $\int(1 + x)dx = x + \frac{1}{2}x^2 + C$. Hence

$$A(10) = 10 + \tfrac{1}{2}(10)^2 + C = 60 + C,$$
$$A(0) = 0 + \tfrac{1}{2}(0)^2 + C = C,$$

and the area $AOB'B = 60 + C - C = 60$ as found in § 9.7.

This example shows that in evaluating an area or definite integral, the arbitrary constant of the indefinite integral may be omitted. If the notation $[A(x)]_a^b$ is used to denote the difference $A(b) - A(a)$, a convenient way of setting out the above work is

$$\text{area } AOB'B = \int_0^{10} (1 + x)\,dx$$
$$= \left[x + \tfrac{1}{2}x^2\right]_0^{10}$$
$$= 10 + \tfrac{1}{2}(10)^2 - 0 - \tfrac{1}{2}(0)^2 = 60.$$

The connection between the limiting value of a sum and integration has therefore made it possible to avoid the summation processes of § 9.7. In the present instance, this is not a matter of much importance for the summations are simple and the area involved (being that of a trapezium) can be otherwise found. In more general cases, in which areas are bounded by *curves*, the summations are more difficult and the areas cannot usually be easily found by geometrical methods. In such cases, integration provides a useful means of carrying out the calculations.

9.11 Some examples of the evaluation of definite integrals and calculation of area

Here we give some examples of the method of setting out the work involved in evaluating a definite integral. Some applications of the integral calculus to the calculation of areas are also given.

Example 21. *Evaluate* $\int_1^2 \left(x - \dfrac{1}{x}\right)^2 dx$. [L.U.]

$$\int_1^2 \left(x - \frac{1}{x}\right)^2 dx = \int_1^2 (x^2 - 2 - x^{-2})\, dx$$
$$= \left[\tfrac{1}{3}x^3 - 2x + \frac{1}{x}\right]_1^2$$
$$= \tfrac{1}{3}(2)^3 - 2(2) + \tfrac{1}{2} - \tfrac{1}{3}(1)^3 + 2(1) - 1$$
$$= -\tfrac{1}{6}.$$

Example 22. *Evaluate* $\int_0^{\pi/4} \tan^2 x\, dx$. [L.U.]

$$\int_0^{\pi/4} \tan^2 x\, dx = \int_0^{\pi/4} (\sec^2 x - 1)\, dx$$
$$= \left[\tan x - x\right]_0^{\pi/4}$$
$$= \tan\frac{\pi}{4} - \frac{\pi}{4} - \tan 0 + 0$$
$$= 1 - \frac{\pi}{4}.$$

Example 23. *Evaluate* $\int_0^{\pi/2} \cos 4x \sin x\, dx$. [L.U.]

$$\int_0^{\pi/2} \cos 4x \sin x\, dx = \tfrac{1}{2}\int_0^{\pi/2} (\sin 5x - \sin 3x)\, dx$$
$$= \tfrac{1}{2}\left[-\tfrac{1}{5}\cos 5x + \tfrac{1}{3}\cos 3x\right]_0^{\pi/2}$$
$$= \tfrac{1}{2}\left\{-\tfrac{1}{5}\cos\frac{5\pi}{2} + \tfrac{1}{3}\cos\frac{3\pi}{2} + \tfrac{1}{5}\cos 0 - \tfrac{1}{3}\cos 0\right\}$$
$$= \tfrac{1}{2}(\tfrac{1}{5} - \tfrac{1}{3}) = -\tfrac{1}{15}.$$

Example 24. *Find the area bounded by the curve* $y = 3x^2 + 2x + 1$, *the axis of* x *and ordinates at* $x = 1$, $x = 3$.

The required area $= \int_1^3 (3x^2 + 2x + 1)\, dx$
$$= \left[x^3 + x^2 + x\right]_1^3$$
$$= (3)^3 + (3)^2 + 3 - (1)^3 - (1)^2 - 1$$
$$= 36 \text{ units.}$$

Example 25. *Calculate the area of the segment of the curve $y^2 = 4x$ cut off by the line $y = x$.* [L.U.]

Fig. 83 shows the graphs of $y^2 = 4x$ and $y = x$. The graphs intersect at the origin O and the point P with coordinates $(4, 4)$. The area of the segment cut off, shown shaded, is the difference between the areas bounded respectively by $y^2 = 4x$ and $y = x$, the axis of x and ordinates at $x = 0$, $x = 4$. Hence the required area

$$= \int_0^4 \sqrt{(4x)}\, dx - \int_0^4 x\, dx = \int_0^4 (2\sqrt{x} - x)\, dx$$

$$= \left[\frac{4}{3} x^{3/2} - \frac{x^2}{2}\right]_0^4 = \frac{4}{3}(4)^{3/2} - \frac{(4)^2}{2}$$

$$= \frac{32}{3} - 8 = \frac{8}{3} \text{ units.}$$

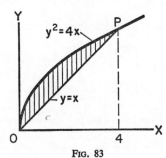

Fig. 83

9.12 Definite integrals by change of variable

Two methods are available for evaluating a definite integral when the integration is performed by change of variable. In the first, the indefinite integral is found and expressed in terms of the original variable and then the limits of integration are inserted. In the second (and usually preferable) method, everything, including the limits, is expressed in terms of the new variable. Both methods are illustrated in Example 26 below; in the remaining examples, only the second method is used.

Example 26. *Evaluate* $\int_0^{\pi/2} \sin^2 x \cos x\, dx$. [L.U.]

Method 1. Put $\sin x = u$, so that $\cos x\, (dx/du) = 1$ giving $dx/du = \sec x$. Hence,

$$\int \sin^2 x \cos x\, dx = \int u^2 \cos x \sec x\, du = \int u^2\, du,$$
$$= \tfrac{1}{3} u^3 = \tfrac{1}{3} \sin^3 x,$$

giving

$$\int_0^{\pi/2} \sin^2 x \cos x\, dx = \left[\tfrac{1}{3} \sin^3 x\right]_0^{\pi/2} = \tfrac{1}{3}\left(\sin^3 \frac{\pi}{2} - \sin^3 0\right) = \tfrac{1}{3}.$$

Method 2. Using the same substitution $\sin x = u$, the indefinite integral

$$\int \sin^2 x \cos x\, dx$$

can as before be reduced to $\int u^2\, du$. At the lower limit of integration $x = 0$, so that since $\sin x = u$, the lower limit of the integral in u will be given by $u = \sin 0 = 0$. Similarly, since $x = \frac{1}{2}\pi$ at the upper limit of the integral in x, the upper limit of the integral in u will be given by $u = \sin \frac{1}{2}\pi = 1$. Hence

$$\int_0^{\pi/2} \sin^2 x \cos x\, dx = \int_0^1 u^2\, du = \left[\tfrac{1}{3}u^3\right]_0^1 = \tfrac{1}{3}.$$

Example 27. *Use the substitution $x = \sin^2 u$ to show that*

$$\int_0^{\frac{1}{2}} \sqrt{\left(\frac{x}{1-x}\right)}\, dx = \tfrac{1}{4}(\pi - 2). \qquad \text{[L.U.]}$$

If $x = \sin^2 u$, $dx/du = 2 \sin u \cos u$. When $x = 0$, $\sin^2 u = 0$ and $u = 0$; when $x = \frac{1}{2}$, $\sin^2 u = \frac{1}{2}$, $\sin u = 1/\sqrt{2}$ and $u = \frac{1}{4}\pi$. Hence the limits in the integral in u are 0 and $\frac{1}{4}\pi$ giving

$$\int_0^{\frac{1}{2}} \sqrt{\left(\frac{x}{1-x}\right)}\, dx = \int_0^{\pi/4} \sqrt{\left(\frac{\sin^2 u}{1 - \sin^2 u}\right)} 2 \sin u \cos u\, du$$

$$= \int_0^{\pi/4} 2 \sin^2 u\, du, \quad \text{since } \sqrt{(1 - \sin^2 u)} = \cos u,$$

$$= \int_0^{\pi/4} (1 - \cos 2u)\, du$$

$$= \left[u - \tfrac{1}{2}\sin 2u\right]_0^{\pi/4} = \frac{\pi}{4} - \frac{1}{2}\sin\frac{\pi}{2}$$

$$= \tfrac{1}{4}(\pi - 2).$$

Example 28. *Evaluate* $\int_{-\pi/4}^{\pi/4} \tan^2 x \sec^2 x\, dx$.

Putting $\tan x = u$, $\sec^2 x(dx/du) = 1$ and $dx/du = \cos^2 x$. When $x = -\pi/4$, $u = \tan(-\pi/4) = -1$ and when $x = \pi/4$, $u = \tan(\pi/4) = 1$. Hence

$$\int_{-\pi/4}^{\pi/4} \tan^2 x \sec^2 x\, dx = \int_{-1}^1 u^2 \sec^2 x \cos^2 x\, du$$

$$= \int_{-1}^1 u^2\, du = \left[\tfrac{1}{3}u^3\right]_{-1}^1$$

$$= \tfrac{1}{3} + \tfrac{1}{3} = \tfrac{2}{3}.$$

Exercises 9 (e)

Evaluate the following definite integrals

1. $\displaystyle\int_1^4 x^{5/2}\, dx.$ [L.U.]   2. $\displaystyle\int_{-2}^2 (x^2 + x)\, dx.$ [O.C.]

3. $\displaystyle\int_{-\pi/4}^{\pi/4} (\sec^2 x - 1)\, dx.$ [O.C.]   4. $\displaystyle\int_1^2 \frac{(x^2 + 1)^2}{x^2}\, dx.$ [L.U.]

5. $\displaystyle\int_1^4 \left(\sqrt{x} + \frac{1}{\sqrt{x}}\right) dx.$ [L.U.]   6. $\displaystyle\int_0^2 \frac{dx}{\sqrt{(4 - x^2)}}.$ [L.U.]

7. $\displaystyle\int_0^{\pi/3} \cos x \cos 3x \, dx.$ [L.U.] 8. $\displaystyle\int_0^{\pi/4} \sin 5x \cos 3x \, dx.$ [L.U.]

9. $\displaystyle\int_0^{\pi/4} (x-1) \sin 2x \, dx.$ [L.U.] 10. $\displaystyle\int_0^{\pi/4} \sin^3 x \cos x \, dx.$ [L.U.]

11. Show that $\displaystyle\int_0^{\pi/4} (\tan^3 x + \tan x) \, dx = \tfrac{1}{2}.$ [N.U.]

12. Prove that $\displaystyle\int_0^{\pi/2} (\sin x + \cos x)^2 \, dx = 1 + \tfrac{1}{2}\pi.$ [N.U.]

13. By means of the substitution $u = \sin^2 x$, prove that

$$\int_0^{\pi/2} \sin^7 x \cos^5 x \, dx = \frac{1}{120}.$$ [O.C.]

14. Evaluate

(i) $\displaystyle\int_0^1 x^2(1+x^3)^2 \, dx,$ (ii) $\displaystyle\int_0^1 \frac{x^2 \, dx}{(1+x^3)^2}.$ [N.U.]

15. Evaluate, by means of the substitution $x = \sec^2 u$,

$$\int_1^2 \frac{dx}{x^2\sqrt{(x-1)}}.$$ [O.C.]

16. Calculate the area enclosed by the curve $y = x^2(1-x)$, the axis of x and ordinates at $x = 0$, $x = 1$. [N.U.]

17. Find the area enclosed by the axis of x and that part of the curve $y = 5x - 6 - x^2$ for which y is positive. [O.C.]

18. Find the area enclosed between the curve $y = \sqrt{(x^3)}$ and the straight line $y = 2x$. [O.C.]

19. Find the area enclosed between the curves $y^2 = 4x$ and $x^2 = 4y$. [O.C.]

20. Show that the area contained by the curve $y = a + bx + cx^2 + dx^3$, the axis of x and the ordinates at $x = \pm h$ is equal to $h(y_1 + y_2)$ where y_1 and y_2 are the values of y when $x = \pm h/\sqrt{3}$. [L.U.]

9.13 Numerical integration

It often happens in practice that the value of the definite integral $\displaystyle\int_a^b \phi(x) \, dx$ is required and that we are unable to find a function whose derivative is $\phi(x)$. Instances in which the values of $\phi(x)$ are only known numerically and not by a formula also often occur. In such cases, an approximate value of the integral can be found by numerical methods and we describe below some of these methods.

Since the definite integral $\displaystyle\int_a^b \phi(x)\,dx$ represents the area enclosed by the graph of $y = \phi(x)$, the x-axis and ordinates at $x = a$, $x = b$, a simple method of evaluating it is to draw a diagram on squared paper and to estimate the area by counting the squares enclosed. To enable reasonable accuracy to be obtained, a large scale graph is usually required.

Example 29. *Plot the graph of $y = 1/(1 + x)$ on squared paper. By counting squares, estimate the area bounded by the curve, the coordinate axes and an ordinate at $x = 1$. Hence deduce an approximate value for the definite integral $\displaystyle\int_0^1 (1 + x)^{-1}\,dx$.*

The values of $y = 1/(1 + x)$ for $x = 0, 0\cdot1, 0\cdot2, \ldots, 0\cdot9, 1\cdot0$ are

x	0·0	0·1	0·2	0·3	0·4	0·5	0·6	0·7	0·8	0·9	1·0
y	1·000	0·909	0·833	0·769	0·714	0·667	0·625	0·588	0·556	0·526	0·500

and these are plotted in Fig. 84. It should be noted that

100 small squares = 1 large square = $0\cdot1 \times 0\cdot1 = 0\cdot01$

and hence that 1 small square = $0\cdot0001$. In estimating the number of squares in the area below the curve it is helpful to draw in the dotted stepped line shown and it is easily found that the area below this occupies 63 large squares. The number of small squares between the curve and the dotted line is, by actual counting, found to be approximately 620. Hence the total number of small squares in the area is $(63 \times 100) + 620 = 6920$. The required area and value of the given definite integral is therefore approximately $6920 \times 0\cdot0001$, that is, $0\cdot692$.

Another method is to use the *trapezoidal rule* which is derived by dividing the area into a number of strips and taking the area of each of these strips to be approximately that of a trapezium. In Fig. 85, the area $AA'B'B$ below the curve $y = \phi(x)$ has been divided into six strips by dividing $A'B'$ into six equal parts. Ordinates y_0, y_1, y_2, y_3, y_4, y_5 and y_6 have been erected at A', B' and at each point of sub-division. We consider the first strip $AA'P'P$ (shown enlarged in Fig. 86) and it is clear that its area is only slightly less than the area of the trapezium $AA'P'P$. We can therefore use the area of this trapezium as an approximation for the area of the strip. The mean height of the trapezium is $\frac{1}{2}(y_0 + y_1)$ and, if we use h for the length $A'P'$ of its base, we therefore have area of strip $AA'P'P \simeq \frac{1}{2}h(y_0 + y_1)$. Treating the other five

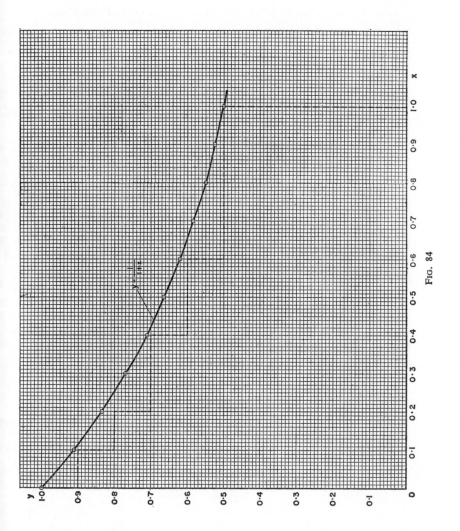

$$y = \frac{1}{1+x^2}$$

Fig. 84

strips of Fig. 85 in the same way, we shall find that the total area of $AA'B'B$ is approximately given by

$$\text{area } AA'B'B \simeq \tfrac{1}{2}h(y_0 + y_1) + \tfrac{1}{2}h(y_1 + y_2) + \ldots + \tfrac{1}{2}h(y_5 + y_6)$$
$$= h\{\tfrac{1}{2}(y_0 + y_6) + y_1 + y_2 + y_3 + y_4 + y_5\}$$

and, since $A'B' = b - a$ and we have used six strips, $h = \tfrac{1}{6}(b - a)$.

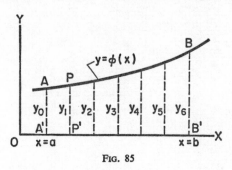

FIG. 85

In the same way, using n strips, we shall find that the area $AA'B'B$, or the definite integral $\displaystyle\int_a^b \phi(x)\,dx$ is approximately equal to

$$h\{\tfrac{1}{2}(y_0 + y_n) + y_1 + y_2 + \ldots + y_{n-2} + y_{n-1}\}$$

where now $h = (b - a)/n$. This formula, which is known as the trapezoidal rule, can be expressed by saying that *if the range of integration from $x = a$ to $x = b$ is divided into n equal parts each of width*

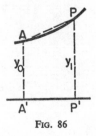

FIG. 86

$h = (b - a)/n$, called the interval, and ordinates to the graph of $y = \phi(x)$ are erected at $x = a$, $x = b$ and at each point of sub-division, then

$$\int_a^b \phi(x)\,dx \simeq \text{interval} \times (\text{half the sum of the first and last ordinates} + \text{the sum of the remaining ordinates}). \qquad (9.24)$$

It should be clear from its method of derivation that the approximation of the trapezoidal rule (9.24) improves as the number of strips used increases. It should also be apparent that the rule over-estimates the value of the integral in those parts of the range where the graph of $y = \phi(x)$ is of the shape shown in Fig. 85 and that it underestimates it if $y = \phi(x)$ is of the shape depicted in Fig. 87.

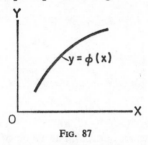

FIG. 87

In deriving the trapezoidal rule, we have replaced arcs of the curve bounding the area by straight lines and the use of this rule is not always most economical in labour. If great accuracy is required, a large number of ordinates are necessary and the amount of numerical work involved may become quite heavy. Another method, known as

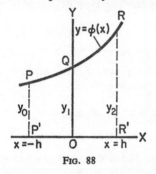

FIG. 88

Simpson's rule, can be set up by replacing arcs of the graph of $y = \phi(x)$ by arcs of the curve $y = Ax^2 + Bx + C$.

In Fig. 88, PQR is an arc of the graph of $y = \phi(x)$ intersecting the axis of y at Q and PP', RR' are ordinates at $x = -h$ and $x = h$ respectively. The lengths PP', QO, RR' are taken as y_0, y_1 and y_2. Since the equation $y = Ax^2 + Bx + C$ contains three constants A, B and C the graph of this function can be made to pass through the three points $P(-h, y_0)$, $Q(0, y_1)$ and $R(h, y_2)$. For this to occur, A, B and C satisfy the equations

$$y_0 = Ah^2 - Bh + C, \qquad y_1 = C, \qquad y_2 = Ah^2 + Bh + C,$$

and it follows that

$$2(Ah^2 + C) = y_0 + y_2, \qquad C = y_1.$$

Provided the widths h of the strips $PP'OQ$, $QOR'R$ are not too large, the area below the curve $y = Ax^2 + Bx + C$ will be a good approximation to the area shown in Fig. 88 and hence

$$\int_{-h}^{h} \phi(x)\, dx \simeq \int_{-h}^{h} (Ax^2 + Bx + C)\, dx$$

$$= \left[\tfrac{1}{3}Ax^3 + \tfrac{1}{2}Bx^2 + Cx \right]_{-h}^{h} = \tfrac{2}{3}Ah^3 + 2Ch$$

$$= \tfrac{1}{3}h(2Ah^2 + 6C) = \tfrac{1}{3}h\{2(Ah^2 + C) + 4C\}$$

$$= \tfrac{1}{3}h(y_0 + y_2 + 4y_1) \tag{9.25}$$

when we substitute for $2(Ah^2 + C)$ and C.

Formula (9.25) gives an approximate value of the integral when the range of integration ($2h$) is divided into two strips each of width h, when y_0, y_2 are the ordinates at the ends and when y_1 is the ordinate at the mid-point of the range. If this formula is applied to the area in Fig. 85, the addition of three pairs of such strips gives

$$\int_{a}^{b} \phi(x)\, dx \simeq \tfrac{1}{3}h(y_0 + y_2 + 4y_1) + \tfrac{1}{3}h(y_2 + y_4 + 4y_3)$$

$$+ \tfrac{1}{3}h(y_4 + y_6 + 4y_5)$$

$$= \tfrac{1}{3}h\{y_0 + y_6 + 4(y_1 + y_3 + y_5) + 2(y_2 + y_4)\}.$$

In a similar way, if the range of integration is divided into an even number $2n$ of strips each of width h,

$$\int_{a}^{b} \phi(x)\, dx \simeq \tfrac{1}{3}h\{y_0 + y_{2n} + 4(y_1 + y_3 + \ldots + y_{2n-1})$$

$$+ 2(y_2 + y_4 + \ldots + y_{2n-2})\} \tag{9.26}$$

where $h = (b - a)/2n$. This formula, known as Simpson's rule, can be expressed thus—*if the range of integration from $x = a$ to $x = b$ is divided into an even number $2n$ of equal parts each of width $h = (b - a)/2n$, called the interval, and ordinates to the graph of $y = \phi(x)$ are erected at $x = a$, $x = b$ and at each point of sub-division, then*

$$\int_{a}^{b} (x)\, dx \simeq \tfrac{1}{3} \times interval \times (sum\ of\ first\ and\ last\ ordinates$$

$$+\ four\ times\ the\ sum\ of\ all\ the\ odd\ ordinates$$

$$+\ twice\ the\ sum\ of\ the\ remaining\ even\ ordinates).$$

Both the trapezoidal and Simpson's rules (9.24) and (9.26) can be used to evaluate definite integrals when the integrand $\phi(x)$ is given by a numerical table or by a mathematical formula. In the latter case, a table given the numerical values of $\phi(x)$ at equal intervals has to be computed. Two examples are given below. In the first, the integrand is given numerically; the second, in which the integrand is $1/(1 + x^2)$, has been chosen so that the approximate results can be compared with the known exact result.

Example 30. *Use the trapezoidal and Simpson's rules to evaluate* $\int_9^{10} y\,dx$ *when y is given in terms of x by the following table*

x	9·0	9·25	9·5	9·75	10·0
y	0·1111	0·1081	0·1053	0·1026	0·1000

A convenient way of setting out the work is as follows

x	First and last ordinates	Odd ordinates	Remaining even ordinates
9·0	0·1111		
9·25		0·1081	
9·5			0·1053
9·75		0·1026	
10·0	0·1000		
Sum	0·2111	0·2107	0·1053

The interval h is 0·25, the sum of the first and last ordinates is 0·2111 and the sum of all the remaining ordinates is 0·2107 + 0·1053, that is, 0·3160. Hence the trapezoidal rule (9.24) gives

$$\int_9^{10} y\,dx \simeq 0\cdot25(\tfrac{1}{2} \times 0\cdot2111 + 0\cdot3160) = 0\cdot10539.$$

Simpson's rule (9.26) yields

$$\int_1^{10} y\,dx \simeq \tfrac{1}{3} \times 0\cdot25(0\cdot2111 + 4 \times 0\cdot2107 + 2 \times 0\cdot1053) = 0\cdot10538.$$

Thus to four places of decimals, the values of the definite integral obtained by the two rules are each 0·1054.

Example 31. *Use the trapezoidal and Simpson's rules with eleven ordinates to find approximate values of* $\int_0^1 \dfrac{dx}{1 + x^2}$. *Compare your results with the exact value of the integral.*

The first step is to tabulate the integrand $1/(1 + x^2)$ for $x = 0\cdot0, 0\cdot1, 0\cdot2, \ldots,$ 0·9, 1·0 and the results are shown in the second column of the table below. The entries in the remainder of this table are similar to those used in Example 30 above and the work proceeds in the same way.

x	$\dfrac{1}{1 + x^2}$	First and last ordinates	Odd ordinates	Remaining even ordinates
0·0	1·0000	1·0000		
0·1	0·9901		0·9901	
0·2	0·9615			0·9615
0·3	0·9174		0·9174	
0·4	0·8621			0·8621
0·5	0·8000		0·8000	
0·6	0·7353			0·7353
0·7	0·6711		0·6711	
0·8	0·6098			0·6098
0·9	0·5525		0·5525	
1·0	0·5000	0·5000		
Sum		1·5000	3·9311	3·1687

Since the interval $h = 0\cdot1$, the trapezoidal rule gives

$$\int_0^1 \frac{dx}{1 + x^2} \simeq 0\cdot1(\tfrac{1}{2} \times 1\cdot5000 + 3\cdot9311 + 3\cdot1687) = 0\cdot7850.$$

By Simpson's rule,

$$\int_0^1 \frac{dx}{1 + x^2} \simeq \tfrac{1}{3} \times 0\cdot1(1\cdot5000 + 4 \times 3\cdot9311 + 2 \times 3\cdot1687)$$
$$= 0\cdot7854.$$

The exact value of the integral is

$$\int_0^1 \frac{dx}{1 + x^2} = \left[\tan^{-1} x \right]_0^1 = \tan^{-1}(1) - \tan^{-1}(0) = \tfrac{1}{4}\pi = 0\cdot7854,$$

so that the result obtained by Simpson's rule is correct to four places of decimals. The value given by the trapezoidal rule is an underestimate: to obtain similar accuracy, more ordinates, and therefore more labour, would be necessary with this rule.

Exercises 9 (f)

1. Values of y for various values of x are given by

x	1·00	1·25	1·50	1·75	2·00
y	2·000	1·024	0·593	0·373	0·250

By plotting a graph of y against x and estimating the area beneath it obtain an approximate value for the definite integral $\int_1^2 y\,dx$.

2. Find approximate values of $\int_1^2 y\,dx$ from the data of Exercise 1 above by using (i) the trapezoidal rule and (ii) Simpson's rule.

3. Use the trapezoidal rule to find the value of the definite integral $\int_0^{240} \phi(x)\,dx$ given that

x	0	40	80	120	160	200	240
$\phi(x)$	0·1	13·5	16·7	17·1	15·4	10·7	0·1

4. Use Simpson's rule to evaluate $\int_0^{240} \phi(x)\,dx$ given that

x	0	24	48	72	96	120	144	168	192	216	240
$\phi(x)$	0·1	8·5	14·5	16·3	17·1	17·1	16·3	14·6	12·1	6·1	0·1

5. Use the trapezoidal rule and an interval of unity to evaluate $\int_0^8 2^x\,dx$.

6. Given that the correct value of $\int_1^3 x^{-1}\,dx$ to four places of decimals is 1·0986, show that the percentage errors in evaluating the integral by Simpson's rule with intervals in x of 1, $\frac{1}{2}$ and $\frac{1}{4}$ are respectively approximately 1·14, 0·13 and 0·01.

7. Equidistant ordinates of a curve are at $x = 1\cdot0000, 0\cdot4444, 0\cdot2500, 0\cdot1600$ and 0·1111. Use Simpson's rule to estimate the area bounded by the curve, the axis of x and the extreme ordinates which are at $x = 0$ and $x = 2$.

8. Corresponding values of x and y are

x	0	1	2	3	4	5	6
y	0	2	2·5	2·3	2	1·7	1·5

Use Simpson's rule to evaluate the definite integral $\pi \int_0^6 y^2\,dx$.

9. Use Simpson's rule and an interval of 0·05 in x to evaluate the definite integral $\int_0^{\frac{1}{2}} \frac{dx}{\sqrt{(1 - x^2)}}$. Compare your result with the exact value of the integral.

10. Use Simpson's rule and an interval of $\frac{1}{6}\pi$ to show that

$$\int_0^\pi \frac{\sin x \, dx}{x} \simeq 1\cdot852.$$

Exercises 9 (g)

1. Integrate $4x(x^2 + 3x + 3)$ with respect to x.

2. Evaluate the indefinite integral $\int\{(3x + 2)^2 + 4\cos x\}\,dx$.

3. Integrate $3x(x^2 - 4)^2$ with respect to x.

4. Show that

$$\int \frac{dx}{2x^2 + 2x + 25} = \frac{1}{7}\tan^{-1}\left(\frac{2x + 1}{7}\right) + C.$$

5. Use the formulae $\sin 3x = 3\sin x - 4\sin^3 x$ and $\cos 3x = 4\cos^3 x - 3\cos x$ to show that

$$\int \cos^3 x \, dx = \sin x - \tfrac{1}{3}\sin^3 x + C.$$

6. Show that $2\sin(x - \frac{1}{3}\pi)\cos(x + \frac{1}{3}\pi) = \sin 2x - \frac{1}{2}\sqrt{3}$ and hence integrate $\sin(x - \frac{1}{3}\pi)\cos(x + \frac{1}{3}\pi)$ with respect to x.

7. Integrate with respect to x
    $$\text{(i) } \sec^2(2x + 1), \qquad \text{(ii) } \sin 2x \cos x.$$

8. Use the substitution $x = \sqrt{u}$ to find
    $$\text{(i) } \int x\sqrt{(1 + x^2)}\,dx, \qquad \text{(ii) } \int \frac{x\,dx}{1 + x^4}.$$

9. Evaluate
    $$\text{(i) } \int (3x + 1)(3x^2 + 2x + 4)^2\,dx, \qquad \text{(ii) } \int \frac{(3x + 1)\,dx}{(3x^2 + 2x + 4)^3}.$$

10. If $t = \tan\frac{1}{2}x$, show that
    $$\text{(i) } \frac{dx}{dt} = \frac{2}{1 + t^2}, \qquad \text{(ii) } 1 - \cos x = \frac{2t^2}{1 + t^2}.$$

     Hence find the value of

$$\int \frac{dx}{1 - \cos x}.$$

11. Show that $\displaystyle\int_\alpha^{2\alpha} \sin 2x \, dx = \sin\alpha\sin 3\alpha$ and find a similar result for $\displaystyle\int_\alpha^{2\alpha} \cos 2x \, dx.$

12. For what value of a is $\displaystyle\int_0^{\pi/2} x \sin x \, dx = \int_0^2 (ax^2 + 2x) dx$?

13. Evaluate the definite integrals

$$\text{(i)} \int_0^1 x(1 - x)^5 dx, \qquad \text{(ii)} \int_0^2 \sqrt{(1 + 2x^2)}\, dx. \qquad \text{[L.U.]}$$

14. Show that $\displaystyle\int_0^{\pi/2} x \sin^2 x \, dx = \frac{1}{16}(\pi^2 + 4)$.   [O.C.]

15. By means of the substitution $x^2 = 1/u$, show that

$$\int_1^2 \frac{dx}{x^2\sqrt{(5x^2 - 1)}} = \tfrac{1}{2}\sqrt{19} - 2. \qquad \text{[O.C.]}$$

16. Evaluate the definite integrals

$$\int_0^{\pi/8} \sec^2 2x \, dx, \qquad \text{(ii)} \int_0^{\pi/2} \sin 2x(1 - \sin 2x)\, dx. \qquad \text{[L.U.]}$$

17. Find the values of the constants a, b, c and d such that

$$\frac{x^4}{1 + x^2} \equiv ax^2 + bx + c + \frac{d}{1 + x^2}.$$

Use these results and the method of integration by parts to show that

$$\int_0^1 x^3 \tan^{-1} x \, dx = \tfrac{1}{6}.$$

18. By means of the substitution $x = \pi - y$ show that

$$\int_0^\pi xf(\sin x) \, dx = \tfrac{1}{2}\pi \int_0^\pi f(\sin x) \, dx.$$

Hence evaluate

$$\int_0^\pi \frac{x \sin^3 x}{1 + \cos^2 x} \, dx. \qquad \text{[N.U.]}$$

19. Calculate the area between the curve $y = 4 + 2x - x^2$ and the line $y = 4$.

20. Show that the area enclosed by the curve $y = \phi(x)$, the axis of y and abscissae at $y = \alpha$, $y = \beta$ is $\displaystyle\int_\alpha^\beta x \, dy$. Hence show that the area between the curve $y = 2x^2$, the y-axis and the lines $y = 1$, $y = 4$ is $(7\sqrt{2})/3$ units.

21. The curve $y = 11x - 24 - x^2$ cuts the axis of x at points A, B and PN is the greatest positive ordinate. Show that $2PN \cdot AB$ equals three times the area bounded by that portion of the curve which lies in the first quadrant.   [L.U.]

9

22. A line of slope m through the origin O meets the graph of $y = 2x - x^2$ at the point P. If the area between the curve and the line OP is half the whole area between the curve and the axis of x, show that $m = 2 - (4)^{\frac{1}{3}}$.

23. The coordinates (x, y) of points on a curve are given by

x	0	5	10	15	20	25	30	35	40	45	50
y	0	10	18	20	19	20	17	7	3	1	0

Use Simpson's rule to find the area between the curve and the axis of x.

24. Using an interval of unity in x, estimate to one place of decimals the value of the definite integral $\displaystyle\int_0^6 \sqrt{(4 + x^3)}\, dx$ by (i) the trapezoidal rule, (ii) Simpson's rule.

25. The function $J_0(z)$ is given by the formula

$$\pi J_0(z) = \int_0^\pi \cos(z \sin x)\, dx.$$

Use Simpson's formula and an interval of $\frac{1}{6}\pi$ to show that $J_0(1) \simeq 0{\cdot}765$.

CHAPTER 10

SOME APPLICATIONS OF THE INTEGRAL CALCULUS

10.1 Introduction

This chapter gives a few of the many applications of the integral calculus. These include the calculation of mean values, volumes, centres of gravity, moments of inertia and some straightforward dynamical applications. As in Chapter 8 on the applications of the differential calculus, the notation adopted is that which occurs naturally in the problem under discussion. The reader must therefore be prepared to use the results given in Chapter 9 with appropriate changes of symbols when these are called for.

10.2 Further examples of the calculation of area

The formula $\int_a^b \phi(x)\,dx$ for the area bounded by the curve $y = \phi(x)$, the axis of x and ordinates at $x = a$, $x = b$ was established in § 9.9, equation (9.23). If the curve $y = \phi(x)$ lies below the axis of x, y is negative and the area obtained for the above definite integral will be negative (see Example 1 below). If therefore the *whole* area enclosed by a curve which crosses the axis of x at points between the two extreme abscissae is required, it is best to appeal to a diagram and to divide the range of integration into appropriate sub-ranges. Such a procedure is illustrated in Example 2.

Example 1. *Calculate the area between the curve $y = 3x(x-4)$ and the axis of x.*

The area required is shown shaded in the rough sketch of the curve shown in Fig. 89. Hence the required area

$$= \int_0^4 y\,dx = \int_0^4 3x(x-4)\,dx$$

$$= \int_0^4 (3x^2 - 12x)\,dx$$

$$= \left[x^3 - 6x^2\right]_0^4 = -32 \text{ units,}$$

and the negative sign is explained by the fact that the curve lies below the axis of x for the range of values of x under consideration.

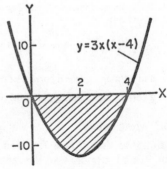

FIG. 89

259

Example 2. *Find the whole area bounded by the curve $y = \cos x$, the axis of x, and ordinates at $x = 0$, $x = \pi$.*

A sketch of the curve is shown in Fig. 90 and it is clear that

$$\text{area } OAB = \int_0^{\frac{1}{2}\pi} \cos x \, dx$$

$$= \left[\sin x \right]_0^{\frac{1}{2}\pi} = 1,$$

$$\text{area } BCD = \int_{\frac{1}{2}\pi}^{\pi} \cos x \, dx$$

$$= \left[\sin x \right]_{\frac{1}{2}\pi}^{\pi} = -1.$$

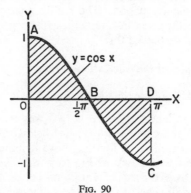

Fig. 90

The whole area, shown shaded, is therefore 2 units and the working could have been set out thus,

$$\text{whole area} = \int_0^{\frac{1}{2}\pi} \cos x \, dx - \int_{\frac{1}{2}\pi}^{\pi} \cos x \, dx = \left[\sin x \right]_0^{\frac{1}{2}\pi} - \left[\sin x \right]_{\frac{1}{2}\pi}^{\pi}$$
$$= 1 - 0 - (0 - 1) = 2.$$

If the range of integration had not been sub-divided at $x = \frac{1}{2}\pi$, the result would have been

$$\text{area} = \int_0^{\pi} \cos x \, dx = \left[\sin x \right]_0^{\pi} = 0,$$

and although this is a correct value of the definite integral $\int_0^{\pi} \cos x \, dx$, it is not a correct interpretation in terms of area.

10.3 Mean values

Suppose that y is a function $\phi(x)$ of x whose graph is shown in Fig. 91 and suppose that the range $A'B'$ from $x = a$ to $x = b$ is divided into n equal sub-ranges each of width δx. Let $y_1, y_2, y_3, \ldots, y_n$ be the values of y at the middle points of these sub-ranges. The arithmetic mean of these n values of y is

$$\frac{1}{n}(y_1 + y_2 + y_2 + \ldots + y_n)$$

and, since $n \, \delta x = b - a$, this can be written

$$\frac{(y_1 + y_2 + y_3 + \ldots + y_n) \, \delta x}{b - a}.$$

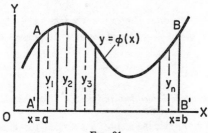

FIG. 91

If this expression has a limiting value as δx approaches zero, this limiting value is

$$\frac{1}{b-a} \int_a^b y \, dx \qquad (10.1)$$

and this is called the "*mean value*" of y over the range $b - a$.

Fig. 92 is a reproduction of Fig. 91 without the details of the sub-ranges. The rectangle $LA'B'M$ has been constructed on the base $A'B'$

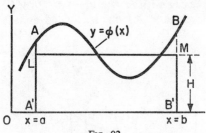

FIG. 92

so that its area is equal to the area enclosed by the curve $y = \phi(x)$, the axis of x and ordinates at $x = a$, $x = b$. The area of the rectangle is therefore $\int_a^b y \, dx$ and, if its height is H, it is also equal to $(b - a)H$.

Hence

$$(b - a)H = \int_a^b y \, dx$$

and, comparison with equation (10.1), shows that H is the mean value of y over the range $b - a$. Thus the geometrical interpretation of the mean value of a function $y = \phi(x)$ over the range $x = a$ to $x = b$ is the height of the rectangle of base $b - a$ whose area is equal to that included between the graph of $y = \phi(x)$, the axis of x and ordinates at $x = a$, $x = b$.

Example 3. *Find the mean value of $\sin x$ over the range $x = 0$ to $x = \frac{1}{2}\pi$.*

Here $y = \sin x$, $a = 0$, $b = \frac{1}{2}\pi$ and formula (10.1) gives for the mean value $\bar{y}$ of y,

$$\bar{y} = \frac{1}{\frac{1}{2}\pi - 0} \int_0^{\frac{1}{2}\pi} \sin x \, dx = \frac{2}{\pi} \left[- \cos x \right]_0^{\frac{1}{2}\pi} = \frac{2}{\pi} = 0.637.$$

Example 4. *A number n is divided into two parts. Show that the mean value of the product of these parts is $\frac{1}{6}n^2$.*

If x is one part into which the number n is divided, the other part is $n - x$ and the product of the two parts is $x(n - x)$. Since x can range from 0 to n, the required mean value of the product is

$$\frac{1}{n - 0} \int_0^n x(n - x) \, dx = \frac{1}{n} \left[\frac{1}{2}nx^2 - \frac{1}{3} x^3 \right]_0^n = \frac{1}{6}n^2.$$

10.4 Volumes of solids of revolution

Another simple application of the integral calculus is the calculation of the volume of the solid formed by the rotation of the curve $y = \phi(x)$ about the axis of x.

Fig. 93 shows the graph of $y = \phi(x)$, again for simplicity shown as positive and increasing with x. As in § 9.8, $PNMQ$ is one of the n strips into which the area $AA'B'B$ is divided and $ON = x$, $PN = y$,

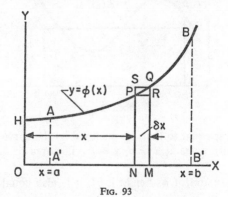

Fig. 93

$NM = \delta x$. The volume formed by the rotation about the axis of x of the strip $PNMQ$ will be greater than the volume formed by the rotation of the rectangle $PNMR$ and less than that formed by the rotation of the rectangle $SNMQ$. The body formed by the rotation of the rectangle $PNMR$ will be a circular cylinder of radius $PN = y$ and length $NM = \delta x$, so that its volume will be $\pi y^2 \delta x$. Similarly the volume formed by the rotation of the rectangle $SNMQ$ will be $\pi(y + \delta y)^2 \, \delta x$ for the radius of this cylinder is $QM = y + \delta y$. Taking the volume formed by the rotation of the area $HONP$ to be $V(x)$, that formed by the rotation of the area $HOMQ$ will be $V(x) + \delta V(x)$ so that, by subtraction, the volume formed by the rotation of the strip $PNMQ$ will be $\delta V(x)$. Hence

$$\pi y^2 \, \delta x < \delta V(x) < \pi(y + \delta y)^2 \, \delta x.$$

Denoting by V the volume of the solid formed by rotating the area $AA'B'B$ we have, since this area is made up of n strips of which $PNMQ$ is typical,

$$\Sigma \pi y^2 \, \delta x < V < \Sigma \pi(y + \delta y)^2 \, \delta x.$$

Using a similar argument to that of § 9.8, these inequalities lead to

$$V = \lim_{\delta x \to 0} (\Sigma \pi y^2 \, \delta x)$$

$$= \int_a^b \pi y^2 \, dx = \pi \int_a^b y^2 \, dx \qquad (10.2)$$

and this is the required formula for the volume of a solid of revolution.

In § 9.8 and in the above, we have derived formulae for area and volume by setting up inequalities for the "elements" of area and volume. Thus we have shown that the element of volume δV lies between $\pi y^2 \, \delta x$ and $\pi(y + \delta y)^2 \, \delta x$ and deduced that the whole volume V is the limiting value of $\Sigma \pi y^2 \, \delta x$ as δx tends to zero. To save repeating these arguments when making other applications of the integral calculus, it is worth noticing that equation (10.2) can be obtained *formally* by saying that the element of volume is *approximately* $\pi y^2 \, \delta x$ and that the whole volume is given from the limiting value of the sum of such elements in the form $\int_a^b \pi y^2 \, dx$.

Example 5. *The area enclosed by the curve $x = 3(y^2 - 1)$ and the lines $x = 0$, $x = 24$ is rotated through four right angles about the axis of x. Find the volume of the solid generated.* [L.U.]

Here $y^2 = 1 + \tfrac{1}{3}x$ and the required volume V is given by

$$V = \pi \int_0^{24} y^2 \, dx = \pi \int_0^{24} (1 + \tfrac{1}{3}x) \, dx$$

$$= \pi \left[x + \tfrac{1}{6}x^2 \right]_0^{24} = \pi \left(24 + \frac{576}{6} \right) = 120\pi \text{ units.}$$

Example 6. *Find the volume of a right circular cone of height h and base radius r.*

In Fig. 94, OP is the straight line through the origin O and the point $P(h, r)$. The slope of OP is r/h and its equation is

$$y = \frac{r}{h} x.$$

A cone of the required dimensions can be formed by rotating this line about the axis of x and its volume V is given by

$$V = \pi \int_0^h y^2 \, dx = \pi \int_0^h \left(\frac{rx}{h}\right)^2 dx$$
$$= \frac{\pi r^2}{h^2} \int_0^h x^2 \, dx = \frac{\pi r^2}{h^2} \left[\frac{1}{3} x^3\right]_0^h = \frac{1}{3}\, \pi r^2 h,$$

as given in § 8.3.

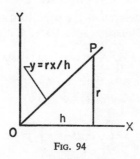

FIG. 94

Exercises 10 (a)

1. Sketch the curve $y = x(x - 1)(x - 2)$ and find the area enclosed by the curve and the axis of x between $x = 0$, $x = 2$.

2. Sketch the curve $y = x(3 - x)$ and find the area contained between the curve, the axis of x and ordinates at $x = 0$, $x = 5$.

3. An ordinate is drawn to the curve $y = x(1 - x^2)$ at $x = 1 + p$ where $p > 0$. Find p so that the area between the axis of x and the curve for x between 1 and $1 + p$ may equal in absolute magnitude the area between the curve and the axis of x for x between 0 and 1.   [L.U.]

4. Find the mean value of the ordinate of the curve $y = 4 - x^2$ over the range $-2 \leqslant x \leqslant 2$.

5. Find the mean values, as x varies from 0 to π, of

   (i) $\sin^2 x$,   (ii) $x \sin x$.

6. The pressure p kilogrammes per square centimetre and the volume v cubic centimetres of a quantity of gas are related by the law $pv^{1\cdot2} = 1000$. Find the mean pressure as the volume of gas increases from 3 cm³ to 8 cm³.

7. The quantities v, x and t are related by the equations

$$v = 2\sqrt{(a^2 - x^2)}, \qquad x = a \sin 2t.$$

Show that the mean value of v, considered as a function of t, between $t = 0$ and $t = \frac{1}{4}\pi$ is $(4a)/\pi$.

8. Find the volume generated when the area enclosed by the axis of x and the curve $y = 3x^2 - x^3$ is rotated about the axis of x. [L.U.]

9. The portion of the curve $xy = 8$ from $x = 2$ to $x = 4$ is rotated about the axis of x; find the volume generated. [L.U.]

10. The area enclosed by the curve $by = b^2 - x^2$, the axis of x and the ordinates $x = \pm a$ $(a < b)$ revolves through four right angles about the axis of x. Show that the volume of the solid formed is

$$\frac{2\pi a}{15b^2} (3a^4 - 10a^2b^2 + 15b^4). \qquad \text{[L.U.]}$$

11. The area between the curve $y = \cos x$ $(0 \leqslant x \leqslant \frac{1}{2}\pi)$ and the coordinate axes is rotated about the axis of x to form a solid of revolution. Find its volume. [L.U.]

12. Sketch the curve $y^2 = (x - 1)(x^2 - 1)$. If the curve is rotated about the axis of x through an angle 2π, show that the volume enclosed by the surface swept out by the loop of the curve is $4\pi/3$. [L.U.]

13. That part of the curve $x^2 + y^2 = a^2$ for which y is positive is rotated through two right angles about the axis of x. Show that the solid so formed is divided by the plane formed by the rotation of the ordinate at $x = \frac{1}{2}a$ into two segments whose volumes are in the ratio $27 : 5$. [O.C.]

14. O is the origin and P the point $(a, 2a)$ on the graph of $y^2 = 4ax$. The area bounded by the chord OP and the arc of the curve between O and P is revolved about the axis of x through four right angles. Find the volume of the solid so generated. [O.C.]

15. The area bounded by the curve $y^2 = 20x$ and the lines $x = 0$ and $y = 10$ is rotated about the axis of y. Show that the volume of the solid obtained is 50π and find the volume of the solid obtained by rotating the same area about the axis of x. [O.C.]

10.5 Centres of gravity

Consider a system of particles lying in a plane whose weights are $w_1, w_2, \ldots, w_n$ and whose positions $P_1, P_2, \ldots, P_n$ have coordinates $(x_1, y_1), (x_2, y_2), \ldots, (x_n, y_n)$ with respect to axes OX, OY (Fig. 95). If the plane OXY is horizontal, the weights of the particles will all act in a direction perpendicular to the plane and* will have a resultant

* The concepts of the resultant of a system of forces and its moment are developed in Chapter 14.

$w_1 + w_2 + \ldots + w_n$. If this resultant acts at the point $(\bar{x}, \bar{y})$, the moment of the resultant about the axis OY is equal to the sum of the moments of the separate weights about this axis and we shall have

$$(w_1 + w_2 + \ldots + w_n)\bar{x} = w_1 x_1 + w_2 x_2 + \ldots + w_n x_n. \quad (10.3)$$

In the same way, by taking moments about OX,

$$(w_1 + w_2 + \ldots + w_n)\bar{y} = w_1 y_1 + w_2 y_2 + \ldots + w_n y_n. \quad (10.4)$$

We have assumed in the above that the weights of the particles form a system of parallel forces. Strictly speaking, these forces act through the centre of the earth's gravitational field but, as the bodies dealt with in practice are usually small compared with the earth, this is a reasonable assumption and one which also allows us to take $w_1, w_2, \ldots, w_n$

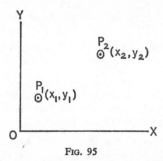

Fig. 95

as being proportional to the masses $m_1, m_2, \ldots, m_n$ of the various particles. In the case therefore of particles distributed over an area small enough for these approximations to be made, we can write equations (10.3) and (10.4) in the form

$$M\bar{x} = N_x, \qquad M\bar{y} = N_y, \quad (10.5)$$

where $M = \Sigma m$, $N_x = \Sigma mx$, $N_y = \Sigma My$ and the sign Σ denotes summation over all the particles of the system. M is the total mass, N_x and N_y are sometimes called the *first moments* with respect to x and y respectively, and the point $(\bar{x}, \bar{y})$ is called the *centre of mass* or the *centre of gravity*.

To obtain an extension from a system of particles to a continuous body, it is natural to replace the particles by "elements" of the body and to use limiting sums (that is, integrals) in place of summations. Before doing this, one general observation should be made. If a uniform body has a centre of symmetry G such that for every particle A of the body there is a corresponding particle A' of equal mass and if G is the mid-point of AA', then the resultant of the weights of A and A' may be taken to act at G. Every other such pair of points can be dealt with similarly and G is therefore also the centre of gravity of the body. Thus the centre of gravity of a uniform thin rod is at its mid-point, that of a uniform parallelogram is at the intersection of its diagonals, that of a uniform circle or sphere is at the geometrical centre, and so on.

Consider first a thin rod of length l and variable density situated along the axis of x with one end of the rod at the origin. Let the density of the rod at a point of abscissa x be ρ. If δM be the mass of an element of the rod for points whose abscissae lie between x and $x + \delta x$, δM lies between $\rho\, \delta x$ and $(\rho + \delta \rho)\, \delta x$. The total mass M can be considered as the limiting value as δx tends to zero of the sum of the approximate elementary masses $\rho\, \delta x$, that is $M = \int_0^l \rho\, dx$. In the same way the first moment δN_x of the element is approximately $x\rho\, \delta x$ so that $N_x = \int_0^l x\rho\, dx$ and the abscissa $\bar{x}$ of the centre of gravity of the rod is given by (10.5) as

$$\bar{x} = \frac{N_x}{M} = \frac{\displaystyle\int_0^l x\rho\, dx}{\displaystyle\int_0^l \rho\, dx}. \tag{10.6}$$

Example 7. *The density of a rod AB varies as the distance from the end A. Find the position of the centre of gravity of the rod if its total length is 2 metres.*

If we take the rod to be along the axis of x with the end A at the origin, the density ρ at a point with abscissa x is kx, where k is a constant. The element of mass is approximately $kx\, \delta x$ and the total mass M is given by

$$M = \int_0^2 kx\, dx = k\left[\tfrac{1}{2}x^2\right]_0^2 = 2k.$$

The first moment of the element is approximately $x \cdot kx\delta x$ and hence

$$N_x = \int_0^2 kx^2 dx = k\left[\tfrac{1}{3}x^3\right]_0^2 = \frac{8k}{3}.$$

The abscissa $\bar{x}$ of the centre of gravity is given by

$$\bar{x} = \frac{N_x}{M} = \left(\frac{8k}{3}\right)\Big/\left(2k\right) = \frac{4}{3},$$

so that the centre of gravity is at 1·333 metres from the end A.

Now consider the centre of gravity of a lamina of *uniform* density bounded by the curve $y = \phi(x)$, the axis of x and ordinates at $x = a$, $x = b$. If ρ is the density, the mass M of the lamina is given by $M = \rho \times \text{area} = \rho \int_a^b y\, dx$. The element $PNMQ$ of Fig. 96 has approximate area $y\, \delta x$ and mass $\rho y\, \delta x$. Its first moment with respect to x is

$x \cdot \rho y \, \delta x$ and the total first moment N_x is given by $\displaystyle\int_a^b xpy \, dx$. Since ρ is constant this can be written $\displaystyle\rho \int_a^b xy \, dx$ and formula (10.5) gives for the abscissa $\bar{x}$ of the centre of gravity

$$\bar{x} = \int_a^b xy \, dx \div \int_a^b y \, dx. \qquad (10.7)$$

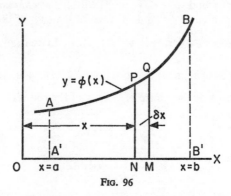

FIG. 96

Since the centre of gravity of the element $PNMQ$ is approximately at a height $\frac{1}{2}y$ above OX, its first moment with respect to y is $\frac{1}{2}y \cdot \rho y \, \delta x$ and we find that the ordinate $\bar{y}$ of the centre of gravity is given by

$$\bar{y} = \frac{1}{2}\int_a^b y^2 \, dx \div \int_a^b y \, dx. \qquad (10.8)$$

The point $(\bar{x}, \bar{y})$, found by assuming uniform density of material over an area, is usually called the *centroid* of the area; when the density is uniform the centroid and the centre of gravity coincide.

Example 8. *The perpendicular to the axis OX from a point $P(2, 6)$ on the curve $y = \frac{3}{4}x^3$ meets OX at Q. Find the coordinates of the centroid of the lamina bounded by the arc OP and the lines OQ, OP.*   [O.C.]

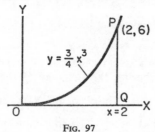

FIG. 97

From Fig. 97, it is clear that the limits a and b of the integrals in (10.7), (10.8) are respectively 0 and 2. Since $y = \frac{3}{4}x^3$,

$$\int_0^2 y\,dx = \frac{3}{4}\int_0^2 x^3\,dx = \frac{3}{4}\left[\frac{1}{4}x^4\right]_0^2 = 3,$$

$$\int_0^2 xy\,dx = \frac{3}{4}\int_0^2 x^4\,dx = \frac{3}{4}\left[\frac{1}{5}x^5\right]_0^2 = \frac{24}{5},$$

$$\frac{1}{2}\int_0^2 y^2\,dx = \frac{9}{32}\int_0^2 x^6\,dx = \frac{9}{32}\left[\frac{1}{7}x^7\right]_0^2 = \frac{36}{7},$$

and (10.7), (10.8) give for the coordinates $(\bar{x}, \bar{y})$ of the centroid,

$$\bar{x} = \tfrac{24}{5} \div 3 = \tfrac{8}{5}, \qquad \bar{y} = \tfrac{36}{7} \div 3 = \tfrac{12}{7}.$$

10.6 Some further examples of centres of gravity

Here we determine the position of the centre of gravity of a triangular lamina, a sector of a circle, a circular arc, a solid hemisphere and a solid cone. These results and also some of those given in Exercises 10(b) will be used in Chapter 15. In all cases, the density of the body considered is assumed to be uniform and is taken as ρ.

(i) *Triangular lamina*

Suppose the base AB of the triangle OAB is of length a and its height OH is h. Take the vertex O as the origin and lines through O parallel

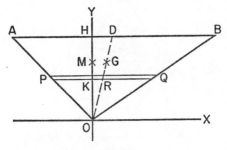

FIG. 98

and perpendicular to AB as the axes of x and y (Fig. 98). PQ is a thin strip parallel to OX; it is at height y above O, of width δy and meets OY at K. It is clear from similar triangles that $PQ/AB = OK/OH$ and this leads to $PQ = ay/h$. The mass of the strip PQ is therefore approximately $\rho ay\,\delta y/h$ and its moment about OX is $\rho ay^2\,\delta y/h$. The total moment about OX is

$$\frac{\rho a}{h}\int_0^h y^2\,dy = \frac{\rho a}{h}\left[\frac{1}{3}y^3\right]_0^h = \tfrac{1}{3}\rho ah^2,$$

and as the area of the triangle is $\frac{1}{2}ah$ and its mass $\frac{1}{2}\rho ah$, the height $\bar{y}$ of its centre of gravity is given by

$$\tfrac{1}{2}\rho ah\, \bar{y} = \tfrac{1}{6}\rho ah^2,$$

leading to $\bar{y} = \frac{2}{3}h$.

Since the centre of gravity of the strip PQ is at its mid-point R, it follows that the centre of gravity G of the whole triangle will lie on the line joining the mid-points of all such strips, that is, on the median OD. If M is a point on OY such that $OM = \frac{2}{3}OH$, we have, by similar triangles,

$$\frac{OG}{OD} = \frac{OM}{OH} = \frac{2}{3},$$

so that *the centre of gravity of the triangle is a point G in the median OD such that $OG = \frac{2}{3}OD$.*

(ii) *Sector of a circle*

Let the sector with centre the origin O have radius r and subtend an angle 2α at O, the axis of x bisecting the sector (Fig. 99). By symmetry, the centroid lies on OX. Consider an element bounded by radii

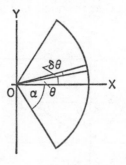

Fig. 99

inclined at angles θ and $\theta + \delta\theta$ to the axis of x. The area of this element is $\frac{1}{2}r^2\,\delta\theta$ and its mass is $\frac{1}{2}\rho r^2\,\delta\theta$. The element is approximately triangular in shape and its centroid is on the median at distance $\frac{2}{3}r$ from O and at distance $\frac{2}{3}r\cos\theta$ from the axis OY. The moment of the element is therefore approximately $\frac{1}{2}\rho r^2\,\delta\theta \times \frac{2}{3}r\cos\theta$, that is $\frac{1}{3}\rho r^3\cos\theta\,\delta\theta$, and the total moment for the whole sector is

$$\int_{-\alpha}^{\alpha} \tfrac{1}{3}\rho r^3\cos\theta\,d\theta = \tfrac{1}{3}\rho r^3 \int_{-\alpha}^{\alpha}\cos\theta\,d\theta = \tfrac{1}{3}\rho r^3\Big[\sin\theta\Big]_{-\alpha}^{\alpha} = \tfrac{2}{3}\rho r^3\sin\alpha.$$

Since the total mass of the sector is $\rho r^2 \alpha$, the abscissa $\bar{x}$ of the centroid is given by $\rho r^2 \alpha \bar{x} = \frac{2}{3}\rho r^3 \sin \alpha$, leading to

$$\bar{x} = \frac{2r \sin \alpha}{3\alpha}.$$

When $\alpha = \frac{1}{2}\pi$, the sector becomes a *semi-circle* and the centroid then lies on the central radius at distance $4r/3\pi$ from the centre.

(iii) *Circular arc*

Fig. 100 shows the arc of a circle of radius r, centre the origin O and subtending an angle 2α at the centre. If the axis OX bisects the arc, it is clear from symmetry that the centroid lies on OX and we require therefore only its abscissa $\bar{x}$. If OA, OB are radii inclined at angles θ and $\theta + \delta\theta$ to OX, the length of the element of arc AB is $r\,\delta\theta$, its

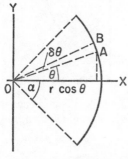

Fig. 100

mass is $\rho r\,\delta\theta$ and the element is at distance $r\cos\theta$ from OY. The moment of the element is therefore $\rho r^2 \cos\theta\,\delta\theta$ and the moment for the whole arc is

$$\int_{-\alpha}^{\alpha} \rho r^2 \cos\theta\, d\theta = \rho r^2 \int_{-\alpha}^{\alpha} \cos\theta\, d\theta = \rho r^2 \left[\sin\theta\right]_{-\alpha}^{\alpha} = 2\rho r^2 \sin\alpha.$$

Since the mass of the arc is $2\rho r\alpha$, $\bar{x}$ is given by $2\rho r\alpha\bar{x} = 2\rho r^2 \sin\alpha$, that is

$$\bar{x} = \frac{r \sin \alpha}{\alpha}.$$

(iv) *Solid hemisphere*

Consider a hemisphere of radius r with its centre at the origin O and with the axis OX as its axis of symmetry (Fig. 101). Consider an element in the form of a circular disc of radius y and thickness δx at distance x from the axis OY. The volume of the element is approximately

$\pi y^2 \, \delta x$ and its mass is $\pi \rho y^2 \, \delta x$. The moment of this mass about the axis OY is $\pi \rho x y^2 \, \delta x$ and, since $x^2 + y^2 = r^2$, the whole moment is

$$\int_0^r \pi \rho x y^2 \, dx = \pi \rho \int_0^r x(r^2 - x^2) \, dx$$

$$= \pi \rho \left[\tfrac{1}{2} x^2 r^2 - \tfrac{1}{4} x^4 \right]_0^r = \tfrac{1}{4} \pi \rho r^4.$$

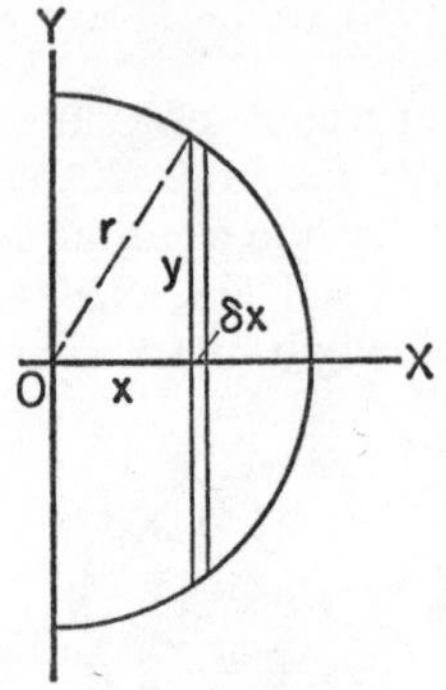

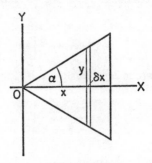

FIG. 101

The mass of the hemisphere is $\tfrac{2}{3} \pi \rho r^3$ and hence the centre of gravity lies on the line OX at a distance $\bar{x}$ from O given by $\tfrac{2}{3} \pi \rho r^3 \bar{x} = \tfrac{1}{4} \pi \rho r^4$, that is,

$$\bar{x} = \tfrac{3}{8} r.$$

(v) *Solid cone*

Fig. 102 shows a right circular cone of semi-vertical angle α with its vertex at the origin O and axis along the axis of x. Consider an element

FIG. 102

again in the form of a circular disc of radius y and thickness δx at distance x from OY. As in (iv) above the mass of such a disc is $\pi \rho y^2 \, \delta x$

and its moment about OY is $\pi \rho x y^2 \, \delta x$. If h is the height of the cone, the whole moment is (since now $y = x \tan \alpha$),

$$\int_0^h \pi \rho x y^2 \, dx = \pi \rho \int_0^h x^3 \tan^2 \alpha \, dx = \pi \rho \tan^2 \alpha \left[\tfrac{1}{4} x^4 \right]_0^h = \tfrac{1}{4} \pi \rho h^4 \tan^2 \alpha.$$

The volume of the cone is $\tfrac{1}{3} \pi h^3 \tan^2 \alpha$ and its mass is $\tfrac{1}{3} \pi \rho h^3 \tan^2 \alpha$, so that the centroid lies on the axis OX at a distance $\bar{x}$ from O given by $(\tfrac{1}{3} \pi \rho h^3 \tan^2 \alpha) \bar{x} = \tfrac{1}{4} \pi \rho h^4 \tan^2 \alpha$, that is

$$\bar{x} = \tfrac{3}{4} h.$$

10.7 Moments of inertia

If $m_1, m_2, \ldots, m_n$ are the masses of a system of particles situated at points $P_1, P_2, \ldots, P_n$ whose perpendicular distances from a given straight line are $r_1, r_2, \ldots, r_n$, the sum of the products of each mass and the *square* of its distance from the line is called the *moment of inertia* of the system with respect to the given line. This moment, sometimes also called the *second moment*, is conveniently denoted by I so that

$$I = m_1 r_1^2 + m_2 r_2^2 + \ldots + m_n r_n^2. \tag{10.9}$$

If we imagine the total mass $M = m_1 + m_2 + \ldots + m_n$ to be concentrated at a point at distance k from the given line such that this single mass has the same moment of inertia about the given line as the system of particles then

$$M k^2 = I = m_1 r_1^2 + m_2 r_2^2 + \ldots + m_n r_n^2. \tag{10.10}$$

The distance k, calculated from this equation, is known as the *radius of gyration* of the system about the given line.

The moment of inertia of a rigid body about an axis is required in Dynamics to express the kinetic energy of the body (see § 21.9) and it is useful to set up two general theorems before discussing the moments of inertia of specific bodies. These are as follows.

(i) *The parallel axes theorem. If the moment of inertia of a system of particles of total mass M about an axis through the centre of mass is Mk^2, the moment of inertia of the system about a parallel axis distant a from the first is $M(k^2 + a^2)$.*

Suppose the particles are of masses $m_1, m_2, \ldots, m_n$ and that they are at distances $r_1, r_2, \ldots, r_n$ from the axis through the centre of mass and at distances $R_1, R_2, \ldots, R_n$ from the second (parallel) axis. Let the two axes meet a plane perpendicular to them in G and O respectively. If this plane passes through the point P_1 occupied by the first particle (Fig. 103), we shall have, since $OG = a$,

$$R_1^2 = r_1^2 + a^2 - 2 a r_1 \cos \theta_1$$

and similar relations between R and r hold for all n particles of the system. The moment of inertia I of the system about the axis through O is given by $I = \Sigma mR^2 = \Sigma m(r^2 + a^2 - 2ar \cos \theta)$ where Σ denotes summation over all the particles of the system and this can be written

$$I = \Sigma mr^2 + a^2\Sigma m - 2a\Sigma mr \cos \theta.$$

Now $\Sigma m = M$, $\Sigma mr^2 = Mk^2$ (the moment of inertia about the axis through G) and $\Sigma mr \cos \theta = 0$ for this latter sum when divided by M

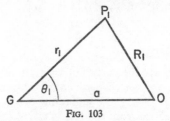

FIG. 103

gives the distance in the direction GO of the centre of mass from the point G. Hence $I = Mk^2 + Ma^2$ and the theorem is proved.

(ii) *If the moments of inertia of a system of particles lying in a plane about two perpendicular axes in the plane meeting in a point O are A and B respectively, the moment of inertia of the system about an axis through O perpendicular to the plane is $A + B$.*

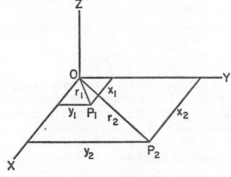

FIG. 104

In Fig. 104, OX, OY are the given perpendicular axes in the plane and OZ is the axis perpendicular to the plane. $P_1, P_2, \ldots, P_n$ are the points $(x_1, y_1), (x_2, y_2), \ldots, (x_n, y_n)$ occupied by particles of masses $m_1, m_2, \ldots, m_n$. Then, since the moments of inertia about OY, OX are respectively A and B, $A = m_1x_1^2 + m_2x_2^2 + \ldots + m_nx_n^2$, $B = m_1y_1^2 + m_2y_2^2 + \ldots + m_ny_n^2$, and, by addition,

$$A + B = m_1(x_1^2 + y_1^2) + m_2(x_2^2 + y_2^2) + \ldots + m_n(x_n^2 + y_n^2).$$

If $OP_1 = r_1$, $OP_2 = r_2$, . . ., $OP_n = r_n$, it is clear from the diagram that $r_1^2 = x_1^2 + y_1^2$, $r_2^2 = x_2^2 + y_2^2$, . . ., $r_n^2 = x_n^2 + y_n^2$, hence

$$A + B = m_1 r_1^2 + m_2 r_2^2 + . . . + m_n r_n^2,$$

and this is the moment of inertia of the system about the axis OZ.

10.8 Some examples of the calculation of moments of inertia

As in the calculation of the position of centres of gravity, an extension from a system of particles to a continuous body can be obtained by replacing the particles by elements of the body and using integrals in place of summations. We give below the calculations for the moments of inertia about specific axes of a thin rod, a circular disc and a sphere, the bodies being of uniform density ρ in all cases.

(i) Thin rod

Suppose (Fig. 105) AB is a thin rod of length $2l$ lying along the axis OX with its mid-point at the origin O. The mass of an element PQ of

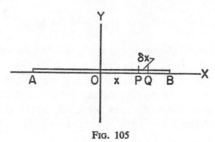

FIG. 105

length δx at distance x from O is $\rho \, \delta x$ and its moment of inertia about the axis of y is $\rho \, \delta x \times x^2$. Hence the moment of inertia I_0 of the whole rod about a line through its centre and perpendicular to its length is given by

$$I_0 = \int_{-l}^{l} \rho x^2 \, dx = \rho \left[\tfrac{1}{3} x^3 \right]_{-l}^{l} = \tfrac{2}{3} \rho l^3.$$

Since the total mass M of the rod is $2\rho l$, this can be written in the form

$$I_0 = \tfrac{1}{3} M l^2,$$

showing that the radius of gyration k is given by $k^2 = \tfrac{1}{3} l^2$.

If the moment of inertia I_A about an axis perpendicular to the length of the rod and passing through the end A is required, the parallel axes theorem gives

$$I_A = I_0 + M l^2 = \tfrac{4}{3} M l^2.$$

(ii) *Circular disc*

The moment of inertia of a circular disc about an axis through its centre O perpendicular to the plane of the disc can be found by considering the ring element bounded by circles of radii r and $r + \delta r$ (Fig. 106). The mass of the element is approximately $2\pi \rho r\, \delta r$ and its

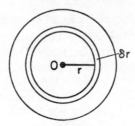

FIG. 106

moment of inertia about the axis is $2\pi \rho r\, \delta r \times r^2$. Hence, if a is the radius of the disc the total moment of inertia I_0 is

$$I_0 = \int_0^a 2\pi \rho r^3\, dr = 2\pi \rho \left[\tfrac{1}{4} r^4 \right]_0^a = \tfrac{1}{2} \pi \rho a^4.$$

Since the total mass M of the disc is $\pi \rho a^2$, this can be written $\tfrac{1}{2} M a^2$.

If the moment of inertia of the disc about a diameter is A, then by symmetry the moment of inertia about a perpendicular diameter is also A. Therefore, by the second of the general theorems of § 10.7, the moment of inertia about an axis perpendicular to the plane of the disc is $2A$ and we have $2A = \tfrac{1}{2} M a^2$ giving $A = \tfrac{1}{4} M a^2$.

(iii) *Sphere*

Let the sphere be of radius r with its centre at the origin O. Consider an element in the form of a circular disc of radius y, thickness δx at distance x from the axis OY (Fig. 107). The mass of this element is

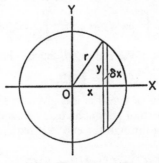

FIG. 107

approximately $\pi\rho y^2\,\delta x$ and, by (ii) above, its moment of inertia about the axis OX is $\frac{1}{2}(\pi\rho y^2\,\delta x) \times y^2$. The moment of inertia about OX of the whole sphere is therefore, since $x^2 + y^2 = r^2$,

$$\int_{-r}^{r} \tfrac{1}{2}\pi\rho y^4\,dx = \tfrac{1}{2}\pi\rho \int_{-r}^{r} (r^2 - x^2)^2\,dx$$

$$= \tfrac{1}{2}\pi\rho \left[r^4 x - \tfrac{2}{3}r^2 x^3 + \tfrac{1}{5}x^5 \right]_{-r}^{r} = \tfrac{8}{15}\pi\rho r^5.$$

Since the mass M of the sphere is $\frac{4}{3}\pi\rho r^3$, this can be written as $\frac{2}{5}Mr^2$.

Example 9. *A uniform lamina is bounded by the curve $y = 8x^3$, the axis of x and an ordinate at $x = 1$. Find its radius of gyration about a line perpendicular to its plane through the origin of coordinates.*

Fig. 108 shows the lamina and an elementary strip of height y and width δx. If ρ is the surface-density of the lamina, the mass of the strip is approximately

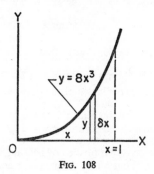

FIG. 108

$\rho y\,\delta x$ and its moment of inertia about the axis of y is $\rho y\,\delta x \times x^2$. Hence the moment of inertia I_y of the whole lamina about the axis of y is given by, since $y = 8x^3$,

$$I_y = \int_0^1 \rho x^2 y\,dx = 8\rho \int_0^1 x^5\,dx = 8\rho \left[\tfrac{1}{6}x^6 \right]_0^1 = \tfrac{4}{3}\rho.$$

The moment of inertia of the strip about the axis of x is, using the result for a thin rod in (i) above, $\rho y\,\delta x \times \frac{1}{3}y^2$, and the moment of inertia I_x of the lamina about the axis of x is

$$I_x = \int_0^1 \tfrac{1}{3}\rho y^3\,dx = \frac{512}{3}\rho \int_0^1 x^9\,dx = \frac{512}{3}\rho \left[\tfrac{1}{10}x^{10} \right]_0^1 = \frac{256}{15}\rho.$$

By the general theorem (ii) the moment of inertia about an axis through O perpendicular to the plane of the lamina is

$$I_x + I_y = \left(\frac{256}{15} + \frac{4}{3} \right)\rho = \frac{92}{5}\rho.$$

As the mass M of the lamina is given by

$$M = \int_0^1 \rho y \, dx = 8\rho \int_0^1 x^3 \, dx = 8\rho \left[\tfrac{1}{4} x^4 \right]_0^1 = 2\rho,$$

the moment of inertia can be written as $\tfrac{46}{5}M$ and the required radius of gyration is therefore $\sqrt{(46/5)} = 3 \cdot 033$.

Exercises 10 (b)

1. OA is a non-uniform rod, of length l, the density of which at distance x from O is $a + 2bx$, where a and b are constants. Prove that the mass of the rod is $l(a + bl)$ and that the distance of its centre of gravity from O is

$$\frac{l(3a + 4bl)}{6(a + bl)}.$$ [O.C.]

2. Find the y coordinate of the centroid of the area in the first quadrant enclosed by the curve $y^2 = 4ax$, the axis of x and the line $x = h$. [O.C.]

3. Find the abscissa $\bar{x}$ of the centre of mass of a lamina of uniform density bounded by the curve $y = 1 + 10x - 2x^2$, the axis of x and ordinates for which $x = 1$ and $x = 5$. Verify that

$$\bar{x} = (y_1 + 12y_2 + 5y_3)/(y_1 + 4y_2 + y_3),$$

where y_1, y_2 and y_3 are ordinates of the curve at $x = 1$, 3 and 5. [O.C.]

4. Find the coordinates of the centroid of the area enclosed between the curve $y = \sqrt{(x^3)}$ and the straight line $y = 2x$. [O.C.]

5. A solid of uniform density is formed by rotating the portion of the curve $y = x^2 - 3x$ which is cut off by the axis of x about that axis. Find the position of the centre of gravity.

6. O is the origin, A is $(a, 0)$, B is (a, a) and $OABC$ is a uniform square lamina $(a > 0)$. Prove that the x coordinate of the centre of gravity of the lamina bounded by AB, BC and the arc AC of the circle with centre O and radius a is $(\tfrac{2}{3}a)/(4 - \pi)$. [O.C.]

7. Find the coordinates of the centroid of the uniform lamina bounded by the curve $y = 2 \sin \tfrac{1}{2}x$ and the axis of x between $x = 0$ and $x = 2\pi$.

8. Show that the centre of gravity of a uniform thin hemispherical shell of radius r is at distance $\tfrac{1}{2}r$ from the plane of its rim.

9. Find the moment of inertia about one of its sides of a square lamina of uniform density ρ and side of length a.

10. The perpendicular to the axis of x from the point $P(2, 6)$ on the curve $y = \tfrac{3}{4}x^3$ meets the axis at Q. Find the radius of gyration about PQ of the uniform lamina bounded by the arc OP and the lines OQ, QP. [O.C.]

11. The area enclosed by the curve $y^2 = 4ax$, the axis of x and the line $x = h$ is rotated through four right angles about the axis of x to form a solid. Find the radius of gyration about the x-axis of this solid. [O.C.]

12. Show that the moment of inertia about its axis of a uniform solid circular cone of mass M and base radius r is $\frac{3}{10}Mr^2$.

13. Find by integration the radius of gyration of a uniform semi-circular disc of radius a about its bounding diameter. Deduce its radius of gyration about a parallel axis through the centroid G of the disc, assuming that G is distant $4a/3\pi$ from the bounding diameter. [O.C.]

14. The smaller of the two areas bounded by the curve $y^2 = 4x$, the line $y = 2$ and the line $x = 4$ rotates through four right angles about the axis of x. Prove that the volume of the solid so formed is 18π and that its radius of gyration about the axis of x is $2\sqrt{2}$. [O.C.]

15. A uniform thin hemispherical shell has mass M and radius r. Show that its moment of inertia about the radius perpendicular to its base is $\frac{2}{3}Mr^2$. [O.C.]

10.9 Some applications from dynamics

If v is the velocity of a body which has travelled a distance x in time t, we have seen in § 8.4 that $v = dx/dt$ and hence, using equations (9.1) and (9.3) with the appropriate changes in notation,

$$x = \int v \, dt. \qquad (10.11)$$

Again, if a is the acceleration of the body at time t, $a = dv/dt$ and it follows that

$$v = \int a \, dt. \qquad (10.12)$$

Example 10. *A body moves along a straight line so that, t seconds after passing a fixed point A in the line, its velocity is $(3t^2 + 2t + 4)$ m/s. If it arrives at a point B in the line 4 seconds after passing A, calculate the distance AB. Show that the body is midway between A and B when its acceleration is 20 m/s^2.* [O.C.]

Here $v = 3t^2 + 2t + 4$ and the distance x travelled in time t is given by

$$x = \int v \, dt = \int (3t^2 + 2t + 4) \, dt = t^3 + t^2 + 4t + C.$$

At time $t = 0$, the body is at A and $x = 0$. Substituting these values of x and t in the above formula we find that the arbitrary constant C is zero and hence

$$x = t^3 + t^2 + 4t. \qquad (10.13)$$

The distance AB is the value of x for which $t = 4$, that is

$$AB = (4)^3 + (4)^2 + 4(4) = 96 \text{ m}.$$

The acceleration a is given by

$$a = \frac{dv}{dt} = \frac{d}{dt}(3t^2 + 2t + 4) = 6t + 2,$$

and when this is 20 m/s^2, we have $6t + 2 = 20$ leading to $t = 3$. The distance travelled when $t = 3$ is given by equation (10.13) as

$$x = (3)^3 + (3)^2 + 4(3) = 48 \text{ m},$$

showing that the body is then midway between A and B.

Example 11. *A particle, moving in a straight line, has an acceleration of $(2t - 9)$ m/s^2 at time t seconds. If its velocity when $t = 0$ is 18 m/s, show that the particle is stationary when $t = 3$ and find the other value of t for which it is stationary.*
[N.U.]

The acceleration $a = 2t - 9$ and hence, by (10.12) the velocity v is given by

$$v = \int a \, dt = \int (2t - 9) \, dt = t^2 - 9t + C.$$

The value of the arbitrary constant C is found from the fact that $v = 18$ when $t = 0$, so that $18 = (0)^2 - 9(0) + C$, giving $C = 18$. Hence $v = t^2 - 9t + 18$ and the particle is stationary when

$$t^2 - 9t + 18 = 0.$$

This quadratic can be written $(t - 3)(t - 6) = 0$, so that the particle is at rest when $t = 3$ and again when $t = 6$.

10.10 Motion with constant acceleration

An important particular case of formulae (10.11), (10.12) occurs when the acceleration a is *constant*. In this case, (10.12) gives

$$v = \int a \, dt = a \int dt = at + C.$$

If u is the *initial* velocity of the body, then $v = u$ when $t = 0$ and substitution gives $u = C$. Hence we have

$$v = u + at. \tag{10.14}$$

The distance x travelled in time t is given by (10.11) as $x = \int v \, dt$ and, substituting for v from (10.14),

$$x = \int (u + at) \, dt = ut + \tfrac{1}{2}at^2 + C'.$$

If the body is initially at the origin, $x = 0$ when $t = 0$ giving $C' = 0$ and

$$x = ut + \tfrac{1}{2}at^2. \tag{10.15}$$

Equations (10.14) and (10.15) respectively give the velocity v and distance travelled at time t for a body starting from the origin with velocity u and moving with constant acceleration a. It is sometimes useful to combine these equations to give alternative formulae as follows. Firstly, (10.15) can be written

$$x = \tfrac{1}{2}ut + \tfrac{1}{2}ut + \tfrac{1}{2}at^2 = \tfrac{1}{2}\{u + (u + at)\}t,$$

and substitution for $u + at$ from (10.14) leads to

$$x = \tfrac{1}{2}(u + v)t. \tag{10.16}$$

Secondly, equations (10.14) and (10.15) can be written $at = v - u$ and

$$2ax = 2a(ut + \tfrac{1}{2}at^2) = 2u(at) + (at)^2.$$

Substituting for at from the first of these in the second,

$$2ax = 2u(v - u) + (v - u)^2 = (v - u)(v + u) = v^2 - u^2.$$

Hence

$$v^2 = u^2 + 2ax. \tag{10.17}$$

Finally, equation (10.14) gives $u = v - at$ and substitution in (10.15) yields $x = (v - at)t + \tfrac{1}{2}at^2$ leading to

$$x = vt - \tfrac{1}{2}at^2. \tag{10.18}$$

The application of these important formulae to practical problems is given in Chapter 16. Here we give a single example which illustrates also a point arising in the calculation of mean values.

Example 12. *A body has an initial velocity of 80 m/s and is subjected to a retardation of 32 m/s². Find the mean value of the velocity of the body during its forward motion.*

Here $u = 80$, $a = -32$ and equation (10.14) gives the velocity v at time t in the form $v = 80 - 32t$. Forward motion ceases when $v = 0$, that is when $t = 80/32 = 5/2$ seconds and hence the mean velocity with respect to the time t is

$$\frac{1}{(5/2) - 0} \int_0^{5/2} (80 - 32t)\, dt = \frac{2}{5} \left[80t - 16t^2 \right]_0^{5/2} = \frac{2}{5}(200 - 100) = 40 \text{ m/s}.$$

In the above we have worked in terms of the time t. Alternatively we could have worked in terms of the distance x moved by the body. In this case equation (10.17) is used to give $v^2 = 80^2 - 64x$ and forward motion ceases when $x = 80^2/64 = 100$ m. The mean velocity with respect to the distance x is therefore

$$\frac{1}{100 - 0} \int_0^{100} \sqrt{(6400 - 64x)}\, dx = \frac{8}{100} \int_0^{100} \sqrt{(100 - x)}\, dx$$

$$= \frac{8}{100} \left[-\tfrac{2}{3}(100 - x)^{3/2} \right]_0^{100}$$

$$= \frac{8}{100} \cdot \frac{2}{3} \cdot 1000 = 53 \cdot 33 \text{ m/s}.$$

The different results obtained in this example for the mean velocity show that, when a quantity can be expressed in terms of more than one variable, it is important to state which is the variable whose range has been sub-divided in calculating the mean.

Exercises 10 (c)

1. A particle starts from rest with acceleration $(30 - 6t)$ m/s² at time t seconds. When and where will it come to rest again?   [O.C.]

2. The velocity v m/s of a particle which travels from rest to rest in a straight line is given at time t seconds by $v = 6t - 3t^2$. Find the total distance travelled.   [N.U.]

3. A particle moves in a straight line so that its acceleration at time t is $(2 - 3t)$ m/s^2. Find the distance x m of the particle from the origin at time t, subject to the conditions that $x = 3$ when $t = 0$ and that the velocity is zero when $t = 1$. At what other instant does the velocity vanish?

4. The velocity v m/s of a particle, moving in a straight line, at time t seconds is given by the equation $v = pt^3 + qt$ where p and q are constants. If $v = 2\frac{1}{3}$ when $t = 1$ and $v = 15$ when $t = 3$, find the values of p and q. Calculate also the distance travelled by the particle in the sixth second.   [N.U.]

5. A body, starting from the origin, moves along a straight line so that its velocity at time t is $6 \sin 2t$. Find a formula giving the distance travelled in time t.

6. A particle moves in a straight line and its acceleration at time t seconds is $(A + 3t)$ m/s^2 where A is a constant. When $t = 0$ its distance from the origin is 5 m and when $t = 1$ it is 13 m from the origin and moving with a velocity of 10 m/s. Find the value of A.

7. A particle moves in a straight line, starting with a velocity of 4 m/s. At time t seconds, its acceleration is $2(3t - 4)$ m/s^2. Find (i) how far the particle moves before first coming to instantaneous rest, (ii) the total time that elapses before the particle returns to the starting point. [N.U.]

8. The acceleration of a body at time t seconds moving in a straight line is $8/t^3$ m/s^2 and its velocity after 1 second is 6 m/s. Find (i) the distance travelled in the time interval $t = 1$ to $t = 2$, (ii) the further time required to travel an equal distance.

9. The retardation at time t of a body starting from the origin with velocity a is $a \sin t$ where a is a constant. Show that the displacement x at time t is given by $x = a \sin t$ and find, in the time interval $0 < t < \frac{1}{2}\pi$, the mean velocity (i) with respect to time, (ii) with respect to displacement.

10. What constant acceleration or retardation is required
    (i) to move a particle 50 m from rest in 5 seconds,
    (ii) to stop a particle moving with velocity 45 m/s in 15 m?

11. Two racing cars A and B pass the same point at the same instant. A is moving at a steady speed of 120 m/s; B then has a speed of 110 m/s but maintains a uniform acceleration of $\frac{1}{6}$ m/s^2. Write down the further distance each travels in t seconds; hence find after what time B will overtake A and what B's speed will then be.

12. A train takes t and $3t/2$ seconds to travel successive distances of x m. Assuming that the train moves with uniform retardation, show that this retardation is $(4x/15t^2)$ m/s^2.

13. A body starts with velocity u m/s and moves with a constant acceleration of 32 m/s^2. It travels 720 m in the first t seconds and 2240 m in the first $2t$ seconds of its motion. Find u and t.

14. Two particles moving in a straight line have, at a given time $t = 0$, velocities u_1 and u_2. The motion of the first particle is uniformly retarded while that of the second is uniform. Prove that by the time the first particle comes to rest, the distances travelled are in the ratio $u_1 : 2u_2$.

15. If x_1, x_2 and x_3 are the distances described by a body moving with uniform acceleration in a straight line in the pth, qth and rth seconds, prove that $x_1(q - r) + x_2(r - p) + x_3(p - q) = 0$.

Exercises 10 (d)

1. Find the whole area enclosed by the curve $y = x^3 - 5x^2 + 6x$ and the axis of x.

2. The curve whose equation is $y = x(x - a)(x - b)$ where $0 < a < b$ cuts the axis of x at O (the origin), A and B in that order. Calculate the area contained between the curve and the portion OA of the axis. If the two areas enclosed between the curve and the axis are equal in magnitude, find the ratio of a to b. [N.U.]

3. Show that the mean ordinate of that part of the curve $y = 3x - x^2$ which lies in the first quadrant is two-thirds of the maximum ordinate.

4. Sketch the curve $x^2 = 4a(a - y)$, where a is positive. If the area bounded by the axis of x and that portion of the curve which lies above it is rotated about the axis of x, show that the volume of the solid formed is $(32\pi a^3/15)$. [N.U.]

5. Calculate the volume of the solid formed when the area bounded by the curve $y = x^2 + 3$, the axis of y and the line $y = 4$ rotates about the axis of y. [N.U.]

6. The area enclosed by the coordinate axes and the curve $y = \cos^2 x$ between $x = 0$ and $x = \frac{1}{2}\pi$ is rotated about the axis of x through four right angles. Find the volume of the solid formed. [L.U.]

7. Sketch the curve $y^2 = x^2(x + 1)(2 - x)$. Find the ratio of the volume obtained by revolving the larger loop of the curve about the axis of x to that obtained by revolving the smaller loop about the same axis, both rotations being through two right angles. [L.U.]

8. The part of the curve $y = \sqrt{(20x - x^2)}$ between $x = 0$ and $x = 10$ is a quadrant of a circle. The arc of the curve from the origin to a point P

whose abscissa is a is revolved about the axis of x. If the volume of the bowl thus obtained is one-half that of the bowl obtained by revolving the whole quadrant, show that $30a^2 - a^3 = 1000$.   [N.U.]

9. Sketch the curve whose equation is $y = (x + 1)(5 - x)$ and find the coordinates of the points A and B where the line $y = 2x + 5$ cuts the curve. Find the area bounded by the chord AB, the axis of x and the intermediate arcs of the curve. Find also the volume produced when this area is rotated about the axis of x through four right angles.   [O.C.]

10. A barrel of circular cross-section is $1 \cdot 2$ m long. Both end sections are of diameter $0 \cdot 6365$ m, the central section is of diameter $0 \cdot 764$ m and sections at $0 \cdot 3$ m from either end are of diameter $0 \cdot 716$ m. Use Simpson's rule to calculate the volume of the barrel.

11. AB is a non-uniform straight rod of length l, the density of which at a distance x from A is $a + bx^2$ where a and b are constants. Prove that the mass of the rod is $\frac{1}{3}l(3a + bl^2)$. Find also the distance of the centre of mass of the rod from A.   [O.C.]

12. Find the volume cut off from the solid obtained by rotating the curve $y^2 = 4ax$ about the axis of x by a plane at distance $5a$ from the origin. If the solid is of uniform density, find also the position of the centre of gravity of this part of the solid.   [O.C.]

13. Find the coordinates of the centroid of the area lying between the curves $y^2 = 2x - 4$ and $y^2 = x$.   [L.U.]

14. A uniform lamina is bounded by that part of the curve $9x^2 + 16y^2 = 144$ which lies in the first quadrant. Show that the centroid is the point $(16/3\pi, 4/\pi)$.

15. The surface density of a circular lamina of radius r varies as the distance from the centre. If the total mass of the lamina is M, show that its moment of inertia about an axis through the centre and perpendicular to its plane is $\frac{3}{5}Mr^2$.

16. A lamina of mass M is bounded by the curve $y = \sin x$ and the axis of x between $x = 0$ and $x = \pi$. Show that the moments of inertia with respect to the axes of x and y are respectively $\frac{2}{9}M$ and $\frac{1}{2}(\pi^2 - 4)M$.

17. Show that the radius of gyration of a uniform triangular lamina of base a and height h about its base is $h/\sqrt{6}$.

18. A uniform lamina is bounded by the chord AB of a circle of radius a and the arc ACB subtends an angle of $90°$ at the centre of the circle. Prove that the radius of gyration of the lamina about the diameter parallel to AB is $\frac{1}{2}a \sqrt{\left(\dfrac{\pi}{\pi - 2}\right)}$.   [O.C.]

19. Show that the radius of gyration k of a uniform circular arc of radius r and angle 2α about an axis through its centre of gravity perpendicular to its plane is given by

$$k^2 = r^2 \left(1 - \frac{\sin^2 \alpha}{\alpha^2} \right).$$

Show also that the radius of gyration k' about a parallel axis through the middle point of the arc is given by

$$(k')^2 = 2r^2 \left(1 - \frac{\sin \alpha}{\alpha} \right).$$

20. The velocity of a body at time t seconds is $6t - t^2$. Show that the distance travelled in the first 3 seconds is equal to that travelled in the next 3 seconds.

21. The velocity v m/s of a body moving in a straight line and starting from a fixed point O is given by $v = 10 + 25t - 4t^2$ where t seconds is the time from O. Calculate (to the nearest metre) the distance travelled during the time for which the velocity is increasing.

22. A particle starting from rest and moving with constant acceleration in a straight line travels 6 metres in the first second of its motion. In the last second of its motion it travels $\frac{5}{9}$ths of the total distance travelled. Find the total time of the motion and the total distance travelled.

23. A body moving in a straight line with constant acceleration passes in succession three points P, Q, R. The distances PQ, QR are respectively b, c and the times from P to Q and from Q to R are each t. Show that the acceleration is $(c - b)/t^2$.

24. The acceleration of a particle moving in a straight line decreases uniformly from 64/15 to 16/15 cm/s² in half a minute. If it starts from rest, find its greatest velocity in this half minute and the distance travelled. Find also the velocity of the particle at the instant when the acceleration vanishes.

25. A train starts from rest with acceleration $1 \cdot 1$ m/s² and this acceleration decreases uniformly to zero in 2 minutes. After this time the train is brought to rest with a uniform retardation of 3 m/s². Find the total distance travelled during the journey.

CHAPTER 11

THE LOGARITHMIC AND EXPONENTIAL FUNCTIONS; EXPANSIONS

11.1 Introduction

In reading § 9.2, the student should have noticed that the result

$$\int x^n \, dx = \frac{x^{n+1}}{n+1} + C$$

was invalid when $n = -1$ and that there was no discussion of $\int x^{-1} \, dx$. We start the present chapter by considering this integral and show how it leads to two functions which are of great importance in mathematics and its applications. Once this integral has been established, it is possible to integrate many more functions, and gaps left in Chapter 9 can be filled in.

The latter part of the chapter deals with the expansion of functions in series by means of the Taylor–Maclaurin theorem.

11.2 The integral $\int x^{-1} \, dx$

Fig. 109 shows the graph of $y = 1/x$ for positive values of x and AA', BB' are ordinates at $x = 1$, $x = u$. Using the results of § 9.9,

$$\text{area } AA'B'B = \int_1^u x^{-1} \, dx$$

and, as the ordinate BB' moves to the right, it is clear that the area

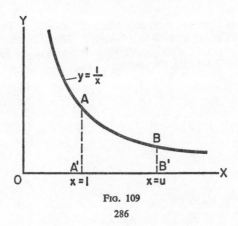

Fig. 109

286

$AA'B'B$ (and therefore the value of the integral $\int_1^u x^{-1}\,dx$) is an increasing function of u. Denoting this by $f(u)$, we therefore have

$$f(u) = \text{area } AA'B'B = \int_1^u x^{-1}\,dx, \tag{11.1}$$

and it should be noticed that when $u = 1$, the ordinate BB' coincides with AA' so that the area $AA'B'B$ is then zero, and hence

$$f(1) = 0. \tag{11.2}$$

Values of $f(u)$ for values of u other than unity can be found by evaluating the integral $\int_1^u x^{-1}\,dx$ by the trapezoidal or Simpson's rules and the reader who has worked Exercises $9(f)$, 6 will in fact have done this for the case $u = 3$. Results of such numerical integrations give

$$f(2) = 0 \cdot 693, \quad f(3) = 1 \cdot 099,$$
$$f(4) = 1 \cdot 386, \quad \ldots$$

and, if these results are plotted, the graph shown in Fig. 110 is obtained.

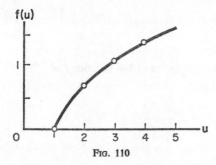

FIG. 110

Fig. 110 shows values of $f(u)$ only for values of u greater than unity. Values of $f(u)$ in the range $0 < u < 1$ can be deduced from those already found as follows. As $0 < u < 1$, then $1/u > 1$ and

$$f\left(\frac{1}{u}\right) = \int_1^{1/u} x^{-1}\,dx.$$

Now change the variable in this integral from x to t where $x = 1/t$ by the method of § 9.12. The limits of integration correspond to values of t of 1 and u and, since $dx/dt = -1/t^2$, we have

$$f\left(\frac{1}{u}\right) = \int_1^u t\left(-\frac{1}{t^2}\right)dt = -\int_1^u t^{-1}\,dt = -f(u). \tag{11.3}$$

Formula (11.3) enables the graph of $f(u)$ to be extended to values of u less than unity. For example, if $u = 2$ the formula gives

$$f(\tfrac{1}{2}) = -f(2) = -0.693$$

and $f(\tfrac{1}{3}), f(\tfrac{1}{4}), \ldots$ can be found in the same way. Fig. 111 shows the

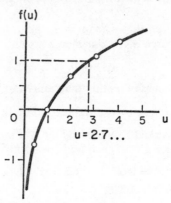

FIG. 111

shape of the graph giving values of $f(u) = \displaystyle\int_1^u x^{-1}\, dx$ for all positive values of u.

11.3 Some further properties of the function $f(u)$

From (11.1), it follows that

$$\frac{d}{du}\{f(u)\} = u^{-1} \tag{11.4}$$

and, if c is a constant, this formula and the rule for differentiating a function of a function gives

$$\frac{d}{du}\{f(cu)\} = (cu)^{-1} \times c = u^{-1}.$$

Hence, by subtraction,

$$\frac{d}{du}\{f(cu)\} - \frac{d}{du}\{f(u)\} = 0$$

showing that

$$f(cu) - f(u) = \text{constant}.$$

The value of the constant can be found by writing $u = 1, f(1) = 0$ and we find

$$f(cu) - f(u) = f(c).$$

This can be written

$$f(cu) = f(c) + f(u) \tag{11.5}$$

and, if we replace u by $1/u$,

$$f(c/u) = f(c) + f(1/u) = f(c) - f(u), \tag{11.6}$$

when use is made of equation (11.3).

One further property of $f(u)$ is required and this is obtained by writing $u = c^n$ in (11.1) so that

$$f(c^n) = \int_1^{c^n} x^{-1}\,dx.$$

Changing the variable in the integral by the substitution $x = t^n$, the limits of integration become 1, c and, since $dx/dt = nt^{n-1}$,

$$f(c^n) = \int_1^c t^{-n}\, nt^{n-1}\, dt = n\int_1^c t^{-1}\, dt = nf(c). \tag{11.7}$$

11.4 The logarithmic function

The properties $f(cu) = f(c) + f(u)$, $f(c/u) = (fc) - f(u)$, $f(c^n) = nf(c)$ and $f(1) = 0$ suggest that there is a connection between the function $f(u)$ and the logarithmic function for which $\log_a (cu) = \log_a c + \log_a u$, $\log_a (c/u) = \log_a c - \log_a u$, $\log_a (c^n) = n \log_a c$, $\log_a 1 = 0$. This connection can be established as follows.

The graph of Fig. 111 shows that $f(u) = 1$ when u is about 2·7 and the precise value of u for which this is so will be denoted by e (it can be shown in fact that $e = 2·718 \ldots$ and this is done in § 11.10). Hence $f(e) = 1$ and, writing $c = e$, $n = x$ in (11.7),

$$f(e^x) = xf(e) = x.$$

Setting $e^x = y$, this gives $f(y) = x$ and a combination of these two results shows that

$$y = e^x = e^{f(y)}. \tag{11.8}$$

Thus $f(y)$ is the power to which the number e must be raised to make it equal to y and hence, by the definition of a logarithm, the function f is the logarithm to base e, that is

$$f(y) \equiv \log_e y. \tag{11.9}$$

The logarithm to base e is called a *natural* or Napierian logarithm and a more modern notation for $\log_e y$ is $\ln y$, the "n" signifying the word "natural".

Changing the variable from y to x in (11.9) and from u to x in (11.4), we have

$$(x) = \log_e x, \quad \frac{d}{dx}\{f(x)\} = \frac{1}{x}$$

so that

$$\frac{d}{dx}\{\log_e x\} = \frac{1}{x}. \tag{11.10}$$

The inverse relation is

$$\int x^{-1}\, dx = \log_e x + C \tag{11.11}$$

and these two results are of fundamental importance.

It should be noticed that, because of the identity between the function f and the logarithm, Fig. 111 gives a graph of the logarithmic function. Also, by writing $a = 10, b = e = 2\cdot718\ldots$ in Example 6 of Chapter 1,

$$\log_e n = \frac{1}{\log_{10} 2\cdot718\ldots} \times \log_{10} n = 2\cdot302\ldots \times \log_{10} n. \tag{11.12}$$

Example 1. *If $y = \log_e \sin x$, find dy/dx.*

Writing $u = \sin x, y = \log_e u$ it follows by (11.10) that $dy/du = 1/u$. The rule for differentiating a function of a function then gives

$$\frac{dy}{dx} = \frac{dy}{du} \times \frac{du}{dx}$$

$$= \frac{1}{u} \times \frac{d}{dx}(\sin x) = \frac{\cos x}{u}$$

$$= \frac{\cos x}{\sin x} = \cot x.$$

11.5 The exponential function

If $x = \log_e y$, the graph of Fig. 111 [with $u = y$ and $f(u) = x$] shows that x is given uniquely for positive values of y. We may also regard y as a function of x and, remembering that x is the power to which the base e must be raised to give y, we have

$$y = e^x, \tag{11.13}$$

or, in a notation which is more convenient when x is replaced by a complicated expression,

$$y = \exp(x). \tag{11.14}$$

y is called the *exponential* function of x and this function is of great importance in mathematics and in its applications. The graph of the exponential function can be obtained from that of Fig. 111 by interchanging the axes and this is shown in Fig. 112.

To find the derivative of e^x, we have from the equation $x = \log_e y$ and (11.10)

$$\frac{dx}{dy} = \frac{d}{dy}(\log_e y) = \frac{1}{y}.$$

But, from (7.18),

$$\frac{dy}{dx} = 1\Big/\left(\frac{dx}{dy}\right),$$

so that

$$\frac{dy}{dx} = 1\Big/\left(\frac{1}{y}\right) = y = e^x,$$

giving the important result

$$\frac{d}{dx}(e^x) = e^x. \tag{11.15}$$

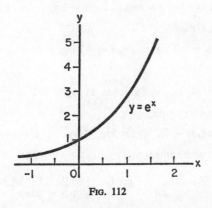

FIG. 112

This shows that the slope of the curve $y = e^x$ at a point whose abscissa is x is equal to the ordinate at this point. The formula for the derivative of a function of a function gives, if a is a constant,

$$\frac{d}{dx}(e^{ax}) = ae^{ax}, \tag{11.16}$$

and the inverse relation is

$$\int e^{ax}\,dx = \frac{1}{a}e^{ax} + C. \tag{11.17}$$

Example 2. *If $y = \tan(e^x - 1)$, show that $y^2 = e^{-x}(dy/dx) - 1$.*   [L.U.]

Writing $e^x - 1 = u$ so that $y = \tan u$ and $du/dx = e^x$, we have

$$\frac{dy}{dx} = \frac{dy}{du} \times \frac{du}{dx} = \sec^2 u \times e^x$$
$$= e^x(1 + \tan^2 u) = e^x(1 + y^2).$$

Hence

$$1 + y^2 = e^{-x}\frac{dy}{dx}$$

and the required result follows immediately by transposing the first term on the left.

Example 3. *Find $\int x\, e^{2x}\, dx$.*

Putting $u = x$, $dv/dx = e^{2x}$ so that $du/dx = 1$ and $v = \frac{1}{2}e^{2x}$, the formula for integrating by parts gives

$$\int x\, e^{2x}dx = x(\tfrac{1}{2}e^{2x}) - \int\{1(\tfrac{1}{2}e^{2x})\}\, dx$$
$$= \tfrac{1}{2}x\, e^{2x} - \tfrac{1}{2}\int e^{2x}dx$$
$$= \tfrac{1}{2}x\, e^{2x} - \tfrac{1}{4}e^{2x} + C.$$

Example 4. *Show that $e^{\log_e x} = x$ and that $e^{-3\log_e x} = 1/x^3$.*

If $y = e^{\log_e x}$, then $\log_e y = \log_e x \cdot \log_e e = \log_e x$, since $\log_e e = 1$.
Hence $y = x$.
If $z = e^{-3\log_e x}$, then

$$\log_e z = -3\log_e x \cdot \log_e e = -3\log_e x = \log_e(1/x^3),$$

so that $z = 1/x^3$.

Exercises 11 (a)

1. Differentiate with respect to x

    (i) $x(\log_e x - 1)$,   (ii) $\log_e(1/x)$,   (iii) $\log_e \sec x$.

2. Differentiate with respect to x

    (i) $\dfrac{x}{\log_e x}$,   (ii) $\log_e\left(\dfrac{\sin x + \cos x}{\sin x - \cos x}\right)$.   [O.C.]

3. Show that the maximum value of the function $x^2\log_e(1/x)$ occurs when $x = 1/\sqrt{e}$.

4. Find the derivative with respect to x of $\log_e\{x/\sqrt{(1 - x^2)}\}$ and show that if $y = \log_e\{1 + \sqrt{(1 - x^2)}\}$ then

    $$\sqrt{(1 - x^2)}\frac{dy}{dx} + x\, e^{-y} = 0.$$ [L.U.]

5. If $y = \cos(\log_e x)$, show that

    $$x^2\frac{d^2y}{dx^2} + x\frac{dy}{dx} + y = 0.$$

6. If $y = x^n e^{ax}$, show that

$$\frac{dy}{dx} - ay = \frac{ny}{x}.$$ [L.U.]

7. Differentiate with respect to x

(i) $e^{-2x^2} \log_e 3x$,   (ii) $e^{2x} \log_e \sec x$,   (iii) $x^2 e^x \tan^{-1} x$.   [O.C.]

8. If $y = (A + Bx) e^{-x}$ where A and B are constants, prove that

$$\frac{d^2y}{dx^2} + 2\frac{dy}{dx} + y = 0.$$ [L.U.]

9. Prove that

$$\frac{d}{dx} (3 e^{3x} \sin x - e^{3x} \cos x) = 10 e^{3x} \sin x.$$

Hence find the area bounded by the curve $y = e^{3x} \sin x$, and the segment of the axis of x between $x = 0$ and $x = \pi$.   [L.U.]

10. Find the maximum and minimum values of the function $(1 + 2x^2) e^{-x^2}$.   [O.C.]

11. If $y = e^{-x} \cos x$, determine the three values of x between 0 and 3π for which $dy/dx = 0$. Show that the corresponding values of y form a geometrical progression with common ratio $-e^{-\pi}$.   [N.U.]

12. Given that $y = e^{ax} \sin bx$ where a and b are real constants, prove that

$$\frac{d^2y}{dx^2} - 2a\frac{dy}{dx}.$$

is a constant multiple of y. Deduce that all positive stationary values of y are maximum values.   [N.U.]

13. Evaluate the following definite integrals

(i) $\int_0^1 e^{-3x} dx$,   (ii) $\int_0^1 (e^x - e^{-x})^2 dx$,   (iii) $\int_0^2 (x - 1) e^x dx$.   [L.U.]

14. Find

(i) $\int e^{x+2} dx$,   (ii) $\int x^2 e^{2x} dx$.   [L.U.]

15. Show that $\int_0^1 x^3 e^{x^2} dx = \frac{1}{2}$.   [O.C.]

11.6 An integral depending on $\int x^{-1} dx$

It has been shown in equation (11.11) that $\int x^{-1} dx = \log_e x + C$ and this result enables some methods of integration which were omitted from Chapter 9 to be discussed. It should first be noted that when x is replaced by the linear expression $(ax + b)$, the above result together with that of equation (9.7) gives

$$\int \frac{dx}{ax + b} = \frac{1}{a} \log_e (ax + b) + C \qquad (11.18)$$

and that, in the particular case in which $a = 1$, this reduces to

$$\int \frac{dx}{x + b} = \log_e (x + b) + C. \qquad (11.19)$$

Equation (11.19) is a particular case of the integral

$$I = \int \frac{f'(x)}{f(x)} \, dx,$$

in which the numerator of the integrand is the derivative with respect to x of the denominator and this integral can be evaluated as follows. Writing $f(x) = u$, so that $f'(x) \cdot (dx/du) = 1$ giving $dx/du = 1/f'(x)$, the rule (9.11) for integration by change of variable yields

$$\int \frac{f'(x)}{f(x)} \, dx = \int \frac{f'(x)}{u} \cdot \frac{1}{f'(x)} \, du = \int \frac{du}{u}$$

$$= \log_e u + C$$

$$= \log_e f(x) + C. \qquad (11.20)$$

Hence *the integral of a fraction in which the numerator is the differential coefficient of the denominator is $\log_e$ (denominator).*

Example 5. *Evaluate* $\int_0^1 \frac{x \, e^{x^2}}{1 + e^{x^2}} \, dx$.

Since $\dfrac{d}{dx} (1 + e^{x^2}) = 2x \, e^{x^2}$, we have

$$\int_0^1 \frac{x \, e^{x^2}}{1 + e^{x^2}} = \frac{1}{2} \int_0^1 \frac{2x \, e^{x^2}}{1 + e^{x^2}} \, dx$$

$$= \frac{1}{2} \int_0^1 \frac{\frac{d}{dx} (1 + e^{x^2})}{1 + e^{x^2}} \, dx$$

$$= \tfrac{1}{2} \left[\log_e (1 + e^{x^2}) \right]_0^1$$

$$= \tfrac{1}{2} \log_e (1 + e) - \tfrac{1}{2} \log_e 2 = \tfrac{1}{2} \log_e \left(\frac{1 + e}{2} \right).$$

Example 6. *Integrate tan x with respect to x.*

$$\int \tan x \, dx = \int \frac{\sin x}{\cos x} \, dx$$

$$= -\int \frac{-\sin x}{\cos x} \, dx$$

$$= -\int \frac{\frac{d}{dx}(\cos x) \, dx}{\cos x}$$

$$= -\log_e \cos x + C.$$

11.7 The integration of rational algebraic fractions

The integration of rational algebraic fractions (those in which the numerator and denominator contain only positive integral powers of the variable and constant coefficients) can often be made to depend on the integral given in (11.18). We give below some examples and it should be noted that where the degree of the numerator is equal to or greater than that of the denominator, the numerator must first be divided by the denominator until the remainder is of lower degree than the denominator.

(i) *Denominator of the first degree*

When the denominator is of the first degree, the remainder after the division has been performed will be independent of the variable and the integral will be given as a sum of terms involving powers of the variable together with a logarithmic term.

Example 7. *Find* $\int \frac{3x \, dx}{x + 2}$. [L.U.]

Here the numerator is of the same degree as the denominator and, dividing $3x$ by $x + 2$ we find

$$\frac{3x}{x + 2} \equiv 3 - \frac{6}{x + 2},$$

the quotient being 3 and the remainder -6. Hence

$$\int \frac{3x \, dx}{x + 2} = \int 3dx - \int \frac{6 \, dx}{x + 2},$$

$$= 3x - 6 \log_e (x + 2) + C.$$

Example 8. *Find* $\int \frac{x^3 \, dx}{4 - 2x}$.

Here the numerator is of higher degree than the denominator and the division process gives

$$\frac{x^3}{4 - 2x} \equiv -\tfrac{1}{2}x^2 - x - 2 + \frac{8}{4 - 2x}.$$

Hence

$$\int \frac{x^3\,dx}{4-2x} = \int (-\tfrac{1}{2}x^2 - x - 2)\,dx + \int \frac{8\,dx}{4-2x}$$

$$= -\tfrac{1}{6}x^3 - \tfrac{1}{2}x^2 - 2x - 4\log_e(4-2x) + C.$$

(ii) *Denominator of the second degree*

When the denominator is of the second degree and when it splits up into a pair of linear factors, the integrand can be resolved into partial fractions by the method of § 2.12. Each partial fraction will produce a logarithmic term when the integration is performed.

Example 9. *Find* $\int \dfrac{2\,dx}{4x^2 - 1}$. [O.C.]

We first factorise the denominator into $(2x - 1)$ and $(2x + 1)$ and write

$$\frac{2}{4x^2 - 1} \equiv \frac{A}{2x - 1} + \frac{B}{2x + 1},$$

where A and B are two constants to be found. The usual method for resolution into partial fractions then gives as the identity from which A and B are to be determined

$$A(2x + 1) + B(2x - 1) \equiv 2.$$

By letting $x = \pm\tfrac{1}{2}$ in turn we find $A = -B = 1$, so that

$$\int \frac{2\,dx}{4x^2 - 1} = \int \frac{dx}{2x - 1} - \int \frac{dx}{2x + 1}$$

$$= \tfrac{1}{2}\log_e(2x - 1) - \tfrac{1}{2}\log_e(2x + 1) + C$$

$$= \tfrac{1}{2}\log_e\left(\frac{2x - 1}{2x + 1}\right) + C.$$

Example 10. *Find* $\int \dfrac{(x^3 - a^2x + a^3)}{(x^2 - a^2)}\,dx$. [O.C.]

Here the numerator is of higher degree than the denominator and division shows that

$$\frac{x^3 - a^2x + a^3}{x^2 - a^2} \equiv x + \frac{a^3}{x^2 - a^2}.$$

The last term on the right is resolved into partial fractions by writing

$$\frac{a^3}{x^2 - a^2} \equiv \frac{A}{x - a} + \frac{B}{x + a}$$

so that the identity for the determination of A and B is

$$A(x + a) + B(x - a) \equiv a^3.$$

By letting $x = \pm a$ in turn we find $A = -B = \tfrac{1}{2}a^2$. Hence

$$\int \frac{x^3 - a^2x + a^3}{x^2 - a^2}\,dx = \int x\,dx + \tfrac{1}{2}a^2\int \frac{dx}{x - a} - \tfrac{1}{2}a^2\int \frac{dx}{x + a}$$

$$= \tfrac{1}{2}x^2 + \tfrac{1}{2}a^2\log_e(x - a) - \tfrac{1}{2}a^2\log_e(x + a) + C$$

$$= \tfrac{1}{2}\left\{x^2 + a^2\log_e\left(\frac{x - a}{x + a}\right)\right\} + C.$$

(iii) *Denominator of higher degree*

When the denominator is of higher degree than the second, resolution into partial fractions is still often useful. A few instances will be found in the examples and exercises which follow.

Example 11. *Find* $\int \dfrac{2\,dx}{x(x^2+1)}$. [O.C.]

Here we write, since (x^2+1) is a quadratic factor of the denominator,

$$\frac{2}{x(x^2+1)} \equiv \frac{A}{x} + \frac{Bx+C}{x^2+1}$$

and A, B, C are found from the identity

$$A(x^2+1) + (Bx+C)x \equiv 2.$$

Equating the coefficients of x^2, x and the terms not involving x gives respectively $A + B = 0$, $C = 0$, $A = 2$ and hence

$$\int \frac{2\,dx}{x(x^2+1)} = \int \frac{2\,dx}{x} + \int \frac{-2x\,dx}{x^2+1}$$

$$= 2\log_e x - \log_e(x^2+1) + C,$$

the second integral on the right being found by the method of § 11.6.

11.8 Further examples of integration by parts

The method of integration by parts (§ 9.6) is often effective when the integrand contains the function $\log_e x$. If this function is taken as u in the formula

$$\int u\frac{dv}{dx}\,dx = uv - \int v\frac{du}{dx}\,dx, \tag{11.21}$$

then du/dx in the integral on the right is $1/x$ and the integral can often be found easily. As a simple example the integral $\int \log_e x\,dx$ can be found by taking $u = \log_e x$, $dv/dx = 1$ so that $du/dx = 1/x$ and $v = x$. Formula (11.21) then gives

$$\int \log_e x\,dx = x\log_e x - \int x\left(\frac{1}{x}\right)dx$$

$$= x\log_e x - \int dx = x\log_e x - x + C.$$

Another example which depends on the work of this chapter is given below.

Example 12. *Find* $\int \tan^{-1} x\,dx$.

Writing $u = \tan^{-1} x$, $dv/dx = 1$ we have $du/dx = 1/(1+x^2)$ and $v = x$. Hence (11.21) gives

$$\int \tan^{-1} x\,dx = x\tan^{-1} x - \int \frac{x\,dx}{1+x^2}$$

$$= x\tan^{-1} x - \tfrac{1}{2}\int \frac{2x}{1+x^2}\,dx$$

$$= x\tan^{-1} x - \tfrac{1}{2}\log_e(1+x^2) + C,$$

the second integral on the right being found by the method of § 11.6.

Exercises 11 (b)

Find the following indefinite integrals

1. $\int \dfrac{x^2\,dx}{x^3 + 4}$.   [O.C.]   2. $\int \dfrac{(x + 2)\,dx}{x^2 + 4x + 10}$.   [O.C.]

3. $\int \left(\dfrac{e^a + e^{-a}}{e^a - e^{-a}}\right) dx$.   4. $\int \left(\dfrac{x^{\theta-1} + e^{a-1}}{x^\theta + e^a}\right) dx$.

5. $\int \left(\dfrac{1 - x}{1 + x}\right) dx$.   [O.C.]   6. $\int \dfrac{(x^2 + 3)\,dx}{2x + 3}$.

7. $\int \dfrac{dx}{x(x - 2)}$.   [O.C.]   8. $\int \dfrac{x\,dx}{(x - 1)(x - 2)}$.   [O.C.]

9. $\int \dfrac{5x\,dx}{(2x + 1)(x - 2)}$.   [O.C.]   10. $\int \dfrac{(x + 6)\,dx}{x^2 + 6x + 8}$.   [O.C.]

11. $\int \dfrac{x^2\,dx}{x^2 - 4}$.   [O.C.]   12. $\int \dfrac{(4x + 3)\,dx}{(x - 3)^2}$.

13. $\int \dfrac{dx}{(x - 1)^2(x^2 + 1)}$.   14. $\int \dfrac{(7x + 5)\,dx}{(x - 3)(x^2 + 4)}$.

Evaluate the following definite integrals

15. $\displaystyle\int_1^{10} \dfrac{(3x + 1)\,dx}{x(3x + 2)}$.   16. $\displaystyle\int_0^1 \dfrac{dx}{(x + 1)(x + 2)}$.

17. $\displaystyle\int_0^1 \dfrac{dx}{4 + x - 3x^2}$.   18. $\displaystyle\int_0^3 \dfrac{2x\,dx}{(1 + x^2)(3 + x^2)}$.

Use the method of integration by parts to find the following integrals

19. $\int x \log_e x\,dx$.   20. $\int x \log_e (x + 4)\,dx$.

21. $\int x^3 \log_e 5x\,dx$.   [O.C.]   22. $\int x \sec^2 x\,dx$.

23. Show that

$$\int \dfrac{x - \sin x}{\cos 2x + 1}\,dx = \tfrac{1}{2}x \tan x + \tfrac{1}{2} \log_e \cos x - \tfrac{1}{2} \sec x + C. \quad \text{[O.C.]}$$

24. Show that $\operatorname{cosec} x = (\tfrac{1}{2} \sec^2 \tfrac{1}{2}x)/(\tan \tfrac{1}{2}x)$ and hence find $\int \operatorname{cosec} x\,dx$. By replacing x by $x + \tfrac{1}{2}\pi$, deduce that

$$\int \sec x\,dx = \log_e \tan (\tfrac{1}{4}\pi + \tfrac{1}{2}x) + C.$$

25. Use the substitution $\sqrt{x} = u$ to find $\int(1 + \sqrt{x})^{-1}\,dx$. Deduce that

$$\int_0^4 \left\{ \dfrac{1}{\sqrt{(1 + x)}} - \dfrac{1}{1 + \sqrt{x}} \right\} dx = 2(\sqrt{5} - 3 + \log_e 3). \quad \text{[L.U.]}$$

11.9 Successive approximations and the Taylor–Maclaurin theorem

Consider first the function $1/(1 + x)$ when $-1 < x < 1$. By actual division we find

$$\frac{1}{1+x} = 1 - \frac{x}{1+x} = 1 - x + \frac{x^2}{1+x} = 1 - x + x^2 - \frac{x^3}{1+x}$$

and so on. Hence 1, $1 - x$, $1 - x + x^2$, . . . are *successive approximations* to the function $1/(1 + x)$, for the respective errors are

$$-\frac{x}{1+x}, \qquad \frac{x^2}{1+x}, \qquad -\frac{x^3}{1+x}, \qquad . . .,$$

and, since $-1 < x < 1$, these errors become progressively smaller. It should be noticed that for $x = 0$, the successive approximations are all equal, from $1 - x$ onwards they all have the same first derivative, from $1 - x + x^2$ onwards they all have the same second derivative and so on.

This suggests the following method of approximating to a function. Let

$$f(h + x) \simeq a_0 + a_1 x + a_2 x^2 + a_3 x^3 + . . . + a_n x^n, \qquad (11.22)$$

and choose a_0, a_1, a_2, a_3, . . ., a_n so that $f(x + h)$ and its first n derivatives have the same values when $x = 0$ as the polynomial on the right and *its* n derivatives. By this procedure it might well be expected that the polynomial will be a successively better approximation to the function as the number of its terms increases.

The first, second and third derivatives of the polynomial on the right of (11.22) are respectively

$$a_1 + 2a_2 x + 3a_3 x^2 + . . . + na_n x^{n-1},$$
$$2a_2 + 3 \cdot 2 a_3 x + . . . + n(n - 1)a_n x^{n-2},$$
$$3 \cdot 2a_3 + 4 \cdot 3 \cdot 2 a_4 x + . . . + n(n - 1)(n - 2) a_n x^{n-3},$$

and so on for the higher derivatives. The values of the polynomial and its first n derivatives are, when $x = 0$, therefore a_0, a_1, $2!a_2$, $3!a_3$, . . ., $(n)!a_n$. Equating these to the values of $f(x + h)$ and its first n derivatives when $x = 0$, we have

$$a_0 = f(h), \ a_1 = f'(h), \ 2!a_2 = f''(h), \ 3!a_3 = f'''(h), \ . . .,(n)!a_n = f^{(n)}(h),$$

and we may expect to be able to write

$$f(x + h) \simeq f(h) + xf'(h) + \frac{x^2}{2!}f''(h) + \frac{x^3}{3!}f'''(h) + . . . + \frac{x^n}{(n)!}f^{(n)}(h).$$

Provided $f(x)$ satisfies certain conditions, it can in fact be proved (but we shall not attempt to do so here) that the non-terminating series

$f(h) + xf'(h) + (x^2/2!)f''(h) + \ldots$ converges and that the limit of its sum is $f(x + h)$. In such cases,

$$f(x + h) = f(h) + xf'(h) + \frac{x^2}{2!}f''(h) + \ldots + \frac{x^n}{(n)!}f^{(n)}(h) + \ldots$$
$$(11.23)$$

and the series on the right of (11.23) is called *Taylor's* series for $f(x + h)$. In the special case of $h = 0$, (11.23) reduces to

$$f(x) = f(0) + xf'(0) + \frac{x^2}{2!}f''(0) + \ldots + \frac{x^n}{(n)!}f^{(n)}(0) + \ldots \quad (11.24)$$

and the series in (11.24) is known as *Maclaurin's* series for $f(x)$.

Example 13. *If x is the radian measure of an angle which is so small that x^3 and higher powers of x can be neglected, show that*

$$\sin\left(\tfrac{1}{6}\pi + x\right) = \tfrac{1}{2} + \tfrac{1}{2}\sqrt{3}\,x - \tfrac{1}{4}x^2. \qquad \text{[O.C.]}$$

Here $h = \tfrac{1}{6}\pi$ and $f(x) = \sin x$, $f(h) = \sin\tfrac{1}{6}\pi = \tfrac{1}{2}$. Hence $f'(x) = \cos x$, $f''(x) = -\sin x$ so that $f'(h) = \cos\tfrac{1}{6}\pi = \sqrt{3}/2$ and $f''(h) = -\sin\tfrac{1}{6}\pi = -\tfrac{1}{2}$. Substituting in (11.23) and neglecting the terms in x^3 and higher powers immediately gives the required result.

11.10 Series for e^x and $\log_e (1 + x)$

As examples of Maclaurin's expansion (11.24), we give below the series for e^x and $\log_e (1 + x)$.

If $f(x) = e^x$, all the derivatives are e^x and we have

$$f(x) = f'(x) = f''(x) \ldots = f^{(n)}(x) = \ldots = e^x,$$

and

$$f(0) = f'(0) = f''(0) = \ldots = f^{(n)}(0) = \ldots = e^0 = 1.$$

Hence, from (11.24),

$$e^x = 1 + x + \frac{x^2}{2!} + \ldots + \frac{x^n}{(n)!} + \ldots \qquad (11.25)$$

and it can be shown, but this is not attempted here, that (11.25) is valid for all values of x. The expression on the right of (11.25) is known as the *exponential* series and has many applications. Here we shall only use it to calculate the value of e a little more accurately than the value taken from the graph of Fig. 111 and given in § 11.4. Thus, with $x = 1$,

$$e = 1 + 1 + \frac{1}{2!} + \frac{1}{3!} + \frac{1}{4!} + \frac{1}{5!} + \frac{1}{6!} + \ldots$$
$$= 1 \cdot 000 + 1 \cdot 000 + 0 \cdot 5000 + 0 \cdot 1667 + 0 \cdot 0417 +$$
$$0 \cdot 0083 + 0 \cdot 0014 + 0 \cdot 0002 + \ldots = 2 \cdot 718 \ldots$$

If $f(x) = \log_e (1 + x), f(0) = \log_e 1 = 0$ and

$$f'(x) = \frac{1}{1 + x}, \quad f''(x) = -\frac{1}{(1 + x)^2}, \quad f'''(x) = \frac{2}{(1 + x)^3},$$

$$f^{1v}(x) = \frac{-6}{(1 + x)^4}, \quad \ldots$$

Hence

$$f'(0) = 1, \quad f''(0) = -1, \quad f'''(0) = 2!, \quad f^{1v}(0) = -3!, \quad \ldots$$

and (11.24) gives

$$\log_e (1 + x) = x - \frac{x^2}{2} + \frac{x^3}{3} - \frac{x^4}{4} + \ldots \tag{11.26}$$

This is the *logarithmic* series and, for reasons which we cannot go into here, it is valid only for the restricted range $-1 < x \leqslant 1$. Hence (11.26) can only be used for calculating natural logarithms for small values of x and, even for values of x approaching unity, many terms of the series have to be used to obtain reasonable accuracy. However, by algebraical manipulation, the series can be recast into a form which permits the calculation of the logarithms of larger numbers and a typical example is given below.

Example 14. *If $x > 1$, show that*

$$\tfrac{1}{2} \log_e \left(\frac{x + 1}{x - 1}\right) = \frac{1}{x} + \frac{1}{3x^3} + \frac{1}{5x^5} + \ldots,$$

and use this result to calculate $\log_e 2$ to three places of decimals.

Since

$$\log_e \left(\frac{x + 1}{x - 1}\right) = \log_e \left(\frac{1 + 1/x}{1 - 1/x}\right) = \log_e \left(1 + \frac{1}{x}\right) - \log_e \left(1 - \frac{1}{x}\right)$$

and since $x > 1$, x can be replaced by $1/x$ and $-1/x$ in turn in (11.26) to give

$$\log_e \left(\frac{x + 1}{x - 1}\right) = \frac{1}{x} - \frac{1}{2x^3} + \frac{1}{3x^3} - \frac{1}{4x^4} + \frac{1}{5x^5} - \ldots$$

$$- \left\{-\frac{1}{x} - \frac{1}{2}\left(-\frac{1}{x}\right)^2 + \frac{1}{3}\left(-\frac{1}{x}\right)^3 - \frac{1}{4}\left(-\frac{1}{x}\right)^4 + \frac{1}{5}\left(-\frac{1}{x}\right)^5 - \ldots\right\}$$

$$= 2\left(\frac{1}{x} + \frac{1}{3x^3} + \frac{1}{5x^5} + \ldots\right),$$

and the required result follows after division by 2. Putting $x = 3$ we have

$$\log_e \left(\frac{4}{2}\right) = 2\left(\frac{1}{3} + \frac{1}{3 \times 3^3} + \frac{1}{5 \times 3^3} + \ldots\right)$$

$$= 2(0 \cdot 3333 + 0 \cdot 0124 + 0 \cdot 0008 + \ldots)$$

and this leads immediately to $\log_e 2 = 0 \cdot 693. \ldots$

11.11 Newton's method of approximation to the root of an equation

An interesting and useful application of Taylor's series is Newton's method of approximating to the root of an equation.

Suppose that $x = \alpha$ is an approximation to a root of the equation $f(x) = 0$ and that the actual value of this root is $\alpha + \varepsilon$ where ε is small. Then $f(\alpha + \varepsilon) = 0$ and, writing $h = \alpha$, $x = \varepsilon$ in (11.23),

$$f(\alpha) + \varepsilon f'(\alpha) + \frac{\varepsilon^2}{2!} f''(\alpha) + \ldots + \frac{\varepsilon^n}{n!} f^{(n)}(\alpha) + \ldots = (0).$$

Neglecting powers of the small quantity ε above the first,

$$f(\alpha) + \varepsilon f'(\alpha) = 0,$$

so that $\varepsilon = -f(\alpha)/f'(\alpha)$ and a better approximation than $x = \alpha$ to the root is

$$\alpha - \frac{f(\alpha)}{f'(\alpha)}. \tag{11.27}$$

Example 15. *Find, correct to three decimal places, the root of the equation* $x^4 - 8x = 60$ *which is nearly equal to* 3.

Here $f(x) = x^4 - 8x - 60, f'(x) = 4x^3 - 8$, so that
$$f(3) = (3)^4 - 8(3) - 60 = -3, f'(3) = 4(3)^3 - 8 = 100.$$

Hence a better approximation than $x = 3$ is

$$x = 3 - \frac{f(3)}{f'(3)} = 3 - \frac{-3}{100} = 3 \cdot 03.$$

A better approximation than $x = 3 \cdot 03$ can be obtained by reworking the above with $3 \cdot 03$ in place of 3. Thus

$$f(3 \cdot 03) = (3 \cdot 03)^4 - 8(3 \cdot 03) - 60 = 0 \cdot 049,$$
$$f'(3 \cdot 03) = 4(3 \cdot 03)^3 - 8 = 103 \cdot 273,$$

and the next approximation is

$$x = 3 \cdot 03 - \frac{f(3 \cdot 03)}{f'(3 \cdot 03)} = 3 \cdot 03 - \frac{0 \cdot 049}{103 \cdot 273} = 3 \cdot 02951$$

$$= 3 \cdot 030 \text{ (to three places)}.$$

Exercises 11 (c)

1. If x is sufficiently small for x^3 and higher order terms to be neglected, show that $\tan(x + \theta) = \tan \theta + x \sec^2 \theta + x^2 \sec^2 \theta \tan \theta$.

2. Assuming the expansions are convergent, show that

$$\sin x = x - \frac{x^3}{3!} + \frac{x^5}{5!} - \ldots, \qquad \cos x = 1 - \frac{x^2}{2!} + \frac{x^4}{4!} - \ldots.$$

3. Prove that the first three terms in the expansion of $\log_e(1 + e^x)$ in a series of ascending powers of x are $\log_e 2 + \frac{1}{2}x + \frac{1}{8}x^2$ and that there is no term in x^3.   [O.C.]

4. Show that the expansion of sec x in a series of ascending powers of x as far as the term in x^4 is $1 + \frac{1}{2}x^2 + \frac{5}{24}x^4$.   [O.C.]

5. If $y = e^{\cos x}$, prove that

$$\frac{d^2y}{dx^2} + \frac{dy}{dx}\sin x + y\cos x = 0$$

and that, if x is so small that x^5 and higher powers can be neglected, then $y = e(1 - \frac{1}{2}x^2 + \frac{1}{6}x^4)$.   [O.C.]

6. If x^5 and higher terms are neglected, show that

$$\log_e \{x + \surd(1 + x^2)\} = x - \tfrac{1}{6}x^3.$$ [O.C.]

7. If $-1 < x < 1$ and $y = x + \frac{1}{2}x^2 + \frac{1}{3}x^3 + \frac{1}{4}x^4 + \ldots$, give an expression not involving a series for y in terms of x. Hence find an expansion for x in powers of y as far as the term in y^4.   [N.U.]

8. Given that $y = (2 + x)^2 e^{-x}$, find the expansion of y in ascending powers of x as far as the term in x^3. Find also the expansion of $\log_e y$ in ascending powers of x as far as the term in x^3 and state the coefficient of x^n.   [N.U.]

9. Prove that

$$\log_e \left(\frac{x+1}{x}\right) = 2\left\{\frac{1}{2x+1} + \frac{1}{3(2x+1)^3} + \frac{1}{5(2x+1)^5} + \ldots\right\},$$

stating the range of values of x for which the series is valid.   [O.C.]

10. Expand $E \equiv \log_e \{(2 - x)/(1 - x)\}$ in ascending powers of x up to x^3. Evaluate E when $x = \frac{1}{3}$ and hence find $\log_e 3$ to three places of decimals, given that $\log_e 2 = 0.6931$.   [O.C.]

11. If α is so small that its cube and higher powers may be neglected, find the values of the constants A, B and C so that

$$\exp(x + \alpha) = A\exp(x) + B\exp(x + \tfrac{1}{2}\alpha) + C\exp(x + \tfrac{1}{3}\alpha).$$

12. If p, q are the roots of the quadratic equation $x^2 - ax + b = 0$, show that for suitable values of x,

$$\log_e (1 + ax + bx^2) = (p + q)x - \tfrac{1}{2}(p^2 + q^2)x^2 + \tfrac{1}{3}(p^3 + q^3)x^3 - \ldots$$

13. Given that a root of the equation $(x^2 + 9)^{3/2} + 8x^2 + x = 258$ is close to 4, find the value of this root correct to three significant figures.   [O.C.]

14. A root of the equation $\sin^3 \frac{1}{2}x + \cos x - \frac{249}{400} = 0$ is approximately $\frac{1}{3}\pi$. Find the value of this root correct to three decimal places.   [O.C.]

15. Use Newton's method of approximating to the root of an equation to find the positive square root of 26 to three decimal places.

Exercises 11 (d)

1. Find the derivative with respect to x of

$$\log_e \left(\frac{3 + 4 \cos x}{4 + 3 \cos x} \right).$$ [O.C.]

2. If $y = e^x \tan x$, show that

$$\frac{d^2y}{dx^2} - 2(1 + \tan x)\frac{dy}{dx} + (1 + 2 \tan x)y = 0.$$ [O.C.]

3. If A, B, k and p are constants and

$$\frac{d}{dx}(Ae^{kx} \sin px + Be^{kx} \cos px) = e^{kx} \sin px$$

for all values of x, find A and B in terms of k and p. Hence evaluate

$$\int_0^{\pi/4} e^{3x} \sin 2x \, dx.$$ [L.U.]

4. With the same axes and scales for both graphs, draw the graphs of $y = e^x$ and $y = 15/(x + 1)$ from $x = 0$ to $x = 3$.
A point $P(x, y)$, where $1 < y < 15$, is taken on the curve $y = e^x$. A rectangle is formed by the lines $x = 0$, $y = 15$ and the perpendiculars from P to these lines. Show that the area of the rectangle is a maximum when $(x + 1)e^x = 15$ and obtain the approximate solution of this equation from your graphs. [L.U.]

5. If $y = e^{4x} \cos 3x$, show that

$$\frac{d^2y}{dx^2} - 8\frac{dy}{dx} + 25y = 0.$$ [O.C.]

6. If $y = Ae^{-x} \cos(x + \alpha)$ where A and α are constants, prove that

(i) $\dfrac{d^2y}{dx^2} + 2\dfrac{dy}{dx} + 2y = 0$,   (ii) $\dfrac{d^4y}{dx^4} + 4y = 0$. [O.C.]

7. Show that

$$\log_e (1 + x + x^2) = \int \frac{dx}{1 - x} - 3 \int \frac{x^2 \, dx}{1 - x^3} + C$$

where C is an arbitrary constant. By expanding the integrands as far as the terms in x^5, find the first six terms of the series for $\log_e (1 + x + x^2)$ for small values of x. [N.U.]

8. Find

(i) $\displaystyle\int \frac{x \, dx}{2x - 3}$,   (ii) $\displaystyle\int \frac{2x + 3}{x + 2} \, dx$,   (iii) $\displaystyle\int \frac{x^3 \, dx}{x - 1}$.

9. Find

(i) $\displaystyle\int \frac{6x\,dx}{x^2 - 4x + 3}$, (ii) $\displaystyle\int \frac{(5x + 8)\,dx}{2x^2 + x - 3}$, (iii) $\displaystyle\int \frac{(3 + 2x)\,dx}{1 - 4x^2}$.

[O.C.]

10. Evaluate

(i) $\displaystyle\int_1^2 \frac{dx}{x^2 + 4x}$, (ii) $\displaystyle\int_1^2 \frac{dx}{x^2(1 + x)}$.

11. Integrate with respect to x

(i) $x^2 \tan^{-1} x$, (ii) $(\log_e x)/(x + 1)^2$.

12. Find by integrating by parts the area bounded by the curve

$$y = (\log_e x)/\sqrt{x},$$

the x-axis between $x = 1$ and $x = e$ and the line $x = e$. [N.U.]

13. Show that

$$\int_1^2 \frac{dx}{e^x - 1} = \log_e (1 + 1/e).$$

[N.U.]

14. Prove that the area enclosed by the curve $y = \tan x$, the x-axis and $x = \frac{1}{3}\pi$ is $\log_e 2$. If the point $(\bar{x}, \bar{y})$ is the centroid of this area, prove that $\bar{y} = (3\sqrt{3} - \pi)/(6 \log_e 2)$ and calculate $\bar{x}$ by means of Simpson's rule with ordinates at intervals of $\frac{1}{12}\pi$, given that $\tan \frac{1}{12}\pi = 2 - \sqrt{3}$.

[O.C.]

15. Prove that if $C = \int e^{ax} \cos bx\,dx$ and $S = \int e^{ax} \sin bx\,dx$ then

$$aC - bS = e^{ax} \cos bx, \qquad aS + bC = e^{ax} \sin bx.$$

Evaluate $\displaystyle\int_0^{\pi/2} e^{2x} \sin 3x\,dx$. [O.C.]

16. A particle is projected with a speed of 3 cm/s along the axis of x towards the origin O from an initial position at a distance of 1 cm from O on the positive side of O. After time t seconds its displacement x cm from O is given by $x = Ae^{-t} + Be^{-2t}$ where A and B are constants. Find the numerical values of A, B and the time at which the particle reaches O. Show that the particle travels beyond O and that the time taken to travel from O to the furthest position reached beyond O is $\log_e 2$ seconds. [N.U.]

17. Sketch the curve $y^2(x + a) + x(x - a) = 0$, where a is a positive constant. Show that the volume enclosed by rotating about the axis of x the part of the curve which lies between $x = 0$ and $x = a$ is

$$\pi a^2(1 \cdot 5 - 2 \log_e 2).$$

18. If $y = \exp(\sin^2 x)$ prove that

$$\frac{dy}{dx} = y \sin 2x, \qquad \frac{d^2y}{dx^2} = \tfrac{1}{2}y(1 + 4\cos 2x - \cos 4x)$$

and obtain the expansion of y as far as the term in x^4. [O.C.]

19. Find the expansion of $(\sin^{-1} x)/\sqrt{(1 - x^2)}$ in ascending powers of x as far as, and including, the term in x^3. [O.C.]

20. If $y = (1 + x)^{-1} \log_e (1 + x)$ prove that

$$(1 + x)\frac{dy}{dx} + y = \frac{1}{1 + x}, \qquad (1 + x)\frac{d^2y}{dx^2} + 2\frac{dy}{dx} = -\frac{1}{(1 + x)^2}.$$

Show also that, if x^5 and higher terms are neglected, then

$$y = x - \tfrac{3}{2}x^2 + \tfrac{11}{6}x^3 - \tfrac{25}{12}x^4. \qquad \text{[O.C.]}$$

21. If $y = (1 + x)^2 \log_e (1 + x)$, evaluate dy/dx and d^2y/dx^2. Prove that, if $n > 2$, then

$$\frac{d^ny}{dx^n} = (-1)^{n-1}\frac{2 \cdot (n - 3)!}{(1 + x)^{n-2}},$$

and deduce that the expansion of y as far as the term in x^4 is

$$y = x + \tfrac{3}{2}x^2 + \tfrac{1}{3}x^3 - \tfrac{1}{12}x^4. \qquad \text{[O.C.]}$$

22. In the equation $x^{2+\lambda} = e^2$, λ is a small quantity whose third and higher powers may be neglected. Prove that

$$\text{(i) } x/e = \exp\left(-\frac{\lambda}{2 + \lambda}\right),$$

$$\text{(ii) } x = e(1 - \tfrac{1}{2}\lambda + \tfrac{3}{8}\lambda^2).$$

23. Prove that $\log_2 e - \log_4 e + \log_8 e - \log_{16} e + \ldots = 1$ where e is the base of natural logarithms. [N.U.]

24. Find, correct to three decimal places, the root of the cubic equation $x^3 + 2 = 9{\cdot}7x$ which is close to 3.

25. Given that $\log_{10} x = 0{\cdot}4343 \log_e x$ and that a root of the equation $x + \log_{10} x = 5$ lies between 4 and 5, find this root to three significant figures.

CHAPTER 12

ELEMENTARY DIFFERENTIAL EQUATIONS

12.1 Introduction

Problems in science and engineering can often be expressed in mathematical form but it is usually necessary to make simplifications and approximations before this is possible. The choice of these simplifications and approximations is a matter of some skill since they must not be so drastic that the mathematical problem does not properly represent the actual problem and, at the same time, they must be chosen so that the resulting equations are reasonably simple.

The translation of an actual physical problem into mathematical form usually starts from well-established physical laws which can be expressed as mathematical equations, and principles which permit the choice of physically acceptable solutions to such equations. Typical examples are that (for a certain range of speeds) the drag of the air on an aeroplane is proportional to the square of its speed and the principle that energy cannot be created or destroyed. The resulting mathematical formulation is often given as an equation involving differential coefficients and in this chapter we give an introduction to the study of the simplest types.

12.2 Some definitions

Equations such as

$$\frac{dy}{dx} = y, \qquad \frac{d^2y}{dx^2} + 4y = 0, \qquad \frac{d^3y}{dx^3} + 2\frac{d^2y}{dx^2} + 3\frac{dy}{dx} + 2y = \cos x,$$

all of which involve differential coefficients, are known as *differential equations*. The *order* of such an equation is defined as the order of the highest differential coefficient appearing in it and the order of the above three equations are therefore respectively first, second and third. Here we shall only be concerned with certain very special forms of first and second order equations. Typical examples are

$$\frac{dy}{dx} = \cos x, \qquad \frac{dy}{dx} = y, \qquad \frac{dy}{dx} = \frac{y^3}{2+x}, \qquad (12.1)$$

$$\frac{d^2y}{dx^2} + 4y = 10, \qquad (12.2)$$

and the *solution* in each case consists of a relation between the two variables x and y, free from differential coefficients.

12.3 First order equations with variables separable

The first order differential equation to be considered in this chapter is one which can be written in the form

$$\frac{dy}{dx} = \frac{f(x)}{g(y)}, \qquad (12.3)$$

where $f(x)$ and $g(y)$ are functions respectively of x and y. That the equations in (12.1) are of this type can be seen by writing them respectively in the forms

(i) $\dfrac{dy}{dx} = \dfrac{\cos x}{1}$, (ii) $\dfrac{dy}{dx} = \dfrac{1}{(1/y)}$, (iii) $\dfrac{dy}{dx} = \dfrac{1/(2+x)}{(1/y^3)}$,

so that, in these three examples, $f(x)$ and $g(y)$ are given by

(i) $f(x) = \cos x, g(y) = 1$, (ii) $f(x) = 1, g(y) = 1/y$,

(iii) $f(x) = 1/(2+x), g(y) = 1/y^3$.

To solve equation (12.3), we first multiply by $g(y)$ to give

$$g(y)\frac{dy}{dx} = f(x).$$

Integration with respect to x of each side of the equation then leads to

$$\int g(y)\frac{dy}{dx}\,dx = \int f(x)\,dx + C \qquad (12.4)$$

where C is an arbitrary constant. In obtaining equation (12.4) the reader should note that it is unnecessary to add arbitrary constants C_1 and C_2 to each indefinite integral. If we did include two such constants, equation (12.4) would be

$$\int g(y)\frac{dy}{dx}\,dx + C_1 = \int f(x)\,dx + C_2$$

and this could be written in the form

$$\int g(y)\frac{dy}{dx}\,dx = \int f(x)\,dx + C_2 - C_1$$

$$= \int f(x)\,dx + C,$$

where $C = C_2 - C_1$ is simply another arbitrary constant. The left-hand side of (12.4) can be simplified to $\int g(y)\,dy$ so that

$$\int g(y)\,dy = \int f(x)\,dx + C. \qquad (12.5)$$

When $f(x)$ and $g(y)$ are given functions and when the integrations have been carried out, equation (12.5) gives a relation between the two variables x and y free from differential coefficients and is the required solution of the differential equation (12.3).

In the solution of the differential equation (12.3), some of the steps described above can be omitted in practice. If we treat dy and dx as separate quantities, the differential equation

$$\frac{dy}{dx} = \frac{f(x)}{g(y)}$$

can, by cross-multiplication, be written

$$g(y)\, dy = f(x)\, dx$$

and everything involving y is on one side of the equation and everything involving x is on the other. In this form, the variables x and y are said to be *separated*. Integration of both sides and the addition of an arbitrary constant then leads to the solution

$$\int g(y)\, dy = \int f(x)\, dx + C$$

as given in (12.5).

Example 1. *Solve the differential equation $dy/dx = \cos x$.*

Here cross-multiplication gives

$$dy = \cos x\, dx$$

and the variables are now separated. Integrating

$$\int dy = \int \cos x\, dx,$$

giving, for the required solution

$$y = \sin x + C.$$

Example 2. *Solve the differential equation*

$$\sec x \frac{dy}{dx} = \surd(1 - y^2).\qquad\text{[O.C.]}$$

Cross-multiplication and integration gives

$$\int \frac{dy}{\surd(1 - y^2)} = \int \cos x\, dx,$$

so that

$$\sin^{-1} y = \sin x + C$$

is the required solution.

In some cases a neater solution to a differential equation is given by taking the arbitrary constant in logarithmic form. The following are typical examples.

Example 3. *Solve the differential equation dy/dx = y.*

Here separation of the variables by cross-multiplication and integration gives

$$\int \frac{dy}{y} = \int dx,$$

and this leads to the solution $\log_e y = x + C$. If we write $C = \log_e A$, where A is therefore another arbitrary constant, the solution is $\log_e y = x + \log_e A$. This can be written

$$\log_e y - \log_e A = x$$

so that

$$\log_e \left(\frac{y}{A}\right) = x,$$

and hence

$$\frac{y}{A} = e^x.$$

The neatest form of the solution is then $y = Ae^x$.

Example 4. *Show that the solution of the differential equation*

$$x \frac{dy}{dx} - y(y + 1) = 0$$

can be written in the form $y = Ax(y + 1)$ where A is a constant.

The given equation can be written

$$x \frac{dy}{dx} = y(y + 1)$$

and separation of the variables by cross-multiplication gives

$$\frac{dy}{y(y + 1)} = \frac{dx}{x}.$$

Integrating

$$\int \frac{dy}{y(y + 1)} = \int \frac{dx}{x} + \log_e A$$

where $\log_e A$ is an arbitrary constant. Resolving $1/\{y(y + 1)\}$ into partial fractions,

$$\int \left(\frac{1}{y} - \frac{1}{y + 1}\right) dy = \int \frac{dx}{x} + \log_e A$$

giving

$$\log_e y - \log_e (y + 1) = \log_e x + \log_e A.$$

This can be written

$$\log_e \left(\frac{y}{y + 1}\right) = \log_e (Ax)$$

so that $y/(y + 1) = Ax$ and hence $y = Ax(y + 1)$.

So far all the solutions obtained have contained an arbitrary constant; such solutions are known as *general* solutions. "Particular" solutions are often required which, as well as satisfying the differential equation, fulfil given relations between the variables. Two examples are given below.

Example 5. *Find a solution of the differential equation*

$$(1 + x^2)\frac{dy}{dx} + xe^{-y} = 0$$

which satisfies the condition $y = 1$ *when* $x = 0$.   [O.C.

Writing the equation in the form

$$(1 + x^2)\frac{dy}{dx} = -xe^{-y},$$

separation of the variables and integration gives

$$\int e^y dy = -\int \frac{x \, dx}{1 + x^2}.$$

This leads to

$$e^y = -\tfrac{1}{2}\log_e(1 + x^2) + C$$

as the general solution. Since $y = 1$ when $x = 0$,

$$e = -\tfrac{1}{2}\log_e(1) + C,$$

giving $C = e$ and the required solution can be written

$$\tfrac{1}{2}\log_e(1 + x^2) = e - e^y.$$

Example 6. *If* $x(1 - y)(dy/dx) + 2y = 0$ *and* $y = 2$ *when* $x = e$, *show that* $x^2 y e^{-y} = 2$.

The differential equation can be written

$$x(1 - y)\frac{dy}{dx} = -2y$$

so that, by cross-multiplication

$$\left(\frac{1-y}{y}\right) dy = -\frac{2 \, dx}{x}.$$

Writing the left-hand side as $\{(1/y) - 1\} \, dy$ and integrating

$$\int \left(\frac{1}{y} - 1\right) dy = -2\int \frac{dx}{x}$$

we have

$$\log_e y - y = -2 \log_e x + C$$

as the general solution. Putting $y = 2$, $x = e$ and remembering that $\log_e e = 1$,

$$\log_e 2 - 2 = -2 + C$$

so that $C = \log_e 2$ and

$$\log_e y - y = -2 \log_e x + \log_e 2.$$

Hence,

$$\log_e y + 2 \log_e x - \log_e 2 = y$$

or

$$\log_e \left(\frac{x^2 y}{2} \right) = y$$

and $\frac{1}{2}x^2y = e^y$, from which the required result follows on cross-multiplication.

Exercises 12 (a)

Find the general solutions of the following differential equations

1. $\dfrac{dy}{dx} = 4x^3.$

2. $\dfrac{dy}{dx} = y^2(1 + x).$

3. $\dfrac{dy}{dx} + \sin x = 0.$

4. $\dfrac{dy}{dx} + e^{-y} = 0.$

5. $\sec x \dfrac{dy}{dx} + \sec y = 0.$

6. $\dfrac{dy}{dx} = 4xy.$

7. $x \dfrac{dy}{dx} - y = xy.$

8. $\dfrac{dy}{dx} - \sin x \tan y = 0.$ [O.C.]

9. $y(1 + x^2) \dfrac{dy}{dx} - 2x(1 - y^2) = 0.$ [N.U.]

10. $\dfrac{dy}{dx} - x^2y = x^2.$

11. $(2y^2 + 1) \dfrac{dy}{dx} - 3x^2y = 0.$

12. $\dfrac{dy}{dx} - x \operatorname{cosec}^2 y = 3 \operatorname{cosec}^2 y.$ [N.U.]

Find the solutions of the following differential equations subject to the conditions stated

13. $\dfrac{dy}{dx} = 4y;\ y = 3$ when $x = 2.$

14. $e^{-x} \dfrac{dy}{dx} = (1 - y)^2;\ y = 0$ when $x = 0.$ [N.U.]

15. $\dfrac{dy}{dx} - y = 1;\ y = 2$ when $x = 0.$

16. $xy \dfrac{dy}{dx} - x = 1;\ y = \sqrt{2}$ when $x = 1.$

17. $2y \dfrac{dy}{dx} - \sin 2x = 0;\ y = 0$ when $x = 0.$

18. $x \dfrac{dx}{dy} - y = 1;\ y = 0$ when $x = 0.$

19. $(x^2 - 1) \dfrac{dy}{dx} + 2y = 0;\ y = 3$ when $x = 2.$ [N.U.]

20. $e^x \dfrac{dy}{dx} = xy^2;\ y = 1$ when $x = 0.$ [O.C.]

12.4 Homogeneous equations

The first order differential equation

$$\frac{dy}{dx} = f\left(\frac{y}{x}\right), \tag{12.6}$$

in which the right-hand side is a function of the ratio y/x, is said to be *homogeneous*. The equation can be reduced to an equation in which the variables can be separated by means of the substitution $y = vx$.

Thus, if $y = vx$, it follows that

$$\frac{dy}{dx} = x\frac{dv}{dx} + v$$

and equation (12.6) becomes

$$x\frac{dv}{dx} + v = f(v). \tag{12.7}$$

This can be written

$$x\frac{dv}{dx} = f(v) - v,$$

and separation of the variables by cross-multiplication gives

$$\frac{dv}{f(v) - v} = \frac{dx}{x}.$$

The general solution of the transformed equation (12.7) then follows by integration and the solution of the original equation (12.6) is then given by substituting y/x for v.

Example 7. *Solve the equation* $x\dfrac{dy}{dx} - y = x.$ [O.C.]

Here $x(dy/dx) = x + y$ and this can be written

$$\frac{dy}{dx} = 1 + \frac{y}{x},$$

so that the equation is of the form (12.6) and is homogeneous. Writing $y = vx$, so that

$$\frac{dy}{dx} = x\frac{dv}{dx} + v,$$

the equation becomes

$$x\frac{dv}{dx} + v = 1 + v.$$

This reduces to

$$x\frac{dv}{dx} = 1$$

and, separating the variables, we have

$$dv = \frac{dx}{x}.$$

Hence

$$\int dv = \int \frac{dx}{x},$$

giving

$$v = \log_e x + \log_e A,$$

where $\log_e A$ has been taken as the arbitrary constant. Substituting $v = y/x$, the solution of the original equation is

$$\frac{y}{x} = \log_e x + \log_e A,$$

and this can be written $y = x \log_e Ax$.

Example 8. *Find the solution of the equation* $(x + y) \dfrac{dy}{dx} + y = x$ *which satisfies the condition* $y = 1$ *when* $x = 3$.

Here

$$\frac{dy}{dx} = \frac{x - y}{x + y} = \frac{1 - (y/x)}{1 + (y/x)},$$

showing that the equation is homogeneous. The substitution $y = vx$ transforms the equation into

$$x \frac{dv}{dx} + v = \frac{1 - v}{1 + v},$$

so that

$$x \frac{dv}{dx} = \frac{1 - v}{1 + v} - v = \frac{1 - 2v - v^2}{1 + v}.$$

Separation of the variables and integration gives

$$\int \frac{(1 + v)dv}{1 - 2v - v^2} = \int \frac{dx}{x}$$

and, since $1 + v = -\frac{1}{2} \dfrac{d}{dv} (1 - 2v - v^2)$, this yields

$$-\tfrac{1}{2} \log_e (1 - 2v - v^2) = \log_e x + \log_e A,$$

where the arbitrary constant has again been taken as $\log_e A$. This can be written

$$\log_e x + \log_e A + \log_e \sqrt{(1 - 2v - v^2)} = 0$$

so that

$$Ax\sqrt{(1 - 2v - v^2)} = 1.$$

Substituting $v = y/x$, the general solution of the original equation is

$$A\sqrt{(x^2 - 2xy - y^2)} = 1$$

and, since $y = 1$ when $x = 3$, we have

$$A\sqrt{(9 - 6 - 1)} = 1$$

giving $A = 1/\sqrt{2}$. Hence the required solution is $x^2 - 2xy - y^2 = 2$.

12.5 An important second order differential equation

The second order differential equation

$$\frac{d^2y}{dx^2} + n^2y = c,$$

in which n and c are constants, has many applications to physical problems and a particular example is given in § 21.2. The general solution of this equation can be found as follows.

First consider the equation

$$\frac{d^2y}{dx^2} + n^2y = 0. \tag{12.8}$$

Writing $v = dy/dx$, we have

$$\frac{d^2y}{dx^2} = \frac{dv}{dx} = \frac{dv}{dy} \cdot \frac{dy}{dx} = v\frac{dv}{dy},$$

and equation (12.8) becomes

$$v\frac{dv}{dy} + n^2y = 0.$$

Separation of the variables and integration gives

$$\int v \, dv = -n^2 \int y \, dy,$$

so that

$$\tfrac{1}{2}v^2 = -\tfrac{1}{2}n^2y^2 + C.$$

Taking the arbitrary constant C as $\tfrac{1}{2}n^2a^2$, this gives $v^2 = n^2(a^2 - y^2)$ where a is another arbitrary constant. Since $v = dy/dx$, we have

$$\frac{dy}{dx} = n\sqrt{(a^2 - y^2)}$$

so that, separation of the variables in this equation and integration leads to

$$\int \frac{dy}{\sqrt{(a^2 - y^2)}} = n\int dx.$$

Hence

$$\sin^{-1}\left(\frac{y}{a}\right) = nx + C'$$

and, if we take the arbitrary constant C' in the form $n\varepsilon$, it follows that

$$y = a \sin n(x + \varepsilon).$$

Next consider the equation

$$\frac{d^2y}{dx^2} + n^2y = c \tag{12.9}$$

in which n and c are constants. Writing $y = (c/n^2) + z$ and noticing that

$$\frac{dy}{dx} = \frac{dz}{dx}, \quad \frac{d^2y}{dx^2} = \frac{d^2z}{dx^2},$$

we have

$$\frac{d^2z}{dx^2} + n^2z = 0$$

of which the solution is, as above,

$$z = a \sin n(x + \varepsilon).$$

Hence the solution of (12.9) is

$$y = \frac{c}{n^2} + a \sin n(x + \varepsilon). \tag{12.10}$$

When the arbitrary constant a is zero, this solution reduces to $y = c/n^2$ and this is called a *particular integral* of the differential equation (12.9).

Example 9. *Solve the equation*

$$\frac{d^2y}{dx^2} + 4y = 10$$

given that $y = dy/dx = 0$ when $x = 0$. [O.C.]

Here $n = 2$, $c = 10$ and the general solution of the differential equation is given by (12.10) as

$$y = \frac{10}{4} + a \sin 2(x + \varepsilon).$$

It follows that

$$\frac{dy}{dx} = 2a \cos 2(x + \varepsilon)$$

and since $y = dy/dx = 0$ when $x = 0$, the arbitrary constants a, ε are given by the equations

$$0 = \frac{10}{4} + a \sin 2\varepsilon, \quad 0 = 2a \cos 2\varepsilon.$$

A solution of these equations is $2\varepsilon = \tfrac{1}{2}\pi$, $a = \tfrac{5}{2}$ so that the required solution of the differential equation is

$$y = \tfrac{5}{2} + \tfrac{5}{2} \sin (2x + \tfrac{1}{2}\pi) = \tfrac{5}{2}(1 - \cos 2x).$$

Exercises 12 (b)

Find the general solutions of the following homogeneous equations

1. $\dfrac{dy}{dx} + \dfrac{y}{x} = 1.$

2. $xy\dfrac{dy}{dx} = y^2 + x^2\,e^{y/x}.$ [O.C.]

3. $2x^2\dfrac{dy}{dx} - xy - y^2 = 0.$

Find the solutions of the following homogeneous equations subject to the conditions stated

4. $2xy\dfrac{dy}{dx} = x^2 - y^2;$ $y = 1$ when $x = 2.$

5. $2xy\dfrac{dy}{dx} - x^2 = 3y^2;$ $y = 0$ when $x = 1.$

6. Show that the general solution of the equation

$$(x - y)\dfrac{dy}{dx} - x = y$$

can be written in the form $\tan^{-1}(y/x) = \log_e\{C\sqrt{(x^2 + y^2)}\}$ where C is an arbitrary constant.

7. If $y = 4$ when $x = 1$ and if y satisfies the equation

$$x^2\dfrac{dy}{dx} + xy - y^2 = 0,$$

find the value of y when $x = 2.$

8. By means of the substitution $y = vx$ reduce the differential equation

$$xy\dfrac{dy}{dx} = y^2 + \sqrt{(x^2 + y^2)}$$

to an equation in v and x. Find the solution, given that $y = 1$ when $x = 1.$ [O.C.]

Solve the following second order differential equations subject to the conditions stated

9. $\dfrac{d^2y}{dx^2} + y = 0;$ $y = 1$ when $x = 0,$ $y = 0$ when $x = \tfrac{1}{2}\pi.$

10. $\dfrac{d^2y}{dx^2} + 4y = 1;$ $y = 0$ and $\dfrac{dy}{dx} = \tfrac{1}{2}$ when $x = 0.$ [O.C.]

11. $\dfrac{d^2y}{dx^2} + 9y = 4;$ $y = 0$ and $\dfrac{dy}{dx} = 2$ when $x = 0.$ [O.C.]

12. $\dfrac{d^2y}{dx^2} + 4y = 10;$ $y = 1$ when $x = 0$ and when $x = \tfrac{1}{4}\pi.$ [O.C.]

12.6 Some applications to practical problems

The first part of this chapter has been concerned with the solution of certain special types of first and second order differential equations. There are, of course, many other types of such equations but these are outside the scope of the present book. However, many practical problems give rise to the differential equations which we have considered and we give below some typical examples and exercises.

Example 10. *A particle is projected with velocity u at time $t = 0$ and moves in a straight line. At time t its velocity is v and the distance travelled is x. The acceleration of the particle is $-kv^n$ where k is a positive constant and n is a constant less than unity. Show that the particle will come to rest when*

$$t = \frac{u^{1-n}}{(1-n)k} \quad and \quad x = \frac{u^{2-n}}{(2-n)k}.$$ [N.U.]

By equation (8.2), the acceleration of the particle at time t is dv/dt so that

$$\frac{dv}{dt} = -kv^n.$$

This is a first order differential equation in which separation of the variables and integration gives

$$\int v^{-n}\, dv = -k\int dt$$

leading to

$$\frac{v^{1-n}}{1-n} = -kt + C.$$

The arbitrary constant C can be found from the fact that $v = u$ when $t = 0$, so that

$$\frac{u^{1-n}}{1-n} = C.$$

Hence

$$kt = \frac{u^{1-n} - v^{1-n}}{1-n}$$

and, since the particle comes to rest when $v = 0$, the time required is given by $t = u^{1-n}/(1-n)k$. The acceleration can also be expressed, see equation (8.4), as $v\, dv/dx$ giving

$$v\frac{dv}{dx} = -kv^n.$$

Separation of the variables and integration now gives

$$\int v^{1-n}\, dv = -k\int dx$$

and

$$\frac{v^{2-n}}{2-n} = -kx + C'.$$

Since $v = u$ when $x = 0$,

$$\frac{u^{2-n}}{2-n} = C'$$

and

$$kx = \frac{u^{2-n} - v^{2-n}}{2 - n}.$$

Writing $v = 0$, the distance travelled when the particle comes to rest is given by $x = u^{2-n}/(2 - n)k$.

Example 11. *The rate of decay of a certain radioactive substance is kx, where x is the fraction of substance remaining at time t and k is a constant. Show that the half-life of the substance is* $(1/k) \log_e 2$.

The rate of increase of x with respect to t is dx/dt so that its rate of *decay* is $-dx/dt$. Hence

$$-\frac{dx}{dt} = kx$$

and separation of the variables in this differential equation and integration gives

$$-\int \frac{dx}{x} = k \int dt.$$

This gives

$$- \log_e x = kt + C$$

and the arbitrary constant C can be found from the fact that $x = 1$ when $t = 0$. This gives $C = 0$ and hence $\log_e x = -kt$. The half-life is the time at which $x = \frac{1}{2}$ and hence

$$\log_e (\tfrac{1}{2}) = -kt$$

leading to $t = (1/k) \log_e 2$.

Example 12. *A curve passes through the point* $(3, 1)$ *and its gradient at the point* (x, y) *is given by* $2\{1 + (y/x)\}$. *Find the equation of the curve.*

Since the gradient of the curve at the point (x, y) is dy/dx, we have

$$\frac{dy}{dx} = 2\left(1 + \frac{y}{x}\right).$$

This is a homogeneous equation and the substitution $y = vx$ transforms it into

$$v + x\frac{dv}{dx} = 2(1 + v).$$

A little simplification, separation of the variables and integration gives

$$\int \frac{dv}{2 + v} = \int \frac{dx}{x},$$

leading to

$$\log_e (2 + v) = \log_e x + \log_e A.$$

Hence $2 + v = Ax$ and, since $v = y/x$, this becomes

$$2x + y = Ax^2.$$

Since the curve passes through the point $(3, 1)$, the arbitrary constant A is given by

$$2(3) + 1 = A(3)^2,$$

so that $A = \frac{7}{9}$. Hence the required equation of the curve is $y = \frac{7}{9}x^2 - 2x$.

Example 13. *A particle starting from rest at the origin O moves along the positive x-axis and its acceleration when at distance x m from O is $(1 - x)$ m/s². Find the distance travelled and the velocity acquired in $\frac{1}{2}\pi$ seconds.*

Since the acceleration of the particle at time t is d^2x/dt^2, we have

$$\frac{d^2x}{dt^2} = 1 - x$$

so that

$$\frac{d^2x}{dt^2} + x = 1.$$

By § 12.5, the general solution of this second order differential equation is

$$x = 1 + a \sin(t + \varepsilon)$$

where a and ε are arbitrary constants. The velocity v at time t is given by

$$v = \frac{dx}{dt} = a \cos(t + \varepsilon)$$

and since both v and x are zero when $t = 0$,

$$0 = a \cos \varepsilon, \qquad 0 = 1 + a \sin \varepsilon.$$

These simultaneous equations are satisfied by $a = 1$, $\varepsilon = \frac{3}{2}\pi$ and we have

$$x = 1 + \sin(t + \tfrac{3}{2}\pi) = 1 - \cos t,$$
$$v = \cos(t + \tfrac{3}{2}\pi) = \sin t.$$

When $t = \frac{1}{2}\pi$, $x = 1 - \cos \frac{1}{2}\pi = 1$ m and $v = \sin \frac{1}{2}\pi = 1$ m/s.

Exercises 12 (c)

1. A condenser of capacity C farads is at voltage v_0 and is discharged through a resistance of R ohms. It is known that the voltage v at time t seconds is given by the differential equation $RC(dv/dt) = -v$. Find a formula giving v in terms of t.

2. A circuit consisting of a resistance R ohms and an inductance L henries is connected to a battery of contant voltage E. The current, i amperes, at time t after the circuit has been closed is known to be given by the differential equation $L(di/dt) + Ri = E$. Show that

$$Ri = E\{1 - \exp(-Rt/L)\}.$$

3. A body moves in a straight line with retardation kv^2, where v is the velocity and k is a constant. If the body starts moving with velocity 10 m/s and after 1 second its velocity is 5 m/s, what is its velocity after 4 seconds?

4. The gradient of a curve at the point (x, y) is $3x^2 - 20x + 25$. If the curve passes through the point $(5, 0)$, find its equation and calculate the area enclosed by the curve and the axis of x.   [L.U.]

5. The height of a tank is 4 m and it is completely full of water. At a given instant a tap is turned on allowing the water to flow out through an

orifice in the base of the tank. If y metres is the depth of water in the tank t seconds after the tap has been turned on and if $75\,dy/dt = -\sqrt{y}$, find the time (in minutes) required to empty the tank.

6. A particle is projected with velocity u and moves in a straight line with retardation kv^3 where v is the velocity of the particle at time t and k is a constant. If s is the distance travelled in time t, show that

$$\frac{1}{v} = ks + \frac{1}{u} \quad \text{and} \quad t = \tfrac{1}{2}ks^2 + \frac{s}{u}.$$

7. In a chemical reaction, the amount x of one substance at time t is related to the velocity dx/dt of the reaction by the differential equation

$$\frac{dx}{dt} = k(3 - x)(6 - x),$$

k being a constant. If $x = 0$ when $t = 0$, express t in terms of x. Determine also the value of k if it is known that $x = 2 \cdot 8$ when $t = 3$.

8. The atmospheric pressure p at height h satisfies the relation $dh/dp = -v$ where v is the volume per unit mass of the atmosphere. Show that, in an isothermal layer in which $pv = RT$ (R and T being constants), $p = p_0 \exp(-h/RT)$ where p_0 is the atmospheric pressure when $h = 0$.

9. In a chemical solution, a substance A is converted into another substance B at a rate which is proportional to the amount unconverted at any time. If 10 out of 100 grammes of A are converted in the first 30 minutes, find the amount converted in the first hour.

10. The population of a certain country was 9 million at the beginning of the 19th century and 100 years later it was 36 million. Assuming that the increase of population per year is proportional to the population, find the population in the year 1970.

11. A curve passes through the point $(0, 1)$ and its slope at the point (x, y) is $2xy/(x^2 - y^2)$. Find the equation of the curve.

12. The acceleration of a particle moving in a straight line is $4(1 - x)$ m/s^2 when it is at distance x m from the origin O. If the particle starts at a distance of 1 m from O and is at a distance of 2 m after $\tfrac{1}{4}\pi$ seconds, find its initial velocity.

Exercises 12 (d)

1. If $dy/dx = 2y^2/x^3$, express y explicitly in terms of x.

2. Show that the general solution of the differential equation

$$x\frac{dy}{dx} + y^2 = y$$

can be written in the form $y = Ax(1 - y)$ where A is an arbitrary constant.

3. Find the general solution of the differential equation

$$\frac{dy}{dx} = \tan^2 x \tan^2 y.$$

4. Find the general solutions of the equations

(i) $e^{-2v}\dfrac{dy}{dx} = x^2 - 1$,   (ii) $(x^2 - 1)\dfrac{dy}{dx} = e^{-2v}$.

5. Find the solution of the equation

$$\cos^2 x\frac{dy}{dx} + y = 1.$$

which satisfies the condition that $y = 0$ when $x = 0$.

6. If

$$\sin y \frac{dy}{dx} + \sin (x - y) = \sin (x + y)$$

and $y = 1$ when $x = \frac{1}{2}\pi$, show that $y = 2 \sin x - 1$.

7. Given that $y = 2$ when $x = 1$ and $(dy/dx) + y^2 = x^2y^2$, express $1/y$ in terms of x.

8. Show that the general solution of the differential equation

$$y - x^2 \frac{dy}{dx} = 1 + x\frac{dy}{dx}$$

can be written in the form $y = 1 + Cx(1 + x)^{-1}$ where C is an arbitrary constant.

9. Find the value of the constant a given that

$$x^3 \frac{dy}{dx} = a - x$$

and that $y = 0$ when $x = 2$ and when $x = 6$.   [L.U.]

10. Use the substitution $z = x + y$ to find the general solution of the differential equation

$$\frac{dy}{dx} = (x + y)^2.$$

11. If $y = \frac{1}{4}$ when $x = 1$ and if

$$\frac{dy}{dx} + \frac{2y}{x} = \frac{1}{x},$$

find the value of y when $x = 2$.

12. Use the substitution $z = xy$ to transform the equation

$$x\frac{dy}{dx} + y + \cot xy = 0$$

into one in which the variables can be separated. Hence show that the general solution of the equation is $\cos xy = Ae^x$ where A is an arbitrary constant.

13. Solve the homogeneous equation

$$x(x + y)\frac{dy}{dx} + y^2 = xy$$

given that $y = 1$ when $x = 1$.

14. Solve the equation

$$y^2(y - 3x)\frac{dy}{dx} - x^3 = y^3$$

subject to the condition that $y = 0$ when $x = 1$.

15. Show that the general solution of the homogeneous differential equation

$$(xy + 2x^2)\frac{dy}{dx} = xy + 2y^2$$

can be written in the form $(y - x)^3 = Cx^2y^2$ where C is an arbitrary constant.

16. Show that the general solution $y = a \sin n(x + \varepsilon)$ to the second order differential equation $(d^2y/dx^2) + n^2y = 0$ can be written in the form $y = A \sin nx + B \cos nx$ where the arbitrary constants a, ε, A and B are related by the equations $a^2 = A^2 + B^2$, $\tan n\varepsilon = B/A$.

17. Solve the equation

$$\frac{d^2y}{dx^2} + 16y = 0$$

subject to the conditions $y = 2$ and $dy/dx = 1$ when $x = 0$.

18. During a fermentation process, the rate of decomposition of a substance at any instant is related to the amounts y of substance and x of active ferment by the law $dy/dt = -\frac{1}{4}xy$. The value of x at time t is $4/(1 + t)^2$ and when $t = 0$, $y = 10$. Express dy/dt in terms of y and t and hence determine y as a function of t.   [N.U.]

19. At time t, the rate of flow of water into a spherical container of radius r is $5rt$. Find the total time required to fill the container.

20. In the adiabatic expansion of a gas, the volume v and pressure p are related by the differential equation

$$c_p\frac{dv}{dp} + c_v\frac{v}{p} = 0$$

where c_p and c_v are respectively the specific heats of the gas at constant pressure and constant volume. Assuming that these specific heats are constant show that $pv^\gamma = $ constant, where $\gamma = c_p/c_v$.

21. By Newton's law of cooling, the surface temperature T at time t of a sphere in isothermal surroundings at temperature T_0 is given by the equation

$$\frac{dT}{dt} = -k(T - T_0)$$

where k is a constant. Show that $T = T_0 + (T_1 - T_0)e^{-kt}$ where T_1 is the initial temperature of the sphere.

22. The retardation of a particle moving in a straight line with velocity v cm/s is av cm/s², where a is a constant. The particle is projected with velocity 386 cm/s and half a second later its velocity is 142 cm/s. Find the value of a.

23. A car is travelling along a straight road. When it is passing a certain position O the engine is switched off. At time t seconds after the car has passed O the speed v m/s is given by the formula $v^{-1} = A + Bt$, where A and B are constants. Show that the retardation is proportional to the square of the speed. If when $t = 0$, the retardation is 1 m/s² and $v = 30$, find A and B. If x m is the distance moved from O in t seconds, express (i) x in terms of t, (ii) v in terms of x.   [N.U.]

24. The acceleration of a motor car at a speed of v m/s is $1 - (v/30)^2$ m/s² If the car starts from rest, state the greatest speed of which it is capable. Find the distance in which half this speed is acquired from rest and the time taken to reach this distance.   [N.U.]

25. Show that the substitution $y = e^{-x}z$ transforms the equation

$$\frac{d^2y}{dx^2} + 2\frac{dy}{dx} + 5y = 0 \text{ into } \frac{d^2z}{dx^2} + 4z = 0.$$

Hence solve the original equation subject to the conditions $y = 2$ and $dy/dx = 0$ when $x = 0$.

CHAPTER 13

ELEMENTARY COORDINATE GEOMETRY OF THE CIRCLE, PARABOLA, ELLIPSE AND HYPERBOLA

13.1 Introduction

It was shown in Chapter 5 that an equation of the first degree in x and y represented a straight line and we used algebraical methods to solve certain problems involving such lines. Here we consider similar methods applied to curves represented by equations in x and y of the second degree. Such curves are the circle, parabola, ellipse and hyperbola and it can be shown, but we shall not attempt to do so here, that all these curves can be formed by the intersection of a right circular cone with a plane. For this reason, the curves discussed in this chapter are called *conic sections*.

13.2 The equation of a circle

Suppose that the radius of the circle is R and that the coordinates of its centre C are (α, β). The circle is the locus of a point which moves so that its distance from the point (α, β) is always equal to R. Hence if P is any point (x, y) on the circle

$$(x - \alpha)^2 + (y - \beta)^2 = R^2, \qquad (13.1)$$

for the left-hand side of this equation is the square of the distance between the two points (x, y) and (α, β). Equation (13.1) therefore represents a circle of radius R and centre at the point (α, β). Writing $\alpha = \beta = 0$, the equation of a circle of radius R and centre the origin is

$$x^2 + y^2 = R^2. \qquad (13.2)$$

The general equation of the second degree in x and y is

$$ax^2 + 2hxy + by^2 + 2gx + 2fy + c = 0, \qquad (13.3)$$

where a, b, c, f, g, h are constants. It should be clear, from the way in which equation (13.1) was formed, that if equation (13.3) is to represent a circle then *the coefficients of x^2 and y^2 must be equal and there can be no term in the product xy*, that is, $a = b$ and $h = 0$. There is no loss of generality in taking $a = 1$ and the general equation of a circle can be written

$$x^2 + y^2 + 2gx + 2fy + c = 0. \qquad (13.4)$$

The radius and the coordinates of the centre of the circle given by the general equation (13.4) can be found as follows. Writing (13.4) in the form

$$(x + g)^2 + (y + f)^2 = g^2 + f^2 - c,$$

325

and comparing it with equation (13.1), which represents a circle of radius R and centre at the point (α, β), we see that the radius of the circle given by (13.4) is $\sqrt{(g^2 + f^2 - c)}$ and its centre is the point $(-g, -f)$.

Example 1. *Write down the equation of the circle whose centre is at the point* $(-2, -3)$ *and whose radius is 4 units.*

The square of the distance of a point (x, y) on the circle from its centre $(-2, -3)$ is $(x + 2)^2 + (y + 3)^2$ and, since this is equal to the square of the radius,

$$(x + 2)^2 + (y + 3)^2 = 4^2.$$

This reduces to $x^2 + y^2 + 4x + 6y - 3 = 0$ and is the required equation.

Example 2. *Find the radius and the coordinates of the centre of the circle* $x^2 + y^2 - 4x - 12y + 4 = 0.$

The given equation can be written in the form

$$(x - 2)^2 + (y - 6)^2 = -4 + 4 + 36 = 6^2,$$

showing that the point (x, y) is always at a distance of 6 units from the point $(2, 6)$. Alternatively, in the given equation $g = -2, f = -6$ and $c = 4$. Hence

$$\text{radius} = \sqrt{(g^2 + f^2 - c)} = \sqrt{(4 + 36 - 4)} = 6,$$

centre, $(-g, -f)$, i.e. $(2, 6)$.

In Fig. 113, A and B are the points (x_1, y_1), (x_2, y_2) at the extremities of a diameter of a circle and P is any point (x, y) on the circle. Since

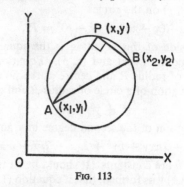

FIG. 113

AB is a diameter, the lines AP and PB are perpendicular. The slopes of AP and PB are respectively

$$\frac{y - y_1}{x - x_1} \quad \text{and} \quad \frac{y - y_2}{x - x_2}$$

and the product of these slopes will be -1. Hence

$$\left(\frac{y - y_1}{x - x_1}\right)\left(\frac{y - y_2}{x - x_2}\right) = -1$$

or

$$(x - x_1)(x - x_2) + (y - y_1)(y - y_2) = 0. \qquad (13.5)$$

Since this relation is satisfied by the coordinates (x, y) of *any* point P on the circle, it is the equation of the circle whose diameter is the join of the points (x_1, y_1) and (x_2, y_2).

Example 3. *The line joining the points* $(-1, 7)$ *and* $(23, 17)$ *is taken as the diameter of a circle. Find the equation of this circle, the length of its radius and the co-ordinates of its centre.* [O.C.]

By (13.5), the required equation is

$$(x + 1)(x - 23) + (y - 7)(y - 17) = 0$$

and this reduces to $x^2 + y^2 - 22x - 24y + 96 = 0$. This equation can be written

$$(x - 11)^2 + (y - 12)^2 = -96 + 121 + 144 = 169 = 13^2,$$

showing that the radius is 13 and the centre is the point (11, 12).

13.3 The tangent to a circle at a given point

Suppose we require the equation of the tangent at the point (x_1, y_1) to the circle

$$x^2 + y^2 + 2gx + 2fy + c = 0. \qquad (13.6)$$

Differentiating this equation with respect to x

$$2x + 2y\frac{dy}{dx} + 2g + 2f\frac{dy}{dx} = 0,$$

so that the gradient of the circle at the point (x_1, y_1) is given by

$$\frac{dy}{dx} = -\frac{x_1 + g}{y_1 + f}.$$

The tangent is the line passing through the point (x_1, y_1) with slope equal to this gradient; its equation is therefore

$$y - y_1 = -\left(\frac{x_1 + g}{y_1 + f}\right)(x - x_1)$$

and this can be written

$$xx_1 + yy_1 + g(x - x_1) + f(y - y_1) = x_1^2 + y_1^2. \qquad (13.7)$$

Since the point (x_1, y_1) lies on the circle,

$$x_1^2 + y_1^2 + 2gx_1 + 2fy_1 + c = 0,$$

and we can replace $x_1^2 + y_1^2$ by $-(2gx_1 + 2fy_1 + c)$. Hence equation (13.7) can be written

$$xx_1 + yy_1 + g(x + x_1) + f(y + y_1) + c = 0. \qquad (13.8)$$

Equation (13.8) is the required equation of the tangent at the point (x_1, y_1). It is worth noting that *the equation of the tangent can be obtained from the equation* (13.6) *of the circle by replacing* x^2 *with* xx_1, y^2 *with* yy_1, $2x$ *with* $(x + x_1)$ *and* $2y$ *with* $(y + y_1)$. This is a particular case of a general rule which enables the equation of the tangent to be written down at sight for any of the curves treated in this chapter.

Example 4. *Find the equation of the tangent to the circle*

$$x^2 + y^2 + 10x - 12y + 11 = 0 \text{ at the point } (2, 7).$$

The required equation is

$$2x + 7y + 5(x + 2) - 6(y + 7) + 11 = 0$$

and this reduces to $7x + y = 21$.

Example 5. *Prove that the equation of the circle passing through the origin O and the points $A(a, 0)$ and $B(0, b)$ is $x^2 + y^2 - ax - by = 0$. Find the equations of the tangents at B and $P(a, b)$. Prove that, if these tangents meet at Q, then $PQ = ra/b$ where r is the radius of the circle.*   [O.C.]

Let the equation of the circle through O, A and B be

$$x^2 + y^2 + 2gx + 2fy + c = 0.$$

Then this equation is satisfied by $x = 0$, $y = 0$, by $x = a$, $y = 0$ and by $x = 0$, $y = b$. Hence

$$c = 0, \quad a^2 + 2ga + c = 0, \quad b^2 + 2fb + c = 0$$

and we have $2g = -a$, $2f = -b$, $c = 0$. The equation of the circle is therefore $x^2 + y^2 - ax - by = 0$ and, since this can be written in the form

$$(x - \tfrac{1}{2}a)^2 + (y - \tfrac{1}{2}b)^2 = \tfrac{1}{4}(a^2 + b^2),$$

the radius r is given by $r^2 = \tfrac{1}{4}(a^2 + b^2)$. The equations of the tangents at $B(0, b)$ and at $P(a, b)$ are respectively

$$x(0) + y(b) - \tfrac{1}{2}a(x + 0) - \tfrac{1}{2}b(y + b) = 0$$

and

$$x(a) + y(b) - \tfrac{1}{2}a(x + a) - \tfrac{1}{2}b(y + b) = 0,$$

and these reduce to $by - ax = b^2$, $by + ax = a^2 + b^2$. The coordinates of Q are given by the values of x and y simultaneously satisfying these equations and these are $x = \tfrac{1}{2}a$, $y = \tfrac{1}{2}(a^2/b) + b$. Hence

$$PQ^2 = (a - \tfrac{1}{2}a)^2 + \left(b - \tfrac{1}{2}\frac{a^2}{b} - b\right)^2 = \tfrac{1}{4}(a^2 + b^2)\frac{a^2}{b^2} = \frac{r^2a^2}{b^2},$$

and $PQ = ra/b$.

Example 6. *Prove that the line $lx + my + n = 0$ is a tangent to the cirlce $x^2 + y^2 = a^2$ if $a^2(l^2 + m^2) = n^2$.*   [L.U.]

The abscissae of the two points of intersection of the line and circle are given by substituting $y = -(lx + n)/m$ in the equation of the circle. This gives

$$x^2 + \frac{(lx + n)^2}{m^2} = a^2$$

or

$$(l^2 + m^2)x^2 + 2lnx + n^2 - a^2m^2 = 0.$$

The line will intersect the circle in two coincident points (and therefore be a tangent) if this quadratic in x has equal roots. The condition for this is

$$(2ln)^2 = 4(l^2 + m^2)(n^2 - a^2m^2)$$

and this reduces to $a^2(l^2 + m^2) = n^2$.

Exercises 13 (a)

1   Find the coordinates of the centre and radius of the circle

$$x^2 + y^2 - 10x + 12y = 0.$$ [O.C.]

2. The coordinates of the points A and B are $(-2, 2)$ and $(3, 1)$ respectively. Show that the equation of the circle which has AB as diameter is

$$x^2 + y^2 - x - 3y - 4 = 0.$$ [N.U.]

3. A point P moves in such a way that the ratio of its distance from the point $A(a, 0)$ to its distance from the point $B(-a, 0)$ is always $1 : 3$. Show that the locus of P is a circle and find its centre and radius. [L.U.]

4. A circle is drawn with the points whose coordinates are $(0, 1)$ and (p, q) as ends of a diameter. The circle cuts the axis of x in two points whose coordinates are $(\alpha, 0)$ and $(\beta, 0)$. Find the values of $\alpha + \beta$ and $\alpha\beta$. [N.U.]

5. Find the coordinates of the centres P, Q of two circles, each of radius 10, which pass through the points $A(-5, 5)$ and $B(9, 3)$. Find the equations of the two circles and prove that only one cuts the x-axis and that both cut the y-axis. [O.C.]

6. A is the point $(1, 3)$ and P is a point which moves so that the mid-point of AP always lies on the circle $x^2 + y^2 = 25$. Find the equation of the locus of P and identify the locus. [L.U.]

7. Find the equation of the circle whose centre lies on the line $y = 3x - 7$ and which passes through the points $(1, 1)$ and $(2, -1)$. [L.U.]

8. Find the equation of the tangent at the point $(3, 2)$ to the circle $(x - 1)^2 + (y + 2)^2 = 20$ and write down the equation of the tangent at the origin to the circle $x^2 + y^2 + 2x + 4y = 0$.

9. Show that the equation of the tangent PT at the point $P(\frac{1}{5}, \frac{3}{5})$ on the circle $x^2 + y^2 + 8x + 10y - 8 = 0$ is $3x + 4y - 3 = 0$. Find the equations of the chords, each of length $4\sqrt{10}$, which are parallel to PT. [O.C.]

10. If A is the point $(-2, 0)$ and B is the point $(2, 0)$, write down the equation of the circle on AB as diameter. Find the equations of the tangents to this circle which are parallel to the line $3x + 4y = 0$ and determine their points of contact. [L.U.]

11. The line $4y = 3x$ is parallel to the diameter PQ of the circle

$$x^2 + y^2 + 6x - 8y = 0.$$

Find the equations of the tangents to the circle at P and Q.   [L.U.]

12. The circles $x^2 + y^2 = a^2$, $(x - 5)^2 + (y - 12)^2 = 64$ touch externally at a point between the origin O and the centre C of the second circle. Find the value of a and the coordinates of the point of contact.   [O.C.]

13. Find the equation of the circle which touches the x-axis at the point $(2, 0)$ and passes through the point $(-1, 9)$.   [L.U.]

14. Prove that the equation of the circle which passes through the three points $(2, 0)$, $(5, 0)$ and $(1, 2)$ is $x^2 + y^2 - 7x - 4y + 10 = 0$. Find the equations of the two tangents to this circle which pass through the origin.   [O.C.]

15. Find the equation of the circle which has its centre at the point $(3, 4)$ and passes through the point $(0, 5)$. Find also the equation of the tangent to this circle at the point $(0, 5)$. If this tangent cuts the axis of x at T, find the equation of the other tangent passing through T.   [O.C.]

16. Find the equations of two circles which touch the x-axis at the origin and also touch the line $12x + 5y = 60$.   [L.U.]

17. The perpendicular bisector of the line joining the points $A(1, 2)$ and $B(3, 3)$ meets the x-axis in L and the y-axis in M. The origin is O. Find the equation of the circle through L, M and O.   [L.U.]

18. A circle is drawn on the line joining the two points $(3, 2)$ and $(-1, 4)$ as diameter. Find the equation of this circle and the length of the chord it intercepts on the y-axis. Find also the equations of the two tangents to this circle which are parallel to the x-axis.   [O.C.]

19. A circle with centre $(3, 2)$ touches the line $4x - 3y + 4 = 0$. Find the equation of the circle and show that it touches the x-axis.   [N.U.]

20. A variable circle passes through the point $A(x_1, y_1)$ and touches the x-axis. Show that the locus of the other end of the diameter through A is given by $(x - x_1)^2 = 4y_1y$.   [L.U.]

13.4 The equation of a parabola

When a point P moves so that its distance from a fixed point S is equal to its perpendicular distance from a fixed straight line AB, the locus of P is called a *parabola*, the point S and the line AB being known respectively as the *focus* and the *directrix* of the parabola.

The equation of a parabola takes its simplest form when the focus S is taken as the point $(a, 0)$ and the directrix AB as the line $x = -a$

(Fig. 114). Let AB meet the x-axis at C so that C is the point $(-a, 0)$ and, if P is the point (x, y), the perpendicular distance PM of P from AB is clearly the sum of the abscissa of P and the distance CO so that $PM = x + a$. Since P and S are respectively the points (x, y) and $(a, 0)$, $PS^2 = (x - a)^2 + y^2$ and since $PM = PS$, we have

$$(x - a)^2 + y^2 = (x + a)^2.$$

This reduces to

$$y^2 = 4ax \qquad (13.9)$$

and is the equation of the parabola with focus the point $(a, 0)$ and directrix the line $x + a = 0$.

To trace the curve we first observe that, since equation (13.9) contains only an even power of y, there is symmetry about the x-axis.

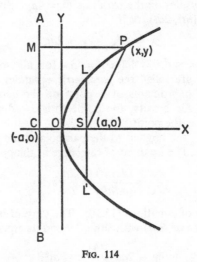

FIG. 114

Also, y is imaginary when x is negative and there is thus no part of the curve to the left of the origin O. This point is called the *vertex* of the parabola. When $x = 0$, $y^2 = 0$ and the y-axis therefore meets the curve in two coincident points at the origin, that is, the y-axis is the tangent to the parabola at its vertex. Finally, as x increases so does y^2 and the general shape of the curve is as shown in Fig. 114.

The double ordinate LSL' drawn through the focus S is known as the *latus-rectum* of the parabola. Since LS is the value of y when $x = a$, equation (13.9) shows that $LS = 2a$ and hence the length of the latus-rectum $= LSL' = 2LS = 4a$.

Example 7. *Find the ordinates of the points in which the straight line* $x + 2y = c$ *meets the parabola* $y^2 = 10x$ *and find the value of* c *when this line is a tangent to the parabola.*   [O.C.]

Since we require the values of y at the points of intersection of the line and the parabola, we substitute $x = c - 2y$ in the equation $y^2 = 10x$. This gives $y^2 = 10(c - 2y)$, or, arranged as a quadratic in y,

$$y^2 + 20y - 10c = 0.$$

The required ordinates are the roots of this equation and these are

$$-10 \pm \sqrt{\{10(10 + c)\}}.$$

The line is a tangent to the parabola when these two roots are equal and this occurs when $c = -10$.

13.5 The parametric equations of a parabola

It is often convenient to be able to write down the coordinates of a point which always lies on the parabola $y^2 = 4ax$. Such a point is one with coordinates $(at^2, 2at)$ for if

$$x = at^2, \qquad y = 2at, \tag{13.10}$$

then $y^2 = (2at)^2 = 4a^2t^2 = 4a(at^2) = 4ax$ for all values of t. The equations (13.10) are called the *parametric equations* of the parabola. They express the coordinates of a point on the curve in terms of a *parameter* t and, for brevity, the point with coordinates $(at^2, 2at)$ is often referred to as the point "t".

The equation of the tangent to the parabola at the point "t" can be found as follows. The gradient of the curve at the point is given by

$$\frac{dy}{dx} = \frac{(dy/dt)}{(dx/dt)} = \frac{2a}{2at} = \frac{1}{t}, \tag{13.11}$$

when use is made of equations (13.10). The tangent is the line passing through the point $(at^2, 2at)$ with slope $1/t$ and its equation is

$$y - 2at = \frac{1}{t}(x - at^2)$$

and this reduces to

$$x - ty + at^2 = 0. \tag{13.12}$$

If (x_1, y_1) is a point on the parabola $y^2 = 4ax$, we have $x_1 = at^2$, $y_1 = 2at$ and the equation (13.12) of the tangent can be written $x - (y_1/2a)y + x_1 = 0$, that is,

$$yy_1 = 2a(x + x_1). \tag{13.13}$$

It should be noted that this equation can be written down by observing the general rule given in § 13.3 that *the equation of the tangent at the point* (x_1, y_1) *is obtained from the equation* $y^2 = 4ax$ *of the curve by replacing* y^2 *by* yy_1 *and* $2x$ *by* $(x + x_1)$.

The *normal* to a curve at a point P is the straight line which passes through P and is perpendicular to the tangent at P. Since the slope of the tangent at the point $(at^2, 2at)$ to the parabola $y^2 = 4ax$ is, by (13.11), equal to $1/t$, that of the normal is $-t$ and the equation of the normal at the point "t" is therefore

$$y - 2at = -t(x - at^2),$$

or,

$$y + tx = 2at + at^3. \tag{13.14}$$

Many problems involving the parabola are best solved by using the parametric equations and the above equations for the tangent and normal are useful in such work. The reader should remember them or, preferably, be able to derive them quickly.

Example 8. *Show that the point of intersection of two perpendicular tangents to a parabola lies on its directrix.*

By (13.12), the equations of the tangents at the points "t_1" and "t_2" to the parabola $y^2 = 4ax$ are

$$x - t_1 y + a t_1^2 = 0 \qquad \text{and} \qquad x - t_2 y + a t_2^2 = 0.$$

Eliminating y from these equations by multiplying respectively by t_1 and t_2 and subtracting, we have

$$(t_2 - t_1)x + a t_1^2 t_2 - a t_2^2 t_1 = 0$$

giving $x = a t_1 t_2$. Since the tangents are perpendicular to each other, the product of their slopes $1/t_1$ and $1/t_2$ is -1 so that $t_1 t_2 = -1$. Hence the abscissa of their point of intersection is given by $x = -a$ and this shows that the point lies on the directrix of the parabola.

Example 9. *If the tangent at P to a parabola meets the axis of the parabola at Q and if S is the focus, show that the triangle PQS is isosceles.*

In Fig. 115, P is the point "t" on the parabola $y^2 = 4ax$ whose focus is S. PT

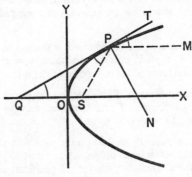

Fig. 115

is the tangent at P meeting the axis of the parabola at Q. Since the coordinates of P and S are respectively $(at^2, 2at)$ and $(a, 0)$,

$$PS^2 = (at^2 - a)^2 + (2at - 0)^2$$
$$= a^2(t^4 - 2t^2 + 1 + 4t^2)$$
$$= a^2(t^2 + 1)^2,$$

so that $PS = a(t^2 + 1)$. The equation of the tangent PT is $x - ty + at^2 = 0$ and this meets the axis $y = 0$ where $x + at^2 = 0$, so that $QO = at^2$. Since $OS = a$, $QS = QO + OS = at^2 + a = a(t^2 + 1)$. Hence $QS = PS$ and the triangle PQS is isosceles.

Example 9 above enables an important property of the parabola to be established. Since the triangle PQS is isosceles, angle PQS = angle SPQ and if (Fig. 115) PM is a line through P parallel to the axis of the parabola, angle TPM = angle PQS = angle SPQ. Hence *the lines PS and PM are equally inclined to the tangent PT and also equally inclined to the normal PN*. Thus, if a ray of light starting from the focus S of a parabolic mirror strikes the mirror at P, the reflected ray, which makes an equal angle with the normal, will be parallel to the axis of the mirror. Since P is any point on the mirror, all incident rays from a source at the focus will be reflected as rays which are all parallel to the mirror's axis. Motor-car headlamps, searchlights and some electric fires are constructed so as to make use of this property.

Exercises 13 (b)

1. Find the equations of the tangents to the parabola $y^2 = 144x$ at the points $(144, 144)$, $(9, -36)$ and show that they are perpendicular. Find also the coordinates of their point of intersection.   [O.C.]

2. If the tangent at the point P to the parabola $y^2 = 4ax$ meets the parabola $y^2 = 4a(x + b)$ at points Q and R, prove that P is the middle point of QR.   [O.C.]

3. Find the coordinates of the points in which the line $y = 8x - a$ meets the parabola $y^2 = 4ax$. Find the equations to the tangents to the parabola at these points and the coordinates of their point of intersection.   [L.U.]

4. Determine the values of the parameter t at the points P and Q in which the line $x - y + a = ak^2$ cuts the parabola $x = at^2$, $y = 2at$. Show that as k varies the locus of the mid-point of PQ is the line $y = 2a$. [L.U.]

5. If the tangent and normal at $P(at^2, 2at)$ on the parabola $y^2 = 4ax$ meet the axis of the parabola at T and G respectively and if S is the focus $(a, 0)$, prove that $ST = SG$.   [L.U.]

6. If the normal at a point $P(at^2, 2at)$ on the parabola $y^2 = 4ax$ meets the x-axis at G and O is the origin, show that $OG = a(2 + t^2)$ and $PG = 2a\sqrt{(1 + t^2)}$. Deduce that, for all positions of P on the curve, PG^2/OG is neither less than $2a$ nor greater than $4a$.   [L.U.]

7. Find the value of λ for which the straight line $y = mx + \lambda$ touches the parabola $y^2 = 4ax$. A tangent to this parabola cuts the x-axis at a distance a from the origin. Find the coordinates of the possible points of contact and of the points in which the possible tangents cut the y-axis.   [L.U.]

8. Prove that the equation of the chord joining the points $P(at^2, 2at)$ and $Q(aT^2, 2aT)$ on the parabola $y^2 = 4ax$ is $2x - (t + T)y + 2atT = 0$ and that, if the chord passes through the focus of the parabola, then $PQ = a(t + t^{-1})^2$.   [O.C.]

9. The tangents to the parabola $y^2 = 4ax$ from the point (h, k) meet the tangent at the vertex O of the parabola at B and C. Prove that the product of OB and OC is independent of k.   [O.C.]

10. Find the equation of the normal to the parabola $y^2 = 4x$ at the point $P(1, 2)$. This normal meets the parabola again at Q. Find the angle between PQ and the tangent at Q.   [L.U.]

11. The tangent at the point $P(at^2, 2at)$ on the parabola $y^2 = 4ax$ cuts the y-axis at T. If S is the point $(a, 0)$ prove that ST and PT are at right angles. Show also that the locus of the centre of the circle through P, T and S is the curve $2ax = a^2 + y^2$.   [L.U.]

12. From the point $P(at^2, 2at)$ on the parabola $y^2 = 4ax$ a chord is drawn through the focus $(a, 0)$ to meet the parabola again at Q. Show that the coordinates of Q are $(a/t^2, -2a/t)$ and that the tangents at P and Q intersect on the directrix $x = -a$.   [L.U.]

13. P is the point $(at^2, 2at)$ on the parabola $y^2 = 4ax$. From a fixed point $Q(h, k)$ a line is drawn perpendicular to the tangent at P to meet, at R, the parallel through P to the x-axis. Find the equation of the locus of R.   [L.U.]

14. The tangents to the parabola $y^2 = 4ax$ at the points $P(at_1^2, 2at_1)$, $Q(at_2^2, 2at_2)$ meet the y-axis in the points H and K respectively. Find the equation of the circle on HK as diameter and prove that this circle passes through the focus $(a, 0)$ if the chord PQ also passes through the focus.   [L.U.]

15. PQ is a variable chord of the parabola $y^2 = 4ax$ passing through the point $K(2a, 0)$. Show that

$$\frac{1}{PK^2} + \frac{1}{QK^2} = \text{constant},$$

and that the point of intersection of the tangents at P and Q is at a constant distance from the directrix.   [L.U.]

16. P is any point on the parabola $y^2 = 4ax$ and N is the foot of the perpendicular drawn from the origin to the tangent at P. Show that, as P varies, the locus of N is the curve $x(x^2 + y^2) + ay^2 = 0$.   [L.U.]

17. C is the mid-point of a variable chord PQ of the parabola $y^2 = 4ax$. The tangents to the parabola at P and Q meet at R. Prove (i) that RC is parallel to the axis of the parabola and (ii) that, if PQ subtends a right angle at the vertex, then the locus of C is $2ax = y^2 + 8a^2$.   [O.C.]

18. Prove that the normals to the parabola $y^2 = 4ax$ at its points of intersection with the straight line $2x - 3y + 4a = 0$ meet on the parabola.   [O.C.]

19. Two parabolae with their vertices at the origin of coordinates and their axes along $y = 0$ have latus-recta of lengths $4a$ and $4b$. A line perpendicular to the axes of the parabolae meets the curves in points A and B. Prove that the tangents to the curves at A and B meet on the line $y = 0$.

20. The parameters of three points A, B and C on the parabola $y^2 = 4ax$ are t_1, t_2 and t_3. The tangents at A and B meet the tangent at C at Q and P respectively; the tangents at A and B meet at R. Prove that, if P is the mid-point of QC, then $2t_2 = t_1 + t_3$. Prove also that RP is parallel to AC.   [O.C.]

13.6 The equation of an ellipse

When a point P moves so that its distance from a fixed point S (the focus) is always in a constant ratio ε (less than unity) to its perpendicular distance from a fixed straight line AB (the directrix), the locus of P is called an *ellipse* of *eccentricity* ε.

The equation of an ellipse takes its simplest form when the focus S is taken as the point $(-a\varepsilon, 0)$ and the directrix AB as the line $x = -a/\varepsilon$.

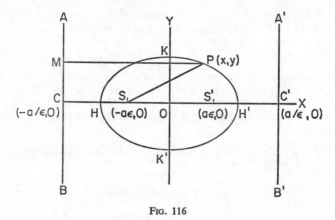

FIG. 116

In Fig. 116, P is the point (x, y) and PM is perpendicular to AB, so that

$$PS = \varepsilon PM.$$

C is the point $(-a/\varepsilon, 0)$ and PM is the sum of the abscissa of P and the length CO so that $PM = x + (a/\varepsilon)$. Since P and S are respectively the points (x, y) and $(-a\varepsilon, 0)$, we have

$$PS^2 = (x + a\varepsilon)^2 + y^2$$

and the relation $PS = \varepsilon PM$ gives

$$(x + a\varepsilon)^2 + y^2 = \varepsilon^2 \left(x + \frac{a}{\varepsilon}\right)^2,$$

that is,

$$(1 - \varepsilon^2)x^2 + y^2 = a^2(1 - \varepsilon^2).$$

This can be written in the form

$$\frac{x^2}{a^2} + \frac{y^2}{b^2} = 1 \qquad (13.15)$$

where

$$b^2 = a^2(1 - \varepsilon^2) \qquad (13.16)$$

and (13.15) is the equation of the ellipse with eccentricity ε, focus the point $(-a\varepsilon, 0)$ and directrix the line $x = -a/\varepsilon$.

In tracing the curve given by (13.15), it is clear that the curve is symmetrical about both the axes of coordinates for only even powers of x and y occur in the equation. From this symmetry we can deduce the existence of a second focus S' at the point $(a\varepsilon, 0)$ and a second directrix $A'B'$ along the line $x = a/\varepsilon$. The curve meets the coordinate axes at four points H', H, K and K' whose coordinates are easily found to be $(\pm a, 0)$, $(0, \pm b)$. By writing equation (13.15) in the form

$$y^2/b^2 = 1 - (x^2/a^2),$$

it is clear that y^2 is negative, and therefore there are no real points on the curve, when $x > a$ or when $x < -a$. Similarly there are no real points when $y > b$ or when $y < -b$. The curve is therefore a closed one and its general shape is shown in Fig. 116.

The points H and H' are called the *vertices* of the ellipse and the lines HH' and KK' are called its *axes*; since $\varepsilon < 1$, equation (13.16) shows that $b < a$ and the axes HH', KK' are referred to respectively as the *major* and *minor* axes. Their lengths are $2a$, $2b$. The origin O is called the *centre* of the ellipse and a chord passing through the centre is called a *diameter*.

Example 10. *Find the eccentricity and the distance between the foci of the ellipse* $3x^2 + 4y^2 = 12$.

The given equation can be written in the form $(x^2/4) + (y^2/3) = 1$ so that, comparing this with the standard equation $(x^2/a^2) + (y^2/b^2) = 1$, the semi major and minor axes a, b are given by $a = 2$, $b = \sqrt{3}$. The eccentricity ε is given by the equation $b^2 = a^2(1 - \varepsilon^2)$ and hence

$$3 = 4(1 - \varepsilon^2)$$

giving $4\varepsilon^2 = 1$ and $\varepsilon = \frac{1}{2}$. The distance between the foci

$$= 2a\varepsilon = 2 \cdot 2 \cdot \tfrac{1}{2} = 2.$$

Example 11. *Show that the sum of the focal distances of any point on an ellipse is equal to the length of the major axis and deduce a simple mechanical method for constructing the curve.*

Using Fig. 116 and the definition of the ellipse, if x is the abscissa of P,

$$PS = \varepsilon PM = \varepsilon \left(\frac{a}{\varepsilon} + x\right) = a + \varepsilon x.$$

Similarly, if PM' is drawn perpendicular to the second directrix $A'B'$,

$$PS' = \varepsilon PM' = \varepsilon \left(\frac{a}{\varepsilon} - x\right) = a - \varepsilon x.$$

The sum of the focal distances PS, PS' is therefore $2a$, the length of the major axis. By fixing pins at S, S' and keeping stretched by a pencil point an endless piece of string passing round the two pins, the pencil will describe an ellipse with S and S' as foci.

13.7 The parametric equations of an ellipse

As with the parabola, it is very often useful to be able to express the coordinates of a point on an ellipse in terms of a parameter. It is easy to verify that the equation (13.15) of an ellipse is satisfied by taking

$$x = a \cos \phi, \qquad y = b \sin \phi \qquad (13.17)$$

and these can be taken as the parametric equations of an ellipse. The parameter ϕ is called the *eccentric angle* of the point $(a \cos \phi, b \sin \phi)$.

The gradient of the ellipse at the point whose eccentric angle is ϕ is given by

$$\frac{dy}{dx} = \frac{(dy/d\phi)}{(dx/d\phi)} = \frac{b \cos \phi}{- a \sin \phi} = - \frac{b}{a} \cot \phi,$$

when use is made of the parametric equations (13.17). The tangent at the point, being a line through $(a \cos \phi, \ b \sin \phi)$ with slope $-(b/a) \cot \phi$, is therefore the line

$$y - b \sin \phi = - \frac{b}{a} \cot \phi(x - a \cos \phi)$$

and this reduces to

$$\frac{x}{a} \cos \phi + \frac{y}{b} \sin \phi = 1. \qquad (13.18)$$

If (x_1, y_1) is the point "ϕ" on the ellipse we have $x_1/a = \cos\phi$, $y_1/b = \sin\phi$ and the equation (13.18) of the tangent can be written in the form

$$\frac{xx_1}{a^2} + \frac{yy_1}{b^2} = 1. \tag{13.19}$$

Again it should be noted that *the equation of the tangent at the point* (x_1, y_1) *can be obtained from the equation* $(x^2/a^2) + (y^2/b^2) = 1$ *of the ellipse by replacing* x^2 *and* y^2 *by* xx_1 *and* yy_1 *respectively.*

The normal to the ellipse at the point with eccentric angle ϕ is the line through the point $(a\cos\phi, b\sin\phi)$ perpendicular to the tangent. The slope of the normal is therefore $(a/b)\tan\phi$ and the equation of the normal is

$$y - b\sin\phi = \frac{a}{b}\tan\phi\,(x - a\cos\phi)$$

which reduces to

$$ax\sec\phi - by\operatorname{cosec}\phi = a^2 - b^2. \tag{13.20}$$

Example 12. *Show that tangents to the ellipse* $(x^2/a^2) + (y^2/b^2) = 1$ *at points whose eccentric angles differ by* $90°$ *meet on the ellipse* $(x^2/a^2) + (y^2/b^2) = 2$.

The tangents at points with eccentric angles ϕ and $(90° + \phi)$ are from equation (13.18) the lines $(x/a)\cos\phi + (y/b)\sin\phi = 1$ and

$$(x/a)\cos(90° + \phi) + (y/b)\sin(90° + \phi) = 1.$$

These can be written

$$\frac{x}{a}\cos\phi + \frac{y}{b}\sin\phi = 1,$$

$$-\frac{x}{a}\sin\phi + \frac{y}{b}\cos\phi = 1,$$

and the locus of the point of intersection (x, y) is obtained by eliminating ϕ between these equations. This can be done by squaring and adding and the result is

$$\frac{x^2}{a^2} + \frac{y^2}{b^2} = 2.$$

Example 13. *O is the centre of the ellipse* $(x^2/a^2) + (y^2/b^2) = 1$ *and QP is the ordinate at P; the normal at P cuts the x-axis at N. Show that* $NQ = (b^2/a)\cos\phi$. *If the normal at P bisects the angle OPQ prove that the eccentricity* ε *satisfies the equation* $\varepsilon^2(1 + \sin^2\phi) = 1$. [O.C.]

In Fig. 117, P is the point $(a\cos\phi, b\sin\phi)$, PT is the tangent and $OQ = a\cos\phi$. The normal PN at P is the line $ax\sec\phi - by\operatorname{cosec}\phi = a^2 - b^2$ and this meets the x-axis where $ax\sec\phi = a^2 - b^2$. Hence

$$ON = \frac{a^2 - b^2}{a}\cos\phi$$

and

$$NQ = OQ - ON$$

$$= a \cos \phi - \frac{a^2 - b^2}{a} \cos \phi = \frac{b^2}{a} \cos \phi.$$

Now $OP^2 = a^2 \cos^2 \phi + b^2 \sin^2 \phi = a^2 \cos^2 \phi + a^2(1 - \varepsilon^2) \sin^2 \phi$
$= a^2(1 - \varepsilon^2 \sin^2 \phi)$, $PQ^2 = b^2 \sin^2 \phi = a^2(1 - \varepsilon^2) \sin^2 \phi$, and if the normal PN bisects the angle OPQ we have $OP/PQ = ON/NQ$. Squaring and substituting for OP^2, PQ^2, ON^2 and NQ^2,

$$\frac{a^2(1 - \varepsilon^2 \sin^2 \phi)}{a^2(1 - \varepsilon^2) \sin^2 \phi} = \frac{(a^2 - b^2)^2 \cos^2 \phi}{b^4 \cos^2 \phi} = \frac{a^4 \varepsilon^4}{a^4(1 - \varepsilon^2)^2},$$

and this reduces to $\varepsilon^2(1 + \sin^2 \phi) = 1$.

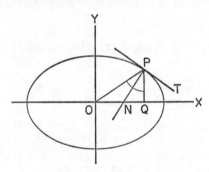

FIG. 117

13.8 The equation of a hyperbola

When a point P moves so that its distance from a fixed point S (the focus) is always in a constant ratio ε (greater than unity) to its perpendicular distance from a fixed straight line AB (the directrix), the locus of P is called a *hyperbola* of *eccentricity* ε.

As with the ellipse, the equation of a hyperbola is here derived when the focus S is taken as the point $(-a\varepsilon, 0)$ and the directrix AB as the line $x = -a/\varepsilon$. In Fig. 118, P is the point (x, y) and PM is perpendicular to AB, so that $PS = \varepsilon PM$. C is the point $(-a/\varepsilon, 0)$ and PM is the sum of the abscissa of P and the length CO so that $PM = x + (a/\varepsilon)$. Since P and S are respectively the points (x, y) and $(-a\varepsilon, 0)$, we have $PS^2 = (x + a\varepsilon)^2 + y^2$ and the relation $PS = \varepsilon PM$ gives

$$(x + a\varepsilon)^2 + y^2 = \varepsilon^2 \left(x + \frac{a}{\varepsilon} \right)^2,$$

that is

$$(\varepsilon^2 - 1)x^2 - y^2 = a^2(\varepsilon^2 - 1).$$

This can be written in the form

$$\frac{x^2}{a^2} - \frac{y^2}{b^2} = 1 \qquad (13.21)$$

where

$$b^2 = a^2(\varepsilon^2 - 1) \qquad (13.22)$$

and (13.21) is the equation of the hyperbola with eccentricity ε, focus the point $(-a\varepsilon, 0)$ and directrix the line $x = -a/\varepsilon$.

Since equation (13.21) contains only even powers of x and y, the hyperbola is a curve which is symmetrical about the axes of coordinates. Because of this symmetry, there is a second focus S' at the point $(a\varepsilon, 0)$ and a second directrix $A'B'$ along the line $x = a/\varepsilon$. The curve

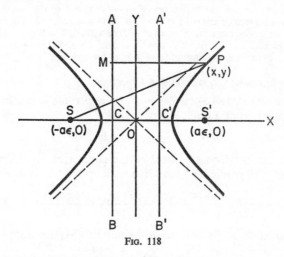

Fig. 118

cuts the x-axis at two points H, H' with coordinates $(\mp a, 0)$ but it does not meet the y-axis in real points. By writing equation (13.21) in the form $y^2/b^2 = (x^2/a^2) - 1$, it is clear that y^2 is negative, and that therefore there is no part of the curve, for values of x which lie between $\pm a$. On the other hand, if the equation is written in the form $x^2/a^2 = 1 + (y^2/b^2)$ it can be seen that points exist on the curve for *all* values of y, and that x^2 increases as y^2 increases. The curve consists of two portions, one of which extends indefinitely in the direction for which x is positive and the other indefinitely in the direction of negative x as shown in the diagram.

The points H and H' are called the *vertices* of the hyperbola and the line HH' is called the *transverse axis*. The origin O is the *centre* of the hyperbola and chords through O are called *diameters*. The line $y = mx$

meets the hyperbola (13.21) at points with abscissae given by $(x^2/a^2) - (m^2x^2/b^2) = 1$ and, if this equation is written in the form

$$\frac{1}{x^2} = \frac{1}{a^2} - \frac{m^2}{b^2},$$

it can be seen that lines through the origin with slopes given by $m^2 = b^2/a^2$ meet the hyperbola in two coincident points at an infinite distance from the centre O. The two lines with such slopes, that is, the lines $y = \pm bx/a$ are called the *asymptotes* of the hyperbola and are shown by dotted lines in Fig. 118.

Example 14. *Find the eccentricity, the coordinates of the foci and the equations of the asymptotes of the hyperbola* $4x^2 - 9y^2 = 36$.

The equation with given equation can be written $(x^2/9) - (y^2/4) = 1$ so that, comparing this with the equation $(x^2/a^2) - (y^2/b^2) = 1$, we have $a = 3, b = 2$. The eccentricity ε is given by the equation $b^2 = a^2(\varepsilon^2 - 1)$ and hence $4 = 9(\varepsilon^2 - 1)$ leading to $9\varepsilon^2 = 13$ and $\varepsilon = \frac{1}{3}\sqrt{13}$. The coordinates of the foci are $(\pm a\varepsilon, 0)$, that is, $(\pm\sqrt{13}, 0)$ and the asymptotes $(y = \pm bx/a)$ are the lines $3y = \pm 2x$.

13.9 The parametric equations of a hyperbola

The equation $(x^2/a^2) - (y^2/b^2) = 1$ of a hyperbola is satisfied by the coordinates (x, y) of a point when

$$x = a \sec \theta, \qquad y = b \tan \theta, \qquad (13.23)$$

and these equations may be used as the parametric equations of the hyperbola. The gradient of the curve at the point "θ" is given by

$$\frac{dy}{dx} = \frac{(dy/d\theta)}{(dx/d\theta)} = \frac{b \sec^2 \theta}{a \sec \theta \tan \theta} = \frac{b \sec \theta}{a \tan \theta},$$

and the equation of the tangent at the point "θ" is therefore

$$y - b \tan \theta = \frac{b \sec \theta}{a \tan \theta} (x - a \sec \theta)$$

or,

$$\frac{x}{a} \sec \theta - \frac{y}{b} \tan \theta = 1. \qquad (13.24)$$

If (x_1, y_1) is the point of contact of the tangent, equation (13.24) can be written $(xx_1/a^2) - (yy_1/b^2) = 1$ and this is yet another example of replacing x^2, y^2 by xx_1, yy_1 to obtain the tangent. The normal at this point is the line with equation

$$y - b \tan \theta = -\frac{a \tan \theta}{b \sec \theta} (x - a \sec \theta)$$

and this reduces to

$$ax \sin \theta + by = (a^2 + b^2) \tan \theta. \qquad (13.25)$$

Example 15. *A and B are respectively the points* $(a \sec \theta, b \tan \theta)$, $(a \sec \phi, b \tan \phi)$ *on the hyperbola* $(x^2/a^2) - (y^2/b^2) = 1$ *and* $\theta + \phi = \frac{1}{2}\pi$. *Show that the normals to the hyperbola at A and B intersect at a point P whose y-coordinate is independent of* θ *and* ϕ. [N.U.]

The normals at A and B are respectively the lines

$$ax \sin \theta + by = (a^2 + b^2) \tan \theta \qquad (13.26)$$

and

$$ax \sin \phi + by = (a^2 + b^2) \tan \phi.$$

Since $\phi = \frac{1}{2}\pi - \theta$, the second of these can be written

$$ax \cos \theta + by = (a^2 + b^2) \cot \theta \qquad (13.27)$$

and the y-coordinate of the point of intersection of the normals is given by eliminating x from equations (13.26), (13.27). This can be done by multiplying the equations by $\cos \theta$, $\sin \theta$ respectively and subtracting to give

$$by(\cos \theta - \sin \theta) = (a^2 + b^2)(\sin \theta - \cos \theta),$$

so that $y = -(a^2 + b^2)/b$ and this is independent of θ and ϕ.

13.10 The rectangular hyperbola

The asymptotes $y = \pm bx/a$ of the hyperbola $(x^2/a^2) - (y^2/b^2) = 1$ are at right angles to each other when $b = a$. In this case the equation of the curve can be written $x^2 - y^2 = a^2$ and the hyperbola is said to be *rectangular*. The equation of a rectangular hyperbola takes a particularly simple form when its asymptotes are taken as the co-ordinate axes and can be derived from the equation $x^2 - y^2 = a^2$ by rotating the axes through 45°. The resulting equation is

$$xy = c^2, \qquad (13.28)$$

where $c^2 = \frac{1}{2}a^2$, and a useful parametric form of this equation is

$$x = ct, \qquad y = c/t. \qquad (13.29)$$

The gradient of this rectangular hyperbola at the point "t" is given by

$$\frac{dy}{dx} = \frac{(dy/dt)}{(dx/dt)} = \frac{-c/t^2}{c} = -\frac{1}{t^2}$$

and the tangent to the curve at this point is the line

$$y - \frac{c}{t} = -\frac{1}{t^2}(x - ct),$$

that is,

$$x + t^2 y = 2ct. \qquad (13.30)$$

The normal at the point "t" is the line through the point $(ct, c/t)$ with slope t^2 and its equation is

$$y - \frac{c}{t} = t^2 (x - ct),$$

or,

$$t^2 x - y = c(t^3 - t^{-1}). \tag{13.31}$$

Example 16. *A variable chord of the hyperbola $xy = c^2$ passes through the fixed point (α, β). Prove that the locus of the mid-point of the chord is given by the equation $2xy = \beta x + \alpha y$.* [O.C.]

The equation of the chord joining the two points $(ct, c/t)$ and $(cT, c/T)$ on the hyperbola is

$$\frac{x - ct}{cT - ct} = \frac{y - (c/t)}{(c/T) - (c/t)}$$

which reduces to $x + tTy = c(t + T)$. If this line passes through the point (α, β) we have

$$\alpha + tT\beta = c(t + T). \tag{13.32}$$

The mid-point (x, y) of the chord is given by

$$x = \tfrac{1}{2}c(t + T), \qquad y = \tfrac{1}{2}c\left(\frac{1}{t} + \frac{1}{T}\right),$$

so that $t + T = 2x/c$ and $tT = x/y$. Substitution in (13.32) then gives

$$\alpha + \beta(x/y) = c(2x/c),$$

that is, $2xy = \beta x + \alpha y$ as the locus of the point (x, y).

Exercises 13 (c)

1. Find the equation of an ellipse whose centre is the origin and whose axes lie along the coordinate axes given that the semi-major axis of the ellipse is 10 and that the length of the minor axis is equal to the distance between the foci.

2. Show that the intercepts made on the coordinate axes by the tangent at the point $(16/5, 9/5)$, to the ellipse $9x^2 + 16y^2 = 144$ are equal. [O.C.]

3. Show that the line $y = mx + c$ is a tangent to the ellipse

$$(x^2/a^2) + (y^2/b^2) = 1 \text{ if } c^2 = a^2m^2 + b^2.$$

Prove also that, if a tangent to the ellipse from the point $(-a\sqrt{2}, 0)$ is perpendicular to a tangent to the ellipse from the point $(0, 13b/5)$, then the eccentricity of the ellipse is $\sqrt{(7/12)}$. [O.C.]

4. Show that the line $lx + my + n = 0$ is a tangent to the ellipse $(x^2/a^2) + (y^2/b^2) = 1$ if $a^2l^2 + b^2m^2 = n^2$ and find the coordinates of the points of contact when this condition is satisfied. Find the points on the ellipse $4x^2 + 9y^2 = 1$ at which the tangents are parallel to the line $8x = 9y$. [L.U.]

5. P and Q are two points on the ellipse $(x^2/a^2) + (y^2/b^2) = 1$ with eccentric angles ϕ and $\frac{1}{2}\pi + \phi$. Prove that the equation of the chord PQ is

$$b(\sin\phi - \cos\phi)x - a(\sin\phi + \cos\phi)y + ab = 0.$$

Prove also that, if the eccentricity of the ellipse is $\frac{1}{2}\sqrt{2}$, then the product of the lengths of the perpendiculars from the foci to that chord for which $\phi = 0$ is $\frac{1}{6}a^2$. [O.C.]

6. The tangent at $P(a\cos\phi, b\sin\phi)$ on the ellipse $(x^2/a^2) + (y^2/b^2) = 1$ cuts the x-axis at T and the normal at P cuts the x-axis at N. If ε is the eccentricity of the ellipse, prove that

   (i) $OT . ON = a^2\varepsilon^2$,
   (ii) $PT/PN = \tan\phi/\sqrt{(1 - \varepsilon^2)}$. [O.C.]

7. P is the point $(a\cos\phi, b\sin\phi)$ on the ellipse $(x^2/a^2) + (y^2/b^2) = 1$. The normal at P to the ellipse meets the x-axis at N. Show that the locus of the middle point of PN is an ellipse whose semi-axes are of lengths $(2a^2 - b^2)/2a$ and $b/2$.

8. The circles with the two parallel chords $x = x_1$, $x = x_2$ of the ellipse $(x^2/a^2) + (y^2/b^2) = 1$ as diameters pass through the focus $(a\varepsilon, 0)$; prove that $x_1 + x_2 = 2a\varepsilon/(2 - \varepsilon^2)$. If one chord is $x = 0$ and the other is PQ, prove that the tangent to the ellipse at P or Q makes an intercept of length $\frac{1}{2}(3\sqrt{2}a)$ on the y-axis. [O.C.]

9. P is the point on the ellipse $(x^2/a^2) + (y^2/b^2) = 1$ with coordinates $(a\cos\phi, b\sin\phi)$ and Q is the point $(a\cos\phi, a\sin\phi)$ on the circle $x^2 + y^2 = a^2$. If S is a focus of the ellipse, show that the length of the perpendicular from S on to the tangent at Q to the circle is equal to PS. [L.U.]

10. The equation of a chord of the ellipse $x^2 + 4y^2 = 260$ is $x + 6y = 50$. Find the coordinates of its middle point. [O.C.]

11. The centre of a hyperbola is at the origin and its transverse axis lies along the x-axis. Find the equation of the hyperbola if the distance between its foci is equal to $4a$, where $2a$ is the length of the transverse axis.

12. A point P moves so that its distance from the point $(5, 0)$ is $5/4$ times its distance from the straight line $x = 3\frac{1}{5}$. Show that the locus of P is the curve $(x^2/16) - (y^2/9) = 1$. Find the coordinates of the four points on the locus at each of which the join of the points $(5, 0)$ and $(-5, 0)$ subtends a right angle. [O.C.]

13. The point $P(a\sec\theta, b\tan\theta)$ on the hyperbola $(x^2/a^2) - (y^2/b^2) = 1$ is joined to the vertices $A(a, 0)$ and $B(-a, 0)$. The lines AP, BP meet the asymptote $ay = bx$ at Q, R respectively. Prove that the x-coordinate of Q is $(a\cos\frac{1}{2}\theta)/(\cos\frac{1}{2}\theta - \sin\frac{1}{2}\theta)$ and that the length of QR is independent of the value of θ. [N.U.]

14. The ordinate at $P(a \sec \theta, b \tan \theta)$ on the hyperbola

$$(x^2/a^2) - (y^2/b^2) = 1$$

meets the asymptote $ay = bx$ at Q. The tangent to the hyperbola at P meets the asymptote at R and the normal at P meets the x-axis at G. Prove that the angle RQG is a right angle. [N.U.]

15. Find the equation of the normal at the point $(3, 4)$ to the rectangular hyperbola $xy = 12$. Find also the coordinates of the point at which the normal meets the curve again.

16. Prove that the normal at the point $P(ct, c/t)$ to the hyperbola $xy = c^2$ meets the curve again at $Q(-c/t^3, -ct^3)$. If R is the opposite end of the diameter of the hyperbola through P, prove that PR is perpendicular to RQ. [N.U.]

17. The chord PQ of the hyperbola $xy = c^2$ meets the x-axis at N and M is the mid-point of PQ. If O is the origin of coordinates, prove that $OM = MN$. [O.C.]

18. Q is the foot of the perpendicular from the origin on to the tangent at any point P to the rectangular hyperbola $xy = c^2$. Find the equation of the locus of Q.

19. The tangents at $P(ct, c/t)$ and $Q(cT, c/T)$ to the hyperbola $xy = c^2$ meet at R. Show that the line joining the origin to R passes through the mid-point of PQ. [O.C.]

20. The normal at P to the rectangluar hyperbola $xy = c^2$ meets the curve again at Q. If O is the origin, show that $c^2 \cdot PQ = OP^3$. [O.C.]

Exercises 13 (d)

1. Prove that the locus of a point which moves so that its distance from the point $(-a, 0)$ is n times its distance from the point $(a, 0)$ is

$$(n^2 - 1)(x^2 + y^2 + a^2) - 2(n^2 + 1)ax = 0.$$

Show that this locus is a circle and find its centre and radius. Show also that the tangent to this circle at a point of intersection with the circle $x^2 + y^2 = a^2$ passes through the origin. [O.C.]

2. A point P moves so that the sum of the squares of its distances from the two lines $ax + by - 1 = 0$ and $ax - by + 1 = 0$ is equal to the square of its distance from the x-axis. Prove that P lies on the locus

$$2a^2x^2 + (b^2 - a^2)y^2 - 4by + 2 = 0.$$

Show that, when $3a^2 = b^2$, this locus is one of two different but equal circles and find the centre and radius of each. [O.C.]

3. A circle C, of radius r, passes through the points $A(a, 0)$, $A_1(-a, 0)$ and $B(0, b)$ where a and b are positive and not equal; a circle C_1, of radius r_1, passes through A, B and $B_1(0, -b)$. Prove that the centre of C is the

point $[0, (b^2 - a^2)/2b]$ and that $r_1/r = b/a$. Find the point of inter-section of the tangents to the circle C at A and A_1. [O.C.]

4. If A and B are the points $(-2, 1)$ and $(4, k)$, find the value of k if the x-axis is a tangent to the circle on AB as diameter. Find also the coordinates of the centre and the length of the radius of the circle.

5. The point $A(-2, 11)$ lies within the circle $x^2 + y^2 - 4x + 2y - 165 = 0$ and is the mid-point of the chord BC of the circle. Find the equation of BC. Hence, or otherwise, determine the coordinates of B and C. [L.U.]

6. If k is real, find the radius and the coordinates of the centre of the circle $x^2 + y^2 + 2kx - 4by = -k^2$. Prove that the circle touches the x-axis and find the equation of another straight line through the origin which touches the circle. Show that there are two values of k for which the circle passes through the point $(-1, 2)$, and that, if $r_1, r_2(r_1 > r_2)$ are the radii of these circles, then $r_1/r_2 = 9 + 4\sqrt{5}$. [O.C.]

7. The circles $x^2 + y^2 = a^2 (a > 0)$ and $x^2 + y^2 - 10x + 9 = 0$ intersect in two distinct points: prove, using a diagram, that $1 < a < 9$. Prove that, if the length of the common chord is $24/5$, then $a = 3$ or $\sqrt{73}$. Prove also that, when $a = 3$, the circles cut at right angles. [O.C.]

8. A circle, with its centre in the first quadrant, touches the y-axis and also touches externally the circle $x^2 + y^2 - 4x = 5$; prove that the co-ordinates (α, β) of its centre satisfy the equation $\beta^2 = 10\alpha + 5$. If the circle also touches the x-axis, prove that the abscissa of the point of contact with that axis is $5 + \sqrt{30}$. [O.C.]

9. If the normal at the point $P(at^2, 2at)$ to the parabola $y^2 = 4ax$ meets the axis of the parabola at Q, show that the locus of the middle point of PQ, as t varies, is the parabola $y^2 = a(x - a)$. [L.U.]

10. O is the origin, P the point $(a, 2a)$ and PQ the chord of the parabola $y^2 = 4ax$ which is the normal at P. PR is drawn parallel to OQ to meet the axis of the parabola at R. Find the coordinates of R. [L.U.]

11. The normal at a point P on the parabola $y^2 = 4ax$ meets the curve again at Q and the tangents to the parabola at P and Q meet at R. Prove that, if P is a variable point on the parabola, the locus of R is the curve

$$y^2(x + 2a) + 4a^3 = 0.$$ [O.C.]

12. The middle point of a variable chord of the parabola $y^2 = 4ax$ lies on the line $y = mx + c$. Find the equation of the locus of the point of intersection of the tangents to the parabola at the ends of this chord. [L.U.]

13. The tangent at the point $P(at^2, 2at)$ on the parabola $y^2 = 4ax$ meets the x-axis in T. The normal at P meets the x-axis in G. Show that (i) the middle point of GT is the focus, (ii) the tangent at the vertex bisects PT. Find the locus of the centroid of the triangle GPT as t varies. [L.U.]

14. The tangents to the parabola $y^2 = 4ax$ at the points P and Q intersect at T. If S is the focus, prove that

   (i) $ST^2 = SP \cdot SQ$ and   (ii) $TP^2/TQ^2 = SP/PQ$.   [L.U.]

15. A line from the point $(2, 0)$ perpendicular to the tangent at the point $(2t^2, 4t)$ on the parabola $y^2 = 8x$ meets that tangent at the point (h, k). Express h and k in terms of t and deduce the equation of the locus of the foot of the perpendicular from the point $(2, 0)$ on to any tangent to this parabola.   [L.U.]

16. The tangent at the point $P(a \cos \phi, b \sin \phi)$ to an ellipse centre O and semi-axes a, b meets the major axis at T. N is the foot of the perpendicular from P on the major axis. Show that $ON \cdot OT = a^2$.   [O.C.]

17. S and S' are the foci of an ellipse of semi-axes a and b. The normal at a point P on the ellipse meets the minor axis at G. Show that the square of the distance of G from either focus is

$$\left(\frac{a^2 - b^2}{b^2}\right) SP \cdot S'P.$$ [O.C.]

18. If the normal at P on an ellipse cuts the major and minor axes at G and H, show that as P moves on the ellipse, the mid-point of GH describes another ellipse of the same eccentricity.   [N.U.]

19. The foci of an ellipse are $S'(a\varepsilon, 0)$ and $S(-a\varepsilon, 0)$. T and K are the feet of the perpendiculars from S' and S respectively on any tangent to the ellipse. Prove that $S'T \cdot SK = b^2$ where $b^2 = a^2(1 - \varepsilon^2)$.   [O.C.]

20. Show that, for any value of m, the lines $y = mx \pm \sqrt{(a^2m^2 + b^2)}$ are tangents to the ellipse $(x^2/a^2) + (y^2/b^2) = 1$. A tangent, whose gradient m is positive, meets the positive x-axis at A and the negative y-axis at B. Prove that the area of the triangle OAB is $(a^2m^2 + b^2)/(2m)$ where O is the centre of the ellipse. Prove also that when the area of the triangle OAB is a minimum, the coordinates of the point of contact of the tangent are $(\frac{1}{2}a\sqrt{2}, -\frac{1}{2}b\sqrt{2})$.   [O.C.]

21. Find the conditions that the line $lx + my + n = 0$ should be (i) a tangent and (ii) a normal to the hyperbola $(x^2/a^2) - (y^2/b^2) = 1$.

22. Show that the line $y = mx + c$ is a tangent to the rectangular hyperbola $x^2 - y^2 = a^2$ if $c^2 = a^2(m^2 - 1)$ and that the coordinates of the point of contact T are $(-ma^2/c, -a^2/c)$. If the line meets the asymptotes at P and Q show that T is the mid-point of PQ.   [N.U.]

23. PN is the perpendicular to an asymptote from a point on a rectangular hyperbola. Prove that the locus of the mid-point of PN is a rectangular hyperbola with the same axes.   [O.C.]

24. The perpendicular from the origin to the tangent at a point P on the rectangular hyperbola $xy = c^2$ meets the curve at Q and R. The chords PQ and PR meet the x-axis at U and V. Prove that the mid-point of UV is the foot of the perpendicular from P on to the x-axis.   [O.C.]

25. PP' is a diameter of the rectangular hyperbola $xy = c^2$. The tangent at P meets lines through P' parallel to the asymptotes in Q and Q'. Prove that P is the mid-point of QQ' and that the equation of the locus of Q is $xy + 3c^2 = 0$.

CHAPTER 14

THE EQUILIBRIUM OF A RIGID BODY

[The student is assumed to have read the part of Chapter 6 dealing with vectors before starting this chapter.]

14.1 Applied mathematics

The term applied mathematics is used to describe any subject in which the methods of pure mathematics are applied to physical problems. Statics and Dynamics, which are treated in this book, are subjects of this kind; in Statics we discuss bodies which are at rest, in Dynamics bodies which are in motion.

Physical situations cannot always be described in exact mathematical terms and in both Statics and Dynamics certain simplifying assumptions are made so that problems may be treated mathematically. Thus bodies are assumed to be made up of a large number of particles of negligible dimensions such that the position of a particle may be considered as that of a mathematical point. Bodies are described as rigid to indicate that the relative positions of the constituent particles are unalterable. Consequently, two bodies can be assumed to have contact at a mathematical point. Similarly, a string may be taken as inextensible and weightless, a surface may be taken as perfectly smooth and pulleys and wheels as frictionless. These assumptions are not exactly true in the physical world as we know it, but the exact definitions make Statics and Dynamics precise mathematical subjects and they are close enough to the truth to allow quite accurate calculations to be made using simple mathematical techniques.

14.2 Force

Force is defined as that which moves or tends to move a body. The effect of force can be seen but the force itself is invisible. It may however be felt, and one of the earliest human experiences is that of the force of gravity.

Force is, in fact, measured in terms of the force of gravity and in the metric system the standard force is that with which the earth attracts a standard bar of platinum whose mass is called one kilogramme. This standard force is called one kilogramme weight and written as 1 kg wt or, sometimes, 1 kgf, the f standing for force. The British unit is one pound weight written as 1 lb wt or 1 lbf.

Other forces are measured by comparison with the standard force, possibly by suspension from a spring balance in which the extension of the spring is known to be proportional to the force. Thus we can measure forces of 1 gramme weight, 1 ton weight, etc.

These are all *gravitational forces* whose magnitude is the earth's attraction of a particular mass. Since the acceleration due to gravity is not the same in different latitudes, the force 1 kg wt which gives this acceleration to a mass of one kilogramme is not the same in different localities and we shall find it necessary in Dynamics to have an absolute measure of force. This is called the *newton* (abbreviation N) and is the force which gives to a mass of 1 kilogramme an acceleration of 1 metre per second per second.

$$1 \text{ kg wt} = 9\!\cdot\!81 \text{ N, approximately.}$$

We shall take all forces as being in newtons, unless otherwise stated. The *mass* of a body will be taken as m or M kilogrammes and its *weight* as W newtons ($W = Mg$).

The forces studied in Statics may be tensions, such as the force in a string by which a weight is suspended, or thrusts, as exerted by a prop supporting a weight. They may be attractions exerted without visible contact, such as the force of gravity, and include reactions which are the equal and opposite forces between two bodies in contact.

If a light string supports a weight W, the tension in the string T balances the weight and $T = W$. This is the force exerted by the string on the weight at the point of contact. If the upper end of the string is attached to a peg, and the weight of the string is negligible in comparison with W, the peg supports the weight W and this force is transmitted to the peg by the string. Thus the tension T is the same all along the string. Similarly, if a weight is supported by a prop of negligible weight, the weight is transmitted through the prop to the ground and the thrust is the same at any point of the prop.

14.3 Forces acting on a particle

We have seen (§ 6.9) that since displacements, velocities and accelerations are vector quantities and, since by virtue of Newton's second law the force on a particle has the same direction as its acceleration, the force acting on a particle is also a vector quantity. Thus two or more forces acting on a particle are equivalent to a single force acting on the particle which is the vector sum of the two forces. Also, a single force acting on a particle can be replaced by component forces in two directions which have the same effect as the single force. Forces which act on the same particle are said to act at a point.

Thus, from § 6.9, forces P and Q acting on a particle in directions which include an angle θ have resultant R in a direction making an angle α with the force P, where

$$R = \sqrt{\{P^2 + Q^2 + 2PQ \cos \theta\}} \tag{14.1}$$

and

$$\sin \alpha = \frac{Q}{R} \sin \theta. \tag{14.2}$$

Also (from § 6.9) a force P acting on a particle in a direction which makes an angle θ with a given direction OX is equivalent to a force $P \cos \theta$ parallel to OX and a force $P \sin \theta$ perpendicular to OX.

A particle is said to be in *equilibrium* if it is at rest (relative to its surroundings) under the action of two or more forces. Thus the condition for its equilibrium is that the resultant of the forces acting on it shall be zero. This is so if the vectors representing the forces form a closed polygon, and this is equivalent to saying the sums of the components of the vectors in two directions are zero.

Example 1. *The resultant of two forces P and Q acting on a particle is equal to P in magnitude; that of forces $2P$ and Q acting in the same directions as before is also equal to P. Find the magnitude of Q and prove that the direction of Q makes an angle of $150°$ with P.* [O.C.]

Let θ be the angle between the directions of P and Q. We have for the magnitude of the resultant in each case, from (14.1),

$$P^2 = P^2 + Q^2 + 2PQ \cos \theta$$
$$P^2 = 4P^2 + Q^2 + 4PQ \cos \theta.$$

Hence, eliminating $\cos \theta$, we find

$$P^2 = -2P^2 + Q^2, \qquad Q = P\sqrt{3}.$$

Also

$$\cos \theta = -\frac{Q}{2P} = -\frac{\sqrt{3}}{2}, \text{ so that } \theta = 150°.$$

Example 2. *The ends of a string of length $2a$ are attached to points A and B at distance a apart at the same level. A small smooth ring of weight W slides on the string and is in equilibrium when held by a horizontal force P directly below B. Prove that $P = \frac{1}{2}W$ and find the tension in the string.*

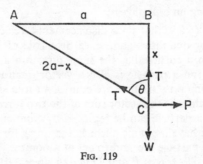

Fig. 119

Let T be the tension in the string so that there will be two forces T acting on the ring at C along the lines CB and CA (Fig. 119). If $BC = x$, $CA = 2a - x$ and $(2a - x)^2 = a^2 + x^2$, so that $x = 3a/4$ and $2a - x = 5a/4$. Hence if the angle

$ACB = \theta$, $\sin\theta = 4/5$, $\cos\theta = 3/5$. Equating to zero the sums of the horizontal and vertical components of the forces acting on the ring at C we have

$$P - T\sin\theta = 0$$
$$T + T\cos\theta - W = 0.$$

Hence
$$T = W/(1 + \cos\theta) = \tfrac{5}{8}W, \qquad P = \tfrac{4}{5}T = \tfrac{1}{2}W.$$

Exercises 14 (a)

1. Forces of 12 N and 9 N act on a particle in directions which include an angle of 60°. Find the magnitude of the resultant and its inclination to the direction of the 12 N force.

2. Forces of 5 N and 7 N acting on a particle have a resultant of 10 N. Find the angles made by the 5 N force and by the resultant with the 7 N force.

3. A particle of mass 10 kg is suspended by two strings inclined to the vertical at angles of 30° and 45° respectively. Find the tensions in the strings.

4. Equal masses of 10 kg are attached to the ends of a light inextensible string which passes over three smooth pegs in a wall. The pegs are the vertices of an equilateral triangle whose base is horizontal. Find the thrust on each peg.

5. Forces of 8 and 5 newton act on a particle in directions N.E. and N.30°W. respectively. Find the components of their resultant in directions N. and E.

6. A particle of mass 10 kg rests in equilibrium on a smooth plane inclined at 30° to the horizontal, being held by a light string inclined at 15° to the line of greatest slope. Find the tension in the string and the reaction of the plane.

7. R is the resultant of forces P and Q acting on a particle, their lines of action being inclined at 30°; if Q acts in the opposite direction the resultant is R_1. Prove that, if the lines of action of R and R_1 are at right angles, then $Q = P$. Find also the ratio $R : R_1$. [O.C.]

8. $ABCDEF$ is a regular hexagon. Forces of 10, 12, 8, 9, P, Q newton act on a particle in directions parallel to the sides AB, BC, CD, DE, EF, FA and the particle is in equilibrium. Find the values of P and Q.

9. ABC is a triangle in which $AB = 7$, $BC = 3$, $CA = 5$. Find (a) graphically (b) analytically the resultant of the following forces acting at a point: 3 N in the direction BC, 9 N in the direction AC, 9 N in the direction BA.

10. Three equal strings are knotted to form an equilateral triangle ABC and a weight W is suspended from C. If the system is supported with AB horizontal by strings attached to A and B, each making an acute angle α with the horizontal, prove that the tension in AB is

$$W \sin(60° - \alpha)/(\sqrt{3}\sin\alpha).$$ [L.U.]

11. The resultant of two intersecting forces P and $2P$ is $P\sqrt{3}$. Find the angle between the forces and the angle made by the resultant with the force of magnitude P.   [L.U.]

12. The ends of a light inextensible string of length l are fastened to points A and B at the same level distance a apart. A smooth ring of weight W slides on the string and a horizontal force X is applied to the ring so that it rests in equilibrium below B. Prove that $X = aW/l$ and the tension in the string is $W(a^2 + b^2)/2l^2$.   [L.U.]

13. Four horizontal wires are attached to a telephone post and exert the following tensions, in newtons, on it: 20 N., 30 E., 40 S.W., 50 S.E. Calculate the resulting pull on the post and find its direction.   [O.C.]

14. A pulley carries a mass of 30 kg and can slide freely up and down a smooth vertical groove. It is held up by a string passing round the pulley so that the two parts of the string make angles of 30° and 60° with the horizontal. Show that the tension in the string is slightly under $22g$ N.   [O.C.]

15. A body of mass 20 kg is suspended from a fixed point by a string and is in equilibrium with the string inclined at 20° to the vertical under the action of a force making an angle of 60° with the downward vertical. Find the magnitude of the force and the tension in the string. Assuming the force remains constant in magnitude but varies in direction, find the greatest possible inclination of the string to the vertical.   [O.C.]

14.4 Forces acting on a rigid body

Plane motion of a body is motion in which each particle of the body moves in a plane. In this case the position of every particle of the body can be found if the position of some plane section of the body which moves in its own plane is known. Thus the plane motion of a rigid body is often described as that of a lamina moving in its plane with all the forces that act on the body, including its weight, acting on the lamina in its plane. Hence, in discussing the motion or equilibrium of a body we need to be able to find the resultant of *coplanar forces* acting on the body.

A force acting on a rigid body will act on some particular particle of the body. The principle of *transmissibility of forces* acting on a rigid body states that the *effect* of a force depends, not on the point at which it is applied, but on the position of the line along which it acts. Thus if a force P is applied to a rigid body at a point A in a direction AB (Fig. 120), the effect of the force on the motion or the equilibrium of the body would be the same if the force were applied at B or at any point of the line AB. This principle follows from consideration of the manner by which force is transmitted from particle to particle within the body. It is easily verified by experiment and is formally proved in Dynamics when the equations of motion of a rigid body are obtained.

Because of its transmissibility, force is sometimes described as a *line localised* vector quantity.

The principle of transmissibility enables us to find the resultant of several coplanar forces acting on a rigid body. Let two of the forces

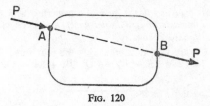

FIG. 120

be P and Q acting on particles at A and B in directions $A'A$ and $B'B$ respectively (Fig. 121). Let the lines $A'A$ and $B'B$ meet at D. Then the forces P and Q may be taken as acting on a particle at D and their resultant X acting at D along the direction DE is obtained as the vector

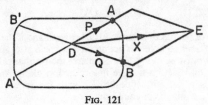

FIG. 121

sum of the vectors representing P and Q. Now let a third force R act at a point C in the direction $C'C$, and let the lines DE and $C'C$ meet at F (Fig. 122). We may take the forces R and X as acting on a particle at F, that is, since X is the resultant of P and Q, we may take the forces

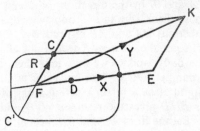

FIG. 122

P, Q and R as acting on a particle at F and obtain by vector summation their resultant Y acting along a line FK. Similarly the resultant of any number of forces acting on a rigid body can be obtained and the resultant will be represented by the vector sum of the vectors representing the forces irrespective of where the forces are applied. This vector sum gives the magnitude and direction of the resultant. The position of its line of action may be obtained by the process described above, but we shall see that it is more easily obtained by summing the turning effects of the forces.

Example 3. *PQRS is a lamina in the form of a trapezium with PQ parallel to SR. Prove that the lamina is in equilibrium under the action of forces completely represented by PS, SQ, QR and RP.* [L.U.]

PS, SQ, QR, RP are vectors representing the four forces in magnitude and direction (Fig. 123) and $PS + SQ = PQ$, $QR + RP = QP = -PQ$, so that

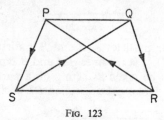

FIG. 123

the vector sum of the forces is zero. Also, the resultant of the forces, represented by PS and SQ may be taken as acting on a particle at S and its line of action parallel to PQ must be along SR. Similarly the resultant of the forces represented by QR and RP must have line of action along RS. Hence, the two resultants being equal and opposite and with the same line of action must balance and the lamina is in equilibrium.

14.5 Resultant of parallel forces

The argument in the previous paragraph would appear to break down when the resultant of forces whose lines of action are parallel has to be found, but this is not so. Let P and Q be two parallel forces acting on a rigid body at A and B in the directions $A'A$ and $B'B$ respectively (Fig. 124). Suppose there were in addition two equal forces R acting at A and B in directions BA and AB respectively. By the principle of transmissibility of force these forces R would not affect the motion or equilibrium of the body, and so we may take them as being applied. By drawing the triangle AGC we find by vector addition the resultant of P and R acting at A as a force X acting along AC; similarly the triangle of forces BHD gives the resultant of Q and R as a force Y acting along BD. Let the lines AC and BD meet at E. Then the forces X and Y may be taken as acting at E and, replacing X and Y by their constituent forces, we have forces R, P, R, Q acting at E, the two forces R being in opposite directions and the forces P and Q in the same direction. The forces R balance each other and the resultant is a single force $P + Q$ acting at E in a direction parallel to that of P and Q.

Let this resultant meet the line AB in F. The triangles with parallel sides AGC and EFA are similar, therefore $P/EF = R/AF$. Similarly, the triangles BHD and EFB are similar so that $Q/EF = R/BF$. From these equations $P/Q = BF/AF$, that is $P/BF = Q/AF$, so that the resultant divides the line AB in the inverse ratio of the forces.

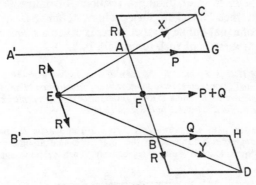

FIG. 124

The same procedure applies when the parallel forces P and Q act in opposite senses. Such forces are called *unlike* parallel forces as opposed to *like* parallel forces when their sense is the same. Introducing equal and opposite forces R acting at A and B along AB (Fig. 125) we have as before triangles AGC and BHD giving by vector addition forces X and

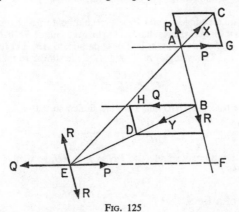

FIG. 125

Y acting along AC and BD respectively. Where their lines of action meet at E, we replace X and Y by their constituent forces, the forces R cancel and we are left with the resultant $P - Q$ acting at E in a direction parallel to that of P.

If the resultant meets the line AB in F, the triangles AGC and EFA are similar, as are the triangles BHD and EFB. Therefore we have as before $P/EF = R/AF$ and $Q/EF = R/BF$, so that again $P/BF = Q/AF$ and the resultant still divides AB in the inverse ratio of the forces but in this case the point of division is external to the line AB.

The above method of finding a resultant of unlike parallel forces breaks down when $P = Q$, for then the lines AC and BD will be parallel; such a pair of equal unlike parallel forces is called a *couple* and we shall discuss the properties of such forces in § 14.8.

Example 4. *ABCD is a lamina in the form of a trapezium with AB parallel to DC. Forces P and Q are represented in magnitude, direction and line of action by AB and DC respectively. Show that the resultant is P + Q parallel to AB and that its line of action divides AD in the ratio Q to P.*

Complete the parallelogram $ADCF$ (Fig. 126) and draw BE parallel to AD. Let AD represent a force R on the same scale and assume that equal and opposite forces R act at A and D respectively. Then AE represents the resultant

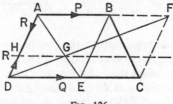

FIG. 126

of forces P and R acting at A and DF the resultant of forces Q and R acting at D. If these lines meet at G the resultant of the forces acting at G will be the resultant of forces P, Q, R and $-R$, that is $P + Q$ parallel to AB. Let its line of action meet AD in H. The triangles AHG and ADE are similar so that

$$\frac{AH}{HG} = \frac{AD}{DE} = \frac{R}{P}.$$

Similarly the triangles DHG and DAF are similar so that

$$\frac{DH}{HG} = \frac{DA}{AF} = \frac{R}{Q}.$$

From these equations we find $Q \times DH = P \times AH$, so that H divides AD in the ratio Q to P.

14.6 Moment of a force

The moment of a force P about a point O is defined as $P \times p$, where p (Fig. 127) is the perpendicular (and shortest) distance from O to the line of action of the force. The moment is taken as positive if, as in the diagram, the force is tending to make the particle on which it acts move in an anti-clockwise direction about O. Thus the moment of the force Q about O is $-qQ$. Strictly the moment is about an axis through O perpendicular to the plane in which the point and the force both lie and is a measure of the turning effect of the force on a body about this axis. The units of a moment are units of force and distance and we may speak of a moment of 10 mN.

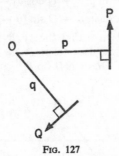

FIG. 127

If a uniform rod is pivoted at its centre O so that it is free to turn in a vertical plane about the pivot, it will balance in a horizontal position if it is placed there (Fig. 128). If equal weights are attached to the rod at equal distances from O the balance will be unbroken. Unequal weights W and W' may also be suspended from the two sides without unbalancing the rod provided that they are correctly placed. It will be found that if the weights W and W' are suspended at distances p and p' respectively from O the rod will balance if, and only if, $Wp = W'p'$, that is if the moments of the weights about O are equal in magnitude and opposite in sign. We shall, in fact, prove later that for the rod to

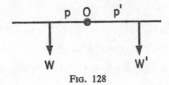

FIG. 128

be in equilibrium the sum of the moments of the forces acting on it about the pivot must be zero.

We shall now prove the important theorem on moments, that the sum of the moments of several forces about a point is equal to the moment of their resultant about the same point.

Let P and Q be forces acting along OA and OC where the angle $AOC = \theta$ and let R be their resultant acting along OB where the angle $AOB = \alpha$ (Fig. 129). Then, from the theory of vectors, R is the sum of components $P + Q \cos \theta$ along OA and $Q \sin \theta$ in the perpendicular direction OY, so that

$$R \cos \alpha = P + Q \cos \theta,$$
$$R \sin \alpha = Q \sin \theta.$$

Hence, if β be any other angle,

$$R \sin(\beta - \alpha) = \sin \beta \cdot R \cos \alpha - \cos \beta \cdot R \sin \alpha$$
$$= \sin \beta (P + Q \cos \theta) - \cos \beta (Q \sin \theta)$$
$$= P \sin \beta - Q \sin(\theta - \beta). \tag{14.3}$$

Now let D be any point such that the angle $AOD = \beta$, and let DL, DM, DN be the perpendiculars from D to the lines OA, OB, OC respectively.   Then $DL = OD \sin \beta$, $DM = OD \sin(\beta - \alpha)$,

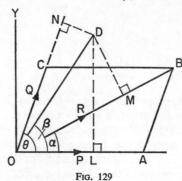

Fig. 129

$DN = OD \sin(\theta - \beta)$. The sum of the moments of the forces P and Q about D is

$$P \times DL - Q \times DN$$
$$= OD\{P \sin \beta - Q \sin(\theta - \beta)\}.$$

The moment of R about D is

$$R \times DM = OD \times R \sin(\beta - \alpha)$$
$$= OD\{P \sin \beta - Q \sin(\theta - \beta)\}, \text{ from (14.3).}$$

Thus the moment of R about D is the sum of the moments of P and Q about D.

Since the resultant of several forces may be obtained by adding one force at a time, the moment of the final resultant about any point will be equal to the sum of the moments of the several forces about the point.

Example 5. *A straight line XY in the plane of a triangle ABC cuts BC at D. Show how to replace a force S acting along XY by forces acting along BC and AD. Deduce that S may be represented by three forces P, Q, R, acting along the sides BC, CA, AB respectively. If p is the perpendicular from A to XY, show that P is of magnitude $p \cdot BC \cdot S/(2\Delta)$, where Δ is the area of the triangle.* [L.U.]

Let **DF** (Fig. 130) be a vector representing S. Draw FG parallel to CB to meet AD in G and draw FE parallel to GD. Draw BH parallel to AC to meet AD in H. Then $\mathbf{DF} = \mathbf{DG} + \mathbf{DE}$ and the forces represented by these vectors act along

AD and BC respectively. Let $DG = \lambda AH$ and $DE = \mu BC$, where λ and μ are scalars. Then the force represented by DG has magnitude λAH and may be taken to act at A, so that it is equivalent to forces represented by λAB and λBH (since $AB + BH = AH$), the force represented by λBH acting along AC. We have, therefore, replaced the force S by forces P, Q, R along BC, CA, AB respectively, where $P = \mu BC$, $Q = \lambda BH$, $R = \lambda AB$.

The sum of the moments of P, Q and R about A will be equal to the moment of their resultant S about A. Q and R have no moments about A and the moment

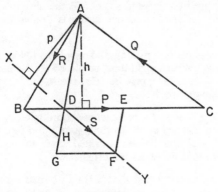

Fig. 130

of P about A is Ph, where h is the length of the perpendicular from A on BC. The moment of S about A is $S \cdot p$, therefore

$$P \cdot h = S \cdot p,$$
$$P \cdot h \cdot BC = S \cdot p \cdot BC,$$

and since $h \cdot BC = 2\Delta$,

$$P = p \cdot BC \cdot S/(2\Delta).$$

Exercises 14 (b)

1. A light triangular lamina ABC is freely suspended by the vertex C and particles of weights P and Q are attached at A and B respectively. The lamina hangs in equilibrium with the internal bisector of the angle ACB vertical. Find the ratio of $P : Q$ in terms of the sides of the triangle.
   [L.U.]

2. $ABCDEF$ is a lamina in the shape of a regular hexagon of side a. Forces $4P$, $5P$, $2P$, $3P$, $6P$, $3P$ act along the sides AB, BC, CD, DE, EF, FA respectively. Show that the resultant of these forces is a force $2P$ and find its moment about A.

3. A non-uniform rod AB of length 20 cm rests horizontally on two supports at C and D, where $AC = BD = 4$ cm. The greatest mass that can be hung from A without disturbing equilibrium is 8 kg, and the greatest mass that can be hung from B is 10 kg. Find the mass of the rod and the distance of its centre of gravity from A. [L.U.]

4. A rod AB, 10 cm in length, is supported horizontally by vertical forces at C and D, where $AC = 1$ cm, $DB = 3$ cm. A mass of 9 gm placed at A will just disturb equilibrium as will a mass of 15 gm placed at B. Find the mass of the rod and the distance of its centre of mass from A.   [L.U.]

5. A uniform plank 9 m long of mass 80 kg is supported horizontally by vertical strings attached at 1 m and 8 m from one end. What mass should be placed on one end so that (i) the tension in one string just vanishes, (ii) the tension in one string is double the tension in the other?   [L.U.]

6. 2·8 metres of a plank 8 m long and weighing 100 kg project over the side of a quay. What weight must be placed on the end of the plank so that a man of mass 75 kg may be able to walk to the other end without the plank tipping over?   [O.C.]

7. A force of $30g$ N acts at a point whose coordinates in metres are $(3, 1)$ in a direction inclined at $30°$ to the x-axis and a force of $6g$ N acts at the point $(5, -1)$ in a direction inclined at $60°$ to the x-axis. Find the sum of their moments about the origin.

8. A heavy non-uniform beam AB, of length l, rests across a fixed peg P and carries equal masses M_1 hung from the ends. In equilibrium with AB horizontal AP is x_1. For another pair of masses M_2 the corresponding distance AP is x_2. Prove that the mass M of the beam is given by

$$(x_1 - x_2)M = (M_1 - M_2)l - 2M_1x_1 + 2M_2x_2.$$ [L.U.]

9. $ABCD$ is a quadrilateral in which $AB = BC = a$, $CD = DA$, A and C are right angles and the angle B is $60°$. Equal forces $\sqrt{3}P$ act along AD and DC, equal forces P act along CB and BA. Find the magnitude of their resultant and show that its moment about a point on BA produced distant a from A is zero.

10. A uniform metal plate of mass 36 kg is in the form of an equilateral triangle. It is supported with its plane horizontal by three vertical strings each attached to the mid-point of a side. A mass P kg is placed at a corner of the plate. Find the value of P if (i) the tension in one string vanishes, (ii) the tensions in the strings are in the ratio $1 : 2 : 2$.   [L.U.]

11. A square lamina $ABCD$ with $AB = 8$ cm rests on a smooth table. Forces of 3, 2, 5, 4 N act along AB, BC, DC, DA respectively. The lamina is held by a smooth pin through a point in the line joining the mid-points of AB and DC and does not move. Find the distance of the pin from AB.

12. A rectangular plate 4 m × 3 m lies on a horizontal surface. The centre of gravity is 1 m from a 4 m edge and 1·5 m from a 3 m edge. The mass of the plate is 120 kg. Determine the vertical force which, applied to each of the four corners in turn would just raise them off the ground.

14.7 Line of action of the resultant

The theorem on moments proved in § 14.6 enables us to find the line of action of the resultant of several forces acting on a rigid body. Let A be a point on the line of action of the resultant R; then the moment of R about A will be zero, therefore the sum of the moments of the forces about A will be zero. The moment of R about any other point B will equal the sum of the moments of the forces about B. Thus having found the magnitude and direction of the resultant by simple vector addition of the forces, the distance of its line of action from some point is found by equating its moment about the point to the sum of the moments of the forces about that point.

This method can be described in terms of Cartesian coordinates. Let forces whose components parallel to axes OX and OY are X_1 and Y_1,

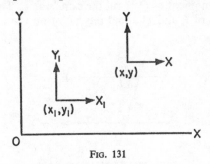

FIG. 131

X_2 and Y_2, . . . act at points (x_1, y_1), (x_2, y_2), . . ., and let their resultant have components X and Y and act at the point (x, y) (Fig. 131). Here (x, y) may be any point on the line of action of the resultant. Then by vector addition we have

$$X = X_1 + X_2 + \ldots, \qquad Y = Y_1 + Y_2 + \ldots.$$

The moment of the first force about the origin is the sum of the moments of its components, that is $x_1Y_1 - y_1X_1$, and a similar expression gives the moment of each of the other forces and of the resultant. Therefore

$$xY - yX = (x_1Y_1 - y_1X_1) + (x_2Y_2 - y_2X_2) + \ldots.$$

Substituting for X and Y we have an equation satisfied by the coordinates of any point (x, y) where the resultant may be taken to act, namely

$$x(Y_1 + Y_2 + \ldots) - y(X_1 + X_2 + \ldots)$$
$$= (x_1Y_1 - y_1X_1) + (x_2Y_2 - y_2X_2) + \ldots.$$

This is the equation of the line of action of the resultant.

We have seen (§ 14.5) that like parallel forces P and Q have a parallel resultant $P + Q$ whose line of action divides any intercept of a line between the lines of action of the forces in the inverse ratio of the forces. Let A and B (Fig. 32) be points on the lines of action of P and Q respectively and let the resultant $P + Q$ pass through a point F on AB. Then

$$\frac{P}{BF} = \frac{Q}{AF},$$

so that $P \times AF = Q \times BF$. Then if θ is the inclination of AB to the direction of P

$$P \times AF \sin \theta = Q \times BF \sin \theta. \qquad (14.4)$$

But $P \times AF \sin \theta$ is the moment (clockwise in Fig. 132) of P about any point on the line of action of the resultant and $Q \times BF \sin \theta$ is the (anticlockwise) moment of Q about the same point. Therefore the sum of the moments of P and Q about any point on the resultant is zero.

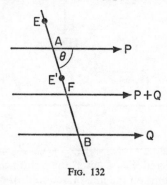

FIG. 132

Further, if E be any other point on AB outside AB, the sum of moments of P and Q about E

$$= P \times AE \sin \theta + Q \times BE \sin \theta$$
$$= P \times (FE - AF) \sin \theta + Q \times (FE + BF) \sin \theta$$
$$= (P + Q) \times FE \sin \theta, \text{ by virtue of } (14.4).$$

Thus the sum of the moments of P and Q about E is equal to the moment of the resultant $P + Q$ about E.

Similarly, if E' is a point between A and B, the sum of moments about E

$$= -P \times AE' \sin \theta + Q \times BE' \sin \theta$$
$$= -P \times (AF - FE') \sin \theta + Q \times (BF + FE') \sin \theta$$
$$= (P + Q) \times FE' \sin \theta, \text{ by virtue of } (14.4),$$

and this is the moment of the resultant about E'.

In the same way if P and Q are unlike parallel forces the resultant is now $P - Q$ through F (Fig. 133) and $P \times AF = Q \times BF$. Then if E be any point on AB the sum of moments about E

$$= P \times AE \sin \theta - Q \times BE \sin \theta$$
$$= P \times (FE + AF) \sin \theta - Q \times (FE + BF) \sin \theta$$
$$= (P - Q) \times FE \sin \theta,$$

which is the moment of the resultant about E.

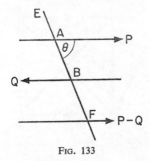

Fig. 133

Example 6. *OABC is a square of side a; OA is taken as the positive x-axis and OC as the positive y-axis. Forces $2P$, $3P$, $4P$, $5P$ and $3P\sqrt{2}$ act along OA, AB, BC, CO and AC respectively. Prove that the resultant is $P\sqrt{(26)}$ and find the equation of its line of action.*   [O.C.]

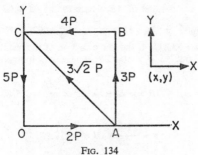

Fig. 134

The force along AC (Fig. 134) has components $-3P$ parallel to OX and $3P$ parallel to OY, so that if X and Y be the components of the resultant

$$X = 2P - 4P - 3P = -5P,$$
$$Y = 3P - 5P + 3P = P,$$

and

$$\sqrt{(X^2 + Y^2)} = P\sqrt{(26)}.$$

If (x, y) be a point on the line of action of the resultant its moment about O is $xY - yX = Px + 5Py$. The sum of the moments of the several forces about O is

$$3Pa + 4Pa + 3\sqrt{2}P \times \frac{a}{\sqrt{2}} = 10Pa.$$

Then

$$Px + 5Py = 10Pa,$$

and the equation of the line of action of the resultant is

$$x + 5y = 10a.$$

Example 7. *Forces of magnitude P, 2P, 3P, 4P act respectively along the sides of a square AB, BC, CD, DA and further forces $8\sqrt{2}P$ act along the diagonals BD and AC. Determine the magnitude of the resultant, the inclination of its line of action to AC and the perpendicular distance of this line of action from A.* [L.U.]

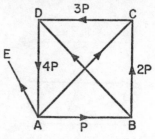

FIG. 135

The sum of the two forces $8\sqrt{2}P$ along the diagonals is a force of $16P$ parallel to AD (Fig. 135). Hence, the sum of all the forces is $P - 3P = -2P$ parallel to AB and $2P + 16P - 4P = 14P$ parallel to AD. The resultant is

$$\sqrt{\{(2P)^2 + (14P)^2\}} = 10\sqrt{2}P$$

and its direction is parallel to AE, where the angle $DAE = \tan^{-1} 2/14$. Then

$$\tan CAE = \tan (45° + \tan^{-1}\tfrac{1}{7}) = \frac{1 + \tfrac{1}{7}}{1 - \tfrac{1}{7}} = \frac{4}{3}$$ and the resultant is inclined at

an angle $\tan^{-1} 4/3$ to AC. If the line of action of the resultant is distant p from A its moment about A is $p \times 10\sqrt{2}P$. The sum of moments of the given forces about A is

$$2P \times AB + 3P \times AB + 8\sqrt{2}P \times \frac{AB}{\sqrt{2}} = 13AB \times P.$$

Therefore

$$p = \frac{13\sqrt{2}}{20} AB = 0.919AB.$$

Example 8. *A system of coplanar forces has moments about the points $O(0, 0)$, $A(4, 0)$ and $B(0, 3)$ in the plane of the forces equal to $+16$, $+4$ and -8 respectively, the anticlockwise direction being taken as positive. Find the equation of the line of action of the resultant R of the system and determine the value of R.* [L.U.]

Let the resultant R have components X and Y parallel to the axis and let (x, y) be any point on its line of action (Fig. 136). The moments of the components taken as acting at (x, y) about O, A and B equated to the given values give

$$xY - yX = 16,$$
$$(x - 4)Y - yX = 4,$$
$$xY - (y - 3)X = -8.$$

Subtracting the second equation from the first and the third equation from the first we find

$$Y = 3, \quad X = -8, \quad R = \sqrt{(9 + 64)} = \sqrt{(73)}.$$

Substituting for X and Y in the first equation we find

$$3x + 8y = 16,$$

and this is the equation of the line of action of R.

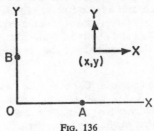

FIG. 136

Example 9. *A uniform beam AB 10 m long and of mass 10 kg rests in a horizontal position on supports at 1 m and 7 m from A. A mass of 2 kg is placed on the beam at B and a mass of 7 kg is moved along the beam from A towards B. Find the reactions at the supports when the 7 kg mass is 3 m from A and its distance from A when the equilibrium is broken.*

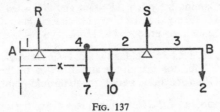

FIG. 137

Let R and S be the reactions of the supports on the beam and let the 7 kg mass be x metres from A (Fig. 137). Since the beam is in equilibrium

$$R + S = 7g + 10g + 2g = 19g.$$

The sum of moments of the forces about any point must be zero, therefore taking moments about the left-hand support,

$$6S = 7(x - 1)g + 10 \times 4g + 2 \times 9g$$
$$S = 8{\cdot}5g + 7xg/6,$$

and hence

$$R = 10{\cdot}5g - 7xg/6.$$

When $x = 3$, this gives $R = 7g$, $S = 12g$ N.
Equilibrium will be broken when $R = 0$, and for this

$$0 = 10{\cdot}5 - 7x/6,$$

giving

$$x = 9,$$

so that the 7 kg mass will be 9 m from A.

Exercises 14 (c)

1. In a rectangular plate $ABCD$, $AB = 5$ cm, $BC = 10$ cm; along the sides AB, BC, CD, DA there act forces of 10, 20, 20, 40 N respectively. Show that their resultant is parallel to one of the diagonals and find the resultant in magnitude and position.　　　　　　　　　　　　　　[L.U.]

2. $OABC$ is a square of side a. Forces of 2, 4, 6, 8 units act along OA, AB, BC, CO respectively and a force P acts along AC. Show that, whatever the value of P the five forces cannot maintain equilibrium or reduce to a couple. If $P = 10\sqrt{2}$ and OA and OC are taken as the x-axis and y-axis respectively, find the magnitude of the resultant and the equation of its line of action.　　　　　　　　　　　　　　[L.U.]

3. The diagonals of a square $ABCD$ of side $2a$ meet in E. Forces 1, 2, 3, 4, 5 N act along AB, BC, CD, DA, AC respectively. Find (i) a force X parallel to BA which when added to the system would give a resultant perpendicular to that of the original system, (ii) the force Y along DB which together with X and the original system would give zero resultant. If the system is in equilibrium with both forces X and Y added, show that the distance of the line of action of X from E is $5(4 + 5\sqrt{2})a/17$.　　　　　　　　　　　　　　[L.U.]

4. Forces $2P$, $5P$, $3P$ and $4P$ act along the sides AB, BC, CD and DA of a rectangular lamina in which $AB = 4a$ and $BC = 3a$, and a force $5P$ acts along AC. Prove that the forces are equivalent to a force $5P$ whose line of action cuts AB produced at $13a/4$ from B.　　　　　　[O.C.]

5. Forces $13P$, $2P$, $3P$, $8P$ act along the sides AB, BC, CD, AD respectively of a square. Find the magnitude and direction of their resultant and prove that its line of action passes through the mid-point of AB.　　[L.U.]

6. Find the resultant of the following forces along the sides of a square: 17 N along DA, 7 N along CB, 19 N along CD, 5 N along BA, and prove that its line of action bisects two sides of the square.　　[L.U.]

7. Forces of 4 N, 3 N, 1 N and 2 N act along the sides AB, CB, CD, AD respectively of a rectangle. $AB = 7a$, $BC = 5a$. If this system of forces is equivalent to a force P acting at A and a force Q acting along DB, find the magnitudes of P and Q and the direction of P. Find also where the line of action of the resultant of the system meets AB.　　[L.U.]

8. ABC is a triangular lamina with $AB = 7a$, $BC = 3a$, $CA = 5a$; forces $3P$, P and $3P$ act along AB, CB and CA respectively. Find the magnitude of their resultant, the angle which its line of action makes with AB and the point O in which its line of action meets AB.　　　　[O.C.]

9. Forces $4P$, P and $2P$ act along the sides BC, CA and BA respectively of an equilateral triangle of side a. Prove that the system is equivalent to a force $3\sqrt{3}P$ in the direction DE, where D is a point in BC at distance $\frac{1}{8}a$ from B and E is the point in CA at distance $\frac{1}{8}a$ from C.　　　[O.C.]

10. *ABC* is an equilateral triangle; forces 4, 2 and 2 N act along *AB*, *AC* and *BC* respectively. Prove that, if *E* is the point where the perpendicular to *BC* at *B* meets *CA* produced and if *F* bisects *AB*, the resultant is $2\sqrt{7}$ N acting along *EF*. [O.C.]

11. *ABC* is an equilateral triangle of side *a* and *AD* is a median. Forces of 4, 3, 3 and 2 N act along *BC*, *CA*, *AB* and *AD* respectively. Find the resultant of the forces in magnitude and direction and the distance from *D* of the point where its line of action intersects *BC* produced. [L.U.]

12. Forces 1, 2, 3, 2, 5 N act along the sides *AB*, *CA*, *FC*, *FD*, *ED* respectively of a regular hexagon *ABCDEF* and forces *P*, *Q* and *R* act along *BC*, *FA* and *FE* respectively. If the system is in equilibrium find the values of *P*, *Q* and *R*.

13. A rectangular lamina *ABCD* lying on a smooth table is acted upon by forces *P* along *AB*, 4 along *CB*, 3 along *CD* and 4 along *AD*. Equilibrium is maintained by a fifth force applied at the middle point of *BC*. If *AB* = 2a and *BC* = 3a, find the magnitude of *P*. [L.U.]

14. An equilateral triangle of side 1 m lies in the plane of a system of forces. These forces have a total anti-clockwise moment of 9 m N about *A*, −3 m N about *B* and 3 m N about *C*. Find the magnitude of the resultant of the system and its moment about the middle point of *AC*. [L.U.]

15. Forces *F*, 2*F*, 3*F*, 4*F* act along the sides *BA*, *BC*, *CD*, *DA* of a quadrilateral. *AB* and *BC* are two sides of a square *ABCE* and *D* is the mid-point of *CE*. Find the magnitude and direction of the resultant and the distances from *B* at which its line of action meets *AB* and *BC*. [L.U.]

14.8 Couples

A couple is defined as a pair of equal and opposite parallel forces acting on a body. Examples of couples are the two forces required to turn a tap and the force exerted at the end of a spanner to turn a nut together with the equal and opposite force exerted by the nut on the spanner. A couple will cause rotation but it will not move things about.

If the resultant is defined in magnitude and direction as the vector sum of forces, the resultant of a couple is evidently zero. Its moment is not, however, zero and we shall show that its moment about any point in the plane of the forces is the same.

Defining the *arm* of a couple as the perpendicular distance between the lines of action of the constituent forces we shall prove the following general theorems on couples:

(i) *The moment of a couple acting on a rigid body about any point in the plane of the forces is the product of its arm and one of the forces.*

Let AB be any line perpendicular to the forces meeting their lines of action in A and B, so that AB is the arm of the couple (Fig. 138). Let C be a point on AB produced outside AB; then the sum of the moments of the forces about C is

$$P \times BC - P \times AC = P \times AB.$$

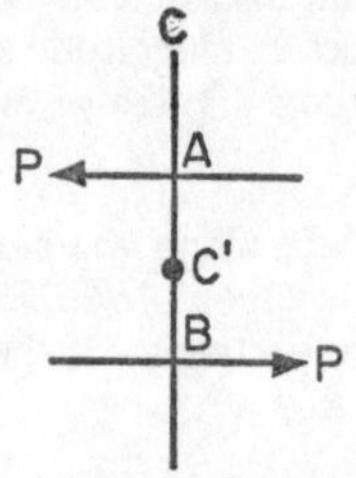

FIG. 138

If C' is another point on AB between A and B the sum of moments about C' is

$$P \times BC' + P \times AC' = P \times AB.$$

Thus the sum of moments about any point is $P \times AB$.

(ii) *Two couples acting on a rigid body in the same plane are equivalent to a single couple whose moment is the sum of their moments.*

Let the forces of the two couples be P and Q respectively and let the lines of action of one pair of forces P and Q meet at A and those of the other pair meet at B. Then if the resultant of P and Q is R we have two unlike parallel forces R acting at A and B forming a resultant couple. The moment of the force R at A about B is equal to the sum of moments of the forces P and Q at A about B, and these moments are those of the resultant couple and of the original couples.

(iii) *The resultant of a single force P and a couple acting in the same plane on a rigid body is a single force P whose line of action is displaced from that of the original force but is parallel to it.*

The effect of a couple of moment M on the body is that of two unlike parallel forces P with distance M/P between their lines of action. If the single force P acts at a point A, one of the forces of the couple may be assumed to act at A in a direction exactly opposite to P while the other acts in the same sense as P at a distance M/P from A. The two forces at A cancel and we are left with the force P whose line of action is distant M/P from A and parallel to that of P.

(iv) *If three forces acting on a rigid body can be represented in magnitude, direction and line of action by the sides of a triangle taken in order, they are equivalent to a couple whose moment is represented by twice the area of the triangle.*

Since the forces are represented by the sides of a triangle taken in order their vector sum must be zero and therefore they reduce to a couple. The moment of the couple about any vertex of the triangle is the moment of the force represented by the opposite side and this force is multiplied by the perpendicular to the opposite side. This is the moment of the couple and it is represented by the product of the perpendicular and the opposite side which is twice the area of the triangle.

Example 10. *A uniform beam AB 20 m long and of mass 200 kg rests in a horizontal position on supports at A and B. An anti-clockwise couple of moment 250g m N is applied at A and a clockwise couple of 750g m N at B. Find the reactions at the supports.*

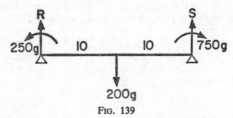

Fig. 139

If R and S be the reactions at the supports (Fig. 139), $R + S = 200g$. The couples are applied at the ends of the beam but their total anti-clockwise moment about any point is $-500g$ m N. Hence, equating to zero the sum of moments about A, we have

$$20 \times S - 10 \times 200g - 500g = 0,$$

and hence $S = 125g$, $R = 75g$ N.

Example 11. *Forces of magnitude 1, 2, 3 and 6 N act along the sides AB, BC, CD and DA of a square of side 2 m. Two other forces P and Q act along the diagonals AC and BD respectively. Determine the values of P and Q in order that the system may reduce to a couple and calculate the moment of the couple.* [L.U.]

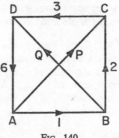

Fig. 140

If the system reduces to a couple the sums of the components of the forces parallel to AB and to BC will be zero (Fig. 140). The components of P and Q, in these directions are $P/\sqrt{2} - Q/\sqrt{2}$ and $P/\sqrt{2} + Q/\sqrt{2}$ respectively, so that

$$P/\sqrt{2} - Q/\sqrt{2} + 1 - 3 = 0$$
$$P/\sqrt{2} + Q/\sqrt{2} + 2 - 6 = 0,$$

and hence $P = 3\sqrt{2}$, $Q = \sqrt{3}$ N.

The moment of the couple will be the same about any point. The sum of moments about A is

$$2 \times 2 + 3 \times 2 + Q \times \sqrt{2} = 12 \text{ m N}.$$

and this is the required moment of the couple.

Exercises 14 (d)

1. $ABCD$ is a square of side 1 m. Forces of 5, 3, 4 and 6 N act along the sides AB, BC, CD and DA respectively and forces of $\sqrt{2}$ N and $2\sqrt{2}$ N act along the diagonals AC and BD respectively. Show that the system of forces is equivalent to a couple and find its moment.

2. The centre of gravity of a gate of weight W N is 1 m from the vertical line containing the two hinges which are 66·7 cm apart. Show that the horizontal components of the action of the hinges on the gate form a couple and find their magnitude.

3. A horizontal beam has one end built into a wall. The masonry pressures on the beam are equivalent to a force of 150 N vertically downwards at 30 cm from where the beam enters the wall at A and a force of 225 N vertically upwards at 12 cm from A. Find the upward force acting at A and the moment of the couple which together with this force is equivalent to the given system.

4. The coupling at the front of a railway wagon in 6 cm higher than that at the rear and the horizontal coupling pull is 2500 N. Find the moment of the couple so formed. If the axles are 96 cm apart and the centre of gravity is mid-way between the axles, find the difference between the loads on the front and rear axles caused by the couple.

5. Forces of 1, 2, 3, 6, 5, 4 units act respectively along the sides AB, CB. CD, ED, EF, AF of a regular hexagon of side a. Prove that the six forces are equivalent to a couple and find its moment.   [L.U.]

6. $ABCD$ is a square of side 2 m. Forces of 4, 3, 2, 1 N act along AB, CB, CD, DA respectively. Calculate the magnitude and direction of the force through A and the moment of the couple which are together equivalent to the given system of forces. Also calculate the distance from A at which the line of action of the single force equivalent to the system intersects AB.   [L.U.]

7. One end of a uniform bar of weight W and length $2a$ is attached to the end of a light inextensible string which hangs freely from a ceiling

A couple of moment G acts on the bar in a vertical plane containing the string. Show that equilibrium is possible only if $G \leqslant Wa$ and find the positions of the rod and string and the tension in the string when this condition is satisfied.   [L.U.]

8. Forces of 3, 13 and 5 N act along OX, OA and OB respectively, where OA and OB are on the same side of the straight line $X'OX$ and rotation from OX to OA and OA to OB is anti-clockwise, $\tan^{-1} AOX = 5/12$, $\tan^{-1} BOX' = 4/3$. A force P forms with the given forces a couple of clockwise moment 90 cm N. Find the magnitude of P and the distance from O of the point where its line of action intersects OX. [L.U.]

9. $ABCD$ is a rectangle in which $AB = 12$ cm, $AD = 5$ cm. Forces of 7 N and 13 N act along AB and BD respectively. Find the magnitude and direction of the force through C and the moment of the couple which together with the given forces will form a system in equilibrium.

     [L.U.]

10. Forces of magnitude 1, 2, 3, P, Q, R units act respectively along the sides AB, CB, CD, ED, EF, AF of a regular hexagon of side a. If the six forces are equivalent to a couple of moment $a\sqrt{3}$, find the values of P, Q and R.

11. Forces of magnitude 2, 3, 5, P, 4 and Q units act along the sides of a regular hexagon taken in order. Determine the values of P and Q in order that the forces may reduce to a couple. If the side of the hexagon is 1 unit, calculate the moment of the couple.   [L.U.]

12. Forces of 1, 2, 3, 5, 4, 2 units act along the sides AB, BC, CD, DE, EF, FA of a regular hexagon of side a. Reduce the system to a force at the centre O of the hexagon and a couple.

14.9 Centre of parallel forces

Let a number of like parallel forces $P_1, P_2, P_3, \ldots$, act on particles of a rigid body at points $A_1, A_2, A_3, \ldots$, (Fig. 141). Then, whatever may be the common direction of the forces, the resultant $P_1 + P_2$ of P_1 and P_2 may be taken to act on a particle at C in A_1A_2 such that

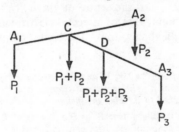

Fig. 141

$P_1 \cdot A_1C = P_2 \cdot A_2C$. Similarly the resultant of this force and P_3, which is $P_1 + P_2 + P_3$, may be taken to act on a particle at D where $(P_1 + P_2) \cdot CD = P_3 \cdot DA_3$. Proceeding in this way we can find the resultant of any number of parallel forces and a point where this resultant may be taken to act. This point is called the *centre of parallel forces* and it should be noticed that its position does not depend on the common direction of the forces and that the particles on which they act need not be in the same plane.

The weights of the constituent particles of a body form just such a system of parallel forces and their centre is called the *centre of gravity* or *centre of mass* of the body. The position of the centre of gravity is therefore independent of the direction in which the weights act and, however the body may be turned, its total weight may be taken as acting vertically downwards through the centre of gravity. Strictly, there is a slight difference between the centre of mass and the centre of gravity; the centre of mass is calculated on the assumption that the gravity forces on the particles of a body are parallel, whereas these forces converge to a point which is the centre of the earth and the true centre of gravity would be the point where these converging forces should be taken to act.

The *centroid* of a lamina is its centre of gravity if the surface has uniform mass, and the position of the centroid is calculated by assuming the mass of each small element of its area to be proportional to that area.

In considering the equilibrium of a rigid body under the action of various forces the weight of the body acting vertically downwards through its centre of gravity must be taken into account. The centroids and centres of gravity of various surfaces and bodies have been found by the methods of the Calculus in § 10.6, and those of composite bodies will be discussed in the next chapter. Here we note that if a body of uniform material has a centre of symmetry G such that to any particle A of the body there corresponds another particle A' in the line AG on the opposite side of G and at the same distance from G, then the resultant of the weights of the particles will pass through G. This will be true for every such pair of particles and hence G must be the centre of gravity of the body. Thus the centre of gravity of a uniform thin rod will be at its mid-point, that of a rectangle or parallelogram at the intersection of its diagonals, that of a circle, ellipse or sphere at its centre and so on.

Example 12. *Masses of weights $2W$, W and W are attached to the vertices A, B and and C respectively of a light equilateral triangle and the triangle is suspended from a string attached to B. Find the inclination of BC to the vertical.*

The centre of the parallel forces W at B and C is at D the mid-point of BC (Fig. 142) and the centre of the three parallel forces is therefore at X the mid-point of the median AD. Thus the total weight may be taken to act at X and as this is supported by the tension of the string, the line BX must be vertical. Now if $AB = a$, $AD = \sqrt{3}a/2$, $XD = \sqrt{3}a/4$, $BD = a/2$ and, since $ADB = 90°$, $\tan XBD = \sqrt{3}/2$; hence BC is inclined at an angle $\tan^{-1}(\sqrt{3}/2)$ to the vertical.

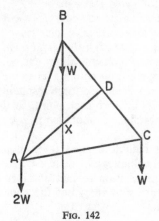

FIG. 142

14.10 Conditions for equilibrium of a rigid body

We have seen that a number of coplanar forces acting on a rigid body is equivalent to a single force with a definite line of action or, in certain cases, to a couple. The single force is the vector sum of the several forces and its component in any direction is the sum of the components of the several forces in that direction. Thus the single force will be zero if the sums of the components of the forces acting on the body in two directions are zero. If the resultant is equivalent to a couple the moment of the couple will be equal to the sum of the moments of the forces about any point and the couple will be zero if this sum of moments is zero. The body will be in equilibrium if the single force and the couple are both zero. Hence, necessary and sufficient conditions for the equilibrium of the body are:

(i) *the sums of the components of the coplanar forces acting on the body in two directions must be zero,*

(ii) *the sum of the moments of the coplanar forces acting on the body about some point in the plane must be zero.*

The solution of problems in Statics is largely a matter of applying these conditions for equilibrium to the forces acting on a body. It will be seen that there are in fact three equations to be obtained, two by equating to zero the sum of components of the forces in two (usually perpendicular) directions and one by equating to zero the sum of moments of the forces about some point. Thus three numerical values can be found by applying these conditions and these may relate to magnitudes of forces or their directions or their lines of action.

The conditions for equilibrium of a rigid body are given in slightly different form in the following theorem.

If a system of coplanar forces acts on a rigid body and the sum of their moments about each of three points in their plane which do not lie in a straight line is zero, then the body is in equilibrium.

The fact that the sum of moments about one point is zero shows that the resultant of the forces is not a couple; when the sum of the moments about two points is zero the single force resultant must be zero or its line of action must pass through each point. If then the third sum of moments is zero the resultant cannot also pass through this point and must be zero.

Application of this condition gives three moment equations from which three numerical values can be deduced. They will not, however, give any additional information to that obtained by equating the resolved parts of the forces to zero, but the equations are sometimes simpler to write down.

Example 13. *A uniform rod AB of length 3 m and mass 8 kg is hinged freely to a fixed pivot at A and is maintained in a horizontal position by a light inextensible string connecting B to a fixed point 5 m vertically above A. Find the tension in the string and the reaction at A. If the breaking tension of the string is 12g N, find the maximum distance from the hinge at which a mass of 7 kg may be placed on the rod with safety.* [L.U.]

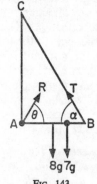

Fig. 143

The string makes an angle α with the horizontal where $\tan \alpha = 5/3$, and $\sin \alpha = 5/\sqrt{(34)}$, $\cos \alpha = 3/\sqrt{(34)}$ (Fig. 143). The sum of the moments of the tension and the weight about A must be zero, and in taking the moment of T it is simpler first to replace T by its components $T \cos \alpha$ and $T \sin \alpha$ since $T \cos \alpha$ has no moment about A. Then

$$T \sin \alpha \times 3 = 8 \times 3/2g,$$

$$T = \frac{4g}{\sin \alpha} = \frac{4\sqrt{(34)}}{5} g \text{ N}.$$

Equating to zero the resolved parts of the forces acting on AB we have, if the reaction R at A makes an angle θ with the horizontal,

$$R \cos \theta = T \cos \alpha = 12/5g,$$
$$R \sin \theta = 8g - T \sin \alpha = 4g,$$

so that

$$R = \sqrt{(4^2 + 2 \cdot 4^2)} = 4 \cdot 66g \text{ N},$$
$$\theta = \tan^{-1}(20/12) = 59° \, 2'.$$

If the 7 kg mass is placed x from A and the tension T is now $12g$ N the equation of moments about A gives

$$12g \, \sin \, \alpha \times 3 = 8g \times 3/2 + 7gx,$$

so that

$$7x = \frac{180}{\sqrt{(34)}} - 12 = 18 \cdot 8,$$

and

$$x = 2 \cdot 69 \text{ m}.$$

14.11 Triangle of forces. Lami's theorem

If three coplanar forces act on a body in equilibrium they must either be concurrent or parallel.

If the forces are not parallel let the lines of action of two of them meet in a point A. Then these forces can have no moment about A and hence, since the sum of the moments of the three forces about A is zero, the moment of the third force about A is zero. Therefore the line of action of the third force must pass through A. In solving problems of equilibrium under the action of three forces we may use the fact that the forces are concurrent instead of equating to zero the sum of moments about a point. Thus the concurrence of the forces and two equations of resolution of forces establish three conditions of equilibrium.

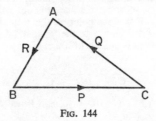

FIG. 144

If a body is in equilibrium when acted upon by three coplanar forces, these forces can be represented by the sides of a triangle taken in order.

This theorem merely states that the vector sum of the forces must be zero and the vector polygon of the forces, now a triangle, must be a closed figure. Thus we have a triangle each of whose sides represents one of the forces in magnitude and direction and sense if the sides are taken in order (Fig. 144). The converse is also true if the three forces are concurrent, since if their vector sum is zero their resultant will be zero. This is a useful theorem in solving statical problems since any triangle which can be found with its sides parallel to the forces taken in order may be called a triangle of forces and the forces are then known to be proportional to the sides of the triangle.

Example 14. *A uniform ladder of length l and weight W rests with its top against a smooth vertical wall and its base against a stop on horizontal ground at distance b from the wall. Find the forces acting on the ladder at the wall and on the ground.*

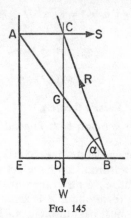

Fig. 145

Let the force at the top be S; since the wall is smooth the direction of S will be perpendicular to the wall (Fig. 145). The weight W acts vertically downwards through the centre G of the ladder. Let the force exerted by the ground and the stop be R in a direction inclined at α to the horizontal. The lines of action of W and S meet at C, therefore the line of action of the third force R must also pass through C. If D is the point on the ground vertically below G the triangle CDB has its sides parallel to the forces W, S and R respectively and may therefore be taken as a triangle of forces giving

$$\frac{W}{CD} = \frac{S}{DB} = \frac{R}{BC}.$$

Now $CD = AE = \sqrt{(l^2 - b^2)}$, $DB = \frac{1}{2}b$, and hence $BC = \sqrt{(l^2 - 3b^2/4)}$, so that

$$R = \frac{BC}{CD} W = \frac{W}{2} \frac{\sqrt{(4l^2 - 3b^2)}}{\sqrt{(l^2 - b^2)}},$$

$$S = \frac{DB}{CD} W = \frac{W}{2} \frac{b}{\sqrt{(l^2 - b^2)}},$$

$$\tan \alpha = \frac{CD}{DB} = \frac{2\sqrt{(l^2 - b^2)}}{b}.$$

Example 15. *A uniform rod AB of length 2a and weight W is pivoted to a fixed point at A. It is held inclined to the horizontal by a light inextensible string of length 2a joining B to a point C which is 2a vertically above A. Find the tension in the string and the magnitude and direction of the force exerted by the pivot on the rod.*   [L.U.]

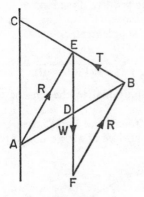

Fɪɢ. 146

The rod (Fig. 146) is in equilibrium under the action of its weight acting at its mid-point D, the tension T acting at B along the line of the string and the force R exerted by the pivot at A. The lines of action of W and T meet at E therefore that of R must pass through E. The triangle ECA has sides parallel to the directions of the forces T, W and R, the forces acting in the senses EC, CA, AE respectively, and is therefore a triangle of forces. Hence

$$\frac{T}{EC} = \frac{W}{CA} = \frac{R}{AE}.$$

Now DE is parallel to the base AC of the equilateral triangle ABC of sides $2a$, so that $EC = AD = a$ and, since the angle AEC is a right angle, $AE = \sqrt{3}a$. Therefore

$$\frac{T}{a} = \frac{W}{2a} = \frac{R}{\sqrt{3}a},$$

and $T = \frac{1}{2}W$, $R = \sqrt{3}W/2$ in a direction inclined at $60°$ to the horizontal.

Lami's theorem is another form of the theorem of the triangle of forces, namely, *if a rigid body is in equilibrium under the action of three forces each force is proportional to the sine of the angle between the directions of the other two.*

Let ABC be the triangle of forces (Fig. 147) with forces P, Q, R represented by the sides BC, CA, AB respectively. Then

$$\frac{P}{BC} = \frac{Q}{CA} = \frac{R}{AB}.$$

The sine rule gives $BC/\sin A = CA/\sin B = AB/\sin C$, so that

$$\frac{P}{\sin A} = \frac{Q}{\sin B} = \frac{R}{\sin C}.$$

The angles between the positive directions of the forces are $180° - A$, $180° - B$, $180° - C$, respectively so that, since the sine of an angle is equal to the sine of its supplement,

$$\frac{P}{\sin(180° - A)} = \frac{Q}{\sin(180° - B)} = \frac{R}{\sin(180° - C)},$$

and each force is proportional to the sine of the angle between the other two.

Both the triangle of forces and Lami's theorem use two of the three conditions for the equilibrium of a rigid body given in § 14.10, namely,

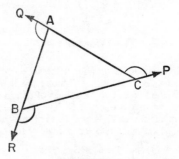

Fig. 147

the two conditions implied in the statement that the vector sum of the forces must be zero. The third condition for equilibrium used with either theorem will usually be that of the concurrence of the three forces. Both theorems apply to the equilibrium of a particle and in this case the concurrence of the forces is evident.

Example 16. *A light inextensible string is attached at one end to a fixed point A and carries at the other end a particle P of weight 20 N. A small smooth pulley B is fixed at the same horizontal level at A and AB = AP. A second light inelastic string is attached to P, passes over the pulley and carries a weight 7 N at its other end. Prove that AP is inclined at an angle* $\cos^{-1}(7/25)$ *to the horizontal and find the tension in the string AP.*   [L.U.]

Let the angle $PAB = \theta$ (Fig. 148) so that, since $AP = AB$,

$$APB = ABP = 90° - \tfrac{1}{2}\theta.$$

PC being vertical, $BPC = 180° - \tfrac{1}{2}\theta$, $APC = 90° + \theta$. Let T_1 be the tension in the string AP. The tension T_2 in the string PB must be the same along its length so that $T_2 = 7$ N. Applying Lami's theorem to the three forces T_1,

T_2 and 20 N acting on P we have

$$\frac{20}{\sin(90° - \tfrac{1}{2}\theta)} = \frac{7}{\sin(90° + \theta)} = \frac{T_1}{\sin(180° - \tfrac{1}{2}\theta)},$$

that is

$$\frac{20}{\cos\tfrac{1}{2}\theta} = \frac{7}{\cos\theta} = \frac{T_1}{\sin\tfrac{1}{2}\theta}.$$

Since $20\cos\theta = 7\cos\tfrac{1}{2}\theta$,

$$40\cos^2\tfrac{1}{2}\theta - 7\cos\tfrac{1}{2}\theta - 20 = 0,$$
$$(5\cos\tfrac{1}{2}\theta - 4)(8\cos\tfrac{1}{2}\theta + 5) = 0,$$

so that $\cos\tfrac{1}{2}\theta = 4/5$ and hence $\cos\theta = 2\cos^2\tfrac{1}{2}\theta - 1 = 7/25$.
Also

$$T_1 = \frac{7\sin\tfrac{1}{2}\theta}{\cos\theta} = \frac{7 \times 3/5}{7/25} = 15 \text{ N, since } \sin\tfrac{1}{2}\theta = 3/5.$$

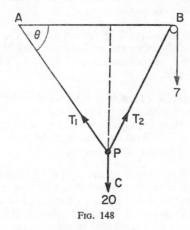

FIG. 148

Exercises 14 (e)

1. A uniform beam AB of length 4 m and mass 10 kg is freely hinged to a fixed pivot at A and supported in a horizontal position by a light string of length 5 m attached to the beam at B and to a point 3 m above A. Find the tension in the string and the magnitude and direction of the reaction at the pivot.

2. A uniform beam AB of length 6 m and mass 20 kg is freely hinged to a fixed pivot at A and supported in a horizontal position by a light string attached to the beam at B and making an angle of 60° with BA. Find the tension in the string and the reaction at the pivot.

3. A uniform beam of length l and weight W is free to turn in a vertical plane about a hinge at A and is supported in a horizontal position by a light string attached to the beam at $l/3$ from A and to a point C at height

b vertically above A. Find the tension in the string and the force at the hinge.

4. A uniform rod AB, mass 10 kg, is smoothly hinged at A and rests in a vertical plane with the end B against a smooth vertical wall. If the rod makes an angle of 40° with the wall, find the pressure on the wall and the magnitude and direction of the reaction at A. [O.C.]

5. AB is a uniform bar of weight W, movable about a smooth horizontal axis fixed at A; to B is attached a light cord which passes over a pulley C fixed vertically above A and supports a weight P at its free end. Show by applying the triangle of forces that in the position of equilibrium $W \cdot CB = 2P \cdot AC$. [L.U.]

6. A uniform rod of mass 10 kg rests with one end against a smooth vertical wall and the other end against a stop on smooth horizontal ground the rod being inclined at 60° to the vertical. Find the reaction at the wall and at the ground.

7. A uniform rod of mass 20 kg rests with one end against a smooth vertical wall and the other end on a smooth plane inclined at 30° to the horizontal. Find the inclination of the rod to the vertical and the reactions at its ends. [O.C.]

8. A uniform lamina of weight W in the form of an isosceles triangle ABC right-angled at B is freely hinged to a fixed point at A and rests with AC vertical and C above A, equilibrium being maintained by a horizontal string attached to C. Find the tension in the string and the magnitude and direction of the reaction at A. [O.C.]

9. A uniform beam AB, 6 m long, has mass 40 kg. The end A, about which the beam can turn freely, is attached to a vertical wall and the beam is kept in a horizontal position by a rope attached to a point of the beam $1\frac{1}{4}$ m from A and to a point on the wall vertically above A. If the tension in the rope is not to exceed $120g$ N show that the height above A of the point of attachment of the rope to the wall must not be less than $1\frac{2}{3}$ m. [L.U.]

10. A ladder 10 m long and 35 kg in mass rests with the end A against a smooth vertical wall and the other end B on smooth ground 6 m from the wall; it is maintained in this position by a horizontal cord attached at B. Find the tension in the cord if the centre of gravity of the ladder is 4 m from B. Find also the magnitude and direction of the force which, applied at A, will keep the ladder in position without the cord. [L.U.]

11. A heavy bar AB whose centre of gravity is at G such that $AG : GB = a : b$, is supported by a string attached at A. The end B is pulled away from the vertical by a horizontal force until the inclination of the string to the horizontal is ϕ. Prove that the inclination θ of the bar to the horizontal is given by $(a + b) \tan \theta = a \tan \phi$. [L.U.]

12. A uniform rod AB of length l rests in equilibrium with the upper end B in contact with a smooth vertical wall and the end A in contact with a smooth concave spherical surface of radius $a\,(2l > a > l)$ whose centre is at O on the wall vertically above B. If AB and OA are inclined to the horizontal at angles θ and ϕ respectively, prove that $\tan\phi = 2\tan\theta$, $\sin\theta = \sqrt{\{(a^2 - l^2)/3l^2\}}$. [L.U.]

Exercises 14 (f)

1. A point P is taken on the circle through the vertices of a rectangle $ABCD$. Show that the resultant of the forces represented by PA, PB, PC, PD is constant in magnitude and passes through the centre for all positions of P on the circle. Find the resultant of the forces represented by PA, PB, CP, DP. [L.U.]

2. Two forces are completely represented by the sides AB, AC of a triangle. Show that their resultant is completely represented by $2AD$, where D is the mid-point of BC. A point O within a given triangle PQR is such that forces completely represented by OP, OQ, OR are in equilibrium. Prove that O is the centroid of the triangle. [L.U.]

3. A particle of weight W is tied by two taut light inelastic strings to two fixed points. The tension in the first string is $\frac{1}{2}W$ and the second is inclined at $60°$ to the horizontal. Find the angle between the strings and the tension in the second string. [L.U.]

4. Forces $4P$, P and $2P$ act along the sides BC, CA and BA of an equilateral triangle of side a. Prove that, if the system is equivalent to a certain force R along BA and a force S along AC together with a couple G in the sense ABC, then

$$R = 6P, \ S = 3P \text{ and } G = 2\sqrt{3}aP.$$ [O.C.]

5. $ABCD$ is a rectangle in which $AB = 4a$, $BC = 3a$. Forces P, $4P$, $2P$, $3P$ act along AB, CB, CD, DA respectively. Prove that the system reduces to a single force Q acting through the point X in AC at $2a$ from A and find the magnitude of Q. If the line of action of Q passes through Y in AB, find the distance AY. [O.C.]

6. $ABCDEF$ is a regular hexagon and O is the intersection of the diagonals. Forces of $1, 2, 3, 4, 5\,\text{N}$ act along AB, BC, CD, DE, EF. Find the magnitudes and senses of the forces acting along the sides of the triangle OAF which are equivalent to the given forces. [O.C.]

7. Forces $3P$, $8P$, $2P$, $4P$ act along the sides AB, BC, DC, AD respectively of a square lamina of side $2a$. Find the magnitude of the resultant and the point E where its line of action meets AB. The lamina is laid on a smooth horizontal table and can turn freely about a point X on BD. Prove that, if it is in equilibrium, the distance of X from B is $12\sqrt{2}a/17$.

8. Forces whose components are $(P, 2P)$, $(-P, P)$ and $(4P, 0)$ act respectively at points whose coordinates are $(a, 0)$, $(a, -a)$ and $(0, a)$. Reduce

the system to a force at the origin and a couple, and deduce that the resultant is a force acting in the line $4y - 3x = 2a$.   [N.U.]

9. ABC is a triangular lamina; $AB = 3a$, $BC = 5a$, $CA = 4a$. D is the foot of the perpendicular from A on BC and H is the mid-point of AD. Forces $2P$, $6P$, $9P$ act along AB, CB, AC respectively and a force P acts through H parallel to BC. Find the magnitude and direction of the resultant R and the point X in AC through which it acts. Find the moment of the couple which must be added so that the new resultant acts through C.   [O.C.]

10. OAB is an equilateral triangle of side a; C is the mid-point of OA. Forces $4P$, P and P act along OB, BA, AO respectively. If OA and OY (parallel to CB) are taken as x and y axes, prove that the resultant R of the forces is $3P$ and its line of action is $3y = \sqrt{3}(3x + a)$. Prove also that R is equivalent to a like parallel force R through the centroid of the triangle together with a couple of moment $aP\sqrt{3}$.   [O.C.]

11. ABC is a triangle right-angled at A, $AB = 4$ cm and $AC = 3$ cm. The moments of a force in the plane of the triangle about A, B and C are respectively 8, -8 and 14 cm N. Calculate the magnitude of the force and the distance from A of the point where its line of action intersects AB.   [L.U.]

12. A beam AB of length 7 m has its centre of gravity 4 m from A. A light string of length 21 m is attached to the ends of the beam which hangs in equilibrium with the string over a smooth peg. Show that the inclination of the beam to the vertical is given by $6 \sin^2 \theta = 5$.   [L.U.]

13. A uniform heavy rod of length $2a$ rests with its lower end in contact with the inside of a smooth hemispherical cup of radius a whose axis is vertical, the upper end of the rod projecting beyond the rim of the cup. Show that the inclination θ of the rod to the horizontal is given by $2 \cos 2\theta = \cos \theta$.   [L.U.]

14. A uniform sphere of radius a is to be kept at rest on a smooth plane inclined to the horizontal at an angle α by means of a string attached to a point on the surface of the sphere, and the tension of the string is not to exceed the weight of the sphere. Prove that the length of the string must not be less than $a(\sec \alpha - 1)$.   [O.C.]

15. A light inextensible string of length l has one end attached to the end A of a uniform heavy rod AB of length $2a$. The other end of the string is attached to a smooth light ring C which slides on the rod. The rod is suspended with the string over a smooth peg P. Show that, in equilibrium, the portion PC of the string is at right angles to AB, and the length x of the portion PA is given by $l(x^2 + a^2) = 2x^3$.   [L.U.]

16. A heavy rod AB is hinged to a wall at A and kept horizontal by a light stay CD joining a point C of the rod to a point D on the wall below A. $AC = 4$ m the angle $ACD = 60°$, the mass of the rod is 20 kg and its

centre of gravity is 8 m from A. Find the thrust in the stay and the reaction at the hinge.   [O.C.]

17. A uniform rod rests with its ends on two smooth planes inclined at angles α and β respectively to the horizontal. Show that, if θ is the inclination of the rod to the horizontal $2 \tan \theta = \cot \alpha - \cot \beta$. [L.U.]

18. The ends of a string of length l are attached to fixed points A and B at the same level a apart. A smooth ring of weight W slides on the string and is in equilibrium under a horizontal force P with W vertically below B. Prove that $P = aW/l$ and find the tension in the string. If now the force on the ring is Q acting in the same direction as P and the part of the string attached to B makes an angle of $45°$ with AB produced, prove that $Q = W(1 + \sqrt{2a}/l)$.   [O.C.]

19. A non-uniform rigid beam AB, of length $3a$ and weight nW, rests on supports P and Q at the same level, where $AP = PQ = QB = a$. When a load W is hung from A the beam is on the point of tilting about P. Find the distance of the centre of gravity of the beam from A. When an additional load W_1 is hung from B the forces exerted on the supports are equal. Find W_1 in terms of n and W. If a couple of moment L acting in the vertical plane through AB is now applied to the loaded beam the reaction at P is increased in the ratio $3:2$. Show that $L = \frac{1}{3}(n + 1)Wa$.   [N.U.]

20. A uniform smooth sphere of weight W and radius a rests on a smooth plane inclined at an angle β to the horizontal. The sphere is held in equilibrium by a light string of length $8a/5$ joining a point on its surface to a point on the plane. Find, in terms of W and β, the tension in the string and the force exerted by the plane on the sphere.   [N.U.]

CHAPTER 15

SOLUTIONS OF SOME PROBLEMS IN STATICS

15.1 Types of problem

In the previous chapters the methods of balancing forces acting on a rigid body were used to establish conditions for equilibrium, and these conditions were applied to simple problems in which not more than three forces acted on the body. In this chapter these same conditions for equilibrium are applied to more complex problems where more than three forces are involved. This sometimes necessitates finding the position of the centre of gravity of bodies which are not symmetrically shaped. The problem of friction between surfaces is dealt with by making certain assumptions as to the nature of this force so that frictional forces can be balanced against the other forces acting on the body. It can then be seen in which cases the frictional forces are insufficient to maintain equilibrium.

Finally, we shall see that when two or more bodies are in contact their equilibrium can be considered as that of a single unit, treating mutual reactions or tensions between the bodies as internal forces of the system. It will be seen, however, that if it is required to find these mutual reactions or tensions the equilibrium of at least one of the bodies must in addition be considered separately.

15.2 Equilibrium under the action of four or more forces

When a rigid body is in equilibrium under the action of four or more forces we can no longer obtain a complete solution by using the triangle of forces or Lami's theorem. We can, however, use the three conditions of equilibrium given in § 14.10 to obtain three equations whose solution will yield three values of unkown quantities, be they forces, directions or lines of action of forces. No further resolution of forces or taking moments will yield additional information.

In problems dealing with the equilibrium of a body it is important that a clear figure be drawn and all the forces acting on the body marked on the figure. Where any body is in contact with another, an unknown reaction must be assumed to act on it which, if the bodies are smooth, will be perpendicular to the common tangent plane. If a body is supported by a string, a tension must be assumed to act in the string and this tension will be unchanged when the string passes over a smooth peg or pulley. If a body is hinged to another body and there is no friction at the hinge the forces there acting on either body may be taken as a single force acting through the centre of the hinge; the direction of this force may be unknown and it is often convenient to represent it by two unknown component forces acting in directions at right angles.

When all the forces have been marked, the three equations giving the conditions of equilibrium should be written down and numbered. If there is more than one body involved the three equations for each body should be set down. When this has been done the statical problem has been solved, although some algebraical manipulation may be required to complete the solution. Geometrical relations between the angles and lengths in the figure may need to be considered so as to simplify the statical equations.

Example 1. *A uniform rod AB of length x m and mass 3 kg per m is hinged at A and is held at 45° to the upward vertical by a horizontal force P acting at B in the vertical plane containing AB. A mass of 24 kg is hung from a point of the rod 9 m from A. Find the value of x for which P is a minimum and find completely the reaction at A for this value of x.*   [L.U.]

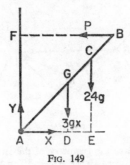

Fig. 149

The arrangement is shown in Fig. 149 where the reaction at A is shown as having components X and Y; a little consideration will show that the unknown force P acts in the sense shown in the figure. We thus have three unknown quantities X, Y and P which we can find from the conditions of equilibrium in terms of x.

The downward gravity forces are $3x$ acting at the mid-point of AB and 24 acting at 9 m from A. Equating to zero the sum of the vertical components of force we have

$$Y - 3gx - 24g = 0. \tag{15.1}$$

Equating to zero the sum of the horizontal components of force,

$$X - P = 0. \tag{15.2}$$

Equating to zero the sum of moments of the forces about A we have, since $AF = x \cos 45°$, $AD = \frac{1}{2}x \cos 45°$ and $AE = 9 \cos 45°$,

$$P \times AF = 3gx \times AD + 24g \times AE,$$

that is

$$Px = 3gx \left(\frac{x}{2}\right) + 9 \times 24g \tag{15.3}$$

and hence

$$P = \frac{3}{2}gx + \frac{216g}{x}.$$

Since $dP/dx = 3g/2 - 216g/x^2$ and $d^2P/dx^2 = 432g/x^3$, we see that P has a minimum value when $x = 12$ and this value $P = 36g$ N.
For these values of x and P we find from equations (15.1) and (15.2)

$$Y = 60g, \qquad X = 36g,$$

and the reaction at A is

$$R = \sqrt{(X^2 + Y^2)} = 12\sqrt{(34)}g \text{ N at } \tan^{-1}(5/3) \text{ to the horizontal.}$$

Example 2. *The figure (Fig. 150) shows a smooth circular wire, centre O and radius r, fixed in a vertical plane; B and C are two small smooth rings, each of weight W, threaded on the wire and through them passes a light endless inextensible string, of total length $9r/4$, which passes through and supports at A a smooth ring of weight W_1. In the position of equilibrium the angle $AOB = 30°$. Prove that $2W = (3\sqrt{3} - 1)W_1$. Prove also that the reaction of the wire on the ring at B is $3W_1$.* [O.C.]

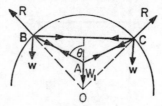

Fig. 150

Consider in the first place the geometry of the string. Since the angle BOC is 60°, $BC = OB = OC = r$. Hence $AB + AC = 5r/4$ and $AB = AC = 5r/8$. D being the mid-point of BC, $BD = \frac{1}{2}r$ so that $\sin DAB = \sin \theta = 4/5$. Also, since angle $AOB = 30°$, angle $OBA = \theta - 30°$. Next consider the forces acting on the ring at A. If T be the tension throughout the string, the forces are T, T and W_1 acting as shown and, equating to zero the vertical components of these forces, we have

$$2T\cos\theta - W_1 = 0,$$

giving, since $\cos\theta = 3/5$,

$$T = \frac{5}{6}W_1. \tag{15.4}$$

No further information can be obtained from the conditions of equilibrium of the ring at A.
Next consider the forces acting on the ring at B. These are the reaction R of the wire (perpendicular to the wire since it is smooth), the weight W and the two tensions in the string at B. Since the force R acts along OB in a direction inclined at 30° to the vertical we have by equating to zero the sums of the horizontal and vertical components of the forces

$$T + T\sin\theta - R\sin 30° = 0, \tag{15.5}$$

$$T\cos\theta + W - R\cos 30° = 0. \tag{15.6}$$

Eliminating R between these equations we have

$$T\{(1 + \sin\theta)\cos 30° - \cos\theta\sin 30°\} = W\sin 30°,$$

and hence

$$T(9\sqrt{3} - 3) = 5W.$$

Substituting for T from (15.4) gives the required relation between W and W_1. The value of R may be obtained from equations (15.5) and (15.6). It can also be obtained by stating that the vertical components of the two reactions support the total weight, that is

$$2R\cos 30° = W_1 + 2W = 3\sqrt{3}W_1,$$

whence

$$R = 3W_1.$$

15.3 Elastic strings

An elastic string is one in which the *strain*, that is the ratio of its extension to its natural unstretched length, is proportional to the tension in the string. Thus if l is the natural length, x the extension and T the tension, we have

$$T = \lambda\frac{x}{l},$$

where λ is a constant for the particular string. This is known as Hooke's Law and is approximately true both for tension and compression of all materials within certain limits. The constant λ depends on the material and is proportional to the cross-sectional area of the string for strings of the same material; λ is called the *modulus of elasticity* and its units will clearly be the same as those of the tension T. A tension λ would, therefore, give unit strain thus doubling the length of the string if Hooke's Law were true for a tension of this magnitude.

Example 3. *A thin uniform rod of weight W and length 6 units is freely hinged about a fixed point at A. The end B is attached by a light elastic string of natural length 5 units to a fixed point C at the same horizontal level as A and 8 units from it. The system hangs in equilibrium. If the angle $CAB = 60°$, find (a) the tension in the string, (b) the modulus of elasticity of the string.* [L.U.]

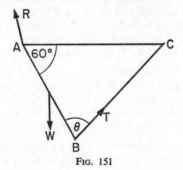

Fig. 151

The three forces acting on the rod are its weight W, the tension in the string T and the reaction R at A (Fig. 151). Let the angle $ABC = \theta$. By the cosine rule $BC^2 = 8^2 + 6^2 - 2 \cdot 8 \cdot 6 \cdot \cos 60° = 52$, $BC = 2\sqrt{(13)}$. By the sine rule

$$\frac{\sin \theta}{8} = \frac{\sin 60°}{2\sqrt{(13)}}, \quad \sin \theta = \frac{2\sqrt{3}}{\sqrt{(13)}}.$$

Equating to zero the sum of moments about A, we have

$$6 \times T \sin \theta = 3 \times W \sin 30°,$$

giving

$$T = \frac{W\sqrt{13}}{8\sqrt{3}} = 0 \cdot 26W.$$

Since $BC = 7 \cdot 212$, its extension is $2 \cdot 212$ and Hooke's Law gives

$$0 \cdot 26W = \lambda \times \frac{2 \cdot 212}{5},$$

$$\lambda = 0 \cdot 59W.$$

Exercises 15 (a)

1. A uniform beam AB 6 m long is free to turn in a vertical plane about a hinge at A. The beam weighs 200 kg and carries a load of 300 kg at B. It is supported with AB horizontal by a rope attached to a point of the beam 4 m from A and to a point 3 m vertically above A. Find the tension in the rope and the reaction at the hinge.

2. A gangway 20 m long which may be considered as a uniform beam of mass 400 kg has one end resting on horizontal ground and the other end on the deck of a ship 3 m above. There is no friction, but the shore end is prevented from moving by a stop. Find the force exerted by the stop and the reaction at each end.

3. An anchor cable from a point A on the bows of a ship is inclined at 30° to the horizontal and a current exerts a horizontal force on the ship which acts along a line 30 m below A. The weight of the ship W acts 120 m aft of A and the vertical force of buoyancy 105 m aft of A. Find the cable pull, the current force and the buoyancy.

4. A uniform bar AB, of mass 40 kg and length 8 m, is hinged at A to a point in a vertical wall and maintained in a horizontal position by a chain joining B to a point in the wall 5 m above A. If the bar carries a load of 20 kg at 6 m from A, calculate the tension in the chain and the magnitude and direction of the action at A.   [L.U.]

5. A lamina $ABCDEF$ is in the form of a regular hexagon and can turn freely in its plane about an axis through A. It is in equilibrium under the reaction at the axis and forces 6 N along BC, 10 N along FC and P N along CD. Find the value of P and the magnitude and direction of the force exerted on the lamina by the axis.   [L.U.]

6. A uniform smooth ladder rests with its extremities against a vertical wall and a horizontal plane and is held by a rope attached to a rung of

the ladder one quarter of the way up and to a point of the base of the wall below the ladder. Show that if the base and top of the ladder are distant a and b respectively from the base of the wall the ratio between the reactions P and Q at the ends of the ladder is given by $Q/P = 3a/5b$.

[L.U.]

7. The ends of a uniform rod 8 cm long and weighing 10 g slide in smooth grooves AO and BO in two planes inclined respectively at 30° and 45° to the horizontal, AO and BO being lines of greatest slope of the planes. Find the weight which should be attached to the rod at 2 cm from the end sliding in AO so that the rod may rest in equilibrium in a horizontal position. [O.C.]

8. A uniform spar AB weighs 200 kg. The end B is pivoted at a point on the ground and the spar is held inclined at 10° to the vertical by a guy rope attached at A and inclined at 30° to the horizontal. A mass of 400 kg is suspended from A. Find the tension in the guy rope and the reaction at the hinge.

9. A non-uniform rod AB of weight W is supported horizontally by two strings CA and BD attached to its ends. C and D are attached to two points at the same level; CA is inextensible, BD is elastic and the directions of the strings are perpendicular. The inclination of BD to the horizontal is α and its natural length is equal to AC. Find the ratio in which the centre of gravity divides AB and the modulus of the elastic string. [L.U.]

10. A uniform rod AB of length $2a$ and weight W is freely hinged to a fixed point at A and the end B is joined to a point C, $2a$ above A, by a light elastic string of modulus W and natural length a. Find the inclination of AB to the vertical in the equilibrium position.

11. A uniform rod OA of weight 6 kg and length 2 m can turn freely about a fixed hinge at O. The rod rests horizontally with A attached to one end of an elastic string of natural length $\sqrt{2}$ m, the other end being attached to a fixed point C, 2 m vertically above O. Find the modulus of elasticity of the string. If a heavy particle is attached to the mid-point of the rod equilibrium is possible when the angle $AOC = 120°$. Find the weight of the particle. [L.U.]

12. One end of a light elastic string of unstretched length 15 cm is attached to a fixed point. To the other end is attached a mass of 8 kg which when hanging freely extends the string to 18 cm. The weight is then held aside from the vertical by a horizontal force of $6g$ N. Find, in the new equilibrium position, the angle which the string makes with the vertical and the horizontal and vertical distances through which the weight has moved. [L.U.]

15.4 Centres of gravity

Centroids and centres of gravity of bodies of various shapes have been obtained in § 10.6. In this section we use the principles of statics to find the centres of gravity of composite bodies and of bodies from which a portion has been removed. If two portions of a body have centres of gravity G_1 and G_2 respectively, the resultant of the two weights acting at these points will act at a point in the line joining G_1 and G_2 and this point will be the centre of gravity of the whole body. Let the weights be W_1 and W_2 and let the coordinates of G_1 and G_2 with respect to axes OX, OY be (x_1, y_1) and (x_2, y_2) respectively (Fig. 152).

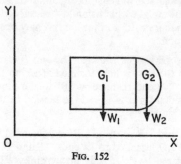

FIG. 152

Since the position of the centre of gravity is unchanged by altering the direction in which the weights act we may take them as acting perpendicularly to the plane XOY. Then if (x, y) be the coordinates of the centre of gravity of the whole body, we have by taking moments about OY and then about OX

$$(W_1 + W_2)x = W_1x_1 + W_2x_2, \qquad (15.7)$$
$$(W_1 + W_2)y = W_1y_1 + W_2y_2. \qquad (15.8)$$

From these equations the values of x and y can be found.

If a portion has been removed from a body, let G_1 and G_2 be the centres of gravity of the whole body and of the removed portion and

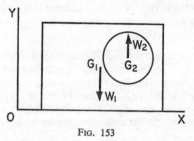

FIG. 153

W_1 and W_2 the weights of the whole and of the removed portion respectively (Fig. 153). Then the weight of the body $W_1 - W_2$ is the resultant of unlike parallel forces W_1 and W_2 acting at $G_1(x_1, y_1)$ and

$G_2(x_2, y_2)$ and the coordinates (x, y) of the centre of gravity are given by the moment equations

$$(W_1 - W_2)x = W_1x_1 - W_2x_2, \qquad (15.9)$$

$$(W_1 - W_2)y = W_1y_1 - W_2y_2. \qquad (15.10)$$

Example 4. *A uniform hemisphere of radius a has its plane face joined to the base of a uniform right circular cone of base radius a and height h. Find the distance of the centre of gravity of the body from the vertex of the cone.*

If ρ be the density of the material the weights of the two parts are

$$W_1 = \tfrac{1}{3}\rho\pi a^2 h \quad \text{and} \quad W_2 = \tfrac{2}{3}\rho\pi a^3.$$

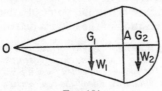

FIG. 154

The centre of gravity of the cone is distant $\tfrac{3}{4}h$ from the vertex O (Fig. 154) and the centre of gravity of the hemisphere is distant $\tfrac{3}{8}a$ from the centre of the base A, and therefore $h + \tfrac{3}{8}a$ from O. Hence, if x be the distance of the centre of gravity of the whole from O,

$$(\tfrac{1}{3}\rho\pi a^2 h + \tfrac{2}{3}\rho\pi a^3)x = \tfrac{1}{3}\rho\pi a^2 h \times \tfrac{3}{4}h + \tfrac{2}{3}\rho\pi a^3(h + \tfrac{3}{8}a),$$

and, dividing by $\tfrac{1}{3}\rho\pi a^2$,

$$(h + 2a)x = \tfrac{3}{4}h^2 + 2a(h + \tfrac{3}{8}a)$$

and

$$x = \frac{3h^2 + 8ah + 3a^2}{4(h + 2a)}.$$

Example 5. *ABCD is a uniform rectangular board with AB = 6 cm, BC = 4 cm. From the board a quadrant of a circle whose centre is C and radius 2 cm is removed. Find the distance of the centre of gravity of the remainder from AD and AB.*

The areas of the rectangle and the quadrant are respectively 24 cm² and π cm² and if ρ be the density, their weights are 24ρ and $\pi\rho$. The centre of gravity of a

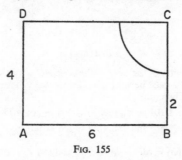

FIG. 155

quadrant of radius r is distant $4r/(3\pi)$ from each of its bounding radii and hence, taking AB and AD as the axes of x and y respectively (Fig. 155), the coordinates of the centre of gravity of the quadrant will be $(6 - 8/3\pi, \ 4 - 8/3\pi)$. The centre of gravity of the rectangle is the point $(3, 2)$ and if (x, y) be the coordinates of the centre of gravity of the remainder

$$(24\rho - \pi\rho)x = 24\rho \times 3 - \pi\rho \times (6 - 8/3\pi),$$
$$(24\rho - \pi\rho)y = 24\rho \times 2 - \pi\rho \times (4 - 8/3\pi),$$

leading to $x = 2{\cdot}68$ cm, $y = 1{\cdot}83$ cm.

If a body is in equilibrium suspended by a string or hinged at a pivot the force in the string or at the pivot must be equal and opposite to the weight of the body acting at its centre of gravity. Hence the centre of gravity must be vertically below the point of attachment of the string or the pivot and the position of the body is determined by this fact.

Example 6. *One end of a uniform cylinder of radius a and height 2h/3 is welded symmetrically to the base of a uniform cone of base radius a and height h made of the same material. The body is suspended from a point on the base of the cone and is in equilibrium with a slant side of the cone horizontal. Prove that the semi-vertical angle α of the cone is given by* $\tan \alpha = \sqrt{5}/6$.   [O.C.]

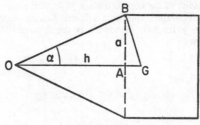

Fig. 156

We first find the position of the centre of gravity G of the composite body (Fig. 156). If x be its distance from the vertex O we have

$$W_1 = \tfrac{1}{3}\rho\pi a^2 h, \ W_2 = \tfrac{2}{3}\rho\pi a^2 h = 2W_1$$

and

$$(W_1 + W_2)x = W_1 \times \tfrac{3}{4}h + W_2 \times \left(h + \frac{h}{3}\right),$$

that is,

$$3x = \tfrac{3}{4}h + \tfrac{8}{3}h = \tfrac{41}{12}h,$$

giving

$$x = 41h/36.$$

Thus if A is the centre of the base of the cone $AG = 5h/36$. If the body is suspended from B, BG must be vertical and since BO is horizontal the angle OBG is a right angle. Therefore

$$\tan GBA = \tan (90° - ABO) = \cot ABO.$$

But $\tan GBA = 5h/(36a)$ and $\cot ABO = a/h = \tan \alpha$.
Hence

$$5h/(36a) = a/h, \ a^2/h^2 = 5/36 \text{ and } \tan \alpha = \sqrt{5}/6.$$

15.5 Toppling problems

A body at rest on a surface will topple about an edge in contact with the surface if the sum of the moments of the forces acting on it about the edge is not zero. At the instant of toppling as part of the body begins to lift clear of the surface the reaction between the body and the surface will, in general, act at the edge and make no contribution to the sum of moments about the edge. Therefore, in the absence of other external forces, a body will topple about an edge if the force of gravity acting through the centre of gravity has a moment about the edge in the sense that will make the body topple. This is equivalent to saying that if the vertical through the centre of gravity passes outside an edge the body will topple.

Example 7. *A crane may be taken as a thin rod of length l and weight W with one end fixed at the centre of a uniform circular disc of radius r and weight W', the centre of gravity of the rod being distant a from the fixed end. The rod is inclined at an angle θ to the vertical and a weight w is suspended from its upper end. Show that the crane will topple when θ exceeds a certain value if*

$$(wl + Wa) > (w + W + W')r.$$

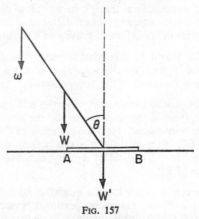

FIG. 157

If the crane topples it will turn about a tangent to the disc at a point A (Fig. 157). When it is on the point of toppling B will be lifting clear of the ground and the reaction of the ground will pass through A. Equating to zero the sum of moments of the gravity forces about A we find

$$w(l \sin \theta - r) - W(r - a \sin \theta) - W'r = 0,$$

giving

$$\sin \theta = \frac{(w + W + W')r}{wl + Wa}.$$

If θ is increased beyond this value the crane will topple. We thus have a critical value of θ at which toppling will begin, provided that the numerator of the fraction is less than the denominator (since $\sin \theta < 1$), that is

$$(wl + Wa) > (w + W + W')r.$$

Exercises 15 (b)

1. The radii of a frustum of a uniform right circular cone are a and $2a$ and its height is h. Find the distance of its centre of gravity from the larger face.

2. $ABCD$ is a square board of side $2a$. A triangular portion is removed by making a straight cut from A to the mid-point of BC. Find the distances of the centre of gravity of the remainder from the edges AD and CD.

3. A piece of solid metal shafting is 10 m long and tapers uniformly from a diameter of 3 m at one end to one of 1 m at the other end. Find the distance of the centre of gravity from the thicker end.   [L.U.]

4. A uniform solid consists of a right-circular cone of slant height 10 cm and base radius 6 cm mounted on the plane face of a hemisphere, also of radius 6 cm. Determine the distance of the centre of gravity from the centre of the hemisphere.   [L.U.]

5. A circular plate, centre O and radius a, is pierced with four circular holes, each of radius c. The centres of these holes are at A, B, C and D, where ABC is an equilateral triangle in a circle of centre O and radius b ($> 2c$), and D is the other end of the diameter of this circle through A. Find the distance of the centre of gravity of the plate from A.   [O.C.]

6. From a cone of height $2h$, a cone of height h having the same circular base is removed; find the distance of the centre of gravity of the remainder from the vertex of the original cone.   [L.U.]

7. A uniform wire $ABCD$ is bent at right angles at B and C in such a way that BA and CD are in the same sense, and the lengths of AB, BC, CD are 6, 4, 2 cm respectively. Find the distances of the centre of gravity from AB and BC. Show that the wire can be suspended with each part equally inclined to the vertical by a string attached to a point P, and give the length of BP.   [O.C.]

8. Show that the centre of gravity of a quadrilateral $ABCD$ is the same as that of three particles of masses proportional respectively to AO, OC, $2AC$ placed at A, C and the mid-point of BD, where O is the intersection of AC and BD.   [L.U.]

9. A rigid framework $ABCDE$ of four equal rods, forming part of a regular hexagon, is suspended from A. Show that the angle made by AB with the vertical is $\tan^{-1}(4\sqrt{3}/7)$.   [O.C.]

10. $ABCD$ is a rectangular plate. $AD = 8$ cm, $BC = 12$ cm and E is the mid-point of BC. If the triangular portion ABE is removed and the remainder is suspended from A, find the inclination of the side AD to the vertical.   [L.U.]

11. A uniform wire of length 44 cm is bent into the form of a closed plane pentagon $ABCDE$ having $AB = BC = AE = ED = 10$ cm,

$BE = 16$ cm, and the angles at C and D equal. If the wire is supported by a vertical string from a point P of AB, find the distance AP if AB is horizontal in the equilibrium position. [L.U.]

12. Two uniform rods AB and BC, each of length l and weight W, are smoothly jointed at B and the ends A and C are joined by a light inextensible string, also of length l. If the system is suspended in equilibrium from A, show that AB is inclined at an angle $\tan^{-1}(\sqrt{3}/5)$ to the vertical. Find the tension in the string. [L.U.]

13. A uniform square lamina $ABCD$ of weight $4W$ is suspended freely from a fixed point A. If the lamina rests in equilibrium with weights W, $2W$, $3W$ attached to B, C, D respectively, find the inclination of AC to the vertical. [L.U.]

14. A frustum is cut from a cone of height h by a plane parallel to the base and distant $\frac{1}{2}h$ from the base. If the frustum can just rest with a generator on a horizontal plane determine the ratio of the diameter of the base of the cone to the height h. [L.U.]

15. A tin made of uniform sheet metal and open at one end is a circular cylinder 30 cm high and 60 cm diameter. Show that the centre of gravity is 10 cm from the base. The tin is pivoted about a diameter of the cross-section 12·5 cm above the base and liquid is steadily poured into the tin. If the metal weighs 4·58 g/cm² and a cubic cm of the liquid weighs 1 g, show that the tin will be on the point of toppling over when the surface of the liquid is 2·5 cm from the top of the tin. [L.U.]

16. An isoceles triangle is cut off a corner of a square lamina. Show that the remainder can stand on a shortened edge if the part cut off is 0·5 of an edge, but not if the part cut off is 0·6 of an edge. [O.C.]

17. A table consists of a 1 cm board, 24 cm square having at its corners legs of the same material 54 cm long and of 4 cm square cross-section. Find the height of the centre of gravity and the greatest angle through which the table can be tilted on two legs without being overturned. [O.C.]

18. A cubical block of edge a rests on a horizontal plane and is gradually undermined by cutting away slices by planes parallel to a horizontal edge, inclined at 45° to the horizontal. Find the centre of mass of the remainder when a length x has been removed from each of four edges, and show that the block will fall when $9x = 5a$, approximately. [L.U.]

15.6 Laws of friction

Smooth surfaces are defined as being such that there is no resistance to sliding over each other. Thus, if two such surfaces are in contact, the action between the surfaces is always perpendicular to their common tangent plane. A smooth surface is a mathematical concept since in fact there is always some friction between bodies in contact tending to prevent or diminish relative motion. The mathematical treatment of friction is based on certain assumptions which are embodied in the so-called *laws of friction* which are found to be in close agreement with experience. These laws are set out below.

Law 1.　When two bodies are in contact the *direction* of the force of friction on either of them at the point of contact is opposite to the direction in which this point tends to move relative to the other body.

Law 2.　If the bodies are in equilibrium the force of friction is *just sufficient* to prevent motion and may be determined by applying the conditions for equilibrium to all the forces acting on each body.

Law 3.　*Limiting friction* is the frictional force which is being exerted when equilibrium is on the point of being broken.

Law 4.　The ratio of limiting friction to the normal reaction depends on the nature of the surfaces in contact. This ratio is called the *coefficient of friction* and is denoted by the Greek letter μ (mu). Thus, if R be the normal reaction, the limiting friction is μR.

Law 5.　The amount of limiting friction is independent of the area of contact between the surfaces.

Law 6.　When motion takes place the direction of friction is opposite to that of relative motion and independent of velocity.

The *angle of friction* is defined as λ (lambda), where $\mu = \tan \lambda$. Thus if R be the normal reaction and the friction is limiting and equal to μR in a direction perpendicular to R, the resultant force at the point of contact is $R\sqrt{(1 + \mu^2)}$ in a direction inclined to the normal reaction at an angle whose tangent is μ. Therefore, the resultant is $R\sqrt{(1 + \tan^2 \lambda)} = R \sec \lambda$, inclined at an angle λ to the normal.

The above laws of friction are confirmed by modern theory which suggests that friction is in fact due to the non-rigidity of bodies. When one body rests on another there is always an *area* of contact rather than a point of contact, and this area may be much smaller than the apparent area of contact. The area of contact will be due to the deformation of the bodies by the normal pressure between them and will be proportional to this pressure. Friction is believed to be caused, at least in the case of some materials, by heat fusion of the materials of the bodies over the area of contact and friction is the resistance of this fusion to breaking before the bodies can move. This makes limiting friction proportional to the true area of contact and therefore proportional to the normal force between the surfaces.

15.7 Equilibrium on an inclined plane

If a body of weight W is placed on a rough plane inclined at an angle α to the horizontal it will slide down a line of greatest slope unless it is prevented by friction, which must therefore act upwards along this line. Let R be the normal reaction and F the force of friction (Fig. 158). The body is in equilibrium under the action of the forces W, R and F, so that, since the weight acts in a direction making an angle $90° - \alpha$ with the line of greatest slope,

$$R = W \cos \alpha$$
$$F = W \sin \alpha,$$

and $$F/R = \tan \alpha.$$

If, however, the body is on the point of moving the friction will be limiting and $F = \mu R = R \tan \lambda$, so that $\tan \alpha = \mu = \tan \lambda$, that is,

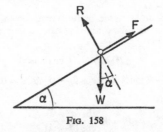

FIG. 158

$\lambda = \alpha$. Therefore the plane of greatest slope on which a body can rest is one inclined at an angle equal to the angle of friction. Also, for a body to rest on a plane of inclination α, the coefficient of friction must be at least $\tan \alpha$. It is assumed here that there is no question of the equilibrium being broken by rolling or toppling.

Example 8. *A small body of weight W is placed on a rough plane inclined at an angle α to the horizontal and the angle of friction is $\lambda (< \alpha)$. Find the least force that must be applied (i) to prevent it sliding down the plane, (ii) to start it moving up the plane.*

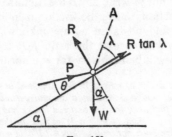

FIG. 159

Let the applied force be P in a vertical plane containing the line of greatest slope and inclined at θ to this line (Fig. 159). In the first case we assume friction to be limiting and to act up the plane; let the normal reaction be R and the friction

$R \tan \lambda$. Equating to zero the resolved parts of the forces normal to and along the plane, we have

$$R - P \sin \theta - W \cos \alpha = 0,$$

$$R \tan \lambda + P \cos \theta - W \sin \alpha = 0.$$

Eliminating R between these equations we find

$$P(\cos \theta + \sin \theta \tan \lambda) = W(\sin \alpha - \cos \alpha \tan \lambda),$$

and hence

$$P = W \frac{\sin (\alpha - \lambda)}{\cos (\theta - \lambda)}.$$

The force P will be a minimum if $\cos (\theta - \lambda) = 1$, that is if $\theta = \lambda$, and in this case $P = W \sin (\alpha - \lambda)$.

If P is just sufficient to start the body moving up the plane the friction will then be acting down the plane and the calculations can be repeated with λ replaced by $-\lambda$, giving

$$R - P \sin \theta - W \cos \alpha = 0$$

$$-R \tan \lambda + P \cos \theta - W \sin \alpha = 0$$

and hence

$$P = W \frac{\sin (\alpha + \lambda)}{\cos (\theta + \lambda)}.$$

In this case P will have its least value when $\theta + \lambda = \pi$, giving

$$P = -W \sin(\alpha + \lambda),$$

that is P has magnitude $W \sin (\alpha + \lambda)$ and acts along OA inclined at an angle λ to the upward direction of the line of greatest slope.

15.8 Problems involving friction

Problems involving friction are solved by applying the conditions for equilibrium to the forces acting on a body, including frictional forces. Care must be taken not to write down the frictional force as μR, where R is the normal reaction, unless the friction is limiting. In general the frictional force should be taken as an unknown quantity F whose direction is usually known and the ratio F/R calculated. Then the inequality $F/R \leqslant \mu$ will be necessary for equilibrium.

Example 9. *A uniform ladder of weight W rests inclined at 45° to the horizontal on rough horizontal ground and against a smooth vertical wall. Show that for equilibrium the coefficient of friction between ladder and ground must not be less than $\frac{1}{2}$. If, however, a man of weight W stands on the bottom, show that the coefficient of friction must not be less than $\frac{1}{4}$. If this man can ascend to the top without it slipping find the least value of the coefficient of friction.* [L.U.]

Let $2a$ be the length of the ladder, R the normal reaction at the ground and S that at the wall (Fig. 160). If the ladder is on the point of slipping the frictional force at B will be μR towards the wall. Equating to zero the horizontal and vertical components of force on the ladder and the sum of their moments about B we obtain the three equations,

$$S - \mu R = 0,$$
$$W - R = 0,$$
$$W . a \cos 45° - S . 2a \cos 45° = 0,$$

so that $W = 2S = R$, and hence $\mu = \frac{1}{2}$.

If now an additional weight W is applied at B, these equations become

$$S - \mu R = 0,$$
$$2W - R = 0,$$
$$W . a \cos 45° - S . 2a \cos 45° = 0$$

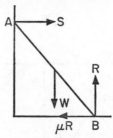

FIG. 160

so that $W = 2S = \frac{1}{2}R$, giving $\mu R = \frac{1}{4}R$ and hence $\mu = \frac{1}{4}$.

If the man has ascended the ladder, his weight W will be applied at A and the equations will become

$$S - \mu R = 0,$$
$$2W - R = 0,$$
$$W . 2a \cos 45° + W . a \cos 45° - S . 2a \cos 45° = 0,$$

so that $W = \frac{2}{3}S = \frac{1}{2}R$, giving $\mu R = \frac{3}{4}R$ and hence $\mu = \frac{3}{4}$.

Example 10. *A small ring A, weight W, is threaded on a fixed rough horizontal wire (coefficient of friction μ). A light inextensible string of length $2l$ is attached to the ring and to the wire at B; a particle of weight $4W$ is attached to the mid-point C of the string. Prove that if the system is in equilibrium with $AB = 2x$, then $x \leqslant 3\mu l/\sqrt{(4 + 9\mu^2)}$. If the ring is about to slide when an additional weight $2W$ is hung from C and when angle $BAC = 60°$, find the value of μ.* [O.C.]

Let T be the tension in the string, the same in both parts by symmetry, R the reaction, F the friction at A and θ the angle BAC (Fig. 161). We know that $\cos \theta = x/l$ and hence $\sin \theta = \sqrt{(l^2 - x^2)}/l$. For the equilibrium of the weight at C we have

$$2T \sin \theta = 4W,$$

and hence

$$T = 2Wl/\sqrt{(l^2 - x^2)}.$$

For the equilibrium of the ring at A,

$$F = T \cos \theta = 2Wx/\sqrt{(l^2 - x^2)},$$
$$R = W + T \sin \theta = 3W,$$

and hence

$$\frac{F}{R} = \frac{2x}{3\sqrt{(l^2 - x^2)}}.$$

The greatest possible value of the ratio F/R is μ, and hence we have

$$\frac{2x}{3\sqrt{(l^2 - x^2)}} \leqslant \mu,$$

$$4x^2 \leqslant 9\mu^2(l^2 - x^2),$$

$$x^2(4 + 9\mu^2) \leqslant 9\mu^2 l^2,$$

and hence

$$x < \frac{3\mu l}{\sqrt{(4 + 9\mu^2)}}.$$

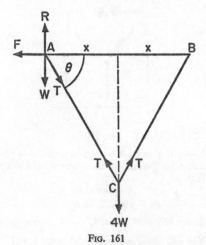

Fig. 161

With the additional weight $2W$ at C and $\theta = 60°$, we have

$$2T \sin 60° = 6W,$$

$$T = 2\sqrt{3}W.$$

Then $F = T \cos 60° = \sqrt{3}W$, $R = W + T \sin 60° = 4W$, $F/R = \sqrt{3}/4$. Since the ring is about to slide, this ratio must be equal to μ, and hence $\mu = \sqrt{3}/4$.

Example 11. *A uniform right circular cone of weight W, height h and base radius a is placed with its base on a rough plank, the coefficient of friction between the bodies being μ. One end of the plank is gradually raised until equilibrium is broken; find the condition that it should be broken by sliding.*

Let α be the inclination of the plank to the horizontal, R the normal reaction and μR the friction in the limiting case (Fig. 162).

If the cone is about to slide for this value of α we have

$$R = W \cos \alpha$$

$$\mu R = W \sin \alpha$$

and hence $\mu = \tan \alpha$.

The cone will, however, topple about the point A if the line of action of its weight passes outside A, and in the critical case this means that the line of action of the weight must be inclined at an angle α to the axis of the cone. Therefore, since the centre of gravity is at $h/4$ from the base, the cone will topple when $\tan \alpha = \dfrac{4a}{h}$. Therefore the cone will slide rather than topple if $\mu < 4a/h$.

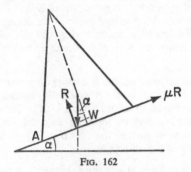

FIG. 162

Exercises 15 (c)

1. A block of wood, mass 4 kg, rests on a horizontal plank 6 m long. It is found that when one end of the plank is raised 2 m the block will just slide; fine the coefficient of friction. If the vertical height of the end is increased to 3 m find the least force perpendicular to the plank which will maintain equilibrium.   [O.C.]

2. Find the least force that will move a mass of 80 kg up a rough plane inclined at 30° to the horizontal when the coefficient of friction is 0·75.   [L.U.]

3. One end of a uniform ladder rests against a rough vertical wall and the other end rests on rough horizontal ground, the coefficient of friction at each contact being $\tan \lambda$. Show that the inclination of the ladder to the vertical when it is on the point of slipping is 2λ.   [L.U.]

4. AB and CD are two opposite edges of a face of a uniform solid cube. The cube is in equilibrium with AB on rough horizontal ground and CD against a smooth vertical wall. Prove that if μ is the coefficient of friction at the ground and θ is the inclination of the face to the horizontal, $\tan \theta$ cannot be outside the range $1/(2\mu + 1)$ to 1.   [L.U.]

5. Two straight wires OA, OB are fixed at right angles in a vertical plane each inclined at 45° to the horizontal, O being the lowest point. Small light rings attached to the ends of a uniform rod can slide one on each wire. The angle of friction for each ring and wire is λ, and $\lambda < 22\frac{1}{2}°$. If the rod rests in limiting equilibrium inclined at an angle α to the horizontal, prove that $\lambda = \frac{1}{2}\alpha$.   [L.U.]

6. A particle of weight W rests on a rough plane, coefficient of friction μ, inclined at α to the horizontal. A horizontal force P parallel to the plane

is applied to the particle which is then in limiting equilibrium. Show that $P^2 = W^2(\mu^2 \cos^2 \alpha - \sin^2 \alpha)$. If the particle is then on the point of moving in a direction making $45°$ with the line of greatest slope, show that $\mu = \sqrt{2} \tan \alpha$. [L.U.]

7. Two small rings each of mass m are threaded on a fixed rough horizontal wire and joined by a light string of length $2a$ and a particle of mass $6m/5$ is attached to the mid-point of the string. Show that, if the coefficient of friction between each ring and the wire is $\frac{1}{2}$, the depth of the particle below the wire when the equilibrium is limiting is $3a/5$. [L.U.]

8. A uniform solid cube of weight W stands on a rough horizontal plane and $ABCD$ is its upper face. A gradually increasing force P in the direction AB is applied to the mid-point of BC. Prove that equilibrium will be broken by sliding or toppling according as the coefficient of friction is less than or greater than $\frac{1}{2}$. If $\mu > \frac{1}{2}$, find the magnitude of P when the cube begins to topple. [L.U.]

9. A rough plane is inclined at α to the horizontal. A weight W just moves up a line of greatest slope when acted on by a force equal to W in this direction. Prove that the angle of friction is $\pi/4 - \alpha/2$. [L.U.]

10. Two equal heavy rings can slide on a fixed rough horizontal rod and are connected by a light inextensible string with a weight equal to that of a ring attached to its mid-point. If in limiting equilibrium each portion of the string is inclined at $30°$ to the vertical, find the coefficient of friction between a ring and the rod. [L.U.]

11. A uniform ladder rests inclined at $60°$ to the horizontal against a smooth vertical wall and on rough horizontal ground (μ being $\frac{1}{4}$). The ladder is 8 m long and has mass 50 kg. A man of mass 100 kg begins to climb. How far can he ascend before the ladder slips? What coefficient of friction is required for him to be able to ascend to the top? [L.U.]

12. A body of mass 1 kg can just be kept from sliding down a rough plane of inclination $\sin^{-1} \frac{4}{5}$ either by a force Pg N acting upwards along a line of greatest slope or by a horizontal force of $1g$ N in the vertical plane containing the line of greatest slope. Show that the ratio of the normal reactions in the two cases is $3 : 7$. Find the coefficient of friction and the value of P. [L.U.]

13. The ends of a light string are attached to a horizontal beam at points C and D, $5a$ apart. The string passes through a small light ring which is attached to the end A of a uniform rod of length $2b$ and weight W; the other end, B, rests in contact with a rough horizontal table, the string and the rod being in a vertical plane. When $AC = 3a$ and $AD = 4a$ the system is in equilibrium and the friction at B is limiting. Prove that, if BA makes an acute angle θ with horizontal, $\tan \theta = (7\mu - 1)/(2\mu)$, where $\mu(> 1/7)$ is the coefficient of friction at the table. [O.C.]

14. A uniform rod AB of length $2a$ rests on a fixed smooth peg P with the end A in contact with a rough vertical wall, AB making an acute angle θ with the upward vertical. If x is the distance of P from the wall and μ the coefficient of friction at the wall, prove that, when the rod is about to slip downwards, $(x - a)\tan^2\theta - \mu a\tan\theta + x = 0$. Deduce that, if $x = 3a/2$, this position of limiting equilibrium is not possible unless $\mu > \sqrt{3}$.   [O.C.]

15. Small rings A and B of weights W and w ($<W$) respectively are threaded on a rough circular wire, of centre O, fixed in a vertical plane, and the rings are joined by a light inextensible string. If, with the string taut, A is on the point of sliding downwards along the wire when OA and OB each make an angle $\theta(< 90°)$ with the upward vertical, prove that $(W - w)/(W + w) = \sin 2\lambda/\sin 2\theta$, where λ is the angle of friction between each ring and the wire.   [O.C.]

16. A particle P, of weight w, is attached to the rim of a uniform circular disc, centre O and weight W; the disc, of radius a, rests in a vertical plane on a rough horizontal floor and against an equally rough vertical wall and is about to slip when P is above the level of O and distant $\frac{1}{2}a$ from the wall. If λ is the angle of friction concerned, prove that $\cos 2\lambda - \sin 2\lambda = W/(W + w)$. Find the value of λ if $w = W(\sqrt{2} - 1)$.
                                                                            [O.C.]

15.9 Problems involving two bodies

When two rigid bodies are in equilibrium together the conditions for equilibrium may be applied to the two bodies considering them as a single unit. In this case the mutual reactions of the bodies at a point of contact or the tension in a string joining the bodies will be treated as an internal force of the system and will not appear in the equations expressing the conditions of equilibrium. To find these internal forces it is necessary to treat one of the bodies as a separate unit in equilibrium under the action of external forces and the internal forces between the bodies. When the conditions for equilibrium of the whole system and of one of the bodies have been written down, no further information will be obtained from the equilibrium of the second body.

Example 12. *A step ladder of weight $2W$ consists of two equal parts freely jointed at the top and held together by a light string joining the mid-points of the parts. When the string is taut the angle between the two parts is 2α, where $\tan \alpha = 6/13$. With the ladder resting on smooth horizontal ground and the string taut, a man of weight $5W$ climbs two-thirds of the way up one side. Find the reactions at the ground, the tension in the string and the reaction at the hinges.*   [L.U.]

Considering the ladder as a single rigid body, let the reactions at the ground be R and S and let each part be of length $2a$ (Fig. 163). The body is in equilibrium under the action of the forces R, S, W, $5W$, W, so that

$$R + S = 7W,$$

and, equating to zero the sum of moments about C,

$$R \times 4a \sin \alpha - W \times 3a \sin \alpha - 5W \times \tfrac{3}{8}a \sin \alpha - W \times a \sin \alpha = 0$$

so that

$$R = \tfrac{13}{8}W, \text{ and hence } S = \tfrac{3}{8}W.$$

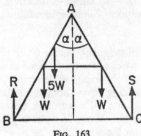

Fig. 163

To find the internal forces between the parts we now consider the equilibrium of the part AC. Let T be the tension in the string and let X and Y be the components of the force exerted on AC by AB at A (Fig. 164). Equating to zero the sum of the moments of the forces about A we have

$$S \times 2a \sin \alpha - W \times a \sin \alpha - T \times a \cos \alpha = 0$$

and hence

$$T = (2S - W) \tan \alpha = \tfrac{13}{8}W \times \tfrac{6}{13}$$
$$= 2W.$$

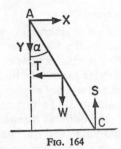

Fig. 164

Equating to zero the horizontal and vertical components of force we have

$$X - T = 0,$$
$$S - W - Y = 0,$$

and hence

$$X = 2W, \qquad Y = \tfrac{5}{8}W.$$

Example 13. *Two uniform beams AB and AC, equal in length and of weights $3W$ and W respectively, are smoothly jointed at A; the system rests in a vertical plane with the ends B and C on a rough horizontal plane, the coefficient of friction being μ. If R and S are the reactions at B and C respectively and the angle BAC is 2θ, prove that $R = \tfrac{3}{2}W$, $S = \tfrac{5}{2}W$ and $\tan \theta < \tfrac{2}{3}\mu$, stating at which point the friction first becomes limiting as θ is increased. Prove also that when $\tan \theta = \tfrac{2}{3}\mu$ the reaction of one beam on the other is inclined at $\tan^{-1}(3\mu)$ to the vertical.*

[O.C.]

Let F and F_1 be the frictional forces at B and C and let $AB = 2a$ (Fig. 165). First we consider the system as a single body in equilibrium under the action of the forces R, S, $3W$, W, F, F_1. Equating to zero the sum of horizontal and vertical components of force and the sum of moments about C, we have

$$F - F_1 = 0,$$
$$R + S = 4W,$$
$$R \times 4a \sin \theta = 3W \times 3a \sin \theta + W \times a \sin \theta$$

and hence

$$R = \tfrac{5}{2}W, \qquad S = \tfrac{3}{2}W.$$

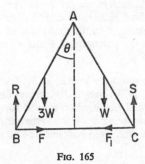

FIG. 165   FIG. 166

Now consider the equilibrium of AC (Fig. 166) under the action of the forces F, $\tfrac{3}{2}W$, W and components of reaction X and Y at A.
Equating to zero the sum of moments about A we have

$$\frac{3W}{2} \times 2a \sin \theta - W \times a \sin \theta - F \times 2a \cos \theta = 0,$$

and hence

$$F = W \tan \theta,$$

and

$$F/S = \tfrac{2}{3} \tan \theta.$$

The end C will therefore slip unless $\tfrac{2}{3} \tan \theta < \mu$. At B we have $F/R = \tfrac{2}{5} \tan \theta$, so that B will slip only when $\tan \theta = \tfrac{5}{2}\mu$ and the friction will first become limiting at C. Equating to zero the sums of the horizontal and vertical components of force on AC we have, when $\tan \theta = \tfrac{3}{2}\mu$,

$$X = F = W \tan \theta,$$
$$Y = \tfrac{3}{2}W - W = \tfrac{1}{2}W,$$
$$X/Y = 2 \tan \theta = 3\mu,$$

so that the reaction at A is inclined at $\tan^{-1}(3\mu)$ to the vertical.

Exercises 15 (d)

1. A ladder consists of two uniform legs of equal length and weights W and $2W$, smoothly hinged at the top with the lower end of the heavier leg attached by a cord to the middle point of the lighter leg. The ladder rests on a smooth horizontal floor with the cord taut and

each leg making an angle of 60° with the floor. Find the tension in the cord. [L.U.]

2. OA and OB are uniform rods of the same length but of weights $2W$ and W respectively. They are freely hinged at O and stand in a vertical plane with A and B on a horizontal plane, the coefficients of friction at A and B being $\frac{1}{2}$ and $\frac{2}{3}$ respectively. Find the smallest angles the rods can make with the horizontal and, if equilibrium is broken, which end slips. [L.U.]

3. Two equal uniform bars AB and AC, each of weight W are freely hinged together at A. They rest in a vertical plane with B and C on a horizontal table held by a light rod joining B to the mid-point of AC, the angle BAC being 120°. Show that the reactions at B and C are equal and the tension in the light rod $\frac{1}{2}W\sqrt{7}$. [L.U.]

4. Two uniform rods AB and BC are smoothly jointed at B. Each rod is of length $2l$, AB is of weight W and BC of weight $2W$. Small light rings are attached to the ends A and C and threaded on a fixed rough horizontal wire, the coefficient of friction being μ. If the system can rest in equilibrium with B below the wire and each rod inclined at α to the vertical, prove that $\mu \geqslant \frac{3}{5} \tan \alpha$. [L.U.]

5. Two equal uniform rods AB and AC, each of length l and weight W, are freely hinged at A. The end C is freely hinged to a point on a rough plane inclined at α to the horizontal; the end B rests on a line of greatest slope through C below C. If angle $ACB = \theta$ when B is about to slip and μ is the coefficient of friction, prove that

$$\mu \tan \alpha \tan^2 \theta + 2 \tan \theta (\mu - \tan \alpha) - 1 = 0. \qquad \text{[O.C.]}$$

6. Two uniform beams AB and BC, each of length $2a$ and weight W, are smoothly hinged at B and a light inextensible string joins A and C. The system is at rest in a vertical plane with A and C in contact with smooth planes each inclined at α to the horizontal. If the angle $ABC = 2\theta$, find the tension in the string and prove that

(i) $\qquad\qquad\qquad \tan \theta > 2 \tan \alpha,$

(ii) the reaction at the hinge is of magnitude $\frac{1}{2}W \tan \theta$. [O.C.]

7. The axis of a fixed right circular cylinder, whose surface is smooth, is horizontal and a section has radius a. A smoothly jointed framework of three rods AB, BC, CD, each of length a and weight W, is placed symmetrically over the cylinder with BC horizontal. Prove that the reaction of the cylinder on BC is $57W/25$, and find the reaction of the hinge at B on AB. [O.C.]

8. AC and BC are uniform rods each of length $2a$ and weights W_1 and W_2 ($<W_1$) respectively, freely jointed at C. A and B are attached to smooth hinges at the same level and C lies below AB with the angle

$BAC = \theta$. If X and Y are the horizontal and vertical components of the reaction of BC on AC at C, prove that $X = \frac{1}{4}(W_1 + W_2)$ cot θ, $Y = \frac{1}{4}(W_1 - W_2)$. Find also the condition that the reactions at A and B should be at right angles. [O.C.]

9. A hollow circular cylinder of internal radius 8 cm, open at both ends, rests with its axis vertical on a rough horizontal plane. Two equal smooth spheres, each of radius 5 cm and weight W, are placed inside the cylinder; show that the two spheres exert a couple on the cylinder and find the moment of this couple. [L.U.]

10. AB and BC are two uniform similar rods, each of weight W, freely hinged at B and carrying small light rings enabling the ends A and C to move without friction on a fixed horizontal wire. The rods include a right angle with B below the wire, and are prevented from closing by a light stay joining the mid-points of the rods. Find the stress in this stay and the reactions at A, B and C. [O.C.]

11. Two uniform rods AB, BC, of equal lengths but of different weights, are freely jointed at B and jointed at A and C to fixed points in the same horizontal line such that ABC is a right angle. Show that the tangent of the angle which the direction of the reaction at B makes with BA is the ratio of the weight of AB to that of BC. [L.U.]

12. Each half of a step ladder is 2 m long and the parts are connected by a cord 70 cm long attached to points 40 cm from their extremities. The half with steps weighs 8 kg and the other half weighs 2 kg. Find the tension in the cord when a man weighing 75 kg is standing on the ladder 50 cm from the top, it being assumed that the reactions at the ground are vertical. [L.U.]

13. Two equal uniform rods AB, BC are freely jointed at B and rest in equilibrium in a vertical plane with A and C on a rough horizontal plane. If μ is the coefficient of friction show that the greatest angle each rod can make with the vertical is $\tan^{-1}(2\mu)$. [L.U.]

14. Two uniform ladders AB, BC of equal lengths and weights W, $W'(W > W')$ are hinged at B and stand on rough ground when containing an angle 2θ. Show that the total reaction at A makes a smaller angle with the vertical than at C. Assuming the coefficients of friction at A and C are each μ, show that, as θ is increased, slipping will occur at C, and that $\mu = \{(W + W') \tan \alpha/(W + 3W')\}$, where α is the value of θ for which slipping occurs. [O.C.]

15. A rigid framework consists of four light rods AB, BC, CD, DA smoothly jointed together and maintained in the form of a trapezium with AB parallel to CD by a fifth light rod BD. Equal and opposite forces of magnitude P, each acting inwards, are applied at A and C parallel to AC. If $2AB = 2BC = 2AD = CD$, find the stresses in the five rods. [L.U.]

Exercises 15 (e)

1. A uniform beam AB, of length $2l$ and weight W, rests tangentially against the rim of a smooth fixed vertical disc of radius a whose plane is the vertical plane through the beam. The lower end A rests on a smooth horizontal plane passing through the lowest point O of the disc. If the end A is acted on by a force T towards O and the beam is inclined to the horizontal at $60°$, prove that $T = Wl/4a$. [L.U.]

2. Five equal weights are attached to a light string which hangs from two points P and Q in the same horizontal. In equilibrium the horizontal projections of the six intervals of the string are all equal to a and the depth below PQ of the lowest weight is $3a$. Show that the inclinations to the horizontal of the parts of the string are $\tan^{-1}(1/3)$, $\pi/4$ and $\tan^{-1}(5/3)$. [O.C.]

3. A uniform bar AB, 3 m long and of mass 4 kg, has a cord 5 m long attached to its ends. The cord passes through a smooth ring O fixed to a smooth vertical wall, and the rod is placed in a vertical plane perpendicular to the wall with A against the wall vertically below O. Prove that the rod will lie in equilibrium if OA is 2 m and show that the tension in the string is $3g$ N. [O.C.]

4. A smooth semicircular wire is fixed in a vertical plane with its diameter horizontal and OA is a smooth vertical wire through the centre O. A small ring P, of weight W is threaded on the semicircular wire and a small ring Q, of weight w on OA, the rings being joined by a string of length l ($<a$). The system is in equilibrium with OP and QP making angles θ and ϕ ($>\theta$) with OA. Prove that $(W + w) \tan \theta = w \tan \phi$. Find also the tension in the string if $W = 3w$ and $l = \frac{1}{2}a$. [O.C.]

5. A uniform rod AB of length $2a$ and weight W is hinged at A and supported horizontally by a string from B to a point C vertically above A; a weight w is hung from B. Prove that, if the reaction of the hinge at A is at right angles to BC, then $AC = 2a\sqrt{(1 + 2w/W)}$. [O.C.]

6. A uniform solid cube of side $2a$ and weight $2W$ has a particle of weight W attached at B, where $ABCD$ is a central cross-section of the cube. The cube is suspended from a fixed point P of a smooth vertical wall by a light inelastic string PA, of length $2a$, attached at A. If the cube is hanging in equilibrium with the edge through D in contact with the wall, determine the inclination of the string to the vertical. [L.U.]

7. AB is the straight edge of a semicircular lamina of radius a. A semicircle of radius r is drawn on the lamina, its centre being on AB at a distance r from A and the area inside this semicircle is cut away. Show that for all values of r ($<a$) the centroid of the remainder lies on a fixed line through A. Find the position which the centroid of the remainder approaches as r tends to a. [L.U.]

8. A uniform wire of length 12 cm forms the perimeter of a triangle ABC in which $BC = 4$ cm, $CA = 5$ cm, $AB = 3$ cm. Find the perpendicular

distance of the centre of gravity of the wire from BC and AB. When freely suspended from a point D in AC there is equilibrium with AC horizontal; prove that $CD:DA = 13:12$. [L.U.]

9. A solid frustum of a right circular cone has base radii $2r$ and r and height $2r$. Show that the centre of mass is $11r/14$ from the larger face. A coaxial cylindrical hole of radius r is bored through the frustum. Find the distance of the centre of mass of the remainder from the base. [L.U.]

10. The density at any point of a thin straight rod of length $2a$ varies directly as its distance from one end. Find the position of the centre of gravity. The rod is bent at its middle point so that the two halves are at right angles and suspended by a wire attached to its middle point. Find the angles which the parts make with the vertical. [L.U.]

11. A uniform lamina $ABCD$, in the shape of a rhombus of side a with angle $BCD = 60°$, consists of two parts hinged along DE, where E is the foot of the perpendicular from D to AB. The portion $EBCD$ is fixed in a horizontal plane and the portion AED is free to rotate about DE. Find the distance of the centroid of $EBCD$ from DE. As the triangle AED rotates show that the centre of mass of the whole lamina can never be nearer than $a/4$ to ED and find the greatest distance from DE. Find also the greatest possible height of the centre of mass above $EBCD$. [L.U.]

12. ABC is a uniform triangular board of weight W in which $BC = a$, $CA = b$, $AB = c$ and the angle ABC is obtuse. The board is placed with its plane vertical and the side BC on a horizontal plane, and a weight w is suspended from A. If the system is in equilibrium, prove that $3(W + w)a^2 \geqslant (W + 3w)(b^2 - c^2)$. [O.C.]

13. A thin uniform wire is bent in the form of a closed pentagon $ABCDE$ in which $AB = BC = AE = ED = 5$ cm, $BE = 8$ cm, $CD = 2$ cm and the angles C and D are equal. Find the distance from A to the centre of mass of the wire. When suspended freely from a point F in AB the wire is in equilibrium with AB horizontal; find the distance AF. [L.U.]

14. Prove that, if from a uniform solid hemisphere of radius a a concentric hemispherical portion of radius ka ($k < 1$) is removed, the centre of gravity of the remainder is at distance $3ak^2/8(1 + k + k^2)$ from that of the original hemisphere. [L.U.]

15. A rough uniform semicircular lamina of mass 4 g is placed in a vertical plane with its curved rim in contact with a horizontal table sufficiently rough to prevent slipping. A particle of mass 1 g is placed on the bounding diameter of the lamina. Find the minimum coefficient of friction between the lamina and the particle necessary to ensure that they remain in equilibrium no matter where the particle is placed on the diameter. [L.U.]

16. P and Q are two fixed equally rough pegs distance a apart, PQ making an angle α with the upward vertical; AB is a uniform rod of length $2l$ and weight W placed over P and under Q, the end B being uppermost. The rod is about to slip when $QB = x$. If R and S are the reactions at P and Q respectively, prove that $R \cos(\lambda + \alpha) = S \cos(\lambda - \alpha)$, and $x = l - \frac{1}{2}a - \frac{1}{2}a \cot \lambda \cot \alpha$, λ being the angle of limiting friction at each peg. [O.C.]

17. A uniform beam AB of length $2a$ and weight W is placed in contact at C with a fixed rough cylinder in a plane at right angles to the axis of the cylinder which is horizontal. When the inclination of AB to the horizontal is θ and the mid-point of AB is at distance x from C, a horizontal force P at B just prevents the beam from slipping downwards. If $\mu \,(= \tan \lambda)$ is the coefficient of friction, prove that $P = W \tan(\theta - \lambda)$; $\mu < \tan \theta$; $x = a \sin \theta \sin(\theta - \lambda) \sec \lambda$. [O.C.]

18. A heavy uniform cube rests in limiting equilibrium with one edge in contact with a horizontal floor and another in contact with a vertical wall; the face containing these edges makes an angle $\theta(<45°)$ with the floor. If the coefficients of friction at the floor and wall are μ and μ' respectively, show that $\tan \theta = (1 - \mu\mu')/(1 + \mu\mu' + 2\mu)$. [N.U.]

19. Two equal uniform rods AB, BC, each of length $2a$ and weight W, are freely jointed at B and rest, in a vertical plane, across two smooth horizontal pegs at the same level a apart. Show that in the position of equilibrium the inclination θ of each rod to the vertical is given by $2 \sin^3 \theta = 1$. Determine the magnitude and direction of the reaction at B. [L.U.]

20. AOB and COD are two uniform rods, each of weight W, freely hinged at O. $AO = CO = a$ and $BO = DO = 3a$. The rods are in equilibrium in a vertical plane, the ends B and D resting on a smooth horizontal plane joined by a light string of length $3a$. Show that the tension in the string is $2\sqrt{3}W/9$, and find the reaction at the hinge. [L.U.]

21. Two uniform rods AB and BC of the same thickness and material and of length 3 m and 2 m respectively, are freely hinged at B and rest in a vertical plane with A and C on a rough horizontal plane. If the greatest value of the angle ABC consistent with equilibrium is $90°$, find the coefficient of friction between the rods and the ground and determine how equilibrium will be broken if the inclination is increased. [O.C.]

22. Two rings of equal weight connected by a light inextensible string can slide on each of two fixed rough rods in the same vertical plane inclined at equal angles of $45°$ in opposite directions to the horizontal. Prove that the extreme angle which the string can make with the horizontal is twice the angle of friction. [L.U.]

23. Two equal uniform rods AB, BC, smoothly joined at B, are in equilibrium with C resting on a rough horizontal plane and A freely pivoted at a point above the plane. Prove that, if α and β are the inclinations of CB

and BA to the horizontal, the coefficient of friction must exceed $2/(\tan \beta + 3 \tan \alpha)$. [O.C.]

24. Two equal particles each of weight W, are placed on a rough horizontal table and connected by a taut inextensible string. Prove that the least horizontal force that can be applied to one of them in a direction inclined at θ to the string so as to cause them both to be on the point of motion is $2\mu W \cos \theta$, where μ is the coefficient of friction. [O.C.]

25. A uniform beam rests over two pegs and is inclined at θ to the horizontal. The angle of friction is λ_1 at the lower peg and λ_2 at the upper, where $\lambda_2 > \theta > \lambda_1$. Show that the beam will just slip when the ratio of the distances from its centre of mass to the lower and upper pegs is $\sin (\lambda_2 - \theta) \cos \lambda_1 / \sin (\theta - \lambda_1) \cos \lambda_2$. [L.U.]

CHAPTER 16

MOTION IN A STRAIGHT LINE

16.1 Velocity and acceleration

We have seen in Chapter 8 that the motion of a particle in a straight line is governed by its velocity and acceleration and that these two quantities are defined at any instant by the limiting processes of the calculus. Thus if a particle is moving in a straight line and at time t is at a distance x from a fixed point of the line, its velocity v is defined as

$$v = \frac{dx}{dt}. \tag{16.1}$$

Similarly, its acceleration a is defined as

$$a = \frac{dv}{dt} = \frac{d^2x}{dt^2} = v\frac{dv}{dx}. \tag{16.2}$$

These are theoretical expressions for the velocity and acceleration and when the actual value of one of these quantities is known it can be equated to a theoretical value and the differential relation can be integrated to give the displacement at any instant.

The methods employed are considered in more detail in this chapter with particular emphasis on the case where the acceleration has a constant value. We shall see that graphical methods can often be useful in analysing the motion whether the acceleration be constant or not.

In dealing with motion in a straight line we need make no distinction between the motion of a particle and that of a rigid body all of whose particles have the same velocity in parallel directions. Thus in describing the motion of the rigid body we describe the motion of some one particle of the body, usually the centre of gravity.

16.2 Units of velocity and acceleration

Units of velocity are units of distance divided by units of time and velocity is usually calculated in metres or centimetres per second or feet per second, or kilometres or miles per hour. The abbreviations m/s, cm/s, ft/s, km/h, mile/h or mph are used. A velocity in miles per hour is expressed in feet per second by multiplying by the factor $5280/3600 = 22/15$. Thus

$$v \text{ mile/h} = \frac{22}{15} v \text{ ft/s} = 0{\cdot}447 \, v \text{ m/s}.$$

Distances at sea are usually given in terms of sea-miles and 1 sea-mile = 1·853 km = 1·152 miles approximately. A speed of one sea-mile per hour is called a *knot*, so that 1 knot = 1·853 km/h = 1·152 mile/h approximately.

A unit of acceleration is a change of velocity in unit time. Thus if velocity is in metres or centimetres per second the unit of acceleration is one metre or centimetre per second in one second. This is written as metres or centimetres per second per second or in short m/s^2 or cm/s^2. If the velocity is in feet per second the acceleration will be in feet per second per second, written as ft/s^2. Similarly we may speak of an acceleration in mph per hour or mph per second.

If a body is falling freely near the surface of the earth it has an acceleration due to gravity directed towards the centre of the earth. This acceleration is denoted by g and its value is approximately 9·81 m/s^2 or 32 ft/s^2. The value of g varies from about 9·780 m/s^2 at the equator to about 9·832 m/s^2 at the poles; in the latitude of England $g = 9·815$ m/s^2 approximately. In many problems sufficient accuracy is obtained by taking $g = 9·81$ m/s^2 or 32 ft/s^2.

The values given for g are those of a particle falling in a vacuum. A body falling in the atmosphere has its acceleration reduced by the resistance of the air.

16.3 Motion with constant acceleration

In Chapter 10, the standard formulae which apply when the acceleration is constant were derived. Writing x as the displacement at time t, v as the velocity at time t, u as the initial velocity (when $t = 0$) and a as the constant acceleration we have

$$v = u + at, \tag{16.3}$$

$$x = \tfrac{1}{2}(u + v)t, \tag{16.4}$$

$$v^2 = u^2 + 2ax, \tag{16.5}$$

$$x = ut + \tfrac{1}{2}at^2, \tag{16.6}$$

$$x = vt - \tfrac{1}{2}at^2. \tag{16.7}$$

These equations apply to any period of time during which the acceleration remains constant, and for a definite period of time t, v is the final velocity and x the final displacement. It will be noticed that each of the above equations involves four of the five quantities u, v, x, t, a, so that if any three of these quantities are known the fourth and fifth can be found by applying the appropriate equations.

Thus the solution of problems involving constant acceleration depends on choosing the appropriate equations to determine the unknown quantities at each stage of the motion. It is useful to draw up a table showing which of the quantities are known and which are to be determined. In a particular case the data might be shown as follows

$$u = 8 \text{ m/s}$$
$$v = ?$$
$$a = 3 \text{ m/s}^2$$
$$x = ?$$
$$t = 4 \text{ sec.}$$

In this case v and x are to be found and appropriate equations are $v = u + at$, $x = ut + \frac{1}{2}at^2$, giving $v = 20$ m/s, $x = 56$ m.

Example 1. *A ball is thrown vertically upwards with a velocity of 29·43 m/s. Neglecting air resistance find its height when it is moving at half this rate and the time between the instants when it is at this height.*

If the distance is measured upwards from the ground, the acceleration due to gravity, which we shall take as 981 cm/s², is downwards and therefore negative. Tabulating the data, we have

$$u = 2943 \text{ cm/s}$$
$$v = 1471·5 \text{ cm/s}$$
$$a = -981 \text{ cm/s}^2$$
$$x = ?$$
$$t = ?$$

To find x we use the formula $v^2 = u^2 + 2ax$, and we have

$$x = \frac{27 \times 981}{8} = 3311 \text{ cm.}$$

To find t we use the formula $x = ut + \frac{1}{2}at^2$, giving

$$4t^2 - 24t + 27 = 0,$$

so that $t = \frac{3}{2}$ or $\frac{9}{2}$. There are thus two values of t for which the height is 33·11 m and their difference is 3 seconds.

Example 2. *A motor-car X uniformly accelerated at 2 m/s² passes a point P on a straight road at 6 m/s; 2 seconds later a motor-car Y uniformly accelerated at 1·5 m/s² and moving in the same direction as X passes P at 15 m/s. Prove that Y overtakes X at a point Q on the road 6 seconds after X passes P, and that X overtakes Y at a point R 12 seconds later still. Prove also that QR = 360 m, and that the maximum distance separating X and Y between Q and R is 9 m.* [O.C.]

Tabulating the data for the two cars and measuring the time from the instant when X passes P, we have

X's motion	Y's motion
$u = 6$ m/s	$u = 15$ m/s
$a = 2$ m/s²	$a = 1·5$ m/s²
$t = T$ seconds	$t = T - 2$ seconds
$x = x_1$ m.	$x = x_2$ m.

Applying the formula $x = ut + \frac{1}{2}at^2$ to each motion we have

$$x_1 = 6T + T^2,$$
$$x_2 = 15(T - 2) + \tfrac{3}{4}(T - 2)^2.$$

Hence we find

$$x_1 - x_2 = \tfrac{1}{4}(T^2 - 24T + 108)$$
$$= \tfrac{1}{4}(T - 6)(T - 18).$$

Thus this distance is zero, first when $T = 6$ and again when $T = 18$. Also

$$x_1 = T(T + 6)$$

and hence $x_1 = 72$ when $T = 6$ and $x_1 = 432$ when $T = 18$, so that $QR = 432 - 72 = 360$ m. Between Q and R, $x_2 - x_1 = \tfrac{1}{4}(18 - T)(T - 6)$. This is a maximum when $T = 12$ and its greatest value is then 9 m.

Example 3. *A train covers the distance between two stations A and B, which is 13·5 kilometres, in 24 minutes. It accelerates uniformly from rest at A, then travels at constant speed V for 12 minutes, finally retarding uniformly to stop at B. Determine the value of V. If the retardation is twice the acceleration in magnitude, obtain their values.* [L.U.]

The data is tabulated as follows

Acceleration	Steady speed	Deceleration
$u = 0$	$u = V$	$u = V$
$v = V$ km/h	$v = V$	$v = 0$
$a = a_1$	$a = 0$	$a = -a_2$
$t = t_1$ h	$t = 0\cdot2$ h	$t = t_2$ h
$x = x_1$ km.	$x = 13\cdot5 - x_1 - x_2$ km.	$x = x_2$ km.

Applying the formula $x = \frac{1}{2}(u + v)t$ to each of the three periods, we have

$$x_1 = \tfrac{1}{2}Vt_1, \qquad 13\cdot5 - x_1 - x_2 = \tfrac{1}{5}V, \qquad x_2 = \tfrac{1}{2}Vt_2.$$

Hence, since $t_1 + t_2 = \frac{1}{5}$, $x_1 + x_2 = \frac{1}{10}V$, and

$$13\cdot5 - \tfrac{1}{10}V = \tfrac{1}{5}V,$$

giving

$$V = 45 \text{ km/h}.$$

Now, if $a_2 = 2a_1$, applying the formula $v = u + at$ to the first and third periods we have

$$V = a_1t_1, \qquad V = 2a_1t_2,$$

so that $t_1 = 2t_2$ and, since $t_1 + t_2 = 12$ minutes, $t_1 = 8$ minutes, $t_2 = 4$ minutes. Hence,

$$a_1 = 2\cdot6 \text{ cm/s}^2, \qquad a_2 = 5\cdot2 \text{ cm/s}^2.$$

16.4 Graphical methods for constant acceleration

When the acceleration has the constant value a the velocity at any instant is given by $v = u + at$. Therefore the graph of velocity plotted against time is a straight line AB (Fig. 167). If this straight line is

14

drawn, the velocity at any instant can be read from the graph. The acceleration is the slope of the straight line and if the acceleration is negative the angle made by the straight line with the T-axis will be obtuse.

The distance moved in time t is given by the formula $s = \frac{1}{2}(u + v)t$ and from the graph it can be seen that this is the area of the trapezium bounded by the ordinates which are the velocities u and v and included

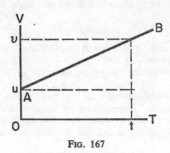

FIG. 167

between the straight line AB and the T-axis. Thus for any value of t the distance moved is the area under the velocity-time graph up to this value of t. Many problems in which the acceleration is constant for various periods of time are simplified if a velocity-time graph is roughly sketched.

Example 4. *A train runs 20 minutes from rest at one station to rest at another station 13 kilometres distant. For the first $\frac{2}{5}$ of a kilometre it has constant acceleration a_1 and for the next kilometre it has constant acceleration $\frac{1}{2}a_1$ then attaining its maximum speed. For the last two kilometres it has constant retardation. Sketch the velocity-time diagram and show that the accelerations $a_1, \frac{1}{2}a_1$ are maintained for equal times. Find the maximum speed in kilometres per hour.* [L.U.]

The motion is divided into four intervals; let their durations be t_1, t_2, t_3, t_4 hours respectively and let V_1 km/h be the speed at time t_1 and V km/h the maximum speed. The velocity-time graph is shown in Fig. 168. The lengths of

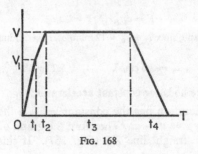

FIG. 168

the four sections are 0·4, 1, 9·6, 2 kilometres and the total time is $\frac{1}{3}$ hour. The tabulated data for the four intervals is as follows

First	Second	Third	Fourth
$u = 0$	$u = V_1$	$u = V$	$u = V$
$v = V_1$	$v = V$	$v = V$	$v = 0$
$t = t_1$	$t = t_2$	$t = t_3$	$t = t_4$
$x = \frac{2}{5}$	$x = 1$	$x = 9\cdot6$	$x = 2$
$a = a_1.$	$a = \frac{1}{2}a_1.$	$a = 0.$	$a = -a_2.$

Applying the formulae $v = u + at$ and $x = ut + \frac{1}{2}at^2$ to each of the first two intervals we have

$$V_1 = a_1t_1, \qquad\qquad V - V_1 = \frac{1}{2}a_1t_2,$$
$$\tfrac{2}{5} = \tfrac{1}{2}a_1t_1^2, \qquad\qquad 1 = V_1t_2 + \tfrac{1}{4}a_1t_2^2.$$

The last two equations give, when V_1 is replaced by a_1t_1,

$$1 = \tfrac{5}{4}a_1t_1^2 = a_1t_1t_2 + \tfrac{1}{4}a_1t_2^2,$$

and hence

$$t_2^2 + 4t_1t_2 - 5t_1^2 = 0.$$

This gives $t_2 = t_1$ and hence $\frac{1}{2}V_1 = V - V_1$, so that $V_1 = \frac{2}{3}V$. Applying the formula $x = \frac{1}{2}(u + v)t$ to each interval we have

$$\tfrac{2}{5} = \tfrac{1}{3}Vt_1,$$
$$1 = \tfrac{5}{6}Vt_2,$$
$$9\cdot6 = Vt_3,$$
$$2 = \tfrac{1}{2}Vt_4,$$

and hence $V(t_1 + t_2 + t_3 + t_4) = 1\cdot2 + 1\cdot2 + 9\cdot6 + 4 = 16$, and, since the total time is $\frac{1}{3}$ hour, $V = 48$ km/h.

Exercises 16 (a)

1. A balloon leaves the ground with a vertical acceleration of $1\cdot33$ m/s². How far has it risen and what is its velocity 30 seconds later? If at this instant some ballast is dropped, how long will this take to reach the ground?

2. A car is timed to take 15 seconds over 220 m and 10 seconds over the next 220 m. Assuming constant acceleration, what is the speed of the car at the end of the observed motion? [O.C.]

3. A body moving in a straight line traverses distances AB, BC, CD of 153 m, 215 m and 217 m respectively in successive intervals of 3, 5 and 7 seconds. Show that these facts indicate a uniform retardation, and find the time and distance traversed when the body comes to rest. [O.C.]

4. The distance between two stations is $4\cdot5$ kilometres. A train starts from rest at the first station and moves with uniform acceleration for 1 kilometre. The speed is then constant for 3 minutes, after which the train is uniformly retarded for 1 minute so that it comes to rest at the

second station. Sketch the velocity-time graph and find the average speed for the journey. Draw also the space-time graph. [L.U.]

5. A train completes a journey of 5 kilometres between two stations A and B in 10 minutes. It starts from rest at A and travels with uniform acceleration a until it reaches 40 km/h. This speed is maintained after which the brakes are applied to give it a uniform retardation $3a$ and bring it to rest at B. Determine the value of a and the time spent in retardation. [L.U.]

6. A and B are points in a vertical line, B being at height h above A. From A a particle is projected vertically upwards with velocity u and, at the same instant, another particle is projected vertically upwards from B with velocity v. Prove that, if the particles collide at a point C above B, $2v(u - v) > gh$ and that $AC = uh/(u - v) - \frac{1}{2}gh^2/(u - v)^2$. [L.U.]

7. A platform is descending with a constant velocity of 4 m/s. A ball is dropped from rest on to the platform from a point 6 m above it. Find the time that elapses before the ball hits the platform. [L.U.]

8. A train accelerates uniformly from rest at one station, attains a uniform speed and then decelerates uniformly to rest at the next station. The magnitude of the deceleration is twice that of the acceleration. If the train covers $\frac{1}{3}$ of the distance at uniform speed show that it will take $\frac{1}{5}$ of the time between stations for this part of the journey. If the distance between stations is 1 kilometre and the time 2 minutes, show that the train will reach a speed of 50 km/h. [L.U.]

9. A point moving in a straight line is retarding uniformly and travels distances a and b in successive time-intervals t and t'. Prove that the retardation is $2(a/t - b/t')/(t + t')$. If the above distances are respectively 56 cm and 69 cm in time intervals of 2 seconds and 3 seconds, find the initial speed and the total distance described before coming to rest. [L.U.]

10. A train travels from rest to rest between stations 1 kilometre apart. Normally the train accelerates to its maximum speed of 40 km/h, continues at this speed and then retards to rest at the second station 100 seconds after starting. Its retardation has twice the value of its acceleration and both are constant. On one occasion after attaining maximum speed the train stopped to comply with signals and on restarting was able to reach only 30 km/h before the brakes were applied for the station. Find how far the train was from the second station when it came to rest for the signal and how long it took after restarting to reach the station. [L.U.]

11. A train leaves a station at 9.45 a.m. and accelerates uniformly from rest to a maximum speed of 60 km/h, after which constant speed is maintained. At 10.05 a.m. another train leaves the same station and accelerates uniformly from rest to 70 km/h. The accelerations of the trains are 4 km/h per minute and 5 km/h per minute respectively and they

travel on parallel tracks towards the same destination. Calculate the time when the second train overtakes the first and the distance from the starting point at this time. [L.U.]

12. The driver of a train, travelling at 45 km/h on a straight level track, sees a signal against him at a distance of 250 m and, putting on the brakes, comes to rest at the signal. He stops for 1 minute and then resumes the journey, attaining the original speed of 45 km/h in a distance of 375 m. Assuming that acceleration and retardation are uniform, find how much time has been lost owing to the stoppage.

13. A motor-car A travelling along a straight road with uniform velocity u passes at X a car B travelling with uniform acceleration a in the same direction, the velocity of B at X being $u_1(<u)$; B overtakes A at Y, thereafter travelling with uniform velocity. Find (i) the maximum distance between the cars between X and Y, and (ii) the uniform acceleration given to A at Y if A overtakes B at Z, where $YZ = XY$. [O.C.]

14. A particle P is thrown vertically upwards from O with velocity V; prove that, neglecting air-resistance, the maximum height H reached above O is given by $V^2 = 2gH$ and that P returns to O after a time $2V/g$. When P reaches a point A, h above O, on its upward flight a second particle is projected upwards from O with velocity V and later collides with P at A. Prove that $9h = 8H$. [O.C.]

15. A body moving in a straight line travels 24 m in the 4th second of its motion, 32 m in the 6th second and 52 m in the 11th second. Prove that these statements are consistent with the fact that the body is uniformly accelerated. When the body has travelled 600 m it is uniformly retarded and comes to rest after travelling a further 1050 m. Find the uniform retardation.

16.5 Differentiation of a graph

The formulae used for constant acceleration cannot be used when the acceleration varies continuously during the motion. This is the case, for example, where air resistance to motion causes a retardation which varies with the speed of a body or where a body is attracted towards some point by a force which varies with the distance from the point.

In such cases the four variables, distance, time, velocity and acceleration will be related in some way and it is sometimes possible to make observations of two of the variables during the motion and to show their relation graphically. Thus we may have a set of values of distance and time and be able to construct a distance-time graph. Then if x be the distance and t the time the velocity v at any instant is (dx/dt), and this is the slope of the tangent to the distance-time curve (Fig. 169). Thus if the tangent to the curve is drawn for a particular value of t, by measuring its slope the velocity for this value of t is found. A series of tangents can be drawn to the curve and a set of corresponding values of velocity and time calculated from which a velocity-time graph can be drawn.

In the same way, by drawing tangents to the velocity-time curve a set of values of (dv/dt), which is the acceleration, can be found.

The process of drawing tangents to a curve and measuring their slopes is called *differentiation of a graph*. For accurate results the graph should be on a large scale and should be a smooth flowing curve. Modern

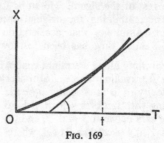

FIG. 169

high speed photography makes this possible with photographs of the displacement of a body taken at intervals of a hundredth of a second or less.

Example 5. *A body starting from rest is timed over successive distances of* 10 *cm with the following results*

distance (cm)	0	10	20	30	40	50	60
time (sec)	0	2·5	3·5	4·3	5.0	5·6	6·3

Plot a space-time graph and find the velocity when the body has moved 20 cm. Show that the acceleration is approximately constant for the first part of the motion and subsequently becomes zero.

The space time graph is shown in Fig. 170.

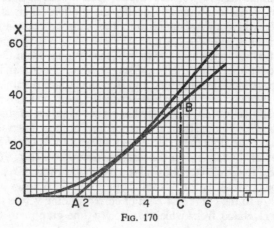

FIG. 170

The tangent is drawn at the point where $x = 20$, $t = 3.5$. This is the line AB which intersects the t-axis at A and the line $x = 40$ at B; C is the foot of the perpendicular from B to the t-axis. Then the slope of AB is the tangent of the angle BAC, that is BC/AC. From the scales $BC = 37.5$ cm, $AC = 3.35$ sec, so that the velocity is $37.5/3.35 = 11.2$ cm/s.

By drawing tangents at other points we obtain the following results

time (sec)	0	1	2	3	4	5	6
velocity (cm/s)	0	3.2	6.4	9.6	12	12	12

Thus for about the first $3\frac{1}{2}$ seconds the velocity increases in proportion to the time showing that the acceleration is constant. After this time the velocity has a constant value and the acceleration is therefore zero.

16.6 Integration of a graph

If observed values are obtained of velocity and time during motion a velocity-time graph can be drawn. Since the velocity is dx/dt, where x is the displacement and t the time, we have

$$\frac{dx}{dt} = v,$$

and on integration between the values $t = t_1$ and $t = t_2$

$$x = \int_{t_1}^{t_2} v\, dt.$$

Now we know that the value of this integral is the area enclosed by the curve, the t-axis and the ordinates at $t = t_1$ and $t = t_2$, the shaded area in Fig. 171. Therefore, by calculating the area under the velocity-time

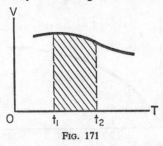

FIG. 171

curve for different values of t we can find the corresponding values of the displacement x. It will be seen that if the units of velocity along the v-axis are cm/s and the units along the t-axis seconds, the unit of area will be centimetres.

The process of finding areas enclosed beneath a curve is called *integration of a graph*. If the graph is drawn on squared paper the area can be found roughly by counting squares, treating squares partially enclosed as halves. If the graph is on a large scale a planimeter may be used. This is an instrument which records the area enclosed by a curve when a pointer is made to follow its boundary closely.

Simpson's rule (see § 9.13) is often used for the calculation of areas. Thus if v_1, v_2, v_3 are the velocities shown by the velocity-time graph corresponding to the values t_1, t_2, t_3 of the time and $t_3-t_2 = t_2-t_1 = \tau$, the area between t_1 and t_3 is approximately

$$x = \frac{\tau}{3}(v_1 + 4v_2 + v_3), \qquad (16.8)$$

and this is the increase of the distance x between the times $t = t_1$ and $t = t_3$.

Example 6. *Values of the speed v km/h and the time t seconds for a train are given in the following table*

v	0	24·6	36·3	43·7	48·3	51·3	53·5
t	0	50	100	150	200	250	300

Find the distance travelled in the 300 seconds.

The velocity-time graph is shown in Fig. 172. Using Simpson's rule with interval $\tau = 50$ seconds to find the area under the graph between $t = 0$ and $t = 300$ we have

$$x = \frac{50}{3}(0 + 4 \times 24{\cdot}6 + 36{\cdot}3) + \frac{50}{3}(36{\cdot}3 + 4 \times 43{\cdot}7 + 48{\cdot}3)$$
$$+ \frac{50}{3}(48{\cdot}3 + 4 \times 51{\cdot}3 + 53{\cdot}5)$$
$$= 11{,}685.$$

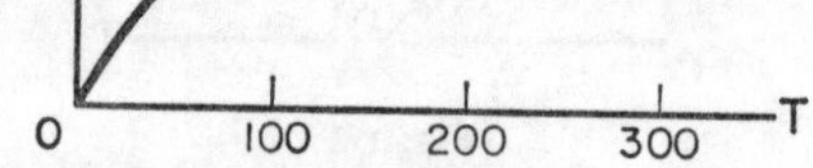

FIG. 172

This is the area in units which are $\dfrac{\text{kilometres}}{\text{hours}} \times$ seconds and must be divided by 3600 to give the distance in kilometres. Thus

$$x = \frac{11{,}685}{3{,}600} = 3{\cdot}25 \text{ kilometres.}$$

16.7 Types of graph

The following types of graph may be encountered

(a) *Time graphs*

  (i) distance-time — differentiation gives a velocity-time graph;
  (ii) velocity-time — differentiation gives an acceleration-time graph;
     integration gives a distance-time graph;
  (iii) acceleration-time — integration gives a velocity-time graph.

(b) *Distance graphs*

If a set of values of velocity and distance is given we may plot a graph of $\frac{1}{2}v^2$ against x, or of $\frac{1}{v}$ against x. Remembering that $a = \frac{d}{dx}(\frac{1}{2}v^2)$ and $\frac{1}{v} = \frac{dt}{dx}$, we find for the following graphs

  (i) $\frac{1}{2}v^2$ against x — differentiation gives an acceleration-distance graph;

  (ii) $\frac{1}{v}$ against x — integration gives a time-distance curve;

  (iii) acceleration-distance — integration gives values of $\frac{1}{2}v^2$ and hence of v.

(c) *Acceleration-velocity graph*

In this case $1/a$ may be plotted against v and since

$$\int \frac{1}{a}\,dv = \int \frac{dt}{dv}\cdot dv = \int dt,$$

integration of the graph leads to a velocity-time graph.

Thus if any two of the four variables distance, time, velocity, acceleration can be connected by a graph, values of the other two variables can be deduced by differentiation or integration.

16.8 Explicit expressions for the acceleration

There are important types of motion in which the acceleration is not constant but is known as a function of the time, the distance or the velocity. Thus, for example, in simple harmonic motion, to be considered in § 21·2, such as occurs when a body is suspended by an elastic string, the acceleration is proportional to the distance from a fixed point. In the motion of a body through the air there is a retardation proportional to the velocity or to some power of the velocity. In such cases a complete knowledge of the motion is obtained when a relation giving the displacement in terms of the time has been found. This is done by equating a theoretical expression for the acceleration, namely $\frac{dv}{dt}$, $\frac{d^2x}{dt^2}$ or $v\frac{dv}{dx}$, to the given function which expresses the acceleration, thus obtaining a differential relation which may be integrated to give expressions for the velocity and distance.

In general, two integrations are required and at each integration an arbitrary constant must be added. The values of these constants can be found if the initial conditions are known, that is the values of the displacement and velocity at the start of the motion. Some examples of this procedure have been given as illustrations of the methods of the Calculus in § 12.6, and a few further examples are given here.

It should be noticed that the velocity given by the expression $\frac{dx}{dt}$ is along a line OX in the direction in which x is increasing and the expressions $\frac{dv}{dt}$, $\frac{d^2x}{dt^2}$ and $v\frac{dv}{dx}$ give the acceleration in this direction.

Example 7. *A body is projected vertically upwards with velocity V and the retardation due to air resistance is kv where v is the velocity and k is a constant. Find expressions for the velocity and height after time t and the time to the highest point reached.*

Let x be the height after time t. Then $v (= dx/dt)$ and dv/dt are measured vertically upwards while the downward acceleration is $kv + g$. Therefore

$$\frac{dv}{dt} = -(kv + g)$$

and

$$\frac{dt}{dv} = -\frac{1}{kv + g}.$$

Integrating with respect to v we have

$$t = -\frac{1}{k} \ln (kv + g) + c \text{ (a constant)}.$$

This equation holds when $t = 0$ and $v = V$, therefore

$$c = \frac{1}{k} \ln (kV + g)$$

and

$$t = \frac{1}{k} \ln \left(\frac{kV + g}{kv + g} \right),$$

so that

$$e^{kt} = \frac{kV + g}{kv + g},$$

giving

$$v = -\frac{g}{k} + \left(V + \frac{g}{k} \right) e^{-kt}.$$

Writing $v = dx/dt$ and integrating with respect to t,

$$x = -\frac{g}{k}t - \frac{1}{k}\left(V + \frac{g}{k}\right)e^{-kt} + d \text{ (a constant)},$$

and, since $x = 0$ when $t = 0$, $d = \frac{1}{k}\left(V + \frac{g}{k}\right)$, and it follows that

$$x = -\frac{g}{k}t + \frac{1}{k}\left(V + \frac{g}{k}\right)\left(1 - e^{-kt}\right).$$

The time to the highest point is that which makes the velocity zero, and this gives

$$\left(V + \frac{g}{k}\right)e^{-kt} = \frac{g}{k},$$

leading to

$$t = \frac{1}{k}\ln\left(1 + \frac{kV}{g}\right).$$

Example 8. *A particle is projected vertically from the earth's surface with velocity V. The acceleration due to gravity when distant x from the earth's centre is gR^2/x^2, where R is the earth's radius. Neglecting air resistance, find the height to which the particle rises.*

The expression $v\,dv/dx$ is the acceleration in the direction of x increasing, that is away from the earth, whereas the acceleration gR^2/x^2 is towards the earth. We have therefore

$$v\frac{dv}{dx} = \frac{d}{dx}(\tfrac{1}{2}v^2) = -\frac{gR^2}{x^2}.$$

Integrating this equation with respect to x,

$$\tfrac{1}{2}v^2 = \frac{gR^2}{x} + c \text{ (a constant)}.$$

Now the initial conditions are that on the earth's surface when $x = R$, $v = V$ therefore

$$\tfrac{1}{2}V^2 = gR + c,$$

and, substituting this value of c, we have

$$v^2 = \frac{2gR^2}{x} + (V^2 - 2gR).$$

At the highest point reached $v = 0$ and at this point

$$x = \frac{2gR^2}{2gR - V^2},$$

and the height above the earth's surface is $x - R$, that is $V^2R/(2gR - V^2)$. We notice that when x is very large so that $2gR^2/x$ is negligible there is a residual velocity v provided that $V^2 - 2gR$ is positive. The velocity given by $V^2 = 2gR$ is called the escape velocity and is the least velocity required for a satellite to go into orbit. Taking $R = 6400$ km and $g = 981$ cm/s^2 this gives $V = 11\cdot2$ kilometres per second approximately.

Exercises 16 (b)

1. Simultaneous values of speed and time for a train are given below Draw the speed-time curve, and find the acceleration at the end of the second minute, and the distance in kilometres passed over in attaining a speed of 50 km/h.

Time (seconds)	0	50	100	150	200	250	300
Speed (km/h)	0	24·6	36·3	43·7	48·3	51·2	53·5

[O.C.]

2. A body starting from rest moves in a straight line and the following observations are taken

Time (seconds)	0	0·2	0·4	0·6	0·8	1·0	1·2	1·4	1·6
Distance (centimetres)	0	0·55	2·1	4·8	8·5	13·2	18·5	23·7	29·0

Determine from the graph the velocity of the body in cm/s at the middle of each interval of time and show that for the first second the acceleration is approximately constant. [O.C.]

3. A motor-car is found to increase its speed from 8 to 80 kilometres per hour in 40 seconds. Find the acceleration (supposed uniform) in centimetre-second units. Plot a space-time graph and from it determine the time taken to travel the last 300 metres of the movement observed. [O.C.]

4. A train starting from rest is timed over successive intervals of 125 m with the following result

Distance (m)	125	250	375	500	625	750
Time (sec)	45	63·6	78	90	100·6	110·2

Plot a space-time graph and a velocity-time graph. What is the average value of the acceleration and at what point was the velocity 30 km/h?

5. The velocity-time diagram of a particle consists of two straight lines AB, BC, where the coordinates of A, B, C are (0, 10), (10, 10), (20, 25), the first coordinate in each case being the time in seconds and the second the velocity in m/s. Describe the motion of the particle and find the total distance covered. [O.C.]

6. A train approaching a station does two successive quarters of a mile in 16 seconds and 20 seconds respectively. Assuming the retardation to be uniform, draw a velocity-time graph for the 36 seconds. Prove that the train runs 1761 ft 10 in further before stopping if the same retardation is maintained. [O.C.]

7. The velocity v km/h of a car t seconds after starting is given by the following table

t	0	5	10	15	20	25	30
v	0	5·8	8·7	10·7	12·2	13·3	14·0

Draw the velocity-time graph and determine from it the distance covered in 30 seconds and the value of the acceleration when $t = 10$.

8. A train is uniformly retarded from 30 km/h to 10 km/h. It travels a certain distance at the latter speed and is then uniformly accelerated until the speed is again 30 km/h, the magnitude of the acceleration being half that of the retardation. The interval from the beginning of retardation until the speed is again 30 km/h is $7\frac{1}{2}$ minutes and the total distance covered is 2 km. Sketch a velocity-time graph and find the distance travelled at 10 km/h. [L.U.]

9. The velocity of a particle at points measured along a straight line from a fixed point are as follows

x m	0	10	20	30	40	50
v m/s	30	20	15	12	10	8·57

Show that the graph of $1/v$ against x is approximately a straight line and find the time taken for the 50 m.

10. The acceleration of a car starting from rest increases uniformly with the distance from an initial value of 0.5 m/s^2 to a value of 2.0 m/s^2 at the end of 150 m. Draw a graph of acceleration against distance and find the final velocity of the car.

11. A particle moves horizontally with retardation kv, where v is the velocity and k is constant. If x is the distance moved at time t and V is the initial velocity, prove that $v = Ve^{-kt}$, $kx = V(1 - e^{-kt})$.

12. A particle moves horizontally with retardation kv^2, where v is the velocity and k is constant. If x is the distance moved at time t and V is the initial velocity, prove that $v = V/(1 + kVt) = Ve^{-kx}$.

13. A particle is let fall from a height h above the earth. Taking the acceleration due to gravity as gR^2/x^2, where R is the earth's radius and x the distance from the centre of the earth, and neglecting air resistance, show that its velocity at the earth's surface will be $\sqrt{\{2ghR/(R + h)\}}$.

14. The acceleration of a particle moving in a straight line is $x + 1/x^3$ towards a fixed point O of the line when x is its distance from O. If it starts from rest when $x = 1$, find its velocity when $x = \frac{1}{2}$.

15. If the retardation of a train is $a + bv^2$, where v is its velocity and a and b are constants, show that it will come to rest from velocity V in a distance l, given by $a + bV^2 = ae^{2bl}$.

Exercises 16 (c)

1. The driver of a train travelling at 60 km/h sees on the same track 200 m in front of him a slow train travelling in the same direction at 20 km/h. What is the least retardation that must be applied to the faster train so as to avoid a collision?

2. Stations A and B are 500 m apart. A train starting from A is uniformly accelerated for 15 seconds to a speed of 30 km/h which is maintained until the train is 100 m from B, when it slows up uniformly and stops at B. Find the values of the accelerations and the time taken.

3. A particle is projected vertically upwards, and at the same instant another is let fall to meet it. Show that, if the particles have equal velocities when they impinge, one of them has travelled three times as far as the other. [O.C.]

4. A car starting from rest at A travels to B with uniform acceleration 0.5 m/s^2; from B to C its speed is constant; at C the brakes are applied, the subsequent retardation being uniform and equal to 0.4 m/s^2. If the total distance travelled is 368.75 m and the total time is 85 seconds, find the time from B to C.

5. Two trains, each of length 75 m, moving in opposite directions along parallel lines, meet when their speeds are 45 km/h and 30 km/h. If their accelerations are 0.33 m/s^2 and 0.67 m/s^2 respectively, find the time they take to pass each other. [L.U.]

6. A particle moving in a straight line with uniform acceleration describes 17 m in the third second of its motion and 29 m in the sixth second. Find the initial speed and the distance described in the tenth second. [L.U.]

7. A particle is projected vertically upwards with a velocity of 30 m/s, and two seconds later another particle is projected vertically upwards from the same point with a velocity of 25 m/s. Find the height above the point of projection at which they meet and the time that has then elapsed. [L.U.]

8. Prove that if a particle starts from rest and moves with constant acceleration, the difference between the distance traversed in successive seconds is constant. If it moves 52 m in the seventh second, find the distance traversed in the tenth second. [L.U.]

9. A cyclist A riding at 10 km/h is overtaken and passed by B riding at 12 km/h. If A immediately increases his speed with uniform acceleration, show that he will catch B when his speed is 14 km/h. If when he has increased his speed to 13 km/h he continues to ride at this speed and catches B after he has gone 41.67 m, find his acceleration. [L.U.]

10. A cage goes down a mine-shaft 750 m deep in 45 seconds. For the first quarter of the distance only the speed is being uniformly accelerated and during the last quarter uniformly retarded, the acceleration and retardation being equal. Find the uniform speed of the cage over the centre portion.   [O.C.]

11. A particle moving in a straight line with uniform acceleration a passes a certain point with velocity u. Three seconds later another particle passes the same point with velocity $\frac{1}{2}u$ and acceleration $\frac{4}{3}a$. The first particle is overtaken by the second when their velocities are respectively 27 and 31 m/s. Find the values of u and a and the distance travelled from the point.   [L.U.]

12. The maximum possible acceleration of a body is 2 m/s² and its maximum possible retardation is 8 m/s². Find the least time in which it can travel 1 kilometre from rest to rest.   [L.U.]

13. A block falls from a mast-head and is observed to take $\frac{2}{5}$ seconds in falling from the deck to the bottom of the hold, a distance of 8 m. Calculate the height of the mast-head above the deck.   [L.U.]

14. A man sees a bus 100 m away starting from rest with constant acceleration. He then runs after it with constant speed and just catches it in one minute. Determine the speed of the man and the acceleration of the bus. If the man's speed is 3 m/s find the nearest he can get to the bus.
                                                                              [L.U].

15. A particle is projected vertically upwards with velocity u and after t seconds another particle is projected vertically upwards from the same point with the same velocity. Prove that they will meet at height $(4u^2 - g^2t^2)/8g$.   [L.U.]

16. The acceleration of a train starting from rest increases uniformly from 0·2 m/s² to 0·7 m/s² in the first 5 seconds, it then increases uniformly to 0·9 m/s² in the next 5 seconds and remains constant at this value for 10 seconds; it then decreases uniformly to zero in 5 seconds. Draw an acceleration-time graph and find the velocity at the end of 25 seconds. Draw a velocity-time graph and find the distance gone in the 25 seconds.

17. A train starts from rest with acceleration 0·2 m/s² which is maintained for 3 minutes. Steam is then gradually shut off reducing the acceleration at a uniform rate until the train is running at full speed 5 minutes after starting. The brakes are then applied and produce a retardation which increases uniformly until the train is brought to rest in 2·5 minutes more. Draw the acceleration-time graph and record (i) the value of full speed, (ii) the value of the retardation at the instant of stopping. Sketch the velocity-time graph.

18. A train starts from a station with acceleration 0·2 m/s² which decreases uniformly with the time for 4 minutes at the end of which time the train is running at full speed. The train is then subject to a constant retardation which brings it to rest at the next station in 1½ minutes. Draw the

acceleration-time graph, finding the values of full speed and the retardation. Find the speed at the end of each successive minute.   [L.U.]

19. The velocity-distance graph of a particle is a straight line joining the points $x = 0$, $v = 10$ to $x = 100$, $v = 20$, where x is in metres and v in m/s. Find the time taken to travel 100 m and the acceleration at $x = 0$ and $x = 100$.

20. A particle moves in a straight line in such a way that at the end of t seconds its distance x from a fixed point of the line is given by $x = 7t + 2 \cos 3t$. Find its acceleration at any instant. Prove that the velocity v never changes in direction but that its acceleration vanishes whenever $v = 13$ or 1.

21. A particle moves in a straight line with acceleration $4t^2$ m/s², where t is in seconds, away from a point O of the line. Initially the particle is passing through O with velocity 2 m/s. Find the velocity and distance moved after 3 seconds.   [O.C.]

22. A particle is projected with a horizontal velocity of 80 m/s in a medium which causes a retardation $v/100$ m/s² when the velocity is v m/s. Find the distance gone in 100 seconds and the velocity after 100 seconds.

23. A particle is projected vertically upwards with a velocity of 100 m/s and the retardation due to air resistance is $v/100$ m/s² when the velocity is v m/s. Find the height to which it rises, given that ln $1\cdot102 = 0\cdot097$.

24. If the retardation caused by the resistances to the motion of a train is $(900 + 7v^2)/7000$ m/s² when the speed is v m/s find the distance travelled with steam cut off when slowing from 72 km/h to 36 km/h.

25. A train running at 45 km/h is brought to rest by a retardation $(7/20 + t/100)$ m/s² where t is the time in seconds. Show that it is brought to rest in 26 seconds in a distance of $0\cdot18$ km.

CHAPTER 17

MOTION IN A PLANE

17.1 Relative motion and parabolic motion

When the pilot of an aeroplane wishes to fly from a point A to a point B it is not sufficient for him merely to find the bearing of B from A and to head the aeroplane in this direction. He must also know the strength of the prevailing wind and make such allowance for his movement due to the wind that his course relative to the ground will be along the line AB. Similarly, if a ship A at sea wishes to come up with a ship B which is in motion the navigator will not steer directly towards B but will ensure that his course relative to B will bring A directly to B. The methods by which these practical problems are dealt with are treated in this chapter under the heading of relative motion.

A second form of motion in a plane is that of a body thrown through the air and moving along a curved path. If it is moving slowly so that the resistance of the air is negligible, its path is a parabola. We shall see that in this case every detail of the motion can be found from simple equations based on the fact that the motion can be separated into up and down motion under the influence of gravity and unimpeded horizontal motion. While not directly applicable to bodies moving at high speeds, certain parts of the theory are of use in determining the trajectories of missiles.

17.2 Frames of reference

We are satisfied that we know the position of a point on the earth's surface if we know its latitude and longitude. Here we are using the earth as a frame of reference and describing the position of the point relative to this. The velocity of a particle at the point, being the rate of change of its position, is given relative to the same frame of reference.

The earth is not the only possible frame of reference. Astronomers prefer to use the sun and the directions from the sun to certain fixed stars and describe motion by reference to this frame. Thus any velocity that we can observe is velocity relative to some frame of reference which we regard as fixed. It is often convenient to take a moving ship or vehicle as a frame of reference and to describe motion with reference to the ship or vehicle. The velocity found is called *relative velocity* with respect to the ship or vehicle.

17.3 Resultant velocity

When a body is moving through the air or through water, the velocity that a person moving with the body can most easily observe is its velocity relative to the air or water. Thus, for example, the air speed indicator on an aeroplane indicates a velocity relative to the air. If the air is also moving, the velocity of the aeroplane relative to the ground is the combination of the air speed and the velocity of the air, that is the vector sum of the air speed and the velocity of the air.

If the air speed is u in a direction OA (Fig. 173) and the velocity of the air is v in a direction OB, the combined velocity is represented in magnitude and direction by the diagonal OC of the parallelogram $OACB$.

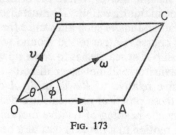

FIG. 173

Denoting the angle AOB by θ, the resultant velocity w is given by (see § 6.4),

$$w^2 = u^2 + v^2 + 2uv \cos \theta, \qquad (17.1)$$

in a direction making an angle ϕ with OA, where

$$\tan \phi = \frac{v \sin \theta}{u + v \cos \theta}. \qquad (17.2)$$

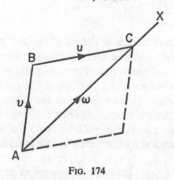

FIG. 174

The resultant velocity can also be found by drawing the vectors and measuring the magnitude and direction of the resultant.

If an aeroplane is to move along a certain course it must be headed in such a direction that the vector sum of its air speed and the air's velocity is along this course. Let AX (Fig. 174) be the desired course; draw AB to represent the air's velocity v. With centre B and radius BC

representing the air speed u describe an arc to cut AX in C. Then AC represents the resultant velocity along the course and BC the direction in which the aeroplane must be headed.

Example 1. *The wind is blowing from due West at* 40 *km/h. An aeroplane whose air speed is* 200 *km/h flies from its base* X *to a point* Y 40 *km East and* 80 *km North of* X *and then returns to its base. Find the direction in which it must be headed for each journey and the total time of flight.*

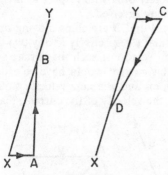

FIG. 175

Draw XY in the appropriate direction (Fig. 175). Taking 1 cm to represent 20 km/h draw XA of length 2 cm to represent the wind's velocity. With centre A and radius 10 cm (the air speed) draw an arc to cut XY in B. Then AB is the direction in which the aeroplane must be headed and by measurement this is found to be North $16\frac{1}{4}°$ East. Also $XB = 10\cdot75$ cm and this represents the true speed of 215 km/h.

A similar construction for the return journey shows that the true speed is 179 km/h and the direction South $36\frac{3}{4}°$ West. The distance XY is $89\cdot44$ kilometres and the time for the double journey is

$$\frac{89\cdot44}{215} + \frac{89\cdot44}{179} = 0\cdot92 \text{ h.}$$

The result may also be found by calculation. Since $\tan BXA = 2$, BXA is $63°\ 26'$, and applying the sine rule to the triangle BXA we have

$$\frac{200}{\sin 63°\ 26'} = \frac{40}{\sin ABX} = \frac{XB}{\sin BAX},$$

giving $XAB = 106°\ 16'$ and $XB = 214\cdot8$. Thus the direction is North $16°\ 16'$ East and the true speed $214\cdot8$ km/h. For the return journey, since CYD is $180° - 63°\ 26'$, we have

$$\frac{200}{\sin 63°\ 26'} = \frac{40}{\sin CDY} = \frac{YD}{\sin DCY},$$

giving $DCY = 53°\ 8'$ and $YD = 179$ so that the direction is South $36°\ 52'$ West and the true speed 179 km/h. The time is

$$\frac{89\cdot44}{214\cdot8} + \frac{89\cdot44}{179} = 0\cdot917 \text{ h} = 55 \text{ minutes.}$$

17.4 Relative velocity

If two bodies A and B are moving along a straight line with velocities u and v respectively in the same direction, where $u > v$, the distance between the bodies is increasing at the rate $u - v$, and this is the relative velocity of A with respect to B. If B is moving in the opposite direction to A with velocity v the distance between them is increasing at the rate $u + v$ and this is the relative velocity of A with respect to B. In both cases the relative velocity of A with respect to B is found by adding to A's velocity B's velocity reversed.

Suppose now that A and B are ships moving on the surface of the sea with velocities u and v respectively in any two directions. Suppose further that a current sets in of such magnitude and direction that it brings B to rest. This current would have velocity v in the opposite direction to B's motion and A's new velocity would be the resultant of its velocity u and the velocity of the current, that is the resultant of

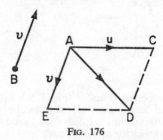

FIG. 176

A's velocity and B's velocity reversed (Fig. 176). This is represented in vector form by the diagonal AD of the parallelogram $ACDE$, and this would be the velocity of A as seen from B whether the current operated or not.

Thus *the relative velocity of A with respect to B is the vector sum of A's velocity and B's velocity reversed.*

To find this relative velocity it is not necessary to know the positions of the two bodies but only the magnitudes and directions of their velocities.

It is evident that the relative velocity of B with respect to A is equal and opposite to the relative velocity of A with respect to B. Also, if the relative velocity is known and the velocity of one of the bodies is known the velocity of the other is easily found.

Example 2. *A cruiser is proceeding due East at 20 knots, and a destroyer whose speed is 30 knots is 10 sea-miles due South of it. In what direction must the destroyer travel in order to meet the cruiser, and when will the meeting occur?*   [O.C.]

The destroyer must travel in such a direction that its velocity relative to the cruiser is directly towards the cruiser, that is due North. Let θ be the bearing of the direction of travel (Fig. 177). The relative velocity will be the sum of the cruiser's velocity reversed, that is 20 knots due West, and the destroyer's velocity. This relative velocity will be due North if

$$30 \sin \theta = 20,$$
$$\sin \theta = \tfrac{2}{3},$$

and hence

$$\theta = 41° 49'.$$

The relative velocity is of magnitude $30 \cos \theta$ and this is, since $\cos \theta = \sqrt{5}/3$, $10\sqrt{5} = 22\cdot36$ knots. The time to the meeting is $10/(10\sqrt{5}) = \tfrac{1}{5}\sqrt{5} = 0\cdot447$ h or $26\cdot8$ minutes.

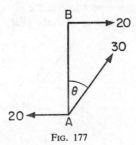

Fig. 177

Example 3. *A ship is steaming at 15 km/h in the direction N 20°E and the wind appears to blow from the direction N 35°W. The ship alters course and steams at the same speed in the direction N 20°W and the wind then appears to blow from the direction N 50°W. Find graphically the magnitude and direction of the true wind velocity.* [L.U.]

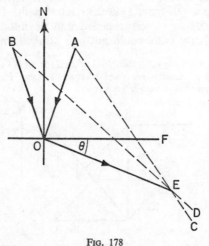

Fig. 178

Draw (Fig. 178) the vectors OA and OB from O each of length 15 units in the directions of the ship's motion in the two cases. From A draw AC in the direction N 35°W, that is inclined at 55° to OA. From B draw BD in the direction

N 50°W, that is inclined at 30° to *OB*. Let *AC* and *BD* meet at *E*; then *OE* represents the velocity of the wind in magnitude and direction. By measurement *OE* = 20·9 units and the angle *EOF* = 19°, therefore the wind's true velocity is 20·9 km/h from the direction N 71°W. It is clear that in each case the sum of the vectors representing the wind's velocity and the ship's velocity reversed gives a relative wind in the appropriate direction.

17.5 Relative path

If the positions of two bodies *A* and *B* at some instant are *P* and *Q* respectively and the relative velocity of *A* with respect to *B* is known, the *relative path* of *A* with respect to *B* is the straight line drawn through *P* in the direction of the relative velocity (Fig. 179). This is the path

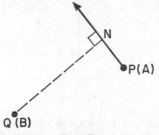

Fig. 179

that *A* would actually follow if a current set in which brought *B* to rest. The nearest approach of *A* to *B* is then the length of the perpendicular distance *QN* from *Q* to the relative path. It is assumed, of course, that the relative velocity is constant in magnitude and direction, otherwise the relative path would not be a straight line.

Example 4. *A ship A is 5 sea-miles due North of a ship B. A is steaming due West at 15 knots and B is steaming due North-West at 10 knots. Find the distance and time of their nearest approach to each other.*

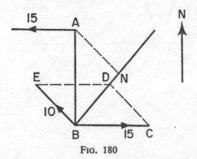

Fig. 180

Plot the positions *A* and *B* 5 sea-miles apart (Fig. 180). At *B* draw *BC* of length 15 units due East, representing *A*'s velocity reversed; draw *BE* of length 10 units due North-West representing *B*'s velocity. Complete the parallelogram

BCDE. Then *BD* represents the relative velocity of *B* with respect to *A* and *BD* is the relative path. By measurement *BD* = 10·6 units and the relative velocity is 10·6 knots. If *AN* is the perpendicular from *A* to *BD*, *AN* = 3·73 sea-miles and *BN* = 3·33 sea-miles. Thus the nearest approach is 3·73 sea-miles and the time to this point is 3·33/10·6 = 0·314 h = 18·8 min.

By calculation, if *v* is the relative velocity and θ its bearing,

$$v = \sqrt{\{15^2 + 10^2 + 2 \cdot 15 \cdot 10 \cos 135°\}} = 10 \cdot 62 \text{ knots,}$$

$$\theta = \tan^{-1}\left(\frac{15 - 10 \cos 45°}{10 \sin 45°}\right) = 48° \, 16',$$

$$AN = 5 \sin 48° \, 16' = 3 \cdot 732 \text{ sea-miles,}$$

$$BN = 5 \cos 48° \, 16' = 3 \cdot 328 \text{ sea-miles,}$$

and the result follows as before.

Example 5. *A ship leaves a certain point and steams North-East at 15 knots; 5 hours later another ship leaves the same port and steams due West at 20 knots. Their wireless instruments can maintain communication up to 225 nautical miles. Find to the nearest nautical mile their distances from port when communication ceases.*
[L.U.]

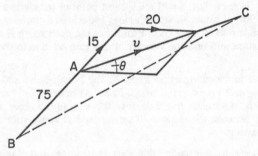

Fig. 181

The initial position shown in Fig. 181 has the second ship *B* in port and the first ship *A* 75 sea-miles to the North-East. The relative velocity of *A* with respect to *B* is *v* in a direction θ North of East, where

$$v^2 = 20^2 + 15^2 + 2 \cdot 20 \cdot 15 \cos 45°, \qquad v = 32 \cdot 38 \text{ knots,}$$

$$\tan \theta = \frac{15 \sin 45°}{20 + 15 \cos 45°}, \qquad \theta = 19° \, 7'.$$

Then, if *C* is a point on the relative path 225 sea-miles from *B*,

$$\frac{225}{\sin (135 + \theta)} = \frac{75}{\sin ACB} = \frac{AC}{\sin ABC},$$

whence

$$\sin ACB = \tfrac{1}{3} \sin 154° \, 7' = 0 \cdot 1455,$$

$$ACB = 8° \, 22', \qquad ABC = 17° \, 31', \qquad AC = 155 \cdot 2.$$

The time is therefore 155·2/32·38 = 4·80 hours and the distances from port are 75 + 15 × 4·80 = 147 sea-miles and 4·80 × 20 = 96 sea-miles.

Exercises 17 (a)

1. A car is travelling due East at 30 km/h and the driver notices that the wind appears to come from a direction 030° (N 30°E). When he drives due West at the same speed the wind appears to blow from 300° (N 60°W). Find, graphically, or otherwise, the true speed and direction of the wind. Find also its apparent direction when he drives due South at 45 km/h. [L.U.]

2. To an observer in a train travelling due East at 80 km/h an aeroplane appears to be travelling due North at 150 km/h. Find the true course and speed of the aeroplane. [O.C.]

3. Falling rain is carried by a horizontal wind. When a man cycles facing the wind at 4 m/s on a horizontal road the apparent direction of the rain is at 45° to the horizontal. When he cycles with his back to the wind at 5 m/s the angle increases to 64°. Calculate the velocity of the wind. [L.U.]

4. Two smooth rods AB, AC of unequal length, are fixed as chords of a vertical circle so that A is at the highest point of the circle and the angle BAC is 90°. Two small smooth rings are released simultaneously from A and slide one on each rod. Prove that the rings reach B and C at the same instant and find the velocity of one ring relative to the other after time t. [L.U.]

5. A ship A is travelling at 23 knots to the North-West and a ship B is travelling at 7 knots to the North-East. At noon A is 17 sea-miles due East of B. Calculate to the nearest half-minute the times at which the distance between the ships is 10 sea-miles, and verify your answer by a scale drawing. [L.U.]

6. At noon a ship A is sailing due East at 10 knots and a ship B, 10 sea-miles due South of A, is sailing in a direction $\cos^{-1} \frac{3}{5}$ East of North at 20 knots. Find the shortest distance between A and B and the time when they are nearest together. [L.U.]

7. Two straight roads intersect at O. At a certain instant a motorist on the first road is 10 kilometres due North of O and travelling towards O at 40 km/h, while a cyclist on the second road is leaving O and travelling at 10 km/h in the direction N 60°E. Assuming their speeds to remain constant find their shortest distance apart and the time that elapses before this is attained. [L.U.]

8. To a motorist driving due North at 30 km/h it appears that the wind comes from the North-East. When he increases his velocity to 40 km/h it appears to come from N 30°E. Find the magnitude and direction of the wind velocity. [L.U.]

9. A motor car is travelling E along a straight road and a second car is travelling NE with the same speed along another straight road; both cars are approaching the junction of the roads. If v is the speed of

either car, find the velocity of the first relative to the second. If the first car is 300 m short of the junction when the second is 400 m short, find to the nearest ten metres how nearly the cars will approach each other.

[L.U.]

10. A submarine sailing on a course 045° (N 45°E) at 10 knots sights a merchant ship 3 nautical miles due East and sailing on a course 300° (N 60°W) at 8 knots. If both ships maintain their courses and speeds find, by scale drawing or otherwise, how long it is before they are first at a distance of one nautical mile apart. Find the bearing of the merchant ship from the submarine at this moment.   [L.U.]

11. Two cars A and B are travelling along straight roads which cross at right angles at O, their constant velocities being 40 km/h westwards and 30 km/h northwards respectively. At the instant when B is passing O, A is 142 m from O and moving towards it. Find the velocity of B relative to A, the least distance between the cars and their distances from O when nearest to one other.   [N.U.]

12. When a motor launch moves northwards at 20 knots a pennant on its masthead points due East. On the return journey when the speed is 20 knots southwards the pennant points N 10° 12′ E. Find the speed and direction of the wind assuming them to be unchanged throughout.

[N.U.]

13. A ship which has a speed 10 knots in still water steams from a point A, which is 5 sea-miles due South of a lighthouse L, to a point B, which is 5 sea-miles due East of L, through a current flowing at 3 knots in the direction 15° North of East. If the course set to take the ship along the line AB is ϕ North of East, prove that $\sin (\phi - 45°) = 3/20$. Find to the nearest minute the times for the run A to B and for the return run from B to A.   [O.C.]

14. A wind is blowing towards the direction N θ E. An aeroplane, on a course N α W, passes over two points A and B, B being due North of A; on arrival over B the course is altered to S β E and the aeroplane passes over C due East of B. Prove that $\tan \theta = \sin \alpha \sec \beta$. If $AB = BC$ and T_1, T_2 are the times taken for flying over the distances AB, BC respectively, prove that $T_1/T_2 = \tan \frac{1}{2} (\alpha + \beta)$.   [O.C.]

15. At 6 a.m. a ship is at A, 8 nautical miles due South of a lighthouse L. Given that the ship's speed in still water is 10 knots find, graphically or otherwise, the course to be steered through a current, flowing in the direction N 30°E at 3 knots, so as to pass through the position K which is 10 nautical miles due East of L. Find also, to the nearest minute, the time of arrival at K. If the current remains unchanged, find how long it will take the ship to go from K to A.   [O.C.]

17.6 Components of velocity and acceleration

When a particle is moving along a curved path in a plane its position at any instant may be specified with reference to fixed rectangular axes

OX, OY by its coordinates (x, y) at time t. Thus we may think of each of the coordinates x and y as quantities which vary with t and may be differentiated with respect to t. In Fig. 182, let A be the initial position of the particle when $t = 0$, P its position at time t and Q its position after a small additional time δt. Denoting by s the distance it has travelled from A to P and by δs the additional distance from P to Q, the average velocity between P and Q is $\delta s / \delta t$ and its velocity V at time t is

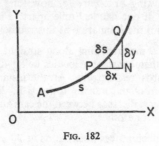

FIG. 182

defined as the limiting value of this average velocity as δt becomes indefinitely small. Thus

$$V = \lim_{\delta t \to 0} \frac{\delta s}{\delta t} = \frac{ds}{dt}.$$

Further, since the limiting direction of the chord PQ and of the arc PQ is that of the tangent to the curve at P, the direction of the velocity is along the tangent at P.

If the coordinates of P and Q are (x, y) and $(x + \delta x, y + \delta y)$ respectively, the average velocities for the period δt in the directions OX and OY are $\delta x / \delta t$ and $\delta y / \delta t$, so that the components of the velocity V parallel to the axes are

$$\lim_{\delta t \to 0} \frac{\delta x}{\delta t} = \frac{dx}{dt} = \dot{x} \text{ and } \lim_{\delta t \to 0} \frac{\delta y}{\delta t} = \frac{dy}{dt} = \dot{y}.$$

The acceleration of the particle is a vector quantity such that its component in any direction is the rate of change of velocity in that direction. Thus if u and v are the components of the velocity V at time t parallel to OX and OY respectively and $u + \delta u$ and $v + \delta v$ the components at time $t + \delta t$, the components of acceleration parallel to OX and OY are

$$\lim_{\delta t \to 0} \frac{\delta u}{\delta t} = \frac{du}{dt} = \frac{d^2 x}{dt^2} = \ddot{x},$$

$$\lim_{\delta t \to 0} \frac{\delta v}{\delta t} = \frac{dv}{dt} = \frac{d^2 y}{dt^2} = \ddot{y}.$$

The quantities $\dot{x}$, $\dot{y}$, $\ddot{x}$ and $\ddot{y}$ are components of velocity and acceleration measured in the positive directions of the axes. Thus if the axis OY is directed vertically upwards and the acceleration is g vertically downwards, we have $\ddot{y} = -g$.

17.7 Parabolic motion

We now consider the two-dimensional motion of a particle which is projected with a given velocity in a given direction. We shall suppose the motion to take place near the earth's surface, so that the acceleration due to gravity may be taken as constant and in a constant direction throughout the motion. We shall suppose also that the resistance of the air is negligible. In practice the resistance of the air is by no means negligible; at high velocities it may cause a retardation much greater than that due to gravity and the range of an artillery shell is often less than one-tenth of what it would be if there were no air resistance. Long range rockets do indeed rise above the greater part of the earth's atmosphere and for most of the trajectory air resistance is negligible. However, at these heights gravity may no longer be taken as constant and the effect of the variation of the gravity acceleration is to make the trajectory approximately an ellipse.

We shall suppose then that the motion takes place in a vacuum, or *in vacuo*, and we shall see that in this case the path of the particle is a parabola.

17.8 Equations governing the motion

Let the particle be projected with initial velocity V from a point O in a direction making an angle α with the horizontal. Let OX and OY be

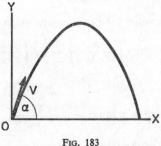

FIG. 183

horizontal and vertical axes of coordinates through O, so that the motion takes place entirely in the vertical plane XOY and the position of the particle at any instant may be described by coordinates (x, y) with respect to these axes (Fig. 183).

The theoretical acceleration at any instant has components $\ddot{x}$ and $\ddot{y}$ parallel to the axes. In fact the only acceleration is $-g$ parallel to the y-axis. Therefore

$$\ddot{x} = 0, \quad \ddot{y} = -g. \tag{17.3}$$

These equations are valid throughout the motion and may therefore be integrated with respect to the time t, giving

$$\dot{x} = \text{constant}, \quad \dot{y} = -gt + \text{constant}.$$

These relations are true for all values of t and in particular when $t = 0$, at which time $\dot{x}$ has the value $V \cos \alpha$ and $\dot{y}$ the value $V \sin \alpha$. Hence the values of the constants of integration are $V \cos \alpha$, $V \sin \alpha$ and we have

$$\dot{x} = V \cos \alpha, \quad \dot{y} = V \sin \alpha - gt. \tag{17.4}$$

Thus the horizontal component of velocity remains constant throughout the motion while the vertical component diminishes with the time and eventually becomes negative.

Integrating again with respect to t,

$$x = (V \cos \alpha)t, \quad y = (V \sin \alpha)t - \tfrac{1}{2}gt^2. \tag{17.5}$$

No constants need be added on integration since both x and y are zero when $t = 0$.

Equations (17.5) give the position of the particle for all values of t and may also be considered as giving the equation of the path of the particle in parametric form. This equation may be written in terms of x and y by eliminating t between these equations. We have

$$t = \frac{x}{V \cos \alpha},$$

and substituting this value for t in the expression for y

$$y = V \sin \alpha \left(\frac{x}{V \cos \alpha} \right) - \frac{1}{2} g \left(\frac{x}{V \cos \alpha} \right)^2,$$

that is

$$y = x \tan \alpha - \frac{gx^2}{2V^2 \cos^2 \alpha}. \tag{17.6}$$

This equation, being of the second degree in x and of the first degree in y, is the equation of a parabola. With some rearrangement it may be written in the more recognisable form

$$\left(x - \frac{V^2 \sin \alpha \cos \alpha}{g} \right)^2 = \left(\frac{-2V^2 \cos^2 \alpha}{g} \right) \left(y - \frac{V^2 \sin^2 \alpha}{2g} \right)$$

showing that the vertex of the parabola is the point

$$[(V^2/g) \sin \alpha \cos \alpha, \ (V^2/2g) \sin^2 \alpha]$$

and the latus rectum is of length $(2V^2/g) \cos^2 \alpha$.

17.9 Range and time

The range R is the distance measured horizontally from O to the point where the trajectory meets the horizontal through O, and the time of flight T is the time taken to reach this point. R is therefore the value of x for which $y = 0$. When $y = 0$, equation (17.5) gives

$$0 = (V \sin \alpha) t - \tfrac{1}{2} g t^2$$

and hence $y = 0$ when $t = 0$ and when $t = \dfrac{2V \sin \alpha}{g}$.

Therefore

$$T = \frac{2V \sin \alpha}{g}. \tag{17.7}$$

The corresponding value of x is $(V \cos \alpha)T$, and hence

$$R = \frac{2V^2 \sin \alpha \cos \alpha}{g}$$

$$= \frac{V^2 \sin 2\alpha}{g}. \tag{17.8}$$

The *maximum range* that can be obtained for a given initial velocity V by varying the angle of projection is easily seen to be V^2/g, since the greatest value of $\sin 2\alpha$ is 1. If $\sin 2\alpha = 1$, $\alpha = 45°$ and this is the angle of projection for maximum range.

To find the angle of projection required to give a certain range R with a given velocity of projection V, we use equation (17.8), giving

$$\frac{V^2 \sin 2\alpha}{g} = R,$$

$$\sin 2\alpha = \frac{gR}{V^2},$$

$$\alpha = \tfrac{1}{2} \sin^{-1} \left(\frac{gR}{V^2} \right). \tag{17.9}$$

This gives a real value of α provided that $gR/V^2 \leqslant 1$, that is, that the desired range is less than or equal to the maximum range. If $gR/V^2 < 1$, since $\sin 2\alpha = \sin (180° - 2\alpha)$, we have either

$$\sin 2\alpha = \frac{gR}{V^2} \quad \text{or} \quad \sin (180° - 2\alpha) = \frac{gR}{V^2},$$

giving

$$\alpha = \tfrac{1}{2} \sin^{-1} \frac{gR}{V^2} \quad \text{or} \quad 90° - \alpha = \tfrac{1}{2} \sin^{-1} \frac{gR}{V^2},$$

and hence the angle of projection may be α or $90° - \alpha$. The corresponding times of flight for these two angles of projection are given by equation (17.7) and are

$$T_1 = \frac{2V \sin \alpha}{g}, \quad T_2 = \frac{2V \cos \alpha}{g}. \tag{17.10}$$

From this it can be seen that the angle of projection greater than $45°$ gives the longer time of flight. Firing guns with angles of projection greater than $45°$ is called *upper register* firing; most mortars can only be fired at angles in the upper register.

An alternative form for the equation of the trajectory is

$$y = x \left(1 - \frac{x}{R}\right) \tan \alpha, \tag{17.11}$$

where R is the range. Since $R = (2V^2/g) \sin \alpha \cos \alpha$, this is equivalent to

$$y = x \tan \alpha - \frac{gx^2 \tan \alpha}{2V^2 \sin \alpha \cos \alpha}$$

$$= x \tan \alpha - \frac{gx^2}{2V^2 \cos^2 \alpha}$$

which is the form given in equation (17.6).

17.10 Vertex and remaining velocity

The *vertex* is the highest point of the trajectory; at this point the particle ceases to rise and begins to descend again. Hence the vertical component of velocity is zero and we have

$$V \sin \alpha - gt = 0,$$

so that

$$t = \frac{V \sin \alpha}{g},$$

and this is the time in which the initial vertical velocity is destroyed by gravity. Thus the time of flight to the vertex is $\tfrac{1}{2}T$. The vertex height is given by

$$y = (V \sin \alpha)\, t - \tfrac{1}{2}gt^2$$

$$= \frac{V^2 \sin^2 \alpha}{2g}, \tag{17.12}$$

and the corresponding value of x is $(V \cos \alpha)\tfrac{1}{2}T = \tfrac{1}{2}R$.

The *remaining velocity* v at time t has components

$$V \cos \alpha \quad \text{and} \quad V \sin \alpha - gt,$$

and is given by

$$v^2 = (V \cos \alpha)^2 + (V \sin \alpha - gt)^2,$$

leading to

$$v = \sqrt{\{V^2 - 2V (\sin \alpha)gt + g^2t^2\}}. \tag{17.13}$$

Its direction is inclined to the horizontal at an angle θ given by

$$\tan \theta = \frac{V \sin \alpha - gt}{V \cos \alpha}. \tag{17.14}$$

It is easily seen that when $t = T$, $v = V$ and $\tan \theta = -\tan \alpha$, so that the final velocity is V inclined at $-\alpha$ to the horizontal.

It is possible that at some instant during its flight the particle is moving in a direction perpendicular to its original direction. If this is so for some value of t, we have

$$\tan \theta = \frac{V \sin \alpha - gt}{V \cos \alpha} = \tan (\alpha - 90°) = -\cot \alpha,$$

so that

$$gt \sin \alpha = V (\cos^2\alpha + \sin^2\alpha),$$

and

$$t = \frac{V}{g \sin \alpha}.$$

For this to be possible we must have $V/(g \sin \alpha) \leqslant T$

that is

$$\frac{V}{g \sin \alpha} \leqslant \frac{2V \sin \alpha}{g}$$

giving

$$\sin \alpha \geqslant \frac{1}{\sqrt{2}},$$

so that the angle of projection must be greater than 45°.

17.11 Projection from a height

If a particle is projected from a height h above the ground at an inclination α to the horizontal, its range R will be the horizontal distance to the point where it hits the ground. This distance is easily found from the trajectory equation (17.6) by putting $y = -h$ when $x = R$, giving

$$-h = R \tan \alpha - \frac{gR^2}{2V^2 \cos^2 \alpha} \tag{17.15}$$

and

$$R^2 - \frac{2V^2 \sin \alpha \cos \alpha}{g} \cdot R - \frac{2V^2 h \cos^2 \alpha}{g} = 0,$$

so that

$$R = \frac{V^2 \sin \alpha \cos \alpha}{g} + \frac{V \cos \alpha}{g} \sqrt{(V^2 \sin^2 \alpha + 2gh)}. \tag{17.16}$$

The negative value of the surd will lead to a negative value of R and is rejected. The time of flight is that required to cover the distance R with velocity $V \cos \alpha$ and is $R/(V \cos \alpha)$.

Equation (17.15) may also be solved to find the value of $\tan \alpha$ for a given range R. Writing $1/\cos^2 a = \sec^2 \alpha = 1 + \tan^2 \alpha$, the equation becomes

$$\tan^2 \alpha - \frac{2V^2}{gR} \tan \alpha - \left(\frac{2V^2 h}{gR^2} - 1 \right) = 0$$

giving

$$\tan \alpha = \frac{V^2}{gR} \pm \frac{1}{gR} \sqrt{(V^4 + 2ghV^2 - g^2R^2)}. \tag{17.17}$$

Thus there is a real value of $\tan \alpha$ if, and only if, $V^4 + 2ghV^2 \geqslant g^2R^2$, and the maximum attainable range occurs when the

$$V^4 + 2ghV^2 = g^2R^2,$$

that is $R = \dfrac{V}{g} \sqrt{(V^2 + 2gh)}$.

In a similar manner the range on an inclined plane of inclination β can be found from the equations

$$y = x \tan \beta \quad \text{and} \quad y = x \tan \alpha - gx^2/(2V^2 \cos^2 \alpha),$$

from which

$$x = \frac{2V^2 \cos^2 \alpha}{g} (\tan \alpha - \tan \beta).$$

The distance measured along the plane is then $x \sec \beta$.

17.12 Condition for a point to lie on the trajectory

If a point whose coordinates are (a, b) lies on the trajectory for a given angle of projection α and initial velocity V, we have from the trajectory equation (17.6)

$$b = a \tan \alpha - \frac{ga^2}{2V^2 \cos^2 \alpha}. \tag{17.18}$$

If α is given, V is easily found from this equation. If V is given, α may be found by replacing $1/\cos^2 \alpha$ by $\sec^2 \alpha = 1 + \tan^2 \alpha$, giving

$$b = a \tan \alpha - \frac{ga^2}{2V^2}(1 + \tan^2 \alpha),$$

and this quadratic can be solved for $\tan \alpha$.

If the trajectory is to pass through two specified points we have two equations of the form (17.18) from which both V and α can be found.

Example 6. *A bomb due to explode in 5 seconds is thrown with velocity 30 m/s at elevation 60°. Find the height, range and velocity of the bomb at the instant of explosion.*

Here $V = 30$ m/s, $\sin \alpha = 0.866$, $\cos \alpha = 0.5$, $V \sin \alpha = 25.98$, $V \cos \alpha = 15$. Then when $t = 5$,

$$x = 5 \times 15 = 75 \text{ m},$$
$$y = 5 \times 25.98 - 4.905 \times 5^2 = 7.28 \text{ m},$$
$$\dot{x} = 15 \text{ m/s},$$
$$\dot{y} = 25.98 - 9.81 \times 5 = -23.07 \text{ m/s},$$
$$v = \sqrt{(\dot{x}^2 + \dot{y}^2)} = 27.5 \text{ m/s},$$

and the inclination of its direction to the horizontal is given by

$$\tan \theta = -\frac{23.07}{15}, \qquad \theta = -56° \, 58'.$$

Example 7. *A particle is projected from a point O with initial speed of 50 m/s in a direction making an angle α with the vertical. At the same instant a particle is projected vertically downwards with the same speed from a point in the plane of the line of flight 100 metres horizontally and 200 metres vertically from O. If the two meet, find α and the time of flight to the point of impact.* [L.U.]

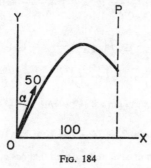

FIG. 184

With reference to horizontal and vertical axes through O (Fig. 184) we have for the coordinates of the first particle at time t, remembering that the initial velocity makes an angle $\frac{1}{2}\pi - \alpha$ with the horizontal,

$$x = (50 \sin \alpha)t, \qquad y = (50 \cos \alpha)t - \tfrac{1}{2}gt^2.$$

If (x_1, y_1) be the coordinates of the second particle at time t we have, since it falls vertically under gravity,

$$x_1 = 100, \qquad y_1 = 200 - (50t + \tfrac{1}{2}gt^2).$$

When the particles meet, $x = x_1$ and $y = y_1$, so that

$$(50 \sin \alpha)t = 100$$
$$(50 \cos \alpha)t = 200 - 50t,$$

whence

$$2 = \frac{1 + \cos \alpha}{\sin \alpha} = \frac{2 \cos^2 \dfrac{\alpha}{2}}{2 \sin \dfrac{\alpha}{2} \cos \dfrac{\alpha}{2}}$$

giving

$$\tan \frac{\alpha}{2} = \frac{1}{2}, \qquad \alpha = 53° \, 8',$$

and

$$t = \frac{2}{\sin \alpha} = 2 \cdot 5 \text{ seconds.}$$

Example 8. *A particle projected from the origin with velocity V passes through the point $P(a, h)$. Prove that there are two possible trajectories if $(V^2 - gh)^2 > g^2(a^2 + h^2)$. If $V^2 = 2ga$ and $a = 2h$, prove that the directions of motion at P in the two trajectories include an acute angle whose tangent is 2, and that the times taken to reach P are in the ratio $\sqrt{5} : 1$.* [O.C.]

The point (a, h) lies on the trajectory given by equation (17.6) if

$$h = a \tan \alpha - \frac{ga^2}{2V^2} \sec^2 \alpha,$$

that is, since $\sec^2 \alpha = 1 + \tan^2 \alpha$, if

$$\tan^2 \alpha - \frac{2V^2}{ga} \tan \alpha + 1 + \frac{2V^2 h}{ga^2} = 0,$$

giving

$$\tan \alpha = \frac{V^2}{ga} \pm \sqrt{\left(\frac{V^4}{g^2 a^2} - \frac{2V^2 h}{ga^2} - 1 \right)}$$

$$= \frac{V^2}{ga} \pm \sqrt{\left\{ \frac{(V^2 - gh)^2}{g^2 a^2} - \left(1 + \frac{h^2}{a^2} \right) \right\}}.$$

This gives two real values of $\tan \alpha$ if $(V^2 - gh)^2 > g^2(a^2 + h^2)$. Since $V^2/ga = 2$, we have

$$\tan \alpha = 2 \pm \sqrt{(4 - 2 - 1)} = 3 \text{ or } 1,$$

so there are two values of α, α_1 and α_2, such that $\cos \alpha_1 = \dfrac{1}{\sqrt{2}}$, $\cos \alpha_2 = \dfrac{1}{\sqrt{10}}$.

If the corresponding times to P are t_1 and t_2

$$(V \cos \alpha_1)t_1 = (V \cos \alpha_2)t_2 = a$$

giving

$$t_1 = \frac{a}{V}\sqrt{2}, \qquad t_2 = \frac{a}{V}\sqrt{10}.$$

Thus the times are in the ratio $\sqrt{5}:1$. The inclination of the velocity at P to the horizontal is given by equation (17.14) of § 17.10, namely

$$\tan \theta = \frac{V \sin \alpha - gt}{V \cos \alpha} = \tan \alpha - \frac{gt}{V \cos \alpha} = \tan \alpha - \frac{gt^2}{(V \cos \alpha)t}$$

$$= \tan \alpha - \frac{gt^2}{a}.$$

Thus

$$\tan \theta_1 = 1 - 1 = 0, \qquad \tan \theta_2 = 3 - 5 = -2,$$

and the angle between the directions is $\tan^{-1} 2$.

Example 9. *A particle is thrown out to sea from the top of a cliff of height h with velocity u at an angle of elevation α and strikes the sea at a distance x from the foot of the cliff. Show that the maximum value of x for a given value of u is $u\sqrt{(u^2 + 2gh)}/g$.* [L.U.]

The particle moves in a parabola whose equation with reference to axes through the point of projection is

$$y = x \tan \alpha - \frac{gx^2}{2u^2 \cos^2 \alpha}.$$

Where it strikes the sea $y = -h$ and we have

$$-h = x \tan \alpha - \frac{gx^2 \sec^2 \alpha}{2u^2},$$

that is

$$gx^2 \tan^2 \alpha - 2u^2 x \tan \alpha + gx^2 - 2u^2 h = 0.$$

Solving for $\tan \alpha$ we find

$$\tan \alpha = \frac{u^2 x \pm \sqrt{\{u^4 x^2 - gx^2(gx^2 - 2u^2 h)\}}}{gx^2}$$

$$= \frac{1}{gx}\{u^2 \pm \sqrt{(u^4 + 2ghu^2 - g^2 x^2)}\}.$$

This gives a real value for α if, and only if,

$$g^2 x^2 < u^4 + 2ghu^2,$$

leading to

$$x < u\sqrt{(u^2 + 2gh)}/g.$$

This gives also the maximum range obtainable for a given value of u, and if this range is attained $\tan \alpha = u^2/gx = u/\sqrt{(u^2 + 2gh)}$).

Example 10. *A, B, C and D are four vertices of a regular hexagon of side a with its plane vertical and its two remaining vertices on the x-axis. If a particle projected from the origin passes through A, B, C and D in that order prove that its range is $a\sqrt{7}$.* [L.U.]

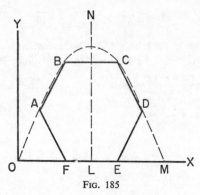

FIG. 185

Let $ABCDEF$ be the hexagon (Fig. 185) and let R be the range. Let L be the mid-point of FE, and LN the vertical through L. The pairs of points A and D, and B and C are symmetrically placed about LN, therefore LN must be the axis of the parabola and hence $OL = LM = \frac{1}{2}R$. The coordinates of A and B are

$$(\tfrac{1}{2}R - a, \tfrac{1}{2}a\sqrt{3}) \quad \text{and} \quad (\tfrac{1}{2}R - \tfrac{1}{2}a, a\sqrt{3}),$$

and these points lie on the parabola $y = x\left(1 - \dfrac{x}{R}\right)\tan\alpha$. Therefore

$$\frac{1}{2}a\sqrt{3} = \left(\frac{1}{2}R - a\right)\left(\frac{1}{2} + \frac{a}{R}\right)\tan\alpha,$$

$$a\sqrt{3} = \left(\frac{1}{2}R - \frac{1}{2}a\right)\left(\frac{1}{2} + \frac{1}{2}\frac{a}{R}\right)\tan\alpha,$$

and hence, eliminating $\tan\alpha$,

$$(R - a)(R + a) = 2(R - 2a)(R + 2a),$$
$$R^2 = 7a^2,$$
$$R = a\sqrt{7}.$$

Exercises 17 (b)

1. A particle is projected from a point O with speed V m/s so that it passes through a point whose horizontal and vertical distances from O are 4 m and 3 m respectively. If $V^2 = 8g$, find the initial angle of elevation. Find also the range on a horizontal plane through O and the greatest height attained. [L.U.]

2. A projectile is fired with a given initial speed from a point in a horizontal plane. Show that for a given range less than the maximum there are two possible angles of projection. If the times of flight for the two paths corresponding to these angles are in the ratio $2:1$, show that the range is $\frac{4}{5}$ of the maximum. [L.U.]

3. A particle is projected from a point O at an angle of elevation α. Prove that, with respect to horizontal and vertical axes through O, the equation of its path is $y = x(1 - x/R) \tan \alpha$, where R is the horizontal range. If $\alpha = 45°$ and the particle just clears the tops of two vertical masts 120 m apart and each 45 m above O, calculate the value of R. [L.U.]

4. A particle projected from a point A with speed u at an elevation α strikes the horizontal plane through A at B. Find the distance AB. If the particle is projected from A with the same elevation but with speed $2u$, find its height above the plane when it passes over B. [L.U.]

5. A particle is projected with speed u from a point O on the ground at angle of elevation α. Prove that the horizontal range is a maximum for $\alpha = 45°$. If R is this maximum range find the two angles of projection necessary to obtain a range $\frac{1}{2}R$ with the same speed, and show that the two times of flight are $(R/2u) \sec 15°$ and $(R/2u) \operatorname{cosec} 15°$. [L.U.]

6. A particle is projected *in vacuo* with initial horizontal and vertical components of velocity u and v respectively. Write down formulae for the horizontal and vertical distances traversed in time t. Prove that the direction of motion of the particle will have turned through a right angle after time $(u^2 + v^2)/gv$, and that the particle will then be above the horizontal plane through the point of projection if $v > u$. [L.U.]

7. A ball is thrown with angle of elevation α, where $\tan \alpha = \frac{4}{3}$ from horizontal ground and just clears the top of a post 24 m high at 45 m from the point of projection. Find the distance between the two points of the trajectory at which the ball is at a height of 24 m. [L.U.]

8. At a range of 100 m *in vacuo* a bullet fired horizontally strikes the target 10 cm below the point at which its initial direction produced would cut the target. Find the initial velocity of the bullet. [O.C.]

9. A projectile is fired from a point on a cliff to hit a mark 200 m horizontally from the point and 200 m vertically below it. The velocity of projection is that due to falling freely under gravity 100 m from rest. Show that the two possible directions of projection are at right angles and that the times of flight are approximately 4·9 and 11·8 seconds.

10. Show that if R be the maximum horizontal range for a given velocity of projection, a particle can be projected to pass through a point whose horizontal and vertical distances from the point of projection are $\frac{1}{2}R$ and $\frac{1}{4}R$ respectively, provided that the tangent of the angle of projection is 1 or 3, and that in the second case the range on the horizontal plane is $\frac{3}{4}R$. [L.U.]

11. A particle is projected from a point at a height $3h$ above a horizontal plane at an angle α to the horizontal. Show that, if the greatest height above the point of projection is h, the horizontal distance travelled before striking the plane is $6h \cot \alpha$.

12. A heavy particle projected from a point O with speed u and elevation α describes a parabola. At a point P on the trajectory the direction of motion is at right angles to the direction of projection. Prove that the time taken to travel from O to P is $u/(g \sin \alpha)$ and calculate the distance OP.   [L.U.]

13. A particle is projected from a point O with horizontal and vertical components of velocity u and v respectively. Show that the radius vector OP will be perpendicular to the direction of motion of the particle at some point of its path if $v \geqslant 2\sqrt{2}u$. If $v = 3u$ find the horizontal distances from O when the path is perpendicular to the radius vector.   [L.U.]

14. A particle P is projected under gravity from a point O. Prove that in the absence of air resistance it describes a parabola. If the line OP meets at Q a fixed vertical line in the plane of motion, show that Q descends with constant velocity.   [L.U.]

15. Two particles A and B are projected simultaneously from the same point with the same velocity u and move in the same vertical plane. If their directions of projection are at right angles, prove that after time t $AB = ut\sqrt{2}$ and that AB makes a constant angle with the horizontal. Show that the particles are moving in exactly opposite directions at the instant when the horizontal distance between them is u^2/g.   [L.U.]

16. A player stands on a tennis court at 12·19 m from the net 0·914 m high and strikes the ball at a height 0·914 m above the ground. The ball travels in a vertical plane perpendicular to the net and just clears the net and hits the ground at 3·05 m beyond it. Find the speed and the direction of flight of the ball on leaving the racquet.   [L.U.]

17. A bowler in a cricket match delivers the ball at a height of 6 ft above the ground at an angle of elevation α; the ball hits the wicket, 22 yd away at 8 in above the ground. If the maximum height of the ball in its trajectory is 9 ft above the ground find the value of $\tan \alpha$ and the angle with the horizontal at which the ball hits the wicket.   [O.C.]

18. A particle is fired horizontally with a velocity of 60 m/s from a point A on the top of a vertical cliff so as to hit a boat B. If A is 200 m above sea level, find the horizontal distance of B from A. Find the angle of elevation and the velocity of projection for a projectile fired from B so as to pass through A horizontally.   [O.C.]

19. A particle P is projected from O with velocity V at angle of elevation α. A and B are two points on the trajectory at a vertical height h above O; at A and at B the acute angle between the direction of motion and the horizontal is θ. Prove that, if H is the height above O reached by the particle, $H \tan^2 \theta = (H - h) \tan^2 \alpha$. If the time in the trajectory between A and B is equal to the time for P to reach height H, prove that $4h = 3H$.   [O.C.]

20. A particle is projected with velocity V at angle of elevation α and the horizontal range is R. Prove that, if $R < V^2/g$, there are two possible angles of projection α_1 and α_2 ($\alpha_2 > \alpha_1$) which give the same range R, and that if T_1 and T_2 are the corresponding times of flight $T_1 T_2 = 2R/g$. Also, if $\alpha_1 = 15°$, prove that $T_2 - T_1 = V\sqrt{2}/g$, and that if two particles are projected simultaneously, one in the α_1 and the other in the α_2 direction, then the distance between them after t seconds is Vt. [O.C.]

Exercises 17 (c)

1. Two football players A and B are running straight down the field in parallel lines 5 m apart. A, who has the ball, is 2 m ahead of B. If both are moving at 20/3 m/s, with what velocity (relative to himself) must A pass the ball to B in order that the pass may just not be "forward", i.e. in order that the ball may travel at right angles to the length of the field? Find also the velocity of the ball relative to the ground. [O.C.]

2. If an aeroplane can travel at 200 km/h in still air and the air is moving from the West at 80 km/h, how long will it take the aeroplane to reach a place 500 kilometres off to the South-West?

3. An aeroplane travels in still air at 200 km/h. It starts from A to reach a point B due North 300 kilometres away. There is a wind blowing due West at 40 km/h, but when half the distance has been covered its velocity increases to 60 km/h. Find the time taken over the flight to the nearest minute.

4. An aeroplane can travel at 160 km/h in still air and the wind is blowing at 60 km/h. Compare the times taken from A to B and back again if the direction of the wind all the time is (i) A to B, (ii) at right angles to AB, (iii) at 45° to AB.

5. A man swims at 3 km/h across a river 125 m wide, flowing at 5 km/h. How long will it take him if he swims so as to reach the opposite bank (a) as quickly as possible, (b) as little downstream as possible? [L.U.]

6. A destroyer, steaming N 30°E at 30 knots, observes at noon a steamer which is steaming due North at 12 knots, and overtakes the steamer at 12.45 p.m. Find the distance and bearing of the steamer from the destroyer at noon. [O.C.]

7. A cruiser which can steam at 30 knots receives a report that an enemy vessel steaming due North at 20 knots is 29 nautical miles away in a direction 30° North of East. Show (i) graphically, (ii) by calculation, that the cruiser can overtake the vessel in almost exactly two hours. [O.C.]

8. Two ships are sailing at speeds of 10 and 12 knots along parallel lines in the same direction. When they are opposite one another and 2 nautical miles apart the faster ship turns its course through 30° in the direction of the other. Find how close they get to one another. [L.U.]

9. If a ship is moving North-East at 15 knots, and a second ship appears to an observer on the first to be moving due East at 7 knots, determine the actual direction and magnitude of the velocity of the second. [L.U.]

10. A vessel A is steaming due North at 18 knots, and a vessel B is steaming South-East at 15 knots. Find, graphically or otherwise, the magnitude and direction of the velocity of A relative to B. If B is initially 30 sea-miles due North of A, find the shortest distance between the two vessels in the subsequent motion. [L.U.]

11. A man who can swim at 2 km/h wishes to cross a river 250 metres wide, flowing at 3 km/h, as quickly as possible. Find by calculation, in what direction with respect to the bank he should head and how many minutes he would take. Also, calculate how far down stream he would land. [L.U.]

12. A man falling vertically by parachute in a steady downpour of rain observes that when his speed is v_1 the rain appears to make an angle α with the vertical. When his speed is v_2 the angle is β. Show that the rain actually falls at an angle θ with the vertical given by

$$(v_2 - v_1) \cot \theta = v_2 \cot \alpha - v_1 \cot \beta.$$ [L.U.]

13. A ship at A which cannot sail at more than 20 knots wishes to intercept a ship at B, 38 sea-miles due East of A, which is sailing at 24 knots in a direction 30° N of W. Prove that in order to intercept, the first ship may steer any course that makes an angle of not more than $\tan^{-1} \frac{4}{3}$ with due North. Calculate the least time in minutes in which she can intercept. [L.U.]

14. To a cruiser C steaming North at V knots an enemy battleship B, distant a sea-miles to the West, appears to be moving South-East at $V\sqrt{2}$ knots. Find the true velocity of B, and show that when the vessels are nearest to one another C is North-East of B. If C is within firing range of B when the vessels are not more than b sea-miles apart, where $b < a$, show that C is liable to be hit at any moment within an interval of $\sqrt{(2b^2 - a^2)}/V$ hours. [N.U.]

15. A and B are two points on the banks of a river 750 metres wide and flowing due East at 3 km/h, B being due North of A. A boat, whose speed in still water is 9 km/h is steered from A in a constant direction $\tan^{-1} \frac{3}{4}$ West of North and reaches the opposite bank at C. Find (i) the distance BC, (ii) the time taken and (iii) the time taken in returning in a straight line from C to A. [O.C.]

16. A particle is projected from a point O with a velocity whose horizontal and vertical components are u and v respectively. If $u = 96$ m/s, $v = 288$ m/s show that at two points the direction of the particle's motion is at right angles to the line joining the particle to O, and find the positions of these points.

17. A shell is observed to explode at the level of the gun from which it is fired after 10 seconds and the sound of the explosion reaches the gun after a further interval of 3 seconds. Assuming motion *in vacuo* find the elevation of the gun and the muzzle velocity. (Take the velocity of sound as 340 m/s.) [O.C.]

18. A mortar bomb fired at elevation 45° on horizontal ground hits a point 50 m beyond a target. When fired at elevation 60° it hits a point 50 m short of the target. Find the correct elevation (> 45°) to hit the target and the time of flight. [O.C.]

19. A particle projected from a point meets the horizontal plane through the point of projection after traversing a horizontal distance a, and attains a greatest height b. Find the horizontal and vertical components of the velocity of projection. Show that when it has described a horizontal distance x it has attained a height $4bx(a - x)/a^2$. [O.C.]

20. A ball is thrown with a velocity whose horizontal component is 12·26 m/s from a point 1·303 m above the ground and 6·13 m away from a vertical wall 4·982 m high in such a way as just to clear the wall. At what time will it reach the ground? [L.U.]

21. A ball is thrown from the top of a tower 29·43 m high with a velocity of 24·525 m/s at an elevation of 30° above the horizontal; find the horizontal distance from the foot of the tower of the point where it hits the ground. [L.U.]

22. A stone is projected horizontally from the top of a tower 36 m high with a velocity of 10 m/s, and at the same instant another stone is projected in the same vertical plane from the foot of the tower with a velocity of 20 m/s at an elevation of 60°. Show that the stones will meet and find the height above the ground and the distance from the tower at this instant. [L.U.]

23. Two particles are projected at the same instant from points A and B on the same horizontal level where $AB = 28$ m, the motion taking place in the vertical plane through AB. The particle from A has an initial velocity of 39 m/s at an angle $\sin^{-1} \frac{5}{13}$ with AB, and the particle from B has an initial velocity of 25 m/s at an angle $\sin^{-1} \frac{3}{5}$ with BA. Show that the particles will collide in mid-air, and find when and where the impact occurs. [L.U.]

24. Two vertical posts, each of height h, stand on a horizontal plane $\frac{3}{2} h$ apart. A particle is projected from a point on the plane at an angle of 45° to the horizontal and just clears the top of each post. Prove that the speed of projection is $3\sqrt{(\frac{1}{2}gh)}$ and find the horizontal distance of the point of projection from the nearer post. [L.U.]

25. A shot is projected from a point on level ground with a speed of 120 ft/s so as just to clear a vertical wall 20 ft high at a distance of 300 ft from the point, and the flatter of two possible trajectories is chosen. Prove that it will hit the ground at about 50 ft beyond the wall. [L.U.]

26. The horizontal distance between two men, A and B, is 16 ft. A cricket ball is thrown by A to B with speed 32 ft/s; B catches it at a point whose vertical height above the point of projection is 8 ft. Show that there are two possible directions of projection and find the time of flight in each case.   [L.U.]

27. A projectile is fired from a point O with a speed due to a fall of 100 m from rest under gravity, and hits a mark 50 m below O and distant 100 m from the vertical through O. Show that the two possible directions of projection are perpendicular and find their inclinations to the horizontal. Determine the time from O to the mark in each case.   [L.U.]

28. When at elevation α, a gun fires a shot to hit a mark P on the horizontal plane through the gun. When the elevation is reduced to 15° the shot falls 100 m short of P, but when the elevation is 45° it falls 400 m beyond P. Show that $\sin 2\alpha = 0.6$ and calculate the distance of P from the gun.   [L.U.]

29. A ball is thrown from a height 1 m above the ground to clear a wall 12 m away horizontally and 5 m high. Show that the velocity of projection must not be less than than acquired by falling under gravity 8·325 m, and, when this is the velocity of projection, find how far beyond the wall it will hit the ground.   [L.U.]

30. A stone projected with velocity V at an angle of elevation α from a point O on the top of a cliff, hits a small object A at a horizontal distance a from O and at distance h below the level of O. A hit is also made if the stone is projected from O with velocity V at an angle of depression of $90° - \alpha$. Prove that $V^2 + ga \cot 2\alpha = 0$, $h + a \tan 2\alpha = 0$. Find also, when $\alpha = 60°$, the tangent of the angle between the two trajectories at impact with A.   [O.C.]

CHAPTER 18

NEWTON'S LAWS; POWER; WORK; ENERGY

18.1 Newtonian mechanics

In previous chapters we have discussed the motion of a body when its acceleration is known; we now discuss the relation between the force acting on a body and its acceleration. This relation is based on the definitions and laws of motion enunciated by Newton in the seventeenth century; these are the foundation of all theoretical work in applied mechanics. Although these laws are incapable of direct proof, they are firmly established by the agreement of predicted results with experience; for example, the time and place of an eclipse can be foretold with accuracy from calculations based on Newton's laws.

The applications of the Newtonian system of mechanics are made easier by the introduction of the concepts of power, work and energy. In the second part of this chapter we shall define these quantities and apply them in the solution of many practical problems.

18.2 Newton's laws

Newton's laws of motion, which form the basis of dynamics, may be stated as follows.

(i) Every body perseveres in its state of rest or uniform motion in a straight line except in so far as it is compelled by applied external forces to change that state.

(ii) The rate of change of momentum is proportional to the applied force and is along the line of action of the force.

(iii) Action and reaction are equal and opposite.

The first law gives, in effect, a definition of force as that which changes the state of motion of the body. A state of uniform motion is considered as not differing essentially from a state of rest, since all motion is relative to some frame of reference which may or may not be itself at rest. This law disposed of some pre-Newtonian theories that force was required to keep a body moving.

The third law states that if a body A exerts a certain force on a body B, then the body B exerts an equal and opposite force on A. These equal and opposite forces are called the *reactions* between the bodies. Such reactions occur between the particles that constitute a rigid body and are called the *internal forces* of the body. Since they occur in pairs, equal and opposite, their sum is zero and we shall see that their effect on the motion of the rigid body is nil. Thus change of motion is caused by the *external forces* acting on the body.

18.3 Newton's second law

The *momentum* of a body is defined as the product of its mass and velocity, that is

$$\text{momentum} = mv. \tag{18.1}$$

Assuming for the moment that for every particle or body there is some constant which is a measure of its mass, we have

$$\text{rate of change of momentum} = \frac{d}{dt}(mv)$$

$$= m\frac{dv}{dt} = ma,$$

where a is the acceleration. Thus Newton's second law states that the product of mass and acceleration is proportional to force. Hence if a force F acts on a particle or body, F is proportional to ma, that is $F = kma$, where k is a constant. By choosing a suitable unit of force it is possible to make the constant k equal to unity and thus we have the fundamental Newtonian equation, in suitable units,

$$F = ma. \tag{18.2}$$

The mass of a body is usually defined as the quantity of matter that it contains. This is not a very helpful definition but it is easily understood that a small body requires less force to give it a certain acceleration than a more massive one.

We may think of the mass of a body as being a number depending on the size and density of the body such that the equation (18.2) is satisfied. A standard piece of platinum is kept as a basis for the measurement of mass and its mass is called *one kilogramme* or 1000 grammes. The masses of other bodies are found by comparison with this standard and the comparison is made by weighing. If a certain mass is double the weight of the standard, the force F due to gravity acting on it is double the force acting on the standard and hence, since the acceleration g due to gravity is the same for both, it follows from equation (18.2) that its mass is two kilogrammes. In the same way the mass of any body can be compared with that of the standard or with other bodies.

We notice here the distinction between the mass of a body and its weight. The weight is a force whereas the mass is a measure of the effect of force. The mass of the standard piece of platinum is unchanged if its latitude is changed, but its weight is altered with its distance from the earth's centre.

In the British system the standard of mass is *one pound*, and

$$1 \text{ pound} = 453 \cdot 39 \text{ grammes}$$

approximately. A piece of platinum whose mass is one pound is kept as a standard.

18.4 Units of force

Having defined masses of one kilogramme and one pound, we next have to consider the units in which the force must be expressed in order to make the equation $F = ma$ true.

A *newton* (abbreviation N) is defined as the force which will give to a mass of one kilogramme an acceleration of one metre per second per second. Thus if F is the force in newton, m the mass in kilogramme and a the acceleration in metre per second per second, we have $F = ma$. Hence a force of 10N acting on a mass of 5 kg in a certain direction will give it an acceleration of 2 m/s² in that direction. The newton is called an *absolute* unit of force.

A mass of one kilogramme falling vertically under gravity has acceleration g (=9·81 m/s² approximately), therefore the force acting on it is g newton. This force is the weight of the body and is called 1 kilogramme force or 1 kilogramme weight (abbreviations kgf or kg wt). This is called a *gravitational* unit of force since it is not independent of the local gravitational attraction.

Therefore 1 kgf = g newton
= 9·81 N, approximately.

Thus, to find the acceleration due to a force F kgf we must first bring the force to newton and write

$$Fg = ma. \tag{18.3}$$

This is the form of equation to be used when the force F is expressed in gravitational units.

The *Système International* (SI), which is recommended by international bodies for eventual adoption by all countries, takes as basic units in dynamics the newton, the kilogramme and the metre and envisages the eventual exclusion of other basic units. Previously the metric system had used the *dyne* as the unit of force, the gramme as the unit of mass and the centimetre as the unit of length, so that F dynes gives to a mass of m grammes an acceleration of a cm/s² in accordance with the equation $F = ma$. A little consideration will show that

$$1 \text{ dyne} = 10^{-5} \text{ newton.}$$

In the British system the absolute unit of force is the *poundal* (pdl) defined as the force required to give a mass of one pound an acceleration of one foot per second per second in accordance with the formula

$F = ma$. The corresponding gravitational unit is the *pound force* or *pound weight* (lbf or lb wt) and

$$1 \text{ lbf} = g \text{ pdl}$$
$$= 32 \text{ pdl (approximately)}$$

if g is taken as 32 ft/s.

Note that 1 pdl $= 0.138$ N and 1 lbf $= 4.448$ N (approximately).

18.5 Motion of a rigid body

If all the particles of a rigid body have the same acceleration a and the force on a particle of mass m_1 of the body is F_1 we have $F_1 = m_1a$. A similar equation holds for every particle of the body and, adding these equations for all the particles, we have

$$\Sigma F_1 = (\Sigma m_1)a. \tag{18.4}$$

Here, Σm_1 is the sum of the masses of all the particles and is therefore the mass of the body, which we denote by M. ΣF_1 is the sum of all the forces, both external and internal, which act on particles in the direction of the acceleration. Since the internal forces occur in equal and opposite pairs (by Newton's third law) their sum is zero, and hence ΣF_1, denoted by F, is the sum of the external forces acting on the body. Thus

$$F = Ma, \tag{18.5}$$

and this basic equation applies to the motion of a rigid body all of whose particles have the same acceleration.

Example 1. *An engine exerting a constant tractive force hauls six 10 tonne trucks (1 tonne = 1000 kg) on the level against a resistance of 6 kgf per tonne and gives them an acceleration of $3cm/s^2$. If one truck is uncoupled and the tractive force is unaltered find the new acceleration of the remaining trucks.*

Since the acceleration is 0.03 m/s² and the mass 6×10^4 kg the accelerating force is

$$F = 6 \times 10^4 \times 0.03 = 1800 \text{ N}.$$

The resistance $= 6 \times 60 \text{ kgf} = 360g = 3531.6 \text{ N}.$

The engine pull $= 1800 + 3531.6 = 5331.6 \text{ N}.$

The resistance to 5 trucks $= 300 \text{ kgf} = 2943 \text{ N}.$

The net accelerating force $= 2388.6 \text{ N}.$

The new mass accelerated $= 5 \times 10^4 \text{ kg}.$

The new acceleration $= \dfrac{2388.6}{5 \times 10^4} = 0.0478 \text{ m/s}^2.$

18.6 The inclined plane

Consider a particle of mass m kilogramme on a smooth plane inclined at an angle α to the horizontal (Fig. 186). The only forces acting on the particle are its weight, mg newton, and the reaction of the plane on the particle, R newton (say). These forces combine to give a force $(R - mg \cos \alpha)$ newton perpendicular to the plane and $mg \sin \alpha$ newton down the plane. Since the acceleration perpendicular to the plane is zero we have

$$R - mg \cos \alpha = 0,$$

and, if a is the acceleration down the plane in metres/s^2

$$mg \sin \alpha = ma,$$

so that $a = g \sin \alpha$.

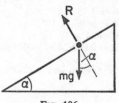

FIG. 186

If the inclined plane is rough and the coefficient of friction is μ, we have in addition, if we assume the body to be in motion, a frictional force μR acting up the plane. In this case

$$R - mg \cos \alpha = 0,$$
$$mg \sin \alpha - \mu R = ma,$$

and hence

$$a = g(\sin \alpha - \mu \cos \alpha).$$

If $\mu \cos \alpha$ were greater than $\sin \alpha$, this expression would give a negative acceleration. In fact, the acceleration would be zero, for the friction would not be limiting but only sufficient to prevent motion. Hence, for the particle to slide down the plane we must have $\mu < \tan \alpha$ or, if $\mu = \tan \lambda$ where λ is the angle of friction, $\lambda < \alpha$, that is the angle of friction must be less than the angle of slope of the plane.

Example 2. *A body is hung from a spring balance suspended from the roof of a lift. When the lift is descending with uniform acceleration 90 cm/s^2, the balance indicates a load of 10 kg. When the lift is ascending with uniform acceleration x cm/s^2 the reading is 12 kg. Find the value of x.*

In each case the body moves under the action of two forces, its weight and the pull of the balance shown by the indicated weight.
This if m kg be the mass of the body, when descending

$$mg - 10g = m \times 0.9,$$

when ascending

$$12g - mg = m \cdot x/100.$$

From the first equation $m = \dfrac{10g}{g - 0.9} = 11.01$

and hence

$$x = \frac{12 - 11.01}{11.01} g = 0.88 \ m/s^2 = 88 \ cm/s^2$$

Example 3. *An engine exerts a force of 3.75×10^3 kgf on a train of mass 2.4×10^5 kg and draws it up a slope of 1 in 120 against track resistance of 7 kgf per 1000 kg. Find the acceleration. Find also the braking force required on the return journey with steam shut off to prevent the acceleration exceeding 0.2 cm/s^2.*

The component of the train's weight down the track is $2.4 \times 10^5 \times \sin \alpha$, where $\sin \alpha = 1/120$, so that

$$\text{slope resistance} = 2.4 \times 10^5 \times 9.81/120 = 1.962 \times 10^4 \text{ N}$$
$$\text{track resistance} = 7 \times 240 \times 9.81 = 1.648 \times 10^4 \text{ N}$$
$$\text{engine pull} = 3.75 \times 10^3 \times 9.81 = 3.679 \times 10^4 \text{ N}$$
$$\text{net accelerating force} = 0.069 \times 10^4 \text{ N}$$
$$\text{mass accelerated} = 24 \times 10^4 \text{ kg}$$
$$\text{acceleration} = 0.069/24 = 0.0029 \text{ m/s}^2.$$

On the return journey let P newton be the braking force required to keep the acceleration to 0.002 m/s^2.
Then

$$-P + 1.962 \times 10^4 - 1.648 \times 10^4 = 24 \times 10^4 \times 0.002$$
$$P \times 10^{-4} = 0.314 - 0.048 = 0.266$$
$$P = 2660 \text{ N}.$$

18.7 Motion of connected masses

We now consider the motion of two or more masses connected by a light inextensible string so that their displacements, velocities and accelerations are equal. The masses may lie on a plane surface or they may hang vertically with the string passing over a smooth pulley. Because of its negligible mass no force is required to move the string and the tension will be the same throughout its length. The accelerations of the masses are related by the fact of their being connected by the string and, if the equation of motion $F = ma$ is written down for each mass, the tension T in the string can be eliminated between the two equations and the accelerations found. The acceleration of either particle being known the tension in the string is easily found.

Example 4. *A light inelastic string passes over a fixed smooth peg. At each end of the string is attached a scale-pan of mass 1 g. A 2 g weight is placed in one scale-pan and two 2 g weights in the other. The system is released from rest with the scale-pans hanging vertically. Calculate the acceleration of the system, the tension in the string, the thrusts the weights exert on each scale-pan and the reaction between the two 2 g weights in the second scale-pan.* [L.U.]

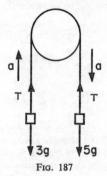

Fig. 187

Let a cm/s^2 be the downward acceleration of one pan and the upward acceleration of the other (Fig. 187). Let T dynes be the tension in the string. Applying
the equation $F = ma$ to each pan we have

$$5g - T = 5a,$$
$$T - 3g = 3a.$$

Adding, we find $a = \frac{1}{4}g = 245$ cm/s^2 and hence, substituting for a in either
equation, $T = 3679$ dynes.

Let R_1 and R_2 gmf be the reactions of the pans on the weights on the two sides
and R_3 the reaction between the two weights on the right-hand side.

Applying the equation $F = ma$ to each of the weights separately we have

$$R_1g - 2g = 2a,$$
$$4g - R_2g = 4a,$$
$$2g - R_3g = 2a,$$

and hence $R_1 = 2 \cdot 5$, $R_2 = 3$, $R_3 = 1 \cdot 5$.

Example 5. *A mass $3m$ is connected by a light inextensible string over a smooth fixed
pulley to a movable smooth pulley of mass m over which passes a second light
inextensible string with masses m and $2m$ attached to its ends. Find the acceleration
of each mass when the system is released and the tensions in the strings.* [O.C.]

Let the masses be in kilogrammes and let T newton be the tension in the first
string and T_1 the tension in the second (Fig. 188). Let a be the upward acceleration of the $3m$ mass and the downward acceleration of the movable pulley;

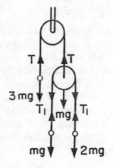

FIG. 188

let a_1 be the downward acceleration of the mass $2m$ and the upward acceleration of the mass m with respect to the movable pulley. Then the total downward acceleration of the $2m$ mass is $a + a_1$ and of the mass m, $a - a_1$.

The forces acting on the masses are

on $3m$,	$T - 3mg$ upwards,
on the pulley,	$2T_1 + mg - T$ downwards,
on $2m$,	$2mg - T_1$ downwards,
on m,	$mg - T_1$ downwards.

Applying the formula $F = ma$ to each mass and to the movable pulley we have

$$T - 3mg = 3ma,$$
$$2T_1 + mg - T = ma,$$
$$2mg - T_1 = 2m(a + a_1),$$
$$mg - T_1 = m(a - a_1).$$

Addition of all four equations and division by m gives

$$g = 7a + a_1.$$

Subtraction of the last two equations gives

$$g = a + 3a_1.$$

Hence, $a = \frac{1}{10}g$, $a_1 = \frac{3}{10}g$, $T = 3\cdot3\ mg$, $T_1 = 1\cdot2\ mg$.

Exercises 18 (a)

1. On a level track the acceleration of a train, consisting of an engine of mass 200 tonnes and a coach of mass 70 tonnes is 3 cm/s². The resistances to the engine and coach are 7 and 5 kgf per tonne respectively. Find the tractive force of the engine and the tension of the coupling between engine and coach. (1 tonne = 1000 kg.) [O.C.]

2. A particle is projected with velocity u from A up the line of greatest slope of a rough plane inclined at α to the horizontal, and at the same time a second particle slides from rest at a distance a from A, the angle of friction λ being less than α. The particles collide at distance $\frac{1}{2}a$ from A. Prove that $u^2 = ag \sin^2 \alpha \cos \lambda / \sin (\alpha - \lambda)$. [O.C.]

3. A and B are two points d apart on a rough plane inclined at 30° to the horizontal, B being above A on a line of greatest slope. A particle P of mass m is placed at B. Prove that if the coefficient of friction is $\sqrt{3}/6$, P moves down the plane with acceleration $\frac{1}{4}g$. P is now attached to one end of a light inextensible string and a particle Q of mass M is attached to the other end; P is placed at A and the string passes over a small smooth pulley at the top of the plane in AB produced, with Q hanging vertically. The system is released and P reaches B with acceleration $\frac{1}{4}g$. Prove that $M = \frac{4}{3} m$. When P reaches B the string is cut. Find the velocity of P on its return to A. [O.C.]

4. A balloon weighing 500 kg is descending at a steady speed of 3 m/s and is 80 m above the ground when 60 kg of ballast is thrown out. Find the acceleration with which the balloon begins to rise and its height when the ballast reaches the ground.

5. A bullet weighing 30 g is fired into a fixed block of wood with a velocity of 294 metres per second and is brought to rest in 1/150 s. Find the resistance exerted by the wood, supposing it to be uniform. [O.C.]

6. A ship of 10 000 tonnes slows, with engines stopped, from 6 knots to 5 knots in a distance of 30 m; assuming the resistance to be uniform, calculate its value. [L.U.]

7. A and B are two particles of mass m and $2m$ respectively lying on a rough horizontal table and connected by a taut light inextensible string; B is connected to a particle C, of mass $3m$, by a similar string which passes over a small fixed smooth pulley at the edge of the table, C hanging vertically and in the vertical plane through AB. If the coefficient of friction between the table and each of the particles A and B is $\frac{1}{2}$, prove that C descends 1·226 m in the first second of its motion. [O.C.]

8. A cord passes over a smooth fixed pulley and supports at one end a mass of 4 kg and at the other end a smooth movable pulley of mass 1 kg. A cord over this pulley supports at one end a mass of 1 kg and at the other end a mass of M kg. The system is released from rest with the masses hanging vertically. Determine M if the 4 kg mass remains at rest. The mass M is removed and the loose end of the cord fastened to a fixed point, the cord being vertical. If the rest of the system is unchanged determine the acceleration of the 4 kg mass when released. [L.U.]

9. A particle of mass 3 kg lies on a rough horizontal table and a taut inextensible string attached to the particle passes over a smooth pulley at the edge of the table and carries a mass of 5 kg hanging vertically. If the system moves from rest and each particle has acceleration 4 m/s² find the coefficient of friction between the first particle and the table. [L.U.]

10. Two scale pans each weighing 20 g are connected by a light inextensible string which passes over a small smooth fixed peg, and masses of 180 and 200 g are placed one in each pan. Find the acceleration of the system when it is released and the reactions between each pan and the mass it carries. [L.U.]

11. Planes inclined at θ and ϕ respectively to the horizontal meet in a crest and AP and BP are lines of greatest slope on the planes. Particles X and Y, of masses m and M respectively, are attached to the ends of a string which passes over a smooth pulley at P and are placed with the string taut on AP and BP respectively. If λ is the angle of friction on each plane, prove that Y will move downwards if

$$M \sin (\phi - \lambda) > m \sin (\theta + \lambda)$$

and find its acceleration. [O.C.]

12. A particle P, of mass 2 kg, is placed on a rough horizontal table at O; a string attached to P passes over a small smooth pulley A at the edge of the table and carries a particle Q of mass 4 kg hanging vertically. The system is released when P is 1 m from A. If the coefficient of friction on the table is $\frac{1}{2}$, prove that P reaches A after 0·64 sec. Prove also that when the particles have been moving for $\frac{1}{4}$ sec the speed of their centre of mass is 0·914 m/s.

13. A light inextensible string passing over a smooth peg O carries a particle A of mass M at one end and a small smooth pulley B of mass m at the other end; a similar string over the pulley carries particles C and D of masses $2m$ and m at its ends. The pulley B is x below O and C is y

below B. Write down equations of motion of each particle and of the pulley. When the system is released with the strings taut A ascends with acceleration $\frac{1}{3}g$. Prove that $M = 11m/6$.   [O.C.]

14. A light string $ABCD$ has one end fixed at A, and, passing under a movable pulley of mass M at B and over a fixed pulley at C carries a mass m at D. The parts of the string are supposed vertical. Show that M descends with acceleration $(M - 2m)g/(M + 4m)$.   [O.C.]

15. A force equal to a weight of 1 kilogramme acts for 3 seconds on a mass of 5 kilogrammes. Find the velocity produced and the space passed over.   [L.U.]

18.8 Work done by a force

The work done by a constant force F acting on a particle while it moves from a position O to a position A, where the direction of the force makes an angle θ with the line OA (Fig. 189), is defined as

$$W = F \times OA \times \cos \theta. \tag{18.6}$$

The work done is therefore the product of the resolved part of F along OA and OA; it is also the product of the force F and the projection of

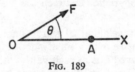

Fig. 189

OA on the line of action of the force. If $\theta = \frac{1}{2}\pi$, W is zero and if $\cos \theta$ is negative W is negative.

We note that W is, in fact (see § 6.8), the scalar product of the vectors representing the force and the displacement, and we may write

$$W = \mathbf{F} \cdot \mathbf{OA}. \tag{18.7}$$

Work being the product of a force and a distance, the units of work will be *newton-metres* in the SI system and a newton-metre is called a *joule* (symbol J). A former measure in the metric system was the *dyne-centimetre*, called an *erg*, and 1 erg $= 10^{-7}$ joule. The corresponding unit in the British system is the foot-poundal; the unit foot-pound (ft lbf) is still widely used. We have

$$1 \text{ ft pdl} = 0 \cdot 0421 \text{ J}$$
$$1 \text{ ft lbf} = 1.356 \text{ J}.$$

If the force F is a variable one, the element of work done by it in an infinitesimal displacement δx alonn the line OX is $\delta W = F \cos \theta \, \delta x$. The work done in a finite displacement from x_1 to x_2 along OX is then

$$W = \int_{x_1}^{x_2} F \cos \theta \, dx. \tag{18.8}$$

As an example of this we shall show that the work done in stretching an elastic string is the product of the extension and the mean of the initial and final tensions.

Let λ be the modulus, a the unstretched length and T the tension in the string when its extension is x. Then

$$T = \frac{\lambda}{a} x.$$

Then using (18.8) with $\theta = 0$ and $\cos \theta = 1$, the work done in increasing the extension from x_1 to x_2 is W, where

$$W = \int_{x_1}^{x_2} T \, dx$$

$$= \frac{\lambda}{a} \int_{x_1}^{x_2} x \, dx$$

$$= \frac{\lambda}{2a} (x_2{}^2 - x_1{}^2)$$

$$= (x_2 - x_1) \frac{1}{2} \left(\frac{\lambda}{a} x_2 + \frac{\lambda}{a} x_1 \right), \qquad (18.9)$$

and this is the product of the extension and the mean tension.

Example 6. *A car of mass* 1000 *kg accelerates uniformly from rest to acquire a velocity of* 50 *km/h on a level road in a distance of* 250 *m against frictional and other resistances of* 30 *kgf. Find the work done by the engine.*

The constant acceleration a is given by

$$\left(\frac{50 \times 1000}{3600} \right)^2 = 2a \times 250,$$

so that

$$a = 0 \cdot 386 \text{ m/s}^2.$$

The force required to give this acceleration is

$$F = 1000 \times 0 \cdot 386 = 386 \text{ N}.$$

The total force required is therefore $386 + 30 \times 9 \cdot 81$ N and the work done is

$$W = 680 \cdot 3 \times 250 = 1 \cdot 7 \times 10^5 \text{ J}.$$

18.9 Work done in lifting a body

We shall now prove that the work done against gravity in lifting a body depends only on the height through which its centre of gravity is raised.

Let $w_1, w_2, \ldots$ be the weights of typical particles of the body and suppose that these particles are raised from height $x_1, x_2, \ldots$ to height $y_1, y_2, \ldots$ above some standard position. The height $\bar{x}$ of the centre of gravity of the body before it is lifted and the height $\bar{y}$ afterwards are given by

$$W\bar{x} = w_1x_1 + w_2x_2 + \ldots,$$
$$W\bar{y} = w_1y_1 + w_2y_2 + \ldots,$$

where W is the total weight. The total work done against gravity is

$$w_1(y_1 - x_1) + w_2(y_2 - x_2) + \ldots$$
$$= (w_1y_1 + w_2y_2 + \ldots) - (w_1x_1 + w_2x_2 + \ldots)$$
$$= W(\bar{y} - \bar{x}),$$

and this is the product of the weight and the height through which the centre of gravity is raised. Thus the work done depends only on the initial and final height of the centre of gravity and is independent of the path followed by the individual particles.

Example 7. *A right circular cone of weight W, base radius a and height h, rests with a generator in contact with a horizontal plane. Find the work done in raising it so that its base is in contact with the plane.*

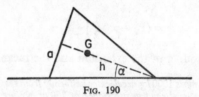

FIG. 190

Let α be the semivertical angle of the cone, so that $\tan \alpha = a/h$ (Fig. 190). Initially the centre of gravity, which is $\frac{3}{4}h$ from the vertex, is at a height $\frac{3}{4}h \sin \alpha$ above the plane and, when raised, it is at a height $\frac{1}{4}h$ above the plane. Therefore the work done is

$$W(\tfrac{1}{4}h - \tfrac{3}{4}h \sin \alpha)$$
$$= \tfrac{1}{4}Wh \left\{1 - \frac{3a}{\sqrt{(a^2 + h^2)}}\right\}.$$

18.10 Work done by a couple

If a couple whose moment is M acts on a rigid body, no work is done by the couple when the body moves without rotation, but if the body rotates through a small angle $\delta\theta$ the work done is $M\delta\theta$.

Let F be the magnitude of each force of the couple acting at a distance d apart, so that $M = Fd$. Let the forces act on particles A and B of the body (Fig. 191). If the body moves without rotation so that A moves to A', then B moves to B' where BB' is equal and parallel to AA' so that the work done by one force F in the displacement AA' is equal and opposite to the work done by the other force F in the displacement BB'. Thus the total work done is zero.

If now the body rotates so that AB is turned through a small angle $\delta\theta$ to the position AB' (Fig. 192), then B has a small displacement

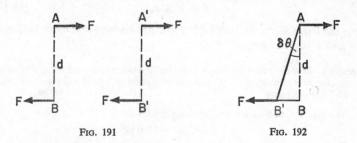

FIG. 191   FIG. 192

relative to A of $BB' = d\delta\theta$ to the first order of small quantities and the element of work done is

$$\delta W = Fd\delta\theta = M\delta\theta.$$

Thus the work done by the couple in a finite rotation of the body through an angle α is

$$W = \int_0^\alpha Md\theta, \qquad (18.10)$$

and, if M is constant,

$$W = M\alpha. \qquad (18.11)$$

18.11 Power

Power is defined as the rate at which work is done. Thus if 30 joule of work is done in 2 seconds the average power is 15 joule per second (15 J/s). A power of 1 joule per second is called a *watt* (symbol W). This is a small unit and that most commonly met is the *kilowatt* which is 1000 W (symbol kW).

The British unit of power is the *horse-power* (abbreviation h.p.), which is defined as a rate of 550 ft lbf/s or 33,000 ft lbf/minute. This represents a rate of working which a strong horse might be able to maintain, for example, when moving steadily at 10 ft/s and exerting a tractive force of 55 lbf.

We have

$$1 \text{ horse-power} = 746 \text{ watt}$$
$$1 \text{ kilowatt} \quad = 1\cdot34 \text{ horse-power}.$$

The French *cheval-vapeur* (symbol C.V.) raises 75 kg through 1 metre in 1 second and is $75 \times 9\cdot81 = 735\cdot75$ W.

If the power is n watt when a force F newton is applied to a body at a point which moves along the line of action of the force at a steady speed of v metre per second, the power exerted in watt is

$$n = F \times v. \qquad (18.12)$$

Thus the force F can be found if n and v are known, and v can be found if n and F are known.

Example 8. *Find the power exerted by a locomotive which keeps a train of 200 tonnes moving at a constant speed of 72 km/h up a slope of 1 in 160 against resistances of 7 kgf per tonne.*

The resolved part of the weight along the track
$$= 2 \times 10^5/160 = 1250 \text{ kgf.}$$

The resistances
$$= 7 \times 200 = 1400 \text{ kgf.}$$

The total tractive force
$$= 2650 \text{ kgf} = 25\,996 \cdot 5 \text{ N.}$$

The work done per second
$$= 25\,996 \cdot 5 \times 20 = 519\,930 \text{ watt.}$$

The power
$$= 520 \text{ kW.}$$

Example 9. *A car of 1000 kg mass whose engine is working at a constant rate of 12 kW can travel at a maximum speed of 45 km/h up a hill of inclination α, where $\sin \alpha = 1/14$. If the resistance is unchanged and the engine works at the same rate, calculate the acceleration of the car up a hill of inclination β, where $\sin \beta = 1/20$, at the moment when the speed is 36 km/h.* [L.U.]

If the tractive force is P newton and the velocity is $12 \cdot 5$ m/s, we have from (18.12)

$$P = \frac{12\,000}{12 \cdot 5} = 960 \text{ N.}$$

The resolved part of the weight down the slope is $1000 \, g \sin \alpha = 700 \cdot 7$ N so that the balance of the tractive force goes to overcome a resistance of $259 \cdot 3$ N. On the second slope the speed is 10 m/s, so that the tractive force is 1200 N. The resolved part of the weight is now $9810/20 = 490 \cdot 5$ N so that the total force opposing motion is $749 \cdot 8$ N. The forward net force is then $450 \cdot 2$ N and the acceleration a is given by

$$450 \cdot 2 = 1000 \, a$$

giving
$$a = 0 \cdot 450 \text{ m/s.}$$

Example 10. *A car of mass 1000 kg tows a second car of equal mass at a uniform speed of 40 km/h on level ground; the resistance to motion of each is 50 kgf. Show that the rate of working is $10 \cdot 9$ kilowatts. The pull of the first car is gradually increased until the tow-rope breaks under a tension of 75 kgf. If the rate of working is then $21 \cdot 8$ kilowatts find how much further the second car then travels before it comes to rest.* [L.U.]

The total pull is 100 kgf when the speed is 40 km/h (100/9 m/s) so that the rate of working is

$$100 \times 9.81 \times \frac{100}{9} = 10.9 \text{ kilowatts.}$$

At the instant when the rope breaks the forward pull on each car will be 75 kg and since the rate of working is then 21·8 kilowatts we have, if v is the speed in m/s,

$$21.8 \times 10^3 = 150 \times 9.81 v,$$
$$v = 14.81 \text{ m/s} = 53.33 \text{ km/h.}$$

The second car is then retarded by the resistance of 50 kgf and the retardation a m/s² is given by

$$50 \times 9.81 = 1000a,$$
$$a = 0.4905.$$

The distance in which it comes to rest is given by the formula $v^2 = u^2 - 2ax$, and hence

$$\left(\frac{53.33 \times 10^3}{3600}\right)^2 = 0.981x,$$
$$x = 224 \text{ m.}$$

18.12 Efficiency

The power of an engine may be measured in two ways. In a piston engine, for example, the thrust of the expanding gases on the piston end can be measured during its motion and the work done by this thrust calculated. The rate at which this work is done is called the *indicated power* of the engine. There is always a loss of power, due to friction and other causes, between the piston and the rotating parts of the engine, and the power measured at a later stage, for example by a brake on the flywheel, gives what is called the *brake power* of the engine. The *efficiency* of the engine is the ratio of the brake power to the indicated power. The efficiency of any mechanical system may be measured in a similar way as the ratio of the output of work to the input of work. Thus, if a weight w is lifted by a pulley system through a height h, the work done is wh and this is the output of work. The input of work is then the work done in hauling on the rope that causes the system to move and, due to friction, this will usually be somewhat greater than the output.

Example 11. *Find the rate of working in kilowatt of an engine which can fill a cistern 70 m above the level of a river with 1.5×10^5 litres of water in 24 hours, assuming that a litre of water weighs 1 kg and that only two-thirds of the work actually done by the engine is available for raising the water.*

The rate at which work is being done in raising 1.5×10^5 kg of water through 70 m in 24 hours is

$$\frac{1.5 \times 10^5 \times 9.81 \times 70}{24 \times 60 \times 60} \text{ watt}$$
$$= 1.192 \text{ kilowatt.}$$

Since the efficiency of the system is ⅔, the power of the engine must be

$$1.192 \times \tfrac{3}{2} = 1.79 \text{ kilowatt.}$$

Exercises 18 (b)

1. A car travels at a uniform speed of 36 km/h on a level road when the engine is working at 8 kW. Prove that the frictional resistance is 800 N. If the total weight of the car is 1250 kg and the frictional resistance varies at the square of the speed find the power required for the car to travel at 18 km/h up a road inclined at $\sin^{-1}$ (0·05) to the horizontal.
   [L.U.]

2. A car of mass 2000 kg is travelling at 45 km/h up an incline of $\sin^{-1}$ (1/14), the resistance to motion being $15g$ N. Show that the engine is working at 19·36 kW. The car reaches level ground and the engine continues to work at the same rate. Assuming that the resistance is proportional to the square of the car's speed, find the maximum speed attainable.
   [L.U.]

3. A car of mass 1 tonne climbs a hill of gradient 1 in 10 at a steady speed of 45 km/h. If the engine is working at 15 kW calculate the road resistance. Assuming the road resistance varies as the square of the speed, find the maximum speed attainable on the level with the same power.
   [L.U.]

4. A car of mass 1000 kg tows a trailer of mass 750 kg. With the engine switched off, they run down a slope of $\sin^{-1}$ (1/112) with constant speed. Calculate the resistance to motion. When the car and trailer run on the level the engine develops 15 kW when the speed is 45 km/h, the resistances remaining unaltered. Calculate the acceleration at this speed and the pull in the tow bar.
   [L.U.]

5. A car of mass 1000 kg travels at a constant speed of 60 km/h on a level road when the engine works at 15 kW. Prove that the resistance to motion is $91·74g$ N. With the same rate of working and the same resistance the car ascends a road inclined at θ to the horizontal at a constant speed of 45 km/h. Find the value of $\sin \theta$.
   [L.U.]

6. A car weighing 840 kg freewheels down a slope of $\sin^{-1}$ (1/14) at uniform speed against road resistances. On level road the engine is switched on and the car accelerates at 2 m/s² from 50 km/h, the road resistances remaining the same. At what rate does the engine work?
   [L.U.]

7. A train weighing 300 tons, including the engine, has a maximum speed of 20 mile/h up an incline of 1°. If the engine can develop a maximum of 1000 h.p. show that the frictional resistance, assumed constant, is approximately 7000 lbf. Find the maximum speed on level ground assuming the frictional resistance to remain unaltered.
   [L.U.]

8. A motor-car of mass 1000 kg runs with constant speed with the brakes released and the engine shut off down a slope inclined to the horizontal at an angle $\sin^{-1}$ (1/20). If the same car ascends the slope at 40 km/h, determine the rate at which the engine must work. Find the acceleration when the car is moving on level ground at the same speed with the engine working at the same rate.
   [L.U.]

9. A cyclist with his machine weighs 100 kg. He free-wheels at uniform speed down a straight road inclined to the horizontal at $\sin^{-1}(1/80)$. Find the rate at which he must work if he cycles up the incline at a constant speed of 18 km/h. On a horizontal road, working at the same rate, the resistance to his motion being unchanged, find his maximum speed and his acceleration when his speed is 18 km/h.

10. A lorry of mass M tonnes, with its engine working at H kW, has a maximum speed on the level of u km/h. If the maximum speed up a road inclined at an angle α to the horizontal is v km/h when the rate of work and the resistance are unchanged, prove that $40H(u - v) = 109 Muv \sin \alpha$.

11. An 8-tonne truck, with the engine working at a constant rate of 20 kW, climbs a road with a gradient of 1 in 40, the resistance being $7g$ N per tonne. Find (a) the maximum speed v attained and (b) the acceleration when the speed is $\frac{1}{2}v$. [O.C.]

12. A man cycles up a hill of inclination α, where $\sin \alpha = \frac{1}{10}$, at a maximum speed of 10 km/h. The combined weight of the man and his bicycle is 100 kg and the resistance to motion is $5g$ N. What power is he developing? On level road he continues to work at the same rate, the resistance remaining unchanged. Find his initial acceleration and his maximum speed on the level. [L.U.]

13. A 500-h.p. locomotive draws a train weighing 200 tonnes (including the locomotive) against a constant resistance. The train can attain a maximum speed of 36 km/h up a slope and a maximum speed of 72 km/h down the same slope. Find the inclination of the slope and the maximum speed on the level. [L.U.]

14 A locomotive working at 500 h.p. pulls a train of 200 tons (including the locomotive) along a level track, the resistance to motion being 16 lbf per ton. When the speed is 30 mile/h, determine its acceleration. At what steady speed will the locomotive pull the same train up an incline of 1 in 100 with the same expenditure of power against the same resistance? [L.U.]

15. A train of 3×10^5 kg is ascending a track at an inclination of 1 in 250 and the frictional and other resistances are $2000g$ N. Find the highest speed of the train when the engine is working at 500 kW. If the engine is also working at this rate when the speed if 30 km/h, find the acceleration. [L.U.]

18.13 Kinetic energy

The *kinetic energy* of a particle is defined as the quantity $\frac{1}{2}mv^2$, where m is the mass of the particle and v its velocity.

If a constant force F acts on a particle along a straight line as the particle moves a distance x along the line, the work done by the force is Fx. The acceleration, which is constant, is given by the equation

$F = ma$, m being the mass of the particle. The initial and final velocities during the motion are given by the formula $v^2 = u^2 + 2ax$, so that

$$\text{work done} = Fx$$
$$= max$$
$$= \tfrac{1}{2}mv^2 - \tfrac{1}{2}mu^2. \qquad (18.13)$$

Thus the work done is equal to the change of kinetic energy and equation (18.13) which expresses this fact is known as the *work equation*. The change of kinetic energy may, of course, be an increase or a decrease according as the work done is positive or negative.

The units in which kinetic energy is measured are the same as the units of work. Thus, if the force F is in absolute units, the units of kinetic energy will be absolute units of work such as joules. If the force F is in gravitational units, then in absolute units the force is Fg and

$$Fgx = \tfrac{1}{2}mv^2 - \tfrac{1}{2}mu^2,$$

so that if the work is expressed in gravitational units, such as m kgf, we have

$$Fx = \frac{1}{2}\frac{m}{g}v^2 - \frac{1}{2}\frac{m}{g}u^2. \qquad (18.14)$$

The kinetic energy in gravitational units is therefore $\dfrac{1}{2}\dfrac{m}{g}v^2$. When the work done is expressed in gravitational units, it is convenient to write w for m in the expression for the kinetic energy as a reminder and to write the work equation as

$$\text{work done} = \frac{w}{2g}v^2 - \frac{w}{2g}u^2. \qquad (18.15)$$

Example 12. *A bullet of mass 5 g moving with speed 400 m/s strikes a fixed block of wood and penetrates 15 cm. Find the resistance of the wood, assuming it to be uniform.*

The kinetic energy of the bullet
$$= \tfrac{1}{2} \times 5 \times 10^{-3} \times (400)^2$$
$$= 400 \text{ J.}$$

If the resistance offered by the wood is constant and equal to F newton, the work done against the bullet in its penetration

$$= F \times 0.15 \text{ J.}$$

This work changes the kinetic energy from its initial value to zero, therefore

$$0.15F = 400,$$

giving

$$F = 2667 \text{ N.}$$

When the force F varies in magnitude during the motion, the work done is

$$\int_0^x F\,dx = m\int_0^x a\,dx$$

$$= m\int_0^x v\,\frac{dv}{dx}\,dx = m\int_0^x v\,dv,$$

$$= m[\tfrac{1}{2}v^2]_0^x = \tfrac{1}{2}mv^2 - \tfrac{1}{2}mu^2,$$

so that the work equation still holds good.

The kinetic energy of a rigid body is the sum of the kinetic energies of its particles. Hence if a body is moving in a straight line, so that all its particles have the same velocity, its kinetic energy is

$$\Sigma\tfrac{1}{2}mv^2 = \tfrac{1}{2}v^2\Sigma m = \tfrac{1}{2}Mv^2,$$

where M is the total mass, and this change in kinetic energy is equal to the work done by the forces acting on the body.

18.14 Kinetic energy and power

In calculating the rate at which an engine is doing work we have to find the work done against resistances or against gravity in a given time. If the velocity changes during this time we must add the work done in increasing the kinetic energy or deduct the work done which represents a decrease of kinetic energy.

Example 13. *An engine in 7 seconds has raised a load of 1000 kg through a height of 1 metre and has communicated to it a speed of 3·5 m/s. At what average rate has it been working?*

The work done in lifting the weight $= 10^3 g = 9810$ J.
The kinetic energy imparted

$$= \frac{1}{2} \times 1000 \times (3·5)^2 = 6125 \text{ J}.$$

The total work done $= 15\,935$ J.
This work is done in 7 seconds so that the rate at which the engine is working

$$= \frac{15\,935}{7 \times 1000} = 2·276 \text{ kilowatts}.$$

Example 14. *An engine raises water from a reservoir to a height of 10 m and delivers it through a circular nozzle of diameter 10 cm at 9 m/s. If the efficiency of the engine is 20 per cent, find the power of the engine.*   [L.U.]

The mass of water delivered in each second is that contained in a tube 10 m long and of 10 cm diameter. Taking the density of water as 1000 kg/m³, this mass is

$$M = \pi\,(·05)^2 \times 10 \times 1000$$
$$= 78·54 \text{ kg}.$$

The work done in raising this mass of water through 10 m is
$$10Mg = 7705 \text{ J.}$$
The work done in giving this mass of water a velocity of 9 m/s is
$$\tfrac{1}{2}M \times 81 = 3181 \text{ J.}$$
The total work done per second is 10 866 J and the useful power is 10·87 kW. Since the efficiency is only 20 per cent the power of the engine must be 5 × 10·87 = 54·4 kW.

18.15 Potential energy

The *potential energy* of a particle is defined as the work which the forces acting on it would do if it moved from its given position to some standard position.

This if a particle of mass m kg is at a height h m above a table, and we take the surface of the table as the standard position, the force of gravity acting on the particle is mg newton and the work which this force would do as the particle fell to the table is mgh joule, and this is the potential energy of the particle. It is clear in this case that as the particle descends potential energy is lost and at the same time work is done by gravity and, in fact, at any stage the loss of potential energy is equal to the work actually done.

From the work equation we know that the increase of kinetic energy is equal to the work done, so that the increase of kinetic energy is equal to the loss of potential energy. In other words, the sum of the kinetic energy and the potential energy remains constant during descent. The equation based on this fact is known as the *energy equation* and is sometimes written as

$$K.E. + P.E. = \text{constant}, \tag{18.16}$$

where $K.E.$ stands for kinetic energy and $P.E.$ for potential energy. In this case, if v m/s is the velocity when the particle has fallen x m, the kinetic energy is $\tfrac{1}{2}mv^2$, the potential energy is $mg(h - x)$ and the energy equation is

$$\tfrac{1}{2}mv^2 + mg(h - x) = c \text{ (a constant).}$$

If the velocity is zero when x is zero the value of c must be mgh and the equation simplifies to

$$\tfrac{1}{2}mv^2 - mgx = 0,$$

so that

$$v^2 = 2gx.$$

Potential energy due to the force of gravity is the most commonly used form of potential energy, but there are other forms such as that of a stretched string where the potential energy is the work that would be done by the elasticity of the string as it returned to its natural length.

The potential energy of a body is, of course, the sum of the potential energies of its particles. We have seen in § 18.9 that the work done in lifting a rigid body is Wh, where W is its weight and h the height through which its centre of gravity has been raised. This is therefore its potential energy in the raised position if the old position is taken as the standard position.

The energy equation (18.16) is an expression of a fundamental scientific principle known as the *principle of conservation of energy* which states that the total amount of energy in the universe is constant. This does not, however, imply that the total amount of mechanical energy is constant since such energy may be converted by friction or the deformation of a body into other forms of energy such as heat or sound.

Example 15. *A light inextensible string passes over a small smooth pulley and carries masses of 4 kg and 6 kg at its ends. Find the velocity of the heavier mass when it has descended 2 m from rest.*

Let v m/s be the velocity of either mass when the 6 kg mass has descended x m from rest (Fig. 193). Then the kinetic energies of the masses are $\frac{1}{2} \times 4v^2$ and $\frac{1}{2} \times 6v^2$, and the total kinetic energy is $5v^2$.

If l is the length of the string, when the 6 kg mass is x below the pulley the 4 kg mass is $l - x$ below it. We can write the potential energies of the masses with reference to a standard level h below the pulley as $6g(h - x) + 4g(h - l + x)$, or taking the pulley as the standard level we put $h = 0$ and have for the potential energy $-6gx - 4g(l - x)$, the difference between the two expressions being constant.

In either case the energy equation is

$$5v^2 - 6gx - 4g(l - x) = c \text{ (a constant).}$$

Since $v = 0$ when $x = 0$, $c = -4gl$ and we find

$$v^2 = \tfrac{2}{5}gx,$$

giving, when $x = 2$, $v = 2 \cdot 80$ m/s.

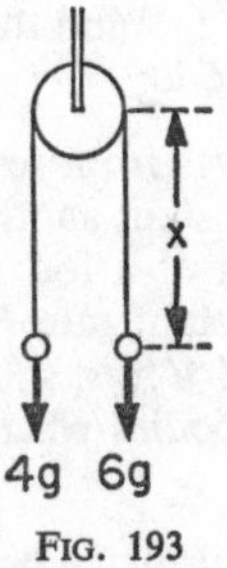

4g 6g

FIG. 193

Exercises 18 (c)

1. A train travelling at 63 km/h begins an ascent of 1 in 75. The tractive force during the ascent is constant and equal to $2 \cdot 5$ tonnes weight; the resistance is constant and equal to $1 \cdot 5$ tonnes weight, and the mass of the

whole train is 225 tonnes. Show that the train will come to a standstill after climbing for 1·76 km.

2. An army tank weighing 10,000 kg in surmounting an obstacle has its speed reduced from 30 km/h to 15 km/h and its centre of gravity raised by 1·2 m. Find the total loss of energy. [L.U.]

3. A motor car of mass 2000 kg arrives at the bottom of a hill 0·8 km long, which rises 1 in 125, with a speed of 30 km/h and arrives at the top with a speed of 15 km/h. If there is a retarding force due to friction of 14 kgf, calculate the work done by the engine in getting the car up the hill. [L.U.]

4. A motor car weighing 1000 kg starts up an incline at 18 km/h. The road rises 125 m in 1 km and at the end of that distance the speed has been reduced to 9 km/h. If the frictional resistances are 40 kgf, find the average power exerted, the time for the km being 4·5 min.

5. A man strikes a block with a 10 kg hammer 33 times a minute. If the velocity of the hammer on striking the block is 8 m/s and the hammer is reduced to rest after each blow, find the average power exerted by the man. [L.U.]

6. A car of mass 3000 kg will just run down a slope of angle $\sin^{-1}$ (1/20) under its own weight. Assuming that the forces resisting its motion are constant and that the engine exerts a constant tractive force, determine the power developed when a speed of 45 km/h is attained from rest on a level track in a time of 4 min. [L.U.]

7. Find the uniform force that will move a mass of 1 kg from rest through 1 m in 1 second. If this force is exerted while the mass moves 100 m from rest, find the work done by the force and the maximum power attained. [L.U.]

8. An engine, pumping water from a well 10 m deep, discharges 20 gallons/ second with a speed of 7 m/s. Find the power of the engine, given that 1 gallon of water weighs 4·5 kg. [O.C.]

9. A body of mass M kg moves from rest under the action of a constant force F kgf. At the same instant another body of the same mass moves from rest under the action of a force in a fixed horizontal direction, which does work at a constant rate P m kgf/s. If after T seconds the bodies have the same speed V m/s, show that $P = \frac{1}{2}FV$. Find the ratio of the speeds of the two bodies when they have been moving for $4T$ seconds. [L.U.]

10. A fire-engine raises water through a height of 10 m from a reservoir and delivers it at 15 m/s through a nozzle of cross-section 25 cm². Neglecting frictional losses, calculate the power at which the engine is working. [L.U.]

11. Find the power of a pump which in 1 min raises 1 m³ of water through 7 m, discharging it at a speed of 2 m/s. [O.C.]

12. The pump of a fire-fighting launch throws a jet of 6 cm diameter at a speed of 30 m/s from the nozzle which is 3 m above the water line. Find the power required to drive the pump. [L.U.]

13. A mass m rests on a smooth plane inclined at α to the horizontal. It is connected by a light inextensible string, parallel to a line of greatest slope, which passes over a smooth pulley at the top of the plane and carries a mass M hanging vertically. Find the velocity of the particle when it has moved a distance c from rest up the plane, assuming $M > m \sin \alpha$.

14. A mass of 3 kg is attached to the middle, and masses of 2 kg to the ends of a light inextensible string which is placed over two smooth pegs 4 m apart at the same level, the 3 kg mass being mid-way between the pegs. If the system is released, find how far the 3 kg mass descends before coming instantaneously to rest.

15. A uniform heavy chain of length $3a$ is placed over a smooth peg with lengths $2a$ and a hanging vertically and released from rest. Write down the kinetic and potential energies of the chain in terms of the velocity v and the length x of the longer section, and prove that $av^2 = \frac{2}{3}g(x^2 - 3ax + 2a^2)$. [O.C.]

Exercises 18 (d)

1. A train weighing 3×10^5 kg is travelling at 80 km/h and the frictional resistances to motion are 0·01 kgf/kg. The train slips a carriage weighing 10^4 kg. How far will the carriage go before coming to rest and what will then be the velocity of the train if the resistance to motion is unaltered?

2. An engine exerting a constant tractive force is pulling seven 10,000 kg trucks and giving them an acceleration of 3 cm/s² on the level the resistances being 0·008 kgf/kg. If one truck is uncoupled and the engine exerts the same tractive force, show that the acceleration is increased by 60 per cent.

3. A lorry travelling on the level at 30 km/h can be stopped by its brakes in 16 m. Find the speed from which it can be brought to rest in the same distance when descending a hill whose angle of slope is $\sin^{-1}(1/15)$.

4. A plumb-line in a ship is seen to be inclined at an angle of 1° 30' to the vertical. Find the acceleration of the ship in cm/s².

5. Find in N per tonne the force exerted by the brakes of a train travelling at 90 km/h, which will bring it to rest in 1 km, and find the time during which the brakes act. [O.C.]

6. The diameter of the low-pressure cylinder of a marine engine is 1·1 m, the average speed of the piston is 250 m/min and the average pressure of the steam on the piston is 22×10^4 N/m². What is the indicated power of the engine? [L.U.]

7. A man with his bicycle has mass 100 kg. He begins to ascend an incline of 1 in 10 at a speed of 25 km/h and with uniform retardation. He has to dismount when his speed is not greater than 5 km/h. If he works at an average rate of 0·15 kW, how far will he ascend? How far would he have ascended if he had not worked at all ?   [L.U.]

8. A light inextensible string has one end attached to the under-side of the edge of a smooth table. It passes through a small smooth ring of weight W and has its other end attached to a weight W' on the table. If the system is held with the string taut and then released, prove that W' will move with acceleration $2Wg/(W + 4W')$.   [O.C.]

9. A particle held at rest on a smooth table is attached by a light inextensible string to a second particle of the same mass which hangs over the edge of the table, the string being taut and at right angles to the edge. If the particle on the table is released, find its acceleration.   [O.C.]

10. Two particles of masses 3 kg and 5 kg respectively are connected by a light inextensible string. The 3 kg particle lies on a plane inclined at 30° to the horizontal, the coefficient of friction between the particle and plane being $\frac{1}{5}$. The string lies parallel to a line of greatest slope and passes over a pulley at the top so that the 5 kg mass hangs vertically. Find the tension in the string when the system is released and the velocity after half a second. If the string then breaks, find the distance the 3 kg mass travels up the plane before stopping.

11. Bodies P and R of masses 3 kg and 1 kg respectively lie on a smooth table joined by a light string which passes through two holes in the table and supports a light pulley Q which carries a load of 6 kg. The hanging parts of the string are vertical. Prove that the magnitudes of the initial accelerations of P, Q, R are in the ratio $1:2:3$. Find the velocities acquired by P, Q, R in the first t seconds of the motion and verify the energy equation at this instant.   [L.U.]

12. A particle of mass 6 kg lies on a rough horizontal table, and a taut string from the particle passes over a smooth pulley at the edge of the table and carries a mass of 10 kg which hangs freely. If the system starts from rest and each particle has acceleration 4 m/s², find the coefficient of friction.   [L.U.]

13. A railway carriage runs down an incline of 1 in 250 and at the foot runs along the level. Find how far it will run on the level if its speed was constant at 20 km/h on the incline and the resistance is unchanged on the level.   [L.U.]

14. A man carrying a bag which has a mass of 30 kg steps into a lift. The lift moves upwards a certain distance with constant acceleration and then comes to rest under its own weight after travelling altogether a distance of 30 m. If the man can only exert a force of 50 kgf, find the shortest time in which the ascent can be made if he holds the bag all the time.   [L.U.]

15. The resistance to a train of 220 tons is 12 lbf per ton. On the level it acquires a speed of 45 mile/h from rest in 5 min. Find the least h.p. of the engine, assuming that the pull of the engine is constant. With this h.p. find the maximum speed of the train up a slope of $\sin^{-1}$ (1/150).
[L.U.]

16. A car of mass 2500 kg is accelerating at 1 m/s² up an incline of 1 in 50, the resistance being $30g$ N. Find the power exerted when the speed is 20 km/h.
[L.U.]

17. A mass of 10⁴ kg is drawn up a slope of 1 in 96 against a resistance of $75g$ N. If 30 kW is used, find the greatest speed that the mass can have.
[L.U.]

18. A train is running at 45 km/h when it is at a distance of 0·5 km from a station. Steam is then shut off and the train runs against a uniform resistance equal to 1/100 of the weight of the train. If the uniform brake force which can be exerted is equal to 1/10 of the weight of the train, find how far from the station the brake must be applied so that the train may stop there.
[L.U.]

19. A car has mass 1500 kg and the greatest driving force that can be exerted on it is 100 kgf. The resistance due to friction is $26 + v^2/128$ kgf, where v is the speed in km/h. Calculate the greatest speed at which it can be driven up a slope of 1 in 40, and the power developed when running at a steady speed of 80 km/h on the level.
[L.U.]

20. A car has a maximum speed of 100 km/h on the level and the engine is then working at 65 h.p. Calculate the total resistance to motion. If the mass of the car is 1000 kg and the tractive force remains unaltered, and the resistance varies as the square of the speed, find the greatest slope up which a speed of 80 km/h could be maintained.
[L.U.]

21. The total mass of a train is 600 tonnes. Find the greatest power the engine can develop on the level if the greatest speed is then 80 km/h and the resistances to motion are 5 kgf/tonne. Find also the maximum speed v km/h attainable up a slope of 1 in 80 if the horse-power then developed is the horse-power on the level multiplied by $(1 - v/32)$.
[L.U.]

22. A train travelling uniformly on the level at 60 mile/h begins an ascent of 1 in 50. The tractive force due to adhesion has a maximum value of 3 tonf, the resistances are 30 cwt and the weight of the whole train is 200 tons. Show that it cannot surmount the incline if this exceeds 11/6 miles in length, and find the horse-power exerted by the engine, (i) just before beginning the ascent, (ii) just after.
[L.U.]

23. A 10 ton tram-car arrives at the foot of an incline of 1 in 15 at a speed of 15 mile/h and commences to climb with a constant tractive effort of 1 tonf, the frictional resistance being 16 lbf/ton. Find the speed of the car and the effective horse-power after 30 seconds. Calculate also the work done by the motors during this time.
[L.U.]

24. A body slides down a rough plane ($\mu = \frac{1}{4}$) a distance of 100 m, the inclination of the plane being 28°. It then runs over a short curved piece and up an equally rough plane inclined at 35° to the horizontal. Find how far it runs up this plane.

25. Three equal weights are attached to the middle and ends of a light cord which is placed over two smooth pulleys at the same level so that the central weight hangs symmetrically between the pulleys and the others hang vertically. If the central weight is pulled down until its connecting cord makes angles of 50° with the horizontal and then let go, find what the angles will be when the weights next come to momentary rest.

[L.U.]

CHAPTER 19

IMPULSE; IMPACT; UNITS

19.1 Introduction

In the previous chapter we have discussed the application of Newton's laws to bodies for finite intervals of time. We shall now consider the application of these laws to what is called impulsive motion in which a large force acts for a very brief time interval. In such cases measurement of the magnitude of the force acting on the body is often impossible, but it is generally possible to measure the resulting change in the momentum of the body. This leads to the enunciation of the important principle of conservation of linear momentum which has many practical applications.

A full discussion of the behaviour of two bodies which collide requires a knowledge of the elasticity of the bodies and of the extent to which their shapes are altered during the collision. However, a simple approximate solution gives the resulting change in the relative motion of the bodies in terms of a coefficient of restitution, and we shall see how this can be applied to the impact of a body with a fixed surface and to the direct impact of two spheres.

In the final section of this chapter a table is given of the quantities used in dynamics and of the units in which these quantities are usually expressed, and rules are given for changing from one system of units to another.

19.2 Impulse and momentum

If a constant force F acts on a particle of mass m for time t, and in that time increases its velocity from u to v along the line of action of the force, we have

$$F = ma,$$

$$v = u + at,$$

so that

$$Ft = mat = mv - mu,$$

$$= \text{change of momentum.} \tag{19.1}$$

If the force F is of variable magnitude,

$$F = m \frac{dv}{dt},$$

$$\int_0^t F \, dt = m \int_0^t \frac{dv}{dt} \, dt,$$

$$= m \, [v]_0^t,$$

$$= mv - mu,$$

$$= \text{change of momentum.} \qquad (19.2)$$

These formulae give the change of momentum for all values of t for which the force F is defined and apply to the motion of a rigid body, in which case F is the external force acting on the body.

The quantity $\int F \, dt$, or Ft if F is constant, is called the *impulse* acting on the particle or body. An impulse is a product of force and time and is therefore measured in newton-seconds or in kgf-seconds, or in corresponding British units. The momentum is measured in the same units as impulse and, with m in kg and v in m/s, the momentum is mv newton-seconds. If F_1 is a force measured in kgf, $F_1 g = ma$ and

$$F_1 g t = mv - mu$$

so that

$$F_1 t = \frac{m}{g} v - \frac{m}{g} u. \qquad (19.3)$$

In this form the impulse is in kgf seconds and the momentum is also in kgf seconds. It is convenient to write w for m in this equation as a reminder that gravitational units are being used and to write

$$F_1 t = \frac{w}{g} v - \frac{w}{g} u. \qquad (19.4)$$

The concept of an impulse is particularly useful when dealing with a large force acting for a very short time, as in the case of a bat striking a ball, a hammer hitting a nail or a charge of ammunition giving velocity to a bullet or shell. In these cases it is usually impossible to obtain accurate measurements of the magnitude of the force or its duration, but the magnitude of the impulse can be found by measuring the change of momentum.

Since velocity is a vector quantity momentum is also a vector quantity with a definite direction, and impulse, being equal to change of momentum is also a vector quantity.

19.3 Collision of particles

If two particles moving in a straight line collide, there is a brief period of contact. During this period each particle exerts on the other a certain force, which may vary in magnitude. At any instant the forces exerted by each particle on the other are, by Newton's third law, equal and opposite. Therefore, the impulses exerted by each particle on the other during the period of contact are equal and opposite.

It follows that the momentum imparted to one particle is equal in magnitude and opposite in direction to that imparted to the other. Hence, the total momentum gained by the two particles is zero.

Let m_1, m_2 be the masses of the particles, u_1, u_2 their velocities before collision and v_1, v_2 their velocities afterwards, all velocities being measured in the same direction in the same sense. Let I be the impulse on m_1 measured in the same sense, so that $-I$ is the impulse on m_2 in the same sense. Then

$$I = m_1v_1 - m_1u_1,$$
$$-I = m_2v_2 - m_2u_2,$$

so that

$$m_1v_1 - m_1u_1 + m_2v_2 - m_2u_2 = 0,$$

that is

$$m_1v_1 + m_2v_2 = m_1u_1 + m_2u_2. \tag{19.5}$$

This equation states that the total momentum in a given direction is the same after the collision as it was before the collision.

This leads to the principle of *conservation of linear momentum*, which states that the total momentum measured in any direction of a system of particles is unaltered by mutual collisions between the particles. This applies to the linear motion of rigid bodies during collision, the line of impact being perpendicular to their plane of contact during the collision. The time of contact is usually assumed to be small, so small that the effect of other forces, such as the force of gravity, which may be acting on the body during the collision can be neglected.

During a collision of two bodies there is always some deformation of their shape. This deformation usually causes the generation of heat, which is a form of energy, and this energy may be lost to the system. It is to be expected then that there will always be a loss of kinetic energy in a collision, and the principle of conservation of energy will not apply.

Example 1. *A railway truck of mass 8000 kg running at 6 km/h is overtaken by a truck of mass 12,000 kg running at 10 km/h. After impact the trucks begin to separate at 1 km/h. Find the speed of the trucks after impact and the loss of kinetic energy in the impact.*

Let v km/h be the speed of the heavier truck after impact, then the speed of the lighter truck will be $v + 1$ km/h. The total momentum after impact will be the same as that before and, since no other quantities are involved, we may write the momentum with the mass in thousands of kilogrammes and the velocity in kilometres per hour, giving

$$12v + 8(v + 1) = 12 \times 10 + 8 \times 6,$$

so that

$$v = 8 \text{ km/h,}$$
$$v + 1 = 9 \text{ km/h.}$$

The loss of kinetic energy is

$$\{\tfrac{1}{2} \times 12 \times 10^3(10^2 - 8^2) + \tfrac{1}{2} \times 8 \times 10^3(6^2 - 9^2)\} \left(\frac{10^3}{3600}\right)^2$$

$$= \frac{10^5}{36 \times 36} \{(6 \times 18 \times 2) - (4 \times 15 \times 3)\}$$

$$= 2 \cdot 78 \times 10^3 \text{ joule.}$$

Example 2. *A shell weighing 12 kg is fired with velocity 800 m/s from a gun barrel weighing 800 kg. Find the impulse caused by the explosion and the velocity of recoil of the barrel, assuming the recoil to be free. If this recoil is taken up by a buffer on the gun carriage which is fixed and the buffer exerts a constant force which brings the barrel to rest in a distance of 45 cm, find this force and also the time of recoil.*

The forward momentum given to the shell is

$$12 \times 800 = 9600 \text{ newton second,}$$

and this is the magnitude of the impulse. Let V m/s be the velocity of recoil of the barrel. Equating the backward momentum of the barrel to the forward momentum of the shell we have

$$800V = 9600,$$

so that

$$V = 12 \text{ m/s.}$$

Let F newton be the thrust of the buffer. This force destroys the kinetic energy of the barrel in a distance of 0·45 m, so that the work equation gives

$$F \times 0 \cdot 45 = \frac{1}{2} \times 800 \times 12^2$$

$$F = 128 \text{ kN.}$$

If the momentum of the barrel is destroyed in t seconds, we have

$$F \times t = 800 \times 12,$$

$$t = \frac{9600}{128\,000} = \frac{3}{40} \text{ seconds.}$$

Example 3. *A bullet of mass 30 g is fired horizontally into a small block of wood of mass 8 kg which is suspended by a string 2 m long. The bullet remains embedded in the wood and the block rises until the string makes an angle of 30° with the vertical. Find the velocity of the bullet.*

This is an example of a ballistic pendulum such as were at one time used to find the velocities of bullets and shells. Let V m/s be the velocity of the bullet before impact and v m/s the velocity of the bullet and block after impact. The momentum equation gives

$$30 \times V = 8030 \times v,$$

so that

$$v = \frac{3}{803} V.$$

Thus the velocity to be measured, that of the block, is considerably smaller than that of the bullet before impact. When the string turns through 30° the block rises a height $(2 - 2\cos 30°)$ m, and the work done against gravity is

$$8.03 \times 2 (1 - \cos 30°) = 2.152 \text{ m kgf.}$$

The kinetic energy of the block has been destroyed by this work, so that

$$\frac{1}{2} \times 8.03 \left(\frac{3V}{803}\right)^2 = 2.152 \times 9.81,$$

giving

$$V^2 = 2.152 \times 2 \times 109 \times 803,$$

$$V = 614 \text{ m/s.}$$

Example 4. *Two particles, A and B, each of mass 4 kg, are joined by a light inextensible string of length 2·5 m and are placed on a smooth horizontal table 1·5 m apart. A is projected along the table at right-angles to the line AB with velocity 10 m/s. Show that when the string tightens B begins to move with velocity 4 m/s. Find the loss of kinetic energy of the system when the string is taut.* [L.U.]

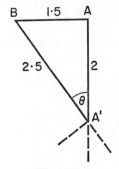

FIG. 194

Let A' be the position of the particle A when the string becomes taut (Fig. 194). Then since $BA' = 2.5$ m, $BA = 1.5$ m and BAC is a right-angle, $AA' = 2$ m, and the angle $AA'B = \theta$ where $\sin \theta = \frac{3}{5}$, $\cos \theta = \frac{4}{5}$. A's velocity of 10 m/s has components

10 cos θ = 8 m/s, along BA',

10 sin θ = 6 m/s, perpendicular to BA'.

The string has an impulsive tension along BA' which brings B into motion along this line, and, if v m/s is the common velocity of the particles in this direction, we have from the momentum equation

$$(4 + 4)v = 4 \times 8,$$

so that

$$v = 4 \text{ m/s.}$$

The velocity of A in the direction perpendicular to the line of the impulse is unchanged, therefore the kinetic energy of the system becomes

$$\frac{1}{2} \times 4 \times 4^2 + \frac{1}{2} \times 4(4^2 + 6^2) = 136 \text{ J}.$$

The kinetic energy initially was

$$\frac{1}{2} \times 4 \times 10^2 = 200 \text{ J}.$$

The loss of kinetic energy is therefore 64 J.

Example 5. *An inelastic pile weighing W kg is driven a metres into the ground by a hammer weighing w kg falling h metres before hitting the pile. Show that the resistance of the ground, supposed uniform, is $W + w + w^2h/\{(W + w)a\}$ kgf.*
[L.U.]

The hammer falling h m acquires a velocity $\sqrt{(2gh)}$ m/s, and after impact with the pile the common velocity of the hammer and pile is V m/s, where

$$(W + w)V = w\sqrt{(2gh)}.$$

The kinetic energy of the hammer and pile is therefore

$$\frac{(W + w)}{2g} V^2 = \frac{W + w}{2g} \cdot \frac{2ghw^2}{(W + w)^2}$$

$$= \frac{w^2h}{W + w}.$$

This kinetic energy is destroyed in a distance a by the resistance of the ground R kgf less the weight $W + w$, so that

$$(R - W - w)a = \frac{w^2h}{W + w}$$

and

$$R = W + w + \frac{w^2h}{a(W + w)}.$$

19.4 Impact of water jets

If a jet of water is played on a fixed surface at right angles to the jet, the momentum of a certain quantity of water is destroyed in each second, and the destroyed momentum is a measure of the impulse on the surface. Now the duration of the impulse is one second, therefore we can find the average thrust on the surface during that second.

Example 6. *Water issues from a circular pipe 6 cm in diameter with a velocity of 15 m/s and strikes a fixed plane at right angles. Find the thrust of the water on the plane.*

The volume of water discharged per second is $1500 \times 9\pi$ cm^3 and the mass discharged per second is $13,500\pi$ g. The momentum of this mass is

$$13.5\pi \times 15 \text{ newton seconds.}$$

This momentum is destroyed by a force F newton in 1 second and

$$F \times 1 = 13 \cdot 5 \pi \times 15,$$

so that

$$F = 636 \text{ newton.}$$

This is therefore the magnitude of the equal and opposite thrust of the water on the surface.

Exercises 19 (a)

1. A bullet of mass m moving horizontally with speed u strikes a small block of mass M lying at rest on a smooth horizontal plane. If the bullet becomes embedded in the block, find (a) the impulse on the block, (b) the loss of kinetic energy at impact. [L.U.]

2. A pile-driver of mass 240 kg falls through 2 m from rest on to a pile of mass 800 kg which is driven 10 cm into the ground by the blow. The pile-driver rebounds through a height of 2 cm. Calculate the resistance offered by the ground to the motion of the pile. [L.U.]

3. A particle of mass m is attached to one end of a string of length $2l$ the other end being attached to a fixed point P. The particle falls from rest at A on the same level as P. If $AP = \sqrt{3}l$, show that the impulse on the string when it tightens is $\frac{1}{2}m\sqrt{(2gl)}$ and find the inclination of the string to the vertical when it first comes to rest. [L.U.]

4. A truck of mass 6000 kg, travelling on a straight level track at 6 m/s, overtakes a truck of mass 4000 kg travelling in the same direction at 1 m/s; at the moment of impact they are automatically coupled together and they then travel 105 m before coming to rest. Find the resistance (assumed uniform) in kilogrammes force.

5. A shell weighing 60 kg is fired from a piece weighing 1500 kg with velocity 500 m/s. Find the impulse of the explosion and the velocity of recoil (assuming the recoil to be free) at the instant when the shell leaves the muzzle. If the recoil is taken up by a constant force in a distance of 1 m, find this force and the time of recoil.

6. A and B are two particles of mass 4 kg and 8 kg respectively, lying in contact on a smooth horizontal table and connected by a string 1 m long. B is more than 1 m from the edge of the table and is connected by a taut string passing over the edge to a particle C of mass 4 kg hanging vertically. If the system is released from rest, find the speed with which A begins to move. [L.U.]

7. Two trucks, of mass respectively 5 tonnes and 3 tonnes, are on the same level set of rails. If the heavier truck impinges on the lighter, which is at rest, with a speed of 5 m/s, and the velocity of the lighter relative to the heavier after they separate is 3 m/s, find the actual speeds of the trucks and the kinetic energy lost by the impact. [O.C.]

8. A truck of mass 5000 kg is moving on level rails at 5 m/s and impinges on a second truck of mass 10,000 kg which is at rest. After impact, the second truck moves on at the rate of 2 m/s. Find the speed of the first truck and the number of joules of kinetic energy lost by the impact.

9. A railway truck of 12,000 kg strikes at 6 m/s a truck of mass 2000 kg which is at rest against a buffer in a fixed frame. The buffer is in the form of a spring of natural length 1 m. The two trucks are brought instantaneously to rest when the spring is compressed to 50 cm. Find the force that would hold the buffer compressed by 25 cm.   [L.U.]

10. A train of trucks is being started from rest and, just before the last coupling becomes taut, the front part has acquired a speed of 15 km/h. If the front part has mass 72,000 kg and the last truck has mass 6000 kg, find the jerk in the coupling in kgf-sec units.   [L.U.]

11. A wooden ball of mass 250 g is moving horizontally at 10 m/s at a height of 50 m above the ground when it is struck centrally by a bullet of mass 20 g moving vertically upwards at 500 m/s. If the bullet emerges vertically with its speed halved, find the magnitude and direction of the velocity of the ball after impact and the time before it reaches the ground, assuming the penetration to be instantaneous.   [L.U.]

12. If a gun of mass M fires horizontally a shot of mass m, find the ratio of the energy of recoil of the gun to that of the shot. If a 500 kg gun discharges a 25 kg shot with a velocity of 400 m/s, find the uniform resistance necessary to stop the recoil in 15 cm.   [L.U.]

13. Water issues from a circular pipe of 6 cm diameter at 5 m/s; find the mass of water discharged per minute. If the water impinges directly on a plane and its momentum is thereby wholly destroyed, what is the pressure of the jet on the plane?   [L.U.]

14. Waves are striking against a vertical sea-wall with a speed of 50 ft/s. Taking a cubic foot of sea-water to weigh 64 lb, show that the pressure on the wall due to the destruction of the momentum of the waves is, very approximately, $34\cdot7$ lbf/in^2.   [O.C.]

15. A 2000 kg mass is raised 3 m above the top of a pile of mass 1000 kg. It is let fall and drives the pile 10 cm into the ground, the weight remaining on top of the pile. Assuming the resistance of the ground to be uniform, find its resistance in kgf and the time in seconds during which the pile moves. What is the loss of kinetic energy in the impact?   [L.U.]

19.5 Coefficient of restitution

When a body strikes a hard fixed surface there is an instant during the impact when the momentum of the body has been destroyed, and at this instant the body has its maximum deformation. After this instant the body begins to regain its shape and some momentum in the reverse direction. There is, therefore, firstly an impulse that destroys momentum and secondly an impulse that restores momentum.

The ratio of the two impulses, that is the ratio of the momentum after impact to the momentum before impact is called the *coefficient of restitution* (or elasticity) and denoted by e. Thus, the mass of the body being unaltered, if we measure the velocities before and after impact *in the same direction*, we have

$$\frac{\text{velocity after impact}}{\text{velocity before impact}} = -e. \qquad (19.6)$$

If $e = 0$ the body is said to be *inelastic*, if $e = 1$ it is *perfectly elastic* in the impact with the given surface.

The theory is most easily applicable to the impact of spheres on smooth surfaces or on each other, so that the impulse during compression and restitution is normal to the surface or to the common tangent plane of the spheres. The theory has its origin in experimental work carried out by Newton, which led him to formulate the law of impact of spheres, namely, *the relative velocity of the spheres along the line of impact immediately after impact is* $-e$ *times the relative velocity before impact*. This theory gives fairly consistent results for hard bodies at low velocities, but it is not easy to find a value of e which does not vary with the velocity of impact. The treatment of this problem in modern work on impact is considerably more complicated.

19.6 Impact of a sphere on a smooth fixed surface

The impact is said to be *direct* when the motion is normal to the surface, *indirect* when it is not. For direct impact, if u is the velocity before impact, e the coefficient of restitution and v the velocity after impact, both velocities being measured in the same direction we have

$$v = -eu. \qquad (19.7)$$

Thus, for example, if a sphere falls from a height h on to a fixed horizontal plane, the velocity before impact is

$$u = \sqrt{(2gh)}.$$

Therefore, the velocity, measured upwards, after impact is

$$v = e\sqrt{(2gh)}.$$

This velocity is destroyed by gravity when the sphere has risen to a height h' given by $v^2 = 2gh'$, so that

$$2gh' = 2ghe^2,$$
$$h' = e^2h,$$

and

$$e = \sqrt{(h'/h)}.$$

Thus the value of e may be found experimentally by measuring the height of rebound.

If the impact of the sphere on the surface is indirect, let u be the velocity before impact in a direction inclined at an angle α to the surface and let v be the velocity after impact in a direction inclined at an angle β to the surface (Fig. 195). Since the impulse is along the normal to the

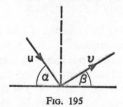

FIG. 195

surface, there is no change in the component of velocity parallel to the surface. Therefore

$$u \cos \alpha = v \cos \beta. \tag{19.8}$$

The components of velocity normal to the surface before and after impact are $u \sin \alpha$ and $v \sin \beta$ in opposite directions, therefore

$$v \sin \beta = eu \sin \alpha. \tag{19.9}$$

From equations (19.8) and (19.9)

$$v^2 = u^2(\cos^2 \alpha + e^2 \sin^2 \alpha),$$

and

$$\tan \beta = e \tan \alpha.$$

The loss of kinetic energy due to the impact, if the mass of the sphere be m,

$$= \tfrac{1}{2}m(u^2 - v^2)$$
$$= \tfrac{1}{2}m(u^2 - u^2 \cos^2 \alpha - e^2 u^2 \sin^2 \alpha)$$
$$= \tfrac{1}{2}mu^2(1 - e^2) \sin^2 \alpha.$$

Thus, there is always a loss of kinetic energy unless $e = 1$.

Example 7. *A ball dropped to the ground from a height of 10 m rebounds to a height of 8 m. Find the height to which it rebounds after a second impact and the time between the second and third impacts.* [O.C.]

As seen in § 19.6, the velocity acquired in falling from a height h is $\sqrt{(2gh)}$. Similarly, the velocity required to rise to a height h' is $\sqrt{(2gh')}$. Therefore, if e is the coefficient of restitution

$$\sqrt{(2gh')} = e\sqrt{(2gh)},$$

giving $e^2 = h'/h = 8/10$. If h'' is the height to which it rebounds after the second impact, we have in the same way,

$$\frac{h''}{h'} = e^2 = \frac{8}{10},$$

whence, since $h' = 8$, $h'' = 6\cdot4$ m. The time to fall to the ground from height $6\cdot4$ m is given by $6\cdot4 = \frac{1}{2}gt^2$, so that

$$t^2 = \frac{2 \times 6\cdot4}{g} = 1\cdot305$$

giving $t = 1\cdot14$ seconds. The time between the second and third impacts is twice this time, that is $2\cdot28$ seconds.

Example 8. *A small ball is projected horizontally with velocity 10 m/s from a point above a smooth horizontal plane. It strikes the plane at a point A, rebounds and strikes the plane again at a point B, 3 seconds after the instant of projection. If AB = 10 m, find the coefficient of restitution between the ball and the plane.*
[L.U.]

Let the ball be projected from a point at a height h m above a point O of the plane. The horizontal velocity remains unchanged throughout at 10 m/s, and hence B is 30 m from O. It follows that A is 20 m from O and that the time to A is 2 seconds. The distance fallen in 2 seconds from rest under gravity is given by the formula $h = \frac{1}{2}gt^2$, and hence $h = 19\cdot62$ m. The vertical velocity acquired in falling is given by the formula $v^2 = 2gh$, and is $19\cdot62$ m/s. After the impact at A the ball rises for $\frac{1}{2}$ second and the velocity u with which it starts to rise is given by the formula $v = u - gt$ with $v = 0$, so that the velocity u is $4\cdot905$ m/s. Therefore the coefficient of restitution is

$$e = \frac{4\cdot905}{19\cdot62} = \frac{1}{4}.$$

19.7 Direct impact of spheres

Let two spheres, assumed to be of equal radii so that their common tangent plane at contact is vertical, have masses m_1 and m_2. Let u_1 and u_2 be their respective velocities before impact and v_1 and v_2 their velocities after impact, all velocities being along the same line and *measured*

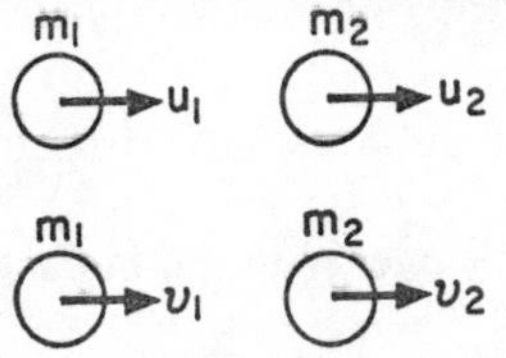

FIG. 196

in the same direction. Fig. 196 shows the spheres and their velocities before impact and after impact. Two equations are needed to determine v_1 and v_2 when u_1 and u_2 are known. The first of these is derived from the fact that the total momentum before impact is the same as that after impact, that is

$$m_1v_1 + m_2v_2 = m_1u_1 + m_2u_2. \tag{19.10}$$

The second equation is given by equating the relative velocity $v_1 - v_2$ after impact to $-e$ times the relative velocity $u_1 - u_2$ before impact, that is

$$v_1 - v_2 = - e(u_1 - u_2). \qquad (19.11)$$

Multiplying equation (19.11) by m_2 and adding to (19.10) we have

$$(m_1 + m_2)v_1 = (m_1 - em_2)u_1 + m_2(1 + e)u_2,$$

and similarly

$$(m_1 + m_2)v_2 = m_1(1 + e)u_1 + (m_2 - em_1)u_2.$$

19.8 Loss of kinetic energy

The velocity V of the centre of gravity of the two spheres before impact is given by

$$V = \frac{m_1u_1 + m_2u_2}{m_1 + m_2},$$

and equation (19.10) shows that this velocity is unchanged by the impact.

The kinetic energy of the two spheres before impact is

$$\tfrac{1}{2}m_1u_1{}^2 + \tfrac{1}{2}m_2u_2{}^2 = \frac{1}{2(m_1 + m_2)} \{m_1{}^2u_1{}^2 + m_2{}^2u_2{}^2 + m_1m_2(u_1{}^2 + u_2{}^2)\}$$

$$= \frac{1}{2(m_1 + m_2)} \{(m_1u_1 + m_2u_2)^2 + m_1m_2(u_1 - u_2)^2\}$$

$$= \tfrac{1}{2}(m_1 + m_2)V^2 + \frac{m_1m_2}{2(m_1 + m_2)} (u_1 - u_2)^2.$$

Similarly, the kinetic energy of the two spheres after impact is

$$\tfrac{1}{2}m_1v_1{}^2 + \tfrac{1}{2}m_2v_2{}^2 = \tfrac{1}{2}(m_1 + m_2)V^2 + \frac{m_1m_2}{2(m_1 + m_2)} (v_1 - v_2)^2.$$

Hence, the loss of kinetic energy in the impact is

$$\frac{m_1m_2}{2(m_1 + m_2)} \{(u_1 - u_2)^2 - (v_1 - v_2)^2\},$$

and, using (19.11), this loss is

$$\frac{m_1m_2}{2(m_1 + m_2)} (u_1 - u_2)^2 (1 - e^2). \qquad (19.12)$$

It follows that there is always a loss of kinetic energy if $e < 1$.

Example 9. *Three smooth spheres A, B and C of equal radii, but of masses m, 2m and 3m respectively, lie at rest in a straight line on a smooth horizontal table. A is projected with speed u so as to impinge directly on B, which subsequently impinges on C. Find the value of the coefficient of restitution if A is brought to rest by its impact with B and, assuming that this coefficient is the same for the second impact, find the final speeds of B and C. Find also the loss of kinetic energy.* [L.U.]

Fig. 197 shows the velocities of A and B before and after the first impact. The momentum equation is

$$mu = 2mv,$$

so that

$$v = \tfrac{1}{2}u.$$

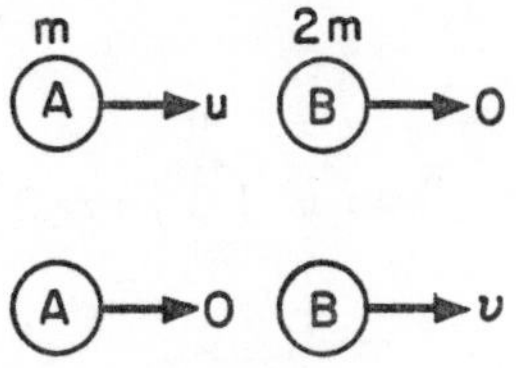

FIG. 197

The relative velocity of A with respect to B is u before impact and $-v = -\tfrac{1}{2}u$ after impact. Therefore

$$\frac{-\tfrac{1}{2}u}{u} = -e,$$

and

$$e = \tfrac{1}{2}.$$

Fig. 198 shows the velocities of B and C before and after the second impact. The momentum equation is

$$2mv_1 + 3mv_2 = mu,$$

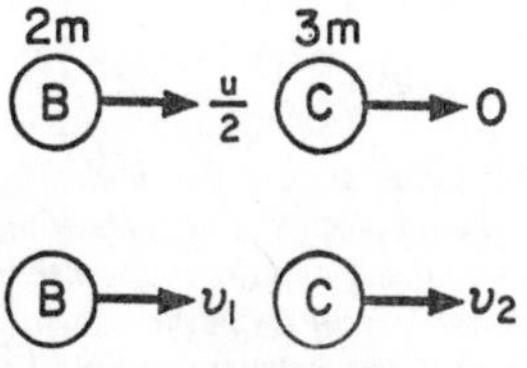

FIG. 198

and the restitution equation is

$$v_1 - v_2 = -\tfrac{1}{2}(\tfrac{1}{2}u).$$

From these equations $v_1 = u/20$, $v_2 = 3u/10$, and these are the final speeds of B and C. The final kinetic energy is

$$\tfrac{1}{2}(2m)\left(\frac{u}{20}\right)^2 + \tfrac{1}{2}(3m)\left(\frac{3u}{10}\right)^2 = \frac{11mu^2}{80}.$$

Since the initial kinetic energy was $\tfrac{1}{2}mu^2$, the loss is $29mu^2/80$.

Example 10. *A particle A, of mass 2m, moving with a velocity u impinges directly on a stationary particle B, of mass m, placed at a distance d from a wall which is at right angles to the direction of motion of A. After B rebounds from the wall a second impact occurs between A and B, T seconds after the first impact. Prove that, if the coefficient of restitution between A and B is ½ and between B and the wall is e, then Tu(1 + 2e) = 2d(1 + e).* [O.C.]

Fig. 199 shows the velocities of the particles before and after the first impact.
The momentum equation gives

$$2mv_1 + mv_2 = 2mu.$$

The restitution equation gives

$$v_1 - v_2 = -\tfrac{1}{2}(u).$$

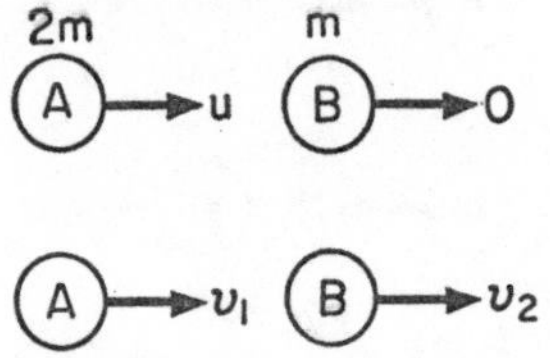

FIG. 199

Solving these equations we find that $v_1 = \tfrac{1}{2}u$, $v_2 = u$. The particle B will hit the wall in time d/u and after impact with the wall its velocity will be eu in the reverse direction. The distance moved by the particles from their initial position after time $T(> d/u)$ will be respectively

$$\tfrac{1}{2}uT \quad \text{and} \quad d - eu\left(T - \frac{d}{u}\right).$$

If the particles are together after time T we have

$$\tfrac{1}{2}uT = d - eu\left(T - \frac{d}{u}\right),$$

giving $Tu(1 + 2e) = 2d(1 + e)$.

Example 11. *Two light inextensible strings OA and OB, each of length a, have one end of each attached to a fixed point O. Particles of mass 2m and m are attached to the strings at A and B respectively and are held so that AOB is a horizontal line of length 2a. The particles are released simultaneously from rest. If the coefficient of restitution is ½, show that the heavier particle is brought to rest by the first impact. Calculate the loss of kinetic energy caused by this impact.* [L.U.]

If a particle swings at the end of a string attached to a fixed point, at the lowest point of the swing it will be moving horizontally and the kinetic energy at this point will be equal to the work done by gravity as it falls from its initial position. The pull of the string, being always at right angles to the direction of motion, will do no work. In this case, the work done on the lighter particle as it falls to its lowest point is mga and if its velocity there is v we have

$$\tfrac{1}{2}mv^2 = mga,$$

and hence

$$v = \sqrt{(2ga)}.$$

It is easily seen that the velocity of the heavier particle at this point is also v, but in the opposite direction. The velocities before and after impact are shown in Fig. 200. The equations of momentum and restitution are

$$2mv_1 + mv_2 = mv$$
$$v_1 - v_2 = -\tfrac{1}{2}(2v).$$

From these equations we find that $v_1 = 0$, $v_2 = v = \sqrt{(2ga)}$. The loss of kinetic energy is

$$\tfrac{1}{2}(2m)v^2 + \tfrac{1}{2}mv^2 - \tfrac{1}{2}mv^2 = mv^2 = 2mga.$$

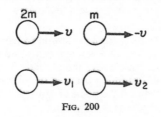

FIG. 200

Exercises 19 (b)

1. A marble dropped on a stone floor from a height of 3 m is found to rebound to a height of 2·5 m. Find the coefficient of restitution to the nearest hundredth. [L.U.]

2. A particle is dropped from a height of 4 m on to an elastic horizontal plane and just before the third impact with the plane it has described a total distance of 6·5 m. Calculate the coefficient of restitution. [L.U.]

3. If sheets of paper are placed on a table, the coefficient of restitution is reduced by an amount proportional to the thickness of the paper. When a ball is dropped on the bare table it rises after impact to three-quarters of the height of fall. When the thickness of paper is 1 cm, it rises to only one-half of the height of fall. What thickness of paper is required in order that the rebound shall be one-quarter of the height of fall? [L.U.]

4. A billiard ball of mass 200g strikes a smooth cushion when moving at 3 m/s in a direction inclined at 30° to the cushion. If the coefficient of restitution is $\tfrac{7}{8}$, find the loss of kinetic energy due to the impact. [L.U.]

5. Hailstones are observed to strike the surface of a frozen pond when moving in a direction inclined at 30° to the vertical and to rebound in a direction inclined at 60° to the vertical. Assuming the contact to be smooth, calculate the coefficient of restitution. Calculate the speed of impact if the hailstones rise to a vertical height of 30 cm after striking the ice. [L.U.]

6. A small sphere hangs freely by a light inextensible string from a point on a smooth vertical plane. It is drawn aside so that the string is taut and makes an angle of 60° with the plane, and released to strike the plane at right angles. After impact the sphere rises until the string makes

an angle of 30° with the plane. Find the coefficient of restitution between the sphere and the plane. [L.U.]

7. A billiard ball of mass m strikes the cushion of a billiard table with speed V at an angle to the cushion and rebounds on to a perpendicular cushion. Show that it rebounds off this cushion in a direction opposite to that in which it started originally. If half the energy is lost after the two rebounds, show that $e = \frac{1}{2}\sqrt{2}$. After the second rebound the ball is brought to rest by direct impact on a stationary ball of the same size but of different weight. If the coefficient of restitution between the balls is also $\frac{1}{2}\sqrt{2}$, show that the loss of energy in the final impact is $(2 - \sqrt{2})mV^2/8$. [L.U.]

8. A ball is projected with speed u at elevation α from horizontal ground at distance a from the foot of a vertical wall. The ball strikes the wall at right angles at a height b above the ground. Prove that $\tan \alpha = 2b/a$. If the coefficient of restitution between the ball and the wall is e, show that the distance between the point of projection and the point at which the ball strikes the ground is $a(1 - e)$. [L.U.]

9. Two spheres which are travelling at the same speed in opposite directions collide directly. Immediately after the collision they move in the same direction with equal momenta. If $e = \frac{1}{2}$, show that the ratio of the masses of the spheres is $(2 + \sqrt{3}):1$. [L.U.]

10. A smooth sphere of mass 1 kg moving at 7 m/s impinges directly on another smooth sphere of mass 2 kg moving in the same sense at 1 m/s. If the lighter sphere is brought to rest by the impact, determine the coefficient of restitution. Find the loss of kinetic energy, due to the impact. [L.U.]

11. Two spheres of masses 3 kg and 2 kg moving in opposite directions with velocities of 4 m/s and 1 m/s respectively impinge directly. If $e = \frac{1}{3}$, find their velocities immediately after impact and calculate the loss of kinetic energy due to the impact. [L.U.]

12. Three equal smooth spheres A, B, C lie at rest on a horizontal table; their centres being in a straight line and B lying between A and C. No two of the spheres are in contact. If A is projected with speed u towards B, show that, after the second collision, the spheres have speeds $\frac{1}{2}(1 - e)u$, $\frac{1}{4}(1 - e^2)u$, $\frac{1}{4}(1 + e)^2u$ respectively, where e is the coefficient of restitution between the spheres. [L.U.]

13. A smooth sphere of mass m impinges directly with speed V on another smooth sphere of equal radius, but of mass $2m$, at rest. The motion takes place on a horizontal plane and $e = \frac{1}{3}$. Show that the velocities after impact are in the ratio $1:4$. After this impact, the heavier sphere impinges directly on a wall. If the coefficient of restitution between the sphere and the wall is $\frac{1}{2}$, show that the impulsive action between them is $\frac{4}{3}mV$. [L.U.]

14. Two elastic particles A and B of equal mass rest on a smooth horizontal floor, the line joining them being at right angles to a vertical elastic wall which is 13 centimetres from the nearest particle B. The coefficients of

restitution between the particles and between B and the wall are each $\frac{2}{3}$. If A is projected directly towards B, show that the second collision between the particles takes place 8 centimetres from the wall. Find what fraction of its original speed A retains after this collision. [L.U.]

19.9 Units and dimensions

The fundamental units used in dynamics are those of length, mass and time which are denoted by L, M and T respectively and the units of all quantities used in dynamics are expressible in terms of these basic units. Thus velocity is a unit of length divided by a unit of time, that is L/T or LT^{-1}, and may be in metres per second, miles per hour, etc. The following table gives the fundamental units of various quantities used in dynamics and the expression of a quantity in terms of these units is called its dimensions.

Dimensions

Velocity	LT^{-1}
Acceleration	LT^{-2}
Force (absolute units)	MLT^{-2}
Force (gravitational units)	M
Energy (absolute units)	ML^2T^{-2}
Energy (gravitational units)	ML
Momentum (absolute units)	MLT^{-1}
Momentum (gravitational units)	MT
Power (absolute units)	ML^2T^{-3}
Power (gravitational units)	MLT^{-1}
Pressure (absolute units)	$ML^{-1}T^{-2}$
Pressure (gravitational units)	ML^{-2}

To change the units of a quantity the dimensions must be considered. Thus, since force (in absolute units) has dimensions MLT^{-2} and 1 lb $= 0.4536$ kg, 1 ft $= 0.3048$ m,

$$\frac{1 \text{ poundal}}{1 \text{ newton}} = \frac{(1 \text{ lb})(1 \text{ ft})(1 \text{ sec})^{-2}}{(1 \text{ kg})(1 \text{ m})(1 \text{ sec})^{-2}}$$

$$= 0.4536 \times 0.3048 = 0.1383$$

and

$$1 \text{ poundal} = 0.1383 \text{ newton}.$$

19.10 SI units

In 1960 the Conférence Générale des Poids et Mesures, the international body which aims at maintaining standards of measurements, formally approved the use of SI units (Système International d'Unités) and the use of these units is being actively encouraged in this country and elsewhere. The main features of the system for use in dynamics are:

1. The basic units of length, mass and time are respectively the metre (symbol m), the kilogramme (symbol kg) and the second (symbol s).

2. The unit of force is the newton (symbol N), which is an absolute unit giving to a mass of 1 kg an acceleration 1 m/s².

3. The unit of energy is the joule (symbol J), which is the product of a newton and a metre, and the unit of power is the watt (symbol W) which is 1 joule/per second.

4. Some other derived SI units are:

Quantity	Dimensions	SI units	Symbol
area	L^2	square metre	m^2
volume	L^3	cubic metre	m^3
density	ML^{-3}	kg per cubic metre	kg/m^3
velocity	LT^{-1}	metre per second	m/s
acceleration	LT^{-2}	metre per second per second	m/s^2
angular velocity	T^{-1}	radian per second	rad/s
pressure	$ML^{-1}T^{-2}$	newton per square metre	N/m^2

In this country a complete change from Imperial units to SI units will have to wait upon the installation of metric machinery and equipment. In the interim period such units as the poundal, the pound per square inch and the horse-power will continue to be widely used.

19.11 Conversion table to SI units

Length:	1 inch	= 0·0254 metre
	1 foot	= 0·3048 metre
	1 mile	= 1609·34 metre
	1 sea mile	= 1853·18 metre
Velocity:	1 foot/sec	= 0·3048 metre/second
	1 mile/hour	= 0·44704 metre/second
	1 knot	= 0·51477 metre/second
	1 km/hour	= 0·2778 metre/second
Mass:	1 pound	= 0·45359 kilogramme
	1 ton	= 1016·05 kilogramme
	1 tonne	= 1000 kilogramme
	1 slug	= 14·594 kilogramme
Force:	1 poundal	= 0·138255 newton
	1 lb force	= 4·44822 newton
	1 ton force	= 9964·013 newton
	1 dyne	= 10^{-5} newton
	1 kg force	= 9·8067 newton
Energy, Work:	1 ft pdl	= 0·042140 joule
	1 ft lbf	= 1·35582 joule
	1 erg	= 10^{-7} joule
	1 metre kgf	= 9·8067 joule
Momentum:	1 pdl sec	= 0·138255 newton sec
	1 lbf sec	= 4·44822 newton sec
Density:	1 lb/in³	= 27 680 kg/(metre)³
	1 lb/ft³	= 16·0185 kg/(metre)³
Pressure:	1 lbf/in²	= 6894·76 newton/(metre)²
	1 gmf/cm²	= 9806·7 newton/(metre)²
	1 millibar	= 100 newton/(metre)²
Power:	1 horse-power	= 745·70 watt
	1 metric h.p.	
	(cheval vapeur)	= 735·48 watt

The following prefixes are used to denote multiples of standard SI units:

10^{12}	tera	T	10^{-1}	deci	d
10^{9}	giga	G	10^{-2}	centi	c
10^{6}	mega	M	10^{-3}	milli	m
10^{3}	kilo	k	10^{-6}	micro	μ
10^{2}	hecto	h	10^{-9}	nano	n
10	deca	da	10^{-12}	pico	p
			10^{-15}	femto	f
			10^{-18}	atto	a

Symbols for units do not take a plural form.

Exercises 19 (c)

1. Assuming atmospheric pressure to be 14·7 lbf/in², calculate its value in dyne/cm², taking 1 kg = 2·205 lb and 1 in = 2·54 cm. Use the same data to determine the number of ergs in a foot-poundal. (Take $g = 32$ ft/s².) [L.U.]

2. Taking 1 kg = 2·205 lb, 1 in = 2·54 cm, $g = 32·2$ ft/s², express a pressure of one bar (10^{6} dyne/cm²) in lbf/in². [L.U.]

3. Given that 1 cm = 0·3937 in, and 1 kg = 2·205 lb, find the number of dynes in a poundal. [L.U.]

4. If a second be the unit of time, the acceleration due to gravity (981 cm/s²) the unit of acceleration, and a kilogramme the unit of mass, find the unit of energy in joule. [L.U.]

5. Find the ratio of (a) the momenta, (b) the kinetic energies, of a mass of 8 oz moving at 1½ miles a minute, and a mass of 10 kg moving at 2 metres per second. (1 lb = 454 g, 1 ft = 30·5 cm.) [L.U.]

6. If a force of 1 newton acts on a mass 1 slug, find the acceleration in ft/s².

Exercises 19 (d)

1. If the coefficient of friction between the tyres of a car and the road surface is ⅔, find the times in which a car can be brought to rest with all wheels locked from a speed of (a) 30, (b) 60 km/h. Find the stopping distance in each case.

2. A ball weighing 125 g and moving at 6 m/s is struck by a bat and rebounds with a velocity of 14 m/s. Find the work done on the ball, and the average pressure on the bat, assuming the bat and ball to be in contact for 0·1 seconds. [O.C.]

3. A small block of mass M is moving with velocity V when it is struck by a bullet of mass m moving with velocity v in the same direction. If the bullet becomes embedded in the block, show that there is a loss of kinetic energy $\frac{1}{2}Mm(V - v)^2/(M + m)$, and find the impulse on the block. [L.U.]

4. A bullet weighing 25 g, when fired from a gun weighing 20 kg has a muzzle velocity of 800 m/s. What is the velocity of recoil of the gun and the total energy of the gun and bullet? If the same bullet were fired from a gun weighing 10 kg, and if the total energy were the same as in the previous case, show that the muzzle velocity of the bullet would be about 0·5 m/s less than before.   [L.U.]

5. Prove that if a horizontal jet of water could be made to issue through a nozzle of 6 cm² orifice at the rate of 6·5 m³/min, it would exert a force about equal to the weight of 2 tonnes against any obstacle placed in its path; and find the power required to produce the jet.   [L.U.]

6. An inelastic vertical pile weighing 500 kg is driven 1 m into the ground by 30 blows of a hammer, weighing 2000 kg, falling through 2 m. Show that the resistance of the ground, supposed uniform, is $9·85 \times 10^4$ kgf.   [L.U.]

7. A billiard table is 6 ft by 8 ft. Find the distance of a point in the shorter side from a corner and the direction of projection, such that a ball thus struck off will describe a rectangle and return to the same spot after rebounding at each of the other three cushions, the ball being smooth and the coefficient of elasticity being $\frac{4}{9}$.   [L.U.]

8. Each step of a flight of smooth steps has width a and depth d. A marble is projected from a point on the highest step with a velocity whose horizontal and vertical components are u and v respectively. After time t it rebounds from the next highest step with a velocity whose vertical component is also v. If e is the coefficient of restitution between the marble and a step, show that $v^2 = 2gde^2/(1 - e^2)$, $t = v(1 + e)/ge$. Show that the marble will continue to strike each successive step at the corresponding place if v^2 has the above value and if, in addition, $2du^2(1 + e) = ga^2(1 - e)$.   [L.U.]

9. Two spheres of masses 60 g and 90 g are moving in their line of centres towards each other with velocities of 8 m/s and 10 m/s respectively, and their coefficient of restitution is $\frac{3}{4}$. Find their velocities after impact and the amount of kinetic energy transformed in the collision.   [L.U.]

10. Two smooth equal balls A and B lie on a smooth table, their line of centres being perpendicular to a smooth vertical wall. The coefficient of restitution between the balls is $\frac{3}{4}$ and between a sphere and the wall is $\frac{1}{2}$. If the ball A, farther from the wall, is given a velocity of 16 m/s towards the centre of B, find the velocities of the balls after their second impact, and show that there will be no more impacts between the balls.   [O.C.]

11. Two particles each of mass m and moving in opposite directions with speeds of 6 m/s and 3 m/s collide directly. Prove that, if $e = \frac{2}{3}$, the kinetic energy of the two particles before impact is twice the kinetic energy after impact.   [O.C.]

12. Two small beads of masses m and $2m$ slide on a smooth circular wire of radius a fixed in a vertical plane. The lighter bead is projected from the top of the wire whilst the heavier bead is at rest at the bottom. Upon impact the two beads coalesce and subsequently the combined mass reaches an extremity of the horizontal diameter of the wire. Find the speed of projection and the loss of kinetic energy at impact. [L.U.]

13. Three spheres A, B and C, of equal radii but of masses m, $2m$ and km respectively, lie at rest on a smooth horizontal table with their centres in a straight line. A is projected with speed u towards B and is brought to rest by the first impact. Determine the coefficient of restitution between A and B. The coefficient of restitution between B and C is $\frac{1}{3}$. Determine the value of k if C's speed after this second impact is $u/12$. Show also that B collides with A again and determine the final speed of A. [L.U.]

14. Two smooth spheres of equal radii but of masses 2 kg and 5 kg lie on a smooth horizontal plane. The lighter sphere is projected on the plane so as to impinge directly on the other, which is at rest; $e = \frac{2}{3}$. After impact the second sphere strikes a fixed barrier at right angles to its path, with which its coefficient of restitution is e. Prove that the first sphere reverses its direction of motion after impact and find the smallest value of e that will ensure a second impact between the spheres. If $e = \frac{3}{4}$, find the ratio of the final velocity of the first sphere to its original velocity. [L.U.]

15. A smooth sphere of mass m moving with speed u impinges directly on another smooth sphere of mass km moving with speed λu in the same sense. If the first sphere is brought to rest by the impact, show that the coefficient of restitution is $(1 + k\lambda)/\{k(1 - \lambda)\}$, and deduce that, for this to be possible, k must be greater than 1. [L.U.]

16. A smooth sphere of mass m, moving with speed u on a smooth horizontal table, impinges directly on an equal sphere of mass M which is at rest, the coefficient of restitution being e. Prove that the kinetic energy after impact is $\frac{1}{2}m(m + Me^2)u^2/(m + M)$. If half the kinetic energy is lost, prove that e is not greater than $\frac{1}{2}\sqrt{2}$. [L.U.]

17. Two beads A, B, of equal mass, are threaded on a smooth circular wire fixed in a horizontal plane. The bead A is projected with speed u towards the bead B which is at rest. If the coefficient of restitution is e, find the speeds of the beads after impact, and show that after the second impact (when B catches up with A) the velocities of A and B are respectively $\frac{1}{2}u(1 + e^2)$ and $\frac{1}{2}u(1 - e^2)$. [L.U.]

18. A sphere of mass m and velocity $2u$ impinges directly on a sphere of mass $2m$ and velocity u, moving in the same direction. Prove that, whatever the value of the coefficient of restitution e, the second sphere must have its velocity increased. Find e if the velocity of the sphere of mass m is halved by the impact. [L.U.]

19. Three balls, A, B, C, of mass $3m$, $2m$, $2m$, and of equal radii, lie on a smooth table with their centres in a straight line. The coefficient of restitution is $\frac{1}{4}$; show that if A is projected with velocity V to strike B, there are three impacts and that the final velocities are $(50, 57, 60)V/128$
[O.C.]

20. A, B, C are three exactly similar small spheres at rest in a smooth, horizontal, straight tube. A is set in motion and impinges on B. Show that A will impinge on B again after B has impinged on C, and show that there will be no more impacts if the coefficient of restitution is not less than $3 - \sqrt{8}$. [O.C.]

21. Two particles of masses m_1, m_2 lie at rest on a smooth horizontal table connected by a light flexible inelastic string of length a. Initially the string is taut and a blow J is given to m_1 in the direction to make it hit m_2. If the coefficient of restitution is e, find the time that elapses before the string is again taut and the common velocity of the particles at this instant. [L.U.]

22. Two particles lie on a smooth horizontal floor between two parallel vertical walls and on a line perpendicular to the walls. One, of mass 8 kg, lies halfway between the walls and the other, of mass 2 kg, is projected along the line to strike it directly. The coefficient of restitution between the particles is $\frac{1}{2}$ and that between the 8 kg mass and the wall which it hits is $\frac{1}{3}$. Calculate the coefficient of restitution between the 2 kg mass and the other wall if the particles again meet halfway between the walls. [L.U.]

23. Two small balls A and B, of equal radii and of masses m and $2m$ respectively, lie at rest on a smooth horizontal table in a line perpendicular to a vertical wall, B being nearer to the wall than A; A is given a velocity u so as to impinge directly on B, and after B rebounds from the wall it is brought to rest on its second impact with A. If the coefficient of restitution between A and B is $\frac{1}{4}$, find the coefficient of restitution between B and the wall. [O.C.]

24. A ball, mass 4 oz, is released when at relative rest from a position 6 ft above the floor of a lift which is descending with a uniform acceleration of 4 ft/s². Prove that if the ball rises to the same position after striking the floor, the impulse on the floor at impact is nearly 9·2 ft-lb-second units, and find the times of ascent and descent of the ball relative to the lift. [O.C.]

25. Three spheres A, B, C, of mass m, $2m$, $4m$ respectively rest on a smooth table with their centres collinear, B lying between A and C. The coefficient of restitution between A and B is equal to that between B and C. A is projected directly towards B with velocity u and C moves with velocity $\frac{1}{4}u$ after it has been struck by B. Prove that A and B are reduced to rest, and find the coefficient of restitution. [L.U.]

CHAPTER 20

MOTION IN A CIRCLE

20.1 Introduction

We know, from Newton's first law, that when a body moves in a straight line with uniform speed it requires no force to keep it going. This is not so when a body is moving along a curved path at uniform speed since, although the speed is constant, the direction of motion is constantly changing, and therefore the velocity is constantly changing. We shall show that for a particle to move in a circle of radius r with constant speed v it must have an acceleration of magnitude v^2/r towards the centre of the circle and there must therefore be a force acting on the particle to give it this acceleration.

There are simple applications of this theory to the conical pendulum and to governors of steam engines. A very practical application concerns the motion of vehicles on a curve. By considering the curve to be approximately circular at any point we can find the limiting speeds at which a vehicle will tend to skid or overturn, and we shall see how the tendency to skid or overturn can be diminished by suitable banking of the road.

We shall also consider motion in a circle with variable velocity and see how the energy equation can be used to determine the speed at any point when the path is a vertical circle.

20.2 Normal acceleration

Suppose that a particle is moving in a circle of radius r with uniform speed v. Let O be the centre of the circle and P and Q two points on the circle such that the angle POQ is θ (Fig. 201). If PT and QS are tangents to the circle at P and Q respectively the angle between PT and QS is also θ. The velocity of the particle at P is of magnitude v and its direction is along PT; at Q the velocity is also v but its direction is along QS.

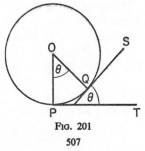

FIG. 201

507

The velocity at Q can be resolved into components $v \cos \theta$, parallel to PT, and $v \sin \theta$, perpendicular to PT. Hence, the change in velocity while the particle moves from P to Q is

$$v \cos \theta - v, \quad \text{parallel to } PT,$$

$$v \sin \theta, \quad \text{perpendicular to } PT.$$

Since the particle is moving with uniform speed v and the length of the arc PQ is $r\theta$, the time taken from P to Q is $r\theta/v$. Hence the average acceleration of the particle in this time has components

$$\frac{v^2}{r} \left(\frac{\cos \theta - 1}{\theta} \right), \quad \text{parallel to } PT,$$

$$\frac{v^2}{r} \left(\frac{\sin \theta}{\theta} \right), \quad \text{parallel to } PO.$$

The limiting values of these quantities as θ tends to zero are the components along and perpendicular to the tangent at P of the acceleration at P. Now

$$\frac{\cos \theta - 1}{\theta} = -\frac{\sin^2 \tfrac{1}{2}\theta}{\tfrac{1}{2}\theta} = -\frac{\sin \tfrac{1}{2}\theta}{\tfrac{1}{2}\theta} \times \sin \tfrac{1}{2}\theta$$

and, since the limiting value of $\sin \tfrac{1}{2}\theta / \tfrac{1}{2}\theta$ as θ tends to zero is 1 and the limiting value of $\sin \tfrac{1}{2}\theta$ is 0, we have

$$\lim_{\theta \to 0} \left(\frac{\cos \theta - 1}{\theta} \right) = 0.$$

Therefore, the component of acceleration along PT is zero.

The component of acceleration parallel to PO is

$$\frac{v^2}{r} \times \lim_{\theta \to 0} \left(\frac{\sin \theta}{\theta} \right) = \frac{v^2}{r}. \tag{20.1}$$

Hence the acceleration at P has magnitude v^2/r and is directed towards the centre of the circle. The acceleration v^2/r towards the centre of the circle is called the *centripetal acceleration* and the particle can not move in a circle unless there is a force acting on it to give it this acceleration.

If s is the length of the arc of the circle, measured from P, which subtends an angle θ at the centre of the circle, $s = r\theta$, where θ is in radians. Therefore

$$v = \frac{ds}{dt} = r \frac{d\theta}{dt} = r\dot{\theta}. \tag{20.2}$$

θ is called the *angular velocity* of the particle about O and is measured in radians per second. The centripetal acceleration can be written in terms of the angular velocity, and we have for its value

$$\frac{v^2}{r} = r\dot{\theta}^2. \tag{20.3}$$

20.3 Effective normal force

The term *effective force* is used to denote the product of the mass and the acceleration of a particle. Thus if a particle of mass m has an acceleration a in a certain direction, we say that it has an effective force ma in that direction. If F be the resultant of the forces acting on the particle, F will have the same magnitude and direction as the effective force ma.

· The equation $F = ma$ applies when the force is in absolute units and hence the effective force ma is in absolute units of force such as newton or poundals. In gravitational units the effective force is $(w/g)a$, where w is written for the mass as a reminder of the units being used.

When a particle of mass m is describing a circle of radius r with uniform speed v, its effective force in absolute units is mv^2/r towards the centre of the circle, and this is called the effective normal force. Thus if the particle is describing the circle on a smooth horizontal table at the end of a string attached to a point O of the table, the tension T in the string must equal the effective normal force and we have

$$T = \frac{mv^2}{r}. \tag{20.4}$$

If the circle is described under the action of a number of forces, the forces acting on the particle and the effective normal force must be equivalent. It is sometimes useful to show the forces and the effective normal force on separate diagrams before writing down equations which state that the resultant of the forces has the same magnitude and direction as the effective normal force.

Example 1. *A particle describes a horizontal circle of radius r at the end of a light string of length l attached at a point A above the centre O of the circle. Find the tension in the string and the velocity of the particle.*

Fig. 202 shows the forces and the effective normal force acting on the particle when it is at a point P of the circle. Then, if the angle APO is α, so that $\cos \alpha = r/l$, we have

$$T \sin \alpha - mg = 0,$$

$$T \cos \alpha = \frac{mv^2}{r}.$$

Hence, since $\sin \alpha = \sqrt{(l^2 - r^2)}/l$, we have

$$T = \frac{mgl}{\sqrt{(l^2 - r^2)}},$$

and

$$v^2 = gr \cot \alpha,$$

$$= \frac{gr^2}{\sqrt{(l^2 - r^2)}}.$$

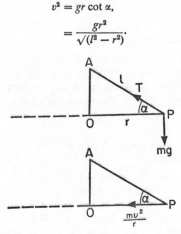

Fig. 202

20.4 Reversed effective force

In Example 1 the forces acting on the particle and the effective normal force are shown on two separate diagrams and the equations of the motion merely state the equivalence of the forces in the two diagrams. It is sufficient, however, to draw just one diagram if the effective normal

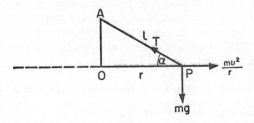

Fig. 203

force is shown on this diagram as acting in the opposite direction to that in which it acts. Thus Fig. 203 shows the forces and the *reversed* effective force for the problem given in Example 1. Now if we consider the particle at P as if it were in statical equilibrium under the action of the three forces shown in the diagram we have, resolving the forces horizontally and vertically,

$$T \sin \alpha - mg = 0, \tag{20.5}$$

$$T \cos \alpha - \frac{mv^2}{r} = 0, \tag{20.6}$$

leading to the same solution as before. Thus by considering the reversed effective force as one of the forces acting on the particle and balancing these forces the problem of motion in a circle becomes a statical one.

The reversed effective force which balances the other forces in the case of uniform motion in a circle is always in a direction *away from the centre* of the circle.

Example 2. *A mass of* 10 *kg rests on a rough horizontal table with coefficient of friction* ½. *It is attached to one end of a light inextensible string which passes through a smooth hole in the table and carries a mass of* 4 *kg hanging vertically. If the 4-kg mass describes a horizontal circle with a uniform speed of* 4 *m/s and the 10-kg mass is then on the point of slipping, find the radius of the circle and the length of string below the table.*

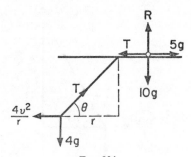

FIG. 204

Let *r* be the radius of the circle and θ the inclination to the horizontal of the string below the table (Fig. 204). The forces (including the reversed effective force) acting on the 4-kg mass are 4g, $4v^2/r$ and T, the tension in the string. Since the 10-kg mass is on the point of slipping $T = 5$ kgf. Therefore, since 5 kgf is 5g newton, where $g = 9.81$ m/s²,

$$5g \cos \theta = \frac{4v^2}{r} = \frac{64}{r},$$

$$5g \sin \theta = 4g,$$

so that $\sin \theta = 4/5$ and, since $\cos \theta = 3/5$, $r = \frac{64}{3g} = 2 \cdot 18$ m. The length of string below the table is $r \sec \theta = 3 \cdot 63$ m.

20.5 Conical pendulum

An arrangement by which a particle attached by a string to a fixed point describes a horizontal circle is called a *conical pendulum* since as the particle describes the circle the string traces out a cone whose semi-vertical angle is the inclination of the string to the vertical. The systems discussed in Examples 1 and 2 are examples of the conical pendulum. We shall consider further examples in which the particle is joined to a vertical axis during rotation by more than one string or by light rods.

If v is the speed with which a circle of radius r is described, the time of a complete revolution is $2\pi r/v$. There will, therefore, be one revolution in $v/(2\pi r)$ seconds and the number of revolutions per minute (denoted by r.p.m.) is given by

$$\text{r.p.m.} = \frac{30v}{\pi r}.$$

Example 3. *A smooth ring of mass m is threaded on a light inextensible string of length 1·5 m. The ends of the string are fixed to two points A and B in the same vertical line 1 m apart. The string and the ring are made to revolve about AB as axis with one part of the string horizontal. Find the tension in the string and the period of rotation.* [L.U.]

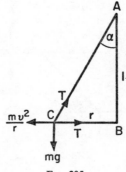

Fig. 205

Let the portion *CA* (Fig. 205) of the string be inclined at an angle α to the vertical. Then since the angle *CBA* is a right angle and $AB = 1$ m, $BC = \tan \alpha$ and $AC = \sec \alpha$, so that

$$\sec \alpha + \tan \alpha = 1\cdot 5.$$

This equation gives the value of α and is easily solved if it is remembered that $\sec^2 \alpha - \tan^2 \alpha = 1$, so that

$$\sec \alpha - \tan \alpha = \frac{1}{\sec \alpha + \tan \alpha} = \frac{2}{3}.$$

From these two equations we find

$$\sec \alpha = \frac{13}{12}, \quad \tan \alpha = \frac{5}{12}.$$

Let T be the tension in each part of the string, v the speed and $r(= \tan \alpha)$ the radius of the circle. Balancing the forces and the reversed effective force on the particle we have

$$T \cos \alpha = mg,$$
$$T + T \sin \alpha = mv^2 \cot \alpha.$$

Hence

$$T = mg \sec \alpha = \frac{13}{12} mg,$$

$$v^2 = g(1 + \sin \alpha) \tan \alpha \sec \alpha$$

$$= 9 \cdot 81 \left(1 + \frac{5}{13}\right) \times \frac{5}{12} \times \frac{13}{12} = 6 \cdot 13,$$

$$v = 2 \cdot 48 \text{ m/s}.$$

The circumference of the circle is $2\pi \tan \alpha = 10\pi/12$, so that the period is $(10\pi/12) \div 2 \cdot 48 = 1 \cdot 06$ seconds.

Example 4. *A conical pendulum consists of a particle of mass m attached to one end A of a light elastic string of natural length l and modulus of elasticity mg. The other end of the string is tied to a fixed point B. The particle describes a horizontal circle with constant angular velocity ω. If the string makes an angle α with the downward vertical, show that $2l\omega^2 = g \sec^2 \frac{1}{2}\alpha$. If $\alpha = 60°$, find the time of revolution of the particle.* [L.U.]

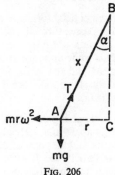

FIG. 206

Let x be the length of the string when the particle is describing the circle (Fig. 206). Then the tension T in the string is given by

$$T = mg \left(\frac{x - l}{l}\right),$$

and the radius of the circle is

$$r = x \sin \alpha.$$

If v is the velocity and ω the angular velocity, $v = r\omega$ and the effective normal force is $mr\omega^2$. Balancing the forces and the reversed effective normal force, we have

$$T \cos \alpha = mg,$$
$$T \sin \alpha = mr\omega^2.$$

From the first and third equations we have, on eliminating T,

$$\cos \alpha = \frac{mg}{T} = \frac{l}{x - l},$$

whence $x = l(1 + \sec \alpha)$. Also $r\omega^2 = g \tan \alpha$, so that

$$\omega^2 = \frac{g \tan \alpha}{l(1 + \sec \alpha) \sin \alpha}$$

$$= \frac{g}{l(1 + \cos \alpha)} = \frac{g}{2l} \sec^2 \tfrac{1}{2}\alpha.$$

When $\alpha = 60°$, $\sec^2 \tfrac{1}{2}\alpha = \frac{4}{3}$, $\omega^2 = \frac{4g}{6l}$, and the time of a revolution is

$$\frac{2\pi}{\omega} = \pi \sqrt{\left(\frac{6l}{g}\right)}.$$

Exercises 20 (a)

1. An inelastic string of length 2 m is fastened at one end to a fixed point O two metres above horizontal ground. At its other end is attached a small bob which describes a horizontal circle in a plane one metre below O. Show that the angular velocity of the bob is 3·13 radians per second. If the string snaps, find the distance of the point where the bob strikes the ground from the vertical through O. [L.U.]

2. A small smooth ring is fixed at height h above a smooth horizontal table. A light inextensible string passes through the ring and carries particles of masses M and m at its ends. M moves on the table in a circle with uniform angular velocity ω while m hangs at rest above the table. Find (i) the reaction between M and the table, (ii) the cosine of the angle between the two parts of the string. Deduce that ω^2 does not exceed the smaller of g/h and $(mg)/(Mh)$. [L.U.]

3. The ends of a light inelastic string of length $2b$ are attached to fixed points A and B, distant $2a$ apart in a vertical line. A heavy particle is attached to the string at its middle point and the system rotates about AB with uniform angular velocity ω. If $a\omega^2 > g$, show that both parts of the string are in tension and find the ratio of the magnitudes of the tensions. [L.U.]

4. A particle of mass m connected by a light inextensible string of length l to a point A, describes with uniform velocity ω a horizontal circle whose centre is vertically below A. If the breaking tension in the string is 4 kgf, the mass of the particle 2 kg and the length of the string 1 m, find the greatest possible speed with which the particle can describe the circle. [L.U.]

5. An elastic string of natural length 1 m has one end fixed and to the other end is tied a small 2-kg mass. This mass rotates uniformly in a horizontal plane, describing a complete circle every second, with the string stretched to 1·5 m. Find the modulus of elasticity of the string, and the angle it makes with the vertical. [L.U.]

6. Four smooth vertical pegs A, B, C, D are fixed in a smooth horizontal plane at the corners of a square of side a. One end of a light inelastic string of length $4a$ is fastened to A and at the other end is attached a particle of mass m. Initially the particle lies at rest on the table at a distance $4a$ from A in DA produced. The particle is given a velocity u in the direction AB. Find the time taken by the particle in reaching A. [L.U.]

7. AC, of length a, and BC are two light rods hinged at C, the mass of the hinge being M. The ends A and B are hinged to two points, A being vertically above B; angle $ACB = 90°$ and angle $BAC = \theta$. If the system revolves with uniform angular velocity ω about AB, prove that both rods are in tension if $a\omega^2 \cos \theta > g$. If either rod can withstand a maximum tension of $5 Mg$, find the maximum value of ω if $a = 1\frac{1}{3}$ and $\theta = 60°$. [O.C.]

8. Two equal particles are connected by a string passing through a hole in a smooth table, one particle being on the table and the other underneath. How many revolutions per minute would the particle on the table have to perform in a circle of radius 15 cm, in order to keep the other particle at rest? [L.U.]

9. A string 2 m long has its ends attached to points A and B, A being 1 m vertically above B. A small heavy ring C is threaded on the string and slides on it without friction. If the ring is made to describe a horizontal circle, find the speed of rotation in revolutions per minute when the radius of the circle is 75 cm.

10. One end of a light inextensible string is attached to a mass of 7·5 kg which is at rest on a rough horizontal table, the coefficient of friction being $\frac{1}{3}$. The string passes through a small hole in the table and supports at its other end a mass of 2 kg which is revolving in a horizontal circle of radius 20 cm. Find the number of revolutions made per minute if the mass on the table is on the point of slipping. [L.U.]

11. A particle of mass 4 kg is whirled round at the end of a string 50 cm long, so as to describe a horizontal circle, making 60 revolutions per minute; calculate the tension in the string and prove that the fixed end of the string is a little less than 25 cm above the centre of the circle. [O.C.]

12. A particle suspended by a fine string from a fixed point describes a circle uniformly in a horizontal plane. If it makes three complete revolutions every two seconds, show that its vertical depth below the fixed point is 11 cm approximately. [O.C.]

13. A particle attached to a fixed point by a string 1 m long describes a circle in a horizontal plane. The string can only support a tension equal to fifteen times the weight of the particle; show that the greatest possible number of revolutions per second is just under two.

14. A particle attached to a fixed point by a light inextensible string describes a horizontal circle with uniform velocity. If the length of the string is 7·62 cm, the weight of the particle is 30 g, and it is inclined at an angle of 60° to the vertical, find the tension in the string and the number of revolutions per minute that the particle is making.

15. A particle P of mass 6 kg is attached by two strings, PQ and PR, of lengths 30 cm and 50 cm respectively to points Q and R, of which R is 40 cm vertically above Q. If the particle describes a horizontal circle with a speed of 4 m/s, both strings being taut, find the tension in each string. Find the minimum speed of the particle in order that both strings may be taut.   [L.U.]

20.6 Vehicles moving in a circle

When a vehicle is moving in a circle with constant speed the forces acting on it, including the reversed effective normal force, must balance. If the forces do not balance the vehicle will overturn or skid.

Let a vehicle of mass M be moving in a horizontal circle whose centre is O with uniform angular velocity ω. The effective normal

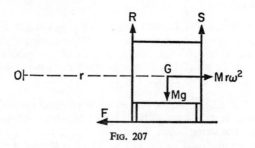

FIG. 207

force on a particle of mass m of the vehicle distant x from the vertical through O, and therefore moving in a circle of radius x, is $mx\omega^2$. For the whole body the effective normal force is $\Sigma mx\omega^2$, and since $\Sigma mx = Mr$ where r is the distance of the centre of gravity of the vehicle from the vertical through O, the total effective normal force is $Mr\omega^2$. When a vehicle is said to be moving in a circle of radius r it is to be understood therefore that its centre of gravity is moving in a circle of radius r.

To examine the balance of forces on the vehicle we must include the reversed effective normal force $Mr\omega^2$ acting outwards from O at the centre of gravity of the vehicle. The forces on the vehicle are (Fig. 207) its weight Mg, the friction F exerted by the track, the reactions R and S at the inner and outer wheels and the effective force $Mr\omega^2$. Let $2a$ be the width of the track of the vehicle and h the height of its centre of gravity G, assumed to be mid-way between the wheels. The statical balance of forces gives

$$R + S = Mg, \tag{20.7}$$

$$F = mr\omega^2, \tag{20.8}$$

and, equating to zero the sum of moments about G,

$$Sa - Ra = Fh. \tag{20.9}$$

From these equations we find

$$R = \frac{1}{2} M \left(g - \frac{h}{a} r\omega^2 \right),$$

$$S = \frac{1}{2} M \left(g + \frac{h}{a} r\omega^2 \right).$$

The vehicle will skid if the friction between the tyres and the road is insufficient, that is, since the maximum friction is $\mu(R + S)$ where μ is the coefficient of friction, if $\mu Mg < Mr\omega^2$, that is if

$$\omega^2 > \frac{\mu g}{r},$$

giving in terms of the speed $v \,(= r\omega)$,

$$v > \sqrt{(\mu g r)}. \tag{20.10}$$

The vehicle will be on the point of overturning when the reaction at the inner wheel vanishes, that is, when $R = 0$. Overturning will occur when

$$\frac{h}{a} \cdot r\omega^2 > g,$$

$$\omega^2 > \frac{ag}{rh},$$

or, in terms if the speed $v \,(= r\omega)$,

$$v > \sqrt{(agr/h)}. \tag{20.11}$$

Thus the vehicle will skid at a lower speed than the overturning speed if

$$\mu g r < agr/h,$$

that is

$$\mu < \frac{a}{h}.$$

Example 5. *A car travels in a curve of 60 m radius on a level road. The wheel base is 150 cm and the centre of gravity is central and 60 cm above the ground. Find the speed at which the car will begin to overturn and the least coefficient of friction between the tyres and the ground to prevent slipping at this speed.*

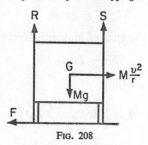

FIG. 208

Let v be the speed, M the mass, F the frictional force, R and S the reactions at the inner and outer wheels (Fig. 208). If $R = 0$, we have by taking moments about the bottom of the outer wheels

$$\frac{Mv^2}{60} \times 60 = Mg \times 75,$$

whence

$$v^2 = 9\cdot81 \times 75, \qquad v = 27\cdot12 \text{ m/s} = 97\cdot7 \text{ km/h}.$$

We have also

$$F = \frac{Mv^2}{6000} = \frac{75}{60} Mg,$$

$$R + S = Mg,$$

so that a large coefficient of friction of $75/60 = 5/4$ would be required to prevent slipping at this speed.

20.7 Banking

A road or railway is usually banked at curves, so that the road is inclined downwards in the direction of the centre of the curve, and on railways the outer track is placed higher than the inner one.

Let α be the inclination of a road towards the centre of the circle that coincides with the curve (Fig. 209). Let R and S be the reactions at the

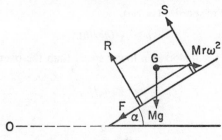

FIG. 209

inner and outer wheels respectively, F the friction and $Mr\omega^2$ the reversed effective force, which is horizontal. Also, let $2a$ be the width of the track of the vehicle and h the height of the centre of gravity, as before. Resolving parallel to and perpendicular to the road, we have

$$R + S = Mg \cos \alpha + Mr\omega^2 \sin \alpha, \qquad (20.12)$$

$$F = Mr\omega^2 \cos \alpha - Mg \sin \alpha, \qquad (20.13)$$

and, taking moments about the centre of gravity,

$$Fh = Sa - Ra. \qquad (20.14)$$

These equations determine the values of F, R and S as before.

If $F = 0$, we have from the second equation,

$$\tan \alpha = \frac{r\omega^2}{g}, \qquad (20.15)$$

and this gives the ideal angle of banking for a speed v ($= r\omega$) with no tendency to skid.

The vehicle begins to overturn if $R = 0$, and this gives

$$a(Mg \cos \alpha + Mr\omega^2 \sin \alpha) = h(Mr\omega^2 \cos \alpha - Mg \sin \alpha),$$

so that

$$v^2 = r^2\omega^2 = gr \left(\frac{a + h \tan \alpha}{h - a \tan \alpha}\right). \qquad (20.16)$$

This gives the overturning speed when the angle of banking is α.

Example 6. *A circular racing track has an effective diameter of 1 kilometre. The track is banked so that a car moving round it at 45 km/h has no tendency to side-slip. Find the tangent of the angle which the track makes with the horizontal. What is the minimum coefficient of friction between the tyres and the track if the car can travel at 90 km/h without side-slip?* [L.U.]

As in § 20.7, the ideal angle of bank α is given by

$$\tan \alpha = \frac{r\omega^2}{g}.$$

Here, $r = 500$ m, $r\omega = 12 \cdot 5$ m/s, so that $r\omega^2 = 0 \cdot 3125$, and

$$\tan \alpha = \frac{0 \cdot 3125}{9 \cdot 81} = 0 \cdot 0319,$$

giving

$$\alpha = 1° \ 50'.$$

With the notation of § 20.7, we have

$$\frac{F}{R + S} = \frac{r\omega^2 \cos \alpha - g \sin \alpha}{r\omega^2 \sin \alpha + g \cos \alpha}$$

$$= \frac{r\omega^2 - g \tan \alpha}{r\omega^2 \tan \alpha + g}.$$

When the speed is 90 km/h $= 25$ m/s, $r\omega^2 = 1\cdot25$, so that

$$\frac{F}{R + S} = \frac{1\cdot25 - 9\cdot81 \tan \alpha}{1\cdot25 \tan \alpha + 9\cdot81}$$

$$= 0\cdot095,$$

and this is the coefficient of friction required.

Exercises 20 (b)

1. A vehicle whose wheel track is 150 cm wide and whose centre of gravity is 90 cm above the road and central takes a curve of radius 45 m on a level road. Find the speed at which the inner wheels would leave the ground. Show that if the centre of gravity were displaced 40 cm towards the inner wheels, the overturning speed would be increased by about 24 per cent.

2. A two-wheeled vehicle has its wheels 165 cm apart and its centre of gravity at a height of 120 cm. If it is travelling round a curve of 100 m radius on a level road at 45 km/h, find the ratio of the normal reactions on the wheels.

3. A car is moving round a curve of 20 m radius on a level road. If the outer wheels do not slip, find the speed at which the inner wheels will leave the ground. Assume the centre of gravity of the car is 60 cm from the ground and that the width of the wheel base is 135 cm.   [L.U.]

4. A railway carriage, of mass 20,000 kg, moves round a curve of radius 240 m with a speed of 36 km/h. The distance between the rails is 140 cm, and the outer rail is raised at such a height above the inner that there is no thrust on the flanges of the wheels. Calculate this height and find the thrust on the flanges when the speed is increased to 54 km/h.   [L.U.]

5. A circular bend on a railway track is of radius 440 yd and the distance between the rails is 4 ft 8½ in. When a train travels round the bend at 36 mile/h there is no lateral thrust on either rail. Show that the outer rail is approximately 3·7 inches higher than the inner one. If an engine of mass 40 tons travels round the bend at 30 mile/h, find the lateral thrust, stating on which rail it acts.   [L.U.]

6. A train of mass 250,000 kg is moving at 48 km/h round a curve of radius 1120 m. If the track is level, find the lateral thrust on the rails. If the width of the track is 144 cm, find the height to which the outer rail must be raised above the inner if there is to be no lateral thrust on the rails at a speed of 64 km/h.   [L.U.]

7. A bicyclist is describing a curve of 20 m radius at a speed of 17·6 km/h; find the inclination to the vertical of the plane of the bicycle. What is the least coefficient of friction between the bicycle and the road, that the bicycle may not side-slip?   [O.C.]

8. The gauge of a railway is 144 cm, and the line runs along an arc of a circle of radius half a kilometre. The average speed of trains on the line is 75 km/h; what should be the height of the oute ɪrail above the inner rail?   [L.U.]

9. A vehicle travels round a curved track of radius 270 m at a speed of 96 km/h. The track is banked at an angle of 10° to the horizontal. Determine the ratio of the normal component of the reaction between the wheels and the track to the component along the line of greatest slope of the track. For what speed would this latter component be zero?

10. A motor track describes a curve of 75 m radius and is sloping downwards towards the inside of the curve at an angle $\tan^{-1} \frac{1}{5}$. At what speed must a car run along it so that there should be no tendency to side-slip?   [N.U.]

11. The shape of a cycle-track at a corner is that of an arc of a circle whose radius is 100 m. Find the angle at which the track should be inclined to the horizontal, so that a rider can take the corner at 48 km/h without any lateral reaction between his bicycle and the track. If a motor-cyclist can take the corner on the banked track safely at 96 km/h, find the least possible value of the coefficient of friction between the track and his tyres.

12. A curve on a railway line is banked up so that the lateral thrust on the inner rail due to a truck moving with speed v_1 is equal to the thrust on the outer rail when the truck is moving with speed v_2 ($> v_1$). Show that there will be no lateral thrust on either rail when the truck is moving with speed $\{\frac{1}{2}(v_1{}^2 + v_2{}^2)\}^{\frac{1}{2}}$.   [O.C.]

20.8 Circular motion with variable velocity

When a particle moves in a circle of radius r with varying velocity v, the acceleration towards the centre of the circle is v^2/r as before, but there is in addition a component of acceleration dv/dt at any point in the direction of the tangent to the circle at the point.

Let P and Q be two positions of the particle on the circle (Fig. 210), and let the angle subtended by PQ at the centre be the small angle $\delta\theta$. Let PT and QS be the tangents at P and Q respectively, the angle

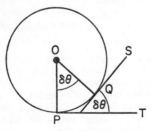

Fig. 210

between the tangents being also $\delta\theta$. Let the velocity at P be v along PT, and at Q, $v + \delta v$ along QS. The components of the velocity at Q along and perpendicular to PT are $(v + \delta v)\cos\delta\theta$ and $(v + \delta v)\sin\delta\theta$. The change of velocity while the particle moves from P to Q is therefore

$$(v + \delta v)\cos\delta\theta - v, \text{ parallel to } PT,$$

$$(v + \delta v)\sin\delta\theta, \qquad \text{perpendicular to } PT.$$

The time in which this change occurs is the time taken to describe the arc PQ of length $r\delta\theta$ and this time is $r\delta\theta/v$, to the first order of small quantities. Hence the average acceleration has components

$$\frac{v}{r\delta\theta}\{v(\cos\delta\theta - 1) + \delta v\cos\delta\theta\}, \text{ parallel to } PT,$$

$$\frac{v(v + \delta v)\sin\delta\theta}{r\delta\theta}, \text{ perpendicular to } PT.$$

The acceleration of the particle at P has components which are the limits of these quantities as $\delta\theta$ tends to zero. Now

$$\lim_{\delta\theta\to 0}\left(\frac{\cos\delta\theta - 1}{\delta\theta}\right) = 0,$$

$$\lim_{\delta\theta\to 0}\left(\frac{v\delta v\cos\delta\theta}{r\delta\theta}\right) = \frac{v}{r}\frac{dv}{d\theta} = \frac{v}{r}\frac{dv}{dt}\frac{dt}{d\theta},$$

and, since $v = r\dot\theta$,

$$\frac{v}{r}\frac{dv}{d\theta} = \frac{dv}{dt}.$$

Also

$$\lim_{\delta\theta\to 0}\left\{\frac{v(v + \delta v)}{r}\frac{\sin\delta\theta}{\delta\theta}\right\} = \frac{v^2}{r}.$$

Therefore the acceleration of the particle at P has components

$$\frac{dv}{dt}, \text{ along the tangent at } P, \tag{20.17}$$

$$\frac{v^2}{r}, \text{ towards the centre of the circle.} \tag{20.18}$$

Example 7. *A particle of mass m is tied to the end B of a light inextensible string AB of length a. The end A is attached to a small fixed peg on a rough horizontal plane. The particle is laid on the plane with the string taut and is then projected in a direction perpendicular to AB. If the coefficient of friction is μ and the particle just describes a semi-circle before coming to rest, find its initial speed and the initial tension in the string. Through what angle will the string have turned when the particle has lost half its initial speed?* [L.U.]

Let v_0 be the initial speed of the particle and v the speed when the string has turned through an angle θ. The forces acting on the particle are the tension T in the string and the frictional force μmg opposing motion and therefore acting along the tangent to the circle. We have therefore

$$m\frac{v^2}{a} = T,$$

$$m\frac{dv}{dt} = -\mu mg.$$

From the second equation we have by integration

$$v = -\mu gt + c \text{ (a constant)},$$

and since $v = v_0$ when $t = 0$, $c = v_0$. It follows that the particle comes to rest when $t = v_0/(\mu g)$. Since $v = a\dot\theta$ we have

$$a\frac{d\theta}{dt} = v_0 - \mu gt,$$

and integrating,

$$a\theta = v_0 t - \tfrac{1}{2}\mu gt^2 + d \text{ (constant)},$$

and since $\theta = 0$ when $t = 0$, $d = 0$. We know that $\theta = \pi$ when $v = 0$ and $t = v_0/(\mu g)$, so that

$$a\pi = \frac{v_0^2}{\mu g} - \frac{1}{2}\frac{v_0^2}{\mu g},$$

giving

$$v_0 = \sqrt{(2\mu ga\pi)}.$$

The initial tension in the string is

$$T_0 = \frac{mv_0^2}{a} = 2\mu mg\pi.$$

The particle has lost half its initial speed when $v = \tfrac{1}{2}v_0$, that is when $t = v_0/(2\mu g)$, and for this value of t

$$a\theta = \frac{v_0^2}{2\mu g} - \frac{v_0^2}{8\mu g},$$

giving, since $v_0^2 = 2\mu ga\pi$,

$$\theta = \tfrac{3}{4}\pi.$$

20.9 Motion in a vertical circle

We next consider the motion of a particle moving in a vertical circle swinging at the end of an inextensible string whose other end is fixed, or sliding on a smooth wire or surface.

Suppose the particle, of mass m, is attached to the end of a light inextensible string of length a the other end of the string being attached to a fixed point O (Fig. 211). Let v_0 be the initial velocity given to the particle when it is at height h_0 above the lowest point of the circle; let v be the velocity and h the height at time t.

The forces acting on the particle are the tension T in the string and its weight mg. Because at any instant the direction of motion of the particle is at right angles to the string the force T does no work as the particle moves in a circle; the work done by gravity as the height changes from h_0 to h is $mg(h_0 - h)$, which is negative if $h > h_0$. Equating the change of kinetic energy to the work done, we have

$$\tfrac{1}{2}mv^2 - \tfrac{1}{2}mv_0^2 = mg(h_0 - h),$$

so that

$$v^2 = v_0^2 + 2g(h_0 - h). \tag{20.19}$$

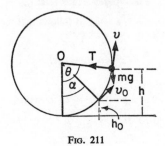

Fig. 211

This equation is sufficient to give the velocity at any point of the path and shows how the velocity diminishes as the particle rises and increases as it falls.

If θ be the inclination of the string at any instant to the downward drawn vertical through O, we have $h = a(1 - \cos \theta)$ and $h_0 = a(1 - \cos \theta_0)$, so that equation (20.19) can be written

$$v^2 = v_0^2 + 2ga(\cos \theta - \cos \theta_0). \tag{20.20}$$

The tension in the string is found from the normal balance of forces, including the reversed effective force, depicted in Fig. 212, giving

$$T = mg \cos \theta + \frac{mv^2}{a}. \tag{20.21}$$

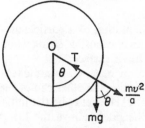

Fig. 212

For the particle to describe a complete circle it must not only have a residual velocity at the highest point of the circle, but also have enough residual velocity at this point to ensure that the string does not become slack. Thus the value of T given by (20.21) must not be negative when $\theta = \pi$, that is

$$\frac{mv^2}{a} \geqslant mg$$

or $v^2 \geqslant ga$ at the highest point. If v_0 is the velocity at the lowest point, that is with $h_0 = 0$, we have from (20.19) for the velocity at the highest point

$$v^2 = v_0{}^2 - 4ga \tag{20.22}$$

and the condition $v^2 \geqslant ga$ gives

$$v_0{}^2 \geqslant 5ga \tag{20.23}$$

for completion of the circle.

If the particle describes the circle attached to a smooth circular wire on which it slides the question of the string becoming slack does not arise and it is sufficient that there should be a residual velocity at the highest point. The condition for this is, from (20.22), $v_0{}^2 > 4ga$.

Example 8. *One end of an inextensible string of length l is attached to a fixed point and the other to a particle. With the string taut and the particle vertically below O, the particle is given a velocity u so as to describe complete circles in a vertical plane through O. At the topmost point of its path the particle strikes and coalesces with an equal particle which is at rest and continues to describe the same circle. Prove that u² must not be less than 8gl.*   [L.U.]

The velocity v of the particle at the topmost point of the circle is given by equation (20.22), namely

$$v^2 = u^2 - 4gl,$$

so that

$$v = \sqrt{(u^2 - 4gl)}.$$

After coalescing with the other particle, which is at rest, the new velocity at the topmost point will be

$$v_1 = \tfrac{1}{2}\sqrt{(u^2 - 4gl)},$$

and this velocity will be the same when the particle has completed another circle. For the string to remain taut we must have, from equation (20.21), $v_1{}^2 \geqslant gl$, so that

$$\tfrac{1}{4}(u^2 - 4gl) \geqslant gl,$$

that is, $u^2 > 8gl$.

Exercises 20 (c)

1. A bob is suspended by a string of length l from a point O. The plane of oscillation is intersected perpendicularly at C by a fixed smooth straight wire, C being at a vertical distance $l - h$ below O ($h < \tfrac{1}{2}l$). The bob B, of mass m, is released from rest with the string taut and OB making an

angle α with the downward vertical. Prove that, if $5h \leqslant 4l \sin^2 \frac{1}{2}\alpha$, B describes a circle about C.   [O.C.]

2. A ring is threaded on a smooth circular wire, centre O and radius a, fixed in a vertical plane. When at the highest point of the wire the ring is given a horizontal velocity $\sqrt{(ga)}$ in the plane of the wire. Prove that the magnitude of the horizontal component of the reaction of the wire on the ring is a maximum when the ring is at a vertical distance $\frac{1}{2}a$ below O.   [O.C.]

3. A bead B of mass m is threaded on a fixed smooth vertical wire, with centre O and radius a, whose plane is vertical. When the bead is at the lowest point of the wire it is projected horizontally with velocity u, and in the subsequent motion B reaches a maximum vertical height of $\frac{1}{2}a$ above O. Prove that $u^2 = 3ga$. Also, if θ denotes the angle which OB makes with the downward vertical, prove that the reaction R of B on the wire is given by $R = mg(1 + 3\cos\theta)$.   [O.C.]

4. A small ring of mass m can slide on a smooth circular wire, radius r and centre O, which is fixed in a vertical plane. From a point on the wire at a vertical distance $\frac{1}{2}r$ above O the ring is given a velocity $\sqrt{(gr)}$ along the downward tangent to the wire. Show that it will just reach the highest point of the wire. Find the reaction between the ring and the wire when the ring is $\frac{1}{2}r$ below O.   [L.U.]

5. A particle of weight W attached to a fixed point by a light rod describes a vertical circle. If the speeds of the particle at the highest and lowest points are u and $3u$ respectively, prove that the tension in the rod when its inclination to the downward vertical is θ is $W(3\cos\theta + 2\cdot5)$. If the length of the rod is $17\cdot5$ cm, determine the speed of the particle when $\theta = 60°$.   [L.U.]

6. A heavy particle in a smooth circular tube, fixed in a vertical plane is slightly disturbed from rest at the top of the tube. Find the ratio of the thrusts on the particle in the two positions when its vertical distance above and below the centre of the tube is half a radius.   [L.U.]

7. A smooth hemispherical bowl, whose lowest point is A, is fixed with its rim uppermost and horizontal. A particle of mass m is projected along the inner surface of the bowl with a speed $\sqrt{(gr)}$ towards A, from a point at a vertical height $\frac{1}{2}r$ above A, so that its motion is in a vertical plane through A. Show that the particle will just reach the top of the bowl, and find the reaction between the particle and the bowl when it is $\frac{1}{2}r$ above A.   [L.U.]

8. A heavy particle, of mass m, oscillates through $180°$ on the inside of a smooth circular hoop of radius a fixed in a vertical plane. Prove that the pressure on the hoop at any point is $3mv^2/(2a)$.   [O.C.]

9. A mass of 1 g, hanging by a string 1 metre long, is swinging as a pendulum through an arc of total magnitude 1 radian. Find the central

acceleration and the tension in the string when the mass is passing
through its lowest point.   [L.U.]

10. A mass m hangs by a string of length a from a fixed point. If the mass
be given a horizontal velocity of $\sqrt{(7ga/2)}$, show that the string will be
about to become slack when it makes an angle of 60° with the upward
vertical. Find the tension in the string when it is inclined at 60° to the
downward vertical.   [L.U.]

11. A heavy particle hanging from a fixed point by a light inextensible string
of length l is projected horizontally with speed $\sqrt{(gl)}$. Find the speed of
the particle and the inclination of the string to the vertical at the instant
of the motion when the tension in the string equals the weight of the
particle.   [L.U.]

12. A ball of mass 6 kg is attached to one end of a thread, 75·5 cm long,
which can just support a mass of 18·2 kg without breaking; the other
end of the thread is fixed. The ball is held with the string taut at a
height of 37·5 cm above the level of the fixed point, and is started at
right-angles to the string with a velocity of 2 m/s. Show that the string
will break when the ball is directly below the starting-point.   [O.C.]

Exercises 20 (d)

1. A particle of mass m lies on a smooth horizontal table and is attached,
by an inextensible string which passes through a smooth hole in the
table, to a particle of mass $2m$ which hangs freely below the table. The
particle of mass m describes a circle of radius 1 m on the table with such
uniform speed that the particle of mass $2m$ remains at rest. Calculate
the speed required.   [L.U.]

2. Three equal particles each of mass 2 kg are at the vertices of an equilateral triangle whose sides are taut inextensible strings of length 15 cm.
If the figure is on a uniform horizontal plane and revolves uniformly
about its centre at the rate of 5 revolutions per second, find the tensions
in the strings.   [L.U.]

3. A particle of mass 6 kg is fastened by a string 150 cm long to a point
90 cm above a smooth horizontal table. How many r.p.m. must the
particle make in horizontal circles so as just to keep clear of the table?
Calculate the thrust between the particle and the table if the speed is
reduced to 25 r.p.m.

4. A small ring of mass m, free to slide on a thin smooth vertical rod, is
attached by a light inelastic string of length $2a$ to a point on the rod.
A particle of equal mass is fixed to the mid-point of the string. Prove
that the system can rotate in steady motion about the rod with each
part of the string inclined to the rod provided the angular velocity
exceeds $\sqrt{(3g/a)}$.   [L.U.]

5. Particles of masses $3m$ and $5m$ are attached to the ends of a light string of
length a which passes through a fixed smooth ring at O. The lighter

particle describes a horizontal circle about the heavier particle (which remains stationary) as centre. Prove that the two particles lie in a horizontal plane at a distance $\frac{3}{8}a$ below O, and that the time of a complete revolution is $\pi\sqrt{(3a/2g)}$.   [O.C.]

6. Two small weights, of 60 g and 30 g respectively, are connected by a light inextensible string, 30 cm long, which passes through a small smooth fixed ring. The 60 g weight hangs 22·5 cm below the ring while the 30 g weight describes a horizontal circle. Show that the plane of this circle is 3·75 cm below the ring, and show also that the 30 g weight makes very approximately 154 r.p.m.

7. A plane horizontal circular disc is constrained to rotate uniformly about its centre, describing two complete revolutions per second. Show that the greatest distance from the centre at which a small object can be placed so as to stay on the disc is, very approximately, $6\cdot22\,\mu$ cm, where μ is the coefficient of friction between the object and the disc.   [O.C.]

8. A rough horizontal circular disc is rotating with uniform angular velocity ω about a fixed vertical axis through its centre. Two particles, of masses M, m, lie on the disc at rest relative to it, being on the same radius and at distances a and $2a$ respectively from the centre. They are connected by a light inextensible string of length a and μ is the coefficient of friction between either particle and the disc. Show that both particles are on the point of slipping outwards if $\omega^2 = \mu g(M + m)/(aM + 2am)$, and find an expression for the corresponding tension in the string.   [O.C.]

9. A steam governor consists of four equal light rods AB, BC, CD, DA, of length 25 cm, freely hinged at their ends and rotating about a vertical axis to which it is hinged at a fixed point A and on which it slides without friction on a light collar attached to the rods at C below A. It carries masses of 6 kg at B and D and is kept in position by a spring at C. Find the number of revolutions being made per minute if the force exerted by the spring is 2 kg downwards and AC equals 30 cm.   [L.U.]

10. The smooth inside surface of a bowl is a segment of a sphere of radius 20 cm, the height of the segment being 10 cm. The bowl has its axis fixed and vertical and is rotated about the axis. Find the greatest possible angular velocity of the bowl, in r.p.m., if a particle placed in it can remain at rest relative to the bowl just within its rim.   [L.U.]

11. A light inextensible string of length l has one end attached to a fixed point and the other end to a particle of mass m which describes a horizontal circle with constant speed u. If the string makes an angle α with the vertical, show that $u^2 = gl \sin^2 \alpha \sec \alpha$. The particle hits an inelastic object which brings it to instantaneous rest. If in the subsequent motion in a vertical plane the greatest speed acquired by the particle is $\frac{1}{2}u$, show that $7 \cos \alpha = 1$. Find the values of the tension in the

string (*a*) just before the blow, (*b*) just after the blow, and (*c*) when the string is vertical. [L.U.]

12. A cyclist turns a corner on a curve of radius 30 m on a level road at a speed of 20 km/h. Find the angle at which he leans from the vertical and the coefficient of friction between the tyres and the road necessary to prevent skidding.

13. A humpback bridge has the shape of an arc of a circle of 40 m radius. Find the greatest speed at which a cyclist can cross the bridge without leaving the road.

14. The width of the track of a car is 46 in and the centre of gravity is 24 in above the road and 3 in to the right of the centre line of the car. The road bends, first to the right and then to the left, the radius of each curve being 40 yd. If the coefficient of friction between the tyres and the road is 0·9, show that if the car were driven too fast it would skid at the first bend and overturn at the second.

15. A cyclist rounds a curve of 30 m radius on a road which is banked at 20° to the horizontal. If the coefficient of friction between the tyres and the road is $\frac{1}{2}$, find the greatest speed at which he can ride without skidding and his inclination to the vertical at this speed.

16. A vehicle rounds a curve of radius *r* at constant speed *v* on a level road on which the angle of friction between the tyres and the road is λ. Show that the car will be on the point of skidding if $(v^2/gr) = \tan \lambda$ and that banking at an angle α will eliminate any tendency to skid at this speed if $\alpha = \lambda$. Show that, if the angle of bank is in fact β, the car will be on the point of skidding when the speed is *V*, where $(V^2/gr) = \tan (\beta + \lambda)$.

17. A vehicle rounds a curve of radius *r* at constant speed *v* on a level road. The shortest line joining the centre of gravity to the outer wheel track is inclined at an angle β to the vertical. Show that the vehicle will be on the point of overturning if $(v^2/gr) = \tan \beta$ and that the reactions at the wheels either side will be equal if the road is banked at an angle β. Show that if the road is banked at an angle α the vehicle will be on the point of overturning when the speed is *V*, where $(V^2/gr) = \tan (\alpha + \beta)$.

18. A stone of mass 1 kg is whirled round on a smooth horizontal table with constant speed in a circle of radius 1 m, at the end of a string whose other end is fixed. If the string can only bear a tension of 8 kgf, find the maximum speed the stone can have. If the same stone is whirled round in a vertical circle of radius 1 m, find the greatest speed the stone can have at the highest point of its path in order that the whole circle can be described without the string breaking. [L.U.]

19. A mass of 1 kg is attached to two fixed points *A* and *B*, which are 18 cm apart in the same horizontal line, by means of two strings each 15 cm in length. The mass is held with the strings taut in the horizontal plane through *AB* and then released. Find the tension in a string when the mass is in the vertical plane through *AB*. [O.C.]

20. A particle hanging at rest from a fixed point by a string of length a is started with velocity $2\sqrt{(ga)}$, and when the string is horizontal it is held at such a point that the particle just completes the circle. At what distance from the particle is the string held?   [L.U.]

21. A particle attached by a light inextensible string of length a to a fixed point is held with the string taut and inclined at an acute angle α to the upward vertical and then released. Show that after the string tightens it will not rise to the level of the fixed end of the string if $\alpha < \frac{1}{4}\pi$, but that, if $\alpha > \frac{1}{4}\pi$, the particle will rise above this level and the string will go slack again when it is at a height $-\frac{2}{3}a \cos \alpha \cos 2\alpha$ above this level.

CHAPTER 21

SIMPLE HARMONIC MOTION. MOTION ABOUT AN AXIS

21.1 Introduction

In this chapter we study in detail the type of motion known as simple harmonic motion which obtains when a particle oscillates to and fro about a central point. This type of motion is of fundamental importance in the study of physical and engineering problems. Many complicated vibrational problems, such as the flutter of aircraft wings, and many problems of structural stability are solved by treating the motion involved in small displacements as being approximately simple harmonic. As a practical example we shall consider small oscillations of a simple pendulum, that is, of a small mass swinging at the end of a light inextensible string.

In the second part of the chapter we shall show how the kinetic energy of a rigid body turning about a fixed axis can be expressed in terms of the moment of inertia of the body about the axis. When this has been done, most problems involving this type of motion can be solved very simply by the use of the energy principle. In this case also we shall show that the small oscillations of a body turning about an axis can be expressed in terms of simple harmonic motion.

21.2 Simple harmonic motion

When a particle moves in a straight line with acceleration always directed towards a fixed point of the line and proportional to its distance from that point, the particle is said to move with simple harmonic motion.

Let O be the fixed point on the straight line $X'OX$ (Fig. 213), and let x be the distance of the particle from O at time t, x being positive

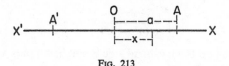

FIG. 213

if the particle is to the right of O. Then we may take the acceleration of the particle along OX as $-\omega^2 x$, where ω^2 is a positive constant. If x is positive this acceleration is directed towards O, and if x is negative $-\omega^2 x$ is positive and it is again directed towards O. A differential relation is obtained by equating one of the theoretical expressions of the acceleration to $-\omega^2 x$, and we have

$$\frac{d^2x}{dt^2} = v\frac{dv}{dx} = -\omega^2 x. \tag{21.1}$$

Let us suppose that the particle starts from rest at A, where $OA = a$. Then the initial conditions required in the solution of the differential equation (21.1) are

$$x = a, \; v = \frac{dx}{dt} = 0 \text{ when } t = 0.$$

We have

$$v\frac{dv}{dx} = \frac{d}{dx}(\tfrac{1}{2}v^2) = -\omega^2 x,$$

and, integrating with respect to x, this gives

$$\tfrac{1}{2}v^2 = -\tfrac{1}{2}\omega^2 x^2 + c \text{ (constant)}.$$

Since $v = 0$ when $x = a$, $c = \tfrac{1}{2}\omega^2 a^2$, and hence

$$v^2 = \omega^2(a^2 - x^2),$$
$$v = \pm\, \omega\sqrt{(a^2 - x^2)}. \tag{21.2}$$

This equation shows that the velocity is zero when $x = a$ and when $x = -a$ and that it has its greatest value $\pm\omega a$ when $x = 0$. The sign is positive when the motion is towards A and negative when it is towards A'. Thus the motion is an oscillation between the values $x = \pm a$. O is called the *centre* of the oscillation and the length a is called the *amplitude*.

Writing $v = dx/dt$ in the equation (21.2) we have

$$\frac{dx}{dt} = \pm\, \omega\sqrt{(a^2 - x^2)},$$

and, separating the variables, we find

$$\pm \int \frac{dx}{\sqrt{(a^2 - x^2)}} = \omega \int dt.$$

Now the integral on the left-hand side is $\sin^{-1}(x/a)$ plus a constant, the sign $\pm$ merely altering the constant, and we have

$$\sin^{-1}\frac{x}{a} = \omega t + \omega\varepsilon \text{ (constant)}$$

or

$$x = a \sin \omega(t + \varepsilon).$$

Then since $x = a$ when $t = 0$, we find $\omega\varepsilon = \pi/2$, and hence

$$x = a \cos \omega t, \tag{21.3}$$

and it follows, by differentiation, that

$$v = - a\omega \sin \omega t. \tag{21.4}$$

Since $\cos (\omega t + 2\pi) = \cos \omega t$ and $\sin (\omega t + 2\pi) = \sin \omega t$, both x and v have the same values when ωt is increased by 2π, that is, when t is increased by $2\pi/\omega$. The quantity $2\pi/\omega$ is called the *period* of the motion and is the time of one complete oscillation starting from any point and ending at the same point moving in the same direction. The *frequency* is the number of oscillations made in unit time. Thus if n the frequency and $2\pi/\omega$ the period

$$n = \frac{\omega}{2\pi}.$$

It will be noticed that the period, or frequency, can be written down directly when the value of ω is known without solving the differential equation. If, in addition, the amplitude a is known the motion is completely determined and is given by equations (21.3) and (21.4) if the time is measured from an instant when the particle is at A.

21.3 Other initial conditions

If the time in a harmonic oscillation is measured from some instant when the particle is not at A, the solution of the equation (21.1) is

$$x = a \sin \omega(t + \varepsilon), \tag{21.5}$$

where ε is a quantity determined by the initial conditions. If the initial conditions are that $x = x_0$ and $v = v_0$ when $t = 0$, we have

$$x_0 = a \sin \omega\varepsilon,$$

and

$$v_0 = a\omega \cos \omega\varepsilon.$$

From these two equations we easily find that

$$a = \sqrt{\left(x_0{}^2 + \frac{v_0{}^2}{\omega^2}\right)},$$

$$\omega\varepsilon = \tan^{-1}\left(\frac{\omega x_0}{v_0}\right).$$

In particular, if $x_0 = 0$, that is if the time is measured from an instant when the particle is at O, we find $a = v_0/\omega$ and $\varepsilon = 0$, and the equation (21.5) becomes

$$x = \frac{v_0}{\omega} \sin \omega t. \tag{21.6}$$

The variation of distance with time, whatever be the initial conditions, is shown in Fig. 214, and is seen to be a sine curve. A portion of the curve for negative t is shown by a broken line.

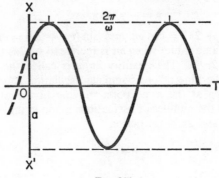

Fig. 214

21.4 Relation to uniform motion in a circle

If a particle is describing a circle of radius a with uniform angular velocity ω, its orthogonal projection on a diameter of the circle moves on the diameter in simple harmonic motion of amplitude a and period $2\pi/\omega$.

Let the time be measured from the instant when the particle is at the end B of any diameter AOB (Fig. 215) which we may take as the x-axis.

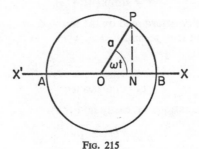

Fig. 215

After time t the particle is at a point P, where the angle $POX = \omega t$. If N be the foot of the perpendicular from P to AB, we have

$$ON = x = a \cos \omega t. \tag{21.7}$$

By comparison with equation (21.3) we see that x varies harmonically and therefore that the point N moves with simple harmonic motion of amplitude a and period $2\pi/\omega$.

Example 1. *A particle is moving in a straight line with simple harmonic motion. Its velocity when at a distance x from a fixed point of the line is given by $v^2 = \pi^2(9 - x^2)$. Find the periodic time and the maximum acceleration. Find also the least time taken by the particle to move between the points given by $x = 3/\sqrt{2}$ and $x = 3/2$, and the value of x for which the kinetic energy is one-third of its maximum value.* [L.U.]

By comparison with the formula $v^2 = \omega^2(a^2 - x^2)$, it is easily seen that $\omega = \pi$ and $a = 3$, so that the periodic time is $2\pi/\omega = 2$. The acceleration $\omega^2 x$ is a maximum when $x = 3$, and the maximum value is $3\pi^2$. Measuring the time t from an instant when $x = 3$, we have from equation (21.3)

$$x = 3 \cos \pi t.$$

Let t_1 and t_2 be the times corresponding to the given values of x, so that

$$\frac{3}{\sqrt{2}} = 3 \cos \pi t_1,$$

$$\frac{3}{2} = 3 \cos \pi t_2,$$

giving $\pi t_1 = \dfrac{\pi}{4}$, $t_1 = \dfrac{1}{4}$ and $\pi t_2 = \dfrac{\pi}{3}$, $t_2 = \dfrac{1}{3}$, so that

$$t_2 - t_1 = \tfrac{1}{3} - \tfrac{1}{4} = \tfrac{1}{12}.$$

The velocity is 3π at the centre of the oscillation and the maximum kinetic energy is $\frac{1}{2}m \, 9\pi^2$. When the kinetic energy is one-third of this $v = \sqrt{3}\pi$ and the corresponding value of x is given by

$$3\pi^2 = \pi^2(9 - x^2),$$

so that $x = \sqrt{6}$.

Example 2. *On a certain day high water for a harbour occurs at 5 a.m. and low water at 11.20 a.m., the corresponding depths being 15 m and 5 m. If the tidal motion is assumed to be simple harmonic prove that, to the nearest minute, the latest time before noon that a ship, drawing 12·5 m, can enter the harbour is 7.6 a.m.* [O.C.]

If the motion is simple harmonic the centre of the oscillation is a depth of 10 m and half its period is $6\frac{1}{3} = \frac{19}{3}$ hours. Then, $\pi/\omega = 19/3$ so that $\omega = 3\pi/19$ and the amplitude is 5 m. Therefore, if x is the depth in excess of 10 m,

$$x = 5 \cos (3\pi t/19),$$

and, when $x = 2·5$,

$$\cos (3\pi t/19) = \tfrac{1}{2} = \cos \pi/3,$$

giving $t = \frac{19}{9} = 2\text{h } 6\frac{2}{3}$ min, bringing the time to 7.6 a.m. The depth will again be 12·5 m when $3 \, \pi t/19 = 5\pi/3$, but this is afternoon.

Example 3. *A particle, describing simple harmonic motion, is 3 m from the central position when its speed is 2 m/s, and 2 m from the centre when its speed is 3 m/s. Find the amplitude and period of the motion. If the two positions are on opposite sides of the centre, show that the particle will take a quarter of a period to travel direct from one position to the other.* [L.U.]

Using the formula $v^2 = \omega^2(a^2 - x^2)$, we have

$$4 = \omega^2(a^2 - 9),$$

$$9 = \omega^2(a^2 - 4),$$

so that $\omega = 1$ and $a = \sqrt{(13)}$. Thus the period is 2π seconds and the amplitude $\sqrt{(13)}$ m. Again, since $\omega = 1$, the distance x from the centre at time t is given by

$$x = \sqrt{(13)} \cos t.$$

If $x = 3$ when $t = t_1$, and $x = -2$ when $t = t_2$, we have

$$\cos t_1 = \frac{3}{\sqrt{(13)}}, \qquad \cos t_2 = -\frac{2}{\sqrt{13}}.$$

It follows that $\sin t_1 = \frac{2}{\sqrt{13}}$ and $\sin t_2 = \frac{3}{\sqrt{13}}$, so that

$$\cos(t_2 - t_1) = \frac{-6 + 6}{13} = 0,$$

giving

$$t_2 - t_1 = \frac{\pi}{2} \text{ seconds,}$$

and this is a quarter of the period.

21.5 The simple pendulum

The simple pendulum consists of a heavy particle attached by a light inextensible string to a fixed point and moving along an arc of a circle in a vertical plane.

Let O be the centre of the circle, l the length of the string, θ the angle which it makes with the downward drawn vertical OA at time t, and m the mass of the particle (Fig. 216). The velocity is $l\dot{\theta}$ along the

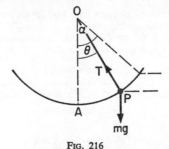

Fig. 216

tangent to the circle. Let α be the inclination of the string to OA when the velocity is zero, then the work done as the particle falls from the position α to the position θ is

$$mg\,(l \cos \theta - l \cos \alpha),$$

so that

$$\tfrac{1}{2} m l^2 \dot{\theta}^2 = mgl\,(\cos \theta - \cos \alpha)$$

and

$$\tfrac{1}{2} l \dot{\theta}^2 = g(\cos \theta - \cos \alpha). \tag{21.8}$$

Differentiating this equation with respect to t, we find

$$l\dot{\theta}\ddot{\theta} = -g \sin \theta \,.\, \dot{\theta}$$

and

$$l\ddot{\theta} = -g \sin \theta. \tag{21.9}$$

When θ is small, so that $\sin \theta = \theta$ approximately, this equation gives

$$\ddot{\theta} = -\frac{g}{l}\,\theta, \tag{21.10}$$

and this is an equation of simple harmonic motion with $\omega^2 = g/l$. Thus θ varies harmonically and the period of the oscillation is T, where

$$T = 2\pi \sqrt{\left(\frac{l}{g}\right)}. \tag{21.11}$$

This is the time of one complete oscillation from the position $\theta = \alpha$ (assumed small) through the position $\theta = 0$ to $\theta = -\alpha$ and back to $\theta = \alpha$.

The *seconds pendulum* is a pendulum whose period is 2 seconds, and whose half-period is 1 second. If l be its length, we have

$$\pi \sqrt{\left(\frac{l}{g}\right)} = 1,$$

so that

$$l = \frac{g}{\pi^2}.$$

Taking $g = 981$ cm/s^2, and $\pi^2 = 9\cdot870$, we find $l = 99\cdot4$ cm $= 39\cdot12$ in.

Example 4. *A pendulum, supposed to beat seconds, is found to lose 50 seconds a day. By what percentage must it be shortened so as to beat seconds accurately?*

The pendulum should beat $24 \times 3600 = 86\,400$ seconds a day and in fact beats $86\,400 - 50$. The time of a beat is therefore

$$\frac{86\,400}{86\,400 - 50} = \left(1 - \frac{50}{86\,400}\right)^{-1}.$$

Hence if l be its length

$$\pi \sqrt{\left(\frac{l}{g}\right)} = \left(1 - \frac{50}{86\,400}\right)^{-1}.$$

If l' be the corrected length, $\pi\sqrt{(l'/g)} = 1$, so that

$$\frac{l'}{l} = \left(1 - \frac{50}{86\,400}\right)^2,$$

$$= 1 - \frac{1}{864}, \text{ approximately,}$$

$$= 0\cdot9988.$$

Hence the pendulum must be shortened by $0\cdot12$ per cent.

Exercises 21 (a)

1. A, O and B are three points in this order on a straight line and $AO = 2\cdot4$ cm, $OB = 2\cdot0$ cm. A particle is projected from A towards O with velocity 7 cm/s and performs simple harmonic oscillations about O as centre. The velocity of the particle at B is 15 cm/s. Show that the amplitude of the oscillations is $2\cdot5$ cm and find the maximum velocity of the particle. [L.U.]

2. A particle of mass m moves in a straight line, being attracted to a fixed point O in the line by a force equal to mk^2 times its distance from O. When at a point P distance b from O its velocity is u towards O. Prove that the particle reaches O in time $(1/k)\tan^{-1}(bk/u)$. [L.U.]

3. A point is moving in a straight line with simple harmonic motion and O is the middle point of its path. If its velocity is u when distant b from O and v when distant c from O, find the amplitude of the motion and its periodic time. [L.U.]

4. A particle moves with simple harmonic motion in a straight line; find the time of a complete oscillation if the acceleration is 4 m/s² when the distance from the centre is 2 m. If the maximum velocity is 8 m/s, find the amplitude.

5. A particle is moving with simple harmonic motion of period 4π about a centre O. It passes through a point 4 m from O with velocity 4 m/s away from O. Find the time which elapses before it next passes through this point.

6. A particle moves in a straight line with simple harmonic motion making 7 complete oscillations in 11 seconds. The velocity is 4 ft/s when the distance from the centre of oscillation is 5 in. Find the amplitude of the motion, the maximum velocity and the maximum acceleration. [L.U.]

7. A particle moving with simple harmonic motion in a straight line has a speed of 6 m/s when 4 m from the centre of oscillation and 8 m/s when 3 m from the centre. Find the amplitude and the shortest time taken by the particle in moving from an extreme position to a point midway between this position and the centre. [L.U.]

8. A particle moves in a straight line with simple harmonic motion, the centre of oscillation being A. When the particle is $1\cdot5$ m from A its velocity is 4 m/s and its acceleration 6 m/s². Find the amplitude and period of the motion and the maximum velocity attained. [L.U.]

9. A piston moving with simple harmonic motion performs three complete oscillations per minute, and its maximum speed is 5 centimetres per second. Find the amplitude of the motion, the velocity when the displacement from the centre is $7\cdot5$ cm, and the maximum acceleration. [L.U.]

10. A particle moving with simple harmonic motion performs 10 complete oscillations per minute and its speed when 20 cm from the centre of oscillation is $\frac{3}{5}$ of its maximum speed. Find the amplitude, the maximum acceleration and the speed when it is 15 cm from the centre. [L.U.]

11. Two particles moving in simple harmonic motion pass through their centres of oscillation at the same instant. They *next* reach their greatest distances from their centres after 2 and 3 seconds respectively, having been at the same distance from these centres after 1 second. Find the ratio of their amplitudes. [L.U.]

12. A particle moving with simple harmonic motion passes through two points A and B, 50 centimetres apart, with the same velocity having occupied 2 seconds in passing from A to B; after another 2 seconds it returns to B. Find the period and amplitude of the oscillation. [L.U.]

13. A pendulum beats seconds at sea-level. How many seconds per day will it lose if taken to the top of a nearby mountain 1 kilometre high? Take the earth's radius as 6400 kilometres. (See § 16.8, Example 8.)

14. A clock regulated by a seconds pendulum loses 10 seconds a day. Find by what percentage the length of the pendulum should be altered to keep correct time, and state whether it should be lengthened or shortened. [L.U.]

15. Calculate the length of a seconds pendulum at a place where $g = 981$ cm/s^2. If a pendulum clock loses 9 minutes a week, find what change is required in the length of the pendulum in order that the clock may keep correct time. [L.U.]

21.6 Forces causing simple harmonic motion

If the acceleration of a particle of mass m at a distance x from a fixed point O is $\omega^2 x$ towards O, the force acting on the particle must be $m\omega^2 x$ towards O, and thus the force is proportional to the distance from O. Simple harmonic motion is, therefore, caused by forces of magnitude proportional to the distance from a point. A simple example is the force in a spring or the tension in an elastic string.

Example 5. *A particle of mass m rests on a smooth horizontal table attached to the end of a light spring of natural length l and modulus of elasticity λ. The particle is displaced a distance a from its equilibrium position O along the axis of the spring and released. Find the period of the oscillation and the maximum velocity of the particle.*

When the particle is distant x from O, the force in the spring is $\lambda x/l$ towards O, and we have

$$m\frac{d^2x}{dt^2} = -\frac{\lambda}{l}x,$$

so that

$$\frac{d^2x}{dt^2} = -\omega^2 x,$$

where $\omega^2 = \lambda/(ml)$. Hence the period is $2\pi/\omega$, and since the velocity is given by

$$v^2 = \omega^2(a^2 - x^2),$$

the maximum velocity is $a\omega$.

Example 6. *A particle of mass m is attached to one end of a light spring of natural length l and modulus of elasticity λ. The spring is suspended with its other end attached to a fixed point and is in equilibrium. If the particle is then given a displacement a vertically downwards and released, find the period of the subsequent oscillation.*

Let O be the position of the particle in equilibrium and let x be its distance below O at any instant in the subsequent motion. If c be the extension of the spring in the equilibrium position, since the tension in the spring balances the weight of the particle, we have

$$\frac{\lambda}{l}c = mg.$$

When the spring is extended a further distance x the tension in the spring is $(\lambda/l)(x + c)$, and the force acting on the particle is

$$\frac{\lambda}{l}(c + x) - mg = \frac{\lambda}{l}x.$$

Thus we have

$$m\frac{d^2x}{dt^2} = -\frac{\lambda}{l}x,$$

and the period is $2\pi/\omega$, where $\omega^2 = \lambda/(ml)$. An oscillation is always about a position of equilibrium and hence it is convenient always to measure the displacement x from a position of equilibrium. If, however, we work in terms of the extension y of the spring, the equation of motion becomes

$$m\frac{d^2y}{dt^2} = -\frac{\lambda}{l}y + mg,$$

$$= -\frac{\lambda}{l}(y - c).$$

This is reduced to the previous form by the substitution $y - c = x$, but the period of the oscillation can be written down without making this substitution, since $\omega^2 = \lambda/(ml)$.

21.7 Suspension by an elastic string

If a particle is suspended by an elastic string and displaced from its equilibrium position, the motion is simple harmonic, just as in the case of the spring, provided that the string does not return to its natural length during the motion; if this happens the string becomes slack and the particle beings to move freely under gravity. Hence, the amplitude of the simple harmonic motion must be less than the extension of the string in the equilibrium position.

The elasticity of a string is often given by stating how much a certain weight stretches it. Thus if a mass m, attached to the end of an elastic string, stretches it a distance c, we have, if l be the natural length and λ the modulus of elasticity,

$$\frac{\lambda c}{l} = mg,$$

so that $\lambda = mgl/c$. Thus if a particle of mass M is now suspended in place of m and oscillates about its equilibrium position, we have the equation of motion

$$M\frac{d^2x}{dt^2} = -\frac{\lambda}{l}x = -\frac{mgx}{c}, \tag{21.12}$$

and the period is $2\pi/\omega$, where $\omega^2 = (mg)/(Mc)$. If the extension of the string in the equilibrium position is now d, we have $\lambda d/l = Mg$, so that $d = Mc/m$, and the amplitude of the oscillation must be less than d.

Example 7. *A light elastic string of natural length $2a$ is fastened at one end to a fixed point. It hangs vertically and carries at its other end a particle of mass m. In the position of equilibrium the length of the string is $9a/4$. Find the period of small vertical oscillations of the particle. If the greatest acceleration during the oscillation is $\frac{1}{2}g$, find the amplitude.* [L.U.]

In the position of equilibrium the extension is $\frac{1}{4}a$, so that

$$\lambda\frac{\frac{1}{4}a}{2a} = mg,$$

and

$$\lambda = 8mg.$$

Then

$$m\frac{d^2x}{dt^2} = -\frac{8mg}{2a}x,$$

so that $\omega^2 = 4g/a$, and the period is $\pi\sqrt{(a/g)}$. If c is the amplitude, the greatest acceleration occurs when $x = c$, and $\frac{1}{2}g = \frac{8gc}{2a}$, giving $c = \frac{1}{8}a$.

Example 8. *Three elastic strings each have one end attached to a particle of mass m. Each string is of natural length a and modulus kmg. A and B are two fixed pegs on a smooth horizontal table $3a$ apart; the free ends of two of the strings are attached to A and the free end of the third string to B. Find the distance of the particle from A in the equilibrium position. If the particle is given a small displacement from its equilibrium position along the line AB and then released, prove that it performs simple harmonic motion and find the period of oscillation.* [L.U.]

If y be the distance of the particle from A in equilibrium, the extensions of the strings are $y - a$, $y - a$ and $3a - y - a$ respectively and, since the tensions in the strings balance,

$$\frac{kmg}{a}(y - a) + \frac{kmg}{a}(y - a) = \frac{kmg}{a}(2a - y),$$

giving $y = 4a/3$. When the particle is displaced a *further* distance x from A, the additional tensions in the strings are $kmgx/a$, $kmgx/a$ and $-kmgx/a$. Therefore, the force back towards A is $3kmgx/a$. Then

$$m\frac{d^2x}{dt^2} = -\frac{3kmg}{a}x,$$

giving $\omega^2 = 3kg/a$, and the period is $2\pi\sqrt{(a/3kg)}$.

Example 9. *A particle of mass* 2 *g is fastened to a horizontal board which is oscillating in a horizontal plane in simple harmonic motion of amplitude* 0·25 *cm;* 10 *complete oscillations are made each second. Find the magnitudes of the greatest and least forces which act between the particle and the board.* [L.U.]

Since the frequency of oscillation is 10, $\omega/2\pi = 10$ and $\omega = 20\pi$ radians/second. If x be the horizontal displacement of the particle from its central position at time t, we have

$$\ddot{x} = -\omega^2 x = -400\pi^2 x,$$

and since the mass of the particle is 2 g = 0·002 kg,

$$m\ddot{x} = -0·8\pi^2 x.$$

This is therefore the force that must be exerted by the board on the particle to make it oscillate, and if x is in metres this force will be in newtons. Therefore the greatest force, when $x = 0·0025$ m, is $2 \times 10^{-3}\pi^2 = 1·974 \times 10^{-2}$ N. When $x = 0$ the force is zero. There is also, of course, in both cases the reaction of the board on the particle which is a force of 0·002g N.

Exercises 21 (b)

1. A particle of mass m is performing simple harmonic motion under a force to a fixed point O. The motion is of period p and amplitude a. Find, in terms of m, p and a, the greatest kinetic energy of the particle, the displacement from O when the speed is $4a/p$, and the greatest rate of working of the force and corresponding displacement from O. [L.U.]

2. OA is a fixed straight line of length $4a$. A particle P of mass m moves along OA under the action of two forces, one of magnitude $mk^2 . OP$ towards O and the other of magnitude $3mk^2 . PA$ towards A. Show that the motion of P is simple harmonic with period π/k and determine the centre of this motion. If the particle is instantaneously at rest at A, what is its speed at the centre of motion? [L.U.]

3. One end of a light elastic string of natural length a is fixed. To the other is attached a particle of mass m which hangs freely at rest, the length of the string then being $5a/4$. Find the modulus of elasticity. The particle is then pulled down through a distance $\frac{1}{4}a$ from its equilibrium position and released from rest. Find the period of oscillation, the greatest speed of the particle and the least tension in the string. [L.U.]

4. A particle of mass m is attached to one end of a light elastic string of natural length l and modulus mg, the other end being fastened to a fixed point A. If the particle is allowed to fall from rest at A, find the greatest extension of the string. [L.U.]

5. A mass m hanging in equilibrium from the lower end of a light elastic string of natural length a causes an extension d. If another mass m is added to the first and the combined mass now released from rest, find the period of the motion and the maximum extension of the string. [L.U.]

6. An elastic string of natural length l is fixed at one end and hangs vertically at rest with a mass m attached to the other end extending the string a distance a. A second mass M is now attached to the first mass and the system is released. Find the greatest extension of the string in the subsequent motion and the period of the oscillations. [L.U.]

7. A particle of mass m is tied to one end of each of two strings each of modulus $4mg$ and unstretched length a. The strings are attached at their other ends to fixed points A and B respectively, in the same vertical line, B being $4a$ below A. Find the depth of the particle below A in the equilibrium position. Also find the period of oscillation of the particle about the equilibrium position. [L.U.]

8. One end of an elastic string of unstretched length l is attached to a fixed point and the other to a mass M. The system hangs in equilibrium with the extension of the string equal to $\frac{1}{4}l$ and a smooth ring of mass m slides down it from rest at its uppermost end. If, after colliding, the ring and load move on together and the further extension to the position of instantaneous rest is $\frac{1}{4}l$, prove that $M = 4m$. [L.U.]

9. A particle P, of mass m, is attached to one end of each of two equal light elastic strings, each of natural length 1 m, the elasticity of each string is such that a force mg produces an extension of 12·5 cm. Two fixed points A and B are 2·5 m apart on a smooth horizontal table and the free ends of the strings are attached to A and B. Initially P is at rest at the mid-point O of AB. P is pulled 12·5 cm towards A and released. Prove that P executes simple harmonic motion about O with period 0·16π seconds. Find the speed of P when equidistant from A and B.

10. One end of an elastic string, of natural length 30 cm, is fixed to a point O; a particle of mass m attached to the other end hangs vertically at rest and extends the string 10 cm. If this particle is replaced by a mass of $\frac{2}{3}m$ which is released from rest at a distance 30 cm below O, find the period and amplitude of the subsequent motion. [O.C.]

11. A particle of mass m kg is fastened to the mid-point O of an elastic string of natural length $2l$; the ends of the string are attached to two fixed points A and B on a smooth horizontal table at a distance $2d$ apart. The particle is pulled a distance c from $O(c < d - l)$ towards B and released. Given that a force 1 kgf stretches the string one-twelfth of its length, prove that the subsequent motion of the particle is simple harmonic of period $\pi\sqrt{(ml/6g)}$. [O.C.]

12. One end of an elastic string, of natural length l and modulus $5mg$, is fixed at O, and to the other end is attached a particle A of mass m.

When A is held at a distance l vertically below O, it is given a downward velocity of $\sqrt{(3gl/5)}$. Prove that the maximum extension of the string is $3l/5$. Find also the acceleration of A when the tension in the string is $\frac{1}{2}mg$.   [O.C.]

13. A small body A, of mass m, is attached to one end of an elastic string, of natural length 3 m, the other end being attached to a fixed point O; when the body is at rest with A vertically below O, the extension is 25 cm. If the body is raised to O and allowed to fall, prove that the maximum extension of the string in the subsequent motion is 1·5 m. When the particle is hanging freely it is given a small displacement downwards and is then released from rest. Prove that the subsequent motion is simple harmonic of period P given by $9·81\, P^2 = 4\pi^2$.

14. A body weighing 12 kg is suspended by a spring and makes three complete oscillations per second. Find how far the spring would be stretched by a load of 10 kg hanging at rest.   [L.U.]

15. A spiral spring supports a carrier weighing 2 kg, and when a 10-kg weight is placed in the carrier the spring extends 2 centimetres. The carrier and its load is then pulled down another 3 centimetres and let go. How high does it rise and what is the period of its oscillation?
                                                           [L.U.]

21.8 Motion of a body about an axis

If a rigid body is turning about a fixed axis, the position of the body at any instant is known if the position of any section of the body perpendicular to the axis is known. The section usually considered is

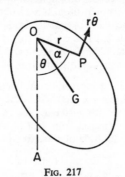

Fig. 217

that containing the centre of gravity of the body, and the motion is equivalent to that of a lamina turning about an axis perpendicular to its plane (Fig. 217). The position of the lamina at any instant is known if the angle which some straight line in the lamina makes with the vertical is known. Let OG be the straight line (Fig. 217), joining the axis of rotation at O to the centre of gravity G and let the position of this line be determined by the angle θ which OG makes with the downward drawn vertical OA.

Let P be any particle of the body such that $OP = r$ and the angle $GOP = \alpha$; the inclination of OP to the vertical is then $\theta + \alpha$, where α is constant. The angular velocity of P about O is

$$\frac{d}{dt}(\theta + \alpha) = \frac{d\theta}{dt},$$

and this is the same for all particles of the body. Since P is moving in a circle about O, its velocity is $r\dot{\theta}$ in a direction perpendicular to OP.

21.9 Kinetic energy of the body

Let the particle P have mass m. Then its kinetic energy is

$$\tfrac{1}{2}mr^2\dot{\theta}^2.$$

A similar expression gives the kinetic energy of each particle of the body, with the same value for $\dot{\theta}$ but with different values of r and m. The total kinetic energy T of the body is then

$$T = \tfrac{1}{2}\dot{\theta}^2\Sigma mr^2,$$

where the symbol Σ denotes the sum of the quantity mr^2 for all particles of the body. This quantity is the moment of inertia of the body about the axis through O, and denoting this sum by I,

$$T = \tfrac{1}{2}I\dot{\theta}^2. \tag{21.13}$$

Moments of inertia of bodies have been considered in §§ 10.7, 10.8 and found for a number of standard shapes of body. The moment of inertia is often written in the form Mk^2, where M is the mass of the body and k is called the radius of gyration about the axis. With this notation we have

$$T = \tfrac{1}{2}Mk^2\dot{\theta}^2. \tag{21.14}$$

Since the kinetic energy of the particle, $\tfrac{1}{2}mr^2\dot{\theta}^2$, is in absolute units, the expressions for T given by (21.13) and (21.14) are also in absolute units such as joules.

Example 10. *Find the kinetic energy of a solid cylindrical flywheel of mass 200 kg and radius 75 cm, rotating at 1200 revolutions per minute.*

The moment of inertia of the flywheel about its axis is (see § 10.8) $\tfrac{1}{2}Ma^2$, where $M = 200$ and $a = 75$ cm. The angular velocity is $20 \times 2\pi$ radians per second, and the kinetic energy is therefore given by

$$T = \frac{1}{4} \times 200 \times \left(\frac{3}{4}\right)^2 \times (40\pi)^2$$

$$= 4 \cdot 44 \times 10^5 \, \text{J}.$$

21.10 The energy equation

Suppose that the body turns about the axis under the action of gravity alone, and let the centre of gravity G be distant h from the axis of rotation at O (Fig. 218). Let M be the mass, Mk^2 the moment of inertia about the axis through O and $\dot{\theta}$ the angular velocity at any instant. If we suppose that the axis is smooth, so that no work is done by friction at O, we may write the potential energy of the body at any instant in terms of the height of the centre of gravity (see § 18.9) above

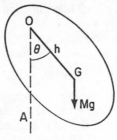

Fig. 218

some standard position, and, taking the lowest position of G during the motion as this standard position, the potential energy is

$$Mg(h - h \cos \theta).$$

Then the energy equation is

$$\tfrac{1}{2}Mk^2\dot{\theta}^2 + Mgh\,(1 - \cos \theta) = \text{constant}. \qquad (21.15)$$

If the initial position and velocity are known, the constant can be evaluated and equation (21.15) then gives the angular velocity $\dot{\theta}$ for any value of θ.

In particular, if the body starts from rest with $\theta = \alpha$, so that $\dot{\theta} = 0$ when $\theta = \alpha$, the value of the constant is $Mgh\,(1 - \cos \alpha)$ and equation (21.15) gives

$$\tfrac{1}{2}Mk^2\dot{\theta}^2 + Mgh(1 - \cos \theta) = Mgh(1 - \cos \alpha),$$

so that

$$\frac{1}{2} \cdot \frac{k^2}{h} \left(\frac{d\theta}{dt}\right)^2 = g(\cos \theta - \cos \alpha). \qquad (21.16)$$

It is clear that this equation represents an oscillatory motion with the body coming instantaneously to rest when $\theta = \alpha$ and when $\theta = -\alpha$.

Example 11. *A uniform circular disc of mass 10 kg and radius 1 m is free to turn in a vertical plane about a horizontal axis through its centre. A particle of mass 2 kg is attached to the highest point of the disc and given a small displacement. Find the greatest angular velocity of the disc in the subsequent motion.*

The moment of inertia of the disc about the axis is $\frac{1}{2} \times 10 \times 1^2$ and that of the 2-kg weight about the same axis is 2×1^2, hence the total moment of inertia is 7 kg m². If θ be the angular velocity when the disc has turned through an angle θ, the loss of potential energy in this position is $2g(1 - \cos \theta)$ and, equating this to the kinetic energy gained, we have

$$\tfrac{1}{2} \times 7\dot{\theta}^2 = 2g(1 - \cos \theta).$$

Hence the maximum velocity, when $\theta = \pi$, is given by

$$\dot{\theta}^2 = \frac{8g}{7} = 11\cdot21,$$

and

$$\dot{\theta} = 3\cdot35 \text{ radians per second.}$$

Example 12. *A uniform rod AB of mass M and length 2a is free to turn about a horizontal axis through A perpendicular to the vertical plane ABC, where C is a point distant 2a from A at the same horizontal level as A. One end of a string is attached to B and the string passes over a smooth peg at C and carries a particle of mass m hanging vertically. The system is released from rest when B is at C. Prove that the angular velocity ω of AB when the rod is vertical is given by* $a(2M + 3m)\omega^2 = 3g(M - 2m\sqrt{2})$. [O.C.]

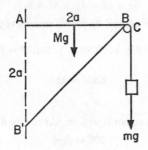

Fig. 219

The figure (Fig. 219) shows the rod AB in the horizontal position and in the vertical position AB'. In the vertical position, the velocity of B' is horizontal and equal to $2a\omega$. The component of this velocity along the line CB' is $2a\omega \cos 45° = a\omega\sqrt{2}$, and this is the velocity at this instant of the end of the string and also of the mass m. The kinetic energy of the system when AB is vertical is therefore, since the moment of inertia of the rod about A is $4Ma^2/3$,

$$\tfrac{1}{2} \cdot \tfrac{4}{3}Ma^2\omega^2 + \tfrac{1}{2}m(a\omega\sqrt{2})^2 = \tfrac{1}{3}(2M + 3m)a^2\omega^2.$$

The loss of potential energy of the rod as it falls is Mga and, since a length of string $2a\sqrt{2}$ has passed over the peg, the potential energy of the mass m has increased by $mg(2a\sqrt{2})$. Hence, the energy equation gives

$$\tfrac{1}{3}(2M + 3m)a^2\omega^2 = Mga - mg(2\sqrt{2}a),$$

so that

$$a(2M + 3m)\omega^2 = 3g(M - 2m\sqrt{2}).$$

Example 13. *Masses of* 4 *g and* 6 *g are attached to the ends of a light inextensible string passing over a rough pulley mounted on a smooth horizontal axle. The pulley is approximately a circular cylinder of mass* 5 *g and radius* 4 *cm. If the masses are released from rest find their acceleration and the tensions in the two parts of the string.*

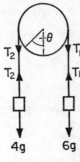

FIG. 220

When the pulley has turned through an angle θ (Fig. 220), the masses have each moved a distance 4θ and the loss of potential energy is

$$6g \times 4\theta - 4g \times 4\theta = 8g\theta.$$

If $\dot{\theta}$ is then the angular velocity, the kinetic energies of the two masses and of the pulley are

$$\tfrac{1}{2} \cdot 4(4\dot{\theta})^2 + \tfrac{1}{2} \cdot 6(4\dot{\theta})^2 + \tfrac{1}{2} \cdot \tfrac{5}{2}(4)^2\dot{\theta}^2 = 100\dot{\theta}^2.$$

Therefore

$$100\dot{\theta}^2 = 8g\theta,$$

giving

$$\dot{\theta}^2 = \tfrac{2}{25}g\theta.$$

If we differentiate this equation with respect to t we find

$$2\dot{\theta}\ddot{\theta} = \tfrac{2}{25}g\dot{\theta},$$

so that

$$\ddot{\theta} = \tfrac{1}{25}g$$

and hence

$$4\ddot{\theta} = \frac{4g}{25}.$$

This is the acceleration of each of the masses. The tensions T_1 and T_2 in the two parts of the string are easily found from the equations of motion of the masses, namely

$$6g - T_1 = 6 \times 4\ddot{\theta} = \tfrac{24}{25}g,$$
$$T_2 - 4g = 4 \times 4\ddot{\theta} = \tfrac{16}{25}g,$$

whence $T_1 = \tfrac{126}{25}g$, $T_2 = \tfrac{116}{25}g$ dynes (taking g in cm/s²).

21.11 The compound pendulum

If we compare equation (21.16) with equation (21.8) of § 21.5 which gives the motion of a simple pendulum, we see that the equations are identical if $k^2/h = l$. The length k^2/h is called the length of the *equivalent simple pendulum*, and, if the oscillations are small, the period of oscillation is as found for the simple pendulum, namely

$$2\pi \sqrt{\left(\frac{k^2}{hg}\right)}. \tag{21.17}$$

Example 14. *A uniform thin rod of length 2a oscillates in a vertical plane about a horizontal axis through one end of the rod. Find the period of small oscillations.*

The moment of inertia of a uniform rod of mass M and length $2a$ about a perpendicular axis through its centre is (§ 10.8) $\frac{1}{3}Ma^2$; about a parallel axis through one end it is $\frac{1}{3}Ma^2 + Ma^2 = \frac{4}{3}Ma^2$. The radius of gyration about this axis is therefore given by

$$k^2 = \frac{4}{3}a^2.$$

The distance of the centre of gravity from the axis is a, therefore, the length of the equivalent simple pendulum is

$$\frac{k^2}{h} = \frac{4}{3}a,$$

and the period is $2\pi\sqrt{(4a/3g)}$.

21.12 Wheel turned by a falling weight

Suppose that a light inextensible string is wrapped around and fastened to a wheel mounted on a horizontal axis and that the free end of

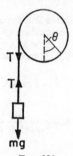

FIG. 221

the string carries a weight hanging clear of the wheel. The descending weight will cause the wheel to rotate.

Let M be the mass, a the radius and k the radius of gyration of the wheel about its axis; let m be the hanging mass and T the tension in the string (Fig. 221). When the wheel has turned through an angle θ, a length $a\theta$ of string has unwound from the wheel and the hanging mass has lost potential energy $mga\theta$. In this position the velocity of the mass m is $a\dot\theta$ and the total kinetic energy of the system is $\frac{1}{2}Mk^2\dot\theta^2 + \frac{1}{2}ma^2\dot\theta^2$.

Equating this kinetic energy to the loss of potential energy we have

$$\tfrac{1}{2}(Mk^2 + ma^2)\dot\theta^2 = mga\theta, \qquad (21.18)$$

and this equation gives the angular velocity of the wheel when it has turned through an angle θ.

The tension in the string is easily found by considering the work done on the mass m separately, namely $(mg - T)a\theta$ as it falls a distance $a\theta$, so that

$$\tfrac{1}{2}ma^2\dot\theta^2 = (mg - T)a\theta. \qquad (21.19)$$

From equations (21.18) and (21.19) we find

$$T = \frac{Mmgk^2}{Mk^2 + ma^2}. \qquad (21.20)$$

The angular acceleration can be found by differentiating equation (21.18) with respect to the time, giving

$$(Mk^2 + ma^2)\dot\theta\ddot\theta = mga\dot\theta,$$

whence

$$\ddot\theta = \frac{mga}{Mk^2 + ma^2}. \qquad (21.21)$$

Example 15. *A flywheel is mounted on a horizontal axle 2 centimetres in diameter. A mass of 10 kg attached to a light string wrapped around the axle falls 3 m from rest in 10 seconds. Assuming the bearings are frictionless, find the moment of inertia of the flywheel and axle.*

Equation (21.21) of § 21.12 shows that the angular acceleration of the wheel is constant and hence that the acceleration of the falling mass is constant. Since it falls 300 cm from rest in 10 seconds we have, from the formula $x = \tfrac{1}{2}at^2$, $300 = 50a$, so that $a = 6$ cm/s². Hence, since the radius of the axle is 1 centimetre,

$$\ddot\theta = 6 \text{ rad/s}^2.$$

From equation (21.21)

$$6 = g\,\frac{10}{Mk^2 + 10},$$

giving

$$Mk^2 + 10 = \frac{10g}{6} = 1635,$$

so that $Mk^2 = 1625$ kg cm².

Exercises 21 (c)

1. A uniform straight rod AB of length $2a$ is smoothly jointed at A to a horizontal table and is allowed to fall from rest when AB makes an angle α with the vertical. Prove that, when the angle which AB makes with the vertical is θ, then $2a\dot\theta^2 = 3g(\cos\alpha - \cos\theta)$. Find also the angular acceleration of the rod just before it becomes horizontal. [O.C.]

2. A uniform circular disc of mass 120 kg and radius 25 centimetres is free to rotate about a horizontal axis through its centre perpendicular to its plane. A particle of mass 30 kg is attached to the highest point of its rim and the equilibrium slightly disturbed. Find the angular velocity, in revolutions per minute, when the particle is passing through its lowest position. [L.U.]

3. Find the kinetic energy of a uniform rigid disc of mass M and radius a rotating with angular velocity ω about an axis through its centre perpendicular to its plane. Prove that if it rotates about a parallel axis at a distance $\frac{1}{2}a\sqrt{2}$ from its centre, with the same angular velocity, its kinetic energy will be twice its previous value. [L.U.]

4. A heavy circular disc of mass 20 kg and radius 1 m is capable of rotating about its centre in a vertical plane. A mass of 10 kg is attached to the rim at its highest point, and the whole slightly displaced. Find the angular velocity when the mass of 10 kg is at the lowest point. [L.U.]

5. A flywheel, 60 cm in diameter and of mass 20 kg, is keyed on to a shaft of 15 cm diameter, which can turn freely in smooth horizontal bearings; a long fine chain is attached to and wrapped round the axle and carries at its other end a mass of 16 kg. The wheel is turned till it acquires a speed of 480 r.p.m. and is then left running. Prove that it will come to rest after about 32 more revolutions. (Neglect the mass of the axle and chain and assume the mass of the wheel to be uniformly distributed round its rim.)

6. A wheel has a cord of length 10 m coiled round its axle; the cord is pulled with a constant force of 25 kgf, and when the cord leaves the axle the wheel is rotating five times a second. Calculate the moment of inertia of the wheel and axle. [L.U.]

7. Masses M_1 and M_2 ($M_1 > M_2$) are attached to the ends of a string which passes over a pulley, of radius a and mass M, with its axis horizontal and rotating in frictionless bearings; the pulley is sufficiently rough to prevent the string from slipping. Initially the masses hang vertically. Prove that when they are released from rest the angular acceleration of the pulley is $2(M_1 - M_2)g/(M + 2M_1 + 2M_2)a$, and that the ratio of the tensions in the two parts of the string is

$$M_1(M + 4M_2)/M_2(M + 4M_1).$$ [O.C.

8. Two equal masses are attached to the ends of a light string passing over a pulley, which may be regarded as a uniform circular disc, whose plane is perpendicular to the edge of a horizontal table, coefficient of friction $\frac{1}{2}$. One mass rests on the table, the other hangs vertically and the mass of the pulley is equal to the mass of each body. Assuming that the string does not slip on the pulley and that the string over the table is parallel to the table, find the acceleration of the system and prove that the ratio of the tensions in the two parts of the string is 7:8. [L.U.]

9. A heavy uniform rod AB of length $2a$ and mass M has a mass m attached to it at B and oscillates about a horizontal axis through A. Prove that the time of a small oscillation is $4\pi\{(M + 3m)a/3(M + 2m)g\}^{\frac{1}{2}}$. [L.U.]

10. A rod AB of length l and negligible weight has two equal weights w attached to the end B and to a point M distant $\frac{1}{3}l$ from B. Find the period of small oscillations about a horizontal axis through A. [L.U.]

11. A uniform circular disc of radius a has a particle of equal mass attached to a point A of the circumference. If the whole can turn freely about a horizontal axis perpendicular to the plane of the disc and through the other end of the diameter through A, find the length of the equivalent simple pendulum. [L.U.]

12. Calculate the period of small oscillations of a uniform rod 6 m long, about a horizontal axis through one end, when a particle of weight equal to that of the rod is attached to its middle point. [O.C.]

13. The end A of the rod AB of mass M and length $2a$ is smoothly hinged to a vertical post and a particle of mass m is attached at B. The system is released from rest when AB is horizontal. Prove that the angular velocity ω of the rod when AB makes an angle θ with the horizontal is given by $2(M + 3m)a\omega^2 = 3(M + 2m)g \sin \theta$. Find also the angular acceleration of the rod when $\theta = 60°$. [O.C.]

14. O is the centre of a uniform circular lamina of mass M and radius a; two particles each of mass m are attached to opposite ends of a diameter PQ. The system is free to rotate about an axis through A, a point on PQ distant b from O, and perpendicular to the plane of the lamina; the system is released from rest with PQ horizontal. If θ is the acute angle between PQ and the vertical and $M = 4m$, prove that the angular velocity of the system about A is given by $\omega^2(2a^2 + 3b^2) = 6gb \cos \theta$. [O.C.]

15. A uniform circular disc of mass M and radius a can rotate about a horizontal axis through its centre perpendicular to its plane. A light inextensible string is wound round the rim with one end attached to the rim; to the other end is attached a particle P of mass m. Prove that, the velocity of P when it has descended through a distance b from rest is $2\{bmg/(M + 2m)\}^{\frac{1}{2}}$. Find also the tension in the string. [O.C.]

Exercises 21 (d)

1. If the period of a simple harmonic motion is 8 seconds and the amplitude 4 m, find the maximum velocity and also the velocity when the particle is 2 m from the central position. [L.U.]

2. A particle is performing a simple harmonic motion of period T about a centre O, and it passes through a point P with velocity v in the direction OP. Prove that the time which elapses before its return to P is

$$(T/\pi) \tan^{-1}\{(vT)/(2\pi \cdot OP)\}.$$ [L.U.]

3. A circle of radius a rolls with uniform angular speed on the inside of a fixed circle of radius $2a$. Prove that any point on the circumference of the moving circle describes a straight line with simple harmonic motion. [L.U.]

4. A particle moving with acceleration $-\mu x$ has coordinates x_1 and x_2 and velocities v_1 and v_2 at any two moments. At the moment midway in time between them its coordinate and velocity are $\bar{x}$ and $\bar{v}$. Show that

$$\frac{x_1 - x_2}{v_2 - v_1} = \frac{\bar{v}}{\mu\bar{x}}, \qquad \frac{x_1 + x_2}{v_1 + v_2} = \frac{\bar{x}}{\bar{v}}.$$ [O.C.]

5. If a be the amplitude and n the frequency in a simple harmonic motion, find the velocity in any position in terms of (i) the distance from the centre, and (ii) the time that has elapsed since the particle was at rest. Show that the time that elapses as the particle moves from the position of maximum velocity to the position in which the velocity is half the maximum is $1/(6n)$ seconds. [L.U.]

6. Calculate the length of a simple pendulum to beat time to a march of 100 paces per minute. In what ratio would the length have to be decreased if the march quickened to 150 paces per minute? [L.U.]

7. Prove that if a pendulum swings from rest n times per second, then $g = n^2\pi^2 l$, where l is the length of the pendulum. In old French measure, the length of the seconds pendulum (for which $n = 1$) at Paris is $3 \cdot 06$ French feet. Calculate the value of g in these units.

8. The period of a simple pendulum consisting of a heavy bob and a thin wire of length l and negligible mass is 1 second when the temperature is 15°C. At a higher temperature the wire expands to a length $l + \Delta l$. Prove that now the pendulum loses approximately $43{,}200\ \Delta l/l$ seconds per day. [O.C.]

9. A body of mass 12 kg is suspended by a spring and makes 3 complete oscillations per second. Find how far the string would be stretched by a mass of 10 kg hanging at rest. [L.U.]

10. A spring loaded with a certain weight is extended 4 cm when in equilibrium. Find the time of oscillation if the weight is pulled down a further distance of two centimetres and let go. Find also the velocity and acceleration when the weight is one centimetre below its equilibrium position. [L.U.]

11. An elastic string of natural length $2a$ can just support a certain weight when it is stretched till its whole length is $3a$. One end of the string is now attached to a point on a smooth horizontal table, and the same weight is attached to the other end and can move on the table. Prove that, if the weight is pulled out to any length and let go, the string will become slack again after time $\frac{1}{2}\pi\sqrt{(a/g)}$. [L.U.]

12. One end of a light elastic string of natural length a and modulus mg is attached to a particle of mass m; the other end is attached to a fixed point O. The particle is released from rest at a point $\frac{1}{2}a$ below O. Prove that it returns to its initial position after a time $(\frac{3}{2}\pi + 2)\sqrt{(a/g)}$. Prove also that the greatest speed attained is $\sqrt{(2ag)}$.   [O.C.]

13. A rough horizontal table moves horizontally in simple harmonic motion, the period being 3 seconds and the maximum speed 4 m/s. A small heavy mass is placed on the table. Find the least coefficient of friction required to prevent the mass from sliding on the table during the motion.

14. A small body A, of mass m, is attached to one end of an elastic string, of natural length 6 m, the other end being attached to a fixed point O; when the body is at rest with A vertically below O, the extension is 50 cm. If the body is raised to O and allowed to fall, prove that the maximum extension of the string during the subsequent motion is 3 m. When the particle is hanging freely it is given a small displacement vertically downwards and is then released from rest. Prove that the subsequent motion is simple harmonic of period P where $gP^2 = 2\pi^2$.   [O.C.]

15. A light elastic string is stretched between two points A and B, distant $2l$ apart, the tension in the string being T. A particle of mass m, attached to the middle point of the string, is displaced a small distance perpendicular to AB and released. Show that the periodic time of an oscillation is $2\pi\sqrt{(\frac{1}{2}ml/T)}$.
(The tension T may be supposed constant throughout and the approximation $\sin \theta = \tan \theta$, where θ is small, may be assumed.)   [L.U.]

16. A non-uniform rod AB of mass M, whose centre of gravity is at C, is free to rotate about a horizontal axis through O in a vertical plane perpendicular to the axis, O lying between A and C; the moment of inertia of the rod about the axis is I and $OC = h$. The rod is released from rest when OA makes an angle α with the upward vertical OV. Prove that, when angle $AOV = \theta$, the angular velocity ω of the rod is given by $I\omega^2 = 2Mgh(\cos \theta - \cos \alpha)$. Deduce that if α is small the period of an oscillation is $2\pi\sqrt{(I/Mgh)}$. This period is the same as that for small oscillations when a particle of mass m is attached to the rod at D, between O and B, the length OD being H. Prove that $I = MhH$.   [O.C.]

17. A uniform rod AB of length $2a$ and mass M can rotate about a smooth horizontal axis through A and perpendicular to the vertical plane ABC, where C is a point at the same horizontal level as A and $2a$ from A. One end of a string, of length greater than $2\sqrt{2}a$, is attached to B and the string passes over a small smooth peg at C carrying at the other end a small particle P of mass m which hangs vertically. The system is released from rest when B is at C. Prove that the angular velocity ω of AB when the rod is vertical is given by

$$a(2M + 3m)\omega^2 = 3g(M - 2m\sqrt{2}).$$ [O.C.]

18. A uniform rod AB of length $2l$ and mass M is welded to a uniform circular disc of radius $a(< 2l)$ and mass M, in the plane of the disc and with the end B at its centre. The system can rotate freely in a vertical plane about a horizontal axis through A perpendicular to the disc. If θ denotes the angle between AB and the downward vertical and the system is released from rest when $\theta = \alpha$, prove that the angular velocity ω of the system in the subsequent motion is given by

$$(32l^2 + 3a^2)\omega^2 = 36gl(\cos\theta - \cos\alpha).$$

Find also the period of small oscillations if $4l = 3a$. [O.C.]

19. A lamina, of mass M, rotates freely about a horizontal axis through O perpendicular to the lamina and I is its moment of inertia about the axis; the centre of gravity G of the lamina is at a distance h from O; OG is produced to L at a distance l from O, and at L a particle of mass m is attached. Prove that if, at time t, OG makes an angle θ with the downward vertical, then $(I + ml^2)\dot\theta^2 - 2g(Mh + ml)\cos\theta = C$, where C is constant. Hence find the period P of small oscillations about the axis. When the particle is detached it is found that the period of small oscillations is again P; prove that $I = Mhl$. [O.C.]

20. A light inextensible string, carrying masses M and $m(< M)$, passes over a uniform solid pulley, of mass $2m$, which can rotate freely about a fixed horizontal axis through its centre O; the groove of the pulley is sufficiently rough to prevent the string from slipping. The system is released from rest when M is at a distance b vertically below O. Prove that when M is at a distance x below O,

$$(M + 2m)\dot x^2 = 2(M - m)g(x - b).$$

Hence find the ratio of the tensions in the parts of the string. [O.C.]

21. AB is a diameter of a uniform circular disc, of radius a and mass M, which can rotate freely in its plane about a horizontal axis through A; a particle of mass m is attached at B and, with B vertically above A, the system is slightly disturbed. Prove that the velocity v of the particle when AB makes an angle θ with the upward vertical is given by

$$v^2 = 16ag(M + 2m)(1 - \cos\theta)/(3M + 8m).$$

Find also the horizontal and vertical components of the linear aceleration of the particle when AB is horizontal and $M = 4m$. [O.C.]

22. The end A of a uniform rod AB, of length $2a$ and mass M, is freely hinged to a fixed point, and a particle of mass $\frac{1}{2}M$ is attached at B. If the system is slightly displaced from rest when B is vertically above A, prove that the angular velocity of the rod when it reaches the horizontal position is $\sqrt{(6g/5a)}$, and find the corresponding angular acceleration. [O.C.]

23. A uniform circular lamina of radius a and mass M is fixed at its centre to one end of a light rod of length b $(b > a)$ in its plane, the other end of the rod being freely pivoted on a horizontal axis perpendicular to the

rod and parallel to a diameter of the lamina. The rod is moved through an angle α from the vertical and then released from rest. If α is small, find the period of oscillation of the approximate simple harmonic motion. [O.C.]

24. A uniform rectangular plate $ABCD$ is free to turn about a smooth horizontal axis coinciding with the edge AB. If $BC = 2b$, show that the time of a small oscillation about the position of equilibrium is $2\pi\sqrt{(4b/3g)}$. Find the position of another horizontal axis, parallel to AB, about which the time of a small oscillation would be equal to that about AB. [L.U.]

25. A uniform circular disc of radius a has a particle of mass equal to that of the disc fixed to its circumference. The disc can turn freely about a fixed horizontal axis through its centre at right angles to its plane. Show that the length of the equivalent simple pendulum for small oscillations of the system about the position of stable equilibrium is $\frac{3}{2}a$. [O.C.]

CHAPTER 22

MATRICES

22.1 Introduction

In this chapter we consider the definitions and elementary uses of matrices. We discuss the multiplication and factorization of matrices and their application to the solution of linear equations. Their use in the specification of mapping processes is also considered.

For simultaneous linear algebraic equations such as

$$\left.\begin{array}{c} ax + by = p \\ cx + dy = q \end{array}\right\} \tag{22.1}$$

we can think of the coefficients of x and y as a group or array of numbers and write the array in the form

$$\mathbf{A} = \begin{bmatrix} a & b \\ c & d \end{bmatrix}. \tag{22.2}$$

Such an array enclosed in square brackets as shown above is called a *matrix* or, more particularly, a square matrix or a 2×2 matrix since it has two rows and two columns. More general arrays with any number m of rows and any number n of columns are called $m \times n$ matrices; for example

$$\mathbf{B} = \begin{bmatrix} 1 & 4 \\ 0 & 2 \\ 3 & 1 \end{bmatrix}$$

is a 3×2 matrix.

A matrix with m rows and only one column, that is a $m \times 1$ matrix is called a *column vector*, or more simply a *vector*. Similarly a $1 \times n$ matrix is called a *row vector* and the set of components of each can, in fact, be thought of as the components of a vector.

We shall see that such arrays can be considered as an extension of the concept of number, much as vectors and complex numbers are, and we shall formulate rules for the addition and multiplication of matrices.

The quantities x and y in equations (22.1) can be shown as a 2×1 matrix or vector denoted by $\mathbf{x}$ and similarly the numbers p and q as a vector denoted by $\mathbf{p}$. Thus

$$\mathbf{x} = \begin{bmatrix} x \\ y \end{bmatrix} \quad \text{and} \quad \mathbf{p} = \begin{bmatrix} p \\ q \end{bmatrix}. \tag{22.3}$$

We define the product of the matrices considered so far as being such that the equation

$$\mathbf{Ax} = \mathbf{p} \tag{22.4}$$

is a short way of writing equations (22.1) since all the information in the equations is known when $\mathbf{A}$, $\mathbf{x}$ and $\mathbf{p}$ are known. We thus have

$$\mathbf{Ax} = \begin{bmatrix} a & b \\ c & d \end{bmatrix} \begin{bmatrix} x \\ y \end{bmatrix} = \begin{bmatrix} ax + by \\ cx + dy \end{bmatrix} = \begin{bmatrix} p \\ q \end{bmatrix} = \mathbf{p}. \tag{22.5}$$

In equation (22.4) $\mathbf{A}$ can be said to *operate* on $\mathbf{x}$ or to *multiply* $\mathbf{x}$; both expressions are used.

These ideas may be extended so that, for example, if we have three simultaneous equations in three unknowns x, y, z, such as

$$\left.\begin{array}{l} a_1x + a_2y + a_3z = p \\ b_1x + b_2y + b_3z = q \\ c_1x + c_2y + c_3z = r \end{array}\right\} \tag{22.6}$$

we may write the equations in the same matrix form

$$\mathbf{Ax} = \mathbf{p} \tag{22.7}$$

where now

$$\mathbf{A} = \begin{bmatrix} a_1 & a_2 & a_3 \\ b_1 & b_2 & b_3 \\ c_1 & c_2 & c_3 \end{bmatrix} \quad \mathbf{x} = \begin{bmatrix} x \\ y \\ z \end{bmatrix} \quad \text{and} \quad \mathbf{p} = \begin{bmatrix} p \\ q \\ r \end{bmatrix}. \tag{22.8}$$

Example 1. *Given that*

$$\mathbf{A} = \begin{bmatrix} 3 & 2 & 1 \\ 0 & -1 & 1 \\ 3 & -2 & 4 \end{bmatrix},$$

write down the full form of the equations $\mathbf{Ax} = \mathbf{p}$. *Find the vector* $\mathbf{p}$ *when*

$$\mathbf{x} = \begin{bmatrix} 1 \\ 2 \\ 3 \end{bmatrix}.$$

The equations are

$$\left.\begin{array}{l} 3x + 2y + z = p, \\ -y + z = q, \\ 3x - 2y + 4z = r. \end{array}\right\} \tag{22.9}$$

Since $x = 1$, $y = 2$, $z = 3$ it follows that

$$p = 3 + 4 + 3 = 10, \quad q = -2 + 3 = 1, \quad r = 3 - 4 + 12 = 11$$

and hence

$$\mathbf{p} = \begin{bmatrix} 10 \\ 1 \\ 11 \end{bmatrix}.$$

Note that when x, y, z are unknowns and $\mathbf{p}$ has this value the solution of equations (22.9) is

$$\mathbf{x} = \begin{bmatrix} 1 \\ 2 \\ 3 \end{bmatrix}.$$

22.2 The product of two 2×2 matrices

The product of the two 2×2 matrices

$$\mathbf{A} = \begin{bmatrix} a_1 & a_2 \\ b_1 & b_2 \end{bmatrix} \quad \text{and} \quad \mathbf{B} = \begin{bmatrix} c_1 & c_2 \\ d_1 & d_2 \end{bmatrix}$$

is defined as the 2×2 matrix

$$\mathbf{AB} = \begin{bmatrix} a_1 c_1 + a_2 d_1 & a_1 c_2 + a_2 d_2 \\ b_1 c_1 + b_2 d_1 & b_1 c_2 + b_2 d_2 \end{bmatrix}. \tag{22.10}$$

The elements in the product are the cross-products of rows of $\mathbf{A}$ and columns of $\mathbf{B}$. Thus the first element is the cross-product, or scalar product (see §6.8), of the *row* $(a_1\, a_2)$ and the column $(c_1 d_1)$, that is $a_1 c_1 + a_2 d_1$. The other elements are similarly formed and may be remembered by the scheme

$$\begin{bmatrix} \text{row 1 col 1} & \text{row 1 col 2} \\ \text{row 2 col 1} & \text{row 2 col 2} \end{bmatrix} \tag{22.11}$$

where in each case rows refer to $\mathbf{A}$ and columns to $\mathbf{B}$.

Example 2. *Find the product $\mathbf{AB}$ where*

$$\mathbf{A} = \begin{bmatrix} 1 & 2 \\ 2 & 3 \end{bmatrix} \quad \text{and} \quad \mathbf{B} = \begin{bmatrix} 3 & 7 \\ 5 & 2 \end{bmatrix}.$$

First fill in the matrix $\mathbf{A}$ twice in the product giving

$$\begin{bmatrix} 1 & 2 & 1 & 2 \\ 2 & 3 & 2 & 3 \end{bmatrix}.$$

Insert in this format the columns of $\mathbf{B}$ giving

$$\begin{bmatrix} 1 \cdot 3 & 2 \cdot 5 & 1 \cdot 7 & 2 \cdot 2 \\ 2 \cdot 3 & 3 \cdot 5 & 2 \cdot 7 & 3 \cdot 2 \end{bmatrix}.$$

Inserting plus signs and completing the arithmetic we obtain the required result as

$$\mathbf{AB} = \begin{bmatrix} 3 + 10 & 7 + 4 \\ 6 + 15 & 14 + 6 \end{bmatrix} = \begin{bmatrix} 13 & 11 \\ 21 & 20 \end{bmatrix}.$$

Notice that a change in the order of a product changes the result and, in general, $\mathbf{AB} \neq \mathbf{BA}$. Thus in the above example

$$\mathbf{BA} = \begin{bmatrix} 3 \cdot 1 + 7 \cdot 2 & 3 \cdot 2 + 7 \cdot 3 \\ 5 \cdot 1 + 2 \cdot 2 & 5 \cdot 2 + 2 \cdot 3 \end{bmatrix} = \begin{bmatrix} 17 & 27 \\ 9 & 16 \end{bmatrix}.$$

In **AB**, **A** is said to *premultiply* **B** or **B** is said to *postmultiply* **A**. The scheme shown in (22.11) applies also to a matrix premultiplying a vector if one remembers that a vector has only one column. Thus

$$\mathbf{A}\begin{bmatrix} x \\ y \end{bmatrix} = \begin{bmatrix} a_1 x + a_2 y \\ b_1 x + b_2 y \end{bmatrix}$$

and the product is itself a vector as seen in §22.1.

Exercises 22 (a)

1. If

$$\mathbf{A} = \begin{bmatrix} 2 & 1 & 3 \\ -1 & 0 & 1 \\ 3 & 4 & 2 \end{bmatrix},$$

write down the value of **Ax**

(a) when $\mathbf{x} = \begin{bmatrix} 1 \\ 1 \\ 1 \end{bmatrix}$, (b) when $\mathbf{x} = \begin{bmatrix} -1 \\ 0 \\ 1 \end{bmatrix}$, (c) when $\mathbf{x} = \begin{bmatrix} 3 \\ 1 \\ 3 \end{bmatrix}$.

2. With the same value of **A** as in Exercise 1 above, write down the value of **AB**

(a) when $\mathbf{B} = \begin{bmatrix} 1 & 1 \\ 1 & 1 \\ 1 & 1 \end{bmatrix}$, (b) when $\mathbf{B} = \begin{bmatrix} 2 & 0 \\ 1 & 1 \\ 0 & 2 \end{bmatrix}$,

(c) when $\mathbf{B} = \begin{bmatrix} 1 & 2 \\ -1 & -1 \\ 2 & 1 \end{bmatrix}$.

3. Find **AB** and **BA** when

$$\mathbf{A} = \begin{bmatrix} 2 & 1 \\ 1 & 2 \end{bmatrix} \quad \text{and} \quad \mathbf{B} = \begin{bmatrix} 3 & 3 \\ 0 & 4 \end{bmatrix}.$$

4. Given

$$\mathbf{A} = \begin{bmatrix} 1 & 3 \\ 2 & 1 \end{bmatrix}, \quad \mathbf{B} = \begin{bmatrix} 1 & 0 \\ 3 & 1 \end{bmatrix}, \quad \mathbf{C} = \begin{bmatrix} 0 & 1 \\ 1 & 3 \end{bmatrix},$$

find **AB**, **AC**, **BC** and **A(BC)**.

5. Find **AB**, **BC** and **CA** when

$$\mathbf{A} = \begin{bmatrix} 1 & 0 \\ 5 & 1 \end{bmatrix}, \quad \mathbf{B} = \begin{bmatrix} 1 & 5 \\ 0 & 1 \end{bmatrix}, \quad \mathbf{C} = \begin{bmatrix} 1 & 2 \\ 2 & 1 \end{bmatrix}.$$

6. Find $\mathbf{A}^2$ and $\mathbf{A}^3$ when

$$\mathbf{A} = \begin{bmatrix} 1 & 2 \\ 3 & 4 \end{bmatrix}$$

and verify that $\mathbf{A}(\mathbf{A}^2) = \mathbf{A}^2(\mathbf{A})$.

7. Given

$$A = \begin{bmatrix} 1 & 3 \\ 2 & 4 \end{bmatrix}, \qquad B = \begin{bmatrix} 4 & 0 & 1 & 2 \\ 2 & 1 & 3 & 4 \end{bmatrix},$$

find **AB**.

8. Find **A(BC)** when

$$A = \begin{bmatrix} 1 & 0 \\ 1 & 1 \end{bmatrix}, \qquad B = \begin{bmatrix} 2 & 1 \\ 3 & 1 \end{bmatrix}, \qquad C = \begin{bmatrix} 1 & 2 \\ 1 & 3 \end{bmatrix}.$$

9. Find $A^2 + B^2$ given that

$$A = \begin{bmatrix} 1 & 0 \\ 1 & 1 \end{bmatrix} \qquad \text{and} \qquad B = \begin{bmatrix} 1 & 1 \\ 0 & 1 \end{bmatrix}.$$

10. Find **AB**, **BC**, **CA** and **A(BC)** where

$$A = \begin{bmatrix} 2 & 0 \\ 0 & 3 \end{bmatrix}, \qquad B = \begin{bmatrix} 1 & 2 \\ 2 & 4 \end{bmatrix} \qquad \text{and} \qquad C = \begin{bmatrix} 1 & 0 \\ 0 & 4 \end{bmatrix}.$$

11. If $x_1 = [x_1, y_1, z_1]$ and $x_2 = \begin{bmatrix} x_2 \\ y_2 \\ z_2 \end{bmatrix}$, find $x_1 x_2$.

12. Calculate **AB**, **BA** and **BB** when

$$A = \begin{bmatrix} 3 & 2 \\ 2 & 3 \end{bmatrix} \qquad \text{and} \qquad B = \begin{bmatrix} 2 & 1 \\ 1 & 2 \end{bmatrix}.$$

22.3 The product of two 3×3 matrices

The product of two 3×3 matrices **A** and **B** is given by the scheme of cross-products

$$AB = \begin{bmatrix} \text{row 1 col 1} & \text{row 1 col 2} & \text{row 1 col 3} \\ \text{row 2 col 1} & \text{row 2 col 2} & \text{row 2 col 3} \\ \text{row 3 col 1} & \text{row 3 col 2} & \text{row 3 col 3} \end{bmatrix} \qquad (22.12)$$

whence if

$$A = \begin{bmatrix} a_1 & a_2 & a_3 \\ b_1 & b_2 & b_3 \\ c_1 & c_2 & c_3 \end{bmatrix} \qquad \text{and} \qquad B = \begin{bmatrix} l_1 & l_2 & l_3 \\ m_1 & m_2 & m_3 \\ n_1 & n_2 & n_3 \end{bmatrix}$$

then

$$AB = \begin{bmatrix} a_1 l_1 + a_2 m_1 + a_3 n_1 & a_1 l_2 + a_2 m_2 + a_3 n_2 & a_1 l_3 + a_2 m_3 + a_3 n_3 \\ b_1 l_1 + b_2 m_1 + b_3 n_1 & b_1 l_2 + b_2 m_2 + b_3 n_2 & b_1 l_3 + b_2 m_3 + b_3 n_3 \\ c_1 l_1 + c_2 m_1 + c_3 n_1 & c_1 l_2 + c_2 m_2 + c_3 n_2 & c_1 l_3 + c_2 m_3 + c_3 n_3 \end{bmatrix}.$$

$$(22.13)$$

Example 3. *Find the product* **AB** *when*

$$A = \begin{bmatrix} 1 & 0 & 1 \\ 2 & 1 & 3 \\ 4 & 2 & 1 \end{bmatrix}, \quad B = \begin{bmatrix} 4 & -1 & 3 \\ 2 & 2 & 2 \\ 3 & 7 & 1 \end{bmatrix}.$$

First fill in the matrix A three times in the product giving

$$\begin{bmatrix} 1 & 0 & 1 & 1 & 0 & 1 & 1 & 0 & 1 \\ 2 & 1 & 3 & 2 & 1 & 3 & 2 & 1 & 3 \\ 4 & 2 & 1 & 4 & 2 & 1 & 4 & 2 & 1 \end{bmatrix}.$$

Insert in this format the three columns of B each in its own column giving

$$\begin{bmatrix} 1.4 & 0.2 & 1.3 & 1.-1 & 0.2 & 1.7 & 1.3 & 0.2 & 1.1 \\ 2.4 & 1.2 & 3.3 & 2.-1 & 1.2 & 3.7 & 2.3 & 1.2 & 3.1 \\ 4.4 & 2.2 & 1.3 & 4.-1 & 2.2 & 1.7 & 4.3 & 2.2 & 1.1 \end{bmatrix}.$$

Inserting plus signs the final result is

$$AB = \begin{bmatrix} 4+0+3 & -1+0+7 & 3+0+1 \\ 8+2+9 & -2+2+21 & 6+2+3 \\ 16+4+3 & -4+4+7 & 12+4+1 \end{bmatrix} = \begin{bmatrix} 7 & 6 & 4 \\ 19 & 21 & 11 \\ 23 & 7 & 17 \end{bmatrix}.$$

Example 4. *If* A *is the* 3 × 3 *matrix in Example* 3 *above, find the product* **AC** *where*

$$C = \begin{bmatrix} 4 & -1 \\ 2 & 2 \\ 3 & 7 \end{bmatrix}.$$

We work as before but remember that the third column of C does not exist. Hence the working is

$$\begin{bmatrix} 1 & 0 & 1 & 1 & 0 & 1 \\ 2 & 1 & 3 & 2 & 1 & 3 \\ 4 & 2 & 1 & 4 & 2 & 1 \end{bmatrix}$$

leading to

$$\begin{bmatrix} 1.4 & 0.2 & 1.3 & 1.-1 & 0.2 & 1.7 \\ 2.4 & 1.2 & 3.3 & 2.-1 & 1.2 & 3.7 \\ 4.4 & 2.2 & 1.3 & 4.-1 & 2.2 & 1.7 \end{bmatrix}$$

and

$$AC = \begin{bmatrix} 7 & 6 \\ 19 & 21 \\ 23 & 7 \end{bmatrix}.$$

The above example shows that matrices of different dimensions can be multiplied *provided* that the number of columns in the premultiplier is equal to the number of rows in the postmultiplier. Such matrices are said to be *conformable* and the product is not defined for matrices which are not conformable. Thus the product **CA** in Example 4 above is meaningless.

22.4 Some general definitions

(i) Multiplication of a matrix by a scalar

The result of multiplying a matrix by a scalar (or number) is defined as being the same matrix with each element multiplied by the scalar.

Thus if

$$A = \begin{bmatrix} 2 & -1 \\ 3 & 0 \end{bmatrix} \quad \text{then} \quad 3A = \begin{bmatrix} 6 & -3 \\ 9 & 0 \end{bmatrix} \quad \text{and} \quad -2A = \begin{bmatrix} -4 & 2 \\ -6 & 0 \end{bmatrix}.$$

(ii) Addition of two matrices

Two matrices of the same shape, i.e. with the same number of rows and columns respectively in each, can be added or subtracted simply by adding or subtracting the elements. Thus if

$$A = \begin{bmatrix} 2 & -1 \\ 3 & 0 \end{bmatrix} \quad \text{and} \quad B = \begin{bmatrix} 4 & 6 \\ 1 & 2 \end{bmatrix}$$

then

$$A + B = \begin{bmatrix} 6 & 5 \\ 4 & 2 \end{bmatrix}, \quad A - B = \begin{bmatrix} -2 & -7 \\ 2 & -2 \end{bmatrix}, \quad A + A = 2A = \begin{bmatrix} 4 & -2 \\ 6 & 0 \end{bmatrix}.$$

It is evident that addition is a commutative operation, i.e. $A + B = B + A$.

(iii) The distributive law

The operations of matrices also satisfy the distributive law both for addition and multiplication, that is

$$(A + B) + C = A + (B + C),$$

the quantities in brackets being added first. Also

$$A(B + C) = AB + AC.$$

(iv) Commutative matrices

In the product of two matrices A and B, the matrices are said to be commutative if, and only if, $AB = BA$. For example with the matrices in (ii) above

$$AB = \begin{bmatrix} 7 & 10 \\ 12 & 18 \end{bmatrix}, \quad BA = \begin{bmatrix} 26 & -4 \\ 8 & -1 \end{bmatrix}$$

so that these two matrices are not commutative.

(v) The power of a matrix

Just as in elementary algebra, the powers of a matrix are defined by products so that

$$A^2 = A \times A, \qquad A^3 = A \times A \times A,$$

and so on.

22.5 Some particular matrices

(*i*) *Diagonal matrices*

A square matrix, that is one with an equal number of rows and columns, whose only non-zero elements occur in the principal diagonal is called a *diagonal matrix.* An example is

$$A = \begin{bmatrix} a & 0 & 0 \\ 0 & b & 0 \\ 0 & 0 & c \end{bmatrix}$$

and this is often written omitting the zeros as

$$A = \begin{bmatrix} a & & \\ & b & \\ & & c \end{bmatrix}$$

or as diag (a, b, c).

(*ii*) *Unit matrices*

A diagonal matrix in which all the non-zero elements are unity is called a *unit matrix.* Thus

$$I_2 = \begin{bmatrix} 1 & \\ & 1 \end{bmatrix}, \qquad I_3 = \begin{bmatrix} 1 & & \\ & 1 & \\ & & 1 \end{bmatrix} \text{ and so on.}$$

The suffices on the I's are often omitted if the order of the matrix is clear. The unit matrix has all the properties of unity in ordinary algebra and it can be easily verified that

$$IA = AI = A,$$
$$I = I^2 = I^3 = \ldots$$

(*iii*) *The null matrix*

A matrix in which all the elements are zero is called a *null matrix,* denoted by **0**, and has the properties of zero in elementary algebra. Thus

$$A0 = A0 = 0.$$

It should be noted however that the equation $AB = 0$ does not imply that either **A** or **B** is **0**. For example $AB = 0$ when

$$A = \begin{bmatrix} 1 & 7 \\ 0 & 0 \end{bmatrix} \quad \text{and} \quad B = \begin{bmatrix} 7 & 14 \\ -1 & -2 \end{bmatrix}.$$

(*iv*) *Triangular matrices*

A square matrix in which all the elements above the principal diagonal are zero is called a *lower triangular matrix* and one in which all the elements below the principal diagonal are zero is called an *upper triangular matrix*. These are usually denoted by **L** and **U** respectively and examples are

$$\mathbf{L} = \begin{bmatrix} 3 & & \\ 4 & 2 & \\ -1 & 4 & 1 \end{bmatrix}, \quad \mathbf{U} = \begin{bmatrix} 3 & 4 & -1 \\ & 2 & 4 \\ & & 1 \end{bmatrix},$$

the omitted elements being all zero. Either is called a *unit triangular matrix* (and usually denoted by the suffix 1) when the elements of the principal diagonal are all unity; examples are

$$\mathbf{L}_1 = \begin{bmatrix} 1 & & \\ 4 & 1 & \\ -1 & 4 & 1 \end{bmatrix}, \quad \mathbf{U}_1 = \begin{bmatrix} 1 & 4 & -1 \\ & 1 & 4 \\ & & 1 \end{bmatrix}.$$

22.6 Determinants

With any square matrix there is associated a number $\triangle$ which is calculated from products of the elements of the matrix. Thus if

$$\mathbf{A} = \begin{bmatrix} a & b \\ c & d \end{bmatrix}, \quad \triangle = |\mathbf{A}| = \begin{vmatrix} a & b \\ c & d \end{vmatrix} \tag{22.14}$$

and $\triangle$ is the number $ad - bc$. Similarly for a 3×3 matrix

$$\mathbf{A} = \begin{bmatrix} a & b & c \\ d & e & f \\ g & h & i \end{bmatrix}, \quad \triangle = |\mathbf{A}| = \begin{vmatrix} a & b & c \\ d & e & f \\ g & h & i \end{vmatrix}$$

and

$$\triangle = a \begin{vmatrix} e & f \\ h & i \end{vmatrix} + b \begin{vmatrix} f & d \\ i & g \end{vmatrix} + c \begin{vmatrix} d & e \\ g & h \end{vmatrix}$$
$$= a(ei - hf) + b(fg - id) + c(dh - ge) \tag{22.15}$$

The value of the associated determinant has often to be calculated when solving simultaneous equations and an example of the calculation so involved is given below.

A matrix **A** is said to be *singular* if the associated determinant $\triangle$ is zero; otherwise it is said to be *non-singular*.

Example 5. *Calculate the value of the determinant*

$$\triangle = \begin{vmatrix} 1 & 2 & 3 \\ 0 & 1 & 3 \\ 2 & -1 & 5 \end{vmatrix}.$$

$$\triangle = 1 \begin{vmatrix} 1 & 3 \\ -1 & 5 \end{vmatrix} + 2 \begin{vmatrix} 3 & 0 \\ 5 & 2 \end{vmatrix} + 3 \begin{vmatrix} 0 & 1 \\ 2 & -1 \end{vmatrix}$$
$$= 1 \times 8 + 2 \times 6 + 3 \times (-2) = 14.$$

22.7 The inverse matrix

The inverse of a square matrix A is a matrix, denoted by A^{-1}, which is such that $A^{-1}A = I$. Thus to solve the simultaneous equations of §22.1, i.e.

$$Ax = p$$

we operate on the equation with A^{-1} giving

$$A^{-1}Ax = A^{-1}p$$

that is

$$Ix = x = A^{-1}p$$

and this is the solution of the equations. It should be noted that the inverse matrix does not exist if the determinant associated with the original matrix is zero.

The following example shows how the inverse matrix may be calculated. This is not a very straightforward way of doing this but less complicated methods will be used later.

Example 6. *Solve the equations $2x + 3y = 8$, $5x - 2y = 1$ by finding the inverse of the matrix*

$$A = \begin{bmatrix} 2 & 3 \\ 5 & -2 \end{bmatrix}.$$

Let

$$A^{-1} = \begin{bmatrix} a & b \\ c & d \end{bmatrix}$$

then, since $A^{-1}A = I$ we have

$$\begin{bmatrix} a & b \\ c & d \end{bmatrix} \begin{bmatrix} 2 & 3 \\ 5 & -2 \end{bmatrix} = \begin{bmatrix} 2a + 5b & 3a - 2b \\ 2c + 5d & 3c - 2d \end{bmatrix} = \begin{bmatrix} 1 & \\ & 1 \end{bmatrix}.$$

Hence $3a - 2b = 0$, $2c + 5d = 0$, $2a + 5b = 1$, $3c - 2d = 1$ giving

$$a = \frac{2}{19}, \quad b = \frac{3}{19}, \quad c = \frac{5}{19}, \quad d = -\frac{2}{19}.$$

Therefore

$$A^{-1} = \frac{1}{19} \begin{bmatrix} 2 & 3 \\ 5 & -2 \end{bmatrix}$$

and

$$\begin{bmatrix} x \\ y \end{bmatrix} = A^{-1} \begin{bmatrix} 8 \\ 1 \end{bmatrix} = \frac{1}{19} \begin{bmatrix} 2 & 3 \\ 5 & -2 \end{bmatrix} \begin{bmatrix} 8 \\ 1 \end{bmatrix}$$

$$= \frac{1}{19} \begin{bmatrix} 2 \cdot 8 + 3 \cdot 1 \\ 5 \cdot 8 - 2 \cdot 1 \end{bmatrix} = \frac{1}{19} \begin{bmatrix} 19 \\ 38 \end{bmatrix} = \begin{bmatrix} 1 \\ 2 \end{bmatrix}.$$

Thus $x = 1$, $y = 2$.

Exercises 22(b)

Given that

$$A = \begin{bmatrix} 1 & 1 & 1 \\ 1 & 1 & 1 \\ 1 & 1 & 1 \end{bmatrix}, \quad B = \begin{bmatrix} 1 & 2 & 0 \\ 0 & 1 & 2 \\ 0 & 0 & 1 \end{bmatrix}, \quad C = \begin{bmatrix} 1 & 2 & 3 \\ 2 & 3 & 4 \\ 3 & 4 & 5 \end{bmatrix},$$

$$D = \begin{bmatrix} 1 & 0 & 1 \\ 0 & 1 & 1 \\ 0 & 0 & 0 \end{bmatrix}.$$

1. Find the values of A^2, B^2, C^2 and D^2.

2. Find ABC and ABCD.

3. Find E^2, F^2 and EF where

$$E = \begin{bmatrix} 1 & & \\ a & 1 & \\ b & c & 1 \end{bmatrix}, \quad F = \begin{bmatrix} 1 & \alpha & \beta \\ & 1 & \gamma \\ & & 1 \end{bmatrix}.$$

4. If

$$A = \begin{bmatrix} a & b & c \\ d & e & f \\ g & h & i \end{bmatrix} \quad \text{and} \quad D = \begin{bmatrix} p & & \\ & q & \\ & & r \end{bmatrix}$$

show that

$$AD = \begin{bmatrix} ap & bq & cr \\ dp & eq & fr \\ gp & hq & ir \end{bmatrix}, \quad DA = \begin{bmatrix} ap & bp & cp \\ dq & eq & fq \\ gr & hr & ir \end{bmatrix}.$$

5. Show that if

$$L = \begin{bmatrix} 1 & & \\ 2 & 1 & \\ 3 & 0 & 1 \end{bmatrix} \quad \text{and} \quad U = \begin{bmatrix} 1 & 2 & 4 \\ & 2 & -2 \\ & & 3 \end{bmatrix}$$

then

$$LU = \begin{bmatrix} 1 & 2 & 4 \\ 2 & 6 & 6 \\ 3 & 6 & 15 \end{bmatrix}.$$

6. If

$$A = \begin{bmatrix} 1 & 2 & -1 \\ 4 & 1 & 2 \\ 3 & 0 & -3 \end{bmatrix} \quad \text{and} \quad D = \begin{bmatrix} 1 & & \\ & -1 & \\ & & 1 \end{bmatrix},$$

show that

$$AD = \begin{bmatrix} 1 & -2 & -1 \\ 4 & -1 & 2 \\ 3 & 0 & -3 \end{bmatrix}, \quad DA = \begin{bmatrix} 1 & 2 & -1 \\ -4 & -1 & -2 \\ 3 & 0 & -3 \end{bmatrix}.$$

7. Prove that

$$\begin{vmatrix} 2 & 1 & 2 \\ 1 & 0 & 1 \\ 2 & 1 & 2 \end{vmatrix} = 0.$$

8. Show that

$$\begin{vmatrix} a & h & g \\ h & b & f \\ g & f & c \end{vmatrix} = abc + 2fgh - af^2 - bg^2 - ch^2.$$

9. Verify that if

$$\mathbf{A} = \begin{bmatrix} 2 & -1 & 1 \\ 1 & -1 & 2 \\ -1 & 1 & -1 \end{bmatrix} \quad \text{then} \quad \mathbf{A}^{-1} = \begin{bmatrix} 1 & 0 & 1 \\ 1 & 1 & 3 \\ 0 & 1 & 1 \end{bmatrix}.$$

10. Prove that the inverse of the matrix product LU is the matrix $\mathbf{U}^{-1}\mathbf{L}^{-1}$ where $\mathbf{U}^{-1}$ and $\mathbf{L}^{-1}$ are the inverses of U and L respectively.

11. Writing $\mathbf{K} = \begin{bmatrix} 0 & 1 \\ -1 & 0 \end{bmatrix}$, show that $\mathbf{K}^2 = -\mathbf{I}$, $\mathbf{K}^3 = -\mathbf{K}$ and $\mathbf{K}^4 = \mathbf{I}$.

12. Prove that

$$\begin{bmatrix} 1 & 2 & 3 \\ 0 & 0 & 0 \\ 0 & 0 & 1 \end{bmatrix} \begin{bmatrix} 2 & 4 & -2 \\ -1 & -2 & 1 \\ 0 & 0 & 0 \end{bmatrix} = 0.$$

22.8 The decomposition of a matrix

A square matrix A can, in general, be expressed as a product of the form

$$\mathbf{A} = \mathbf{L}_1\mathbf{U} \qquad (22.16)$$

where U is an upper triangular matrix and $\mathbf{L}_1$ is a lower unit triangular matrix. The combination $\mathbf{U}_1\mathbf{L}$ is also possible and, as a further step when required, U can be replaced by $\mathbf{DU}_1$, D being a diagonal matrix and $\mathbf{U}_1$ an upper unit triangular matrix. It can be shown that the decomposition is unique.

The decomposition of a matrix in this way is not difficult to perform and when it has been expressed in the form (22.16) it is a much simpler process to find the inverse matrix $\mathbf{A}^{-1}$ and hence to solve the equation $\mathbf{Ax} = \mathbf{p}$.

Example 7. *Express the matrix*

$$\mathbf{A} = \begin{bmatrix} 2 & 3 \\ 5 & -2 \end{bmatrix}$$

in the form $\mathbf{L}_1\mathbf{DU}_1$.

Write $\mathbf{A} = \mathbf{L}_1\mathbf{U}$, that is

$$\begin{bmatrix} 2 & 3 \\ 5 & -2 \end{bmatrix} = \begin{bmatrix} 1 & 0 \\ a & 1 \end{bmatrix} \begin{bmatrix} b & c \\ 0 & d \end{bmatrix}$$

where a, b, c and d have to be found. Carrying out the multiplication we have

$$\begin{bmatrix} 2 & 3 \\ 5 & -2 \end{bmatrix} = \begin{bmatrix} 1.b+0.0 & 1.c+0.d \\ a.b+1.0 & a.c+1.d \end{bmatrix} = \begin{bmatrix} b & c \\ ab & ac+d \end{bmatrix}.$$

Hence $b = 2$, $c = 3$, $ab = 5$ giving $a = 5/2$, $ac + d = -2$ giving $d = -19/2$ and we thus have

$$\begin{bmatrix} 2 & 3 \\ 5 & -2 \end{bmatrix} = \begin{bmatrix} 1 & \\ 5/2 & 1 \end{bmatrix}\begin{bmatrix} 2 & 3 \\ & -19/2 \end{bmatrix}.$$

A further decomposition, if required, is found by writing

$$\begin{bmatrix} 2 & 3 \\ & -19/2 \end{bmatrix} = \begin{bmatrix} e & \\ & f \end{bmatrix}\begin{bmatrix} 1 & g \\ & 1 \end{bmatrix} = \begin{bmatrix} e & eg \\ & f \end{bmatrix}.$$

Thus $e = 2$, $f = -19/2$, $eg = 3$ so that $g = 3/2$ and we have

$$\begin{bmatrix} 2 & 3 \\ 5 & -2 \end{bmatrix} = \begin{bmatrix} 1 & \\ 5/2 & 1 \end{bmatrix}\begin{bmatrix} 2 & \\ & -19/2 \end{bmatrix}\begin{bmatrix} 1 & 3/2 \\ & 1 \end{bmatrix},$$

and this is of the required form.

Example 8. *Express in the form* $A = L_1U$ *the* 3×3 *matrix*

$$A = \begin{bmatrix} 1 & 2 & 4 \\ 2 & 6 & 6 \\ 3 & 6 & 15 \end{bmatrix}.$$

Write

$$\begin{aligned}
A &= \begin{bmatrix} 1 & & \\ a & 1 & \\ b & c & 1 \end{bmatrix}\begin{bmatrix} d & g & h \\ & e & i \\ & & f \end{bmatrix} \\
&= \begin{bmatrix} 1.d+0.0+0.0 & 1.g+0.e+0.0 & 1.h+0.i+0.f \\ a.d+1.0+0.0 & a.g+1.e+0.0 & a.h+1.i+0.f \\ b.d+c.0+1.0 & b.g+c.e+1.0 & b.h+c.i+1.f \end{bmatrix} \\
&= \begin{bmatrix} d & g & h \\ ad & ag+e & ah+i \\ bd & bg+ce & bh+ci+f \end{bmatrix}.
\end{aligned}$$

Hence d, g, h take the values 1, 2, 4 respectively, that is the values of the first row of A. This is always the case. Then

$$\begin{array}{llll}
ad = 2 & \text{giving} \ \ a = 2, & bd = 3 & \text{giving} \ \ b = 3, \\
ag + e = 6 & \text{giving} \ \ e = 2, & bg + ce = 6 & \text{giving} \ \ c = 0, \\
ah + i = 6 & \text{giving} \ \ i = -2, & bh + ci + f = 15 & \text{giving} \ \ f = 3.
\end{array}$$

Therefore

$$A = \begin{bmatrix} 1 & & \\ 2 & 1 & \\ 3 & 0 & 1 \end{bmatrix}\begin{bmatrix} 1 & 2 & 4 \\ & 2 & -2 \\ & & 3 \end{bmatrix}.$$

22.9 The inverse of a unit diagonal matrix

Provided that the determinant associated with the matrix is not zero, the inverse of a unit diagonal matrix is easily found as may be seen in the following examples.

Example 9. *Find the inverse of* $L_1 = \begin{bmatrix} 1 & \\ k & 1 \end{bmatrix}$.

Writing $L^{-1}_1 = \begin{bmatrix} a & b \\ c & d \end{bmatrix}$ we must have

$$\begin{bmatrix} a & b \\ c & d \end{bmatrix}\begin{bmatrix} 1 & \\ k & 1 \end{bmatrix} = \begin{bmatrix} 1 & \\ & 1 \end{bmatrix}$$

and this gives

$$\begin{bmatrix} a.1+b.k & a.0+b.1 \\ c.1+d.k & c.0+d.1 \end{bmatrix} = \begin{bmatrix} a+bk & b \\ c+dk & d \end{bmatrix} = \begin{bmatrix} 1 & \\ & 1 \end{bmatrix}.$$

Hence $b = 0$, $a = 1$, $d = 1$, $c + k = 0$ leading to $c = -k$ and we have

$$\mathbf{L}_1^{-1} = \begin{bmatrix} 1 & \\ -k & 1 \end{bmatrix}.$$

That $\mathbf{L}_1^{-1}$ is also a unit lower triangular matrix is not surprising and this form might have been assumed at the start.

Example 10. *Find the inverse of*

$$\mathbf{L} = \begin{bmatrix} 1 & & \\ \alpha & 1 & \\ \beta & \gamma & 1 \end{bmatrix}.$$

Assuming that $\mathbf{L}_1^{-1}$ is a unit lower triangular matrix we write

$$\mathbf{L}_1^{-1} = \begin{bmatrix} 1 & & \\ a & 1 & \\ b & c & 1 \end{bmatrix}$$

and

$$\begin{bmatrix} 1 & & \\ a & 1 & \\ b & c & 1 \end{bmatrix}\begin{bmatrix} 1 & & \\ \alpha & 1 & \\ \beta & \gamma & 1 \end{bmatrix} = \begin{bmatrix} 1 & & \\ & 1 & \\ & & 1 \end{bmatrix}.$$

This gives

$$\begin{bmatrix} 1.1+0.\alpha+0.\beta & 1.0+0.1+0.\gamma & 1.0+0.0+0.1 \\ a.1+1.\alpha+0.\beta & a.0+1.1+0.\gamma & a.0+1.0+0.1 \\ b.1+c.\alpha+1.\beta & b.0+c.1+1.\gamma & b.0+c.0+1.1 \end{bmatrix}$$

$$= \begin{bmatrix} 1 & 0 & 0 \\ a+\alpha & 1 & 0 \\ b+c\alpha+\beta & c+\gamma & 1 \end{bmatrix} = \begin{bmatrix} 1 & & \\ & 1 & \\ & & 1 \end{bmatrix}.$$

Hence $a = -\alpha$, $c = -\gamma$, $b = -c\alpha - \beta = \alpha\gamma - \beta$ and

$$\mathbf{L}_1^{-1} = \begin{bmatrix} 1 & & \\ -\alpha & 1 & \\ \alpha\gamma - \beta & -\gamma & 1 \end{bmatrix}.$$

22.10 Reduction of a system of equations

When a system of equations can be expressed in the form $\mathbf{L}_1\mathbf{U}\mathbf{x} = \mathbf{p}$ and the inverse $\mathbf{L}_1^{-1}$ of $\mathbf{L}_1$ can be found (and this implies that $|\mathbf{L}_1| \neq 0$), the equation can be reduced as follows. Operate on both sides of the equation with $\mathbf{L}_1^{-1}$, giving

$$\mathbf{L}_1^{-1}\mathbf{L}_1\mathbf{U}\mathbf{x} = \mathbf{L}_1^{-1}\mathbf{p},$$

that is

$$\mathbf{I}\mathbf{U}\mathbf{x} = \mathbf{U}\mathbf{x} = \mathbf{L}_1^{-1}\mathbf{p} \qquad (22.17)$$

and this is the reduced equation.

Example 11. *Reduce the simultaneous equations* $2x + 3y = 8$, $5x - 2y = 1$ *to the above form and hence solve the equations.*

The matrix of the coefficients is $\begin{bmatrix} 2 & 3 \\ 5 & -2 \end{bmatrix}$ and this, by Example 7, can be written

$$\begin{bmatrix} 1 & \\ 5/2 & 1 \end{bmatrix} \begin{bmatrix} 2 & 3 \\ & -19/2 \end{bmatrix}.$$

Hence

$$L_1 = \begin{bmatrix} 1 & \\ 5/2 & 1 \end{bmatrix} \quad \text{and} \quad U = \begin{bmatrix} 2 & 3 \\ & -19/2 \end{bmatrix}.$$

Now, by Example 9 with $k = 5/2$,

$$L_1^{-1} = \begin{bmatrix} 1 & \\ -5/2 & 1 \end{bmatrix}$$

and so equation (22.17) becomes

$$\begin{bmatrix} 2 & 3 \\ & -19/2 \end{bmatrix} \begin{bmatrix} x \\ y \end{bmatrix} = \begin{bmatrix} 1 & \\ -5/2 & 1 \end{bmatrix} \begin{bmatrix} 8 \\ 1 \end{bmatrix} = \begin{bmatrix} 8 \\ -19 \end{bmatrix}.$$

The reduced equations are therefore

$$2x + 3y = 8, \quad -\frac{19}{2}y = -19,$$

giving $y = 2$ and $x = 1$.

Example 12. *Solve the equations*

$$\begin{bmatrix} 1 & 2 & 4 \\ 2 & 6 & 6 \\ 3 & 6 & 15 \end{bmatrix} \begin{bmatrix} x \\ y \\ z \end{bmatrix} = \begin{bmatrix} 2 \\ 3 \\ 1 \end{bmatrix}.$$

Using the result of Example 8, the equations can be written $L_1 U x = p$ where

$$L_1 = \begin{bmatrix} 1 & & \\ 2 & 1 & \\ 3 & 0 & 1 \end{bmatrix} \quad \text{and} \quad U = \begin{bmatrix} 1 & 2 & 4 \\ & 2 & -2 \\ & & 3 \end{bmatrix}.$$

From Example 10 with $\alpha = 2$, $\beta = 3$, $\gamma = 0$, the inverse of L_1 is given by

$$L_1^{-1} = \begin{bmatrix} 1 & & \\ -2 & 1 & \\ -3 & 0 & 1 \end{bmatrix}$$

so that, since $Ux = L_1^{-1}p$,

$$\begin{bmatrix} 1 & 2 & 4 \\ & 2 & -2 \\ & & 3 \end{bmatrix} \begin{bmatrix} x \\ y \\ z \end{bmatrix} = \begin{bmatrix} 1 & & \\ -2 & 1 & \\ -3 & 0 & 1 \end{bmatrix} \begin{bmatrix} 2 \\ 3 \\ 1 \end{bmatrix} = \begin{bmatrix} 2 \\ -1 \\ -5 \end{bmatrix}.$$

Hence

$$x + 2y + 4z = 2,$$
$$2y - 2z = -1,$$
$$3z = -5.$$

The third equation gives $z = -5/3$, the second $y = -13/6$ and the first then leads to $x = 13$ and this is the required solution of the equations.

22.11 Alternative method of reduction of the system of equations

A system of equations $\mathbf{Ax} = \mathbf{p}$ may be reduced to the form $\mathbf{Ux} = \mathbf{L}_1^{-1}\mathbf{p}$ by the traditional method of successive elimination of the unknowns, and this method is often the better way of dealing with a large number of equations especially when desk calculating machines are available. The method is outlined in the following example for the case of three equations in three unknowns.

Example 13. *Solve the equations* $2x + 5y - 3z = 5$, $x - 4y + z = -5$ *and* $4x + 3y - z = 10$.

First reduce each equation by dividing by the coefficient of x (if this coefficient is not zero) and so obtain the equations

$$x + 2{\cdot}5y - 1{\cdot}5z = 2{\cdot}5, \tag{22.18}$$

$$x - 4y + z = -5, \tag{22.19}$$

$$x + 0{\cdot}75y - 0{\cdot}25z = 2{\cdot}5. \tag{22.20}$$

By subtracting equation (22.19) from (22.18) and then (22.20) from (22.19) we have

$$6{\cdot}5y - 2{\cdot}5z = 7{\cdot}5, \tag{22.21}$$

$$-4{\cdot}75y + 1{\cdot}25z = -7{\cdot}5. \tag{22.22}$$

Then reduce the coefficient of y to unity in each of these equations to give

$$y - 0{\cdot}385z = 1{\cdot}154, \tag{22.23}$$

$$y - 0{\cdot}263z = 1{\cdot}579. \tag{22.24}$$

Subtraction then yields

$$0{\cdot}122z = 0{\cdot}425$$

and

$$z = 3{\cdot}48. \tag{22.25}$$

Equations (22.18), (22.23) and (22.25) can be written in matrix form as

$$\begin{bmatrix} 1 & 2{\cdot}5 & -1{\cdot}5 \\ & 1 & -0{\cdot}385 \\ & & 1 \end{bmatrix} \begin{bmatrix} x \\ y \\ z \end{bmatrix} = \begin{bmatrix} 2{\cdot}5 \\ 1{\cdot}154 \\ 3{\cdot}48 \end{bmatrix}$$

and this is of the form $\mathbf{U}_1\mathbf{x} = \mathbf{p}$. The values of x, y and z are easily deduced as $x = 1{\cdot}56$, $y = 2{\cdot}49$, $z = 3{\cdot}48$. It should be noticed that accuracy is often sacrificed when dividing unless a large number of figures are retained in the calculation. In this case the accurate solution is $x = 1{\cdot}5$, $y = 2{\cdot}5$, $z = 3{\cdot}5$.

22.12 Matrices as transforms

If the coordinates of a point P are (x, y) referred to coordinate axes OX, OY and (x', y') referred to new axes OX', OY' obtained by rotating OX, OY through an angle α (Fig. 222), the relations between the two sets of coordinates are obtained by projecting OP on the axes OX and OY giving

$$x = x' \cos \alpha - y' \sin \alpha,$$
$$y = x' \sin \alpha + y' \cos \alpha.$$

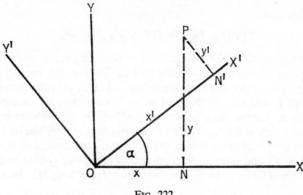

FIG. 222

By projecting OP on OX' and OY' we obtain similarly the inverse relations

$$x' = x \cos \alpha + y \sin \alpha,$$
$$y' = -x \sin \alpha + y \cos \alpha.$$

In matrix notation these results are

$$\begin{bmatrix} x \\ y \end{bmatrix} = \begin{bmatrix} \cos \alpha & -\sin \alpha \\ \sin \alpha & \cos \alpha \end{bmatrix} \begin{bmatrix} x' \\ y' \end{bmatrix} \qquad (22.26)$$

$$\begin{bmatrix} x' \\ y' \end{bmatrix} = \begin{bmatrix} \cos \alpha & \sin \alpha \\ -\sin \alpha & \cos \alpha \end{bmatrix} \begin{bmatrix} x \\ y \end{bmatrix} \qquad (22.27)$$

and it is evident that one matrix is the inverse of the other, that is

$$\begin{bmatrix} \cos \alpha & -\sin \alpha \\ \sin \alpha & \cos \alpha \end{bmatrix} \begin{bmatrix} \cos \alpha & \sin \alpha \\ -\sin \alpha & \cos \alpha \end{bmatrix} = \begin{bmatrix} 1 & \\ & 1 \end{bmatrix}.$$

Again if a second rotation through an angle β gives new axes OX'', OY'' with reference to which the coordinates of P are (x'', y''), it is clear that

$$\begin{bmatrix} x'' \\ y'' \end{bmatrix} = \begin{bmatrix} \cos \beta & \sin \beta \\ -\sin \beta & \cos \beta \end{bmatrix} \begin{bmatrix} x' \\ y' \end{bmatrix}$$

$$= \begin{bmatrix} \cos \beta & \sin \beta \\ -\sin \beta & \cos \beta \end{bmatrix} \begin{bmatrix} \cos \alpha & \sin \alpha \\ -\sin \alpha & \cos \alpha \end{bmatrix} \begin{bmatrix} x \\ y \end{bmatrix}$$

$$= \begin{bmatrix} \cos (\alpha + \beta) & \sin (\alpha + \beta) \\ -\sin (\alpha + \beta) & \cos (\alpha + \beta) \end{bmatrix} \begin{bmatrix} x \\ y \end{bmatrix}.$$

More generally if the scale is changed in addition to the rotation of axes we may have a relation of the form

$$\begin{bmatrix} x' \\ y' \end{bmatrix} = \begin{bmatrix} p & q \\ & p-q \end{bmatrix} \begin{bmatrix} x \\ y \end{bmatrix}$$

and in this case

$$(x')^2 + (y')^2 = (p^2 + q^2)(x^2 + y^2).$$

The mapping of a point on a plane is sometimes given as the reflection of the point in some line. If this line passes through the origin the mapping is found in matrix form as follows. Let (x, y) be the coordinates of a point P and (x', y') those of its reflection Q in the straight line $y = x \tan \alpha$. Let the polar coordinates of P be (r, θ); with the line $y = x \tan \alpha$ as a new initial line the polar coordinates of P will be $(r, \theta - \alpha)$. With respect to this new initial line the polar coordinates of Q will be $\{r, -(\theta - \alpha)\}$ and therefore the polar coordinates of Q with respect to the x-axis will be $\{r, -(\theta - \alpha) + \alpha\}$, that is $(r, -\theta + 2\alpha)$. Hence

$$x' = r \cos (2\alpha - \theta) = r \cos \theta \cos 2\alpha + r \sin \theta \sin 2\alpha$$
$$= x \cos 2\alpha + y \sin 2\alpha,$$

$$y' = r \sin (2\alpha - \theta) = r \cos \theta \sin 2\alpha - r \sin \theta \cos 2\alpha$$
$$= x \sin 2\alpha - y \cos 2\alpha,$$

and therefore

$$\begin{bmatrix} x' \\ y' \end{bmatrix} = \begin{bmatrix} \cos 2\alpha & \sin 2\alpha \\ \sin 2\alpha & -\cos 2\alpha \end{bmatrix} \begin{bmatrix} x \\ y \end{bmatrix}.$$

Example 14. *Show that the matrices that correspond to the reflection of a point in the lines $y = -x \tan \alpha$ and $y = x \tan \alpha$ are respectively*

$$\mathbf{M}_1 = \begin{bmatrix} \cos 2\alpha & -\sin 2\alpha \\ -\sin 2\alpha & -\cos 2\alpha \end{bmatrix} \quad \text{and} \quad \mathbf{M}_2 = \begin{bmatrix} \cos 2\alpha & \sin 2\alpha \\ \sin 2\alpha & -\cos 2\alpha \end{bmatrix}.$$

Show further that the combination of these reflections in the order first $\mathbf{M}_1$ and then $\mathbf{M}_2$ is equivalent to a counter-clockwise rotation about the origin through an angle 4α.

The value of $\mathbf{M}_2$ has been given above and that for $\mathbf{M}_1$ is obtained by writing $-\alpha$ in place of α. The matrix for the combined transform in the required order is

$$\mathbf{M}_2 \mathbf{M}_1 = \begin{bmatrix} \cos 2\alpha & \sin 2\alpha \\ \sin 2\alpha & -\cos 2\alpha \end{bmatrix} \begin{bmatrix} \cos 2\alpha & -\sin 2\alpha \\ -\sin 2\alpha & -\cos 2\alpha \end{bmatrix}$$

$$= \begin{bmatrix} \cos^2 2\alpha - \sin^2 2\alpha & -2 \sin 2\alpha \cos 2\alpha \\ 2 \sin 2\alpha \cos 2\alpha & \cos^2 2\alpha - \sin^2 2\alpha \end{bmatrix}$$

so that

$$\begin{bmatrix} x' \\ y' \end{bmatrix} = \begin{bmatrix} \cos 4\alpha & -\sin 4\alpha \\ \sin 4\alpha & \cos 4\alpha \end{bmatrix} \begin{bmatrix} x \\ y \end{bmatrix}$$

and this, from equation (22.26), corresponds to a rotation of 4α about the origin.

Exercises 22(c)

1. Express in the form $\mathbf{L}_1 \mathbf{U}$ the matrix

$$\begin{bmatrix} 1 & 4 \\ 7 & 9 \end{bmatrix}.$$

2. Find the inverse of the matrix
$$\begin{bmatrix} 1 & & \\ 2 & 1 & \\ 3 & 4 & 1 \end{bmatrix}.$$

3. Assuming it also to be a unit upper triangular matrix, find the inverse of
$$\begin{bmatrix} 1 & 2 & 3 \\ & 1 & -1 \\ & & 1 \end{bmatrix}.$$

4. Express in the form L_1DU the matrix
$$\begin{bmatrix} 2 & -2 & 2 \\ 4 & -2 & 4 \\ 6 & -4 & 7 \end{bmatrix}.$$

5. Reduce the simultaneous equations $x + 3y = 4$, $3x + 2y = 5$ to the form $Ux = L^{-1}p$ and hence solve the equations.

6. Reduce the simultaneous equations $x + y + z = 2$, $2x + 3y - z = 8$ and $4x + 5y + 3z = 10$ to the form $Ux = L^{-1}p$.

7. Solve by the method of §22.11 the equations $2x - y + 5z = 27$, $3x - 2y - z = -3$, $4x + 3y + 2z = 24$.

8. Solve by the method of §22.11 the equations $2y + 3z = 13$, $4x - 4y + 5z = 19$, $2x + y - z = 1$.

9. Show that the reflection of the point (x, y) in the line $y = x \tan \alpha$ is given by $x' = Ax$ where
$$A = \begin{bmatrix} \cos 2\alpha & \sin 2\alpha \\ \sin 2\alpha & -\cos 2\alpha \end{bmatrix}.$$
Find the reflection of the line $y = x$.

10. The transformation $A = \begin{bmatrix} 3 & 1 \\ 4 & 3 \end{bmatrix}$ maps the point (x, y) of a plane on to the point (x', y'), i.e. $x' = Ax$. Find the equation of the line onto which the line $x + y = 0$ is mapped. Find also the values of m for which the line $y = mx$ is mapped onto itself.

Exercises 22(d)

1. Evaluate as a single matrix the product diag (a_1, b_1, c_1) diag (a_2, b_2, c_2).

2. Evaluate as a single matrix $A^2 - 4A$ where
$$A = \begin{bmatrix} 1 & 2 & 2 \\ 2 & 1 & 2 \\ 2 & 2 & 1 \end{bmatrix}.$$

3. If
$$A = \begin{bmatrix} 2 & 1 & 2 \\ 1 & 2 & -2 \\ 2 & -2 & -1 \end{bmatrix}$$
show that $A^3 = 9A$.

4. Find the possible pairs of values of x and y which satisfy the equation
$$\begin{bmatrix} x & y & 1 \\ 2y & x & -x^2 \end{bmatrix} \begin{bmatrix} x \\ -y \\ 1 \end{bmatrix} = \begin{bmatrix} 2 \\ -2 \end{bmatrix}.$$

5. Find the inverse of the matrix

$$A = \begin{bmatrix} 1 & 0 & 0 \\ 2 & -1 & 0 \\ 5 & -6 & -1 \end{bmatrix}.$$

6. By solving the equations

$$\begin{bmatrix} 1 & 3 & 2 \\ 0 & 1 & 1 \\ 0 & 0 & 1 \end{bmatrix} \begin{bmatrix} x \\ y \\ z \end{bmatrix} = \begin{bmatrix} a \\ b \\ c \end{bmatrix}$$

find the inverse of the matrix

$$B = \begin{bmatrix} 1 & 3 & 2 \\ 0 & 1 & 1 \\ 0 & 0 & 1 \end{bmatrix}.$$

7. If the matrices A and B are those given in Exercises 5 and 6 above, find the inverse of the product AB.

8. Express as a product of linear factors the determinant

$$\begin{vmatrix} a & b & c \\ b+c & c+a & a+b \\ bc & ca & ab \end{vmatrix}.$$

9. Evaluate the determinants:—

(i) $\begin{vmatrix} 1 & 1 & 1 \\ 4 & 5 & 6 \\ 8 & 9 & 10 \end{vmatrix}$, (ii) $\begin{vmatrix} 1 & 1 & 1 \\ 1 & 1+a & 1 \\ 1 & 1 & 1+b \end{vmatrix}.$

10. Express as a product of linear factors

$$\begin{vmatrix} 4 & a+1 & a+1 \\ a+1 & (a+2)^2 & 1 \\ a+1 & 1 & (a+2)^2 \end{vmatrix}.$$

11. Find A^{-1} when

$$A = \begin{bmatrix} 1 & -3 & 0 \\ 2 & 0 & 1 \\ 4 & 1 & 3 \end{bmatrix}$$

and hence solve the simultaneous equations $x - 3y = a$, $2x + z = b$, $4x + y + 3z = c$.

12. If $a + 2b + c = p$, $b + 2c = q$, $3a + 4c = r$ find a 3×3 matrix A such that

$$A \begin{bmatrix} p \\ q \\ r \end{bmatrix} = \begin{bmatrix} a \\ b \\ c \end{bmatrix}.$$

13. If $A = \begin{bmatrix} a & b \\ c & d \end{bmatrix}$ show that

$$A^{-1} = \begin{bmatrix} d & -b \\ -c & a \end{bmatrix} \div |A|$$

and hence find A^{-1} when $a = 2$, $b = 3$, $c = 4$, $d = 8$.

14. Find the inverse of the matrix

$$\begin{bmatrix} 1 & 0 & 0 \\ 2 & 1 & 0 \\ 4 & 3 & 1 \end{bmatrix}$$

and hence solve the simultaneous equations $x = a$, $2x + y = b$, $4x + 3y + z = c$ in the cases

$$\begin{bmatrix} a \\ b \\ c \end{bmatrix} = \begin{bmatrix} 1 \\ 5 \\ 7 \end{bmatrix} \quad \text{and} \quad \begin{bmatrix} 2 \\ 3 \\ 8 \end{bmatrix}.$$

15. If $X = \begin{bmatrix} 1 & 1 \\ 4 & -1 \end{bmatrix}$ and $Y = \begin{bmatrix} 1 & -1 \\ 2 & -1 \end{bmatrix}$ show that $X^2 + Y^2 = (X + Y)^2$.

16. Show that

$$\frac{1}{a^2}\begin{bmatrix} -a & -a & -a \\ 0 & a & 0 \\ 0 & 0 & a \end{bmatrix}^2 = \frac{1}{a^3}\begin{bmatrix} 0 & a & 0 \\ -a & -a & -a \\ 0 & 0 & a \end{bmatrix}^3 = I.$$

17. If

$$M(\alpha) = \begin{bmatrix} \cos\alpha & \sin\alpha \\ -\sin\alpha & \cos\alpha \end{bmatrix},$$

show that

(i) $M(\alpha)M(\beta) = M(\beta)M(\alpha) = M(\alpha + \beta)$,

(ii) $M^2(\alpha) = M(2\alpha)$,

(iii) $M(\alpha)M(-\alpha) = I$.

18. If x is a single column matrix with elements x, y, z, x' is a single row matrix with the same elements, and

$$A = \begin{bmatrix} a & h & g \\ h & b & f \\ g & f & c \end{bmatrix},$$

show that

$$x'Ax = ax^2 + by^2 + cz^2 + 2fyz + 2gzx + 2hxy.$$

19. Solve the simultaneous equations $2x + 3y + z = 9$, $x + 2y + 3z = 6$, $3x + y + 2z = 8$.

20. If A' is the matrix obtained from a square matrix A by interchanging its rows and columns and if $\bar{A}'$ is the matrix obtained from A' by replacing its elements by their complex conjugates, the matrix A is said to be *Hermitian* if $\bar{A}' = A$. Show that

$$A = \begin{bmatrix} 1 & 1-i & 2 \\ 1+i & 3 & i \\ 2 & -i & 0 \end{bmatrix}$$

is Hermitian.

ANSWERS TO THE EXERCISES

EXERCISES 1 (a) (p. 16)

1. (i) y^3, (ii) a/c^4, (iii) 0.
2. (i) $6xy^2$, (ii) $3x^2y$.
3. (i) $\dfrac{2a^2y^4}{9b^2x^3}$, (ii) $\dfrac{1}{a^{2/3}x^{a/3}}$.
4. (i) 100, (ii) 8.
5. (i) 2, (ii) 4, (iii) 3/5.
6. 1·2, 1, 0·833, 0·44.
7. $-3/2$.
8. $x = 1 + y$.
9. (i) 2, (ii) $\frac{1}{2}$, (iii) $-\frac{1}{4}$.
10. 216.
11. 256/81.
13. (i) $(a - 1)^2$, (ii) 1.
14. 4.

EXERCISES 1 (b) (p. 19)

1. 4, $\frac{1}{3}$.
5. 3·2.
6. 3.
7. 512.
8. 1.
9. (i) 30, (ii) 1000, (iii) 3.
10. (i) 8, (ii) 1.
11. $\bar{1}$·920819.
12. $y = 100x^{-2/3}$.
13. 1·468.
14. 5, 4·192.
15. $3 - 10 \log 2, 4 - 13 \log 2$.

EXERCISES 1 (c) (p. 23)

1. (i) 2, 3, (ii) 4/3, -3.
2. (i) 1, 3, (ii) 2, $-2/7$.
3. 1, 3.
4. (i) 1·44, 5·56, (ii) 1·18, $-0·85$.
5. (i) 8/7, $-1/3$, (ii) 3/2, 3/2.
6. $\frac{1}{2}$, 11/10; $\frac{1}{2} < k < \frac{11}{10}$.
7. 3/2, 6.
9. $k > 6$ and $k < 2$.
11. 52/9, 4.
12. $x^2 - 2(p^2 - 2q)x + p^2(p^2 - 4q) = 0$
14. (i) 25/8, (ii) $16x^2 - 42x + 9 = 0$.

EXERCISES 1 (d) (p. 26)

1. 64, -1.
2. $-2, -1, 1/3, 4/3$.
3. $-3, -1, -1, 1$.
4. $-4/5, 9/8$.
5. 4, 7.
6. $x = -7, y = 3; \ x = 3, y = -7$.
7. $x = \pm 2, y = \mp 3$.
8. $x = -2, y = 1; \ x = 4/3, y = 6$.
9. $x = 4, y = 1; \ x = 5, \ y = 2; \ x = -11, y = -4; \ x = -44/5, y = -13/5$.
10. $x = 8, y = 64; \ x = 64, y = 8$.
11. $x = 3, y = -2; \ x = 2, y = -3$.
12. 1·53.
13. 1, -2.
14. 0, 0·861.
15. $x = 2·71, y = 1·71$.

EXERCISES 1 (e) (p. 30)

1. -10.
2. 3.
3. $A = -13, B = -26$.
4. $\lambda = -6, \mu = 0$; third factor $= x$.
5. $b = \frac{3}{4}, c = \frac{1}{4}$, third factor $= \frac{1}{4}(3x - 2)$.
6. 0, $-\frac{1}{8}p$.
7. $a = 2, b = -5; \ x = -3, \frac{1}{2}, 5$.
8. $3(x - y)(y - z)(z - x)$.
9. $-(x + y + z)(x - y)(y - z)(z - x)$.
12. $A = 1, B = 3, C = 1$.
14. $A = 1, B = -1, C = -3$.
15. $a = -2, b = 1$.

EXERCISES 1 (f) (p. 31)

4. 4; $x = 10, y = 1$; $x = 1, y = 10$.　　5. 0·934.

7. 16.　　　　　　　　　　　　　　9. $k < 1$ and $k > 9$.

10. $p^2 - 1 = 4q$; $k = -3, 2$.　　11. $4b^2 = 25ac$.

12. $x^2 + (\lambda + \mu)ax + \lambda\mu a^2 + (\lambda - \mu)^2 b = 0$; 1/5, 5.

13. $k < (19/17), k > 3$; $-1/3, 1$; (i) $k = 3$, (ii) $k = 7/5$.

14. $\frac{1}{5}$, 1, 1, 3.　　　　　　　　15. (i) $-1, 2$, (ii) $-2, 0$.

16. (i) 2, 8, (ii) 4, 7.　　　　　　　17. $-3, -1·175, \frac{1}{2}, 1·275$.

18. (i) $x = \frac{1}{2}, y = 3$; $x = -\frac{1}{8}, y = 7$, (ii) $x = y = a$.

20. $A = P(0), B = P(1) - P(0)$.　　21. $b = -3, c = 2$; $x^2 - 2x + 2$.

22. $c = -11$; $-1, -1, -\frac{1}{2}, 3$.　　24. 6, 66.

25. $a = 2$; $(x + 2)(x - 1)$.

EXERCISES 2 (a) (p. 38)

1. (i) 1, 4, 7, 16, (ii) 1, 4, 16, 1024, (iii) $-1, 1, -1, 1$, (iv) 2, 3/2, 4/3, 7/6.

2. 2353.　　　　　3. $\frac{1}{2}(c - a), 9(2c - a)$.　　4. $-69, -510$.

5. 34.　　　　　　6. $\frac{1}{2}n(3n + 13)$, 14.　　7. $2\frac{1}{4}, 1\frac{1}{2}$.

8. $(3a - c)/(a + c)$.　　10. 3/2, 729/8.　　11. $3^{30} - 1$.

12. 8, 3/2.　　　　13. 3/2, 3; $-1, 2$.　　14. 2.

15. $(b/a)^{1/(n-1)}, a^{n/2}b^{n/2}$.　　16. $\frac{1}{2}$, 2.　　20. 3/2, 211/5; 6; 2673.

EXERCISES 2 (b) (p. 41)

1. 54, 162.　　　　　　　　　　　2. 4/27, 160/27.

6. (i) $x > 0$, (ii) $x > 0, x < -\frac{1}{2}$.　　7. 3/4, 1/3.

8. 7.　　　　　　　　　　　　　　9. $\frac{1}{2}x^3(1 - x)^{-1}(2 - x)^{-3}$.

10. $\frac{1}{2}(1 \pm \sqrt{5}), \sqrt{5} - 1$.

EXERCISES 2 (c) (p. 47)

1. 24, 6.　　　　　2. 364.　　　　3. 216.　　　　4. 1120.

5. 127.　　　　　　6. 36.　　　　　7. 256, 711 040.　　8. 665 280, 9 979 200.

9. 2940, 1080.　　10. 16/21.　　　11. 2/15.　　　12. 11/24.

13. 5/18.　　　　　14. 7, 4/7.　　　15. 3/14.

EXERCISES 2 (d) (p. 51)

1. $x^6 - 3x^5 + \frac{15}{4}x^4 - \frac{5}{2}x^3 + \frac{15}{16}x^2 - \frac{3}{16}x + \frac{1}{64}$.

2. 0·9230.　　　　　　3. 672.　　　　5. 28.　　　　6. 5.

7. 11, 55, 165, 330.　　8. 16.　　　　10. 3, 2, 6.　　11. 7, 14.

14. $-9, 46$.

EXERCISES 2 (e) (p. 57)

1. $5x^3/81$, 10·03322.　　　　　2. 0·49753.

3. $1 - 2x + 5x^2 - \frac{40}{3}x^3$; 1·0205.　　4. $1 + \frac{1}{6}x - \frac{1}{36}x^2$, 2·080.

7. $-\frac{3}{4}, -\frac{5}{4}, \frac{1}{2}; \frac{5}{4}, \frac{3}{4}, -\frac{1}{2}.$ 8. 1, −3; 1, 0.

10. $b^2 = 8(a^2 + 1).$ 11. $4n^2 + 2.$

12. (i) $\dfrac{1}{x+2} - \dfrac{1}{x+3}$, (ii) $\dfrac{1}{4}\left\{\dfrac{2}{(x-1)^2} + \dfrac{1}{x-1} - \dfrac{1}{x+1}\right\}$,

   (iii) $\dfrac{1}{3}\left\{\dfrac{1}{x-1} - \dfrac{x+2}{x^2+x+1}\right\}.$

13. (i) $1 + \dfrac{4}{3(x-1)} - \dfrac{1}{3(x+2)}$, (ii) $\dfrac{3}{x-1} + \dfrac{2}{x+1} + \dfrac{1}{x^2+1}.$

14. $\dfrac{3}{(x+2)^2} - \dfrac{1}{x+2} + \dfrac{1}{x-2}$, $-\frac{1}{4} - \frac{3}{4}x + \frac{5}{16}x^2 - \frac{3}{8}x^3 + \frac{11}{64}x^4$, $-1 < x < 1.$

15. $\dfrac{2x+4}{x^2+1} - \dfrac{2}{x+3}$, $\frac{10}{3} + \frac{20}{9}x - \frac{110}{27}x^2 - \frac{160}{81}x^3$, $-1 < x < 1.$

EXERCISES 2 (f) (p. 58)

1. 3/2.   3. (a) 1, (b) 0.

4. $\frac{1}{2}n(n+1)a + \{5r(1-r^n)\}/(1-r)$; $a = 8, r = 2$; 10 670.

5. $m(6m - 1).$ 6. 3.

8. $(1 - ar + ar^2)/\{(1-r)(1-ar)\}.$ 9. (i) 360, (ii) 144.

10. 60, 60.   11. 354, 282.

12. 11/21.   13. (i) 3/44, (ii) 12/44, (iii) 29/44.

14. 1 to 242.   16. −1, −80, 432.

17. $1 - \frac{1}{4}x - \frac{3}{32}x^2 - \frac{7}{128}x^3$, 2·9623.   19. 1, 4, 1.

20. 0, 1, 1.   21. $1 + \frac{1}{2}x - \frac{1}{8}x^2, 1 - \frac{1}{2}x + \frac{3}{8}x^2.$

22. $1 - \frac{1}{2}y + \frac{3}{8}y^2 - \frac{5}{16}y^3$; $c_1 = \cos\theta$, $c_2 = \frac{1}{2}(3\cos^2\theta - 1)$,
    $c_3 = \frac{1}{2}\cos\theta(5\cos^2\theta - 3).$

23. $\frac{1}{2}, \frac{3}{4}, \frac{1}{16}.$

24. $\dfrac{1}{x-3} - \dfrac{x}{x^2+x+1}$, $-\frac{1}{3} - \frac{10}{9}x + \frac{26}{27}x^2 - \frac{1}{81}x^3.$

25. $\dfrac{1}{x+2} - \dfrac{3}{(x+2)^2} + \dfrac{1}{x-3}.$

EXERCISES 3 (a) (p. 68)

1. (i) 155° 29′, 335° 29′, (ii) 143° 4′, 216° 56′.

2. (i) 176° 42′, (ii) 265° 17′.   3. 36° 52′, 216° 52′; 216° 52′.

4. (i) 60°, 300°, (ii) 60°, 300°.   5. 30°, 150°, 210°, 330°.

6. $x(y^2 - 1) + 2 = 0.$ 8. 30°, 210°.

EXERCISES 3 (b) (p. 71)

2. 210°, 330°.   4. 90°, 180°, 270°.   9. 1·88, −0·35, −1·53.

10. 37° 46′, 14° 28′.   13. a.   14. 24/25, 24/7, 336/625.

15. $\pm(1 + \tan\frac{1}{2}\theta)(3 + \tan\frac{1}{2}\theta)(1 + \tan^2\frac{1}{2}\theta)^{-1}.$

EXERCISES 3 (c) (p. 75)

1. $R = \sqrt{2}$, $\alpha = 45°$, $\pm\sqrt{2}$.
2. $R = W(1 + \mu^2)^{1/2}$, $\tan\beta = 1/\mu$.
3. $S = 29$, $\beta = 133° 36'$.
4. $90°, 306° 52'$.
5. $36° 52', 126° 52'$.
6. $36° 52', 241° 56'$.
7. $81°, 199° 24'$.
8. $80° 44', 234° 2'$.
13. $20°, 90°, 100°, 140°$.
15. $\theta = 149° 20'$, $\phi = 98° 1'$.

EXERCISES 3 (d) (p. 80)

1. $\pi/180$.
3. 5.
6. 117 111 km.
7. $87° 55'$.
8. $0\cdot00795$.
10. $\frac{1}{4}\pi, \frac{5}{6}\pi, -1\cdot107, \frac{1}{3}\pi$.
14. 1/6.
15. $0, \pm\frac{1}{2}$.

EXERCISES 3 (e) (p. 81)

1. (i) $90° 24', 198° 24', 306° 24'$, (ii) $15°, 75° 195°, 255°$.
5. $\frac{1}{4}(\sqrt{5} - 1)$.
6. 7/8.
7. $\frac{1}{2}, 1/a$; $53° 8', 60°$.
8. $R = 5$, $\alpha = 36° 52'$; $66° 52'$.
9. $R = 5$, $\tan\alpha = (4\tan\beta - 3)/(4 + 3\tan\beta)$.
10. $45°, 165° 58', 225°, 345° 58'$.
12. $131° 48', 11° 48'$; $168° 12', 48° 12'$.
13. $\cot(5\alpha/2)$; $36°, 90°, 108°, 180°, 252°, 270°, 324°$.
16. $25° 15', 128° 11'$.
17. $0, \frac{1}{6}\pi, \frac{5}{6}\pi, \frac{3}{2}\pi, 2\pi$.
20. $31', 3\cdot09 \times 10^{13}$ km.
22. $0\cdot7391$.
25. (i) $\sqrt{(a^2 + b^2)}$, (ii) $\pm\sqrt{2}$.

EXERCISES 4 (a) (p. 87)

13. $45°$.
15. $120°$.

EXERCISES 4 (b) (p. 91)

3. $0\cdot181$ m.
6. $0\cdot26, 0\cdot30$ m.

EXERCISES 4 (c) (p. 98)

1. $a = 14\cdot35$, $b = 13\cdot0$, $C = 51° 44'$.
2. $b = 122\cdot2$ m, $c = 95\cdot08$ m, $C = 49° 13'$.
3. $b = 6\cdot295$ cm, $c = 5\cdot395$ cm, $A = 72°$.
4. No solution.
5. No solution.
6. $a = 3$, $A = 36° 52'$, $B = 90°$.
7. $b = 36$, $B = 67° 23'$, $C = 90°$.
8. $a = 5\cdot7$ cm, $A = 32°$, $C = 28° 54'$.
9. $b = 0\cdot7026$ m, $A = 11° 18'$, $B = 40° 1'$.
10. $a = 100\sqrt{3}$, $A = 90°$, $C = 60°$; $a = 50\sqrt{3}$, $A = 30°$, $C = 120°$.
11. $b = 64\cdot44$ m, $A = 45° 40'$, $B = 100°$; $b = 12\cdot85$ m, $A = 134° 20'$, $B = 11° 20'$.
12. $a = 6$, $B = 38° 56'$, $C = 70° 32'$.
13. $c = 35$ km, $A = 21° 47'$, $B = 98° 13'$.
14. $A = 35° 6'$, $B = 64° 38'$, $C = 80° 16'$.
15. $A = 20° 56'$, $B = 26° 30'$, $C = 132° 34'$.

EXERCISES 4 (d) (p. 101)

4. 95 m.   5. N 10° 54′ E, 1149 a.m.   6. 60°, 70 m, 3° 38′.

7. (i) 19 m, (ii) 3 m.   11. $d = 6h \tan \alpha/(3 + \tan^2 \alpha)$.   14. 13° 46′.

15. 35° 16′.

EXERCISES 4 (e) (p. 104)

4. $180° - 2A$, $180° - 2B$, $180° - 2C$.   10. 47° 5′, 68° 27′, 76·54 m².

11. 36° 1′.   12. 79°.

14. 56° 11′, 43° 49′, 3·61 km.   15. 76° 9′, 16° 9′.

17. $\frac{1}{2}\sqrt{3}$.   18. 116° 8′, 11° 52′, 3·91 m, 17·09 m.

20. 1011 m.   21. 60·1 m.

EXERCISES 5 (a) (p. 115)

1. (i) $(1, 1)$, (ii) $(-1, \sqrt{3})$, (iii) $(-1, -1)$, (iv) $(2, -2\sqrt{3})$.

2. (i) $(\sqrt{2}, \frac{1}{4}\pi)$, (ii) $(\sqrt{13}, 146° 12′)$, (iii) $(\sqrt{13}, 213° 48′)$, (iv) $(\sqrt{2}, \frac{7}{4}\pi)$.

3. $\frac{1}{2}\sqrt{10}, \frac{1}{2}\sqrt{2}, \sqrt{2}$.

4. (i) $(\sqrt{3}, -\sqrt{3})$, $(-\sqrt{3}, \sqrt{3})$, (ii) $(4 + \sqrt{3}, 4 - \sqrt{3})$, $(4 - \sqrt{3}, 4 + \sqrt{3})$.

5. $6 + 2\sqrt{3}$.   6. $(13/3, 8/3)$.   7. $(4/3, -2/3)$, $(0, -10)$.

8. $3 : 5$.   9. 18·8, 9·5, 13.   11. (i) 10, (ii) 15.

12. $\frac{1}{4}(8 - 3\sqrt{3})$.   13. 10.   14. 4.

15. 7.

EXERCISES 5 (b) (p. 119)

1. $20x + 6y = 109$.   2. $x^2 + y^2 + 6x + 8y = 75$.

3. $x^2 + y^2 - 6x - 12y + 6 = 0$.   4. $3x + y = 19$.

5. $x^2 + y^2 - 8x - 5y + 16 = 0$.   6. $y = \pm 3x$.

7. $(0, 0)$, $(1, 2)$, $\sqrt{5}$.   8. $(4, -1)$, $(4, -2)$, $(4, -3/2)$.

9. $(0, 2)$, $(2, 6)$, $(6, 4)$.   10. $a = 6, b = 3, AB = 1/12$.

11. $(3, 3)$, $(2, 4)$, $(4, 6)$, $(3, 5)$.   12. $x = \frac{1}{2}, 2x - 5y + 4 = 0, (\frac{1}{2}, 1), \frac{1}{2}\sqrt{(145)}$.

EXERCISES 5 (c) (p. 124)

1. (i) $3x + 4y = 0$, (ii) $x - 2y + 4 = 0$, (iii) $x + y + 2 = 0$.

2. (i) $\frac{3}{4}$, (ii) 4, −3.   3. $(2, -2)$, $5x - 2y = 14$.

4. $x - 2y + 2 = 0$, $4x - y = 6$.   5. $(19, 8)$, $4x + 3y = 50$.

6. $3x - 4y = 7$, $35/12$, $(7/6, -7/8)$.   7. $3x + 4y = 5a$.

8. $4x + 3y = 35$, $x + 7y + 10 = 0$, $(11, -3)$, 25.

10. $6x - y = 27$, $2x - 3y + 15 = 0$, $2x + y = 5$.

11. $y + mx = 0$, $(a + b/m)y - bx + ab = 0$, $\left(\dfrac{ab}{am + 2b}, \dfrac{-mab}{am + 2b}\right)$.

12. $3x + y = 12$, $x + 3y = 12$.   13. $4/7$, $-4/13$.

14. $\frac{1}{2}$; 3, −3/2.   15. $(c/3, 0)$, $\frac{2}{3}c - 8$, $12 - \frac{1}{2}c)$; 12.

EXERCISES 5 (d) (p. 132)

1. $135°$.

2. $(AB) 3x + 4y = 19$, $(BC) x - 3y = 2$, $(CA) 5x - 2y + 3 = 0$; $13/9, 13/11$.

3. $x - y + 1 = 0$, $(2, 3)$, $x + y = 5$.

4. (i) $7x - 2y = 7$, (ii) $3x + y = 2$, (iii) $(11/13, -7/13)$.

5. $y - 2x = 3$.   7. $(29/13, 15/13)$, $(45/13, -9/13)$.

9. $y + \sqrt{3}x = 2 + \sqrt{3}$, $1 + \frac{1}{2}\sqrt{3}$.   10. An escribed circle.

11. $x^2 + y^2 - 8x - 14y = 3$.   12. $2x - 5y = 18$.

13. $43x - 29y = 71$.   14. $x + 7y = 31$, $7x - y = 17$.

15. $x + y = 0$, $4\sqrt{5}/5$.

EXERCISES 5 (e) (p. 137)

1. $a = 0·031, b = 2·5$.   2. $m = 2·3, c = -10$.

3. $a = \frac{1}{2}, b = -2$.   4. $\alpha = \frac{1}{3}, c = 4$.

5. $a = 2, b = 0$; $\mu = 0·044$.   6. $k = 12·7, n = \frac{1}{2}$.

7. $A = 0·2, n = \frac{1}{2}$.

8.

x	0	0·4	1·0	1·5	3	6
y	0	1·265	2·000	2·449	3·464	4·898

9. $k = 210, n = 0·3$.

10. $A = \frac{3}{2}, n = \frac{1}{2}$; $m = \frac{1}{2}, c = 1$; $x = 1$ and 4.

11. $A = 2·5, k = 3$.   12. $a = 0·58, b = 2·2$.

EXERCISES 5 (f) (p. 140)

1. $(-14, -10)$.   2. $5·35$.

3. $(6, 10), 52$.   4. $60, (2, -3)$.

5. $(11/3, 13/3)$, $(29/6, 14/3)$.   7. $x^2 + y^2 - 6x - 10y + 9 = 0$.

10. $6\frac{1}{2}, 4\frac{1}{3}$.   11. $x - 5y + 11 = 0$, $5x + y = 23$.

12. $(hx/a^2) + (ky/b^2) = 1$, $\left\{ \dfrac{a^2(b - k)}{hb - ka}, \dfrac{b^2(h - a)}{hb - ka} \right\}$.

13. $7y - x + 18 = 0$.   14. $(3, -4)$.

15. $a \cos \frac{1}{2}(\alpha - \beta)$.   16. $2\sqrt{5}/5$.

17. $43° 40', 2·31$.   19. $\left\{ \dfrac{2(2\lambda - 1)}{5\lambda + 3}, \dfrac{\lambda + 5}{5\lambda + 3} \right\}, \dfrac{7}{3}$.

20. $8x - y = 7$, $x + 8y = 9$.   23. $K = 0·0021, n = \frac{1}{2}$.

24. $1·13, 1·41$.   25. $a = 5·99, b = 1·20$.

EXERCISES 6 (a) (p. 153)

2. $13\{(5/13)i + (12/13)j\}$.   3. $3i - 2j, \sqrt{(13)}$.   5. $1/2$.

7. $6·5$.   13. $120°, 90°$.   14. $3·6$ N, $29° 26'$.

15. $2AB$ at $60°$ to AB.

EXERCISES 6 (b) (p. 162)

1. $3 + 4i$; $18 - i$; $-i$; -4.   2. $-1 - i$; $-2, \frac{1}{2}i$; $7/10 - i/10$.

3. $2\sqrt{2}, 225°$; $1/2, 90°$; $5\sqrt{5}, 116° 34'$; $25, 106° 16'$.

4. $5/34$; $\sqrt{(13)}/3$.   6. $1/2, (1 \pm i\sqrt{3})/2$.

7. $\pm(3 + 2i)$.   9. $x^2 + x + 1 = 0$.

10. $(\pm\sqrt{3} \pm i)$.   11. 3; $60°, 180°, 300°$.

12. $\sqrt{5}, 296° 34'$; $5, 36° 52'$.   13. $\pm\sqrt{2}, \pm\sqrt{2}i, (\pm 1 \pm i)$.

15. $\frac{1}{2}\sqrt{2}, 5\pi/4$; $\sqrt{2}, 3\pi/4$; $\frac{1}{2}\sqrt{(10)}, 161° 34'$.

EXERCISES 6 (c) (p. 163)

1. $97\cdot13$ km, $297° 50'$.   3. $\sqrt{(61)}$ m at $86° 18'$ to AC.

7. $\sqrt{7}$ N.   8. $14\cdot14$ km/h from N.W.

9. 3771 N, N $47° 44'$ E.   11. $2\sqrt{2}, 45°$; $2\sqrt{5}, 26° 34'$.

12. $0\cdot4(3 + 4i)$.   14. $2/3, \pm 2i/\sqrt{3}$.

15. $5\sqrt{5}$; 1.   16. $1/4 + i$; $\sqrt{(17)}/4$.

18. $5, 126° 52'$; $6\cdot5, 292° 37'$; $\frac{1}{2}\sqrt{(17)}, 255° 58'$; $32\cdot5, 59° 29'$.

19. $(1 + i)/2$; $\sqrt{2}/2$.

EXERCISES 7 (a) (p. 172)

1. $0, -3$; $\frac{1}{2}, -2$.   2. $0, 8\cdot402, 29\cdot61$.

3. $x^2 + 6x + 8$.   4. $x^2 + 3x + 1$.

5. $-1, (x + h - 1)/(x^2 + 2hx + h^2 + 1)$.

7. $\pm\frac{1}{2}\sqrt{(2x - x^2)}, (-1 \pm \sqrt{5})(x/2)$.   8. 9.

9. $0, -10$.   10. 8.

11. 5.   12. $-\frac{1}{4}$.

13. $1, -1$.   14. $(4, -2)$.

15. 2.

EXERCISES 7 (b) (p. 176)

1. $3x^2$.   2. $2x + 3$.   3. $4x^3 - 2x$.   4. $-2/x^3$.

5. $-3/x^4$.   6. $-1/(x + 1)^2$.   7. $1/(1 - x)^2$.   8. $-2/(2x + 1)^2$.

9. $1 + \cos x$.   10. $3 \cos 3x$.   11. $-\sin ax$.   12. $\sec x \tan x$.

13. $\sec^2 x$.   14. $-5 + 8x - 3x^2$.   15. $6 + (4/x^2)$.   16. $1 - (1/x^2)$.

17. $-1 - \sin x$.   18. 1.   19. $4x - (8/x^3), 15\frac{7}{8}$.   20. $-3/(x + 1)^2$.

EXERCISES 7 (c) (p. 181)

1. $5x(x^3 + 4x^2 + 4)$.   2. $20x^3 + \sin x$.

3. $9x^2 + (2/x^3)$.   4. $x^{-1/2} - x^{-3/2}$.

5. $3x^2 + 4x + 3$.   6. $-2x(1 + 4x^2)$.

7. $4x(x^2 - 3)$.   8. $3x^2 - 2 - (1/x^2)$.

9. $-3(1 - 2x + x^2)$.   10. $9(9x^2 + 12x + 4)$.

11. $1 - 2x$.

12. $\cos^2 x - \sin^2 x$.

13. $x \cos x$.

14. $\tfrac{1}{2}x^2 \cos x$.

15. $2x \tan x + (x^2 + 1) \sec^2 x$.

16. $\sec x(\sec^2 x + \tan^2 x)$.

17. $- \operatorname{cosec} x(\operatorname{cosec}^2 x + \cot^2 x)$.

18. $\sec x + x \sec x \tan x - \sin x$.

19. $(1 + x^2)/(1 - x^2)^2$.

20. $(1 + 2x - x^2)/(1 - x)^2$.

21. $(x^2 - 4x)/(x^2 + x - 2)^2$.

22. $(4x)/(5 - 2x^2)^2$.

23. $(4x^3)/(x^4 + 1)^2$.

24. $(x \cos x - \sin x)/x^2$.

25. $1/(1 + \cos x)$.

26. $(-16 \cos x)/(3 + 5 \sin x)^2$.

27. $(-11 \sin x)/(3 + 5 \cos x)^2$.

28. $(\cos x - \sin x \tan^2 x)/(1 + \tan x)^2$.

29. $\cot x - x \operatorname{cosec}^2 x$.

30. $(4x^3)/(1 + x^2)^3$.

EXERCISES 7 (d) (p. 185)

1. $6(2x - 3)^2$.

2. $1/\sqrt{(2x - 1)}$.

3. $-3 \sin 3x$.

4. $2x \cos (x^2)$.

5. $2 \sec^2 (2x + 1)$.

6. $3x^2 \sec (x^3) \tan (x^3)$.

7. $2(\cos^2 2x - \sin^2 2x)$.

8. $(-1/2\sqrt{x}) \operatorname{cosec} \sqrt{x} \cot \sqrt{x}$.

9. $3(1 + x^{-2})(x + 1 - x^{-1})^2$.

10. $4 \tan x \sec^2 x$.

11. $3 \sin^2 x \sin 4x$.

12. $(1 + 2x^2)/\sqrt{(1 + x^2)}$.

13. $1/(1 + x^2)^{3/2}$.

14. $(2x^2 - 3)/\{x^4\sqrt{(1 - x^2)}\}$.

15. $(x^3 - 2)/\{2x^2\sqrt{(1 + x^3)}\}$.

16. $-2/[\sqrt{(1 + x^2)}\{\sqrt{(1 + x^2)} + x\}^2]$.

17. $(\sin x \cos x)/\sqrt{(1 + \sin^2 x)}$.

18. $3(1 + x)^2\{\tan 3x + (1 + x) \sec^2 3x\}$.

19. $4 \sec^2 x \tan^3 x$.

20. $- \sin x \cos (\cos x)$.

21. $\sin^{m-1} x \cos^{n-1} x(m \cos^2 x - n \sin^2 x)$.

22. $2 \sec x (\tan x + \sec x)^2$.

23. $x^{n-1} \cos x(n \cos x - 2x \sin x)$.

24. 0.

EXERCISES 7 (e) (p. 191)

1. $1/\{x\sqrt{(x^2 - 1)}\}$.

2. $-1/(1 + x^2)$.

3. $2/\sqrt{(1 - 4x^2)}$.

4. $1/\{(1 + x)\sqrt{x}\}$.

5. $2\sqrt{(1 - x^2)}$.

6. $(2 \sin x \cos x)/(1 + \sin^4 x)$.

7. $1/t$.

10. (i) $(1 - 3x^2y^2)/(2x^3y)$, (ii) $(\tfrac{1}{2}y^2)/(\sin 2y - xy)$.

11. $-(2x + y)/(x + 3y^2)$.

12. $2a^2 \sec^2 ax \tan ax$.

13. $-4 \cos 2x, 8 \sin 2x$.

17. $(1 - 4x - x^2) \sin x + 4(2 + x) \cos x$.

19. $9/4$.

20. $(- \tfrac{5}{8}t^{3/2})/(1 + t^2)$.

EXERCISES 7 (f) (p. 193)

1. $4x^2 + 3x + 1, 23, 19$.

2. $a = b = 1; 1, -1$.

3. $-3, 2, -6$.

4. $-1/(x + 2)^2$.

5. (i) $x \cos x$, (ii) $6x - 10$.

6. (i) $(2 \sec^2 x)/(1 - \tan x)^2$, (ii) $(2x + 4)/(1 - x)^3$, (iii) $1/(1 - x^2)^{32/}$.

10. (i) $x(2 \sin 3x + 3x \cos 3x)$, (ii) $(x^2 - 2x - 3)/(x - 1)^2$, (iii) $(1/x^2) \sin (1/x)$.

14. (i) $-1/(1 + x^2)$, (ii) $(-2x)/(1 + x^4)$.

22. $(x \cos x - 2 \sin x)/x^3$, $\{(6 - x^2) \sin x - 4x \cos x\}/x^4$.

23. $x(6 - x^2) \sin x + 6x^2 \cos x$.   25. $\tan \frac{1}{2}\theta$, $(1/4a) \sec^4 \frac{1}{2}\theta$.

EXERCISES 8 (a) (p. 200)

1. $14 \cdot 33$ m³/min.
2. $0 \cdot 0119$ cm/s.
3. $(4k^3/b)$ cm²/s.
4. (i) $1 \cdot 587$ m, (ii) $0 \cdot 0331$ m/h.
6. 2 cm/min.
7. $1 \cdot 86 \times 10^9$ m³/s.
8. $(180v/\pi h) \sin^2 \theta$ deg/s.
9. $18° 26'$.
10. $4 \cdot 5$ cm/min.
11. $1 \cdot 6$ mm/s.
12. $2\pi x^2(6 + \frac{1}{3}x)$ m³.
13. $60°$.
14. (i) $4 \cdot 91$, (ii) $7 \cdot 07$; $1 \cdot 44$.

EXERCISES 8 (b) (p. 203)

1. 67 m/s, 96 m/s².
2. $c = 4, d = -1$; 1 m/s².
4. $-2 \cdot 24$ m/s.
6. $a, 2a$.
9. $\frac{1}{3}\pi, \frac{2}{3}\pi$ seconds; $\frac{1}{2}\pi$ seconds.
10. $0 \cdot 8$.
11. $0 \cdot 38$ cm³.
13. $0 \cdot 0041$ seconds.
14. $\pm 0 \cdot 857$.

EXERCISES 8 (c) (p. 210)

1. 0 (min.), $4/27$ (max.).
2. 3 (min.), $7/3$ (max.).
3. $a = 3, b = -12$; $x = -2$; 20.
5. $(1, 5)$ (max.), $(-4, -5/4)$ (min.).
6. $2 \cdot 38$ (max.), $2 \cdot 32$ (min.).
7. $0 \cdot 362$ (max.), $12 \cdot 20$ (min.).
9. 125.
10. Max. at $x = \frac{1}{4}\pi$, min. at $x = \frac{5}{4}\pi$.
11. 0 (min.), 1 (max.).
12. 25.
13. 2.

EXERCISES 8 (d) (p. 214)

1. 2 radians, 625 m².
3. 48 m²,
4. $6 \cdot 365$ km.
6. $0 \cdot 042$ m².
8. $2 : 1$, more efficient.
9. $4\pi a^2 \sin \theta \cos^2 \theta$.
10. (i) $\frac{1}{2}d^2$, (ii) $\frac{1}{4}\sqrt{3}d^2$.
11. $7 \cdot 023$ m.
12. Each $0 \cdot 15$ m.
13. 8 kilometres.
14. $0 \cdot 224$ m³.

EXERCISES 8 (e) (p. 219)

1. $-\frac{1}{3}, 2$.
3. $-0 \cdot 443, 1, 1 \cdot 693$.
4. $(2n + 1)\pi$, n an integer.
5. $x = -2$ a minimum, $x = 2$ a point of inflexion.

EXERCISES 8 (f) (p. 220)

1. -3 cm³/s.
2. $0 \cdot 316$ m/min.
3. $1 \cdot 333$ cm/min.
4. $47 \cdot 13$ m³/s, $0 \cdot 104$ m/s.

5. 0.743 m.

6. 48 m.

10. 1.155.

11. $a^2/(a + b)$, min.; $a^2/(a - b)$, max.

13. 1 (min.), -1 (max.).

14. $a = -3$, $b = 0$; 0 (max.), 1 (min.).

15. $\pi/3$ (max.), $5\pi/3$ (min.).

16. 2 (max.), 0 (min.).

17. $a = 1$, $b = 2$; $x = -4$.

18. $64/x^2$, $2x^2 + (256/x)$.

19. 26.3 m.

20. (i) $2\frac{1}{4}$, $4\frac{1}{2}$, (ii) 3, 6.

21. $(32\sqrt{3})/9$.

22. $36° 52'$.

23. $a = 1$, $b = -3$.

24. $\frac{1}{2}$ (max.), $-\frac{1}{2}$ (min.).

EXERCISES 9 (a) (p. 226)

1. $\frac{3}{5}x^{5/3} + C$.

2. $(-3/x) + C$.

3. $4x - 3x^2 - \frac{1}{5}x^5 + C$.

4. $3x^3 + 3x^2 + x + C$.

5. $\frac{2}{3}x^{3/2} + 2x^{1/2} + C$.

6. $\frac{1}{5}x^5 + 2x - \frac{1}{3}x^{-3} + C$.

7. $\frac{1}{5}x^5 + x^2 - x^{-1} + C$.

8. $\frac{1}{5}x^5 - 2x^2 - 4x^{-1} + C$.

9. $2x^{1/2} + 2x + \frac{2}{3}x^{3/2} + C$.

10. $\frac{3}{2}x^2 - 2\cos x + 4\tan x + C$.

11. $\frac{1}{3}x^3 + 2\tan^{-1} x + C$.

12. $x + 3\tan^{-1} x + C$.

13. $x^3 - \frac{1}{2}x^2 + 7x + C$.

14. $\frac{1}{2}ax^2 + \frac{1}{3}bx^3 + \frac{1}{4}cx^4 + C$.

15. $-\frac{1}{2}x^{-2} - x^{-1} - 4x + C$.

16. $-\cos x - 3\cot x + C$.

17. $\frac{2}{3}x^{3/2} - \frac{4}{5}x^{5/2} + \frac{2}{7}x^{7/2} + C$.

18. $\frac{1}{3}x^3 - x^{-1} + C$.

19. $\frac{3}{2}x^2 + 2\sin^{-1} x + C$.

20. $\frac{1}{3}x^3 + 2x - x^{-1} + C$.

21. $\tan x - x + C$.

22. $\frac{1}{2}(x - \sin x) + C$.

24. (i) and (ii) $\frac{1}{3}x^3 - \frac{1}{2}x^2 + x + C$.

25. $4\sin^{-1} x + C$.

EXERCISES 9 (b) (p. 230)

1. $\cos(1 - x) + C$.

2. $\frac{1}{4}\sin 4x + C$.

3. $-\frac{1}{6}(1 - 4x)^{3/2} + C$.

4. $2(x + 2)^{1/2} + \frac{2}{3}(x + 2)^{3/2} + C$.

5. $-\frac{1}{6}(2 - x)^6 + C$.

6. $\frac{2}{5}\sqrt{(5x - 7)} + C$.

7. $-(2x - 3)^{-1/2} + C$.

8. $\frac{1}{3}(1 + 2x)^{3/2} + C$.

9. $-\frac{1}{2}(x - 1)^{-2} - \frac{1}{2}(2 - x)^{-2} + C$.

10. $\frac{1}{3}\tan^{-1}(x/3) + C$.

11. $\sin^{-1}(x/4) + C$.

12. $\frac{1}{2}\tan 2x + C$.

13. $\frac{1}{6}\tan^{-1}(3x/2) + C$.

14. $\sin^{-1}\left(\dfrac{x - 3}{4}\right) + C$.

15. $\frac{1}{4}\sin^{-1}(4x/5) + C$.

16. $\frac{1}{6}\tan^{-1}\left(\dfrac{3x + 1}{2}\right) + C$

17. $\sin^{-1}\left(\dfrac{2x - 1}{2\sqrt{3}}\right) + C$.

18. $\dfrac{1}{\sqrt{(17)}}\tan^{-1}\left(\dfrac{3x - 2}{\sqrt{(17)}}\right) + C$.

19. $x + \frac{1}{2}\cos 2x + C$.

EXERCISES 9 (c) (p. 234)

1. $-\frac{1}{3}(1 - x^2)^{3/2} + C$.

2. $\frac{1}{6}(1 + x^2)^{5/2} + C$.

3. $2\sqrt{x} - 2\tan^{-1}\sqrt{x} + C$.

4. $\frac{2}{3}x^3 + x + \frac{2}{3}(1 + x^2)^{3/2} + C$.

5. $\frac{2}{3}(a^3 + x^3)^{1/2} + C$.

6. $\frac{1}{4}\tan^{-1}(x^4) + C$.

7. $\frac{1}{2}\tan^2 x + C$.

8. $\frac{1}{3}\sin^{-1}(x^3) + C$.

9. $\frac{1}{6}\tan^{-1}(x^2/3) + C$.

10. $\sqrt{(x^2 + 2x - 9)} + C$.

11. $\frac{1}{3}\sin^3 x - \frac{1}{5}\sin^5 x + C$.

12. $-\frac{1}{5}\cos^5 x + \frac{1}{7}\cos^7 x + C$.

13. $-\frac{1}{6}\cos^6 x + \frac{1}{8}\cos^8 x + C$.

14. $\sin x - \frac{1}{3}\sin^3 x + C$.

15. $-\cos x + \frac{2}{3}\cos^3 x - \frac{1}{5}\cos^5 x + C$.

16. $\sec x + \cos x + C$.

17. $-\frac{1}{2}\cos 2x + \frac{1}{6}\cos^3 2x + C$.

18. $2\sqrt{(\sin x)} + C$.

19. $\tan^{-1}(\sin x) + C$.

20. $-\frac{1}{3}\sin^{-1}(3x) - \frac{1}{9}\sqrt{(1 - 9x^2)} + C$.

EXERCISES 9 (d) (p. 238)

1. $\frac{1}{2}\sin x + \frac{1}{10}\sin 5x + C$.

2. $-\frac{1}{4}\cos 2x - \frac{1}{8}\cos 4x + C$.

3. $\frac{1}{2}\sin x - \frac{1}{10}\sin 5x + C$.

4. $\frac{1}{4}\cos 2x - \frac{1}{12}\cos 6x + C$.

5. $x \sin x + \cos x + C$.

6. $\frac{2}{15}(3x - 2)(1 + x)^{3/2} + C$.

7. $\frac{2}{105}(15x^2 - 12x + 8)(1 + x)^{3/2} + C$.

8. $x \sin^{-1} x + \sqrt{(1 - x^2)} + C$.

9. $x - \sqrt{(1 - x^2)}\sin^{-1} x + C$.

10. $-\frac{1}{2}x \cos 2x + \frac{1}{4}\sin 2x + C$.

11. $(2 - x^2)\cos x + 2x \sin x + C$.

12. $-\frac{1}{3}(\pi - x)\cos 3x - \frac{1}{9}\sin 3x + C$.

13. (i) $\frac{1}{2}x - \frac{1}{2}\sin x \cos x + C$, (ii) $\frac{1}{2}\sin^2 x + C$.

EXERCISES 9 (e) (p. 246)

1. $254/7$.

2. $16/3$.

3. $2 - \frac{1}{2}\pi$.

4. $29/6$.

5. $20/3$.

6. $\frac{1}{2}\pi$.

7. $\sqrt{3}/16$.

8. $\frac{1}{4}$.

9. $-\frac{1}{4}$.

10. $1/16$.

14. (i) $7/9$, (ii) $1/6$. 15. $\frac{1}{4}(\pi + 2)$.

16. $1/12$.

17. $1/6$.

18. $16/5$.

19. $16/3$.

EXERCISES 9 (f) (p. 254)

1. 0.75.

2. $0.779, 0.752$.

3. 2940.

4. 2965.

5. 94.5.

7. 0.67.

8. 74.8.

9. 0.5235.

EXERCISES 9 (g) (p. 256)

1. $x^4 + 4x^3 + 6x^2 + C$.

2. $3x^3 + 6x^2 + 4x + 4\sin x + C$.

3. $\frac{1}{2}x^6 - 6x^4 + 24x^2 + C$.

6. $-\frac{1}{4}(\cos 2x + \sqrt{3}x) + C$.

7. (i) $\frac{1}{2}\tan(2x + 1) + C$, (ii) $-\frac{1}{2}\cos x - \frac{1}{6}\cos 3x + C$.

8. (i) $\frac{1}{3}(1 + x^2)^{3/2} + C$, (ii) $\frac{1}{2}\tan^{-1}(x^2) + C$.

9. (i) $\frac{1}{6}(3x^2 + 2x + 4)^3 + C$, (ii) $-\dfrac{1}{4(3x^2 + 2x + 4)^2} + C$.

10. $-\cot\frac{1}{2}x + C$.

11. $\cos 3\alpha \sin \alpha$.

12. $-9/8$.

13. (i) $1/42$, (ii) $13/3$.

16. (i) $\frac{1}{2}$, (ii) $1 - \frac{1}{4}\pi$.

17. $a = 1, b = 0, c = -1, d = 1$.

18. $\frac{1}{2}\pi(\pi - 2)$.

19. $4/3$.

23. 577.

24. (i) 39.3, (ii) 39.0.

EXERCISES 10 (a) (p. 264)

1. $\frac{1}{2}$. 2. 79/6. 3. $\sqrt{2} - 1$. 4. 8/3.

5. (i) $\frac{1}{2}$, (ii) 1. 6. 142 kg/cm^2. 8. $729\pi/35$. 9. 16π.

11. $\frac{1}{4}\pi^2$. 14. $\frac{2}{3}\pi a^3$. 15. 250π.

EXERCISES 10 (b) (p. 278)

2. $\frac{3}{4}\sqrt{(ah)}$. 3. 85/31.

4. $\bar{x} = 40/21$, $\bar{y} = 10/3$. 5. $\bar{x} = 3/2$, $\bar{y} = 0$.

7. $\bar{x} = \pi$, $\bar{y} = \frac{1}{4}\pi$. 9. $\frac{1}{8}\rho a^4$.

10. $2/\sqrt{(15)}$. 11. $\frac{2}{3}\sqrt{(3ah)}$.

13. $\frac{1}{2}a$, $\{a\sqrt{(9\pi^2 - 64)}\}/(6\pi)$.

EXERCISES 10 (c) (p. 281)

1. After 10 seconds, 500 m from starting point.

2. 4 m. 3. $x = 3 - \frac{1}{2}t + t^2 - \frac{1}{2}t^3$; $\frac{1}{3}$ second.

4. $p = \frac{1}{3}$, $q = 2$; 66·9 m. 5. $3(1 - \cos 2t)$.

6. 2. 7. (i) 32/27 m, (ii) 2 seconds.

8. (i) 8 m, (ii) 0·86 seconds. 9. (i) $2a/\pi$, (ii) $\pi a/4$.

10. (i) 4 m/s^2, (ii) $-67·5$ m/s^2.

11. $120t$, $110t + \frac{1}{12}t^2$; 120 seconds, 130 m/s.

13. 64 m/s, 5 seconds.

EXERCISES 10 (d) (p. 283)

1. 37/12. 2. $\frac{1}{12}a^3(2b - a)$; 1 : 2.

5. $\frac{1}{2}\pi$. 6. $3\pi^2/16$.

7. 176 : 13. 9. (0, 5), (2, 9); $34\frac{2}{3}$; $(3592\pi/15)$.

10. 0·4775 m^3. 11. $\dfrac{3l(2a + bl^2)}{4(3a + bl^2)}$.

12. $50\pi a^3$; $\bar{x} = 10a/3$, $\bar{y} = 0$. 13. $\bar{x} = 8/5$, $\bar{y} = 0$.

21. 113 m. 22. 3 seconds, 4·5 m.

24. 80 cm/s, 1440 cm, 85·3 cm/s. 25. 6006 m.

EXERCISES 11 (a) (p. 292)

1. (i) $\log_e x$, (ii) $-1/x$, (iii) $\tan x$. 2. (i) $(\log_e x - 1)/(\log_e x)^2$, (ii) $2 \sec 2x$.

4. $1/\{x(1 - x^2)\}$.

7. (i) $e^{-2x^2}\{(1/x) - 4x \log_e 3x\}$, (ii) $e^{2x}(2 \log_e \sec x + \tan x)$,
   (iii) $x(x + 2)e^x \tan^{-1} x + x^2 e^x (1 + x^2)^{-1}$.

9. $\frac{1}{16}(e^{8\pi} + 1)$. 10. 1, $2/\sqrt{e}$. 11. $\frac{3}{4}\pi$, $\frac{7}{4}\pi$, $\frac{11}{4}\pi$.

13. (i) $\frac{1}{3}(1 - e^{-9})$, (ii) $\frac{1}{2}(e^2 - e^{-2}) - 2$, (iii) 2.

14. (i) $e^{x+2} + C$, (ii) $\frac{1}{4}e^{2x}(2x^2 - 2x + 1) + C$.

EXERCISES 11 (b) (p. 298)

1. $\frac{1}{3}\log_e(x^3 + 4) + C$.

2. $\frac{1}{2}\log_e(x^2 + 4x + 10) + C$.

3. $\log_e(e^x - e^{-x}) + C$.

4. $(1/e)\log_e(x^e + e^x) + C$.

5. $-x + 2\log_e(1 + x) + C$.

6. $\frac{1}{4}x^2 - \frac{3}{4}x + \frac{21}{8}\log_e(2x + 3) + C$.

7. $\frac{1}{2}\log_e(x - 2) - \frac{1}{2}\log_e x + C$.

8. $2\log_e(x - 2) - \log_e(x - 1) + C$.

9. $2\log_e(x - 2) + \frac{1}{2}\log_e(2x + 1) + C$.

10. $2\log_e(x + 2) - \log_e(x + 4) + C$.

11. $x + \log_e(x - 2) - \log_e(x + 2) + C$.

12. $4\log_e(x - 3) - 15/(x - 3) + C$.

13. $-\frac{1}{2}(x - 1)^{-1} - \frac{1}{2}\log_e(x - 1) + \frac{1}{4}\log_e(x^2 + 1) + C$.

14. $2\log_e(x - 3) - \log_e(x^2 + 4) + \frac{1}{2}\tan^{-1}(\frac{1}{2}x) + C$.

15. $3\log_e 2$.

16. $\log_e(4/3)$.

17. $(3/7)\log_e 2$.

18. $\frac{1}{2}\log_e(5/2)$.

19. $\frac{1}{4}x^2(2\log_e x - 1) + C$.

20. $(\frac{1}{2}x^2 - 8)\log_e(x + 4) - \frac{1}{4}x^2 + 2x + C$.

21. $\frac{1}{16}x^4(4\log_e 5x - 1) + C$.

22. $x\tan x + \log_e \cos x + C$.

24. $\log_e \tan \frac{1}{2}x + C$.

25. $2\sqrt{x} - 2\log_e(1 + \sqrt{x}) + C$.

EXERCISES 11 (c) (p. 302)

7. $y = -\log_e(1 - x)$, $x = y - \frac{1}{2}y^2 + \frac{1}{6}y^3 - \frac{1}{24}y^4$.

8. $y = 4 - x^2 + \frac{1}{3}x^3$, $\log_e y = 2\log_e 2 - \frac{1}{4}x^2 + \frac{1}{12}x^3$, $(-1)^{n-1}/(n \cdot 2^{n-1})$.

9. $x < -1$ and $x > 0$.

10. $\log_e 2 + \frac{1}{2}x + \frac{3}{8}x^2 + \frac{7}{24}x^3$; $E = 2\log_e(3/2)$ or $\log_e 2 + \dfrac{352}{3000}$; $1 \cdot 098$.

11. $A = 2, B = 8, C = -9$.

13. $4 \cdot 01$.

14. $1 \cdot 052$.

15. $5 \cdot 099$.

EXERCISES 11 (d) (p. 304)

1. $(-7\sin x)/\{(3 + 4\cos x)(4 + 3\cos x)\}$.

3. $A = k/(k^2 + p^2)$, $B = -p/(k^2 + p^2)$; $\frac{1}{15}(3e^{3\pi/4} + 2)$.

4. $1 \cdot 7$.

7. $x + \frac{1}{2}x^2 - \frac{2}{3}x^3 + \frac{1}{4}x^4 + \frac{1}{5}x^5 - \frac{1}{3}x^6$.

8. (i) $\frac{1}{2}x + \frac{3}{4}\log_e(2x - 3) + C$, (ii) $2x - \log_e(x + 2) + C$,

   (iii) $\frac{1}{3}x^3 + \frac{1}{2}x^2 + x + \log_e(x - 1) + C$.

9. (i) $9\log_e(x - 3) - 3\log_e(x - 1) + C$,

   (ii) $\frac{13}{5}\log_e(x - 1) - \frac{1}{10}\log_e(2x + 3) + C$,

   (iii) $\frac{1}{2}\log_e(1 + 2x) - \log_e(1 - 2x) + C$.

10. (i) $\frac{1}{4}\log_e(5/3)$, (ii) $\frac{1}{2} + \log_e(3/4)$.

11. (i) $\frac{1}{3}x^3 \tan^{-1} x - \frac{1}{6}x^2 + \frac{1}{6}\log_e(x^2 + 1) + C$,

   (ii) $\left(\dfrac{x}{x + 1}\right)\log_e x - \log_e(x + 1) + C$.

12. $4 - 2\sqrt{e}$.

14. $(15 + \sqrt{3})\pi^2/(324\log_e 2)$.

15. $(3 - 2e^\pi)/13$.

16. $A = -1, B = 2$; $\log_e 2$ seconds.

18. $1 + x^2 + \frac{1}{6}x^4$.   19. $x + \frac{2}{3}x^3$.

21. $(1 + x)\{1 + 2 \log_e (1 + x)\}$, $3 + 2 \log_e (1 + x)$.

24. $3 \cdot 006$.   25. $4 \cdot 36$.

EXERCISES 12 (a) (p. 312)

1. $y = x^4 + C$.   2. $-(1/y) = x + \frac{1}{2}x^2 + C$.

3. $y = \cos x + C$.   4. $e^y = C - x$.

5. $\sin y = C - \sin x$.   6. $y = Ce^{2x^2}$.

7. $y = Cxe^x$.   8. $\log_e \sin y + \cos x = C$.

9. $(1 + x^2)\sqrt{(1 - y^2)} = C$.   10. $y + 1 = Ce^{\frac{1}{3}x^3}$.

11. $y^2 + \log_e y = x^3 + C$.   12. $y - \frac{1}{2}\sin 2y = x^2 + 6x + C$.

13. $y = 3e^{4(x-2)}$.   14. $y = 1 - e^{-x}$.

15. $y = 3e^x - 1$.   16. $\frac{1}{2}y^2 = x + \log_e x$.

17. $y^2 = \frac{1}{2}(1 - \cos 2x)$.   18. $x^2 = y^2 + 2y$.

19. $y = (x + 1)/(x - 1)$.   20. $y = e^x/(x + 1)$.

EXERCISES 12 (b) (p. 317)

1. $x^2 - 2xy = C$.   2. $(x + y)e^{-y/x} + x \log_e Cx = 0$.

3. $(y - x)^2 = Cxy^2$.   4. $x^3 - 3xy^2 = 2$.

5. $y^2 = x^3 - x^2$.   7. -4.

8. $\sqrt{(x^2 + y^2)} = x(\sqrt{2} + 1) - 1$.   9. $y = \cos x$.

10. $4y = 1 - \cos 2x + \sin 2x$.   11. $9y = 6 \sin 3x + 4(1 - \cos 3x)$.

12. $2y = 5 - 3(\cos 2x + \sin 2x)$.

EXERCISES 12 (c) (p. 320)

1. $v = v_0 \exp (-t/RC)$.   3. 2 m/s.   4. $y = x(x - 5)^2$; 625/12.

5. 5.   7. $3kt = \log_e \{(6 - x)/(6 - 2x)\}$, $k = 0 \cdot 231$.

9. $19 \cdot 0$ g.   10. 95 million.   11. $x^2 + y^2 = y$.   12. 2 m/s.

EXERCISES 12 (d) (p. 321)

1. $y = x^2/(1 - Cx^2)$.   3. $\tan x + \cot y - x + y = C$.

4. (i) $-\frac{1}{2}e^{-2y} = \frac{1}{3}x^3 - x + C$, (ii) $e^{2y} = \log_e \{(x - 1)/(x + 1)\} + C$.

5. $y = 1 - \exp (-\tan x)$.   7. $y^{-1} = x - \frac{1}{3}x^3 - \frac{1}{6}$.

9. 3.   10. $y = \tan (x + C) - x$.

11. 7/16.   13. $xy = \exp \{(x/y) - 1\}$.

14. $x^4 + 4xy^3 - y^4 = 1$.   17. $y = \frac{1}{4}\sin 4x + 2 \cos 4x$.

18. $y = 10 \exp \{-t/(1 + t)\}$.   19. $2r\sqrt{(2\pi/15)}$.

22. 2.

23. $A = 1/30$, $B = 1/30^2$, $x = 30^2 \log_e \{1 + (t/30)\}$, $v = 30 \exp (-x/30^2)$.

24. 30 m/s, $129 \cdot 5$ m, $16 \cdot 5$ seconds.   25. $y = e^{-x} (\sin 2x + 2 \cos 2x)$.

EXERCISES 13 (a) (p. 329)

1. $(5, -6)$; $\sqrt{61}$. 　　3. $(\tfrac{2}{4}a, 0)$; $\tfrac{3}{4}a$. 　　4. $\alpha + \beta = p$, $\alpha\beta = q$.

5. $(1, -3)$, $(3, 11)$; $x^2 + y^2 - 2x + 6y = 90$, $x^2 + y^2 - 6x - 22y + 30 = 0$.

6. $x^2 + y^2 + 2x + 6y = 90$; circle centre $(-1, -3)$, radius 10.

7. $x^2 + y^2 - 5x - y + 4 = 0$. 　　8. $x + 2y = 7$, $x + 2y = 0$.

9. $3x + 4y + 47 = 0$, $3x + 4y + 17 = 0$.

10. $x^2 + y^2 = 4$, $3x + 4y = \pm 10$, $(\pm 6/5, \pm 8/5)$.

11. $4x + 3y = \pm 25$. 　　12. $a = 5$, $(25/13, 60/13)$.

13. $x^2 + y^2 - 4x - 10y + 4 = 0$. 　　14. $12y = (14 \pm 5\sqrt{10})x$.

15. $x^2 + y^2 - 6x - 8y + 15 = 0$, $y - 3x = 5$, $53y - 9x = 15$.

16. $x^2 + y^2 + 15y = 0$, $3(x^2 + y^2) - 20y = 0$.

17. $4x^2 + 4y^2 - 13x - 26y = 0$.

18. $x^2 + y^2 - 2x - 6y + 5 = 0$, 4, $y = 3 \pm \sqrt{5}$.

19. $x^2 + y^2 - 6x - 4y + 9 = 0$.

EXERCISES 13 (b) (p. 334)

1. $x - 2y + 144 = 0$, $2x + y + 18 = 0$, $(-36, 54)$.

3. $(a/16, -a/2)$, $(a/4, a)$, $16x + 4y + a = 0$, $4x - 2y + a = 0$, $(-a/8, a/4)$.

4. $1 \pm k$. 　　7. a/m, $(a, \pm 2a)$, $(0, \pm a)$.

10. $x + y = 3$, $26°\,34'$. 　　13. $xy = (h - 2a)y + 2ak$.

14. $x^2 + y^2 - a(t_1 + t_2)y + a^2 t_1 t_2 = 0$.

EXERCISES 13 (c) (p. 344)

1. $x^2 + 2y^2 = 100$. 　　4. $(-la^2/n, -mb^2/n)$, $(\pm\tfrac{2}{5}, \mp\tfrac{1}{5})$.

10. $(5, 15/2)$. 　　11. $3x^2 - y^2 = 3a^2$.

12. $(\pm 4\sqrt{(34)}/5, \pm 9/5)$. 　　15. $3x - 4y + 7 = 0$, $(-16/3, -9/4)$.

18. $(x^2 + y^2)^2 = 4c^2 xy$.

EXERCISES 13 (d) (p. 346)

1. $\{(n^2 + 1)a/(n^2 - 1), 0\}$, $2na/(n^2 - 1)$. 　　2. $(0, \pm\sqrt{3}/a)$, $\sqrt{2}/a$.

3. $[0, 2a^2 b)/(a^2 - b^2)]$. 　　4. 9, $(1, 5)$, 5.

5. $3y = x + 35$, $(-5, 10)$, $(1, 12)$. 　　6. $(-k, 2k)$, $2k$; $3y = 4x$.

10. $(4a, 0)$. 　　12. $2ay = m(y^2 - 2ax) + 2ac$.

13. $9y^2 + 8a^2 = 12ax$. 　　15. $h = 0$, $k = 2t$; $x = 0$.

21. $a^2 l^2 - b^2 m^2 = n^2$, $(a^2/l^2) - (b^2/m^2) = (a^2 + b^2)^2/n^2$.

EXERCISES 14 (a) (p. 353)

1. $18 \cdot 25$ N, $25°\,17'$. 　　2. $68°\,12'$, $27°\,41'$.

3. $5 \cdot 18$, $7 \cdot 32g$ N. 　　4. $5 \cdot 18g$, $17 \cdot 32g$, $5 \cdot 18g$ N.

5. $9 \cdot 99$, $3 \cdot 16$ N. 　　6. $5 \cdot 18g$, $7 \cdot 32g$ N.

7. $2 + \sqrt{3} : 1$. 　　8. 13, 7.

9. 6 N at 60° to BA.   11. 120°, 90°.

13. 57·26 N, E 49° 39′ S.   15. 10·64g N, 26·95g N, 32° 8′.

EXERCISES 14 (b) (p. 361)

1. $a : b$.   2. $21\sqrt{3}a\,P/2$.   3. 6 kg, 9·33 cm.   4. 9 gm, 2 cm.

5. 280 kg, 28 kg.   6. 17·3 kg.   7. 48 g mN.   9. 2P.

10. 12, 4.   11. 2 cm.   12. 75, 45, 40, 40g N.

EXERCISES 14 (c) (p. 368)

1. $10\sqrt{5}$ N at 15 cm from A in BA.   2. $2\sqrt{(58)}$, $7y + 3x = 10$.

3. $5\sqrt{2} - 4, 5 - 2\sqrt{2}$ N.   5. $10\sqrt{2}P$, parallel to AC.

6. $24\sqrt{2}$ N at 45° to a side.

7. 1·30, 3·93 N, 81° 9′ to AB, 16a from A.

8. 2P, 60°, 5a/2 from A.   11. $\sqrt{5}$ N, 63° 26′ to BC, $(3\sqrt{3}/4)a$.

12. $2 + 2/\sqrt{3}, -9, -11 - 2/\sqrt{3}$ N.   13. 7/3.

14. 12 N, 6 m N.   15. 6F, $\tan^{-1}(5\sqrt{5} - 9)/8$ to AB, 4·17 AB, 1·14 BC.

EXERCISES 14 (d) (p. 372)

1. 9 m N   2. 1·5W N.

3. 75 N, 18 m N.   4. 150 m N, 312·5 N.

5. $3\sqrt{3}a/2$.

6. $2\sqrt{5}$ N, $\tan^{-1} 2$ to AB, 2 m N, 0·5 m.

7. rod $\sin^{-1}(G/aW)$ to vertical, W.   8. 15 N, 10 cm.

9. $5\sqrt{2}$ N, 45° to CD, 25 cm N.

10. $P = 5$, $Q = 4$, $R = 3$.   11. 1, 4, $19\sqrt{3}/2$.

12. $\sqrt{(31)}$ at 51° 3′ to OD, $17\sqrt{3}a/2$.

EXERCISES 14 (e) (p. 381)

1. 25/3g, 25/3g N, $\tan^{-1} 3/4$ to AB.   2. 20/$\sqrt{3}g$, 20/$\sqrt{3}g$ N, 60° to AB.

3. $W\sqrt{(l^2 + 9b^2)}/(2b)$, $W\sqrt{(l^2 + b^2)}/(2b)$, $\tan^{-1} b/l$ to beam.

4. 4·20g, 10·85g N, 67° 13′ to horizontal.

6. $5\sqrt{3}g$, $5\sqrt{7}g$ N, $\tan^{-1}(2/\sqrt{3})$ to ground.

7. 40/$\sqrt{3}g$, 20/$\sqrt{3}g$ N, $\tan^{-1}(2/\sqrt{3})$.

8. $W/6$, $W\sqrt{(37)}/6$, $\tan^{-1} 6$ to horizontal.

10. 10·5g N, 14g N vertically.

EXERCISES 14 (f) (p. 383)

1. 2DA through the centre of the circle.

3. 90°, $W\sqrt{3}/2$.   5. $Q = 5\sqrt{2}P$, 10a/7.

6. AO, 15; OF, 21; FA, 15 N.   7. 13P, $AE = a$.

8. (4P, 3P), $-2Pa$.

9. $5\sqrt{2}P$ at 45° to AB, 66a/25 from A, $-34Pa/5$.

11. $2\sqrt{5}$ N, 2 cm.

16. $80/\sqrt{3}g$ N, $20\sqrt{(7/3)}g$ N at 40° 54′ to horizontal.

18. $W(l^2 + a^2)/2l^2$. 19. $a(1 + 1/n)$, $W(1 + n)/3$.

20. $(13/12)W \sin \beta$, $W(5 \sin \beta + 12 \cos \beta)/12$.

EXERCISES 15 (a) (p. 390)

1. $1000g$ N, $100\sqrt{(65)}g$ N at $\tan^{-1}(1/8)$ to AB.

2. $29 \cdot 7g$, $198g$, $205g$ N. 3. $0 \cdot 190W$, $0 \cdot 165W$, $1 \cdot 095W$.

4. $66 \cdot 04g$ N; $61 \cdot 33g$ N at $\tan^{-1}(25/56)$ to horizontal.

5. $P = 2$, $8\sqrt{3}$ N at 150° to AB. 7. $20/\sqrt{3}$ g.

8. $113 \cdot 3g$ N, $663 \cdot 8g$ N at 81° 30′ to horizontal.

9. $\sin^2 \alpha : \cos^2 \alpha$; $W \sin \alpha/(\cot \alpha - 1)$. 10. $\cos^{-1}(7/9)$.

11. $3\sqrt{2}g$ N, $6 - 2\sqrt{6}$ kg. 12. $\tan^{-1}(3/4)$, $11 \cdot 25$ cm, 3 cm.

EXERCISES 15 (b) (p. 396)

1. $11h/28$. 2. $8a/9$, $7a/9$. 3. $3 \cdot 46$ m.

4. $0 \cdot 55$ cm. 5. $b(a^2 - 5c^2)/(a^2 - 4c^2)$. 6. $5h/4$.

7. $4/3$, $5/3$, 3 cm. 10. $\tan^{-1}(16/33)$. 11. $4 \cdot 31$ cm.

12. $3\sqrt{7}W/14$. 13. $\tan^{-1}(1/6)$. 14. $\sqrt{(17/7)}$.

17. 47 cm, 27° 3′. 18. $(3a^3 - 3ax^2 + x^3)/3(2a^2 - x^2)$ from a face.

EXERCISES 15 (c) (p. 403)

1. $0 \cdot 35$, $2 \cdot 19g$ N. 2. $73 \cdot 6g$ N. 8. $\frac{1}{2}W$.

10. $\sqrt{3}/9$. 11. $3 \cdot 2$ m, $0 \cdot 48$. 12. $1/7$, $5/7$.

16. $7\frac{1}{2}°$.

EXERCISES 15 (d) (p. 407)

1. $\frac{3}{4}W$. 2. $\tan^{-1}(6/7)$, A.

6. $\frac{1}{2}W(\tan \theta - 2 \tan \alpha)$. 7. $4W/5$ parallel

8. $\cot^2 \theta = 3 + 4W_1W_2/(W_1 + W_2)^2$. 9. $6W$.

10. W, W, W, W. 12. $8 \cdot 6g$ N.

15. $2P/\sqrt{3}$, $P/\sqrt{3}$, $P\sqrt{3}$, $P\sqrt{3}$, P.

EXERCISES 15 (e) (p. 410)

4. $w\sqrt{5}$. 6. $\tan^{-1}(1/2)$.

7. $y = 4x/(3\pi)$; $x = 3a/2, y = 2a/\pi$. 8. 1 cm, $1 \cdot 5$ cm.

9. $5r/8$. 10. $4a/3$ from end, $\tan^{-1}(5)$, $\tan^{-1}(1/5)$.

11. $7a/18$, $a/3$, $a/24$. 13. $3 \cdot 59$ cm, $2 \cdot 15$ cm.

15. $3\pi/16$. 19. $W \cot \theta$, horizontal.

20. $2\sqrt{3} \ W/9$, horizontal. 21. $30/59$, A slips.

EXERCISES 16 (a) (p. 419)

1. 600 m, 40 m/s, 15·9 seconds.
2. 24·9 m/s.
3. 27 seconds, 729 m.
4. 45 km/h.
5. 0·049 m/s², 1·25 min.
7. 1·59 sec.
9. 30 cm/s, 225 cm.
10. 62·5 m, 15 seconds.
11. 12·09 p.m., 136·5 km.
12. 110 seconds.
13. $(u - u_1)^2/2a$, $(2u - u_1)a/u$.
15. 2·33 m/s².

EXERCISES 16 (b) (p. 428)

1. 3·98 cm/s², 2·3 km.
2. 2·7, 7·8, 13·4, 18·5, 23·5, 26·5, 26·5, 26·5 cm/s².
3. 50 cm/s², 16·6 seconds.
4. 12·3 cm/s², at $t = 67·5$ seconds.
5. accel. 0 and 1·5 m/s², 275 m.
7. 81·1 m, 12·6 cm/s².
8. ½ km.
9. 3·75 seconds.
10. 19·36 m/s.
14. ½√(15).

EXERCISES 16 (c) (p. 430)

1. 0·31 m/s².
2. 0·56, 0·35 m/s², 79·5 sec.
4. 62·5 sec.
5. 6⅔ seconds.
6. 7 m/s, 45 m.
7. 31·6 m, 4·76 sec.
8. 76 m.
9. 0·1 m/s².
10. 25 m/s.
11. 3, ½, 720 m.
12. 35·35 seconds.
13. 16·6 m.
14. 3·33 m/s, 0·056 m/s², 19 m.
16. 17·5 m/s, 216·7 m.
17. 48 m/s, 0·64 m/s².
18. 24 m/s, 0·267 m/s²; 10·5, 18, 22·5, 24, 8 m/s.
19. 6·93 seconds, 1 m/s², 2 m/s².
20. −18 cos 3t.
21. 38 m/s, 33 m.
22. 5060 m, 29·4 m/s.
23. 484 m.
24. 391 m.

EXERCISES 17 (a) (p. 440)

1. 30 km/h, 330°; 038° 16′.
2. N 28° 4′ E, 170 km/h.
3. 13·6 m/s.
4. gt.
5. 36 min, 28 min.
6. 20 sea-miles, 12·40 p.m.
7. 1·89 km, 12·86 min.
8. 21·3 km/h, N 39° 54′ W.
9. 0·77v, E 67½° S, 90 m.
10. 9 min, 117° 37′.
11. 50 km/h; 85 m, 51 m, 68 m.
12. 21·25 mile/h, N 19° 48′ E.
13. 34 min, 58 min.
15. N 57° 36′ E, 7 a.m., 108 min.

EXERCISES 17 (b) (p. 452)

1. $\tan^{-1} 2$, 6·4 m, 3·2 m.
3. 240 m.
4. $u^2 \sin 2\alpha/g$, $3u^2\sin^2 \alpha/2g$.
5. 15°, 75°.
7. 15 m.
8. 700 m/s.
12. $u^2 \operatorname{cosec}^2 \alpha/2g$.
13. $4u^2/g$, $5u^2/g$.
16. 16·2 m/s, 13° 30′ to horizontal.
17. 8/33, $\tan^{-1} (40/99)$.
18. 383 m, 46·° 15′, 86·7 m/s.

EXERCISES 17 (c) (p. 455)

1. 17·95 m/s, 16·67 m/s.
2. 3·70 h.
3. 93 min.
4. 29 : 27 : 28.
5. 2·5 min, $3\frac{1}{8}$ min.
6. 15·38 sea-miles, E 43° N.
8. 0·131 nautical miles.
9. E 31° 4′ N, 20·5 knots.
10. 30·5 knots, N 20° 20′ W, 10·4 sea-miles.
11. 90°, $7\frac{1}{2}$ min, 375 m.
13. 62 min.
14. V, due E.
15. 250 m, $6\frac{1}{4}$ min, 5 min.
16. (3754, 3754), (4694, 2347).
17. 25° 41′, 113·2 m/s.
18. 55° 33′, 14·4 seconds.
19. $a\sqrt{(g/8b)}$, $\sqrt{(2gb)}$.
20. $2\frac{1}{8}$ seconds.
21. 85 m.
22. 20·8, 14·8 m.
23. $t = \frac{1}{2}$ second, $x = 18$ m, $y = 6\cdot27$ m.
24. $\frac{3}{4} h$.
26. $\frac{1}{2}\sqrt{2}$, $\frac{1}{2}\sqrt{10}$ seconds.
27. 76° 43′, −13° 17′, 9·82, 2·32 seconds.
28. 600 m.
29. 4·49 m.
30. $\sqrt{3}/12$.

EXERCISES 18 (a) (p. 466)

1. 25·27, 19·73 kN.
3. $\sqrt{(5gd/6)}$.
4. 1·34 m/s², 78·2 m.
5. 1·32 kN.
6. 486 kN.
8. 3, $\frac{1}{9}$ g.
9. 0·58.
10. $g/21$, $4g/21$, $33g/175$.
11. $\dfrac{M \sin(\phi - \lambda) - m \sin(\theta + \lambda)}{(M + m) \cos \lambda}$ g.
15. 5·89 m/s, 8·83 m.

EXERCISES 18 (b) (p. 474)

1. 4·07 kW.
2. 98·6 km/h.
3. 219 N, 79·3 km/h.
4. 153·3 N, 0·6 m/s², 514 N.
5. 0·0306.
6. 31·5 kW.
7. 53·6 mile/h.
8. 10·9 kW, 0·49 m/s².
9. 123 W, 36 km/h, 0·123 m/s².
11. 28·7 km/h, 0·314 m/s².
12. 410 W, 0·981 m/s², 30 km/h.
13. 1 in 210, 48 km/h.
14. 0·218 ft/s², 24·4 mile/h.
15. 57·3 km/h, 0·135 m/s².

EXERCISES 18 (c) (p. 480)

2. $1\cdot427 \times 10^5$ J.
3. $1\cdot832 \times 10^5$ J.
4. 8 h.p.
5. 179 W.
6. 20·3 kW.
7. 2N, 200 J, 40 W.
8. 11·0 kW.
9. 2.
10. 7·9 kW.
11. 1·18 kW.
12. 40·7 kW.
13. $\{2gc(M - m \sin \alpha)/(M + m)\}^{\frac{1}{2}}$.
14. 6·857 m.

EXERCISES 18 (d) (p. 482)

1. 2·52 km, 82·7 km/h.
3. 25·1 km/h.
4. 25·7 cm/s².
5. 312, 80 seconds.
6. 871 kW.
7. 37·3 m, 23·6 m.
9. $\frac{1}{2}g$.
10. 30·8 N, 1·82 m/s, 25·1 cm.
11. $\frac{1}{3}gt$, $\frac{2}{3}gt$, gt.
12. 0·58.
13. 0·39 km.
14. 3·92 s.
15. 723 h.p., 45·7 mile/h.
16. 18·2 kW.
17. 61·5 m/s.
18. 29·7 m.
19. 68·35 km, 16·6 kW.
20. 178 kgf, 1 in 15·6.
21. 654 kW, 13·3 km/h.
22. 537·6 h.p., 1075·2 h.p.
23. 32·14 mile/h, 50$\frac{2}{7}$ h.p., 1037 ft tonf.
24. 32 m.
25. 5° 2′.

EXERCISES 19 (a) (p. 491)

1. $Mmu/(M + m)$, $\frac{1}{2}Mmu^2/(m + M)$.
2. 17·1 kN.
3. 82° 49′.
4. 77·7 kgf.
5. 3 × 10⁴ newton seconds, 20 m/s, 300 kN, 0·1 seconds.
6. 1·92 m/s.
7. 2 m/s, 5 m/s, 15 × 10³ J.
8. 1 m/s, 4 × 10⁴ J.
9. 92·5 kN.
10. 2·35 × 10³ kgf seconds.
11. 22·4 m/s, at 63° 26′ to horizontal, 5·83 seconds.
12. m/M, 6·67 × 10⁵ N.
13. 848 kg, 70·5 N.
15. 4·3 × 10⁴ kgf, 0·039 seconds, 1·962 × 10⁴ J.

EXERCISES 19 (b) (p. 499)

1. 0·91.
2. $\frac{1}{2}$.
3. 2·3 cm.
4. 5·27 × 10⁻² J.
5. $\frac{1}{8}$, 8·41 m/s.
6. 0·52.
10. $\frac{3}{4}$, 5·25 J.
11. 1$\frac{1}{3}$ m/s, 3 m/s, 13·3 J.
14. 47/108.

EXERCISES 19 (c) (p. 503)

1. 1·01 × 10⁶, 4·22 × 10⁵.
2. 14·5.
3. 13 825.
4. 96·2.
5. 0·457, 9·2.
6. 0·225 ft/s².

EXERCISES 19 (d) (p. 503)

1. 1·27, 2·55 seconds, 5·31 m; 21·23 m.
2. 14·5 J, 25 N.
3. $mM(v - V)/(M + m)$.
4. 1 m/s, 8·01 × 10³ J.
5. 1750 kW.
7. 4·4 ft, tan⁻¹ (1·5).

9. 10·9, 2·6 m/s; 2·55 J.

10. 0·875 m/s, 5·875 m/s.

12. $\sqrt{(14ga)}$, 6 mga.

13. $\frac{1}{2}$, 14, $u/12$.

14. $e > 2/5$, 7/18.

17. $\frac{1}{2}(1 - e)u$, $\frac{1}{2}(1 + e)u$.

18. $\frac{1}{2}$.

21. $m_1 a(1 + e)/Je$, $J/(m_1 + m_2)$.

22. 3/5.

23. 2/7.

24. $\sqrt{(3/7)}$ seconds, $\sqrt{(3/7)}$ seconds.

25. $\frac{1}{2}$.

EXERCISES 20 (a) (p. 514)

1. 3 m.

2. $Mg - Mh\omega^2$, $Mh\omega^2/mg$.

3. $(a\omega^2 + g) : (a\omega^2 - g)$.

4. 3·84 m/s.

5. 2·37 × 10² N, 80° 28′.

6. $5\pi a/u$.

7. 12 rad/s.

8. 77·2 r.p.m.

9. 48·8 r.p.m.

10. 57·9 r.p.m.

11. 8·05 kgf.

14. 0·59 N, 153 r.p.m.

15. 73·5 N, 276 N, 1·49 m/s.

EXERCISES 20 (b) (p. 520)

1. 69 km/h.

2. 0·624.

3. 53·5 km/h.

4. 5·9 cm, 1·04 × 10⁴ N.

5. 0·8 tonf, outer rail.

6. 3970 N, 2·35 cm.

7. 6° 57′, 0·122.

8. 12·7 cm.

9. 11·4, 77·8 km/h.

10. 43·7 km/h.

11. 10° 16′, 0·48.

EXERCISES 20 (c) (p. 525)

4. 3·5 mg.

5. 2·45 m/s.

6. 1 : 7.

7. 2 mg.

9. 240 cm/s², 12·2 mN.

10. 3 mg.

11. $\sqrt{(\frac{1}{3}gl)}$, $\cos^{-1}\frac{2}{3}$.

EXERCISES 20 (d) (p. 527)

1. 4·43 m/s.

2. 9·87 × 10 N.

3. 31·5 r.p.m., 2·18 × 10 N.

8. $\mu Mmg/(M + 2m)$.

9. 89 r.p.m.

10. 94·6 r.p.m.

11. 7 mg, $\frac{1}{7} mg$, 19 $mg/7$.

12. 5° 59′, 0·1.

13. 71·3 km/h.

15. 63·5 km/h, 46° 34′.

18. 8·86 m/s, 5·43 m/s.

19. 18·4 N.

20. $\frac{2}{3}a$.

EXERCISES 21 (a) (p. 538)

1. 25 cm/s.

3. $\sqrt{\{(b^2v^2 - c^2u^2)/(v^2 - u^2)\}}$, $2\pi\sqrt{\{(b^2 - c^2)/(v^2 - u^2)\}}$.

4. $\pi\sqrt{2}$ seconds, $4\sqrt{2}$ m.

5. $4\cos^{-1}(1/\sqrt{5})$.

6. 13 in, $4\frac{1}{3}$ ft/s, $17\frac{1}{3}$ ft/s^2.

7. 5 m, $\pi/6$ seconds.

8. 2·5 m, π seconds, 5 m/s.

9. 15·9 cm, 4·41 cm/s, 1·57 cm/s^2.

10. 25 cm, 27·4 cm/s^2, 20·9 cm/s.

11. $1:\sqrt{2}$.

12. 8 seconds, 35·35 cm.

13. 13·5 seconds.

14. shortened 0·02 per cent.

15. 99·40 cm, shortened 0·18 per cent.

EXERCISES 21 (b) (p. 542)

1. $2ma^2\pi^2/p^2$, $a\sqrt{(1 - 4/\pi^2)}$, $4ma^2\pi^3/p^3$, $a/\sqrt{2}$.

2. $3a$ from O, $2ka$.

3. $4mg$, $\pi\sqrt{(a/g)}$, $\frac{1}{2}\sqrt{(ag)}$, 0.

4. $l(1 + \sqrt{3})$.

5. $2\pi\sqrt{(2d/g)}$, 3d.

6. $a(1 + 2M/m)$, $2\pi\sqrt{\{(M + m)a/(mg)\}}$.

7. $17a/8$, $2\pi\sqrt{(a/8g)}$.

9. 1·57 m/s.

10. $\pi/6$ seconds, 6·67 cm.

12. $\frac{1}{2}g$.

14. 2·3 cm.

15. 6·075 cm, 0·31 seconds.

EXERCISES 21 (c) (p. 550)

1. $3g/4a$.

2. 69·1 r.p.m.

3. $\frac{1}{4}M_a^2\omega^2$.

4. 4·43 rad/s.

6. 4·97 kg m^2.

8. $\frac{1}{8}$ g.

10. $2\pi\sqrt{(13l/15g)}$.

11. $11a/6$.

12. 3·75 seconds.

13. $3(M + 2m)g/8(M + 3m)a$.

15. $Mmg/(M + 2m)$.

EXERCISES 21 (d) (p. 552)

1. π m/s, $\frac{1}{2}\pi\sqrt{3}$ m/s.

5. $2\pi n\sqrt{(a^2 - x^2)}$, $2\pi na \sin 2\pi nt$.

6. 35·8 cm, 4:9.

7. 30·2 ft/s^2.

9. 2·3 cm.

10. 0·40 seconds, 27·1 cm/s, 245 cm/s^2.

13. 0·854.

18. $2\pi\sqrt{(14a/9g)}$.

19. $2\pi\sqrt{\{(I + ml^2)/(Mh + ml)g\}}$.

20. $3M:(2M + m)$.

21. $12g/5$, $6g/5$.

22. $3g/5a$.

23. $\pi\sqrt{\{(a^2 + 4b^2)/bg\}}$.

24. $4b/3$ from AB.

EXERCISES 22 (a) (p. 560)

1. (a) $\begin{bmatrix} 6 \\ 0 \\ 9 \end{bmatrix}$, (b) $\begin{bmatrix} 1 \\ 2 \\ -1 \end{bmatrix}$, (c) $\begin{bmatrix} 16 \\ 0 \\ 19 \end{bmatrix}$.

2. (a) $\begin{bmatrix} 6 & 6 \\ 0 & 0 \\ 9 & 9 \end{bmatrix}$, (b) $\begin{bmatrix} 5 & 7 \\ -2 & 2 \\ 10 & 8 \end{bmatrix}$, (c) $\begin{bmatrix} 7 & 6 \\ 1 & -1 \\ 3 & 4 \end{bmatrix}$.

3. $AB = \begin{bmatrix} 6 & 10 \\ 3 & 11 \end{bmatrix}$, $BA = \begin{bmatrix} 9 & 9 \\ 4 & 8 \end{bmatrix}$.

4. $AB = \begin{bmatrix} 10 & 3 \\ 5 & 1 \end{bmatrix}$, $AC = \begin{bmatrix} 3 & 10 \\ 1 & 5 \end{bmatrix}$, $BC = \begin{bmatrix} 0 & 1 \\ 1 & 6 \end{bmatrix}$, $A(BC) = \begin{bmatrix} 3 & 19 \\ 1 & 8 \end{bmatrix}$.

5. $AB = \begin{bmatrix} 1 & 5 \\ 5 & 26 \end{bmatrix}$, $BC = \begin{bmatrix} 11 & 7 \\ 2 & 1 \end{bmatrix}$, $CA = \begin{bmatrix} 11 & 2 \\ 7 & 1 \end{bmatrix}$.

6. $A^2 = \begin{bmatrix} 7 & 10 \\ 15 & 22 \end{bmatrix}$, $A^3 = \begin{bmatrix} 37 & 54 \\ 81 & 118 \end{bmatrix}$.

7. $\begin{bmatrix} 10 & 3 & 10 & 14 \\ 16 & 4 & 14 & 20 \end{bmatrix}$. 8. $\begin{bmatrix} 3 & 7 \\ 7 & 16 \end{bmatrix}$. 9. $\begin{bmatrix} 2 & 2 \\ 2 & 2 \end{bmatrix}$.

10. $\mathbf{AB} = \begin{bmatrix} 2 & 4 \\ 9 & 12 \end{bmatrix}$, $\mathbf{BC} = \begin{bmatrix} 1 & 8 \\ 2 & 16 \end{bmatrix}$, $\mathbf{CA} = \begin{bmatrix} 2 & 0 \\ 0 & 12 \end{bmatrix}$, $\mathbf{A(BC)} = \begin{bmatrix} 2 & 16 \\ 6 & 48 \end{bmatrix}$.

11. $x_1 x_2 + y_1 y_2 + z_1 z_2$.

12. $\mathbf{AB} = \begin{bmatrix} 8 & 7 \\ 7 & 8 \end{bmatrix}$, $\mathbf{BA} = \begin{bmatrix} 8 & 7 \\ 7 & 8 \end{bmatrix}$, $\mathbf{B}^2 = \begin{bmatrix} 5 & 4 \\ 4 & 5 \end{bmatrix}$.

EXERCISES 22 (b) (p. 567)

1. $\mathbf{A}^2 = 3\mathbf{A}$, $\mathbf{B}^2 = \begin{bmatrix} 1 & 4 & 4 \\ 0 & 1 & 4 \\ 0 & 0 & 1 \end{bmatrix}$, $\mathbf{C}^2 = \begin{bmatrix} 14 & 20 & 26 \\ 20 & 29 & 38 \\ 26 & 38 & 50 \end{bmatrix}$,

$\mathbf{D}^2 = \begin{bmatrix} 1 & 0 & 2 \\ 0 & 1 & 2 \\ 0 & 0 & 1 \end{bmatrix}$.

2. $\mathbf{ABC} = \begin{bmatrix} 16 & 23 & 30 \\ 16 & 23 & 30 \\ 16 & 23 & 30 \end{bmatrix}$, $\mathbf{ABCD} = \begin{bmatrix} 16 & 23 & 69 \\ 16 & 23 & 69 \\ 16 & 23 & 69 \end{bmatrix}$.

3. $\mathbf{E}^2 = \begin{bmatrix} 1 & 0 & 0 \\ 2a & 1 & 0 \\ 2b + ca & 2c & 1 \end{bmatrix}$, $\mathbf{F}^2 = \begin{bmatrix} 1 & 2\alpha & 2\beta + \alpha\gamma \\ 0 & 1 & 2\gamma \\ 0 & 0 & 1 \end{bmatrix}$,

$\mathbf{EF} = \begin{bmatrix} 1 & \alpha & \beta \\ a & a\alpha + 1 & a\beta + \gamma \\ b & b\alpha + c & b\beta + c\gamma + 1 \end{bmatrix}$.

EXERCISES 22 (c) (p. 574)

1. $\mathbf{L}_1 = \begin{bmatrix} 1 & 0 \\ 7 & 1 \end{bmatrix}$, $\mathbf{U} = \begin{bmatrix} 1 & 4 \\ 0 & -19 \end{bmatrix}$.

2. $\begin{bmatrix} 1 & & \\ -2 & 1 & \\ 5 & -4 & 1 \end{bmatrix}$. 3. $\begin{bmatrix} 1 & -2 & -5 \\ & 1 & 1 \\ & & 1 \end{bmatrix}$.

4. $\begin{bmatrix} 1 & & \\ 2 & 1 & \\ 3 & 1 & 1 \end{bmatrix}\begin{bmatrix} 2 & & \\ & 2 & \\ & & 1 \end{bmatrix}\begin{bmatrix} 1 & -1 & 1 \\ & 1 & 0 \\ & & 1 \end{bmatrix}$.

5. $\begin{bmatrix} 1 & 3 \\ & -7 \end{bmatrix}\begin{bmatrix} x \\ y \end{bmatrix} = \begin{bmatrix} 4 \\ -7 \end{bmatrix}$; $x = 1, y = 1$.

6. $\begin{bmatrix} 1 & 1 & 1 \\ & 1 & -3 \\ & & 2 \end{bmatrix}\begin{bmatrix} x \\ y \\ z \end{bmatrix} = \begin{bmatrix} 1 & & \\ -2 & 1 & \\ -2 & -1 & 1 \end{bmatrix}\begin{bmatrix} 2 \\ 8 \\ 10 \end{bmatrix}$.

7. $x = 2, y = 2, z = 5$. 8. $x = 1, y = 2, z = 3$.

9. $y' \cos 4\alpha + x'(1 - \sin 4\alpha) = 0$. 10. $x' = 2y'$; $m = \pm 2$.

EXERCISES 22 (d) (p. 575)

1. diag $(a_1 a_2, b_1 b_2, c_1 c_2)$. 2. $5\mathbf{I}$.

4. $x = 2/\sqrt{3}, y = -1/\sqrt{3}$; $x = -2/\sqrt{3}, y = 1/\sqrt{3}$.

5. $\begin{bmatrix} 1 & 0 & 0 \\ 2 & -1 & 0 \\ -7 & 6 & -1 \end{bmatrix}$. 6. $\begin{bmatrix} 1 & -3 & 1 \\ 0 & 1 & -1 \\ 0 & 0 & 1 \end{bmatrix}$.

7. $\begin{bmatrix} -12 & 9 & -1 \\ 9 & -7 & 1 \\ -7 & 6 & -1 \end{bmatrix}$.

8. $-(a + b + c)(b - c)(c - a)(a - b)$.

9. (i) 0, (ii) ab.

10. $2(a + 1)(a + 3)^3$.

11. $x = \frac{1}{5}(-a + 9b - 3c)$, $y = \frac{1}{5}(-2a + 3b - c)$, $z = \frac{1}{5}(2a - 13b + 6c)$.

12. $\frac{1}{13}\begin{bmatrix} 4 & -8 & 3 \\ 6 & 1 & -2 \\ -3 & 6 & 1 \end{bmatrix}$.

13. $\frac{1}{4}\begin{bmatrix} 8 & -3 \\ -4 & 2 \end{bmatrix}$.

14. $\begin{bmatrix} 1 & & \\ -2 & 1 & \\ 2 & -3 & 1 \end{bmatrix}$, $\begin{bmatrix} 1 \\ 3 \\ -6 \end{bmatrix}$, $\begin{bmatrix} 2 \\ -1 \\ 3 \end{bmatrix}$.

19. $x = 35/18$, $y = 29/18$, $z = 5/18$.

INDEX

Abscissa, 107

Acceleration, 152, 196, 201, 279, 414; components of, 441; constant, 280, 415, 417; explicit expressions for, 425; normal, 507; units of, 414

Addition formulae, 66, 110

Ambiguous case for triangle, 93

Amplitude in simple harmonic motion, 532

Angle between two lines, 125

Approximations, 203

Area, as integral, 240; as limit of sum, 238; calculation of, 244, 259

Area of triangle, formula for, 89; in terms of coordinates, 113

Argand diagram, 158

Asymptotes, of hyperbola, 342

Banking, 518

Binomial theorem, for fractional and negative indices, 52; for positive index, 48

c.g.s. units, 461

Cartesian coordinates, 107

Centre of gravity, 265, 269, 374, 391

Centre of mass, 266, 374

Centroid, 268, 374, 391

Change of units, 501

Circle, equation of, 325; on given diameter, 326; tangent to, 327

Circular motion, 507, 516; in vertical circle, 523; with variable velocity, 521

Coefficient, of friction, 398; of restitution, 492

Collision of particles, 486

Combinations, 42; with similar and repeated objects, 44

Complex numbers, 154; algebra of, 155; conjugate, 156; modulus and amplitude of, 156; products and quotients of, 157

Compound pendulum, 548

Conical pendulum, 512

Conservation, of energy, 479; of momentum, 487

Coordinates, Cartesian, 107; of point dividing join of two points, 111; polar, 108; relation between, 109

Cosine formula for triangle, 86

Couples, 369

Cube roots of unity, 160

Curve sketching, 217

Definite integral, 242, 244

Demoivre's theorem, 161

Derivative, 173

Determinants, 565

Differential coefficient, 173; of a constant, 177; of a function of a function, 182; of a product, 178; of a quotient, 179; of a sum, 177; of e^x, 291; of inverse functions, 186; of $\log_e x$, 290; of parametric and implicit functions, 188; of $\sin x$ and $\cos x$, 176; of $\tan x$, etc., 180; of x^n, 175

Differential equations, 307; applications of, 318; first order, 308; homogeneous, 313; second order, 315

Differentiation of a graph, 421

Dimensions, 501

Directrix, of ellipse, 336; of hyperbola, 340; of parabola, 330

Distance between points, 110; of point from line, 129

Dyne, 461

Eccentricity, of ellipse, 336; of hyperbola, 340

Effective normal force, 509; reversed, 510

Efficiency, 473

Elastic strings, 389, 540

Ellipse, equation of, 336; normal to, 339; parametric equations of, 338; tangent to, 338

Empirical laws, 134

Energy, conservation of, 479; kinetic, 476; potential, 478; units of, 476

Energy equation, 479, 546

Equation $a \cos x + b \sin x = c$, 73

Equilibrium, 352, 405; conditions for, 375; with four or more forces, 386

Equivalent simple pendulum, 549

Erg, 468

Explicit functions, 167

Exponential function, 290; derivative of, 291

Exponential series, 301

Focus, of ellipse, 336; of hyperbola, 340; of parabola, 330

Force, 350; as vector, 152, 355; on a particle, 351; on a rigid body, 354; units of, 350

Frames of reference, 433

Frequency, 533

Friction, angle of, 398; coefficient of, 398; laws of, 397; problems on, 400

Functions of a variable, 166

Gradient, 168

Graphical methods in dynamics, 417, 425

Half-angle formulae for triangle, 88

Heights and distances, 99

Higher derivatives, 190

Homogeneous differential equations, 313

Hooke's law, 389

Horse-power, 471; brake, 473; indicated, 473

Hyperbola, equation of, 340; normal to, 342; parametric equations of, 342, 343; rectangular, 343; tangent to, 342

Imaginary parts of a function, 162

Impact, 490, 493, 495; energy loss in, 496

Implicit functions, 167

Impulse, 485

Inclined plane, 398, 462

Included angle formula for triangle, 90

Increment notation, 170

Indefinite integral, 223

Indices, 13; fractional, 15; negative, 15; positive, 13

Induction, method of, 49

Inflexion, points of, 215

Integral, as limit of a sum, 240; definite, 242, 244; indefinite, 223; of e^{ax}, 291; of $f'(x)/f(x)$, 293; of rational algebraic fractions, 295; of x^{-1}, 286

Integration, by change of variable, 231, 245; by parts, 236, 297; numerical, 247; of a graph, 423; of products of sines and cosines, 235

Inverse trigonometrical functions, 79

Kilowatt, 472

Kinetic energy, 476; loss in impact, 496; of rotating body, 545

Lami's theorem, 377

Latus rectum, of parabola, 331

Limiting value of $(\sin x)/x$, 78

Loci, 116; intersection of, 118

Logarithmic function, 289; derivative of, 290

Logarithmic series, 301

Logarithms, 17; common, 19

m.k.s. units, 461

Maclaurin's series, 300

Matrices, 557; decomposition of, 568; determinant associated with, 565; general definitions of, 562; inverse of, 566; inverse of unit diagonal, 569; particular, 564; product of, 559, 561; use in reducing a system of equations,

570; use in solution of simultaneous equations, 572
Maxima and minima, 205; applications of, 211
Mean values, 260
Mensuration formulae, 199
Modulus of elasticity, 389
Moments of a force, 358
Moment of inertia, 273, 275; of lamina, 274
Momentum, 460, 485; conservation of, 487; units of, 486
Motion, about an axis, 544; circular, 507; of connected masses, 464; of rigid body, 462; parabolic, 443; relative, 433; simple harmonic, 531; with constant acceleration, 280, 415, 417

Napierian logarithm, 289
Newton (unit of force), 461
Newton's approximation, 302
Newton's laws of motion, 459, 460
Normal acceleration, 507
Numerical integration, 247
Numerical solution of triangles, 91

Ordinate, 107
Overturning of vehicles, 516

Parabola, equation of, 330; normal to, 333; parametric equations of, 332; tangent to, 332
Parabolic motion, 443; equations of, 443; remaining velocity in, 446; vertex height in, 446
Parallel axis theorem, 273
Parallel forces, 356; centre of, 373
Parallel lines, 127
Parametric equations, 332, 338, 342, 343
Partial fractions, 54
Pascal's triangle, 50
Pendulum, compound, 548; conical, 512; equivalent simple, 549; seconds, 537; simple, 536
Period, 533
Permutations, 42

Perpendicular lines, 127
Polar coordinates, 108
Potential energy, 478
Poundal, 461
Power, 471; units of, 471
Probability, 46
Progression, arithmetical, 35; convergent geometrical, 40; geometrical, 37

Quadratic equations, 20; equations leading to, 24; functions of roots, 22
Quadratic functions, 20

Radius of gyration, 273
Range, in parabolic motion, 445
Rate measurer, 196
Real part of a function, 162
Rectangular hyperbola, 343
Reduction of a system of equations, 570; alternative method of, 572
Relative motion, 433, 436
Relative path, 438
Remainder theorem, 27
Resultant, 351; line of action of, 363
Resultant velocity, 433, 436

Scalar product, 151, 468
Second derivative, 190
Seconds pendulum, 537
Separation of variables, 308
Sequences, 34
Series, 34; for e^x, 300; for $\log_e (1 + x)$, 301
Simple harmonic motion, 531; amplitude in, 532; forces causing, 539; frequency in, 533; initial conditions in, 533; period in, 533; relation to circular motion, 534; with elastic string, 540
Simple pendulum, 536
Simpson's rule, 251
Sine formula for triangle, 84
Slug, 502
Solution of triangles, 91
Standard differential coefficients, 188
Standard integrals, 214, 227

Straight line, equation of, 199; in terms of intercepts, 122; in terms of slope and coordinates of a point, 121; in terms of slope and intercept on y-axis, 120; passing through intersection of given lines, 131; passing through two given points, 122

Système International, 461, 502

Taylor-Maclaurin theorem, 299
Time of flight, 445
Toppling problems, 395
Trajectory, 446, 449
Transformation of $a \cos x + b \sin x$, 72
Transmissibility of force, 354
Trapezoidal rule, 248
Triangle of forces, 377
Trigonometrical, addition formulae, 66, 110; factor formulae, 74; half-angle formulae, 72
Trigonometrical ratios, definitions of, 62; for general angle, 63; graphs of, 65; of multiple angles, 69; of small angles, 76
Turning points, 205

Undetermined coefficients, 29
Unit vectors, 144
Units, 414; absolute, 461; change of, 501; gravitational, 461; of energy, 476; of force, 461; of mass, 460; of momentum, 486; of power, 471; of work, 468; table of, 502
Units and dimensions, 501

Vector algebra, 147
Vector quantities, 152
Vectors, 143; addition of, 144, 150; components of, 149
Velocity, 152, 196, 201, 279, 414; components of, 441; relative, 433, 436; units of, 414
Volumes, by integration, 262

Watt, 472
Wheel, rotation of, 549
Work, 468; done by a couple, 470; in lifting body, 469; in stretching elastic string, 469; units of, 468
Work equation, 476